Aesthetics of Music

Volume 1

Books by David Whitwell

Philosophic Foundations of Education
Foundations of Music Education
Music Education of the Future
The Sousa Oral History Project
The Art of Musical Conducting
The Longy Club: 1900–1917
A Concise History of the Wind Band

The History and Literature of the Wind Band and Wind Ensemble Series

Volume 1 The Wind Band and Wind Ensemble Before 1500
Volume 2 The Renaissance Wind Band and Wind Ensemble
Volume 3 The Baroque Wind Band and Wind Ensemble
Volume 4 The Classic Period Wind Band and Wind Ensemble
Volume 5 The Nineteenth-Century Wind Band and Wind Ensemble
Volume 6 A Catalog of Multi-Part Repertoire for Wind Instruments or for Undesignated Instrumentation before 1600
Volume 7 Baroque Wind Band and Wind Ensemble Repertoire
Volume 8 Classic Period Wind Band and Wind Ensemble Repertoire
Volume 9 Nineteenth-Century Wind Band and Wind Ensemble Repertoire
Volume 10 A Supplementary Catalog of Wind Band and Wind Ensemble Repertoire
Volume 11 A Catalog of Wind Repertoire before the Twentieth Century for One to Five Players
Volume 12 A Second Supplementary Catalog of Early Wind Band and Wind Ensemble Repertoire
Volume 13 Name Index, Volumes 1–12, The History and Literature of the Wind Band and Wind Ensemble

www.whitwellbooks.com

David Whitwell

Aesthetics of Music

VOLUME 1
AESTHETICS OF MUSIC IN ANCIENT CIVILIZATIONS

EDITED BY CRAIG DABELSTEIN

WHITWELL BOOKS • AUSTIN, TEXAS, USA

Aesthetics of Music in Ancient Civilizations
Aesthetics of Music, Volume 1
Second Edition

Dr. David Whitwell
Edited by Craig Dabelstein
www.whitwellbooks.com

Whitwell Publishing
815-A Brazos Street #491
Austin, TX 78701
USA

Composed in Minion Pro
Published in the United States of America

Aesthetics of Music, volume 1 (PAPERBACK) ISBN 978-1-936512-21-8

FOREWORD

We define Music to be that form of music performed live before listeners. We define Aesthetics in Music to be a study of the nature of the perception of music by the listener.

The first philosopher to address the impact which Art has on an observer was Aristotle, in his *Poetics*, in which he first considers the nature and contribution of each of the specific components of Tragedy in his typically methodical style. His great contribution, however, comes when he has completed this discussion, for he then goes beyond the material form of the play itself to discuss the observer. He makes it clear that not only is the end purpose of the elements of the play to produce a specific experience in the observer, but that the nature of this experience is what distinguishes Tragedy from other dramatic forms, such as Spectacle. It was in this moment that he created a new branch of Philosophy known today as 'Aesthetics.'

Our purpose is to provide a source book of representative descriptions of actual performances, observations by philosophers, poets and other commentators which contribute insight to our understanding of what Music meant to listeners during the ancient civilizations.

In this series, we also present material on aesthetics in other forms which might offer insight to aesthetics in music by association. Views on the drama, for example, are important, for drama, like music, has both a written and a performance form. Drama critics focused on the difference between Art and Entertainment, which is also central to aesthetics in music. And poetry, aside from its actual connection with music, was also a medium for the ear which, like music, focused on the direct expression of emotions. We believe, therefore, that study of contemporary views on such forms as drama and poetry help clarify the aesthetic values of the environment in which music was composed and performed.

For the same reason, we are also interested in contemporary views on the physiology of knowing, especially with regard to the relationship of the senses and Reason, and related psychological ideas, such as Pleasure and Pain and the Emotions.

In our discussion of all early music treatises in this series of books, we concentrate only on those passages which offer insights relative to the aesthetics of music and musical performance, while omitting discussion of the usual technical subjects such as scales, modes and counterpoint.

For our initial discussion on the definition of aesthetics we take the last great comprehensive philosopher who addressed this topic at length, Benedetto Croce, as our point of departure.

David Whitwell
Austin, 2011

CONTENTS

PART 1: THE PHYSIOLOGY AND PHILOSOPHY OF AESTHETICS   1

  1   *On Philosophical Problems in the General Field of Aesthetics*   3
  2   *Aesthetics in Music*   19

PART 2: AESTHETICS IN THE MUSICAL PRACTICE OF THE ANCIENT CIVILIZATIONS OF THE NEAR EAST   59

  3   *Mesopotamia*   61
  4   *Egypt*   73
  5   *Ancient Hebrew Music*   85

PART 3: AESTHETICS IN THE MUSICAL PRACTICE OF ANCIENT GREECE   101

  6   *A Preface to the Music of Ancient Greece*   103
  7   *The Epic Poets of the Ninth Century*   113
  8   *The Early Lyric Poets*   123
  9   *Historians of the Fifth Century*   141
 10   *Fifth Century Philosophy Before Plato*   153
 11   *The First Great Dramatists*   169
 12   *Plato*   191
 13   *Aristotle*   249
 14   *The Alexandrian Period of Ancient Greece*   273
 15   *The Alexandrian Philosophers*   281
 16   *Alexandrian Poets*   293
 17   *The Roman Period of Ancient Greece*   303

PART 4: AESTHETICS IN THE MUSICAL PRACTICE OF ANCIENT ROME   341

 18   *Music Before the Republic*   343
 19   *The Republic*   351
 20   *Republican Philosophy*   369
 21   *The Augustan Age*   401
 22   *The Augustan Lyric Poets*   423
 23   *The Empire*   459
 24   *Imperial Philosophers*   477
 25   *Imperial Poets*   499

     Epilogue   511
     Bibliography   515
     Index   521
     About the Author   527

ACKNOWLEDGMENTS

This new edition would not have been possible without the encouragement and help of Craig Dabelstein of Brisbane, Australia. His experience as a musician and educator himself has contributed greatly to his expertise as editor of this volume.

David Whitwell
Austin, 2011

PART 1

The Physiology and Philosophy of Aesthetics

1 ON PHILOSOPHICAL PROBLEMS IN THE GENERAL FIELD OF AESTHETICS

Will Durant, in his review of the twentieth-century classic work, *Aesthetic*, by Benedetto Croce, concludes,

> As to the *Aesthetic*, let others judge. At least one student cannot understand it. Is man an artist as soon as he forms images? Does the essence of art lie only in the conception, and not in the externalization? Have we never had thoughts and feelings more beautiful than our speech? How do we know what the inward image was, in the artist's mind, or whether the work that we admire realizes or misses his idea?[1]

1   Will Durant, *The Story of Philosophy* (New York: Simon & Schuster, 1961), 356. He refers to Benedetto Croce, *Aesthetic* (New York: Noonday, 1958).

This instance of one famous philosopher failing to understand another only illustrates that the first difficulty in the discussion of Aesthetics is language itself. First of all, language is of the rational left hemisphere of the brain whereas the essence of any art has very much to do with the experiential side of ourselves. Because words have an agreed upon rational, conceptual definition, making ordinary speech possible, we often forget that many of the words used in daily conversation are also subject to being understood in the light of the listener's own personal experience. Therefore when we use a word like 'beauty' in a sentence, while it has a general meaning making some level of communication possible, it will have a different meaning to each listener and none of them will be identical with the meaning of the speaker. And this, of course, is one reason why we have Art, in order to communicate with each other beyond what words can express.

Upon reflection one will come to realize that all words lack a universal precision. Precision is found only in the definitions of Science, Science being nothing but a series of definitions. Because the definition that 'two plus two equals four' has universal precision, however, it therefore forfeits all opportunity for individual expression. Thus Science, in creating the only universally precise concepts, ironically speaks in a language devoid of humanity.

Science goes from the known to the unknown. Art, in its capacity to take the observer through contemplation to understanding, goes from the unknown to the known. But herein lies another great difficulty in forming a definition of the Aesthetic. Each observer,

as he observes an art work from the perspective of a unique experiential viewpoint, will have a unique understanding of any art
work. Therefore, if everyone views it differently, how can we hope
to agree on the aesthetic nature of any individual art work? Can
any theory of Aesthetics *prove* that Beethoven's Ninth Symphony
is good *or* bad? If everyone has an individual viewpoint of an art
work, does popularity then represent a measure of aesthetic consensus? No, certainly not in the case of Music, where popularity is
often synonymous with vulgarity.

Similarly, while we speak of the 'art of painting' or the 'art of
music,' we do not mean by this that *technique* is synonymous with
the Aesthetic. An aesthetically rewarding violin recital may have
little to do with violin playing. Thus, with regard to Mr. Durant's
first question, above, we might answer, Yes, a man is an *artist* as
soon as he forms images, but this in and of itself does not address
the question of Aesthetics.

We expect that these questions, which we will resolve below, will
give the reader some introduction to the difficulties and complexi-
ties of this branch of philosophy. Before we can present a practical
discussion of Aesthetics in Music, we must first consider several
additional questions which reoccur in the philosophical literature on aesthetics. These questions are important because to some
extent they are both a prerequisite to, and form the perimeter of,
the discussion of the more specific subject of aesthetics in music.

WHAT IS MEANT BY 'BEAUTY' IN ART?

As mentioned above, our first problem in discussing 'Beauty' in
art is one of language. Aside from the fact that such a word will
mean different things to different persons, it *is* a term appropriate
to aesthetics. In practice, however, it is often uttered colloquially in
an inaccurate usage, as for example in, 'a beautiful golf shot,' when
we may really mean, 'an *accurate* golf shot.' Secondly, with regard to
art, the expression, 'a beautiful painting,' is inherently paradoxical,
because the perception of 'beautiful' is actually in the eye of the
beholder, not in the object, the painting itself. The reason for this is
because it is the experiential history of the individual viewer which
contributes to his perception of a painting as being beautiful. A
different person may not find the same painting 'beautiful' at all.

At the same time, one must acknowledge the possibility of the perception of what we might call 'natural' or 'physical beauty,' as in a beautiful landscape. There is no question that 'natural beauty' can be a stimulus to the artist in his attempt to communicate beauty in art. Indeed, in the case of painters, artists often have the physical model before them. It is interesting to read, for example, among the notes which Leonardo wrote in his notebook while working on the Last Supper,

> Giovannina, weird face, is at St. Catherine's, at the Hospital; Cristofano di Castiglione is at the Pieta, he has a fine head; Christ, Giovan Conte, of Cardinal Mortaro's suite.[2]

2 Quoted in Croce, *Aesthetic*, 107.

But it would be wrong to suppose that it was ever Leonardo's intent to paint Castiglione's face. The most we can say is that the face inspired him to think in some direction. The real issue here is, would everyone have thought Castiglione had a 'fine head?'

The fact is, there is no such thing as 'natural beauty.' That is, there are no 'principles of art' in nature that everyone can agree are synonymous with beauty. Even though the academic world finds and teaches such 'principles,' they are non-existent illusions. They are at most representative of a single viewpoint. For Croce the idea of 'naturalistic laws of the beautiful' makes no more sense than astrology!

> Artists sometimes adopt empirical canons, such as that of the proportions of the human body, or of the golden section, that is to say, of a line divided into two parts in such a manner that the less is to the greater as is the greater to the whole line. Such canons easily become their superstitions, and they attribute to them the success of their works. Thus Michael Angelo left as a precept to his disciple Marco del Pino da Siena that 'he should always make a pyramidal serpentine figure multiplied by one two and three,' a precept which did not enable Marco da Siena to emerge from that mediocrity which we can yet observe in many of his paintings that exist here in Naples. Others took Michael Angelo's words as authority for the precept that serpentine undulating lines were the true *lines of beauty*. Whole volumes have been composed on these laws of beauty, on the golden section and on the undulating and serpentine lines. These should in our opinion be looked upon as the *astrology of Aesthetic*.[3]

3 Ibid., 110.

Thus, nothing could be more incorrect than to suppose that an artist is merely someone with excellent technique, who finds beauty and then copies it on canvas. By 'beauty' in art we refer to the world of the spirit and to the artist's inner vision. He may be inspired by natural beauty, but he forms his own inner concept of beauty, which is what he paints. It is his vision which guides his technique and results in the art 'object.' Thus it was that Michelangelo made his famous observation, 'One paints with the mind, not the brush.'

These considerations are even more strongly delineated in the art of music. To begin with, no words whatsoever can describe the essence of music, which is a form of emotional communication. Even the physical grammar of music, such as notes, chords, instrumentation, etc., is quite inadequately served by language. A term such as 'a dominant chord,' is [1] a label, which [2] represents a technical concept relating to the relationship of tones, which, finally, [3] must represent a sound. Further, since such a chord is normally found in the context of music in which it is merely *one* element, and in which aesthetic meaning is found in the sum of *all* its elements, the label itself seems almost unrelated to the experience of the listener. This, of course, is what we would expect given the duality of the brain, the label, being language, of the left hemisphere and the emotional perception of the sound, as music, being right hemisphere. In fact, one can say that the moment one substitutes a linguistic label for the sound, one has left the world of music. This detached relationship is confirmed in the experience of the majority of listeners who have no idea what the technical terms are for what they are hearing, yet are genetically prepared to *understand* perfectly what they are hearing.

There is nothing equivalent in music for the expression, 'natural beauty,' because all music is man made. When we use the term 'beauty' with respect to music we are hearing, we can only refer to *feeling*. When we say, 'that was a beautiful symphony,' we actually mean the composer touched us and made us feel this way. Further confusion arises because we speak of the elements of music as being beautiful, as in a beautiful tone, beautiful harmony, a beautiful melody, but these are all misnomers as none of them really have meaning by themselves. That is to say, just as in the case of painting, there are no *natural* laws of beauty associated with the elements of music. No one can define in words what is beautiful about a single tone, especially if we disregard the attack, nor what constitutes a beautiful melody or a beautiful harmony. We are using words to try to describe how we, as individuals, are made to *feel* by the music, and these feelings are not capable of description by language.

In music, Beauty has to do with the spirit. Because music is in its essence a form of emotional communication, it, as with art in general, is also found 'in the eye of the beholder.' Because its perception is conditioned by the experiential history of the listener, can we suppose that some listener might misunderstand completely or not hear beauty at all? The answer is no. Because music deals with the communication of genetically acquired and universally shared emotions, the experiential history of the listener only conditions the *degree* of his awareness. But if the listener fails to perceive this communication, the fault will be found in the failure of the communication, which may lie at the doorstep of either the composer or the performance.

When we do find 'beauty' in music it must refer to the highest truths of our experiential nature which are revealed to us through music. This is what was meant when the famous conductor, Sergiu Celibadache, observed,

> Anyone who still hasn't got past the stage of the beauty of music still knows nothing about music. Music is not beautiful. It has beauty as well, but the beauty is only the bait. Music is true.[4]

4 Quoted in *Los Angeles Philharmonic Notes*, April 1989.

What is meant by 'Imitation of Nature' in Art?

If it is not the purpose of the artist to duplicate the beauty he sees in nature, what is meant by the familiar expression, 'Art imitates Nature?' This phrase was introduced by Aristotle when he observed, in his *Poetics*, that imitation seems to be an instinct implanted in man from childhood. In practice, in theater it came to mean plots based on believable, life-like actions. In painting, a more appropriate expression might be 'idealization of nature.'

The one thing the term never means in art is what it implies, a duplication of nature. Although the phrase seems to suggest that the artist paints what he sees in nature, he in fact does the reverse. Even though as mentioned above he may be inspired by nature, he never turns a natural object into an aesthetic idea. Rather, he turns an aesthetic idea into an object, the canvas.

The term would seem inappropriate with regard to music. The only 'natural' thing which music can express are feelings and emotions, but these are never *imitations* of these feelings and emotions. Music is unique among the arts in that the emotions it expresses are the *real* emotions and not symbols or representations of emotions.

In another sense, however, there is something here which is very relevant to the art of music. If we were to say, 'Imitation of Life,' or 'Imitation of Nature,' by which we mean the broad characterization of a culture, then it is quite accurate, for music will always represent the culture from which it springs. The general musical practice of a people can never rise above the culture of the people; primitive people will always be represented by primitive music. It is here that some American music educators make the unbelievable error of treating the art music of Western Europe as a mere category among the music of the world's people. The implication they suggest is that all music is equal, since it is all music. But this is not true. An igloo is not the Chartres Cathedral and they differ not so much in architectural description as they do in the levels of culture they represent.

The fact is that the cultural heritage of Western Europe is not 'the culture of a certain time and place,' as educators label it. It is rather the accumulation of the experience of Western man himself. The nineteenth-century masterpieces of music of Western Europe are not just representatives of nineteenth-century Western Europe, they are the highest chapter of development in something which began four thousand years earlier with equal roots in Greece, Rome, Egypt and the Near East. It is the art music of *all* Western men. To call nineteenth-century German music 'German,' is to betray a poor understanding of Western Civilization. For teachers to not want to pass on the *highest* achievements of man to the next generation, is a dereliction of duty.

WHAT IS MEANT BY 'EMOTION' IN ART?

Philosophers since the ancient Greeks have been aware that there is another dimension to man than the whole of what we call Reason. However since language is the language of Reason, it fails when attempting to explain that which is outside its domain. While the ancient Greeks were fully aware of the existence of pleasure and pain, sensations and emotions, since they found linguistic characterization so difficult they inevitably retreated and declared Reason the most significant characteristic of man.

Today, modern brain research having unlocked the mystery of our twin brain hemispheres, we know that there is literally another half of man which cannot be associated with Reason. But this other half of ourselves, the 'real us' by the way, the seat of the perception of our feelings, also needs an outlet. Since the right hemisphere is entirely mute and cannot speak, what is its outlet? How can we then communicate this part of ourselves or experience introspection?

It is because we have these needs that we have Art, however, Art education makes the mistake of going the opposite direction. It declares Art good and proposes the student should therefore know about it. But the student does not want to know *about* it, he wants to *experience* it. Failing to find this in our classes, the student abandons them, or avoids them, and seeks his experiences where he can find them. Education having failed to prepare him to deal with the feelings he encounters through the arts, he takes the path of least resistance, the path which is least troubling to his feelings. Hence it is to meet emotional needs on this primitive level that has resulted in our culture being filled with vulgar art.

Feelings and emotion are the essence of art, but what does that mean? The early philosophers spoke mostly of pleasure and pain as positive and negative poles of our experience, but their error was in trying to subject experience to the logic of reason. Hence they worried over such questions as, is one merely the absence of the other, or which can be called morally good. They were aware we had senses, but they misunderstood how they worked and knew nothing of where they were seated.

Simple sensations are how we deal with the outside world, we see it, we feel it, we hear it, etc. But while these are inseparable from us, they do not seem to be *us*. They seem more like responses to the outside world, as is clear when you touch a hot stove. After we touch the hot stove we experience 'pain,' and this *does* seem part of us. After a certain number of experiences with pain, we develop a non-verbal, abstract understanding of pain, but it is always a definition personal to us, formed from our own personal experience. It is such understanding, developed through evolution and passed to us genetically, that we call Emotions. These are so clearly defined, even before birth, that we can communicate much of them precisely through the face to anyone on earth, regardless of their language or other cultural characteristics.

But while we communicate them, do we understand them? It is clear that simple sensation was important, with respect to evolution, for survival of the species. 'Feeling,' exists on its most primitive level in association with sensation, which we might call simply an awareness. But, like sensation, this is not associated with the conscious recognition of self. Dogs communicate primitive expressions of feelings in response to their master's voice. Many lower human types live their lives only reacting to feelings at nearly this level.

By 'Emotion' we mean feeling at a much higher level of self awareness, something which is clearly part of *knowing* on the experiential side of ourselves, which is primarily in the right hemisphere. 'Feeling,' at its higher level is probably the same thing, although we, through linguistic practice, use 'feeling' or 'emotion' in different contextual situations. No word is accurate, of course, when we ask language to speak of emotions, because we are literally asking the left hemisphere to speak of something which it knows nothing about. But, in any case, we use expressions like 'awareness' and 'knowing' because emotions are something we can use at will. We purposely color our left hemisphere language with right hemisphere emotional content in order to define the intent of the language.

Emotions are recognizable on both a universal level, which others can read, and on a personal level, defined by our experiential history. Because there is this fundamental personal quality to emotions, they are sometimes placed in the category of the egotistic or hedonistic—as opposed, for example, to 'Morals' which are rational concepts first learned from others. It is interesting, however, that the preacher uses the pain (right hemisphere) of Hell to sell us on his morals (left hemisphere). He has found, over the centuries, that he has been remarkably unsuccessful in trying to do this through Reason (left hemisphere); church laws are easily broken. Although the Church has not yet discovered it, Music is probably the most effective means of connecting the individual with the unfathomable (a sign in a German opera house reads, 'God gave us Music that we might pray without words').

How do we speak of Emotion in the arts? Croce summarizes what some have theorized in earlier times.

> What is called the activity of feeling is nothing but that more elementary and fundamental practical activity which we have distinguished from the ethical activity and made to consist of the apparition and volition for some individual end, apart from any moral determination.
>
> If feeling has been sometimes considered to be an organic or natural activity, this has happened just because it does not coincide either with logical, aesthetic or ethical activity. Looked at from the

standpoint of those three, it has seemed to lie *outside* the true and real spirit, spirit in its aristocracy, and to be almost a determination of nature, or of the soul in so far as it is nature. From this too results the truth of another thesis, often maintained, that aesthetic activity, like ethical and intellectual activities, is not feeling …

But if the activity of feeling in the sense here defined must not be substituted for all the other forms of spiritual activity, we have not said that it cannot *accompany* them. Indeed it accompanies them of necessity, because they are all in close relation both with one another and with the elementary volition form …

A question often asked is thus answered at the same time, one which has correctly seemed to be a matter of life or death for aesthetic science, namely, whether feeling and pleasure precede or follow, are cause or effect of the aesthetic fact. We must widen this question to include the relation between the various spiritual forms, and answer it by maintaining that one cannot talk of cause and effect and of a chronological before and after in the unity of the spirit.[5]

5 Croce, *Aesthetic*, 75ff.

In the first part of his comments, Croce maintains that feeling is something apart from the actual aesthetic activity. Restricting ourselves to the art of music, we must note a well-known statement by Stravinsky seems to support this idea.

I consider that music is, by its very nature, powerless to express anything at all, whether a feeling, an attitude of mind, a psychological mood, a phenomenon of nature, etc … if, as is nearly always the case, music appears to express something, this is only an illusion, and not a reality.[6]

6 Igor Stravinsky, *Chronicle of My Life* (London: Victor Gollancz, 1936), 91–2.

Paul Hindemith seems to agree in discussing this question with respect to the act of aesthetic creation.

Music cannot express the composer's feelings. Let us suppose a composer is writing an extremely funereal piece, which may require three months of intensive work. Is he, during this three-month period, thinking of nothing but funerals? Or can he, in those hours that are not devoted to his work because of his desire to eat and sleep, put his grief on ice, so to speak, and be gay until the moment when he resumes his sombre activity? If he really expressed his feelings accurately during the time of composing and writing, we would be presented with a horrible motley of expressions, among which the grievous part would necessarily occupy but a small space.[7]

7 Paul Hindemith, *A Composer's World: Horizons and Limitations* (Garden City: Doubleday, 1961), 35–6.

These views are simply incorrect. Music, in so far as it implies communication to a listener, communicates nothing but emotions and feelings. Stravinsky was speaking only of the grammar of music and in this respect he is correct. Hindemith's discussion is quite silly, for it is obvious that an artist is capable of putting himself into the mood of the piece he is working on, for the duration of his work.

Croce, in another place, writes that while there may be feelings expressed in an art work, they are not the same as *real* feelings.

> A category of *apparent* aesthetic feelings has been formed in modern Aesthetic, not arising from the form, that is to say, from the works of art as such, but from their content. It has been remarked that artistic representations arouse pleasure and pain in their infinite shades of variety. We tremble with anxiety, we rejoice, we fear, we laugh, we weep, we desire, with the personages of a drama or of a romance, with the figures in a picture and with the melody of music. But these feelings are not such as would be aroused by the real fact outside art; or rather, they are the same in quality, but are quantitatively an attenuation of real things. Aesthetic and *apparent* pleasure and pain show themselves to be light, shallow, mobile ...
>
> But there is, in fact, an abyss between a man who is the prey of anger with all its natural manifestations and another man who expresses it aesthetically; between the appearance, the cries and contortions of some one grieving at the loss of a dear one and the words or song with which the same individual portrays his suffering at another time; between the grimace of emotion and the gesture of the actor. Darwin's book on the expression of the emotions in man and animals does not belong to Aesthetic; because there is nothing in common between the science of spiritual expression and a *Semiotic*, whether it be medical, meteorological, political, physiognomic, or chiromantic.
>
> Expression in the naturalistic sense simply lacks *expression in the spiritual sense*, that is to say, the very character of activity and of spirituality, and therefore the bipartition into the poles of beauty and ugliness. It is nothing but a relation between cause and effect, fixed by the abstract intellect.[8]

8   Croce, *Aesthetic*, 8off, 95.

With regard to music, Croce is simply wrong. Music *does* communicate feelings and emotions and while they may be in a universal form, to be understood in an individual form by the listener, as we will discuss below, they are none the less precise and not an illusion or merely apparent. An observation by Mendelssohn is much more to the point of what really happens in music.

People usually complain that music is so ambiguous; that it is so doubtful what they ought to think when they hear it; whereas everyone understands words. With me it is entirely the converse. And not only with regard to an entire speech, but also with individual words; these, too, seem to me to be so ambiguous, so vague, and so easily misunderstood in comparison with genuine music, which fills the soul with a thousand things better than words. The thoughts which are expressed to me by a piece of music which I love are not too indefinite to be put into words, but on the contrary too definite.[9]

In the second part of his discussion, above, Croce mentions the chronology or cause and effect relationship of feelings to the aesthetic work. The question is, do feelings produce art or does art produce feelings. While both are obviously true, that answer does not do justice to the complexity of a relationship that does change in chronology. The great composer begins with feeling and struggles to transmit these feelings through a symbolic language that is incapable of expressing feelings. That is to say, while musical notation has symbols for loud and soft, accentuation, etc., it has none whatsoever for feeling.[10] The listener, through contemplative listening, has his own feelings raised to the level of the great composer's and in the process comes to understand his own feelings in a more defined form. Also regarding chronology, we should remind the reader that it is a significant distinction between music and the other arts, that in performance the feeling–experience of the observer occurs precisely in the present tense with its expression in the music.

Finally, we must return to a question raised earlier: If music is feelings and emotions, should the question of hedonism be raised? Can one enjoy music too much? Can a piece of music have too much feeling? Can a listener be affected adversely by too much feeling? This sounds important, but it is actually the wrong question.

Each listener comes to a performance with a unique experiential history which, in turn, makes each listener somewhat unique in his sensibility to the feelings of the music. It is *sensibility* which is the key. The listener who is *receptive* to great passionate feelings will always be a listener whose experiential life history has made this level of sensibility possible. The listener whose experiential life history has resulted in a lower threshold of sensibility will simply not understand the feelings of the music. He will not be harmed by something which goes by him unfelt.[11]

9 Felix Mendelssohn, Letter to Marc Andre Souchay, October 5, 1842.

10 The writer has seen an experimental notational system which attempted to notate feeling, resulting in a notation in which each single note had six or eight stems going off in all directions. Curiously enough, the first impression one had in seeing examples of music in this notation was not whether a musician would be able to learn how to read the new notation, but why he would *want* to.

11 It should, of course, be the primary purpose of music education to raise this threshold of sensibility in the student.

So the real question is not can there be too much feeling in music, but can there be too much sensibility in a listener. This, of course, is absurd, as Mendelssohn once pointed out.

> There is no such thing as an excess of sensibility, and what is called 'too-much' is always rather 'too-little.' The soaring, elevated emotions inspired by music—so welcome to the listeners—are no excess; let him, who is capable of emotions, feel them to the utmost of his capacity—and more so, if possible.[12]

12 Mendelssohn, Letter to Pastor Bauer, March 4, 1833.

WHAT IS MEANT BY 'FORM AND CONTENT' IN ART?

There can be no question that in Music it is the *content*, the expressive content, which the general audience responds to in a work of art. One can go further and say that in the greatest art every element is so perfectly crafted that form and content seem one and inseparable. Also content comes first, for whatever is important about form can only be discovered when the work is fully completed.

Why then do critics and teachers talk so much of form and formal aspects of art? The reason is that while it is very difficult, impossible really, to describe in words the non-rational expressive content of the highest art, it is considerably easier to speak of the formal deficiencies of a less successful work, especially those which can be described as having 'form but no content.' Much 'Art' is similar to that described by Croce.

> Somebody who has nothing definite to express may try to conceal his internal emptiness in a flood of words, in sounding verse, in deafening polyphony, in painting that dazzles the eye, or by heaping together great architectural masses which arrest and astonish us without conveying anything whatever.[13]

13 Croce, *Aesthetic*, 98.

This kind of art should perhaps be more accurately described as *dishonest* art. This is not the same thing that one often finds in the art of comedy, where the observer is led to expect one thing only to be surprised by something quite different. In what Croce is talking about the audience is led to expect something and receives *nothing*.

The present writer attended such a concert recently, an annual church choir Christmas concert. The forty-minute work was called a Cantata, and consisted of groups of four brief works for choir, with an occasional solo aria, separated by various actors dressed and speaking as Mary, Joseph, and other characters of the Christmas story.

The music for choir consisted of primarily unison scoring of music utterly without distinction, accompanied by clever quotations of familiar Christmas music in the organ part.

The faces of the audience were not the faces of persons emotionally involved as contemplative listeners of great music. They were faces of people day-dreaming, telling their children to be quiet, etc. Only at the conclusion, when the congregation was invited to join in the singing of three carols, did the faces come alive.

How does one describe this 'concert,' this music? This was music in the form of a Cantata, but was music devoid of content. It was representative of an enormous amount of American music, music of the church, school, and public life. It might be called 'constructed' music, as opposed to 'inspired' music.

The most generous characterization of this music, aesthetically, would be to say that if Art imitates Nature, or Life, this 'Cantata' was an imitation of an imitation. It was imitation music and it reminded this listener of Hotel Art, which is also usually not paintings, but imitations of paintings.

But a more accurate characterization would probably be that of Croce who writes that such inexpressive music, 'can never form part of the aesthetic fact, being, on the contrary, its *antithesis*.'[14] He is correct, because terms such as 'inexpressive art' or 'dishonest art,' are contradictions. Genuine art is synonymous with the expressive and the honest.

Why would anyone want to perform such music? Why would American Protestant churches not want to perform the greatest Protestant music ever written, the music of Bach, Purcell, Telemann and Handel, to name only one period of such music.

The reason lies in the fact that music is a *performance* medium and as such there is a level of enjoyment in just performance for the sake of performance. It is possible for a group of musicians to perform away mindlessly, with the greatest enthusiasm, music of no substance whatsoever—especially if they don't know any better, if they have never been exposed to anything else. For such performance it is always the case, in our experience, that the blame lies at the door of education and not with the performers.

The very same thing can be said for the world of the left hemisphere. It is perfectly possible for people to live their lives with poor vocabulary, improper English, and never having known Shakespeare. But should we blame them, or their education?

14 Croce, *Aesthetic*, 88.

What is meant by 'Universality' in Art?

By Universality is meant the ability of the creator of a work of *high art* to express something which seems to be deeply understood by the broad public. Jan Meyerowitz, himself a gifted composer, defined the universality of Beethoven as,

> The composer's capacity to say the strongest, the weirdest, even the most complicated things in such simple terms that even the 'man in the gallery' can comprehend, is one of the reasons Beethoven occupies his supreme position.[15]

15   Jan Meyerowitz, 'Do We Overestimate Beethoven?,' *High Fidelity Magazine*, January 1970, 79.

We use the term 'universality' in distinction with 'popularity' and the difference is in the content and its reception by the listener. 'Universality' suggests that the music reaches the listener on a deep, human, level. A work of little inherent value, which appeals to an audience superficially, is said to be 'popular.'

But, Universality also implies a contemplative listener, since the contemplative listener is inseparable from the definition of high art. The circumstances of the performance therefore is a factor and accordingly it is possible for an art work to be performed in a venue, and under such circumstances, as to reduce it to 'popular music.' The reverse, however, is never possible. No insignificant work of music can ever, under any circumstances, be made more than it is.

It is important to remember, however, that the audience is prepared *by nature* to be drawn into either a universal experience of high art or to participate in a less exalted experience, according to the nature of what is set before them. In music this 'preparation' is the result of the universal emotional makeup which is passed on genetically to the species. For something like the theater we are all prepared by the fact that we engage in an act of creativity in prose every time we form a sentence. Thus, although we say that the artist, or his art work, has universality, perhaps it would be more accurate to say the universality is already there in the public waiting to be engaged. Croce wrote, in this regard,

> Each of us, as a matter of fact, has in him a little of the poet, of the sculptor, of the musician, of the painter, of the prose writer: but how little, as compared with those who bear those names, just because they possess the most universal dispositions and energies of human nature in so lofty a degree![16]

16   Croce, *Aesthetic*, 11.

The irony is that given this genetically prepared mass audience, it is often the broad public, and not the critics, who, by its response, identifies the masterpieces of art. As Debussy once observed, '*fame is a gift of the masses who know nothing.*' He is wrong, of course, for the masses know everything important about music, their knowledge failing only in the left hemisphere descriptions. If it were not so, great art could not have universality. Because it *is* so, the greatest composers know exactly what is universal in their art. Thus Mozart could predict with complete confidence,

these passages are written in such a way that the less learned cannot fail to be pleased, though without knowing why.[17]

17 Wolfgang Amadeus Mozart, Letter to his father, December 28, 1782.

2 AESTHETICS IN MUSIC

Although music is usually associated with the other arts, painting, sculpture, acting, etc., it is actually quite unique, beginning with the fact that it is the only art you cannot see. Before we attempt to formulate a theory of aesthetics in music, we should first like to demonstrate how music stands apart from, and must have a separate definition of aesthetics from, the other arts.

Unlike painting and acting, for example, which are representations of something else, music is not a representation, nor a symbol, nor a metaphor of anything else. It is more accurately a language, a special non-rational language of our brain, through which we communicate the experiential side of our nature. For the listener, it is this musical language which allows him to communicate directly with the composer's original inner idea and through contemplation learn more about himself.

The distinction, for example, between painting and music works like this:

Object → Painter → Technique → *Canvas*

The painter often has an object, say a vase of flowers, from which he develops an inner artistic vision, which through the technique of oils, brushes, etc., he turns into the work of art, a canvas.

Composer → Technique → Notation → *Performance*

The composer has no comparable object, but rather begins directly with an inner artistic vision, which through music notation he turns into a score, the notated form of music. But this notated form, the score, is not music and neither is it the art work. Written music, like English, is only a symbolic language, symbolic of something else—which in the case of music is the composer's more complete inner idea, which comes into existence in the re-creation of the music in a live performance. The challenge for the composer is expressing his inner vision, which nearly always has an emotional identity, in a notational language which has no symbols at all for emotions.

Equally important is the process of the observer, who goes in the opposite direction. In the performance of music, the listener *experiences* the music immediately and has an *instantaneous* connection with the inner artistic idea of the composer.

An extra step is required of the observer of a canvas because he must first employ *exclusively* the eye. He must get past the experience of the eye before he can get to the experience of the artist.

But there are additional important distinctions. First, the art work of the painter is 'frozen' in time. In this way it is like a photograph. If you think of someone you know well, you can 'see' in your mind much of his features. But if you happen to have a photograph of that person, when you look at that a much more vivid picture of the person comes to mind. But the picture *never becomes the real person*. A recording, by the way, has this same relationship with music.

In the case of the performance of music, the direct experience through which the listener communicates with the composer is always in the present tense, and seems so even when one listens to older music. For example you can listen to thirteenth-century dance music and with little effort 'see' in your mind the palace room, the dancers, and, through meter and rhythm, often the actual dance steps, as if you were actually present. Looking at a thirteenth-century painting of a dance scene would give you none of this, indeed a thirteenth-century painting would appear to be little more than a cartoon.

A final important distinction lies in the nature of the existence of the art work. A finished canvas exists as a work of art even if it is hanging in a closed museum where no one can see it. A composition, on the other hand, exists *as genuine music* only in performance, which implies the presence of a listener—as there would be no purpose in a performance if there were no one to hear it. Therefore in a musical performance the listener is not an observer at all, but a *participant* in a live aesthetic experience.

THE AESTHETICS OF MUSIC

Unlike a painting which is, and may be judged as, a finished art object, music exists only in a live, present-tense experience. It follows, therefore, that the difficulty in formulating a meaningful and universal theory of aesthetics in music is that it must take into account not only the product of the composer, but the circumstances through which it is re-created in performance and heard. Because composer, performer and listener all play a role in determining the final aesthetic experience in music, we must begin by carefully examining each of the constituent parts of the musical experience: the composer and his inner idea, which through his technique in writing music he expresses in the form of a notated score, which is re-created in the form of a live performance, which is perceived by a listener:

THE COMPOSER AND HIS INNER IDEA

Composer → Technique → Notation → Performance → Listener

If music were a static art, if there were no performances of music and instead one examined a score on display and *imagined* the music, as one examines a painting and imagines the artist's inner idea, then all of 'aesthetics in music' would be centered here in the study of the composer's idea. While this is not the case, everything that we mean by aesthetics in music begins here with an original idea which will be communicated through performance to a listener. Let us consider the nature of this inner idea.

Does only the 'genius' have the ideas from which great music is constructed? When Mozart died, his wife immediately sold all his completed works, thinking she would get the best price while he was still remembered. But, interestingly enough, she *saved* his incomplete works and sketches for her two children, reasoning that if one of them wanted to be a composer he would be guaranteed success by having Mozart's melodies to use! It certainly would be a good place to begin, but great music is the product of more than just great melodies. One only has to see the sketches of Beethoven to observe how a composer can begin with a rather mundane idea and gradually shape it into something special. So the answer to this question is, No!

Are great composers born and not made? They certainly seem to be people with remarkable innate mental gifts. But there is a danger in thinking of this gift being in their genes for it is demonstrated over and over again in cases where father and son are composers: genius does not transfer, nor is it inherited. And the same thing is true in the brain's left hemisphere disciplines, as the example of Einstein demonstrates.

It does seem that the Mozarts and the Einsteins are born with their genius and no amount, or absence, of education seems to contribute to the quality of their genius. But if we accept the idea that some men are simply born different, born with genius, how do they differ from us? They probably have much more in common with the rest of us than we might suppose. For, as Croce points out, it is only because we have so much in common that we are able to recognize their genius.

> Nor can we admit that the word *genius* or artistic genius, as distinct from the non-genius of the ordinary man, possesses more than a quantitative signification. Great artists are said to reveal us to ourselves. But how could this be possible, unless there were iden-tity of nature between their imagination and ours, and unless the difference were only one of quantity? It were better to change *poets are born* into *men are born poets*, some men are born great poets, some small. The cult of the genius with all its attendant superstitions has arisen from this quantitative difference having been taken as a difference of quality. It has been forgotten that genius is not some-thing that has fallen from heaven, but humanity itself. The man of genius who poses or is represented as remote from humanity finds his punishment in becoming or appearing somewhat ridiculous. Examples of this are the *genius* of the romantic period and the *superman* of our time.
>
> But it is well to note here, that those who claim unconsciousness as the chief quality of an artistic genius, hurl him from an eminence far above humanity to a position far below it. Intuitive or artistic genius, like every form of human activity, is always conscious; otherwise it would be blind mechanism. The only thing that can be wanting to artistic genius is the reflective consciousness, the superadded consciousness of the historian or critic, which is not essential to it.[1]

1   Croce, *Aesthetic*, 14.

We recognize a part of ourselves in every composer and in every composition and this is because of the common emotional characteristics which are passed down to us genetically. We differ, both in ordinary life and in art, in the quality of the expression and in the meaning of these emotions as understood through varying individual experiential histories.

The idea that the greatest composers are 'born and not made' should not disturb us as each of us through our life experiences arrive at an individual level of 'intelligence,' which can presum-ably be increased by mental activity. It certainly seems the case that right hemisphere 'intelligence' is the sum of our experience and that further experience expands that experiential base. Surely there is no stronger justification in performing only the best music than in permitting ourselves the opportunity to grow through the communication with great minds.

In any case, the artist begins with an *inner* idea; art begins with thought. In music this 'thought' is associated with right hemisphere and hence the word 'thought' itself is a problem as it is usually associated with reason, or the left hemisphere. The word most often substituted is 'intuitive,' but this seems vague to us and we prefer just 'thought,' with the understanding that we mean non-rational thought.

But art begins, as we said, in the mind as is perfectly illustrated in the engaging anecdote of Leonardo, who shocked the prior of the Convent of the Graces by standing for days gazing at *The Last Supper*, without ever touching it with a brush. His response to the prior addressed our point most succinctly.

> The minds of men of lofty genius are most active in invention when they are doing the least external work.[2]

2 Quoted in Croce, *Aesthetic*, 10.

In this regard, Croce takes the very rigid position that this inner thought is everything. He maintains that the formulation of this inner idea is synonymous with the finished art work and that if the idea is not perfectly defined it cannot be expressed in art.

> One often hears people say that they have many great thoughts in their minds, but that they are not able to express them. But if they really had them, they would have coined them into just so many beautiful, sounding words, and thus have expressed them. If these thoughts seem to vanish or to become few and meager in the act of expressing them, the reason is that they did not exist or really were few and meager. People think that all of us ordinary men imagine and intuit countries, figures and scenes like painters, and bodies like sculptors; save that painters and sculptors know how to paint and carve such images, while we bear them unexpressed in our souls. They believe that any one could have imagined a Madonna of Raphael; but that Raphael was Raphael owing to his technical ability in putting the Madonna on canvas. Nothing can be more false than this view.[3]

3 Ibid., 9.

We must forgive Croce's error here for he lived too early to profit from the medical research which finds us bicameral, with language in the left hemisphere and emotions centered in the right. Any lover who has ever tried to write a love letter knows this question, for these feelings, which can be very profound and precise, are never satisfactorily communicated in words. Music is the same. The experience of music is right hemisphere while musical notation, a symbolic language just like English, can never satisfactorily communicate the composer's complete inner idea.

How can we then determine who is a good composer and what is good music? We must first assume that if some composers are persons of greater depth and universality and are also capable of communicating their inner ideas, even if imperfectly, that we are capable of recognizing this form of communication due to our inheritance of a common genetic understanding of the emotions—which is the language of music in so far as the listener is concerned. This is what Croce was thinking about when he added that the first place to measure the success of varying artists in communicating universals of the spirit is in our own spiritual nature.

> The whole difference, then, is quantitative, and as such is indifferent to philosophy, *scientia qualitatum*. Certain men have a greater aptitude, a more frequent inclination fully to express certain complex states of the soul. These men are known in ordinary language as artists. Some very complicated and difficult expressions are not often achieved, and these are called works of art …
>
> We must hold firmly to our identification, because among the principal reasons which have prevented Aesthetic, the science of art, from revealing the true nature of art, its real roots in human nature, has been its separation from the general spiritual life, the having made of it a sort of special function or aristocratic club.[4]

4   Ibid., 13ff.

Having said this, what do we look for in the composer and his composition? How do we find high quality in music?

We must begin, once again, by avoiding the pitfalls of language. Because in English all music is included under one word, 'Music,' some have made the mistaken conclusion that all music is therefore somehow equal. A wide variety of music is available to us which uses the same notational language, but to say this makes all music equal in significance is just as absurd as saying Shakespeare and comic books are equal in significance because they both use letters of the alphabet or words of the same language. The reason great literature and great musical literature are more significant than less significant works has to do not with the language (although, of course, Shakespeare and Mozart *did* use beautiful language), but with what it is that the language represents.

One characteristic of the very best music is universality—music which speaks so clearly and compelling that it is understood on a wide level. It was this that Rossini was thinking of in answer to a question from Ferdinand Hiller regarding whether poetry and music could ever arouse an equal interest at the same time. Rossini replied,

> If the magic of tone has really seized the hearer, the word undoubtedly will always come off second best. But if the music doesn't seize the hearer, what is the good of it? It is useless then, if not superfluous or even detrimental.[5]

5   Quoted by Wagner in 'A Fragment on Rossini' (1869) in Richard Wagner, *Richard Wagner's Prose Works*, trans. William Ashton Ellis (New York: Broude Brothers, 1966), 8:377.

A nice summary of some additional qualities of good music is given by Percy Scholes:

> First, good music has vitality and bad music often has not. It is easier to recognize this characteristic than to define it. A melody which wanders aimlessly is not vital. Compare with such a melody the opening phrase of anyone of Beethoven's sonatas, symphonies or string quartets—a phrase which in every instance arrests the attention … We feel ourselves at once to be in the presence of *life*. And in a 'good' piece of music this feeling continues to the end of the composition …
>
> Originality. We may say that good music is 'individual' and 'personal.' Music lacking vitality is generally found to be a diluted extract of that of some other composer, or perhaps of so many other composers that no one composer can be named …
>
> There is no acid test for 'goodness' in music. The thoughtful consideration of a trained taste must be applied, directed by some such method of analysis as that indicated above. It may not be possible by such means to prove a composition to be a masterpiece, but at all events great masses of second-rate music can thus be put aside …
>
> Not all short-lived music is to be utterly condemned, for soundly-written journalism is a kind of literature. But it *must* be soundly written. There is, in fact, no excuse (beyond the commercial) for really 'bad' music in any place or for any purpose.[6]

6   Percy A. Scholes, *The Oxford Companion to Music*, 7th ed. (London: Oxford University Press, 1947), 770–773.

The 'commercial music' Scholes mentions in closing is music we call *constructed* music, music being turned out in great abundance by educational publishers today. This music is designed for a certain portion of the educational market, designed for mass sales, and is carefully written to meet the technical needs of that market. But it is certainly not inspired music. It is exactly the kind of music Mendelssohn had in mind when he wrote,

7 Mendelssohn, Letter to his Family, September 2, 1831.

Music composed with a purpose will never reach the heart, because it does not come from the heart.[7]

This kind of music has been around for a long time and for centuries serious musicians have made the same complaint. This example by Liszt can serve as the representative of numerous others.

A work which offers only clever manipulation of its materials will always lay claim to the interest of the immediately concerned—of the artist, student, and connoisseur—but, despite this, it will be unable to cross the threshold of the artistic kingdom. Without carrying in itself the divine spark, without being a living poem, it will be ignored by society as though it did not exist at all, and no people will ever accept it as a leaf in the breviary of the cult of the beautiful.[8]

8 Franz Liszt, Letter to August Kiel, September 8, 1855.

Wagner found this same lack of inspiration in much of the music of Meyerbeer, his much more popular rival in Paris.

In Meyerbeer's music there is so appalling an emptiness, shallowness and artistic nothingness, that—especially when compared with by far the larger number of his musical contemporaries—we are tempted to set down his specific musical capacity at zero.

However, Wagner notes, there are moments here and there when, inspired by the libretto, Meyerbeer would rise to moments of great beauty and inspiration. In these passages, Wagner, in 'sincerest joy and frank enthusiasm,' acknowledges these moments as examples of,

9 'Opera and the Nature of Music' (1851), quoted in Wagner, *Richard Wagner's Prose Works*, 2:100ff.

that genuine art-creation which must come to even the most corrupted music-maker, so soon as he treads the soil of a necessity stronger than his self-seeking caprice; of a necessity which suddenly guides his erring footsteps, to his own salvation, into the paths of sterling art.[9]

To discover good music the musician must first have cultivated good taste himself, as Croce implied above. He must then have the integrity to select the best music available to him and to reject everything else. Archibald T. Davison, the famous conductor of the Harvard University Glee Club, made this argument with regard to educational music in 1945.

The most serious demand is for teachers whose knowledge and experience of music is wide enough to guarantee a sound musical taste. Only when there is intelligent revolt against much educational material that now passes for music will there be hope for a productive music education in this country.[10]

10   Quoted in Willi Apel, *Harvard Dictionary of Music* (Cambridge: Harvard University Press, 1947), 472.

Having the good taste to understand the difference between good music and inferior music is probably more common than having the honesty and integrity to engage in what Davison calls, 'intelligent revolt.' Schumann was another who called upon musicians to fight this fight.

> You ought not help to spread bad compositions, but, on the contrary, help to suppress them with all your force.[11]

11   Robert Schumann, 'Maxims for Young Musicians,' 1848.

Does this kind of integrity in the selection of music really matter? Yes, but we must nevertheless recognize that in matters of art there will never be unanimity. Because we each approach any art work from the perspective of our own experiential and emotional background we will each always have a somewhat personal judgment. Croce expressed this as follows:

> Nevertheless, variety of judgments is an indubitable fact. Men disagree as to logical, ethical, and economical valuations; and they disagree equally or even more so as to the aesthetic.[12]

12   Croce, *Aesthetic*, 123.

Surely there is an obligation for education here in helping the student raise his perspective. It was here that Wagner also was placing blame.

> Why make such a fuss about the falsification of artistic judgment or musical taste? Is it not a mere bagatelle, compared with all the other things we falsify: commercial goods, sciences, food, public opinions, State culture-tendencies, religious dogmas, clover seeds, and what not? Are we to grow virtuous all of a sudden in Music? …
>
> The acceptance of the empty for the sound is stunting everything we possess in the way of schools, academies, and so on, by ruining the most natural feelings and misguiding the faculties of the rising generation … But that we should pay for all this, and have nothing left when we come to our senses … this, to be frank, is abominable![13]

13   Quoted in Wagner, *Richard Wagner's Prose Works*, 6:146ff.

Wagner was particularly critical of composers who take no ethical responsibility. In a parody of a familiar Protestant Credo, Wagner proposes the punishment he prefers for those who willingly propagate poor music.

> I believe in God, Mozart and Beethoven, and likewise their disciples and apostles;
>   I believe in the Holy Spirit and the truth of one, indivisible Art;
>   I believe that this Art proceeds from God, and lives within the hearts of illumined men;
>   I believe that he who once has bathed in the sublime delights of this high Art, is consecrated to Her forever, and never can deny Her;
>   I believe that through this Art all men are saved; ...
>   I believe in a last judgment, which will condemn to fearful pains all those who in this world have dared to play the huckster with chaste Art, have violated and dishonored Her through evilness of heart and ribald lust of senses; I believe that these will be condemned through all eternity to hear their own vile music.[14]

14   Ibid., 7:66ff.

THE COMPOSER AND HIS TECHNIQUE

Composer →*Technique* → Notation → Performance → Listener

The inspired composer's original inner idea is usually at heart one associated with *feeling*. It is not something he could express very well in words and in its first, intuitive, form it might even be something he could not express very well in music (Mozart excepted!). At some point the composer decides to communicate his ideas with others through musical composition. To do this, whether well or poorly, depends on the *technique* of composition, the next step in the aesthetic chain (*idea–technique–score –performance–listener*) in music.

   What do we mean by technique in terms of communicating ideas through music? Technique in composition in music exists on two primary levels, the first of which is purely *knowledge*. This is a highly technical form of knowledge that deals not only with every aspect of how to write music, but also with a whole range of technical information regarding the acoustic and performance considerations upon which music depends. Some of this knowledge is very specialized and absorbed through what we might call the composer's *practical* experience. A case in point is the composer's understanding of how music carries the listener along in time. When is a sense of movement in time desired and when is a 'sense of arrival' appropriate? One composer who understood perfectly how to combine his aesthetic ideas with these kinds of practical considerations was Beethoven, as the distinguished composer, Jan Meyerowitz, observes.

> Even with very little training we can place any short quotation from a Beethoven movement in the exact spot where it belongs in the piece, where it fulfills a very definite function in the whole structure. You can recognize whether it is a first or a second theme, an episode, a transition or a retransition, a coda, a beginning, a climax, the end of a development, etc. Each passage, each motif is so clearly devised for its very special, exclusive function that we can place it in its correct spot *in a composition we do not even know!*[15]

15   Meyerowitz, 'Do We Overestimate Beethoven?,' 79.

Of course, technique has its limits, for, in the end, all the technique in the world does not produce beautiful music. And, of course, the reverse is true: one may have beautiful ideas, but lacking technique one's ideas can never be turned into music.

But, there is a more significant limitation to technique: technique is a form of *knowledge*, that is to say, it is *rational*, it can be taught and learned. Thus we immediately encounter an aesthetic paradox: music is the communication of feelings (right hemisphere) and feelings are not rational (left hemisphere). Therefore, there must be an entirely different definition of 'technique' in composition and this has to do with the composer's ability to communicate feelings through a symbolic language which has no specific symbols for feeling. In order to achieve some understanding of what we mean by *this* kind of technique, we must consider briefly the development of symbolic languages themselves.

The earliest writing we know of early man are the pictures in the caves of France, dating from the last Ice Age. In a written language composed of pictures, as one also finds in the Egyptian tomb paintings, and in the ancient Asian languages, you have a language in which the written symbol is synonymous with one's experience (the symbol for 'cat' is a picture of a cat).

With regard to the development of left hemisphere language, a fundamental change occurred with the introduction of the much more efficient phonetic writing (now 'c–a–t' represents a cat, but does not look like a cat). This had the effect of putting a barrier between man's experience and his language, as explained by Marshall McLuhan.

The phonetic alphabet did not change or extend man so drastically just because it enabled him to read. Tribal culture had already coexisted with other written languages for thousands of years. But the phonetic alphabet was radically different from the older and richer hieroglyphic or ideogrammic cultures. The writing of Egyptian, Babylonian, Mayan and Chinese cultures were an extension of the senses in that they gave pictorial expression to reality, and they demanded many signs to cover the wide range of data in their societies—unlike phonetic writing which uses semantically meaningless letters to correspond to semantically meaningless sounds and is able, with only a handful of letters, to encompass all meanings and all languages. This achievement demanded the separation of both sights and sounds from their semantic and dramatic meanings in order to render visible the actual sound of speech, thus placing a barrier between men and objects and creating a dualism between sight and sound. It divorced the visual function from the interplay with the other senses and thus led to the rejection from the consciousness of vital areas of our sensory experience and to the resultant atrophy of the unconscious. the balance of the sensorium—or *Gestalt* interplay of all the senses—and the psychic and social harmony it engendered was disrupted, and the visual function was overdeveloped. This was true of no other writing system.[16]

16   Marshall McLuhan, 'An Interview,' *Playboy*, March 1969.

Once man turned to this new kind of writing, where the language–picture no longer corresponds with experience, things in our rational world become confusing.

Verbal identifications and confused abstractions begin at a tender age … Language is no more than crudely acquired before children begin to suffer from it, and to misinterpret the world by reason of it.[17]

17   Stuart Chase, *The Tyranny of Words* (New York: Harcourt, Brace, 1938), 56.

Another very important point is that from that moment we needed an intermediary, a teacher, to connect *us* with *our* language. Someone has to answer our questions, 'Why isn't *gnat* spelled with an *n*?' or 'When do we use *to, too,* or *two*?'

The development of our *right* hemisphere language, music, followed much the same course. Although early man had no pictorial equivalent for his music, his music *was* a means of directly communicating his feelings. This was such an effective system of communication that no further 'improvements' were needed over a great period of time.

The 'improvement' which came was music's equivalent of a phonetic alphabet, and we call it musical notation. In the case of instrumental music of Western Europe, this period was relatively recent and as with left hemisphere language, once notation arrived it also required an intermediary to connect the musician's experience with the notation, to show him how you really play what is on paper. But as Wagner points out, until the nineteenth century the composer was also present to tell the players how the music should *really* be played, a role now given over almost entirely to the conductor.

> Even today, although we have accustomed ourselves to a most minute notation of the nuances of phrasing, the more talented conductor often finds himself obliged to teach his musicians very weighty, but delicate shadings of expression by *viva voce* explanation; and these communications, as a rule, are better understood and heeded, than the written signs.[18]

In another place,[19] Wagner discusses the development of the dominance of the left hemisphere, and the separation of man from his feelings, in terms remarkably similar to McLuhan. 'Understanding,' by which he means what we call today the rational left hemisphere,

> through the process of imagination acquired a language by which it would make itself intelligible *alone* and in a direct ratio: as the rational man became more intelligible the feeling man became less. In modern Prose we speak a language which we do not understand as being related to Feeling, since its connection with the objects, whose impression on our faculties first generated the roots of speech (pictures), has become lost to us.

It is very difficult to speak objectively of the technique by which a composer communicates *feelings* through musical notation because, unlike the more academic kind of technique, *this* technique is a very personal one. Indeed, Wagner once said that the composer has to actually invent this kind of technique for himself. A musical thought, he says, is not something physically real, but,

> is something which has made in *im*pression on our feeling and which, in order to communicate it to others, we must invent an *ex*pression.

Wagner, in another place, defines more precisely how the composer does this. He points out that the poet, who deals in words, must go into more and more detail to define his meaning, while the composer does the reverse. The composer must concentrate his

18   Wagner, *Richard Wagner's Prose Works*, 4:192.

19   Ibid., 2:230ff.

emotional ideas into the most condensed and refined form, which he refers to as the *Melos*.

> To address the Feeling to any degree, the Poet wandered into that vague diffuseness in which he became the delineator of a thousand details, intended to set a definite shape before the imagination as clearly as possible. But the imagination, bombarded by a host of motley details, only master the proffered object by trying to grasp these perplexing details one by one, thereby losing itself in the function of pure Understanding … The composer's purpose, on the other hand, is to condense an endless element of Feeling into a definite point in order that it might be understood.[20]

20 Ibid., 2:277ff.

Presently we shall speak of how the performer and the listener find *personal* meaning in the *Melos*, but for the moment we should only like to point out that this form of feeling in music, that which we call the *Melos*, is the aspect of emotion in music which might be called 'Universal.' For example, nearly everyone, we believe, would find it emotionally 'wrong' to sing *Crucifixus* in place of *Hallelujah* in Handel's 'Hallelujah Chorus.' Why does it sound 'wrong?' It is not just because we are used to the word we know, it is because the *inherent* emotion of this music does not correspond to the word *Crucifixus*. Music, in other words, *does* have its own inherent emotional meaning. The composer must have the sensibility to create music which accurately reflects the emotional content of his inner aesthetic idea.

For the inspired composer, it is the world of feeling in which he dwells and nearly always he finds it very difficult to say anything important about his music through language. We see an interesting example of this problem in an unpublished diary, in which Wagner made some very private comments in 1864, when he first encountered the C♯ Minor Quartet, op. 131, of Beethoven. In these notes for himself, he did not write of the beginning key and where it modulated to, nor of the elements of melody, harmony, or rhythm, nor of counterpoint, scoring, articulations or dynamics.

This is what he wrote:

> (Adagio) Melancholy morning-prayer of a deeply suffering heart: (Allegro) graceful apparition, rousing fresh desire of life. (Andante and variations). Charm, sweetness, longing, love. (Scherzo) Whim, humor, high spirits. (Finale) Passing over to resignation. Most sorrowful renunciation.[21]

21 Ibid., 8:386.

Of course, since words themselves cannot describe very personal feelings, these particular words of Wagner will not suffice to describe this Beethoven composition for anyone else, even though these words do offer us an important insight into the nature and direction of his thoughts. We are confident that Wagner would agree that the end of the composer's technique is not to write music, but to express aesthetic ideas and feelings.

THE COMPOSER'S SCORE

Composer → Technique → *Notation* → Performance → Listener

> It is usual to distinguish the internal from the external work of art: the terminology seems to us infelicitous, for the work of art (the aesthetic work) is always *internal*; and what is called *external* is no longer a work of art.[22]

22 Croce, *Aesthetic*, 50–51.

What Croce reminds us here is very important. Although the score is a vital step, even an irreplaceable step in art music, the score is not to be considered *music*.[23] The score is a document in symbolic language which only *represents* the composer's original aesthetic inner idea. No matter to what degree of detail the composer notates his ideas on paper, no matter how much time and effort he expends, the score can never be considered as synonymous with his inner musical idea. We will discuss the primary reasons for this below, but the most important is because of the incapacity of the notational system itself, especially in its failure to account for the emotions.

23 In German this distinction is clear, for there is one word, *Die Noten*, for the notation and a separate word, *Die Musik*, for music.

Furthermore, in the case of music, even if another musician is capable of looking at the score and reading it while simultaneously 'hearing' in his mind the very detail of what he sees, he still cannot take this written document as being synonymous with the composer's inner idea. Croce mentions this and reminds us that it is not the score which is beautiful, only that which it represents.

> Writings are not physical facts which arouse directly impressions answering to aesthetic expressions; they are simple *indications* of what must be done in order to produce such physical facts. A series of graphic signs serves to remind us of the movements which we must execute with our vocal apparatus in order to emit certain definite sounds. If, through practice, we become able to hear the words without opening our mouths and (what is much more dif-

ficult) to hear the sounds by running the eye along the stave, all this does not alter in any way the nature of the writings, which are altogether different from direct physical beauty. No one calls the book which contains the *Divine Comedy,* or the score with contains *Don Giovanni,* beautiful in the same sense in which the block of marble which contains Michael Angelo's *Moses,* or the piece of colored wood which contains the *Transfiguration,* is metaphorically called beautiful.[24]

24   Croce, *Aesthetic*, 100–101.

Why can the score never be the same as the music? First, as we have said, the score is written in a left hemisphere symbolic language. It is being asked to represent the composer's right hemisphere musical idea, which is something it cannot by nature do. Since each hemisphere is oblivious to what the other knows, and perhaps even denies the very existence of the other, the left hemisphere simply does not understand music, save the rational aspects of it which can be notated.

Second, musical notation is not capable of precision. We have, for example, only one way of writing a dotted eighth-note followed by a sixteenth-note, while in the actual practice of performance this figure is played with great variety, under the influences of tempo, articulation and style. And in this regard, we skip over symbols such as dynamic markings, which are not only incapable of precision, but were never intended to be precise.

Having said all this, we must not lose sight of the fact that the score is, nevertheless, the special step in the chain of the aesthetic experience in music, which makes *real* music possible. The score remains the only way a composer can try to transmit his ideas and it is the only place the performer can look to discover the composer's inner idea. But the problem remains: musical notation cannot completely notate all there is to music. Furthermore, it will be read by performers, all of whom have different experiential histories and all of whom, therefore, will tend to see this notational language differently.

Finally, we must, however, assume that the score represents the composer's idea as precisely as the notation is capable or as precisely as the composer intended. That is, we must assume that it *is* the physical representation of the composer's idea.[25] If, therefore, a performance fails to communicate the composer's inner idea, the blame will always be assigned to the performer and not to the score.

25   We omit here the sins of editors and publishers who change the notation without telling us.

THE PERFORMANCE

Composer → Technique → Notation → *Performance* → Listener

It seems very odd to make this point, but music is for the ear! The fact is that since singers and instrumentalists read music on paper many of them begin to think of the eye as having the key to answers to problems in interpretation. More important to our discussion here is that if it is understood that music is something to be listened to then the end of music is the experience of the listener. For this reason performance must lie at the heart of any theory of aesthetics in music, for only in performance does music actually exist in the present tense.

At the same time, if we presume, as a matter of artistic integrity, that the performer's goal is to re-create the composer's original aesthetic idea, then it follows that we must assume the performer is indeed capable of doing this. Croce bases his assumption that the performer can do this on the following reasoning. The faculty of the composer which we call *genius* has its corollary in what we might call the *taste* of the performer. He says these are 'substantially identical' characteristics of artistic discernment.[26]

26 Croce, *Aesthetic*, 120.

We prefer to base the assumption that the performer should be able to re-create the composer's aesthetic idea on the shared emotional characteristics of the species together with the genetic aspects of music. In any case, we must assume this goal of the performer is possible, otherwise re-creation in performance would be inconceivable.

On the other hand, we must acknowledge that in saying the performer *should* be able to achieve this goal, we can not say he always does. We know all too well that with respect to left hemisphere language one may speak or write well, but based on erroneous concepts. In the same way, a performer may perform well, yet distort the composer's intent. Certainly it is wrong to think of a beautiful *performance* as the aesthetic goal. As Liszt once observed,

> A successful performance cannot as a rule be considered as a criterion of artistic worth.

It is rather the performance of the *composer's* beautiful idea which is the aesthetic goal.

Thus, by a 'poor performance' we mean not only that which is technically deficient, but also that which fails in its obligation to the composer. There are many ways this can result. In the performance of older music this may simply result from a lack of knowledge of performance practices.

Equally misinformed is the viewpoint that the performer should simply play the music as written, 'letting the music speak for itself.' The error in this viewpoint lies in the false notion that the work of art is the score, when in fact the work of art is that which the score *represents*. Koussevitzky, in particular, complained about those who failed to understand this.

> Nowadays we can often hear 'authorities' exclaim, in reviewing a performance: 'Let the music speak for itself!' The danger of this maxim lies in its paving the way for mediocrities who simply play a piece off accurately and then maintain that they 'let they music speak for itself.' Such a statement is not right, in any event, because a talented artist renders a work as he conceives it, according to his own temperament and insight, no matter how painstakingly he follows the score markings. And the deeper the interpreter's insight, the greater and more vital the performance.
>
> A perfect rendition of a work can have two different aspects which are equally faithful to the score. One part can be called mechanically perfect, the other organically perfect. The first gives the listener the beauty of mathematical balance, symmetry and clarity, the second the complete, vital, pulsing *elan vital* of the composition. The one wants to present a pretty facade, while in the other the musical creation—its basic idea—comes to life. The one may be compared to a completely symmetrical building, the other to a great Gothic cathedral, in parts asymmetrical and yet an organic unit. The one is always friendly and pleasant, but always retains something superficial, like a lively stage set. The other touches the listener, arouses him, fuses him with the reality of the basic idea, and allows him to experience the *elan vital* of the composition.[27]

27   Quoted in Carl Bamberger, *The Conductor's Art* (New York: McGraw-Hill, 1965), 144.

Closely related to this is the error made by the performer who thinks of his responsibility as one of 'understanding' the score in a rational sense, or an academic sense. By this we mean looking at a score as an accumulation of forms, types of melody, harmonic practice, etc. In doing so, he 'fails to see the forest because of the trees.' The trees in this metaphor is the notation, much of it mere grammar. The 'forest' in this metaphor is *feeling*, as Wagner reminds us.

> An artist addresses himself to Feeling, and not to Understanding. If his work is discussed in terms of Understanding, then it might as well be said he has been misunderstood.[28]

28   Wagner, 'Eine Mitteilung an meine Freunde,' 1851.

We do not ignore these theoretical aspects of the language of music, but, as the great pianist, Alfred Brendel, suggests, in doing so we must not lose our focus on *feeling.*

> Although I find it necessary and refreshing to *think* about music, I am always conscious of the fact that *feeling* must remain the Alpha and Omega of a musician; therefore my remarks proceed from feeling and return to it.[29]

29 Quoted in *The New Yorker*, May 30, 1977.

Wagner criticized the school of interpretation led by Mendelssohn on these very grounds.

> At a time when I came into contact with a young musician who had been in Mendelssohn's company, I was perpetually told of the master's one piece of advice: In composing never think of making a sensation or effect, and avoid everything likely to lead to it. That sounded beautiful and right enough, and in fact not a single faithful pupil of the master's has ever chanced to produce a sensation or effect ... I imagine all the teachings of the Leipzig Conservatory are founded on that negative maxim, for I have heard that the young folk there are plagued to death with its warning, whilst the most promising talents can gain them no favor with their teachers unless they forswear all taste for music not in strict accordance with the Psalms ...
>
> Once I begged one of the most reputed older musicians and comrades of Mendelssohn to play me the Eighth Prelude and Fugue from the first part of the Well-tempered Klavier, as that piece had always had such a magical attraction for me; I must admit that seldom have I felt so great a shock as that experienced from his friendly compliance. At any rate there then was no question of gloomy German Gothic ... under the hands of my friend the piece flowed over the keyboard with such a 'Grecian gaiety' ... that involuntarily I saw myself seated in a neo-Hellenic synagogue, from whose musical rites every trace of the Old Testament accentuation had been decently purged away. That singular reading was still ringing in my ears, when one day I begged Liszt to cleanse my musical feelings from the painful impression. He played for me the Fourth Prelude and Fugue. Now, I knew what to expect from Liszt at the pianoforte ... but I never expected what I learnt that day. For then I saw the difference between study and revelation; through his rendering of this single fugue Liszt revealed the whole of Bach to me, so that I now know of a surety where I am with him, can take his every bearing from this point, and conquer all perplexity and every doubt by power of strong faith.[30]

30 Wagner, *Richard Wagner's Prose Works*, 4:344.

The performance which is most objectionable is that by the performer who simply substitutes his own interpretation without any consideration for the composer at all. This is usually a matter of excess. Certainly it is the performer's duty to seek the *Melos* of the composition and certainly no two performers will arrive at exactly the same understanding of this, but we speak of the performer who goes too far and simply creates the music after his own image. Wagner found the performers who were most guilty of this excess to be conductors.

> Lo there is the man who certainly thinks least about himself, and to whom the personal act of pleasing has surely no place, the man beating time for an orchestra. He surely fancies he has bored to the very inside of the composer, yes, he has drawn him on like a second skin! You won't tell me that *he* is plagued with the Upstart-devil, when he takes your tempo wrong, misunderstands your expression marks, and drives you to desperation at listening to your own composition.
>
> Yet *he* can be a virtuoso too, and tempt the public by all kinds of spicy nuances into thinking that it after all is he who makes the whole thing sound so nice. He finds it neat to let a loud passage be played quite soft, for a change, a fast one a wee bit slower. He will add for you, here and there, a trombone effect, or a dash of the cymbals and triangle. But his chief resource is a drastic cut, if he otherwise is not quite sure of his success. Him we must call a virtuoso of the Baton.[31]

31   Ibid., 7:114.

We must then ask, where is the line between a personal interpretation of the composer's intent and a performance in which the personality of the performer replaces the intent of the composer? How does the performer maintain integrity to the composer's original inner idea? What is the proper relationship between the performer and the score?

The highest aesthetic goal in performance is reached when the performer comes to understand that the score is not the work of art, but is only a left hemisphere document written in a left hemisphere symbolic language. However, unlike other types of left hemisphere documents, including the entire range from newspapers to legal briefs, this document is written in a symbolic language in which the symbols themselves lack precision. The symbols require interpretation. By interpretation we mean, what did the composer hear, or have in mind, when he chose these symbols?

In other words, the highest aesthetic goal in performance *begins* when the performer comes to understand that not *all* the music is found on the score page. This is what is meant when some of the greatest musicians of all time observed:

Gustav Mahler:
   The important things in music are not found in the notes.

Felix Weingartner:
   There are musicians who only see the notes and those who see *behind* the notes.

Franz Liszt:
   With notes alone nothing can be accomplished; one thirsts for soul, spirit, and actual life.

Bruno Walter:
   The performer's duty is to recreate the spirit of the score, not the letter of the score.

The 'missing' music they are describing is that which could *not* be notated in left hemisphere symbols. It is the central core of feeling, or emotional meaning, which Leopold Stokowski called, 'the inner spirit of the music and all the potentialities lying dormant on the printed page of the score,' Koussevitzky called the *elan vital*, and Weingartner, 'the spiritualizing internal factor that gives the music its very soul.'

It is when *this* is missing in performance that the re-creation of the music fails to achieve its highest aesthetic end. It is when the performer fails in this responsibility that the composer suffers, for he knows his most important and beautiful ideas have not been communicated. It is interesting, in this regard, to read Verdi's anguished cry regarding performances he heard of his opera, *Aida*.

For my part, I vow that no one has ever, ever, ever, ever even succeeded in bringing out all the effects that I intended ... No one!! Never, never ... Neither singers nor conductors!![32]

32 Bamberger, *The Conductor's Art*, 312.

In contrast, it is also interesting to read Weingartner's testimony that he found Wagner to be the model of what the contribution of the performer should be.

He obviously aimed in his own performances not only at correctness, but at bringing out that to which the sounds and notes are only the *means* ...

He sought the unifying thread, the psychological line, the revelation of which suddenly transforms, as if by magic, a more or less indefinite sound-picture into a beautifully shaped, heart-moving vision, making people ask themselves in astonishment how it is that this work, which they had long thought they knew, should have all at once become quite another thing ... Out of the garment of music there emerges the *spirit of the artwork*; its noble countenance, formerly only confusedly visible, is now unveiled, and enraptures those who are privileged to behold it. Wagner calls this form, this quintessence, this spirit of the artwork its *melos*.[33]

33 Quoted in ibid., 98ff.

This is the performer's great contribution, to communicate *this* to the listener. But how does he find the 'music' that is not written in the score?

His goal must be to hear what the composer heard, not see what the composer wrote. To do this he must learn not to initially fix his concentration on the notation itself, but rather learn to see the notation somewhat passively, giving the notation (the composer) a chance to speak to him before he begins to apply his own personality to the notation. We are reminded of the old European rule of etiquette regarding conversation with a royal person: 'Don't speak until spoken to.' The great conductor, Eugen Jochum, describes this process perfectly.

I take care first of all to have, so to speak, a passive attitude toward the work; that is, to establish a lack of bias, a receptiveness that will allow the work of art to best develop its own reality. First I abandon myself to the work, which I read through again and again ... without my thinking of particulars. What is this tempo? How does it relate to later tempi? What is the nature of the themes? How do they relate to one another? These questions are left for later.

In this manner the tempo focuses 'by itself,' the piece becomes so self-evident that it begins to live its own life, still practically completely withdrawn from my conscious will and shaping impulses. The condition described as passivity now reveals itself as having many layers; only the intellectual layers of consciousness are actually passive. The possessive, forming will is only excluded by the thinking mind. On the other hand, the deeper layers of consciousness are vibrantly awake, straining toward the work, so that an emotional field of tension is formed in which the 'spark leaps over.' This is the decisive point. When it is reached, conscious work of the greatest precision can and must begin. It is only important that the impulse of the will and conscious control do not take over too soon, and that one's own personality is not brought in at the wrong moment. It is thus a question of humble acceptance of a law, of listening to an inner meaning.[34]

34 Quoted in ibid., 260.

This is as it should be, for the symbols themselves are not the music, they are for the most part little more than grammar. We might add, finally, that we believe memorization is the most immediate tool for discovering the music which is not on the page. Memorization allows the performer to mentally stand aside, so to speak, to hear the music in his mind, eliminating the intrusion of our most dominant sense, the eye, and its strong tendency to fix on the left hemisphere form of the music, the symbolic notation itself. Ironically, memorization, not needing to *see* the score, helps the performer to 'see' more of the *music*. This wisdom is engagingly expressed in a famous Sufi parable.

> A student was walking through the village, whereupon he came to the house of his teacher. There he saw his teacher, on his hands and knees, apparently looking for something in the grass.
>
> 'Master, what are you looking for?'
>
> 'I am looking for my house key,' his teacher replied, 'Come and help me look for it!'
>
> The student joined his teacher in the grass, but after a time he concluded that there was probably no key in the grass at all and that this was intended as some sort of lesson.
>
> 'OK, Master, where did you actually lose your house key?'
>
> His teacher answered, 'Well, actually I lost it somewhere inside my house.'
>
> 'Why,' said the student, 'are we looking out here in the grass?'
>
> 'Because there is more light here,' reassured the teacher.

Once he has found the full meaning of the music, to the best of his integrity, the performer is now ready to participate in the re-creation of the music. But here there remains a personal role, which is inevitable and unavoidable, for the performer's perspective will always be influenced by his own experiential history. We think of this subsequent relationship between performer and the score as being somewhat analogous to you and your banker both having a necessary key to open your safe deposit box. The score is certainly the most important 'key,' but without the 'key' of the performer, music would never exist in its true form.

The Listener

Composer → Technique → Notation→ Performance → *Listener*

Both the composer's efforts to transmit his inner aesthetic ideas into a notated form and the efforts required to re-create these ideas through performance imply the expectation of a listener. Indeed, as two great composers observed, would music even make sense without a listener?

> Music remains meaningless noise unless it touches a receiving mind.[35]
> [Hindemith]

> Music is a means of communicating with people, not an aim in itself.
> [Moussorgsky]

The experience of the listener is the logical end of the aesthetic chain in music. This being the case, the question follows, what does the contemplative listener experience in music? This question should also be at the heart of the goals of music education.

There are two broad areas of personal development affected when the contemplative listener experiences music. First, as with the case of any other kind of intellectual exchange, we profit from the exposure to superior minds. By 'superior minds,' in this case, we mean that the great composer differs with us not so much in kind, as in degree. As Croce expresses this,

> What is generally called par excellence art, collects intuitions that are wider and more complex than those which we generally experience.[36]

By contemplative listening the listener is able to place himself in the perspective of the composer, to experience through his experience. By this process we are lifted to a higher level of insight, as Croce again explains:

> To judge Dante, we must raise ourselves to his level: let it be well understood that empirically we are not Dante, nor Dante we; but in that moment of contemplation and judgment, our spirit is one with that of the poet, and in that moment we and he are one thing. In this identity alone resides the possibility that our little souls can echo great souls, and grow great with them in the universality of the spirit.[37]

35   Hindemith, *A Composer's World*, 18.

36   Croce, *Aesthetic*, 13.

37   Ibid., 121.

Because listeners vary greatly in their experiential histories, this opportunity for growth may be easy for some and more difficult for others. It was for this reason that Bruno Walter once observed that it is the special duty of musicians to remember those most in need of this kind of development.

> There are people for whom life begins anew every morning. It is they who are ever more deeply touched by every renewed encounter with Schubert's *Unfinished*, it they whom the perusal of a familiar Goethe poem moves with the force of a first impression; people over whom habit has no power; people who, in spite of their increasing years and experience, have remained fresh, interested, and open to life. And there are others who, when they watch a most glorious sunset or listen to the Benedictus in Beethoven's *Missa Solemnis*, feel scarcely more than 'I know this already'; and who are upset by everything new and unusual—in other words, people whose element is habit and comfort. It is for the former that our poets have written, our artists created, and our musicians composed; and it is for them, above all, that we perform our dramas, our operas, oratorios, and symphonies. As regards the latter, we artists must try, time and time again, to burst open the elderly crust they have acquired, or with which many of them may have been born; our youthful vigor must call upon theirs or revive whatever is left of it.[38]

38 Bruno Walter, quoted in Bamberger, *The Conductor's Art*, 176ff.

The second area of personal development for which the contemplative listener has access through music includes special and unique opportunities for self-discovery. It is here that the concept of the Melos of the music achieves a personal meaning. As we have described above, it is the Melos, the concentrated, pure form of emotion, which is communicated through performance. Each listener then takes in this form of the emotion, sifts it through his own experiential understanding of that emotion, and in the process comes to understand in a more defined sense this aspect of himself. It is this experience in music which is comparable to what Aristotle called *Catharsis* with respect to Tragedy.

Wagner says this is the great value of music, to allow us to 'gaze into the inmost Essence of ourselves.' In addition to this very important observation, Wagner, in the following, also points out that music *is* the means by which the feeling part of us communicates, a part of us which cannot otherwise speak; that music, unlike painting, does this directly; and that the quality of a composition is determined by the degree to which it does this.

Music, who speaks to us solely through quickening into articulate life the most universal concept of the inherently speechless Feeling, in all imaginable gradations, can once and for all be judged by nothing but the category of the *sublime*; for, as soon as she engrosses us, she transports us to the highest ecstasy of consciousness of our infinitude. On the other hand what enters only *as a sequel* to our contemplation of a work of plastic art ... the required effect of *beauty* on the mind, is brought about by Music by her very *first entry*; inasmuch as she withdraws us at once from any concern with the relation of things outside us, and—as pure Form set free from Matter—shuts us off from the outer world, as it were, to let us gaze into the inmost Essence of ourselves and all things. Consequently our verdict on any piece of music should be based upon a knowledge of those laws whereby the effect of Beauty, the very first effect of Music's mere appearance, advances the most directly to a revelation of her truest character through the agency of the Sublime. It would be the stamp of an absolutely empty piece of music, on the contrary, that it never got beyond a mere prismatic toying with the effect of its first entry, and consequently kept us bound to the relations presented by Music's outermost side to the world of vision.[39]

39   Wagner, *Richard Wagner's Prose Works*, 5:77.

The reason why this is so important is because only in the right hemisphere, in which music is our most effective language, can we understand our emotions. We know the left hemisphere cannot do this. Language is one of our most important forms of communication, but anyone who has tried to write a love letter knows that language is quite inferior in the realm of the expression of emotions. Furthermore, when it comes to our most sensitive feelings we often don't want to talk about them at all! Here language fails us.

Everybody knows that language is a very poor medium for expressing our emotional nature. It merely names certain vaguely and crudely conceived states, but fails miserably in any attempt to convey the ever-moving patterns, the ambivalences and intricacies of inner experience, the interplay of feelings with thoughts and impressions, memories and echoes of memories, transient fantasy, or its mere runic traces, all turned into nameless, emotional stuff. If we say that we understand someone else's feeling in a certain matter, we mean that we understand why he should be sad or happy, excited or indifferent, in a general way; that we can see due cause for his attitude. We do not mean that we have insight into the actual flow and balance of his feelings, into that 'character' which 'may be taken as an index of the mind's grasp of its object.' Language is quite inadequate to articulate such a conception. Probably we would not impart our actual inmost feelings even if they could be spoken. We rarely speak in detail of entirely personal things.[40]

40   Susanne K. Langer, *Philosophy in a New Key* (New York: Mentor Books, 1948), 92.

In another place, Langer concludes,

> Language and music are similar in that both are means for express-
> ing something. The difference is that language is principally a means
> for expressing ideas, and music is principally a means for expressing
> feelings.[41]

41 Susanne K. Langer, 'The Cultural Importance of the Arts,' *The Journal of Aesthetic Education* 1, no. 1 (Spring 1966): 5–12.

Two additional writers expressed this same truth as follows:

> Language is not subtle enough, tender enough to express all we
> feel, and when language fails, the highest and deepest longings are
> translated into music.
> [Robert Ingersoll]

> Where words fail, music speaks.
> [Hans Christian Anderson]

Most especially Science will never come to our aid on the subject
of emotions, because emotions are *individual* and Science is only
interested in the *general*. This represents a basic difference between
the left hemisphere world of science and the right hemisphere of
art. Even in the case of the study of human nature itself, science
takes as significant only the general, the average (which represents
no one in particular) and avoids the individual, which is in every
case unique. The psychologist who studies aggressive behavior, for
example, is interested only in those characteristics which create a
syndrome of aggression, but can draw no useful conclusion from
any one individual aggressive person. Art is just the reverse. We
might say: The scientist dreads the presence of individuality as the
death of science; the artist dreads the loss of individuality as the
death of art.

> The reason why scientific description, so far from helping expres-
> sion, actually damages it, is that description generalizes. To describe
> a thing is to call it a thing of such and such a kind; to bring it under
> a conception, to classify it. Expression on the contrary, individual-
> izes … Expressing an emotion has something to do with becoming
> conscious of it.[42]

42 Robin George Collingwood, *Principles of Art* (Oxford: Clarendon, 1938), 112.

Indeed, Liszt points out that it is one of the values of Music that
it relieves us briefly from our left hemisphere dominant world.

> Only in music does feeling, actually and radiantly present, lift the
> ban which oppresses our spirit with the sufferings of an evil earthly

43   Liszt, Letter to August Kiel,
September 8, 1855.

power and liberate us with the white-capped floods of its free and warmth-giving might from 'the demon Thought,' brushing away for brief moments his yoke from our furrowed brows.[43]

In summary, as the distinguished conductor Celibidache points out, it is this personal relationship with our feelings that gives Music its universality.

> Music is the shortest way to expressing how little music has to do with the notes. The notes are physical, coarse textured phenomena. But in its relationship to another note, a note can become something which finds an echo in the human emotions. The reasons for this can be experienced in phenomenology, and demonstrated wonderfully. If it weren't for this relationship between the physical phenomenon of sound and the emotional reaction, no one would want to make music, no one would have any interest in it. But it wakens something in us, and we sing and play to liberate ourselves again [through] this responsiveness.[44]

44   Sergiu Celibidache, quoted in
Los Angeles Philharmonic Notes,
April 1989.

Within this general topic of the individual's personal development through the contemplation of music, there are two other opportunities for personal insight which deserve consideration. First, since it is evident that the two hemispheres of our brain differ so dramatically in the nature of their specialization, it may well be that there are separate forms of understanding unique to the right hemisphere for which music may function as a means of introduction. Because the right hemisphere is mute, and because the left hemisphere tends to deny its existence, there may be forms of right hemisphere understanding which we rarely 'think' of, but are nevertheless a part of our daily lives. We offer, as a single example, the pleasure which we experience in the right hemisphere in returning to something we already know. In music we experience this in recapitulations and *da capi*, but this differs only in kind from seeing a town we used to live in, or an old friend, after some years. But there is nothing comparable to this in the left hemisphere. Numbers begin at one and never return and we would find little pleasure in coming to the end of a novel and finding the instruction to go back and re-read the first five chapters!

Next, the contemplation of music may aid in awakening the listener to his innate relationship to Nature and his environment. There is a very common phrase we use, 'human nature,' which serves to remind us, in the juxtaposition of these two words, of our being inescapably a part of Nature. Man, from the earliest of times, has not been content to take Nature as he found it. Rather, he has reached out to know it better, to improve upon it through new sounds, new colors, new shapes, etc. It is in this reaching out to know Nature that man became human.

> There is, however, no group of human beings which has not culti-vated devices for enriching contact with the sensory world ... The word ordinarily used to describe this class of satisfactions ... is aes-thetic ... the potentials for becoming a human being, as compared with a less complex kind of animal, lie largely in this enrichment and elaboration of the sensory and motor ranges of experience.[45]

45 Gardner Murphy, *Human Potentialities* (New York: Basic Books, 1958), 34.

For early man, education consisted of a lifelong interaction with nature and his environment. After the introduction of language, especially reading, education began to rapidly move from the expe-riential to the conceptual. Today we have an educational world which is almost completely oriented to the left hemisphere. Many critics have pointed out that one consequence of this one-sided education has been the loss of an understanding of one's relation-ship with nature.

> It is no mere coincidence that this devouring sense of alienation from nature and one's fellow man—and from one's own essential self—becomes the endemic anguish of advanced industrial societ-ies. The experience of being a cosmic absurdity, a creature obtruded into the universe without purpose, continuity or kinship, is the psychic price we pay for scientific 'enlightenment' and technologi-cal prowess.'[46]

46 Theodore Roszak, *Where the Wasteland Ends* (New York: Doubleday, 1972), 168.

> Because of the influence of scientific objectivity on our culture, we no longer have any sense of participation or involvement in the world around us or in our own lives. We not only feel removed from our environment but also sense an alienation from the nonintel-lectual and irrational parts of ourselves. Western man has forgotten that what science can measure is actually only a small portion of what man can know.[47]

47 Sam Reese, 'Discovering the Nonintellectual Self,' *Music Educators Journal*, May 1974.

It is curious to us that we have adopted so narrow a concept of education. It takes no more than common sense to realize that a very great part of our behavior is still genetically rooted in sys-tems which are experiential in character. As Ornstein points out, this part of our nature is little concerned with being educated in scientific objectivity.

All animals' 'world-processing systems' highlight events that inspire action. For human beings, such an event might be a sudden noise heard over the normal clamor of traffic; one person in a crowd of faces with a gun; a few coughs interspersed among the hundreds of thousands of breaths you take. Our evolved system simplifies everything that happens, to make sense out of an enormous amount of shifting and chaotic external and internal information and to adapt to the world sufficiently well to survive. There are only a few features of the millions of possible features in the world that we need notice. We simply discard the rest.

Everything outside goes inside into the world processor; what comes out are a few features of the world, features that usually kick off our reactions and our percepts. And the system usually works. When was the last time you bit into a nice hard rock? When was the last time you decided to run straight into a wall?

The neural underpinnings of the mind evolved in part to select only that which is of use to survival. Consequently, the mind tends not to care too much about frills that modern, well-educated human beings are trained to think important, such as self-understanding and accurate perception.[48]

48   Robert Ornstein, *The Evolution of Consciousness* (New York: Prentice Hall, 1991), 165.

It seems clear that for most people it is the right hemisphere, our experiential hemisphere, which connects us with our environment.

UCLA psychologists in a series of hearing tests found that when normal 'right-handed people are given these listening tests with verbal stimuli, a slight right-ear advantage emerges. However, when the tests use environmental sounds—such as a car starting—the right hemisphere does the processing, giving the advantage to the left ear.[49]

49   Craig Buck, 'Knowing the LEFT from the RIGHT,' *Human Behavior*, June 1976.

We even know *which* part of the right hemisphere does this.

It turns out that the right hemisphere plays a dominant role in man's perception of his environment …

One can conclude that the posterior part of the right hemisphere is involved in the direct analysis of information about the external environment.[50]

50   Doreen Kimura, 'The Asymmetry of the Human Brain,' *Scientific American*, 1973, 228.

We also know that feeling and emotion and Music are for the most part processed in the right hemisphere. Does this suggest that Music may in some way serve as a bridge between man and his natural world? Wagner believed there was an immediate relationship.

We have called Music the revelation of the inner vision of the Essence of the world.[51]

51 'Beethoven' (1870), quoted in Wagner, *Richard Wagner's Prose Works*, 5:108.

The way the listener connects with his environment through Music, Wagner describes in this way. He defines the artistic faculty as primarily one of receptivity. The inartistic person is one whose education has cut him off from impressions from the outside; he looks at the world in its relation to him, rather than in his relation to it. The artistic person is one who has learned to 'give himself up without reserve to the impressions which move his emotional being.'[52]

52 Ibid., 1:286.

The value, according to Wagner, is not that the music imitates nature, as in Aristotle's phrase 'Art mirrors Nature,' but that the listener interprets it and synthesizes it with his own experiential vision.

> When we described the relation of the merely imitative Mime to the truly poetic 'interpretative' artist as resembling that of the monkey to the man, nothing was farther from our mind than an actual belittlement of the Mime's qualities …
>
> What scares the plastic and poetic artists from contact with the mime, and fills them with a repugnance not entirely unakin to that of the man for the monkey, is not the thing wherein they differ from him, but that wherein they resemble him. Moreover what the one imitates, and the other 'interprets,' is one thing and the same: Nature; the distinction lies in the How, and in the means employed.[53]

53 Ibid., 4:79.

Liszt saw a much more fundamental relationship between man, his art, and Nature.

> Man stands in inverse relations to art and to nature; nature he rules as its capstone, its final flower, its noblest creature; art he creates as a second nature, so to speak, making of it, in relation to himself, that which he himself is to nature. For all this, he can proceed, in creating art, only according to the laws which nature lays down for him, for it is from nature that he takes the materials for his work, aiming to give them then a life superior to that which, in nature's plan, would fall to their lot. These laws carry with them the ineradicable mark of their origin in the similarity they bear to the laws of nature, and consequently, for all that it is the creature of man, the fruit of his will, the expression of his feeling, the result of his reflection, art has none the less an existence not determined by man's intention, the successive phases of which hold the world in

54   Franz Liszt, 'Berlioz and his "Harold" Symphony,' *Neue Zeitschrift fur Music* (1855), 43.

its course, and, like the world, it is impelled toward an unpredicted and unpredictable final goal in perpetual transformations that can be made subject to no external power.[54]

For the contemplative listener, foremost among 'the laws which nature lays down for him,' of which Liszt speaks, there one which is truly fundamental to music. Everything the musician does, and the listener experiences, is at one with a physical law of nature—the overtone series.

In addition, the contemplation of music may help the listener to understand a sense of community, within his broader environment. As explained in a recent publication,

> Decrying the ascendancy in America of 'an MBA civilization, in which the ability to run a business is considered the highest skill a man could possibly have,' [Robert] Marsh made a significant point: Commerce does not create civilizations, art does, because that task requires grappling with the deepest questions of human life and meaning. In this light, he argued, music is a *moral* force, binding communities together in unique ways.[55]

55   The Report of the National Commission on Music Education (Reston: menc, 1991), 5.

Finally, since music communicates so intimately with the experiential part of our nature, one has to wonder to what extent the contemplation of music might actually induce changes in us. In the matter in which it is so evident that 'we are what we eat,' can the same be inferred with respect to experiences? It is in this regard that our attention was drawn to a comment by Schumann.

> No children can be brought to healthy manhood on candy and pastry. Spiritual like bodily nourishment must be solid. The masters have provided it; cleave to them.

The fact is there is even extraordinary clinical evidence to suggest that something similar to 'you are what you eat' happens with respect to our brain's response to our experiences. Experiences actually change the brain physically! Thus the choice the listener makes, with respect to the quality of music he listens to, is a very serious responsibility, for it *literally* changes his brain.

> The brain's neurons change the communication pathways among themselves in response to experience, says Dartmouth's Bharucha. Working with a computer model of brain cells called a neural network, Bharucha found that as he exposed the model to music, the layer of brain cells responsible for processing individual notes sent

signals to another layer whose cells gradually became specialized for recognizing specific groups of notes, or chords. These cells in turn signaled a third layer of cells that gradually became responsible for recognizing groups of chords as belonging to particular keys. This hierarchical grouping occurred even though Bharucha gave the brain model no explicit instructions as to how the cells should connect themselves. Instead, the network simply organized itself in a manner that reflected the intrinsic organization of music itself.[56]

We have seen that a definition of aesthetics in music must include, as equally influential, the participation of the composer and his expression through the score, the re-creation of the composer's ideas through performance, and the reception by a contemplative listener.

But this has all been expressed in an idealized state, whereas in real life the conditions under which one encounters music may have an impact on the nature of the aesthetic experience. Croce discusses this factor with respect to art in general.

When speaking of the stimuli of reproduction we have added a caution, for we said that reproduction takes place, if all the other conditions remain equal. Do they remain equal? Does the hypothesis correspond with reality?

It would appear not. In order to reproduce an impression several times by means of a suitable physical stimulus it is necessary that this stimulus be not changed, and that the organism remain in the same psychical conditions as those in which was experienced the impression that it is desired to reproduce. Now it is a fact that the physical stimulus is continually changing, and in like manner the psychological conditions.

Oil paintings grow dark, frescoes fade, statues lose noses, hands and legs, architecture becomes totally or partially a ruin, the tradition of the execution of a piece of music is lost, the text of a poem is corrupted by bad copyists or bad printing. These are obvious instances of the changes which daily occur in objects or physical stimuli. As regards psychological conditions, we will not dwell upon the cases of deafness or blindness, that is to say, upon the loss of entire orders of psychical impressions; these cases are secondary and of less importance compared with the fundamental, daily, inevitable and perpetual changes of the society around us and of the internal conditions of our individual life. The phonetic manifestations or words and verses of Dante's *Commedia* must produce a very different impression on an Italian citizen engaged in the politics of the third Rome, from that experienced by a well-informed and

56   William F. Allman, 'The Musical Brain,' *U. S. News & World Report*, June 11, 1990. Diana Deutsch, of the University of California, San Diego, has found some evidence to suggest that we hear the octave as such a pure interval due to the channeling of nerve impulses to the same nerve cell in the brain. See David Stipp, 'What Happens When Music Meets the Brain,' *Wall Street Journal*, August 30, 1985.

intimate contemporary of the poet. The Madonna of Cimabue is still in the Church of Santa Maria Novella; but does she speak to the visitor today as to the Florentines of the thirteenth century? Even though she were not also darkened by time, must we not suppose that the impression which she now produces is altogether different from that of former times? And even in the case of the same individual poet, will a poem composed by him in youth make the same impression upon him when he re-reads it in his old age, with psychic conditions altogether changed?[57]

57   Croce, *Aesthetic*, 123–124.

In fact the conditions under which we perceive music *can* affect its aesthetic quality. Together with this is another qualification, which must also be considered as a 'condition' of the musical experience. This is the fact that a composer's aesthetic aim is also conditioned by the intent of his own purpose and by the function his music fulfills. Therefore, in addition to an abstract definition of aesthetics in music, we also need a means of correlating the principles of that definition with the practical usage of music.

CLASSES OF MUSIC AND CONDITIONS OF PERFORMANCE

We believe the performance of music in actual practice falls naturally into four classes: Art Music, Educational Music, Functional Music and Entertainment Music. Music of high aesthetic quality is *possible* in each class, subject to the conditions of the performance.

We begin our discussion by defining Art Music, the highest aesthetic, the highest quality of experience. We believe Art Music is the most unequivocal in definition. The other three classes, in turn, seem to us more clearly defined in how their conditions and functions differ with Art Music.

I. ART MUSIC

Art Music we believe is defined by four conditions, *all* of which *must always be present.* These are:

1. Art music is inspired.

Art music is music in which it seems evident that the composer has made an honest attempt to communicate genuine feelings. Feelings, which may range from lofty and noble to superficial and vulgar, must be presumed to be generally recognizable in music, as they are in any other art form, including painting, sculpture, dance, and architecture. In Art Music, lofty and noble feelings are paramount.

Due to the common genetically understood nature of emotions, it must also be understood that in music emotions or feelings can not be 'faked.' They will always be recognized as such by any contemplative listener. Croce adds the following observation.

> For by sincerity may be meant, in the first place, the moral duty not to deceive one's neighbor; and in that case it is foreign to the artist. For indeed he deceives no one, since he gives form to what is already in his soul.[58]

58   Croce, *Aesthetic*, 53.

2. Art Music has no purpose other than the communication of its own aesthetic content.

Art Music is free of any purpose or function, save the spiritual communication of pure beauty. As Croce points out,

Art is independent both of utility and of morality, as also of all practical value. Without this independence, it would not be possible to speak of an intrinsic value of art, nor indeed to conceive an aesthetic science, which demands the autonomy of the aesthetic fact as its necessary condition.[59]

59   Ibid., 116.

3. Art Music is that which enjoys a performance faithful to the intent of the composer.

4. Art Music must have a listener capable of contemplation.

If any of these conditions are missing, the performance must result in a lesser aesthetic experience. For example, the Ninth Symphony of Beethoven played in a stadium, during the half-time of a professional football game, would fail for the lack of the presence of Condition Number Four. The same Symphony heard in a concert hall, but in a poor performance, not faithful to the intent of the composer, would fail for the lack of the presence of Condition Number Three.

II. Educational Music

Educational Music may or may not have the same conditions as Art Music, excepting Condition Number Two; it may or may not occur within an educational institution. Educational Music is didactic music, music which has the specific and *additional* aim to educate.

III. FUNCTIONAL MUSIC

Functional Music is music put at the service of something else. We include here, for example, all kinds of religious music, music for weddings, music for the military, and occupational music. Functional Music may share the same conditions as Art Music, excepting Condition Number Two.

One may ask, How can a Mozart Mass be called Functional Music, and not Art Music? Indeed, for Croce, some art may be functional.

> The extrinsic purpose is not necessarily, precisely because it is such, a limit or impediment to the other purpose of being a stimulus to aesthetic reproduction. It is therefore quite false to maintain that architecture, for example, is by its nature imperfect and not free, since it must also obey other practical purposes; in fact, the mere presence of fine works of architecture is enough to dispel any such illusion.[60]

60   Croce, *Aesthetic*, 102.

In the case of music we disagree and do so because of the role of the listener, as we have defined it. If the observer were not contemplatively listening to the music, but were rather contemplating religious thoughts, then the Mozart Mass becomes merely a very high level of Functional Music. If, on the other hand, the observer is a contemplative listener of music, forgetting about religion, then the Mozart Mass is Art Music, but has failed in its purpose as church music.[61] Even Croce, in spite of his opinion above, admits that aesthetic contemplation can hinder functional purpose.

61   Such works as the Verdi Requiem, or the Mozart Requiem, are performed today as Art Music and are almost never used at anyone's funeral.

> It cannot however be denied that aesthetic contemplation sometimes hinders practical usage. For instance, it is a quite common experience to find certain new objects ... so beautiful, that people occasionally feel scruples in maltreating them by passing from their contemplation to their use. It was for this reason that King Frederick William of Prussia showed such repugnance to sending his magnificent grenadiers, so well adapted to war, into the mud and fire of battle.[62]

62   Croce, *Aesthetic*, 102.

Military and wedding music are examples of music in which the contemplative listener is missing entirely. How about airport, supermarket and elevator music where there is no listener at all? According to the definitions we have given, recorded music without listeners is not to be considered music at all.

IV. ENTERTAINMENT MUSIC

Entertainment Music is music with no purpose other than to please, which is missing Condition Four, the contemplative listener. For this reason, Entertainment Music may be inspired music, but the composer is unlikely to be inspired by lofty and noble emotions, knowing there will be no contemplative listener.

It is for these reasons that Entertainment Music can never be Art Music. But, one might protest, when a tired businessman goes to the opera at the end of his work day, is this not for him Art Music which is also a very high level form of Entertainment Music? Franz Josef of Austria once posed this very question. When Mahler was music director of the State Opera in Vienna, he once became frustrated because of the disruption of those arriving late. Therefore he began a policy of having all late arrivals placed in a separate room until the first intermission. When informed of this, the emperor was puzzled and observed, 'But after all, the theater is meant to be a pleasure.'[63]

The answer is No, Entertainment Music and Art Music can never be the same thing because of Condition Number Two: Art Music has no purpose other than the communication of its own aesthetic content. It is inconsistent with the nature of great art to have any extrinsic purpose, including the purpose to entertain.

At the beginning of the nineteenth century most listeners of Art Music were found in very small numbers in usually small 'music rooms' in aristocratic palaces. The very environment was conducive to the contemplative listener. But after the fall of Napoleon there was a movement, beginning with military bands playing outdoors, toward large public audiences. This introduced new aesthetic questions and Wagner was one of the first important critics to write about this with respect to public music. It might be interesting to see how he viewed this question at that time. First, he states the principle mentioned above, as follows:

> The highest principle of aesthetics [is that] the 'objectless' alone is beautiful, because being an end in itself, in revealing its nature as lifted high above all vulgar ends it reveals at like time that to reach whose sight and knowledge alone makes ends of life worth following; whereas everything that serves an end is hideous, because neither its fashioner nor its onlooker can have aught before him save a disquieting conglomerate of fragmentary material, which is first to gain its meaning and elucidation from its employment for some vulgar need.[64]

63   Quoted by Alma Mahler, *Gustav Mahler* (New York: Viking, 1969), 136ff.

64   Quoted in Wagner, *Richard Wagner's Prose Works*, 4:107.

It therefore follows, he adds, that even having the mere purpose of 'to please' must remove a composition of the category of the highest art.

> Thus is born what alone we can term the *Good in art*. This is exactly like the *Morally good*; for this, as well, can spring from no intention, no concern. On the contrary, we might define the Bad as the sheer aim-to-please both summoning up the picture and governing its execution. As we have had to accord our public no developed sense of artistic form, and hardly anything beyond a highly varying receptivity, aroused by the very desire of entertainment, so we must recognize the work that merely aims at exploiting this desire as certainly bare of any value in itself, and closely approaching the category of the morally bad in so far as it makes for profit from the most questionable attributes of the crowd.[65]

Wagner was quite adamant about this, writing in another place,

> I assert that it is impossible for anything to be truly good if it is reckoned in advance for presentation to the public and this intended presentation governs the author in his sketch and composition of an artwork.[66]

And yet again,

> Popularity: the curse of every grand and noble thing.[67]

The great musicians have always understood a certain duty in their art, which was to lead the public to higher aesthetic purpose by way of example. Liszt once wrote a beautiful thought in this regard, a plea to all musicians to think higher.

> Let us ... cast out all but the noblest ambitions, to concentrate our concerns on efforts that dig a deeper furrow than the fashion of the day! Let us renounce, too, for ourselves, in the dreary time in which we live, all that is unworthy of art, all that lacks permanence, all that fails to shelter some grain of eternal and immaterial beauty which art must lighten gloriously in order to glow itself, and let us remember the ancient prayer of the Dorians, whose simple formula was so reverently poetic when they petitioned the gods: 'to give them Good through Beauty!' Instead of laboring so to attract and please listeners at any price, let us rather strive ... to leave a celestial echo of what we have felt, loved, and endured! Let us learn ... to demand of ourselves whatever ennobles in the mystical city of art rather than to seek from the present, without regard to the future, those easy crowns which, scarce assumed, are at once dulled and forgotten![68]

65   Ibid., 6:67.

66   Ibid., 6:55.

67   Ibid., 7:74.

68   Franz Liszt, *Chopin* (Paris, 1852).

It takes great courage and conviction to pursue the highest goals in music when the public is so easily satisfied by a diet of only entertainment. No one knew this better than Wagner.

> To take a last look back upon the picture afforded us by the Public ... we might compare it with a river, as to which we must decide whether we will swim against or with its stream. Who swims with it, may imagine he belongs to constant progress; because it is so easy to be borne along, and he never notices that he is being swallowed in the ocean of vulgarity. To swim against the stream must seem ridiculous to those not driven by an irresistible force to the immense exertions that it costs.[69]

69 Wagner, *Richard Wagner's Prose Works*, 6:94.

In this book we shall seek to define what sense of aesthetics shaped the musical performances of the ancient world. Our procedure will be to examine the classes of music and the conditions of performance as reflected in the descriptions and comments made by the people who actually heard and experienced those performances. Our hope is that, in following the chronological development of their descriptions and definitions with respect to the experience of music, we may help the reader come to a broad understanding of the development of the role and meaning of the performance of music in society.

We shall also consider how the earlier philosophers struggled in an attempt to describe music on a physiological level and as well their aesthetic discussions of Pleasure and Pain, and of Beauty, in those cases where they might contribute to our understanding of their theories of aesthetics in music.

With regard to those peoples before the Christian Era, while we can gain perhaps some insights from iconography, especially in the case of the Egyptian tomb paintings, our greatest resource is the literature through which early peoples described the musical practice as they knew it. As we are therefore limited to extant literature, the musical practice of Greece and Rome must of necessity be the focus of this volume.

Our interest in the musical practice of these ancient civilizations is limited to aesthetics as expressed in actual performance. We should therefore note that it is for this reason that we do not delve into the technical descriptions of ancient instruments or the theoretical practices of tuning systems, descriptions of scales, etc., which are the primary subjects most books on ancient music discuss in detail.

PART 2

Aesthetics in the Musical Practice of the Ancient Civilizations of the Near East

3 MESOPOTAMIA

For the ancient civilizations of Greece and Rome we are fortunate to have a considerable extant literature to help us judge what these ancient peoples themselves thought about music and music practice. Even in the case of the ancient Hebrew peoples we have the Old Testament which, even though it has its limits as an historical document, provides important clues to the role of a wide variety of music.

With respect to Egypt and the countries of the Eastern Mediterranean there is very little extant literature, save clay tablets. Here we must call upon deduction based on iconography, but no matter how logical our conclusions seem, we must remember these icons represent thousands of years of experience which we really can never know.

A common characteristic of most of the oldest civilizations is that music was always associated with the gods.[1] It is clear that the earliest peoples did not associate music with the other arts, such as painting and sculpture, as we do today. Perhaps it was simply that music is the only art you can not see. It is easy to understand how painting, for example, could be thought of as a craft, for in looking at a painting you can immediately see the craft. But music is different. While it can not be seen, it can be immediately understood on an experiential level even by people with no training in music. No doubt it was this mysterious aspect, something which you could experience but not see, which reminded them of the gods.

In nearly all early societies dancing is associated with music and so, for example, the Greek choruses danced when they sang. The most reasonable explanation for this association is that they considered dance as the part of music which you *could* see. Dance was *visual music* long before it became a separate art form. It may be entirely inaccurate, therefore, to describe music as 'accompanying' the dance in these early periods.

1 Alfred Sendrey, in *Music in the Social and Religious Life of Antiquity* (Rutherford: Fairleigh Dickinson University Press, 1974), 31, points out that among the most ancient civilizations, only China and the Hebrews did not ascribe music to divine origin. This book is the finest book on the subject and we are frequently indebted to it. The fact that there is a disproportionate amount of information about temple music for this period only reflects the fact that 'history' was written by the priests.

Sumeria and Akkad (3000 bc)

The area of the Near East which we call Mesopotamia consisted first of isolated city-states, among the oldest of which were Ur, Susa, and Kish. The area known as Babylonia consisted of Sumeria to the south and Akkad to the north. During the third millennium bc these peoples were united by the Semitic king, Sargon I.

Based on the surviving evidence, Sumeria is the oldest civilization we know which developed a sophisticated tradition of music. Since they believed music was of divine origin, they created temples for a number of gods, all of whom they believed had to be entertained, to keep them in good spirits, by singing and playing of instruments.[2] Among these gods was one called Enlil, the father of humanity, who governed with a musical instrument called *al*.

The diffusion of this musical culture can be seen in a stone slab (ca. 800 bc) which lists titles and first lines for religious songs, royal songs, festival songs, songs that recount heroic deeds, folk songs for shepherds and craftsmen, and love songs.[3]

Art Music

As might be expected, the little information we have of musical practice among these earliest of civilizations centers on the music of the temple and the banquet. It is difficult to know how often music was listened to for its own sake, as art music. We can only hope to look for its presence through clues in language, sometimes the language of mundane documents. For example, we are interested in a seal cylinder, a financial record of the Sumerian king, Gudea of Sumeria (2600 bc), which tells of a payment to a peasant flute player. It is apparent that he was being paid to improve himself in order to be able to perform a higher level of music than his usual functional music. The clay cylinder reads,

> Enlulim, the shepherd of the lulim-kids, for the Lord Ningirsu, was given a share in his cult to cultivate diligently flute playing to fill the forecourt of Eninnu with joy.[4]

An even more beautiful description of what Art Music must have been to these people is found on a clay cylinder from 2400 bc.[5]

2 Sendrey, *Life of Antiquity*, 31.

3 Ibid., 32.

4 Curt Sachs, *The History of Musical Instruments* (New York: Norton, 1940), 71.

5 Francis Galpin, *Music of the Sumerians* (Westport, CT: Greenwood Press, 1970), vii.

To fill with joy the Temple court
And chase the city's gloom away,
The heart to still, the passions calm,
Of weeping eyes the tears to stay.

The musicians employed by the kings to play such music no doubt enjoyed many privileges, but also certain drawbacks. The excavations of Ur have uncovered mass graves documenting that the king was buried with his entire court, in one case seventy-four people! In one of these mass graves the musical instruments were found together with female skeletons. Drinking cups found by each skeleton suggest an obligatory mass suicide.[6]

6 Sendrey, *Life of Antiquity*, 35.

FUNCTIONAL MUSIC

The stone slab mentioned above gives not only the titles of actual psalms used in the temple, but also specific instructions regarding accompanying instruments, some of which are quoted by Farmer.[7]

> The precentors a chant to the drum shall sing.
> To the sacred timpani [*lilis*] shall sing.
> To the aulos and tambourine shall sing.

7 Henry G. Farmer, 'The Music of Ancient Mesopotamia,' *The New Oxford History of Music* (London: Oxford University Press, 1966), 234.

We gain some idea of the scope of the activity of temple music in an account which lists the names of one hundred and sixty-four liturgical singers for a single year. Another document lists sixty-four female temple slaves for the temple at Lagash.[8] The titles of some of these musicians indicate one was in charge of supervising the choir and another responsible for the rehearsal of the choir. Farmer mentions a similar document from Akkad in which some temple musicians are described as those who 'know the melodies' and are 'masters of the musical movements.'[9] The latter is perhaps a reference to dance.

8 Sendrey, *Life of Antiquity*, 32.

Sendrey describes what this temple music may have been like.

9 Farmer, 'The Music of Ancient Mesopotamia,' 235.

The earliest orders of the sacred service were simple. They consisted of sacrifices, in which supplications to the gods were supported by musical ceremonies. The songs were accompanied by flutes, aulos, and lyres. Certain ceremonies required accompaniment of sacred drums. Later, this simple religious service developed into a complicated pattern of liturgical actions. It contained four or more hymns, performed with choir singing and instrumental accompaniment. In coeval records we find a minute description of the liturgical ceremony, as it was performed during the full bloom of Sumerian culture.

First of all, a chosen priest applied the magic formula necessary for the purification and consecration of the participants. Then the psalmists had to sustain the opening supplication with their singing; a professional musician (*nar*) furnished the required instrumental accompaniment. The principal psalmist (a sort of 'high priest') chanted a hymn to the gods Ea, Shamash and Marduk, to the accompaniment of the aulos. Sacred services ended with the singing of an epic poem, which must have been well known to everyone, since the entire congregation took part in it.[10]

10　Sendrey, *Life of Antiquity*, 33.

Probably the country people had their own gods which they also worshiped with music. There is an interesting reference to shepherds not acknowledging the god of the city of Kullab, Dumuzi.

11　Ibid., 32.

The shepherds do not play flutes and pipes before him.[11]

There is of course evidence of military music and it is assumed that some kind of trumpet is meant when its sound is compared 'to the howling of the storm and the roaring of the bull.'[12]

12　Ibid.

Entertainment Music

Given the rather stark realities of life at this time it is easy to understand that the very word for music in the Akkadian language, nigutu or ningutu, also has the connotation of 'joy' and 'merry-making.' This aim of music can also be seen in one of the oldest Sumerian art works, the Standard of Ur (twenty-fifth century BC) pictures a singer and a harp player at a royal banquet, which was planned to 'dispel gloom.'[13]

13　Farmer, 'The Music of Ancient Mesopotamia,' 236.

The most important secular festival was the annual New Year festival, which included banquets with music and dance. A fragment of a very ancient vase, dating from 3200 BC, shows such a scene, with two lyre players accompanying a dance.

Babylonia (2000–562 bc)

Soon after the beginning of the second millennium the Amorites invaded Sumeria, ending the Sumerian Empire. From the Sumerian capital, Babylon, we take the name of the people of the next period. The Babylonians were extraordinary people, excelling in mathematics, astronomy, geography and medicine. They founded schools in which they taught cuneiform writing and they first introduced the 354 day calendar with twelve hour days.

With respect to culture, the Babylonians seemed to have little of their own and we can therefore understand that they absorbed completely that of the Sumerians, including their musical traditions. We find a new god, however, Ea, who was god of the mysteries and arts, especially associated with the flutist-psalmist.

Art Music

The stone slab of Assur, mentioned above, mentions the titles of twelve 'royal hymns' and five solemn songs in honor of Ishtar, the god of love and temple prostitution. Since these kinds of songs do not seem appropriate either to the temple or as entertainment for the banquet, they were possibly serious songs which were listened to.

Included also in this category are the songs of lament, which sing the deep sorrow of the fleeting nature and mortality of man. Perhaps this hymn of lamentation will serve as an example.

> O temple, thy skilled master is not present; thy fate who decrees?
> The psalmist, who knows the song, is not present; thy fate to the drum he chants not!
> He that knows how to touch the drum is not present, thy fate he sings not![14]

We are told such lamentations were sung with 'flutes of crystal' and harps during the Festival of Tammuz.[15] This festival also included some epic productions which told of the marriage, death and resurrection of the god Tammuz, sung antiphonally by choirs.[16]

Toward the end of this Babylonian period we come to Nebuchadnezzar and his court music ensemble, which is described in detail in the Book of Daniel, 3:5 and 3:15, of the Old Testament. This account illustrates the problem one encounters in attempting

14 Quoted in Galpin, *Music of the Sumerians*, 54.

15 Sendrey, *Life of Antiquity*, 55.

16 Ibid., 58.

to consider the older parts of the Old Testament as literal history. The Book of Daniel was written four hundred years after the events it describes and so it is prone to all the mistakes and exaggerations of oral tradition.

Furthermore, the actual instruments mentioned in Daniel, *karna, mashrokita, kathros, sambyke, pesanterin,* and *sumponyah,* are expressed in several languages, including Greek, and at least two of them have no agreed upon modern meaning.[17] In view of these difficulties, the modern translator has tended to simply make up names of instruments which might be familiar to his readers. Thus the King James Version gives us a typical renaissance band, consisting of cornett, flute, harp, sackbut, psaltery, and dulcimer! The Revised Standard Version (1952) invents an ensemble of horn, pipe, lyre, trigon, harp, and bagpipe.

FUNCTIONAL MUSIC

The same music, instruments, and even the language, used by the Sumerians in the temple are continued by the Babylonians.

> Their priests took over in their own liturgy the Sumerian hymns, litanies and prayers, and recited or sang them in the old language, just as Hebrew chants are still sung in our days' synagogues in the original language.[18]

Sendrey finds that their hymn and psalm singing seemed to be mostly responsive, a tradition continued by the Hebrews.[19]

The stone slab of Assur also includes psalms of the Babylonians, as well as songs for craftsmen, shepherds, and festival songs intended to encourage crops to grow.[20]

ENTERTAINMENT MUSIC

The Assur slab contains titles of many love songs, including a group curiously titled, '24 songs of the breast for the flute.'[21]

17   Sachs, *The History of Musical Instruments,* 83ff.

18   Carl Bezold, *Ninive und Babylon* (Bielefeld: Velhagen & Klasing, 1926), 148.

19   Sendrey, *Life of Antiquity,* 53.

20   Ibid., 54.

21   Ibid.

ASSYRIAN EMPIRE (750–606 BC)

The Assyrians, who took their name from the god Ashur, were a fierce and warlike collection of tribes who conquered Babylonia. They built the great capital city of Nineveh and began to develop unusual skills in the art of sculpture.[22] Indeed, if it were not for the great stone-reliefs now in the British Museum this empire would probably never be mentioned today, for after their defeat in 612 BC they disappeared from history.

Aside from the stone-reliefs, we can see these feared warriors had also some appreciation for music in the fact that whenever they put a city to the sword, they spared the musicians who, with the rest of the valuable booty, were sent back to Nineveh.[23]

FUNCTIONAL MUSIC

Most of the famous stone-reliefs seem to picture welcomes for the returning armies. The most interesting of these shows a reception for Ashur-Idanni-Pal (668–626 BC) by the city of Susiana, in Elam. Here we see three male harp players, two of whom are dancing while playing; a man playing a kind of dulcimer, who is also dancing; a male aulos player; four female harp players; female players of an aulos and a drum; together with thirteen singers.

ENTERTAINMENT MUSIC

The most notable reference to banquet music of this period is a story involving the above mentioned king. As the story goes, when Assyria was invaded by Teumman, the Elamite king, Ashur-Idanni-Pal consulted the goddess Ishtar, who calmed his fears and recommended he turn to music and feasting. We are told that while he was thus enjoying himself, the news of the defeat of Teumman arrived.[24]

22 Carl Engel, *The Music of The Most Ancient Nations* (London: Reeves, 1909), 24ff.

23 Farmer, 'The Music of Ancient Mesopotamia,' 237.

24 Ibid.

The Persians (600–330 bc)

The final chapter in the progression of independent Mesopotamian empires comes with the rule of the Persians. A series of kings, Cyrus II, Cambyses II, Darius I, and Xerxes, ruled over a powerful and civilized empire. While our small amount of surviving information, especially that written by the Greeks, does not portray these years in their best light, it is nevertheless clear the the Persians absorbed and continued the cultural traditions of Babylon and Assyria.

Educational Music

As we shall see below, the early Greeks believed music was a means of teaching bravery, courage and noble ideals. However, when we approach the Christian Era we begin to find writers who say the opposite, that music inculcates 'effeminacy.' This attitude must have been present much earlier in some areas, for when Cyrus wanted to change a defeated people from warlike to harmless subjects, we read that his solution was to take away their arms and replace them with musical instruments. According to Herodotus, when Cyrus heard that the Lydians had revolted, he consulted with Croesus, who advised him,

> Pardon the Lydians, but lay upon them these edicts, that they may revolt no more nor be any danger to you: send them an injunction that they carry no more arms; bid them wear tunics under their cloaks and soft slippers on their feet; and give them orders that they themselves shall play the flute and the lyre and educate their children to be shopkeepers. Soon enough, my lord, you shall see them become women instead of men, so that they will be no further threat to you as rebels.[25]

25   Herodotus, *Histories*, 1.155. Plutarch, in 'The Apophthegms of Kings and Great Commanders,' told essentially the same story, but regarding Xerxes and the Babylonians, commanding they should practice 'singing and playing on the aulos.'

At the beginning of the Christian Era, however, Strabo, describes an educational system in which music played an important role.

> From five years of age to twenty-four they are trained to use the bow, to throw the javelin, to ride horseback, and to speak the truth; and they use as teachers of science their wisest men, who also interweave their teachings with the mythical element, thus reducing that element to a useful purpose, and rehearse both with song and without song the deeds both of the gods and of the noblest men.

And these teachers wake the boys up before dawn by the sound of brazen instruments, and assemble them in one place ... They require them also to give an account of each lesson, at the same time training them in loud speaking and in breathing, and in the use of their lungs.[26]

26 Strabo, *The Geography of Strabo*, trans. Horace Leonard Jones (Cambridge, MA: Harvard University Press, 1959), 15.18.

FUNCTIONAL MUSIC

While the use of trumpets for playing military signals is extensively documented in these early civilizations, it is possible this practice had evolved into something more artistic with the Persians. According to Kastner the armies of the Persian Empire began their battles by lifting their trumpets and playing a 'war hymn.'[27]

27 Georges Kastner, *Manuel général de musique militaire à l'usage des armées françaises* (Paris, 1848), 23, 30.

ENTERTAINMENT MUSIC

Our most descriptive accounts of the entertainments of the Persians are written by their rivals the Greeks and thus they emphasize the extravagant aspects of court life. Athenaeus records two anecdotes relative to the dinner music of the court of Cyrus the Great (585–529 BC). First he quotes the *Persian History* by Heracleides of Cumae,

> In most cases the king breakfasts and dines alone, but sometimes his wife and some of his sons dine with him. And throughout the dinner his concubines sing and play the lyre; one of them is the soloist, the others sing in chorus.[28]

28 Athenaeus, *Deipnosophistae*, 4.145.

Athenaeus does not mention how many concubine musicians performed for these dinners here, but in another place he says 'three hundred women watch over him.'[29] Annarus, the viceroy under Cyrus, wore women's clothes and ornaments, according to Athenaeus, and, although he himself was technically a slave of the king, his dinners were always accompanied by a hundred and fifty women, playing on harps and singing.[30]

29 Ibid., 12.514.

30 Ibid., 12.530.

Presumably this tradition continued for two centuries, for several accounts mention that when the Greeks finally brought an end to this empire by the defeat of Darius III in 330 BC, they carried away 329 concubine musicians from the court.[31]

It is not clear if Plutarch's reference to these kings refers to these older ones or kings of his generation, but it sounds as if he

31 Farmer, 'The Music of Ancient Mesopotamia,' 239.

is retelling a tale told many times and improved upon each time with the telling.

> The Persian kings, when they contain themselves within the limits of their usual banquets, suffer their married wives to sit down at their tables; but when they once design to indulge the provocations of amorous heats and wine, then they send away their wives, and call for their concubines, their gypsies, and their songstresses, with their lascivious tunes and wanton galliards. Wherein they do well, not thinking it proper to debauch their wives with the tipsy frolics and dissolute extravagances of their intemperance.[32]

32 Plutarch, 'Conjugal Precepts.'

Finally, we should point out that in all the earliest civilizations for which some form of records are extant we find music already developed as an 'international language.' That is, we do not find traditions specific to each country, but rather the same traditions and usages of music in all countries. This tells us, if we did not suppose it to be true for other reasons, that we are not seeing in these most remote records a description of the beginnings of music, but descriptions of music already long established. We see this most clearly in the instruments themselves, where we see the same instruments in every country, not instruments indigenous to each country. Moreover, we see these instruments in seemingly late stages of development. The first pictures of string instruments are pictures of sophisticated instruments and the only types of flutes known today (transverse, blocked and panpipes) are the same, and only, types already found in the earliest specimens.

Thus, in these earliest accounts of music in civilization we find practices familiar to our own experience, not practices remote and distant to us. The same can be said for aesthetics, or at least for the purpose of music. The purposes of music mentioned in Sumera, 2400 BC, describe ways we use music today: for joy, to dispel gloom, to calm and to comfort whose who are sad. For these ancient peoples, as for us, music has to do with our emotions and spirits. It is no surprise to us that the word for music in the ancient Akkadian language also meant 'joy.'

Although the extant accounts of music speak little of what we call art music, that there may have been more art music than we can document. Surely the Babylonian songs which sing of the fleeting nature and mortality of man must have been attentively listened to. And surely it must have been for the value of such music, and not for the background functional music, that musicians enjoyed sufficient social importance that the invading Assyrian warriors, while killing everyone else, spared them.

It is with regard to the choral music of the temple that we find evidence that genuine education in music must have existed. There can be no other alternative explanation when a temple official is identified as being in charge of the choral rehearsals. These are not singers who repeat a simple refrain week after week, something which would require no rehearsal. And surely whatever it was they rehearsed, it was a music far more sophisticated than that of the primitive military trumpet which is described as 'howling' and 'roaring.'

Toward the end of the Mesopotamian civilizations the aesthetic values clearly change. Instead of reports of the 'joy' of music, we now read of 'wanton' and 'lascivious' music. The values of listening to music are lost in the lavish entertainments which follow wealth—the hallmark of a 'successful' civilization. In such an environment sensitivity is not esteemed and thus we see music come to be associated with the effeminate. It is a term meant to reflect a lack of respect for music and it is a term we will find in all countries in the century before the Christian era.

4   EGYPT (2686–52 BC)

In Egypt, as in other ancient civilizations, the spiritual nature of music caused it to be linked in myth with the gods. We find this especially interesting with respect to the limited hieroglyphic language of Egypt. For example, the symbol which represents the god who created earth is also used to represent the god Hesu, who created music.[1] Another dual god, Hathor, was both the goddess of love and the goddess of music. A hymn to Hathor found in the temple of Dandera, seems to refer to the 'music of the spheres,' a familiar notion among the ancient philosophers, most notably Pythagoras.

> To thee, the heaven and its stars make music,
> Sun and moon sing praises to thee,
> The whole earth is making music for thee.[2]

There is an extraordinary painting from the more recent Greco-Roman temple at Medamund, north of Thebes, which includes a complete hymn to the god Hathor. We see a group of female musicians, with harp, drum, and lute, beneath a hieroglyph description:

> The members of the choir take up their instruments and play them. The songstresses in full number adore the Golden Goddess and make music to the Golden Goddess: they never cease their chanting.

The text of the hymn is written behind the lutanist and a singer. We take notice especially of the aim of this music, 'nourishment for the heart.'

> Come, O Golden Goddess, the singers chant
> for it is nourishment for the heart to dance the *iba*,
> to shine over the feast at the hour of retiring
> and to enjoy dance at night.
>
> Come! The procession takes place at the site of drunkenness,
> this area where one wanders in the marshes.
> Its routine is set, the rules firm:
> nothing is left to be desired.

1 Sendrey, *Life of Antiquity*, 37. We believe this is the best single book ever written on ancient music. Accordingly much of this chapter is in debt to Sendrey.

2 Quoted in Lise Manniche, *Music and Musicians in Ancient Egypt* (London: British Museum Press, 1991), 12. This is another outstanding book from which we have much profited.

The royal children satisfy you with what you love
and the officials give offerings to you.
The lector priest exalts you singing a hymn,
and the wise men read the rituals.

The priest honors you with his basket,
and the drummers take their tambourines.
Ladies rejoice in your honor with garlands
and girls with wreaths.

Drunkards play tambourines for you in the cool night,
and those they wake up bless you.
The Bedouin dance for you in their garments,
and Asiatics with their sticks.

The griffins wrap their wings around you,
the hares stand on their hind legs for you.
The hippopotami adore with wide open mouths,
and their legs salute your face.[3]

3 Ibid., 61.

In yet another painting celebrating Hathor, no fewer than twenty-nine female musicians are pictured with percussion instruments.

Another goddess, Merit, was considered to be the personification of music. And then there was the strange dwarf god Bes, usually associated with childbirth but who, nevertheless, is usually pictured playing a variety of musical instruments.

All in all, what we see in these myths is a special significance given to music from the earliest of times.

Beginning with the Old Kingdom (2686–2181 BC) we can see a testimonial to the importance of individual musicians simply from the fact that they were allowed to have their tombs in the vicinity of the royal ones. Also, the hieroglyphic texts which accompany the tomb paintings speak of the importance of these musicians in their very titles: 'royal music director,' 'leader of ritual music,' and 'inspector of vocal music.' Through this entire period the hieroglyphics tell us of numerous actual names of musicians, male and female,[4] professional and amateur alike.

4 Some female musicians carry a tattoo on their thighs of the god Bes, the significance of which is not known.

As with the countries to the East, the earliest extant evidence of music which has come down to us introduces us not to the beginnings of musical tradition but to one already well-developed. The primary evidence for this suggestion comes from the instruments themselves. Even in the twenty-fifth century BC we find not primitive instruments made from bones, but sophisticated instruments such as harps and double-reeds.

Art Music

We use this term, even though so little is known of Egyptian music, as compared to the greater knowledge we have of the musical instruments, simply because there are so many tomb paintings which seem to show people listening to the musician. In one remarkable painting a female musician plays the trumpet for the god Osiris, who is pictured shedding tears.[5]

Most frequently pictured among these persons who seem to be listening is the so-called 'chironomist,' who is always positioned directly facing one or more musicians. Many theories have been advanced regarding the hand signals of this figure: that he was a singer, that he was a kind of conductor, or that he was merely an attentive listener. The hieroglyph used to describe what this figure is doing means 'singing,' but it is always qualified by another hieroglyph in the form of a human arm, suggesting a more definite definition of 'singing with the arm.'[6] Given the fact that ancient Egyptian music apparently had no notated form, we are inclined to the theory that he supplied to the player a kind of visual notation. This view is strengthened by a painting from the Eighteenth Dynasty (1580–1320 BC) in which we see one of these 'conductors' supplying the rhythm as well, with the heel of his foot while snapping a thumb and finger of each hand. Manniche adds an important observation,[7] however, that this figure appears regularly in the paintings of the Old Kingdom, rarely in the those of the Middle Kingdom and disappears during the New Kingdom. Therefore the question remains: if there were no notation, how did the musicians gradually learn to do without him?

According to Farmer[8] all music in ancient Egypt went under the name *hy*, which meant 'joy,' or 'gladness.' Clearly this is an association with the listener and the impact the music had on him. This is again evident in the text of the 'Song of the Harper.'

> Let there be music and singing before thee,
> Cast behind thee all cares, and mind thee of joy,
> Till there cometh that day,
> When we journey to the land that loveth silence.

Another interesting reference to the harp singer is found in a papyrus scroll from the end of the Eighteenth Dynasty. Here one reads of, 'a song which is written before the singing harpist in the house of King Antef.'[9]

5 Manniche, *Music and Musicians in Ancient Egypt*, 58.

6 Ibid., 30.

7 Ibid. She also points to one painting which shows five musicians and six chironomists!

8 Henry G. Farmer, 'The Music of Ancient Egypt,' *New Oxford History of Music* (London: Oxford University Press, 1966), I, 262. An additional suggestion of harmony can be inferred from of a painting of a giant harp played by two musicians at the same time.

9 Manniche, *Music and Musicians in Ancient Egypt*, 97.

10 W. Chappell, *The History of Music* (London, 1874), 2. He also points out (p. 67) that some tomb paintings picture as many as four or five different musical instruments together.

According to Chappell,[10] during the period twenty-five centuries BC there were already remarkable 'concerts' of harmonized music.

Those Egyptians had bands that played with harps and aulos in concert—not in unison, as might have been supposed, but in harmony. This is made manifest by at least one of the representations on the tombs of the fourth dynasty of Egypt. Three aulos players have a conductor beating time for them, and their instruments are of such different lengths, that it is mathematically impossible they could have been playing in unison. Further, it may be proved to demonstration, that the ordinary Egyptian lute had then a compass of two octaves. The hieroglyphic for 'good' makes this evident. It is a lute with a neck, which is from two to three times the length of the body.

One king, Amenophis IV (also known as Amenhotep IV and later as Akhenaten or Ikhnaton), seems to have been an especially enthusiastic sponsor of music. One extraordinary painting from ca. 1570 BC pictures an actual music school, with four rooms used for the storage of musical instruments and three teaching studios in which we see a variety of music instruction in progress. Another painting from his court shows a concert by a double ensemble, which includes foreign guest artists (apparent by their dress).

It is during the reign of this king, by the way, in which we see court scenes with apparently blind, or blindfolded, musicians. The significance of this is not known to modern scholars, some speculating that the blindfolds prevented slave musicians from seeing what was going on in the palace and others that the musician, being of a lower social order, was not permitted to look upon a god. We might add that it could also be the artist's way of reminding the observer that music is the one art you cannot see.

11 Strabo, *The Geography of Strabo*, trans. Horace Leonard Jones (Cambridge, MA: Harvard University Press, 1959), 7.1.11.

According to Strabo,[11] one of the last rulers, Ptolemy Auletes (81–52 BC), was an accomplished aulos player and participated in contests with professional musicians, so we know these kinds of contests existed in Egypt as well as Greece.

Sendrey states that the performances outside the temple were characterized by virtuosity and he quotes Pythagoras, who studied in Egypt, as reporting that the temple musicians 'were violently opposed to this abuse of musical art.'[12]

12 Sendrey, *Life of Antiquity*, 49.

EDUCATIONAL MUSIC

With all the musical activities we see in the tomb paintings, we can assume the existence of formal music education. Indeed, the hieroglyphs actually tell us the names of some of these educators and two of them are the most ancient music educators known by name: Nikaure, 'instructor of the singers of the pyramid of King Userkaf,' and Rewer, 'teacher of the royal singers,' who lived during the Fifth Dynasty (2563–2423 BC). The discovery of the tombs of Nufer and Kaha at Saqqara introduce us to two men who were 'director of singers,' as well as teachers. The information given here confirms what Herodotus suggests, that some professions such as music were maintained by family birthright.

> Their heralds and aulos players, and cooks inherit the craft from their fathers … no others usurp their places … they ply their craft by right of birth.[13]

13 Herodotus, *The History*, trans. David Grene (Chicago: Chicago University Press, 1987), 2.59.

Regarding the tomb of Nufer and Kaha, Manniche points to Nufer as being the head of such a family.

> Kaha was both 'director' and 'instructor' of singers. He also held a title as priest of the 'southern Merit,' the music goddess, and the inscriptions mention that he was 'unique' among the singers and had a beautiful voice. Nufer, as well as being director of singers, was also instructor in the royal artisans' workshops. Three of his sons were 'instructors of singers,' and a fourth was 'director of singers in the palace.' Four other male relatives were 'instructors of singers,' and two of them were also priests of Merit.[14]

14 Manniche, *Music and Musicians in Ancient Egypt*, 122.

During the Sixth Dynasty we find several musicians named Snefrunufer, one of whom had a tomb at Giza which identifies him as 'instructor of singers in The Great House.'

A remarkable painting from the Middle Kingdom tomb of an 'instructor of singers' and 'overseer of prophets' named Khesuwer, located at Kom el-Hisn in the Delta, pictures the instructor actually teaching. We see him teaching ten ladies in sistrum-playing and in another scene teaching ten ladies in hand-clapping.

Strabo, writing during the first years of the Christian Era, says that the Egyptians instructed their children with music established by the government and that musicians were in charge of the development of character in the young.

The musicians in giving instruction in singing and playing the lyre or aulos considered this virtue as essential, since they maintain that such studies are destined to create discipline and develop the character.[15]

15   Quoted in, ibid., 41.

Plato also paid tribute to this educational system and no doubt it was the model for the similar system he proposed for his ideal Greek society. Speaking of Egypt, a character in his *Laws* reports,

Long ago they appear to have recognized the very principle of which we are now speaking—that their young citizens must be habituated to forms and strains of virtue. These they fixed, and exhibited the patterns of them in their temples; and no painter, no other representative artist is allowed to innovate upon them, or to leave the traditional forms and invent new ones. To this day, no alteration is allowed either in these arts, or in music at all. And you find that their works of art are painted or molded in the same forms which they had ten thousand years ago;—this is literally true and no exaggeration,—their ancient paintings and sculptures are not a bit better or worse than the works of today, but are made with just the same skill.[16]

16   Plato, *Laws*, trans., Benjamin Jowett (Oxford: Clarendon Press, 1953), 656d.

Lise Manniche summarizes the deductions which can be made regarding music education in Egypt, from both this passage and the hieroglyphic texts associated with the tomb paintings.

According to Plato, musical theory did exist in ancient Egypt, and was hedged round by a rigid system of laws. Poems and hymns, which are known to have been chanted or performed with some musical accompaniment, may contain clues about musical forms. Patterns of set rhythms or lengths of phrases might be deduced from the words of the text. Repeated lines suggest repeated musical phrases. The wording of a hymn may even suggest antiphonal singing, either by two solo performers, two choirs, or one soloist with choir.[17]

17   Manniche, *Music and Musicians in Ancient Egypt*, 11.

The tomb of an official named Mereruka, in the necropolis of Sakkarah, contains a painting of children engaged in a dance, which the hieroglyphic calls 'the crushing of the grapes,' a title which sounds very much like the educational dances one finds in Greece.

By the last century BC, according to Diodorus Siculus, the 'virtues' of this kind of education were no longer respected.

Music was not, in those days, a part of normal education, since it was thought not only useless but morally injurious, in that it created effeminacy.[18]

18 Quoted by Farmer, in 'The Music of Ancient Egypt,' 265.

This would seem to be contradicted by Athenaeus, writing in the third century of the Christian Era, for at least in Alexandria he found a remarkable knowledge in music which extended to everyone.

I would have you know that there is no record in history of other people more musical than the Alexandrians, and I am not speaking merely of singing to the harp, for even the humblest layman among us, even one who has never learned his ABC's, is so familiar with that, that he can immediately detect the mistakes which occur in striking the notes; no, even when it comes to woodwinds, they are most musical.

FUNCTIONAL MUSIC

In the oldest tomb paintings, those of the Old Kingdom (2686–2181 BC), we can see musicians included in scenes associated with the worship of the gods.

In later periods we also learn the names of some of the musicians are also identified as having positions related to the worship of these gods. One of these, Amenemhab, who appears several times in the Eighteenth Dynasty is described in a stela as having 'followed the king's footsteps in foreign lands.' He is identified as holding a very high office, 'overseer of the singers of the North and South,' and he describes his role as a performer in the temple:

I purify my mouth. I adore the gods. I exalt Horus who is in the sky. I adore him. The Ennead listens, the inhabitants of the Underworld rejoice. They appear at my voice.

In a tomb painting he is called, 'chief of singers of Amun,' and appears singing to the sun god the following beautiful song.

Praise to you millions and millions of times!
I have come to you, adoring your beauty.
Your mother Nut [the sky] embraces you.
You are joyful as you traverse the sky and the earth.

> May the gods of the Underworld [as the sun passes underneath the
>   earth] worship you and sing your praise when you hear my words
>   which worship you every day,
> So that you endow me with a burial in peace after enduring old
>   age and my *ba* being among my ancestors, following the king.[19]

19 Quoted in ibid., 59.

When female musicians appear in the New Kingdom (1567–1085
BC), some of them also have apparent positions in the temple, with
titles such as 'Chief of the Singers.'

The tomb painting tells us of music in the temple by both solo
and choral singers, dances accompanied by instruments, and processions around the altar. The tendency toward string instruments
in temple scenes leads Sendrey to speculate regarding the character
of the temple music:

> We must consider its character solemn and sedate; from this we may
> conclude that their sacred music must have been rigid and formal,
> similar to the ceremonies of their ritual.[20]

20 Sendrey, *Life of Antiquity*, 49.

The literature of the more recent periods speak of observances
of religious-cult which were much less somber. The early historian,
Herodotus, for example, describes two such festivals.

> When they travel to Bubastis, this is what they do. They sail thither,
> men and women together, and a great number of each in each boat.
> Some of the women have rattles and rattle them, others play the
> aulos through the entire trip, and the remainder of the women and
> men sing and clap their hands. As they travel on toward Bubastis
> and come near some other city, they edge the boat near the bank,
> and some of the women do as I have described. But others of them
> scream obscenities in derision of the women who live in that city,
> and others of them set to dancing, and others still, standing up,
> throw their clothes open to show their nakedness. This they do at
> every city along the riverbank. When they come to Bubastis, they
> celebrate the festival with great sacrifices, and more wine is drunk
> at that single festival than in all the rest of the year besides. There
> they throng together, man and woman (but no children), up to the
> number of seven hundred thousand, as the natives say.[21]

21 Herodotus, *The History*, 157.

...

> On the eve of the festival of Dionysus, each one of them cuts
> the throat of his pig in front of the doorway and then gives it, to
> take away, to the swineherd who has sold it to him. For the rest of
> the festival in honor of Dionysus, except for the dance choruses,
> the Egyptians celebrate it almost in everything like the Greeks.

But instead of phalluses they have another invention, which are eighteen-inch-high images, controlled by strings, which the women carry round the villages; these images have a penis that nods and in size is not much less than all the rest of the body. Ahead there goes an aulos player, and the women follow, singing in honor of Dionysus.[22]

Athenaeus,[23] speaking of the period of Ptolemy (285–246 BC), quotes a reference to a 'choral band of six hundred men,' with three hundred harp players participating in the music for a festival.

Regarding music for workers, a scene from ca. 1365 BC pictures a group of women, accompanying a hunter, scaring birds in a forest by beating drums. From a relief in the tomb of Kahif at Giza we see an aulos player making music for the workers in the field.

While again no music survives, the texts for some songs of workers is extant, among them songs for shepherds, the thrasher, and the sedan-chair bearer. One of these, sung by thrashers to the oxen treading on the corn, goes,

Thrash ye for yourselves,
Thrash ye for yourselves, O oxen,
Thrash ye for yourselves,
Thrash ye for yourselves,
The straw which is yours,
The corn which is your master's.

We also see in the tomb paintings scenes of military music. In Tomb 90 of the Theban necropolis (ca. 1425–1405 BC) we see a trumpet player in his helmet and in Tomb 74 two trumpeters marching with their instruments over the shoulder.[24] The only actual surviving trumpets, by the way, were found in the famous tomb of Tutankhamun. When one of these was blown in a trial, it was the only instance that people of our own time have heard the sounds the ancient Egyptians heard.

The percussion instruments of the military are also present and Manniche quotes from a Seventeenth Dynasty text which tells a nice story about one of these players.

A certain Emhab had been practicing his drum secretly, keeping his fingers strong and supple to extract a variety of sounds from his instrument. Then one day he was invited to an audition to try his skills against those of another contestant. Emhab beat his rival by performing no fewer than seven thousand 'lengths.' The nature of

22 Ibid., 152.

23 Athenaeus, *Deipnosophistae*, 5.201.

24 The third century BC inventor, Stesibius, made for Ptolemy's queen, Arsinoe, a water-powered clock, with sounding trumpets.

such a 'length' is not explained, but this must be a technical term, perhaps describing a 'figure' or rhythmical phrase. Having gained the position as army drummer, Emhab spent a whole year drumming every single day, following his king on his campaigns and bravely executing every command until, finally, he was rewarded with a female slave, purchased for him by the king himself.[25]

25   Manniche, *Music and Musicians*, 75. Manniche says sticks were never used on drums in ancient Egypt, but this is incorrect as such sticks actually survive in Berlin and are pictured by Carl Engel in *The Music of The Most Ancient Nations*, 219.

ENTERTAINMENT MUSIC

There exists a two thousand year old papyrus contract for a musician to play for the delight of those who cried, 'Let there be music and singing!'[26] Perhaps this contract was for the kind of banquet scene represented in a fresco now in the British Museum, which is described as follows.

26   Farmer, 'The Music of Ancient Egypt,' 266.

> A number of guests, men and women, are seated on chairs, while women servants are handing wine to them, and female musicians, sitting on the ground, play to them, and women dance before them. Many of the guests hold a lotus flower, and one man a handkerchief as a mark of refinement. The servants and dancers are unclothed with the exception of a slight band.[27]

27   Samuel Sharpe, *Egyptian Antiquities in the British Museum* (London, 1862), 49.

Such banquet scenes with music are frequently seen, as might be expected. Manniche summarizes the elements seen in these paintings.

> Although the banquet scenes in which the ensembles are depicted appear to be secular—feasts like those which must have taken place in real life—they represent the 'idea' of a feast rather than any specific event. Right up to the New Kingdom the basic components change little: men and women in their finest outfits; food and drink; music, song and sometimes dance. In the New Kingdom, and in the 18th Dynasty in particular, there is a marked change of character in these scenes, which begin to show a wealth of detail with a distinctly erotic significance: lotus flowers, mandrake fruits, wigs, unguent cones, semi-transparent garments, and the gestures of the participants. It is clear that the underlying intention is to create a climate propitious to the rebirth of the tomb owner. Music played a vital part in this process: in the New Kingdom it accompanied songs which expressed the possibility of renewed life explicitly; in the Old Kingdom we can trace a similar message in the gestures of dancing girls moving to the music.[28]

28   Manniche, *Music and Musicians*, 24.

The few texts which survive together with the singing pictured in these banquet scenes clearly identify the entertainment nature of the music. Two examples will suffice.

Can it be the goddess Maat
in whose face there is a desire for getting drunk?

...

The beauty of your face shines, you appear, you come in peace.
One gets drunk by looking at you,
You who are as beautiful as gold, O Hathor.
May I be given a fresh mouth with the water you have provided.[29]

29 Ibid., 50.

There is a very interesting example where music entertainment seems to cross over into music therapy. The prince of Byblos had sent a member of the court to obtain a load of precious wood from Lebanon, where he encountered endless problems and delay. When the prince heard of this he sent to him,

two measures of wine and a sheep, as well as his songstress to sing to him and chase away his gloomy thoughts.[30]

30 Ibid., 126.

Finally, there are also tomb paintings, some even dating from the end of the Old Kingdom, which show a tradition of music making by the family, in the home.

In summary, from ancient Egypt we have an extraordinary collection of iconography, in the tomb paintings. While we have little descriptive literature comparable to that of Greece and the Near East, here we can *see* depictions of musical performance. What we see here not only seems to correspond to, and even clarify, references to music in early Greek and Near East literature, but in some cases reveals aspects of musical practice which would be otherwise unknown to us.

These pictorial references to music in the tombs of Egypt are all the more important because we know from the testimony of Plato and others that the musical traditions of Greece were based on the earlier practice in Egypt. In an example we have quoted in this chapter, one can see that the concept of the 'music of the spheres,' which modern writers have always identified with Pythagoras, was actually an idea already present earlier in Egypt.

As with Mesopotamia, the aesthetic purpose of music in Egypt is described as instilling joy and dispelling gloom. But we also find here a broader range of purpose, for example 'nourishment for the heart,' which suggests something more far reaching than mere 'joy.' Certainly a new dimension of musical communication is present when the listener is described as being in tears.

The tomb paintings offer additional insights regarding the value which was given music in this society. First, the very placement of these tombs is important, for we find respected musicians buried in the vicinity of the nobles and not with the slaves. We see real audiences of people listening and applauding. And we cannot fail to notice that the hieroglyph for 'good' was a musical instrument.

The importance of music in the temple, together with the 'divine' character assigned to these musicians, also reflects the importance of music itself to this society. And now we find a whole group of gods which are associated with music, gods worshiped by all levels of society.

The presence of music education is also a mark of the value a society assigns to music. Evidence of a highly disciplined system of music education is witnessed by the fact that temple musicians both sing *and* play instruments. The sophisticated string instruments, the pictures of ensembles which infer multi-part music, the contests held even for percussion players, and the virtuosity upon which the temple musicians frowned, all suggest high levels of musical instruction. This is confirmed by the painting of a music school, sixteen centuries before the Christian Era, as well as those music educators identified by name.

Finally, as in the case of the Near East, when we study this society in the years before the Christian Era we find a general decay in the environment of musical expression. Religious music now begins to accompany cult-erotic ceremonies. At this time entertainment music is also associated with the erotic and the texts found on some paintings of these scenes now mock the gods associated with music in the past.

One writer in the last century before the Christian Era tells us that music was no longer part of general education, since it was then considered, 'useless, morally injurious, and created effeminacy.'

5 ANCIENT HEBREW MUSIC

One of our primary sources of knowledge of the early Hebrew people is, of course, one of man's great works of literature, the Old Testament. But the value of the Old Testament as an historical document is limited by the fact that it is evidently a compilation of earlier works written centuries later than the events described, not to mention considerable linguistic problems.[1]

As history, the Old Testament is a particular problem with respect to the years before the Egyptian period of these peoples. As Sendrey points out, 'The Bible condenses 800 years of the early history of the Jews in a few short sentences.'[2] Sendrey also makes the interesting observation that much of Genesis may have originally existed as sung epic poetry, perhaps in the tradition of the epics of Homer, before it was set down in the form of prose.[3] In this regard we might add that literature which is passed down over long periods of time in an oral form is also subject to the natural tendency to improve the story by exaggeration. A typical example of this can be seen in Josephus's account of Solomon's dedication of the first Temple. Josephus assures us that the ceremony included a performance by 200,000 trumpets![4] This would surely have exceeded all the trumpets of antiquity.

While we know these people were originally wandering desert tribes, we are told very little of their culture during these years, and certainly very few hints of their musical practice. Since water is of paramount importance to desert life, perhaps we can assume the 'Well Song' in Numbers at least reflects on those nomadic years.

> Spring up, O well!—Sing to it!—
> the well which the princes dug,
> which the nobles of the people delved,
> with the scepter and with their staves.[5]

Perhaps another reflection of the earliest times is found in Psalm 81, which sings of a truly pagan festival—something uniquely 'out of place' in the Old Testament.

> Raise a song, sound the timbrel,
> the sweet lyre with the harp.
> Blow the trumpet at the new moon,
> at the full moon, on our feast day.

1 For example the various superscriptions before the Psalms. See Sendrey, *Music in the Social and Religious Life of Antiquity*, 108–137, for a wonderful summary of these terms in their original language, together with their attempted solution by a wide selection of scholars. We also recommend Sendrey's book as the best general discussion of music and instruments found in the Old Testament.

2 Ibid., 77. As Sendrey also points out, the 'invention' of musical instruments given in Genesis 4:21 refers to instruments which are actually already of a rather advanced stage of development.

3 Ibid., 138.

4 Josephus, *Jewish Antiquities*, 8.95.

5 Numbers 21:17. All references are taken from the Revised Standard Version (New York: Nelson, 1952).

While the years the Hebrews spent in Egypt form a critical role in the drama of the Old Testament story, few actual details of this 430-year period are supplied. It is clear that most of this time the Hebrews lived freely in Egypt and were 'captives' in only the final eighty years of this period. During the first 350 years they were apparently free enough to conduct their own 'border wars,'[6] independent of the Egyptians, enjoyed the economic freedom to maintain their own large herds of cattle,[7] and enjoyed sufficient cultural respect that one of them actually married the daughter of a Pharaoh.[8] We can assume therefore that during this long period they were free to absorb much from the older Egyptian culture, including musical practices. In the case of Moses, we are told he 'was instructed in all the wisdom of the Egyptians.'[9]

In a famous instance of the absorption of Egyptian culture which Moses distinctly did not approve of, the singing and dancing around the statue of the golden calf, the singing and general celebration was so loud that Joshua, hearing them from the distance, thought a war had broken out in the camp![10]

The Old Testament also fails to give us much information about the period of captivity in Babylonia, after the destruction of Solomon's Temple in 537 BC. Again, it appears they were not 'captives' in the modern sense of the word, for when the 42,000 of them were allowed to return they brought back with them 7,337 slaves of their own, in addition to 245 male and female [slave] singers![11] One of the apocryphal books also mentions that they returned with all their musical instruments.[12]

It is evident, in any case, that the Hebrews preserved their musical heritage during this period, as we can read in some of the most beautiful lines of the Old Testament.

> By the waters of Babylon,
> there we sat down and wept,
> when we remembered Zion.
> On the willows there
> we hung up our lyres.
> For there our captors
> required of us songs.[13]

6 1 Chronicles 7:21.

7 Exodus 9:6–7; 10:9.

8 1 Chronicles 4:18.

9 Acts 7:22.

10 Exodus 32:17.

11 Nehemiah 7:67 and 1 Esdras 5:42. Ezra 2:65 gives 200 singers.

12 1 Esdras 5:2. The apocryphal books appear in the early Septuagint and Vulgate versions of the Old Testament, but are considered spurious by the modern Jewish and Protestant faiths.

13 Psalm 137.

ART MUSIC

By the definition given at the beginning of our book, no doubt much of the music heard in the Temple would be considered as art music in so far as it was music of substance and contemplatively listened to, but because its primary purpose was to serve the religious service we consider it functional music.

The Old Testament does not discuss directly any music which might be true art music outside the church. However, we wonder if perhaps there were not at this time secular festivals similar to those practiced by the Greeks. Does not the following suggest such festival singing?

He will exult over you with loud singing as on a day of festival.[14]

14 Zephaniah 3:18

Additionally, since the Greek festivals were always held in the Spring, perhaps the following is also a reference to such festivals.

The flowers appear on the earth,
the time of singing has come.[15]

15 Song of Solomon 2:12.

EDUCATIONAL MUSIC

We can assume that the early Hebrews maintained schools for the training of those who performed the music in the Temple, as did other peoples of this time, including the Egyptians.[16] Further, the constant reference in the Old Testament to the importance of the performance of instruments in the Temple by the Temple officials presupposes some ongoing discipline of instruction. Sendrey believes there must have been organized 'schools' of music, carrying on musical traditions many of which the Hebrews may have first learned in Egypt.

16 Engel, *The Music of the Most Ancient Nations*, 323, finds Old Testament references to music schools at Bethel, Naioth, Jericho, Gilgal, and Jerusalem.

One cannot help assuming the existence of one or several such 'schools' when one finds in the biblical text a sudden and unexplained upsurge of large choirs and orchestras, consisting of thoroughly organized and trained musical groups, which would be virtually inconceivable without lengthy, methodical preparation. Similar schools of music are know to have existed among other nations of Antiquity, far back in times of Sumeria.[17]

17 Sendrey, *Life of Antiquity*, 94–95 and 86. Sendrey speculates on the nature of this music education on pages 95–97.

This seems especially evident in passages such as the following, from Psalm 33, where we read of *skillful* performance on a rather sophisticated instrument, not to mention the suggestion of ability in composition.

> Praise the Lord with the lyre,
> > make melody to him with the harp of ten strings!
> Sing to him a new song,
> > play skillfully on the strings, with loud shouts.

The Old Testament itself does not discuss the actual educational process, but does seems to suggest the heads of the major families were in charge of at least the administrative aspects. In such a reference to the family of Heman we also encounter the word 'skillful' once again.

> God had given Heman fourteen sons and three daughters. They were all under the direction of their father in the music in the house of the Lord with cymbals, harps, and lyres ... The number of them who were trained in singing to the Lord, all who were skillful, was two hundred and eighty-eight.[18]

A similar passage[19] mentions, 'Chenaniah, leader of the Levites in music, should direct the music, for he understood it.' An apocryphal book says specifically that these leaders instructed the people in both music and writing.

> Leaders of the people by their counsels, and by their knowl-
> > edge of learning meet for the people, wise and eloquent in
> > their instructions:
> Such as found out musical tunes, and recited verses in writing.[20]

In only one place in the modern versions of the Old Testament is there a clear reference to teaching music to people other than the professional musicians of the Temple. Moses is told, 'write this song, and teach it to the people of Israel.' And indeed we are told he did this in the same day![21] A similar command in Jeremiah,[22] 'teach to your daughters a lament, and each to her neighbor a dirge,' is probably meant rhetorically.

There are also two references in the Psalms which make us wonder if perhaps the early Hebrews went beyond merely contending, as did the Greeks, that music forms character in the young, to actually teaching specific moral principles, and even laws, through music.

18   1 Chronicles 25:5ff.

19   1 Chronicles 15:16ff.

20   Ecclesiasticus 44:4ff.

21   Deuteronomy 31:19, 22.
22   Jeremiah 9:20.

I will sing of loyalty and of justice.[23]

…

Thy statutes have been my songs.[24]

FUNCTIONAL MUSIC

The Old Testament is rich in its detail of the music of the Temple. The apocryphal book of Ecclesiasticus gives credit to David for the formal establishment of this tradition.

> In all his works he praised the Holy One most high with words of glory; with his whole heart he sang songs, and loved him that made him.
> He set singers also before the altar, that by their voices they might make sweet melody, and daily sing praises in their songs.[25]

Regarding the actual organization of the music of the Temple, the Old Testament several times mentions surprisingly large numbers.[26] Indeed, in one place we are told that 'those who offer praises to the Lord with instruments' numbered four thousand![27] We are given actual names for players of trumpet, harps, lyres, and cymbals,[28] the fact that they must be thirty years of age to fully participate in the service,[29] and even such details as the name of the wood the string instruments were constructed of.[30]

One would assume some rotation of these forces took place, but we have no specific information regarding this. Indeed, there is only an occasional reference, such as the two priests who were 'to blow continually before the ark of the covenant,'[31] to any specific role performed by these musicians.

The general role of these musicians is clear, however, and that was to lead in the praise of the Lord. This is nowhere more evident than in Psalm 150:

Praise him with the [shofar] sound;
Praise him with lute and harp!
Praise him with strings and pipe!
Praise him with sounding cymbals;
Praise him with loud clashing cymbals!

23 Psalm 101.

24 Psalm 119.

25 Ecclesiasticus 47:8ff.

26 1 Chronicles 15:16ff; 25:5ff; Ezra 2:40, 65; and Nehemiah 7:43. 1 Esdras 7:22 says the Temple musicians paid no taxes!

27 1 Chronicles 23:5.

28 1 Chronicles 15:16ff; 16:5ff, 42; Nehemiah 12:34ff.

29 1 Chronicles 23:3. Sendrey, *Life of Antiquity*, 104ff discusses the relationship of children to this musical environment, including a quotation from the Mishnah which suggests children could stand with their elders and sing, but not play instruments.

30 Almug wood is specified in 1 Kings 10:12 and Algum wood in 2 Chronicles 9:11. Can we find a hint of the sound of the lyre in two passages which read, 'my soul moans like a lyre' [Isaiah 17:11 and Jeremiah 48:36]?

31 1 Chronicles 16:5ff.

That these large forces sometimes performed together is evident in an extraordinary description of praise associated with thanksgiving.

> … and all the Levitical singers, Asaph, Heman, and Jeduthun, their sons and kinsmen, arrayed in fine linen, with cymbals, harps, and lyres … with a hundred and twenty priests who were trumpeters; and it was the duty of the trumpeters and singers to make themselves heard in unison in praise and thanksgiving … and when the song was raised, with trumpets and cymbals and other musical instruments, in praise to the Lord.[32]

By 'unison' here we believe is meant rather 'together,' for it is unlikely the great numbers of singers and instruments were always heard in unison. This supposition seems confirmed by the reference to a 'great variety *of sounds*' in the following description of the Temple music:

> The singers also sang praises with their voices, with great variety of sounds was there made sweet melody.[33]

Another passage[34] speaks of cymbals, harps, lyres, trumpets, and singing altogether in the service. Perhaps these large forces are also intended by several references to 'Make a joyful *noise*.'[35]

But what are we to make of the form of praise represented by the following?

> And David and all the house of Israel were making merry before the Lord with all their might, with songs and lyres and harps and tambourines and castanets and cymbals.[36]

We assume 'making merry … with all their might' must have included dancing, which probably would not have been unusual even in the Temple at this time. On the other hand, there are certainly references to praising the Lord outside the Temple. A notable example is the song sung by Moses as the waters came together killing all the Egyptians.

> I will sing to the Lord, for he has triumphed gloriously; the horse and his rider he has thrown into the sea.[37]

The richest body of songs of praise are, of course, found in the Book of Psalms. While one hundred and fifty-one[38] have come down to us, it is evident that this is but a very small portion of what

32 2 Chronicles 5:12ff. Other references to songs of thanksgiving are found in 1 Chronicles 16:7, Nehemiah 12:27ff ('with singing, with cymbals, harps and lyres'), Psalm 26:7, Psalm 95, Psalm 107, Isaiah 51:3ff, which gives the complete text of a thanksgiving song, 1 Maccabees 13:51 and 1 Esdras 5:59ff.

33 Ecclesiasticus 50:18.

34 2 Chronicles 29:25ff.

35 Psalm 95 and Psalm 100.

36 2 Samuel 6:5. An almost identical passage is found in 1 Chronicles 13:8, which adds the trumpet.

37 Exodus 15.

38 All modern scholars consider the Book of Habakkuk to be a 'misplaced' Psalm.

must have been a great literature unto itself. In the case of King Solomon, for example, who is represented by no more than two psalms in the Old Testament, we are told elsewhere that he alone composed a thousand and five psalms.[39]

Another specific kind of music mentioned in the Old Testament in regard to the practice of religion is processional music. Once again, with regard to the ark of the covenant, we read of a procession 'to the sound of the horn, trumpets, and cymbals, and made loud music on harps and lyres.'[40] Psalm 68 even gives us the order of the procession: singers in front, then 'maidens playing timbrels,' and finally the instrumentalists. These processions may have also been rather joyous affairs, for once we read of David 'dancing' to the sound of the [ram's] horn.[41]

There was also music of the bridal processions.[42] In a description of one of these we read,

The bridegroom came forth, and his friends and brethren, to meet them with drums, and instruments of music.

only to be slaughtered by Jonathan.

Thus was the marriage turned into mourning, and the noise of their melody into lamentation.[43]

There were also funeral processions, the latter no doubt implied in various references to the singing of laments and dirges.[44] One such passage suggests that there were also professionals in 'wailing,' for we read this was left to 'those who are skilled in lamentation.'[45]

Certainly the most unusual musical practice in the service of their religion is the Old Testament's mention of the Hebrew's use of music for prophesy. Twice we read of the request for a musician for this purpose. Saul said, 'seek out a man who is skillful in playing the lyre,' in this case turns out to be David, who 'took the lyre and played it with his hand.'[46] And again, Jehoshaphat, King of Israel, says,

Now bring me a minstrel. And when the minstrel played, the power of the Lord came upon him.[47]

In a few instances we are told the names of those who specialize in this art. For example in one place we are told that it is the sons of Asaph, Heman and Jeduthun, 'who should prophesy with lyres, with harps, and with cymbals.'[48] It may seem odd to read of

39 1 Kings 4:32. We refer the reader once again to Sendrey's outstanding discussion, *Life of Antiquity*, 108–137, of the superscripts which contain information relative to the singing of these psalms, as well as the term *Selah* which appears throughout them.

40 1 Chronicles 15:28.

41 2 Samuel 6:13.

42 Jeremiah 7:34, in 'the streets of Jerusalem.'

43 1 Maccabees 9:39ff.

44 2 Chronicles 35:25 and Amos 8:3 and 10.

45 Amos 5:16.

46 1 Samuel 16:16. In 1 Samuel 18:10 we are told David practiced everyday on his lyre. In Amos 6:5 we are told he also invented musical instruments.

47 2 Kings 3:15.

48 1 Chronicles 25.

49   Exodus 15:20.

cymbals associated with prophesy, but then Miriam, the sister of Aaron is identified as 'the prophetess,' as well as a percussionist.[49]

A separate, but very extensive, category of functional music mentioned in the Old Testament is the use of the trumpet as a signal instrument. Of all the literature of antiquity, the book of Numbers contains the most extraordinary single description of trumpet signals.

> The Lord said to Moses, 'Make two silver trumpets; of hammered work you shall make them; and you shall use them for summoning the congregation, and for breaking camp. And when both are blown, all the congregation shall gather themselves to you at the entrance of the tent of meeting. But if they blow only one, then the leaders, the heads of the tribes of Israel, shall gather themselves to you. When you blow an alarm, the camps that are on the east side shall set out. And when you blow an alarm the second time, the camps that are on the south side shall set out. An alarm is to be blown whenever they are to set out. But when the assembly is to be gathered together, you shall blow, but you shall not sound an alarm. And the sons of Aaron, the priests, shall blow the trumpets. The trumpets shall be to you for a perpetual statute throughout your generations. And when you go to war in your land against the adversary who oppresses you, then you shall sound an alarm with the trumpets, that you may be remembered before the Lord your God, and you shall be saved from your enemies.

50   Examples of this use of the trumpet can be found in Numbers 29:1, 2 Chronicles 29:25 and Leviticus 23:24 and 25:9.

51   Numbers 10:1ff.

> On the day of your gladness also, and at your appointed feasts,[50] and at the beginnings of your months, you shall blow the trumpets over your burnt offerings and over the sacrifices of your peace offerings.[51]

First of all, we see here the silver trumpet, not the ram's horn instrument. Although the dating of all the material in the Old Testament is problematic, one can generally assume the the silver trumpets were carried away from Egypt, for these would be impossible to make in the desert. Over time, of course, these instruments would become worn out and the ram's horn became their surrogate.

52   A rare exception is found in 2 Samuel 20:1, where we read, 'Now there happened to be there a worthless fellow, whose name was Sheba, the son of Bichri, a Benjaminite; and he blew the trumpet.'

With the signals being so influential as to cause great masses of people to move, it is easy to understand why we are told here that only the high priests can play them.[52] And what a variety of signals we have here, with even the implication of two-part signals, for two trumpets playing in unison would be indistinguishable from one trumpet heard from a distance.

These instruments must have produced enough sound to be heard for a considerable distance. In one place we read of a very impressive progression of trumpet volume, 'a long blast,' followed by 'a very loud blast,' and then 'the sound of the trumpet grew louder and louder.'[53] Perhaps an additional clue to the potential volume of sound capable of being produced by these early trumpets can be found in several symbolic references to the instrument. When, for example, all the scattered people will be called back from the various nations, how is this to be done?—'In that day a great trumpet will be blown.'[54] Or again, 'Cry aloud, spare not, lift up your voice like a trumpet.'[55]

The most frequent mention of trumpet signals in the Old Testament are those used in military circumstances, among which are two familiar stories. The first tells of blowing down the walls of Jericho.[56]

And seven priests shall bear seven trumpets of ram's horns before the ark; and on the seventh day you shall march around the city seven times, the priests blowing the trumpets. And when they make a long blast with the ram's horn, as soon as you hear the sound of the trumpet, then all the people shall shout with a great shout; and the wall of the city will fall down flat.

The second is the story of Gideon's famous surprise attack when, at night, he surrounded the enemy and gave them the impression that a much greater army was accompanying him. As it was, he had three hundred trumpet players.[57]

So Gideon and the hundred men who were with him came to the outskirts of the camp at the beginning of the middle watch, when they had just set the watch; and they blew the trumpets and smashed the jars that were in their hands. And the three companies blew the trumpets and broke the jars, holding in their left hands the torches, and in their right hands the trumpets to blow; and they cried, 'A sword for the Lord and for Gideon!' They stood every man in his place around about the camp, and all the army ran; they cried out and fled. When they blew the three hundred trumpets, the Lord set every man's sword against his fellow and against all the army; and the army fled.

Aside from the functional use of trumpets for signal purposes during battle, we can assume the effect of this music also instilled in the soldiers a raised sense of excitement, as the story of Gideon

53 Exodus 19:13ff.

54 Isaiah 27:12.

55 Isaiah 58. In another symbolic trumpet reference, in Zechariah 9:14, 'the Lord God will sound the trumpet.' In Psalm 105, however, he is described as a leader of singing.

56 Joshua 6:4ff. The Dead Sea Scrolls contain extensive discussion of the military trumpets.

57 Judges 6:34ff. Other examples of the use of military trumpet signals can be found in Numbers 31:6, 2 Samuel 2:28, 2 Chronicles 13:12, Jeremiah 4: 19ff, Jeremiah 6, Jeremiah 42:14, Hosea 8, Joel 2:1 and 15, Amos 3:6, and Zephanian 1:16.

suggests. We also get an indirect allusion to this heightened state of readiness in a description of the effect the trumpet had on the horses.

> His majestic snorting is terrible.
> He paws in the valley, and exults in his strength; he goes out to meet the weapons.
> He laughs at fear, and is not dismayed; he does not turn back from the sword.
> Upon him rattle the quiver, the flashing spear and the javelin.
> With fierceness and rage he swallows the ground; he cannot stand still at the sound of the trumpet.
> When the trumpet sounds, he says 'Aha!'
> He smells the battle from afar, the thunder of the captains, and the shouting.[58]

Other kinds of trumpet signals mentioned are a welcome for King Solomon,[59] for the coronation of a king,[60] and for the taking of an oath.[61]

There are numerous references to the civic watchman, usually associated with a watch tower, as in the Middle Ages in Europe. We would expect him to also be a player of trumpet signals, but in only one place do we find the instrument actually mentioned, there he 'blows the trumpet and warns the people.'[62]

While some ancient writers make frequent mention of music sung or played by workers of various professions, there are only two such references in the Old Testament. The first is a reference to the shepherds 'piping to flocks'[63] and the second is merely an inference, 'and in the vineyards no songs are sung.'[64]

A final example of Functional Music is music to accompany punishment. Even though this reference is symbolic, it would not serve as a symbol if the practice were not known. The use of civic musicians to accompany punishment in the Middle Ages is well documented.

> And every stroke of the staff of punishment which the Lord lays upon them will be to the sound of timbrels and lyres.[65]

58   Job 39:20ff.

59   1 Kings 1:34ff.

60   2 Kings 9:13. Another reference to the trumpet, now with singers, in a coronation ceremony can be found in 2 Chronicles 23:12 .

61   2 Chronicles 15:14.

62   Ezekiel 33:2ff.

63   Judges 5:16.

64   Isaiah 16:10. Perhaps another inference is found in Isaiah 5, 'Let me sing for my beloved a love song concerning his vineyard.'

65   Isaiah 30:32.

ENTERTAINMENT MUSIC

As one would expect, there is little attention given in the Old Testament to the banquet music, especially that played by the prostitute girls, which is so widely discussed in other ancient literature.[66] But here and there are hints that the aristocracy may have enjoyed the same kinds of entertainments found in neighboring countries. As even the wise King Solomon admits,

> I also gathered for myself silver and gold and the treasure of kings and provinces; I got singers, both men and women, and many concubines, man's delight.[67]

It is this type of female singer that is meant when we read,

> Use not much the company of a woman that is a singer, lest thou be taken with her attempts,[68]

and again,

> and one rises up at the voice of a bird, and all the daughters of song are brought low.[69]

Psalm 149 also has an unmistakable reference to the couches which guests reclined on during banquets of the ancient world.

> Sing to the Lord a new song …
> Let them praise his name with dancing,
>   making melody to him with timbrel and lyre! …
> Let them sing for joy on their couches.[70]

One interesting reference to banquet music describes a scene similar to a Greek *symposium*.[71]

> The mirth of the timbrels is stilled, the noise of the jubilant has ceased, the mirth of the lyre is stilled.
> No more do they drink wine with singing.[72]

And speaking of the similarity with Greek banquets, there is a very interesting passage in one of the books left out by the redactors of the Old Testament which reminds us of Aristotle's complaint that the musical entertainers at banquets prevented good conversation.

66   We omit here Nebuchadnezzar's ensemble [Daniel 3:5 and 15], which we have discussed earlier.

67   Ecclesiastes 2:8.

68   Ecclesiasticus 9:4.

69   Ecclesiastes 12:4.

70   A similar scene of music and dancing is found in the New Testament in Luke 15:25.

71   In Greek this word meant 'drinking-party.'

72   Isaiah 24:8ff.

Here, however, it is the reverse: don't talk while the music is being performed, for the music is the highpoint of a good banquet.

> If thou be made the master of a feast, lift not thyself up, but be among them as one of the rest, take diligent care for them, and so sit down.
> And when thou hast done all thy office, take thy place, that thou mayest be merry with them, and receive a crown for thy well-ordering of the feast.
> Speak, thou that art the elder, for it becometh thee, but with sound judgment; and hinder not the music.
> Pour not out words where there is a musician, and [thus] show not forth wisdom out of time.
> A concert of music in a banquet of wine is as a signet of carbuncle set in gold.
> As a signet of an emerald set in a work of gold, so is the melody of music with pleasant wine.[73]

A final reference to banquet music is found in the course of a warning:

> Woe to those … who tarry late into the evening till wine inflames them!
> They have lyre and harp, timbrel and flute and wine at their feasts; but they do not regard the deeds of the Lord.[74]

Aside from banquets, there are several references to general merry-making which seem clearly to be of entertainment music. Typical is the command,

> Again you shall adorn yourself with timbrels and shall go forth in the dance of the merrymakers.[75]

There are accounts of entertainment music for those departing,[76]

> with mirth and songs, with tambourine and lyre

and for welcoming those arriving.

> And all the people went up after him [King Solomon], playing on pipes, and rejoicing with great joy, so that the earth was split by their noise.[77]

In one example of welcome music, after David kills Goliath, we are given the text of the song which was sung. King Saul is met,

73 Ecclesiasticus 32:1ff.

74 Isaiah 5:12.

75 Jeremiah 31:4. Another reference to singing and dancing is found in Exodus 32:18.

76 Genesis 31:27.

77 1 Kings 1:40. Returning armies are welcomed with 'harps, lyres and trumpets' in 2 Chronicles 20:28.

with timbrels, with songs of joy, and with instruments of music.
And the women sang to one another as they made merry,
   Saul has slain his thousands,
   And David his ten thousands.[78]

One welcome with music had a tragic end. Jephthah had made a promise to God that if victorious in battle he would offer the life of the first person who enters his door. This turned out to be his daughter who came 'to meet him with timbrels and with dances.'[79]

We find only one reference in the Old Testament to a genuine love song.

You are to them like one who sings love songs, with a beautiful voice and plays well on an instrument, for they hear what you say, but they will not do it.[80]

There is also one reference to the music of prostitutes, apart from those who sung at banquets.

Take a harp, go about the city, O forgotten harlot!
Make sweet melody, sing many songs, that you may be remembered.[81]

Finally, two references to entertainment music in the Old Testament take the form of moral warnings.

It is better for a man to hear the rebuke of the wise than to hear the song of fools.[82]

     ...

Your pomp is brought down to Sheol, the sound of your harps; maggots are the bed beneath you, and worms are your covering.[83]

In closing we remind the reader that the primary historical document of the ancient Hebrews, the Old Testament, represents an amalgamation of earlier books selected, and combined, much later than the time of the actual events described. As this redactor, whom some scholars believe to be Jeremiah, wished to make the religion of the Hebrews the focus of the resulting work, we are left with a much more narrow view of these peoples than one would expect to find in a general history. Certainly with respect to early music, the loss of detail is to be regretted.

We wish we had a much more complete account of the Egyptian period of these peoples. We are told that Moses 'was instructed in all the wisdom of the Egyptians' and we might assume, but are not told, that this must have included elements of the musical culture.

---

78   1 Samuel 18:6.

79   Judges 11: 34.

80   Ezekiel 33:32.

81   Isaiah 23:15ff.

82   Ecclesiastes 7:5.

83   Isaiah 14:11.

Interesting sounding secular festivals are mentioned, but without detail. Even the references to ceremonies in the Temple acknowledge the presence of musicians, but tell us almost nothing of what they performed or even the exact nature of their contribution. Little, also, is supplied regarding the role of music in the instances where the musician was called to help with prophesy, although we recognize this as another form of the 'divine connection' which musicians enjoyed in Egypt and the Near East.

If there was genuine art music, and accompanying philosophies of aesthetics, as there must have been, no reference to it can be found in the Old Testament. One of the early Hebrew books the redactor left out, Ecclesiasticus, does refer to the kind of art music performed at the end of banquets, not to be confused with background music during the banquet itself. Here it is very clear that art music was performed on such occasions and that it was music to be listened to in silence. 'Don't interrupt the music,' the writer insists, 'and no talking when the musician is present!' That this kind of performance was very highly valued is documented by analogy: it is the precious stone set in the gold ring, i.e., the capstone of the banquet.

There can be no doubt that a high level of musical performance was heard in the Temple, as the Old Testament refers to the skill of these players, it calls some 'expert,' and there is an implication that ability in composition was required. It follows there there must have been systems of music education and an apocryphal book specifically says that the music teachers were 'wise and eloquent in their instructions.'

The Old Testament perhaps gives us the name of a conductor, Chenaniah. We are told he 'should direct the music, for he understood it.' We especially mourn the absence of detail here, for it might have given us the correct interpretation of the 'chironomist' seen in Egyptian tomb paintings.

We wish, also, that we were provided examples of the music which was used to teach laws and serve political ends, which are mentioned twice. One finds the use of music for the ends of government again during the French Revolution and under Mao in China.

The unusually rich details of military music only reflect the environment of constant battle in which all of these early societies found themselves. Among all early accounts, there is no greater insight into the use of trumpet signals than that which we find in the Book of Numbers.

The Old Testament descriptions of entertainment music and banquets, with their prostitutes, couches and drinking, do not differ from other societies and are remarkable only because they are mentioned here.

PART 3

Aesthetics in the Musical Practice of Ancient Greece

6 A PREFACE TO THE MUSIC OF ANCIENT GREECE

The relations between Egypt and Greece can be documented to very remote times, as, for example, in the case of Danaus, a probable brother to Amunoph III, who left Egypt and founded Argos, where he died in 1,425 BC. With the reign of Psammetichus I, Egypt, which had been a rather closed society, was opened to Greek travelers and settlers and from this date many notable Greek philosophers, from Thales and Solon to Plato spent time there. It is no surprise, therefore, that the earliest Greek musical traditions we know of seem quite similar to those of the older Egyptian culture. When we read the writings of the early Greeks and look at the icons of the Egyptians we sense a common ground. Indeed, when Herodotus visited Egypt, he was astonished when he heard a song there which he had believed was a famous song of Greek origin.

These kinds of relationships we can see more clearly than could the early Greeks, thanks to the perspective of a very considerable amount of time. The early Greeks themselves were wont to find their origins in what we call their Myths. These myths, while only colorful stories to us, were for the early Greeks at the very least an important handed down oral tradition. While we can't think of them as genuine oral history, perhaps there may yet be embedded in these stories small nuggets of historical possibilities passed down from a time too remote to have writing. Consider, for example, the myth of the sea god, Triton, and his 'invention' of the trumpet. He, we are told, in the war against the giants, blew into a sea conch producing sounds so new and frightening that the giants, thinking they had encountered a terrible and ferocious monster, took flight. Well, if we leave out the part about the giants, it certainly is easy to imagine this as a possible scenario for the discovery of the trumpet-type instrument. That is to say, some distant man walking along the shore and picking up a large conch and blowing through it to remove the water and sand he subsequently producing a frightening sound. Or, when Ovid relates a mythical musical contest between Pan and his panpipes and Apollo with his lyre,[1] a contest which the latter wins, could not this be viewed as an allegorical testament to the transformation of Greek music from more ancient rural roots to the much more sophisticated music of the lyric poets?[2]

1 Ovid, *Metamorphoses*, bk. 11.

2 Athenaeus, in *Deipnosophistae*, 9.390, quotes Chamaeleon of Pontus as saying, 'The men of old devised the invention of music from the birds singing in solitary places; by way of imitating them, men instituted the art of music.'

In addition, Strabo points out that there was an important educational purpose in the retention of the myths.

> In the first place, I remark that the poets were not alone in sanctioning myths, for long before the poets the states and the lawgivers had sanctioned them as a useful expedient, since they had an insight into the natural affections of the reasoning animal; for man is eager to learn, and his fondness for tales as a prelude to this quality. It is fondness for tales, then, that induces children to give their attention to narratives and more and more to take part in them. The reason for this is that myth is a new language to them—a language that tells them, not of things as they are, but of a different set of things. And what is new is pleasing, and so is what one did not know before; and it is just this that makes men eager to learn. But if you add thereto the marvelous and the portentous, you thereby increase the pleasure, and pleasure acts as a charm to incite to learning.[3]

3 Strabo, *The Geography of Strabo*, trans. Horace L. Jones (Cambridge, MA: Harvard University Press, 1960), 1.2.8.

The real problem with the history of Greek music is that we have a great deal of myth and history but very little music. Because so little actual Greek music survives, many aspects of this music which would be of the most interest today are forever lost to our understanding, in particular what is meant by the Greek 'modes.' We know that these names, like 'Dorian,' were first the names of particular societies before they became systems for tuning the lyre, at a time when the Greeks had no names for the actual notes of music. Several centuries later, Aristoxenus, a pupil of Aristotle, coined the term *tonos*, suggesting that perhaps they had become somewhat more like modern scales. But none of this tells us anything about the music itself.[4]

4 Neither does the description *in words* by Athenaeus tell us anything about the *taste* of the 'Phrygian figs,' or the 'Lydian figs,' or the *smell* of the 'Phrygian odor' [*Deipnosophistae*, 3. 75, 76 and 14.626].

Plato mentions Ionian, Dorian, Phyrgian and three kinds of Lydian (but omits Aeolian!), but why does he say that the tenor Lydian and the bass Lydian should be banned from education? Aristotle intrigues us even more when he defines Dorian as 'music of a moderate and settled temper … grave and manly'; Mixolydian 'makes men sad and grave … woeful and quiet'; Hypodorian as 'magnificent and steadfast'; whereas Phrygias is 'exciting and orgiastic [and] inspires enthusiasm.'[5] This reminds us of one of the most frequently told tales regarding the character of these modes, an incident involving Alexander the Great. As Plutarch retells this moment,

5 Aristotle, *Problemata*, 19.48; *Politica*, 8.5, 7.

> Even Alexander himself, when Antigenides played before him in the Harmatian mode, was so transported and warmed for battle

by the charms of lofty melodies, that leaping from his seat all in his clattering armor he began to lay about him and attack those who stood next him, thereby verifying to the Spartans what was commonly sung among themselves,

> *The masculine touches of the well-tuned lyre*
> *Unsheathe the sword and warlike rage inspire.*[6]

And what are we to think of the contention of Theophrastus of Eresus (372–287 BC), a disciple of Aristotle, who wrote that a person suffering from sciatica would always be free from attacks if one played the aulos in the Phrygian mode over the part of the body affected?[7]

The fact is that these modes are more appropriately thought of as 'styles' of music and because virtually all of the music is lost we can not know what the Greeks recognized in these styles. Even in their own time, according to Plutarch, these various peoples doubted the ability of other peoples to understand their music.

> Indeed it is much questioned among the Dorians themselves, whether the enharmonic composers be competent judges of the Dorian songs.[8]

To merely know, therefore, how the lyre was tuned for the various modes actually tells us nothing of the style of music then played. Thus, when Aeschylus writes,

> Through me too, sorrow runs
> Like a strange Ionian song[9]

we can know the tuning, but nothing of the true nature of the music, or what he could mean by 'strange.' It is as if two thousand years from now someone were speaking of nineteenth-century music and commented on German music being different from French music. We could accept that statement at face value, but if no nineteenth-century music were extant we could not know what the statement actually means musically.

By the way, the idea which the Greeks have suggested of relating 'modes' to specific emotions reappears from time to time until the present day. But if their modes are understood as 'scales,' there is no possible logical foundation for such ideas, since there was no standardized pitch before the twentieth century. How could people agree on the correspondence of emotions with pitch if there were no agreed upon pitch?

6 Plutarch, 'The Second Oration Concerning the Fortune or Virtue of Alexander the Great.'

7 *On Inspiration*, quoted in Athenaeus, *Deipnosophistae*, 14.624. Plutarch, in 'Concerning the Virtues of Women,' also tells of a sickly woman who was healed by the study of music.

8 Plutarch, 'Concerning Music.'

9 Aeschylus, *The Supplices*, 69–70.

It is very clear that the musician who accompanied the singer of ancient Greece did not always play the same notes as the singer, but to what degree there was anything like harmony as we know it, no one can say. Certainly, it is difficult to imagine that comments such as the following one by Aristotle refers only to unisons and octaves.

> We delight in concord because it is the mingling of contraries which stand in proportion to one another.[10]

10   Aristotle, *Problemata*, 19.38.

And what about the reference by Athenaeus to players of the five-string *magadis*, 'Each man ringing out a different tone from the other.'?[11]

Similarly, nearly all scholars who mention rhythm in early Greek music speculate little further than presuming that the rhythms of the music must have been similar to those of poetry. We believe, however, that suggestions can be found which raise the possibility of some kind of meter, or organized beat, in the modern sense. For example, in an anonymous poem dating ca. 800 BC, we find a procession of people singing and *beating time*.

11   Athenaeus, *Deipnosophistae*, 14.637.

> They set out to go, and the lord Apollo, son of Zeus, led the way,
> his step high and stately, and with the lyre in his hands
> played a lovely tune. The Cretans followed him
> to Pytho, beating time and singing the Iepaieon
> in the fashion of Cretans singing a paean when the divine
> Muse has put mellifluous song in their hearts.[12]

12   Homer, 'To Apollon,' 514–519, trans. Apostolos N. Athanassakis, *The Homeric Hymns* (Baltimore: Johns Hopkins University Press, 1976).

In another place, Plutarch seems to suggest the presence of a clear, regular beat structure within melody, in describing the fleet carrying the ashes of Demetrius (337–283 BC) as part of his funeral obsequies.

> The most famous aulos player of the time, Xenophantus, was sitting close to it playing a solemn melody, to which the rowers kept time in rhythm. The beat of their oars, like funeral mourning, answered the strains of the aulos.[13]

13   Plutarch, *Lives*, 'Demetrius,' 53.

The fact that so little actual music survives also prevents us from fully understanding the role of music in Greek society, no matter how vivid a description we may have of it. How we wish, for example, we could hear the music which corresponded to Plutarch's fascinating discussion of the Spartans.[14]

14   Plutarch, 'Customs of the Lacedaemonians.' Plutarch also notes that when it was necessary to punish one, the guilty one had to parade around the city singing a satire of his own composition which reflected on the folly of his crime.

They spent a great part of their studies in poetry and music, which raised their minds above the ordinary level, and by a kind of artificial enthusiasm inspired them with generous heats and resolutions for action. Their compositions, consisting only of very grave and moral subjects, were easy and natural, in a plain dress, and without any paint or ornament, containing nothing else but the just commendations of those great personages whose singular wisdom and virtue had made their lives famous and exemplary, and whose courage in defense of their country had made their deaths honorable and happy. Nor were the valiant and virtuous only the subject of these songs; but the better to make men sensible of what rewards and honors are due to the memory of such, they made invectives in them upon those who were signally vicious and cowards, as men who died with as much contempt as they had lived with infamy. They generally concluded their poem with a solemn profession of what they would be, boasting of their progress in virtue, agreeable to the abilities of their nature and the expectations of their age.

At all their public festivals these songs were a great part of their entertainment, where there were three companies of singers, representing the three several ages of nature. The old men made up the first chorus, whose business was to present what they had been after this manner:

> *That active courage youthful blood contains*
> *Did once with equal vigor warm our veins.*

To which the chorus, consisting of young men only, thus answers:

> *Valiant and bold we are, let who will try:*
> *Who dare accept our challenge soon shall die.*

The third, which were of young children, replied to them in this manner:

> *Those seeds which Nature in our breast did sow*
> *Shall soon to generous fruits of virtue grow;*
> *Then all those valiant deeds which you relate*
> *We will excel, and scorn to imitate.*

And when Plutarch says of them, 'That music was ever accounted among them the best, which was most grave, simple, and natural,' we wish we could also hear the music against which this comparison was made.

Plutarch says the reason the Greeks 'were so careful to teach their children music,' was,

for they deemed it requisite by the assistance of music to form and compose the minds of youth to what was decent, sober, and virtu-

15   Plutarch, 'Concerning Music.'

ous; believing the use of music beneficially efficacious to incite to all serious actions.[15]

Strabo gives a slightly different explanation for the use of music to form character. The ancient Greeks, he said,

> assumed that every form of music is the work of the gods ... And by the same course of reasoning they also attribute to music the upbuilding of morals, believing that everything which tends to correct the mind is close to the gods.[16]

16   Strabo, *The Geography of Strabo*, 10.3.10.

If music was considered this important to education, it stands to reason that someone must oversee the quality of the music itself. Much as Plato would recommend later for his utopian city, Plutarch suggests that the music used in education was subject to civic censors.

> They adjudged it necessary for the preservation of that gravity and seriousness of manners which was required of their youth for the attainments of wisdom and virtue, never to admit of any light and wanton, any ludicrous or effeminate poetry; which made them allow of no poets among them but such only who for their grave and virtuous compositions were approved by the public magistrate; that being hereby under some restraint, they might neither act nor write any thing to the prejudice of good manners, or to the dishonor of their laws and government.[17]

17   Plutarch, 'Customs of the Lacedaemonians.'

But we also know there was a more pragmatic use of music and dance to prepare young men for the requirements of the soldier. In the *pyrrhiche*, danced to the aulos, for example, the first part consisted of very fast feet movement, needed to chase the enemy, or escape its pursuit. The second part was a simulated combat and the third part consisted of leaping movements, as might be needed to leap over walls and ditches, etc.[18] It is no doubt for this reason that Socrates is quoted as having said, 'The best dancer makes the best warrior.'[19]

18   Georges Kastner, *Manuel général*, 9ff.

19   Athenaeus, *Deipnosophistae*, 14.628. Athenaeus, in 1.20, says Socrates himself was a dancer.

Even the wise Socrates was fond of the 'Memphis' dance, and was often surprised in the act dancing it, according to Xenophon. He used to say to his acquaintances that dancing was exercise for every limb.

The primary values of the use of music in education were moral in character, not those having to do with the inherent value of music itself. Thus while we find gods who played instruments, we find almost no Greek leaders, or members of the aristocracy, who do. No doubt they looked upon players as members of the craft class and, as Lord Chesterfield would recommend to his son centuries later, 'Eat meat, but don't be your own butcher,' they no doubt approved listening to music, but not actually playing it. Indeed, there is a story of Philip II, father to Alexander the Great (a rare aristocratic musician), who, after hearing his son perform a composition in a charming and skillful manner, said to him, 'Are you not ashamed, son, to play so well?'[20] Given this attitude, it is easy to believe another story about Philip, again told by Plutarch. Apparently Philip was debating with a musician over some aspect of music and the player responded, with respect to the difference in their stations, 'May never so great a misfortune befall thee, O King, as to understand these things better than I do.'[21] We conclude this was the general consensus when we read Plutarch's remark that Antisthenes was absolutely correct when he said, upon being told that one Ismenias was an excellent piper,

20 Plutarch, Lives, 'Pericles.'

21 Plutarch, 'Second Oration Concerning the Fortune or Virtue of Alexander the Great.'

> It may be so, but he is but a wretched human being, otherwise he would not have been an excellent piper.[22]

22 Plutarch, *Lives*, 'Pericles.'

Plutarch provides another insight into the lack of personal participation in performance by the Greek aristocracy when he discusses the education of Alcibiades.

> When he began to study, he obeyed all his other masters fairly well, but refused to learn upon the aulos, as a sordid thing, and not becoming a free citizen; saying, that to play on the lute or harp does not in any way disfigure a man's body or face, but one is hardly to be known by the most intimate friends, when playing on the aulos. Besides, one who plays on the harp may speak or sing at the same time; but the use of the aulos stops the mouth, intercepts the voice, and prevents all articulation. 'Therefore,' said he, 'let the Theban youths pipe, who do not know how to speak, but we Athenians, as our ancestors have told us, have Minerva for our patroness, and Apollo for our protector, one of whom threw away the aulos, and the other stripped the aulos-player of his skin.' Thus, between raillery and good earnest, Alcibiades kept not only himself but others from learning, as it presently became the talk of the young boys, how Alcibiades despised playing on the aulos, and ridiculed those who studied it. In consequence of which, it ceased to be reckoned amongst the liberal accomplishments, and became generally neglected.[23]

23 Plutarch, *Lives*, 'Alcibiades.'

By virtue of the surviving literature, histories, and poetry, even without actual music specimens, we can nevertheless appreciate the fact that music played a role in all the celebrations of Greek daily life, the weddings, social gatherings, entertainments, funerals, and a variety of cult festivals. As representative of the latter, Athenaeus describes some of the music heard during the three-day celebration by the Spartans of their 'Feast of Hycinthia':

> Boys with tunics girded high play the lyre or sing to aulos accompaniment while they run the entire gamut of the strings with the plectrum; they sing the praises of the god in anapaestic rhythm and in a high pitch. Others march through the theater mounted on gaily adorned horses; full choirs of young men singing some of their national songs, and dancers mingling among them go through the figures in the ancient style, accompanied by the aulos and the voice of the singers.[24]

24 Athenaeus, *Deipnosophistae*, 4.139.

Strabo mentions the celebrations of the Dionysus cult on the Island of Crete, with 'tambourines and similar noisy instruments and with war dance and uproar,' and in another place,

> Bacchic revelry with the high-pitched, sweet-sounding breath of Phrygian flutes ... and joined it to the choral dances of the Trieterides, in whom Dionysus takes delight.[25]

25 Strabo, *The Geography of Strabo*, 10.3.11 and 13.

In addition to the lyre, which is so fully documented in the extant literature, another instrument which would have been well known to the early Greeks was the long, straight trumpet, called *salpinx*.[26] This instrument is frequently mentioned in its military connection, from the fifth century BC. The various trumpet signals which are described were apparently sufficiently recognized that on occasion we read of some general fooling the enemy by the deliberate use of incorrect signals.

26 The trumpet is rarely mentioned in early Greek poetry. Homer, for example, never mentions it in his otherwise vivid battle descriptions.

But there was an interesting appearance of the trumpet which literature rarely mentions and that is the trumpet contests which began with the 96th Olympiad of 396 BC. These seem to have been more physical contests, rather than musical, and perhaps the modern Olympic motto, *citius, altius, fortius* (faster, higher, stronger) describes them well. We know the names of a few of the famous and the information about them reads like a description of sumo wrestlers. We are told, for example, that Heradorus of Megara consumed, in a typical meal, six pints of wheat bread, twenty pounds of meat and six quarts of wine! We also know of a women trumpeter who participated in these contests, Aglais, the daughter of Megacles. She wore a wig with a plume on her head and had an appetite similar to the male trumpeter, eating in a typical meal twelve pounds of meat, four pints of wheat bread and a pitcher of wine![27]

27 Athenaeus, *Deipnosophistae*, 10.414.

The most important wind instrument was of course the aulos, the double-pipe instrument which is so often pictured in vases of this period. Although usually called a 'flute' in English literature, it was unquestionably a reed, and probably double-reed, instrument. As Alcibiades suggested above, this instrument apparently required some exertion to play as it is usually pictured with the player wearing a leather band to support his cheeks. The myth he referred to was that of the goddess Minerva, who invented the aulos, but threw it away as she observed, when looking in a river, how the exertion in playing it deformed her face!

The aulos is described in the earliest accounts of the Greek armies, as for example in the twelfth century BC battle when the Heracleidae defeated Eurystheus of Argos, claiming the Peloponnesus Island. Tradition says it was the aulos players marching in front of the troops, playing a 'rhythmic chant,' which enabled the soldiers to keep their ranks and defeat the enemy.[28]

28 Kastner, *Manuel général*, 26.

The aulos was probably nearly as loud as the narrow bore trumpet, but its great advantage, of course, was its ability to play melodies. Thus, an eyewitness of the troops of Lycurgus (ninth century BC) marveled,

> It was a magnificent and terrible sight to see them marching to the tune of the aulos, with no gap in their lines and no terror in their souls, but calmly and gaily led by music into the perilous fight. Such men were not likely to be either panic stricken or over-reckless, but steady and assured, as if the gods were with them.[29]

29 Plutarch, *Lives*, 'Lycurgus,' 22.

Indeed the gods *were* with them, or at least so an oracle informed the Spartans—so long as they marched to the sound of the aulos. In their famous battle of Leuctra, in 371 BC, against the Thebans, they failed to use the aulos, for they had traditionally recruited these players from Thebes itself. They lost this battle and while modern historians speak only of the greater tactics of the Thebes, for the ancient historians the failure to use the aulos was sufficient reason to explain the defeat.[30]

30 Kastner, *Manuel général*.

But, as we shall read below, the aulos was familiar to all areas of early Greek life. It had its own contests and Plutarch tells us that Alexander the Great organized aulos contests because he had little interest in the usual boxing and wrestling contests.[31] Aristotle argued against these contests[32] and Strabo describes an actual repertoire piece from the contests at Delphi, one in which the aulos player personifies a battle between Apollo and a dragon which

31 Plutarch, *Lives*, 'Alexander,' 4.

32 Aristotle, *Politica*.

33   Strabo, *The Geography of Strabo*, 9.3.10.

34   Athenaeus, *Deipnosophistae*, 4.184 and 14.634.

35   Persaeus of Citium, *Convivial Notes*, quoted in Athenaeus, *Deipnosophistae*, 13.607. Plutarch gives, in 'Concerning the Cure of Anger,' a particularly sordid reference to the single-pipe girl.

Wherefore, when we go to the houses of drunkards, we may hear a wench playing the aulos betimes in the morning, and behold there, as one said, the muddy dregs of wine, and scattered fragments of garlands, and servants drunk at the door.

36   Philetaerus, *The Aulos Lover*, quoted in Athenaeus, *Deipnosophistae*, 14.633.

37   Matthew 9:24. As usual, aulos here often appears in English translations as 'flute.'

ends with the player, 'imitating the dragon as breathing its last in hissings.'[33] Where there are contests there will be teachers and Athenaeus mentions a number of famous teachers and their (now lost) treatises as well as famous aulos schools at Olypiodorus and Orthagoras.[34]

Another frequently mentioned early Greek reed instrument, no doubt related to the aulos, was that played by the so-called, 'single-pipe girls.' As far as we can judge from the extant literature, this instrument was played exclusively by female entertainers, primarily prostitutes who would be auctioned off to the highest bidder after the banquet or drinking party. Persaeus gives an interesting anecdote of such a party which he attended in the third century BC.

There was a philosopher drinking with us, and when a single-pipe girl entered and desired to sit beside him, although there was plenty of room for the girl at his side, he refused to permit it, and assumed an attitude of insensibility. But later, when the single-pipe girl was put up for the highest bidder, as is the custom in drinking-bouts, he became very vehement during the bargaining, and when the auctioneer too quickly assigned the girl to someone else, he expostulated with him, denying that he had completed the sale, and finally that insensible philosopher came to blows, although at the beginning he would not permit the single-pipe girl even to sit beside him.[35]

Finally, as the ancient Greeks found their past in myths, so they looked for their future in myths. For example, Philetaerus, in the fourth century BC, cites a myth that if one goes to Hades, but is a recognized lover of good music, one is permitted 'to revel in love affairs,' whereas 'those whose manners are sordid, having no knowledge of music,' are condemned to spend eternity carrying water in a fruitless effort to fill 'the leaky jar.'[36] Thus Philetaerus exclaims, 'Zeus, it is indeed a fine thing to die to the music of the aulos!' By this he meant arranging to have these musicians playing as one dies so as to demonstrate to the gods that one truly appreciated good music.

It is in the context of this myth that we understand a line in Menander's play, *Old Cantankerous*. The character, Getas, enters the stage from a shrine as an aulos player begins to play for him. Getas tells the aulos player to stop playing, 'I'm not ready for you yet!' And similarly, before Jesus could perform one of his miracles of raising a girl from the dead, he had to first chase the aulos players out of the house, saying, 'Depart, for the girl is not dead but sleeping.'[37]

7 THE EPIC POETS OF THE NINTH CENTURY

With the works of Homer, who flourished ca. 850 BC, and Hesiod, who flourished ca. 800 BC, Western European literature begins. Indeed, their works may have been preserved for a time in an oral fashion, for scholars believe the works of Hesiod coincided with, and the epics of Homer preceded, the introduction of the alphabet to Greece and the beginning of writing in that language.[1] These works are described by most scholars as oral poetry, meaning they were recited, but not sung. If this were the case, however, the recitation was done by one called a rhapsodist, whose form of speech apparently included definite melodic elements. How near this style was to actual singing we can not know, but Geoffrey S. Kirk, of the University of Cambridge, points out that 'the Homeric word for a poet is *aoidos* or singer, one who accompanies himself on the lyre-like instrument.'[2] This scholar makes another interesting observation, in his argument for the singing poet:

> Rarely a Homeric verse will begin with a word whose first syllable is by nature short ... and its explanation (so it seems to me) is almost certainly that the missing weight was supplied by a strong musical chord accompanying the first syllable.[3]

Whether singer or rhapsodist, in the case of Homer it is presumed his lengthy epics were performed as a series of smaller successive rhapsodies, due to their great length.

As for the general musical environment, Plutarch observes of this period,

> But among the more ancient Greeks, music in theaters was never known, for they employed their whole musical skill in the worship of the Gods and the education of youth; at which time, there being no theaters erected, music was yet confined within the walls of their temples, as being that by which they worshiped the supreme Deity and sang the praises of virtuous men.[4]

1 Friedrich A. Wolf, *Prolegomena*, 1795, believed writing was not introduced until 700 BC.

2 Geoffrey S. Kirk, *The Songs of Homer* (Cambridge: The University Press, 1962), 56.

3 Ibid., 89.

4 Plutarch, 'Concerning Music.'

ART MUSIC

The last purpose which Plutarch mentions above represents a kind of performance we believe falls within the definition of art music for this early period. While this is not really educational music, nevertheless the singer who 'sang the praises of virtuous men' was performing a role which had obvious moral and educational implications. Homer gives us a picture of one of these singers, a famous one he says, whose music is wondrous, if 'woeful.' It is an important characteristic of art music that the audience be able to listen in contemplation to the music. Homer makes clear, in this case, that the audience is listening in silence, and indeed one is moved to tears and requests music of a lighter character.

> For them the famous minstrel was singing, and they sat in silence listening; and he sang of the return of the Achaeans—the woeful return from Troy which Pallas Athene laid upon them. And from her upper chamber the daughter of Icarius, wise Penelope, heard his wondrous song, and she went down the high stairway from her chamber ... She stood by the doorpost of the well-built hall, holding before her face her shining veil ... Then she burst into tears, and spoke to the divine minstrel:
>
> 'Phemius, many other things thou knowest to charm mortals, deeds of men and gods which minstrels make famous. Sing them one of these, as thou sittest here, and let them drink their wine in silence. But cease from this woeful song which ever harrows the heart in my breast, for upon me above all women has come a sorrow not to be forgotten ...'
>
> Then the wise Telemachus answered her: 'My mother, why dost thou begrudge the good minstrel to give pleasure in whatever way his heart is moved? It is not minstrels that are to blame, but Zeus ... With this man no one can be wroth if he sings of the evil doom of the Danaans; for men praise that song the most which comes the newest to their ears.'[5]

5 Homer, *The Odyssey*, trans. Augustus Taber Murray (London: Heinemann, 1960), 1.325ff.

A short while later, Telemachus observes, 'This is a good thing; to listen to a minstrel such as this man is, like to the gods in voice.' Somewhat later, when it is time to dance, the character of the music changes and is described as 'gladsome song.'

Later in *The Odyssey* we find another description of one of these singers of epic poetry. The setting is now a banquet, but, as this extraordinary passage makes clear, this is not the usual banquet music—this is again music to be listened to. Indeed, we are told that only when everyone stopped eating and drinking did the singer begin to play and sing. In this case the singer is the blind Demodocus, 'to whom above all others has the god granted skill in song.' He is requested to 'give delight in whatever way his spirit prompts him to sing.'

> For him, the herald, set a silver-studded chair in the midst of the banqueters, leaning it against a tall pillar, and he hung the clear-toned lyre from a peg close above [the singer's] head, and showed him how to reach it with his hands. And beside him he placed a basket and a beautiful table [of food], and a cup of wine, to drink when his heart should bid him. So they put forth their hands to the good cheer lying ready before them. But when they had put from them the desire of food and drink, the Muse moved the minstrel to sing of the glorious deeds of warriors.[6]

Again a listener, now Odysseus [Ulysses], is moved to tears.

> This song the famous minstrel sang; but Odysseus grasped his great purple cloak with his stout hands, and drew it down over his head, and hid his comely face; for he had shame [that his guests, the Phaeacians, should see him] as he let fall tears from beneath his eyebrows. Yea, and as often as the divine minstrel ceased his singing, Odysseus would wipe away his tears and draw the cloak from off his head ... But as often as he began again, and the nobles of the Phaeacians bade him sing, because they took pleasure in his song [lay], Odysseus would again cover his head and moan. Now from all the rest he concealed the tears that he shed.

Later, Demodocus is sent for again, for the purpose of having him play music for a dance. When the artist arrives, however, he 'struck the chords in prelude to his sweet song and sang of the love of Ares and Aphrodite,' forcing the guests to listen rather than dance.[7]

A third time[8] Demodocus is brought before the guests to perform and again Homer notes that the performance waited until the eating had stopped. Because of the impact Odysseus received from the first performance, he now begs the singer to 'change thy theme' and sing no more of the fate of the Achaeans, but rather of the 'building of the horse of wood.' This request the singer complies with, but apparently in such a way that Odysseus was again moved to tears.

> This song the famous minstrel sang. But the heart of Odysseus was melted and tears wet his cheeks beneath his eyelids. And as a

6 Ibid., 8.60ff.

7 Ibid., 8.250ff.
8 Ibid., 8.470ff.

woman wails and flings herself about her dear husband, who has fallen in front of his city and his people, seeking to ward off from his city and his children the pitiless day; and as she beholds him dying and gasping for breath, she clings to him and shrieks aloud, while the foe behind her smite her back and shoulders with their spears, and lead her away to captivity to bear toil and woe, while with most pitiful grief her cheeks are wasted: even so did Odysseus let fall pitiful tears from beneath his brows. Now from all the rest he concealed the tears that he shed, but Alcinous alone marked him and took heed, for he sat by him and heard him groaning heavily.

Finally this Alcinous says, 'Let the minstrel cease, that we may all make merry.'

Before leaving these performances by this blind poet, we must also point out that some scholars believe Homer himself was a blind poet. Another blind poet-singer is found in an anonymous poem, ca. 800 BC, called, 'To Apollo.' In this poem the poet first gives us an interesting description of the talents of these poets, as well as a brief autobiographical note.

> After they first praise Apollo with a hymn
> and now again Leto and arrow-pouring Artemis,
> they tell of men and women who lived long ago
> and sing a hymn, charming the races of men.
> The tongues of all men and their noisy chatter
> they know how to mimic; such is their skill in composing the song
> that each man might think he himself were speaking.
> But now may Apollo and Artemis be propitious;
> and all you maidens farewell. I ask you to call me to mind
> in time to come whenever some man on this earth,
> a stranger whose suffering never ends, comes here and asks:
> 'Maidens, which of the singers, a man wont to come here,
> is to you the sweetest, and in whom do you most delight?'
> Do tell him in unison that I am he,
> a blind man, dwelling on the rocky island of Chios,
> whose songs shall all be the best in time to come.[9]

9   'To Apollon,' in Homer, *The Homeric Hymns*, trans. Apostolos N. Athanassakis (Baltimore: Johns Hopkins University Press, 1976), 158–173.

Hesiod also remarks on the impact which this form of singing 'the praises of virtuous men' had on the listener.

> A man may have some fresh grief over which to mourn,
> and sorrow may have left him no more tears, but if a singer,
> a servant of the Muses, sings the glories of ancient men
> and hymns the blessed gods who dwell on Olympus,

the heavy-hearted man soon shakes off his dark mood,
   and forgetfulness
soothes his grief, for this gift of the gods diverts his mind.[10]

10   Hesiod, *Theogony, Works and Days, Shield*, trans. Apostolos N. Athanassakis (Baltimore: Johns Hopkins University Press, 1983), *Theogony*, 98–103.

There is a very interesting anonymous poem, whose date is unknown, but probably early, which also describes the singing of past glories. Here, however, we have a god, Hermes, singing to a god, Apollo, of past gods.

Upon his left arm he took
the lyre and with the plectron struck it tunefully, and under his hand
it resounded awesomely. And Phoibos Apollon laughed
for joy as the lovely sound of the divine music
went through to his heart and sweet longing seized him
as he listened attentively. Playing sweetly on the lyre,
the son of Maia boldly stood to the left
of Phoibos Apollon and to the clear-sounding lyre
he sang as one sings preludes. His voice came out lovely,
and he sang of the immortal gods and of black earth,
how they came to be, and how each received his lot.
Of the gods with his song he first honored Mnemosyne,
mother of the Muses, for the son of Maia fell to her lot.
And the glorious son of Zeus honored the immortals
according to age, and as each one had been born,
singing of everything in due order as he played the lyre on his arm.[11]

11   'To Hermes,' in Homer, *Homeric Hymns*, 418–433.

Following this, in an extraordinary passage, Hermes, in giving the gift of music to Apollo, gives him advice on the use of music. The choice he holds out to Apollo is the same choice offered to musicians today.

You may choose to learn whatever you desire,
but since your heart is so eager to play the lyre,
sing and play the lyre and minister to gay festivities,
receiving this skill from me and, friend, grant me glory.
Sing well with this clear-voiced mistress in your arms,
since you have the gift of beautiful and proper speech.
From now on in carefree spirit bring it to the well-provided feast,
the lovely dance, and the revel where men vie for glory,
as a fountain of good cheer day and night. Whoever
with skill and wisdom expertly asks, to him
it will speak and teach him all manner of things
joyful to the mind, being played with a gentle touch,
for it shuns toilsome practice. But if anyone should
in ignorance question it at first with rudeness,

12 Ibid., 474–489. The translator observes, 'The artistic sensitivity and the truly genteel nature of the advice that Hermes gives Apollo are remarkable. It is small wonder that the best practitioners of the art of singing and playing the lyre were called *theioi* (divine).'

to him in vain it will chatter high-flown gibberish forever. You may choose to learn whatever you desire.[12]

One further passage in Homer describes a different kind of art music. Here, in *The Iliad*, we find Achilles performing for himself, for the purpose of 'delighting his soul,' as Homer mentions twice. Only one friend is listening, again in silence, and so involved is Achilles in his music that he does not notice the arrival of strangers and is startled.

> And they came to the huts and the ships of the Myrmidons, and found [Achilles] delighting his soul with a clear-toned lyre, fair and richly wrought, with a bridge of silver; this had he taken from the spoil when he laid waste the city of Eetion. Therewith was he delighting his soul, and he sang of the glorious deeds of warriors; and Patroclus alone sat over against him in silence, waiting until Aeacus's son should cease from singing. But the twain came forward and goodly Odysseus led the way, and they took their stand before his face; and Achilles leapt up in amazement with his lyre in his hand, and left the seat whereon he sat.[13]

13 *Iliad*, 9.185ff.

Finally, we should also mention a passage in Hesiod that caught the eye of Plutarch.[14] Hesiod says that when a man sees his wealthy neighbor planting and plowing with zeal, it makes him too 'long for work' and that this form of competition is good. However, artists should not compete, nor create for the market place.

14 Plutarch in 'How to Profit by our Enemies,' notes, 'Neither doth Hesiod approve of one potter or one singer's envying another.'

> Then potters eye one another's success and craftsmen, too; the beggar's envy is a beggar, the singer's a singer. Perses, treasure this thought deep down in your heart, do not let malicious [competition] curb your zeal for work [only] so you can see and hear the brawls of the market place.[15]

15 Hesiod, *Works and Days*, 25–29. Aethenaeus, in *Deipnosophistae*, 7.310, mentions a singing contest at this time in which the prize was 'a lad with the fair bloom of youth,' for the enjoyment of the winner!

EDUCATIONAL MUSIC

When these rhapsodists sung after banquets, there was often a certain educational purpose implied in their performance. Singing of the great men of the past had this purpose, in part, but also, according to Athenaeus, it seems the noble guests depended on these singers to restore balance in their character.

> It is plain that Homer observes the ancient Greek system when he says, 'We have satisfied our souls with the equal feast and with

the lyre, which the gods have made the companion of the feast,' evidently because the art is beneficial also to those who feast. And this was the accepted custom, it is plain, first in order that every one who felt impelled to get drunk and stuff himself might have music to cure his violence and intemperance, and secondly, because music appeases surliness; for, by stripping off a man's gloominess, it produces good-temper and gladness becoming to a gentleman ... It is plain, therefore, that while most persons devote this art to social gatherings for the sake of correcting conduct and of general useful-ness, the ancients went further and included in their customs and laws the singing of praises to the gods by all who attended feasts, in order that our dignity and sobriety might be retained through their help. For, since the songs are sung in concert, if discourse on the gods has been added it dignifies the mood of every one ... It is plain, therefore, in the light of what we have said, that music did not, at the beginning, make its way into feasts merely for the sake of shallow and ordinary pleasure, as some persons think.[16]

16   Aethenaeus, *Deipnosophistae*, 14.627ff.

In another place,[17] Athenaeus points to the Odyssey (8.475), in which Agamemnon leaves a rhapsodist behind with Clytaemnestra.

17   Ibid., 1.14.

His business was first to dilate on the virtues of women and inspire emulation for uprightness, and secondly, to furnish pleasant enter-tainment to divert her mind from low thoughts.

ENTERTAINMENT MUSIC

There are several other descriptions of banquet music in Homer which are lacking only the emphasis on the *attentive* audience, thus we presume these to be more entertainment in character. One such scene, at the beginning of *The Odyssey*, also gives us the name of another poet-musician.

Now after the wooers had put from them the desire of food and drink, their hearts turned to other things, to song and to dance; for these things are the crown of a feast. And a herald put the beautiful lyre in the hands of Phemius, who sang perforce among the wooers; and he struck the chords in prelude to his sweet tale.[18]

18   Homer, *The Odyssey*, 1.148ff. Similar banquet scenes with music in *The Odyssey* are found in 13.25ff (where Demodocus appears again) and in 21.432.

In *The Iliad* there are two banquet scenes of the gods. In one Apollo plays the lyre while the Muses sang, 'replying one to the other with sweet voices,'[19] and in the other they sing and dance.[20]

19   Homer, *The Iliad*, 1.600.

20   Ibid., 16.182.

Hesiod, in his *Theogony*, also has a banquet of the gods with 'enchanting song.'[21]

In their references to wedding music, these epic poets always mention music as part of the entertainment, not as part of the service itself. In *The Odyssey*, for example, Homer describes two acrobats performing during the music.

> ...and among them a divine minstrel was singing to the lyre, and two tumblers whirled up and down through the midst of them, as he began his song.[22]

Homer describes a marriage procession, with aulos and lyres in *The Iliad*.

> ...by the light of the blazing torches they were leading the brides from their bowers through the city, and loud rose the bridal song. And young men were whirling in the dance, and in their midst aulos and lyres sounded continually; and there the women stood each before her door and marveled.[23]

An almost identical description is given by Hesiod.

> And far in the distance
> the light of bright torches
> in the hands of serving maids
> danced in the night,
> and the maids themselves,
> brimming with festive verve,
> pressed on,
> trailed by bands of minstrels and singers.
> And all about there echoed
> the men's smooth song
> to the sound of the shrill pipes,
> while the girls' voices,
> filled with longing,
> took up the lead.
> On the other side young men
> reveled to the sound of the aulos,
> some playfully dancing and singing,
> while others ran ahead,
> and their laughter rang
> in unison with the trills of the aulos.[24]

In discussing the period, Athenaeus provides a brief description of dancing presented as entertainment during a banquet. The

21 Hesiod, *Theogony*, 917.

22 Homer, *The Odyssey*, 4.18.

23 Homer, *The Iliad*, 18.490.

24 Hesiod, *Shield*, 274–284.

music is provided the dancers by the famous blind poet mentioned in *The Odyssey.*

> For Demodocus sang while 'boys in their first bloom' danced, and in the Forging of the Arms a boy played the lyre while others opposite him 'frisked about to the music and the dance.'[25]

Finally, at the beginning of book 10 of *The Iliad*, Homer describes an evening lull in battle, with the entertainment music of the soldiers heard drifting over the battle field.

> So often as [Agamemnon] gazed toward the Trojan plain, he marveled at the many fires that burned before the face of Ilios, and at the sound of aulos and pipes, and the din of men.

FUNCTIONAL MUSIC

Two references to functional music in the works of these epic poets are interesting because they both refer to music associated with occupations. Hesiod mentions workers in the vineyards working to music supplied by an aulos player.[26] Homer tells of two herdsmen (who were soon unfortunately killed!) playing their traditional panpipes.[27] The name of this traditional shepherd instrument is taken from the goat-footed god, Pan, of course. An early anonymous poem describes the playing of this mythical figure.

> Then only at evening
> he shouts as he returns from the hunt and on his pipes of reed
> he gently plays sweet music. In song he could even outdo
> that bird which sits among the leaves at flower-rich springtime
> and, pouring forth its dirge, trills honey-voiced tunes.[28]

Thus we can see by the extant material of the ninth century, it would appear that there was a very clear sense of aesthetics with regard to this sung poetry. This was art music with values strikingly similar to the highest art music today. Not only do we read of the demand that it be listened to in silence, but once we are told of a performer so deeply involved in his performance that he was startled when a person came near him.

The critical thing with respect to art music is the contemplative listener and here already we notice the deep emotional impact

25 Athenaeus, *Deipnosophistae*, 1.15.

26 Ibid., 299.

27 Homer, *The Iliad*, 18.526.

28 Nr. 19,'To Pan,' perhaps fifth century BC, in *The Homeric Hymns*, trans. Apostolos Athanassakis.

this music produced in the listener, several times provoking tears. Once the listener moaned and covered his face to hide his tears. On another occasion the listener produced 'pitiful' tears, so heartfelt that his emotion was compared to that felt by a woman upon seeing her dying husband. Beyond this extraordinary impression caused by the highest art music, we are told of additional purposes of music: to give delight and pleasure, to soothe grief, to evoke 'sweet longing,' and to dignify the listener. All in all, these are the highest values which one could ask of music of any era.

In addition we find these early Greeks had a clear sense of the universal quality of Art Music. We are told that the most skillful composers created music of such empathy that 'every man might think he himself were speaking.'

While we find references to the association of the musician to the divine, as in Egypt and the Near East, here the musician is also described as a 'servant of the Muses.' This we take to signify an awareness of music as an art, as if to say the musician is a 'servant of the art.' At the same time there is a clear awareness of the breadth of musical performance and one poet cautions a would-be musician that what he becomes is up to him, 'You may choose to learn whatever you desire.' There is a similar suggestion of an awareness of both old and new repertoire, with the interesting comment that new music is most praised.

There is also here a clear sense of the power of music to educate, to even transform the character of the listener. We are told music could cure violence and even intemperance. In Homer, Agamemnon leaves a musician with Clytaemnestra to 'inspire emulation for uprightness' and 'divert her mind from low thoughts.' We are not surprised at the power of music, but is is amazing to find such testimony from so early a period of Greek history.

These poets sing of the loftiest values of music.

O sacred voice of the Pierian choir,
Immortal Pindar! Oh, enchanting air,
Of sweet Bacchylides! Oh, rapturous lyre,
Majestic graces of the Lesbian fair!
Stesichorus, thy full Homeric stream!
Soft elegies by Cea's poet sung!
Persuasive Ibycus, they glowing theme!
Sword of Alcaeus, that with tyrant's gore
Gloriously painted, lift'st thy point so high!
Ye tuneful nightingales, that still deplore
Your Alkman, prince of amorous poesy—
Oh yet impart some breath of heavenly fire
To him, who venerates the Grecian lyre.

This anonymous poem pays tribute to a group of seventh and sixth centuries BC poets who are known as 'lyric poets.' The name 'lyric poet' is coined to reflect the fact that this poetry was sung. We must remember that even though we speak here of a very ancient period, the late Bronze Age, in the long span of man this is still a very recent period. The true origin of this type of sung literature is too distant to be known. Nagy, in his brilliant book on the work of these lyric poets, gives a lengthy hypothesis on the development of both poetry and prose from earlier song forms.[1] He also makes the interesting suggestion that the retention of melody with poetry, as in the case of these lyric poets, may have been in part for the purpose of aiding the memory of the performer.

1   Gregory Nagy, *Pindar's Homer* (Baltimore: Johns Hopkins University Press, 1982), 38ff.

> Melody can be an important feature in the mnemonics of oral tradition in song, as we know from the studies of folklorists who scrutinize the transmission and diffusion of song: melody helps recall the words.[2]

2   Ibid., 50. The logic of this lies in the fact that both music and emotions are primarily in the right hemisphere of the brain and in the clinical evidence that emotions are the key to recall.

Our study of these lyric poets is frustrated by the fact that the extant body of their work is very incomplete. For Archilochus, for example, we have not a single complete poem and for all of them we have numerous fragments, sometimes fragments consisting of only a single word. A large number of these fragments survived in the wrappings of mummies, resulting in the irony of our debt to the dead, not the living, for their preservation, as Davenport points out.

We have brief quotations by admiring critics; and we have papyrus fragments, scrap paper from the households of Alexandria, with which third-class mummies were wrapped and stuffed. All else is lost. Horace and Catullus, like all cultivated readers, had Archilochos complete in their libraries. What the living could not keep, the dead and the dullest of books have preserved.[3]

The most important of these poets are:

Archilochus, of the first half of the seventh century BC, was a very creative person. He invented the iambic verse, wrote the first animal fable and is the author of the oldest fragment of a love lyric in Greek.[4] A professional soldier (his name means, 'First Sergeant'), we are not surprised at the barracks eroticism of some of his poetry. He was known by the ancients, however, as 'The Satirist.' His works were banned by the Spartans, because of their mockery of uncritical bravery, and it is said that his tomb bore the inscription, 'Hasten on, Wayfarer, lest you stir up the hornets.'[5]

Sappho (ca. 640–550 BC) is said by Plutarch[6] to have been the first to introduce the mixolydian, which the ancients heard as melancholic. An early writer said she was a harp player from Mytilene in Lesbos. An early writer says she was the first to use the pectis.[7]

Alkman (ca. 640–600 BC) was a slave and choral conductor. He was admired by Goethe and Aristotle said he suffered terribly from lice. Chamaeleon says Alkman 'led the way as a composer of erotic songs, and was the first to publish a licentious song, being prone in his habits of life to the pursuit of women and to poetry of that kind.'[8]

Alcaeus (ca. 640–550 BC), together with Sappho and Ibycus, specialized in lyric love poetry.

Stesichorus of Himera (ca. 610–550 BC) was the creator of the epic hymn.

Anacreon of Teos (ca. 550–500 BC) was surpassed only by Sappho in the lyrical quality of his poetry. He is described by one early writer as, 'flame of drinking parties, cheater of women, of the aulos the foe, lover of the lyre, full of delight, healer of pain.'[9]

Ibycus of Rhegium (ca. 550–500 BC) specialized in choral odes.

3 Guy Davenport, *Archilochos, Sappho, Alkman* (Berkeley: University of California Press, 1980), 2. Plutarch, in 'Concerning Music,' lists some additional lyric poets whose works are now lost to us: Thamyras the Thracian, Demodocus the Corcyraean, and Phemius of Ithaca.

4 Ibid., 5.

5 Ibid., 3.

6 Quoted in Plutarch, 'Concerning Music.'

7 Menaechmus of Sicyon, quoted in Athenaeus, *Deipnosophistae*, 14.635.

8 Chamaeleon, quoted by Archytas of Mytilene, quoted by Athenaeus, *Deipnosophistae*, 13.600.

9 Critias, quoted by Athenaeus, *Deipnosophistae*, 13.600.

Simonides (b. ca. 556 BC) was considered by Pindar to be a mere imitator.[10] Somewhat of an epicurean, he is quoted as having said, 'What life among mortals is desirable without pleasure?'[11]

Pindar (b. ca. 518 BC) wrote the largest variety of forms[12] among these poets and is widely respected as the most talented.

Bacchylides, a contemporary of Pindar, and nearly as talented. He was known to ancient writers for his erotica.

This body of literature was performed in public by the solo singer with lyre (kitharoidos), the solo singer with aulos[13] (auloidos) and by both professional and non-professional choirs (khoros). According to Athenaeus, these singers traditionally had few facial expressions, but were more active with the feet, 'both in marching and in dance steps.'[14]

Although contests in instrumental and vocal music were more ancient, it was the festivals held in connection with the Olympiad for which most of the extant lyric poetry was composed.[15] These particular festivals began in 582 BC when the traditional Python festival in honor of Apollo was transformed into one given in the third year of each Olympiad. Two years later the Isthmian festival of Poseidon, in celebration of Spring, began to be held in the second and fourth year of each Olympiad. During these years the festival of the Neiman Zeus was also held. The fourth of these festivals, and the most ancient, dating from 776 BC, was the Olympian festival of Zeus, held each four years according to a lunar cycle.[16] The honoring of the athletes through the music of these lyric poets seems to have preceded somewhat the tradition of their being honored by statues, the earliest sculptors being documented from about 520 BC.[17]

In these public athletic festivals the performance of music centered in competition, called krisis, judged by adjudicators called, kritai. No doubt we may assume that kritai will be critics, for a fragment by Archilochus responds to some criticism he received.

> Upbraid me for my songs:
> Catch a cricket instead,
> And shout at him for chirping.[18]

According to comments by Pindar himself, the choral competition at these festivals was one among professionals.[19] This seems to be the meaning of a fragment of Bacchylides as well.

10 Plutarch, in 'Apophthegms of Kings and Great Commanders,' relates that when Simonides wanted Themistocles to render an unjust sentence, the latter replied, 'You would not be a good poet if you should sing out of tune; nor I a good governor, if I should give judgment contrary to law.'

11 Athenaeus, *Deipnosophistae*, 12.512.

12 Epinikia, enkomia, hymns, paeans, hyporchemes, dithyrambs, prosodia, partheneia, skolia, and dirges.

13 The aulos was the double-pipe familiar in Greek vases. Although it was clearly a reed, and probably a double reed, instrument, much English literature persists in calling it a 'flute.'

14 Athenaeus, *Deipnosophistae*, 1.22.

15 Not all Odes were performed at the festival; some were performed in procession, some in banquets at the palace, and some in serenade at the homes of the victors.

16 Additional information on these festivals can be found in Bacchylides, *The Poems and Fragments*, trans. Richard C. Jebb (Hildesheim: Georg Olms, 1967), 35, and Nagy, *Pindar's Homer*, 116ff.

17 Bacchylides, *The Poems and Fragments*, 37.

18 Davenport, *Archilochos, Sappho, Alkman*, 76.

19 Nagy, *Pindar's Homer*, 342.

The keenly-contested gifts of the Muses are not prizes open to all,
which the first comer may win.[20]

20   Bacchylides, *The Poems and Fragments*, 423.

Pindar also tells us in one ode that the music lovers of Aegina
loved these competitions.

For his city is one of music lovers,
The sons of Aeacus, bred to the clash of spears;
And glad are they to embrace a spirit, that shares
Their love of contest.[21]

21   *Ode for Sogenes of Aegina, Winner of the Boys' Pentathlon*, in Pindar, *The Odes of Pindar*, trans. Geoffrey S. Conway (London: Dent, 1972), 204. All Pindar quotations are from this translation

Indeed, one of the extant odes of Pindar was written for 'Midas of
Acragas, Winner of the Aulos Playing Contest,' composed for the
Pythian festival of 490 BC.

In addition to these great public festivals there were apparently
more intimate performance sites called *symposia*, where, much like
concerts today, the works of the older lyric poets were performed
as 'Classics.'[22] Indeed, we find evidence of this tradition for the
performance of older repertoire in *The Clouds* by Aristophanes,
produced in 423 BC.

22   Ibid., 113.

STREPSIADES. I bade him
    Take up his lyre and give me the good song
    Of old Simonides, 'The ram was shorn.'[23]

23   Aristophanes, *The Clouds*, 1355–1358.

These symposia offered the opportunity as well for both solo and
choral performance by non-professionals.[24]

24   Nagy, *Pindar's Homer*, 342.

Plutarch provides us with a nice story about Damonidas, a
member of one of these choruses. When the chorus master placed
him in the lowest place for the choral dance, Damonidas is said to
have responded, 'Well, sir, you have found a way to make this place,
which was infamous before, noble and honorable!'[25]

25   Quoted in Plutarch, 'Laconic Apophthegms.'

These choruses should be thought of as representatives of their
cities. Indeed, the Spartans actually called the interior civic space
the *Khoros*. Nagy explains this civic association.

As a representative of the polis, the chorus is concerned partly
with local interests, and it can therefore serve as a formal vehicle
of ritual … which constitute part of the ritual chain of athletics.
The range, however, of choral self-expression in matters of ritual is
certainly not limited to the Games. Besides epinician odes, a given
chorus in a given polis may perform a wide variety of other kinds
of compositions related to various local or civic rituals.

…

As a microcosm of society, it is equally important to note the khoros is also a microcosm of social hierarchy. Within the hierarchy that is the chorus … a majority of younger members act out a patter of subordination to a minority of older leaders; this acting out conforms to the role of the chorus as an educational collectivization of experience … the concept of older leaders, within the hierarchy of the chorus, is in most instances embodied in the central persona of the *khoregos* 'chorus leader.'[26]

26   Ibid., 399, 345.

The evidence is that most of the choral odes included dancing. However, it was clearly dancing reflecting the music, and not music for dancing, as is clarified in Pindar's *Ode for Hieron of Aetna, Winner of the Chariot Race.*

O glorious lyre, joint treasure of Apollo
And of the Muses violet-tressed,
Your notes the dancers' step obeys.[27]

27   Pindar, *The Odes of Pindar*, 81.

In addition to the performances of solo singers it is reasonable to assume that sometimes the solo performer performed together with the chorus. In one of the poems of Alkman, for example, the singer complains that he is too old and weak to dance with the chorus.[28]

28   Nr. 42, in Davenport, *Archilochos, Sappho, Alkman.*

While the 'classic period' of these choral performances coincided with the sixth-century lyric poets, the tradition continued for a time in the choral schools of Melanippides (ca. 450–413 BC), Philoxenus (435–380 BC) and Timotheus (end of the fifth and beginning of the fourth centuries BC).

In the lyric poetry performed by the solo singer, he was accompanied by either the lyre or the aulos. In the tradition of the Greek myths, the Greeks seemed compelled to assign the beginning of everything to a specific god. In the case of the lyre, the inventor was said to be Hermes, however some Greek writers said it was invented by Hermes, the son of Zeus and Maia, daughter of Atlas, while others assigned its origin to the Egyptian Hermes, or Thoth, the god of learning.[29] Plutarch, on the other hand, says that the lyre used by these lyric poets was invented by a student of Terpander.

29   Chappell, *The History of Music*, 1:27.

As to the form of the lyre, it was such as Cepion, one of Terpander's students first caused to be made, and it was called the Asian lyre, because the Lesbian lyre players bordering on Asia always made use of it. And it is said that Periclitus, a Lesbian by birth, was the last lyre player who won a prize by his skill, which he did at one of the Spartan festivals called Carneius; but he being dead, that succession of skillful musicians which had so long continued among the Lesbians, expired.[30]

30   Quoted by Plutarch in 'Concerning Music.'

31   Chappell, *The History of Music*, 32. We can assume this practice was actually much older, in view of the icons we seen in the Egyptian tombs. Bacchylides, *The Poems and Fragments*, 28, says Terpander founded a school of cithara performance in Lesbos which continued for several centuries.

32   Plutarch, in 'Concerning Music.'

33   Ibid.

34   Ibid.

35   Nagy, *Pindar's Homer*, 89. Strabo, *The Geography of Strabo*, 13.2, 13.4.

36   *Ode for Pytheas of Aegina, Winner of the Youths' Pankration*, Pindar, *The Odes of Pindar*, 193.

This musician called Terpander of Lesbos, who flourished ca. 710–670 BC, is said to have won the first music contest at the Feast of Carneius, in Sparta, in 676 BC, and to have invented the practice of lyre singing.[31] Plutarch, however, passes on to us the older belief that the invention of this practice belonged to the gods.

> Heraclides in his *Compendium of Music* asserts, that Amphion, the son of Jupiter and Antiope, was the first that invented playing on the lyre and lyric poetry, being first instructed by his father; which is confirmed by a small manuscript, preserved in the city of Sicyon, wherein is set down a catalog of the priests, poets, and musicians of Argos.[32]

Terpander is also said to have broadened the rhythmic practice associated with accompanying poetry, specifically that he 'introduced an elegant manner, that gave it much life.'[33] Plutarch also comments, in passing, that Terpander, by the power of his music, once appeased a sedition among the Lacedaemonians.[34]

Several early writers, including Strabo and Plutarch, also credit Terpander for being the one who introduced the seven-string lyre, replacing the earlier three- and four-string instruments.[35] Pindar, however, gave credit to Apollo for this instrument.

> Yet for these men the Muses' peerless choir
> Glad welcome sang on Pelion, and with them
> Apollo's seven-stringed lyre and golden quill.[36]

The introduction of additional strings to the lyre was not welcomed by those whose philosophy was to maintain the ancient musical traditions and Plutarch relates how Terpander was punished for this.

> And indeed so great an esteem and veneration had they for the gravity and simplicity of their ancient music, that no one was allowed to recede in the least from the established rules and measures of it, insomuch as the Ephori, upon complaint made to them, laid a severe mulet upon Terpander (a musician of great note and eminency for his incomparable skill and excellency in playing upon the lyre, and who, as he had ever professed a great veneration for antiquity, so ever testified by his eulogiums and commendations the esteem he always had of virtuous and heroic actions), depriving him of his lyre, and (as a peculiar punishment) exposing it to the censure of the people, by fixing it upon a nail, because he had added one string more to his instrument than was the usual and stated number,

though done with no other design and advantage than to vary the sound, and to make it more useful and pleasant.[37]

Plutarch also tells of a musician named Phrynis who had a nine-string lyre only to have Emprepes, one of the Ephors, cut out two strings with a hatchet, saying, 'Do not abuse Music!'[38] Artemon tells of a similar story.

> Timotheus of Miletus is held by most authorities to have adopted an arrangement of strings with too great a number … wherefore he was even about to be disciplined by the Lacedaemonians for trying to corrupt their ancient music, and some one was on the point of cutting away his superfluous strings when he pointed to a small image of Apollo among them holding a lyre with the same number and arrangement of strings as his own, and so was acquitted.[39]

It is understood that the purpose of expanding the number of strings on the lyre was to facilitate moving, if not modulation, from one mode to another. Indeed, Plutarch points to one composer, Sacadas, who composed a choral ode with the first strophe in Dorian, the second in Phrygian, and the third 'after the Lydian manner; and this style was called Trimeres (or threefold) by reason of the shifting of the modes.'[40] Plutarch also observes that at the time the lyre took on the extra strings, the wind instruments began to perform more complex accompaniments as well.[41]

Terpander is also said to have invented yet another string instrument, the barbiton.[42] We find this instrument named in a fragment, consisting of only three words, by Sappho.

> Barbitos, Baromos. Barmos.[43]

We get a glimpse of the rigid training the professional lyre players received as boys in *The Clouds* by Aristophanes. Those were the days, he says, when students were quiet and had discipline. They studied only the best music and the student who showed disrespect for the music by improvising was repaid for his efforts with lashes from the whip!

> CHORUS. Applaud the discipline of former days,
>   On your I call; now is your time to show
>   You merit no less praise than you bestow.
> DICAEOLOGOS. Thus summon'd, I prepare myself to speak
>   Of manners primitive, and that good [old] time
>   Which I have seen, when discipline prevail'd.

37   Quoted in Plutarch, in 'Customs of the Lacedaemonians.'

38   Quoted in Plutarch, in 'Laconic Apophthegms.'

39   Quoted in Athenaeus, *Deipnosophistae*, 14.636.

40   Quoted in Plutarch in 'Concerning Music.' Athenaeus (*Deipnosophistae*, xiv, cap. 31) says that Pronomus, the Theban, was the first who played three kinds of music upon one aulos; and that before him players used separate instruments for each.

41   Ibid.

42   Athenaeus, *Deipnosophistae*, 14.635.

43   Fragment 175, Davenport, *Archilochos, Sappho, Alkman.*

And modesty was sanctioned by the laws,
No babbling then was suffer'd in our schools;
The scholar's test was silence. The whole group
In orderly procession sallied forth
Right onwards, without straggling, to attend
Their teacher in harmony; though the snow
Fell on them thick as meal, the hardy brood
Breasted the storm uncloak'd: their lyres were strung
Not to ignoble melodies, for they were taught
A loftier key, whether to chant the name
Of Pallas, terrible amidst the blaze
Of cities overthrown, or wide and far
To spread, as custom was, the echoing peal.
There let no low buffoon intrude his tricks,
Let no capricious quavering on a note,
No running of variations high and low
Break the pure stream of harmony; no Phrynis
Practicing wanton warblings out of place—
Woe to his back that so was found offending!
Hard stripes and heavy would reform his taste.[44]

44   Aristophanes, *The Clouds*, 961ff.

The tradition of aulos singing, on the other hand, is credited by Plutarch to Clonas, 'an elegiac and epic poet' who also invented the Prosodia, a processional song sung with the aulos. He also mentions that some writers give credit, instead, to Ardalus the Troezenian. Finally, to be thorough, Plutarch passes on the opinion of some that it was a mythical player called Olympus, to whom this credit should go.

First they say, that Olympus, a Phrygian player upon the aulos, invented a certain melodic form in honor of Apollo, which he called Polycephalus, or of many heads. This Olympus, they say, was descended from the first Olympus, the student of Marsyas, who invented several forms of composition in honor of the Gods; and he, being a boy beloved of Marsyas, and by him taught to play upon the aulos, first brought into Greece the laws of harmony.[45]

45   Plutarch, in 'Concerning Music.'

Apparently the performance skills of the aulos players gradually began to usurp the attention of the public, as we notice several writers, Plato among them, vigorously complaining over liberties being taken by the aulos player. Pratinas, in 500 BC for example, reminded his listeners that the Muse had ordained that the song should be the mistress and the aulos the servant, and not the other way around![46]

46   Bacchylides, *The Poems and Fragments*, 46.

For out-of-doors performances, especially of the choral odes, one would assume that multiple aulos performers were involved, as was the tradition in the Greek military. There are poems by Sappho [47] and Bacchylides [48] which use the plural form, but also the poetry itself sometimes hints of multiple players in its choice of adjectives. This seems particularly evident in the case of references to loud playing, which a single aulos could not easily accomplish—especially, as in the following example by Pindar, when the result is still called 'sweet.'

> Let us now as Apollo bids, O Muses,
> From Sicyon lead our chant of triumph
> To Aetna, the new founded city,
> And Chromius' house of happy fortune,
> Whose doors, flung wide, brim over with the stream of guests.
> For him, then, play aloud
> The sweet notes of your praise.[49]

While the performances of this body of lyric poetry were sung with only the lyre and aulos, the poetry itself mentions other instruments familiar to ancient Greece, including the trumpet,[50] the horn-type instrument,[51] and drums [52] and cymbals.[53]

It would seem logical to suspect that the lyric song with lyre or aulos was more common in the seventh century, with the choral works (which continue in later dramatic works) becoming more prevalent in the sixth century BC.

The forms of this lyrical poetry are numerous.[54] The most lengthy was the ode, called *epinikion*, such as the ones by Pindar composed in celebration of various victors in the athletic contests. The later performance, with the lyre, of 'classic' compositions by past masters were called *skolion*. The *dithyramb* was a poem consisting of a narrative of heroes, often one of the Gods. It was this form which developed into the later tragedies. There was the *prosodion*, a processional hymn, and the nearly related dirges. The *hyporcheme* was particularly associated with dance, and Plutarch points to the excellence of Xenodamus in this form.[55] And, of course, there were entertainment forms, including love songs, either *erotica* or *skolia*.

The extant poetry rarely mentions modes, but when they are mentioned, they are familiar names: Pindar mentions only Lydian, Dorian, and Aeolian; Anacreon mentions Lydian.

With this introduction, we now turn to the question of aesthetics. What hints can we find in this body of lyric poetry which might illuminate to some degree the philosophical views on music of these poet–composers?

47 Sappho, Nr. 14:

> A long parade sings its way from the sea.
> The auloi are keen and the drums tight.

48 Bacchylides, *Ode for Automedes of Phlius*, victor in the pentathlon at Nemea.

> Now is the ancient city of Asopus filled with revelry for victory,
> And with the blended strains of auloi and lyres.

49 Pindar, *Ode for Chromius of Aetna*, Winner of the Chariot Race.

50 Archilochus, fragment 109 in Davenport, *Archilochos, Sappho, Alkman*, and Bacchylides, *Choral Ode to Theseus*.

51 Archilochus, fragment 211, ibid., which reads in entirety:

> There goes
> That horn player.

52 Sappho, Nr. 14, in Davenport, *Archilochos, Sappho, Alkman*.

53 Pindar, *Ode for Strepsiades of Thebes*, Winner of the Pankration.

54 Plutarch, in 'Concerning Music,' says that Anthes of Anthedon in Boeotia was the first to compose hymns and that Pierus of Pieria was the first to write in praise of the Muses.

55 Ibid.

Art Music

We regard most of the odes written for the Olympiad festivals as being art music. Excepting the processional works, they do not seem functional in nature and neither do they seem to have entertainment for their aim. We believe these works were listened to. Pindar mentions the listener in a poem in which he also comments on his work being carefully written.

56   Pindar, *Ode for Pytheas of Aegina*, Winner of the Youth's Pankration.

And touched your ears with fine-wrought melody ...[56]

Moreover, descriptions of the listeners are not of those reacting with superficial enthusiasm to entertainment, but rather imply a more internal experience:

57   Pindar, *Ode for Theron of Acragas*, Winner of the Chariot Race.

Gladdened with songs ...[57]

The case for these odes being art music is nowhere more clearly stated than by Bacchylides who defines his music as a gift of the Muses,

58   Bacchylides, *Ode for an Athenian*, Winner of the Foot Races at Isthmus.

a monument not made with hands, [that it] might be a common joy for mankind.[58]

From the lyric poet's perspective, we read several times of the importance of the poet being inspired. In Pindar for example,

Pisa too enjoins
My speech, for from her bidding come to men
The songs inspired of heaven.[59]

59   Pindar, *Ode to Theron of Acragas*, Winner of the Chariot Race.

and Bacchylides,

... for the inspired prophet of the violet-eyed Muses is ready to sing.[60]

60   Bacchylides, *Ode for Automedes of Philius*, Victor in the Pentathlon at Nemea.

Pindar adds that this inspiration from the Gods is a gift for which the poet must maintain respect.

61   Pindar, *Ode for Epharmostus of Opous*, Winner of the Wrestling Match.

For to insult the gods is a fool's wisdom,
A craft most damned, and unmeasured boasting
Is music for mad minds. Let no voice babble
Such follies.[61]

Bacchylides once specifically mentions that his song is 'newly composed,'[62] and in addition makes the observation that it is not easy to compose an original song.

> … for sooth 'tis no light task to find the gates of virgin song.[63]

It seems certain that Pindar would agree with this, for he drew a distinction between original genius and imitation. He accused Simonides of imitation, observing the true poet has a *fertile* mind, whereas those who have only *learned* chatter like crows.[64]

We believe all of this suggests a serious creator who was conscientious in his art. This being the case, we are not surprised to read Pindar's plea that we not forget his song.

> For from the gods comes every skilled endeavor
> Of mortal quality, be it
> Wisdom, or strength of arm, or eloquence.
> So when the praise I purpose
> Of this great man, let not
> My song fall like a bronze-tipped javelin
> Flung from the hand astray outside the line,
> But may a lengthy throw outstrip
> Its every rival.[65]

And in another poem he laments,

> The measured moments of my song
> Have all too brief a span.[66]

Regarding the musical nature of these odes, Plutarch writes that it was Archilochus who invented the idea of playing interludes on the lyre during a song, whereas the ancients played only during the singing.[67] Pindar suggests that his odes had an instrumental prelude for the purpose of giving the singers the pitch.

> And the singers heed your bidding,
> When on the vibrant air your prelude strikes,
> To guide the harmonies of choral song.[68]

The adjectives most often used by the poets to describe this lyric poetry are 'rich' and 'sweet.' Pindar, on five occasions, even calls the effect 'honey-sweet,' as in the following example.

> … and if some spell to charm his soul
> Lay in the honeyed sweetness of my songs …[69]

62 Bacchylides, *Ode for Pytheas of Aegina*, Victor in the Pancration at Nemea.

63 Bacchylides, Fragment 4, *The Poems and Fragments*, 413.

64 Quoted in Bacchylides, *The Poems and Fragments*, 15.

65 Pindar, *Ode for Hieron of Aetna*, Winner of the Chariot Race.

66 Pindar, *Ode for Herodotus of Thebes*, Winner of the Chariot Race.

67 Plutarch, in 'Concerning Music.'

68 Pindar, *Ode for Hieron of Aetna*, Winner of the Chariot Race.

69 Pindar, *Ode for Hieron of Syracuse*. In his *Ode for Diagoras of Rhodes*, Winner of the Boxing Match, Pindar refers to his music as 'the sweet fruit of the mind.'

In another poem in which Pindar uses this description, he adds the important qualification that the serious composer is not one who composes for money nor is a mere hired craftsman.

> For then the Muse had not yet bowed to love of gain,
> Or made herself a hireling journeyman;
> Nor in the market clad in masks of silver
> Did honey-tongued Terpsichore barter
> Her gentle-voiced and sweetly-sung refrains.
> But now she bids us pander to that word
> The Argive spoke, too sadly near the truth:
> 'Money, money makes [the] man' said he
> By gods and friends alike deserted.[70]

We know from these odes that the lyre or aulos player did not merely accompany note for note the vocal part, but rather played an independent role.[71] Simonides, in his poem, 'Anacreon's Tomb,' speaks of the 'tuneful lyre.'[72] No doubt this is what Pindar also meant when he wrote,

> How many a note would he have plucked, linking
> His lively lyre with this my song …[73]

The independent instrumental and vocal parts argue for some form of harmony, an argument strengthened by several descriptions of the result being 'blended.' Pindar, for example, writes,

> Not for him sounds the blended harmony,
> Under the roof-trees echoing to the lyre,
> Of children's lips in soft refrain.[74]

And certainly harmony must have been the what Bacchylides meant when he described the music as,

> the blended strains of auloi and lyres.[75]

Finally, Chappell points out several early Greek harpists who were known to play chords on their instrument.[76]

In conclusion, we find in these odes all the important characteristics of art music which one would find in any age: music which is inspired, carefully written, for the common joy for mankind, and listened to by a receptive audience. Interestingly enough, we even find in one of these early poets an awareness of the irony that

70   Pindar, *Ode for Xenocrates of Acragas*, Winner of the Chariot Race.

71   Athenaeus, *Deipnosophistae*, 5.180, says they also functioned as 'leaders,' or conductors, especially when dance was included.

72   Nathan Haskell Dole, *Odes of Anacreon*, trans. W. Shepard (Boston: Priv. Print. by N. H. Dole, 1903), 132.

73   Pindar, *Ode for Timasarchus of Aegina*, Winner of the Boy's Wrestling Match.

74   Pindar, *Ode for Hieron of Aetna*, Winner of the Chariot Race. The translation of Pindar's *Ode for Aristocleides of Aegina*, Winner of the Pankration, actually uses the word, 'chord.'
Of song grant, of my skill, full measure. Strike,
O daughter of the lord of cloudcapped heaven,
Chords to his honor.

75   Bacchylides, *Ode for Automedes of Philius*, Victor in the Pentathlon at Nemea.

76   Chappell, *The History of Music*, 149.

art composed for posterity may *not* enjoy wide popularity with the masses.

> And this is what everyone will say: 'These are the words of Theognis of Megara, whose name is known among all mortals,'
>   But I am not yet able to please all the townspeople.[77]

77   Quoted in Nagy, *Pindar's Homer*, 375.

Functional Music

In Bacchylides' *Ode to Hieron*, Victor in the Horse Race at Olympia, written in 476 BC, we read the following praise of Hieron, who became the ruler of Syracuse in 478 BC.

> Readily am I wont to send Hieron the song that tells forth his fame
> Without swerving from the path of justice;
> For by such praise it is that happy fortunes,
> Once firmly planted, flourish.

We must not mistake the insertion of such praise in these odes as meaning they were primarily functional, that is, that they existed for this purpose. Rather, this is only the same kind of political dues payment that one finds in the dedications of music during the Classical Period. Probably the poet was happy if he were lucky enough to work for a tyrant who appreciated music, as not all did. Plutarch, for example, tells us of such a one.

> Ateas, king of the Scythians, having taken Ismenias the musician prisoner, commanded him to play during one of his royal banquets. And when all the rest admired and applauded his music, Ateas swore that the neighing of a horse was more delightful to his ears.[78]

78   Plutarch, 'Second Oration concerning the Fortune or Viture of Alexander the Great.'

One of Pindar's odes, that for Sogenes of Aegina, was composed for a religious festival at Delphi, but it seems to be an art work and not intended to serve the purpose of religion. In several fragments by Alkman, on the other hand, we recognize music of religious purpose. First, an individual's song,

> O choirmaster,
> I am a mere girl,
> I sing like the rafter owl,
>   yet I sing
> to welcome the goddess of the dawn …

and in another fragment, soldiers singing a religious hymn,

> Eating and singing and the soldiers
> Nearby begin a hymn to Apollo

and, finally, a very interesting fragment.

> Sing, O Muse, sing high and clear
> O polytonal many-voiced Muse,
> Make a new song for girls to sing.
> About the towered temple of Therapne.

In a fragment of thirteen lines by Bacchylides we have part of a prayer to the gods for peace. It speaks of 'flowers of honeyed song,' and the music of auloi. Quite a different adjective is used for the war trumpet.

> No blast of bronze trumpet is heard; sleep of gentle spirit, that comforts the heart at dawn, is not stolen from the eyelids.[79]

79   Bacchylides, Fragment Nr. 3, *The Poems and Fragments.*

While the dirge was apparently a common form, in the extant poems of these lyric poets we find only two places, both in Pindar, where we are offered musical insight regarding this form.

> That long ago Pallas Athene invented,
> Weaving in music's rich refrain
> The ghoulish dirge of the fierce-hearted Gorgons.
> ......
> The manifold melodies of the aulos, to make
> In music's notes an image of the shrill
> Lamenting cries, strung from Euryale's
> Ravening jaws.[80]

80   Pindar, *Ode for Midas of Acragas,* Winner of the Flute Playing Contest.

> Nor even in death was he of songs forsaken, but the maids
> Of Helicon stood by his pyre and grave,
> And poured o'er him their dirge in chorus. Thus
> Even the immortals ruled
> That to a brave man, though he be no more,
> The songs of goddesses be given.[81]

81   Pindar, *Ode for Cleandrus of Aegina,* Winner of the Pankration.

Finally, in one of Pindar's odes we are given a brief description of another type of functional music, wedding music.

She waited not to see the marriage feast,
Nor stayed to hear
The sound of swelling bridal hymns,
Such notes as maiden friends of a like age are wont
To spread in soothing songs upon the evening air.[82]

82 Pindar, *Ode for Hieron of Syracuse*. Several of Sappho's poems seem to be for weddings, but they do not describe music.

ENTERTAINMENT MUSIC

One of the most frequently mentioned forms of entertainment music before the twentieth century is table music. Pindar gives us an example of a private dinner during which the guests sing light music.

In Sicily, land of rich flocks, and culls
Of all things excellent the noblest fruit;
Made glorious too by the fine flower
Of music's utterance—
Such strains as men will often blithely sing
Where we sit round the table of a friend.
Come then, take from its peg the Dorian lyre.[83]

83 Pindar, *Ode for Hieron of Syracuse*, Winner of the Horse Race.

Somewhat less elegant was the music of the prostitute, the single-pipe player mentioned in a fragment by Archilochus.

She could get her wine down
At a go,
Without taking a breath,
While the pipe
Played a certain little tune.[84]

84 Fragment 146, in Davenport, *Archilochos, Sappho, Alkman*.

Perhaps it was this same professional girl who is referred to in a fragment by Alkman, which in its entirety reads,

She shall play the pipe,
We shall sing the song.[85]

85 Alkman, Fragment 19, in ibid.

There must have been innumerable love songs then, as now. A fragment of such music by Anacreon attracts our curiosity: Was this harp rendered 'noble' for being in the Lydian style or by the nature of the music which could be created with this number of strings?

O Leucastis, I play
Upon a Lydian harp
A noble harp of twenty strings
And thou art in thy youthful prime.[86]

86   Quoted in Dole, *Odes of Anacreon*, 19.

In summary, when one reads the repertoire left by these singer–poets, one is struck by the remarkable, even extraordinary, level of aesthetic activity involving music. There were adjudicated competitions among both professional choirs and instrumentalists and public performances ranging from large out-of-doors festivals to smaller indoor concerts. The quality of these performances must have been high, for we can document both civic and individual pride in the level of artistry—the latter beautifully represented by the singer who, when asked to take the 'last chair' in a chorus, responded that by placing him there the position had been made 'noble and honorable.'

Underlying all this musical activity there appears to have been long established, and rigidly observed, traditions and beliefs regarding performance. These conservative attitudes are symbolized in the example of Terpander, a famous artist of the lyre, who was censured by the public for adding a single string to his instrument. Another artist had an extra string cut with a hatchet, while being warned, 'Do not abuse Music!'

These kinds of attitudes are also reflected in the strict philosophies of music education, which emphasized order and discipline. Music extolling great men of the past was programmed for modeling purposes. Only music of high quality was used and all improvisation was prohibited. The students sat in silence and breaking the rules resulted in 'hard stripes' on the back.

What aesthetic principles can we deduce from this body of poetry? First, the highest art was regarded as inspired, one poet saying by 'heaven' and another saying by the 'Muses.' Even the music performed for the dead is called by Pindar, 'The songs of goddesses.'

Second, Pindar states that original music was more valued than imitation and Bacchylides adds that it is not easy to write original music ('tis no light task to find the gates of virgin song.'). Pindar, in another place, describes his music as carefully written ('fine-wrought melody').

Third, among the aesthetic purposes of art music we find, 'to gladden the listener' and 'for the common joy of mankind.' Such music is once described as 'sweet fruit of the mind.' Implied values for the character of the music may perhaps be found in its descriptions: sweet, glorious, tuneful and blended harmony. Music was surely included, when Simonides observed, 'What life is desirable without pleasure.'

It is easy to imagine the influence such values must have had on society. We are nevertheless surprised to read Plutarch's assertion that the power of music once 'appeased a sedition among the Lacedaemonians.

Entertainment music is not frequently discussed by these lyric poets. A typical reference to the music of a private banquet describes the guests as 'blithely' singing. Even in the case of the prostitute entertainers, we do not find objections to the *quality* of the music.

Following the reforms of Cleisthenes, who created in Athens the first real democratic government in history, in 508 BC, the period begins which represents the cultural highpoint of early Greek society. Although much of the fifth and fourth centuries included internal and external wars, it was nevertheless an era of unprecedented prosperity and cultural achievement.

We begin our discussion of this period with three famous fifth-century historians because they not only describe contemporary aspects of Greek music but because they also discuss certain traditions which have continuity with the earlier eras. The first of these was Herodotus of Halicarnassus (ca. 484–425 BC), whom some call the 'father of history.' He traveled extensively and his writing is valuable for his commentary on what he observed.

Thucydides of Athens (ca. 470–398 BC) was also a general and thus the focus of his writing is a history of the Peloponnesian Wars, although he includes a few important observations relative to our subject.

Xenophon of Athens (ca. 434–355 BC) was also a soldier, but as a friend of Socrates he gives us some important views of the latter which are not found in Plato.

ART MUSIC

We find no reference to art music by Herodotus, although there is one reference to the life of the aesthetic in his mention of a play given in Athens which made 'the whole audience at the theater burst into tears.'[1]

Xenophon provides us with some enlightening details of the choral competitions held as part of the festivals which have been mentioned by the epic and lyric poets in the pages above. First of all, he attributes competition itself as the essential catalyst which brings about the highest levels of performance. He credits Lycurgus as having instituted this philosophy.

1 Herodotus, bk 6.21. He does tell, in bk 1.24, the mythical story of Arion who was forced to jump ship and was rescued by a dolphin. The ship's crew was the audience for a song by Arion, before he jumped, and they seem to be described as genuine listeners.

> They for their part thought what a pleasure it would be for them to hear the greatest singer in the world, and so they retreated from the stern of the boat to amidships.

He saw that where the spirit of rivalry is the strongest among the people, there the choruses are most worth hearing and the athletic contests afford the finest spectacle. [2]

2 'The Lacedaemonians,' 4, in Xenophon, *Scripta minora*, trans. E.C. Marchant (Cambridge: Harvard University Press, 1956).

Xenophon also tells us that long periods of training and large sums of money were necessary to prepare a chorus for competition and he seems almost perplexed that they do this when the goal is only a 'paltry' prize. He apparently failed to realize that it is the honor of winning which propels the competition, not the value of the trophy the winner receives. In a conversation with a political leader, Hiero, Xenophon speaks through the character of Simonides, one of the lyric poets.

In case you fear, Hiero, that the cost of offering prizes for many subjects may prove heavy, you should reflect that no commodities are cheaper than those that are bought for a prize. Think of the large sums that men are induced to spend on horse races, gymnastic and choral competitions, and the long course of training and practice they undergo for the sake of a paltry prize. [3]

3 'Hiero,' 9, in ibid.

The chief end of this 'long course of training,' which he sees in terms of artistic value, is discipline.

There is nothing so convenient nor so good for human beings as order. Thus, a chorus is a combination of human beings; but when the members of it do as they choose, it becomes mere confusion, and there is no pleasure in watching it; but when they act and sing in an orderly fashion, then those same men at once seem worth seeing and worth hearing. [4]

4 'Oeconomicus,' 8, in Xenophon, *Memorabilia and Oeconomicus*, trans. E.C. Marchant, (Cambridge: Harvard University Press, 1953).

Xenophon, now in the voice of Socrates, also tells us that the most successful choruses are those which have as their leaders, 'the best experts.' [5] Although speaking of a battle in another place, he also gives an interesting clue as to how these choruses may have stood when they performed.

5 'Memorabilia,' 3, in ibid.

They took position in lines of about a hundred each, like the choral dancers ranged opposite one another. [6]

6 'The Anabasis of Cyrus,' 5, in Xenophon, *Anabasis*, trans. Carleton L. Brownson and O.J. Todd (Cambridge: Harvard University Press, 1947).

As we have seen above, these choral performances often were accompanied by an aulos player. Socrates, speaking on the subject of imposture, gives us a picture of this aulos player which suggests that some of them must have played the role of the prima donna.

Suppose a bad aulos player wants to be thought a good one, let us note what he must do. Must he not imitate good players in the accessories of the art? First, as they wear fine clothes and travel with many attendants, he must do the same. Further, seeing that they win the applause of crowds, he must provide himself with a large claque. But, of course, he must never accept an engagement, or he will promptly expose himself to ridicule as an incompetent player and an impostor to boot.[7]

Finally, in another discussion relative to war, Xenophon mentions in passing the fact that musicians of his experience were both performing older compositions and creating new ones.

However, my son, since you are desirous of learning all these matters, you must not only utilize what you may learn from others, but you must yourself also be an inventor of stratagems against the enemy, just as musicians render not only those compositions which they have learned but try to compose others also that are new. Now if in music that which is new and fresh wins applause, new stratagems in warfare also win far greater applause, for such can deceive the enemy even more successfully.[8]

Thucydides also mentions these choral competitions, in a brief reference to the festival of Delia, held by the Ionians of Delos every fifth year. He quotes a 'Hymn to Apollo' which speaks of 'music's magic' in reference to the listener, suggesting to us that the audiences were still listening to these performances as music, and not as entertainment.

In Delos, Phoebus, lies thy chief delight,
Thy isle's warm landscapes cheer thy gladden'd sight,
When long-rob'd Ions throng around thy fane,
Whose blushing spouses swell the festal train,
Whose ruddy children's lisping accents sound thy name.
Thy feast to celebrate the leapers vig'rous bound,
The champions box, the dancers' footsteps beat the ground,
While music's magic echoes wide resound.[9]

Finally, in a work called the 'Symposium,'[10] the subject of the rhapsodists, the specialists in the singing-recitation of epic poetry, is introduced in a conversation with Socrates. The tenor of his objection seems to indicate that he felt these artists lacked depth.

7 'Memorabilia,' I, in Xenophon, *Memorabilia and Oeconomicus.*

8 'Cyropaedia,' 1, in Xenophon, *Cyropaedia*, trans. Walter Miller (Cambridge: Harvard University Press, 1960).

9 Thucydides, *The History of Thucydides*, trans. Samuel Thomas Bloomfield (London: Longman, Rees, Orme, Brown, and Green, 1829), bk 3, civ.

10 The Greek word *symposion*, usually translated as 'banquet,' meant literally 'drinks-party.'

NICERATUS. My father was anxious to see me develop into a good man and as a means to this end he compelled me to memorize all of Homer; and so even now I can repeat the whole of Iliad and the Odyssey by heart.

ANTISTHENES. But have you failed to observe that the rhapsodists too, all know these poems?

NICERATUS. How could I, when I listen to their recitations nearly every day?

ANTISTHENES. Well, do you know any tribe of men more stupid than the rhapsodists?

NICERATUS. No, indeed, not I, I am sure.

SOCRATES. No, and the reason is clear: they do not know the inner meaning of the poems. [11]

11 'Banquet,' 3, in Xenophon, *Anabasis.*

This discussion occurred during a private banquet during which another interesting exchange takes place informing us that at least some aulos performances were attended by 'absolutely quiet' listeners. We also read of Socrates' preference for songs accompanied by this instrument.

HERMOGENES. My definition of 'convivial unpleasantness' is the annoying of one's companions while they are drinking.

SOCRATES. Well, do you realize that at the present moment you conform to the definition by annoying us with your taciturnity?

HERMOGENES. What! while you are talking?

SOCRATES. No, but in the intervals.

HERMOGENES. Why, don't you see that a person could not insert even a hair in the interstices of your talk, much less a word?

SOCRATES. Callias, could you come to the rescue of a man hard put to it for an answer?

CALLIAS. Yes, indeed, we are absolutely quiet every time the aulos is played.

HERMOGENES. Is it your wish that I should converse with you to the accompaniment of an aulos, the way the actor Nicostratus used to recite tetrameter verses?

SOCRATES. In Heaven's name, do so, Hermogenes. For I believe that precisely as a song is more agreeable when accompanied on the aulos, so your discourse would be embellished somewhat by the music. [12]

12 Ibid., 6.

Before leaving the subject of art music, we should mention that one of the great political leaders of fifth century Athens, Pericles, was educated in music. According to Plutarch,

The master that taught him music, most authors are agreed, was Damon. Although Aristotle tells us that he was thoroughly practiced in all accomplishments of this kind by Pythoclides.[13]

13 Plutarch, *Lives*, 'Pericles.'

Finally one of the important clues to the appreciation of real art music in ancient Greece were the existence of concert halls. One of the early writers who mentioned these halls, Plutarch, also mentions his sponsorship of music competitions and his construction of a special hall for the performance of music.

The Odeum, or concert hall, which in its interior was full of seats and ranges of pillars, and outside had its roof made to slope and descend from one single point at the top, was constructed, we are told, in imitation of the king of Persia's Pavilion …

Pericles, also, eager for distinction, then first obtained the decree for a contest in musical skill to be held yearly at the Panathanaea, and he himself, being chosen judge, arranged the order and method in which the competitors should sing and play on the aulos and harp. And both at that time, and at other times also, they sat in this music room to see and hear all such trials of skill.

FUNCTIONAL MUSIC

The references to functional music by the three historians is primarily limited to ceremonies of a religious-cult nature. Herodotus mentions a festival new in his time honoring two Hyperborean girls, named Arge and Opis, who died at Delos. He mentions newly composed music, as well as the composer's name.

The Delian women, they say, collected gifts for [the girls], giving them names in the hymn that Olen, a Lycian, made for them. It was from Delos that the islanders and Ionians learned to sing in honor of Opis and Arge, calling them by these names and collecting gifts for them. This Olen made other of the old hymns that are sung in Delos, when he came there out of Lycia.

The celebration of this festival included the burning of thigh bones on the altar and the casting of the ashes on the graves of the girls.[14] In reference to a later Delphi festival, Herodotus mentions that the town of Chians sent a choir of one hundred young men to celebrate the festival but ninety-eight caught the plague and died and only two returned home.[15] Thucydides implies the festivals at Delos

14 Bk 4, 35. Plutarch describes, in *Lives*, 'Aristides,' the Eleutheria cult festival which included the burning of a black bull. The only music he mentions is a trumpet which announces the processional.

15 Bk. 6, 29

16 Thucydides, *The Peloponnesian War*, 11.103.

were very ancient as suggested in a hymn to Apollo (here called Phoebus) by Homer.[16]

> Phoebus, where'er thou strayest, far or near,
> Delos was still of all thy haunts most dear.
> Thither the robed Ionians take their way
> With wife and child to keep thy holiday,
> Invoke thy favor on each manly game,
> And dance and sing in honor of thy name.

Finally, Herodotus describes an unusual festival held by the Epidaurians in a place called Oea where female singers and dancers performed in an abusive and satirical manner aimed at other women. For this purpose ten choral conductors (*choregi*) were appointed to pay and train the dancers.[17]

17   Herodotus, bk 5, 85.

With regard to military music there are numerous accounts of the Greek armies marching to melodies played by the auloi. Thucydides in describing a military engagement involving the Spartans gives us an important detail on the actual placement of these musicians in battle. In this case, as their foes, the Argives, 'marched on with vehement impetuosity,'

> the Argives and their allies advancing with haste and fury, the Lacedaemonians slowly and to the music of many aulos players— a standing institution in their army, that has nothing to do with religion, but is meant to make them advance evenly, stepping in time, without breaking their order, as large armies are apt to do in the moment of engaging.[18]

18   Thucydides, bk 5, xvii, 70. Athenaeus, in *Deipnosophistae*, 12.520, gives some extraordinary instances where an enemy was defeated by a spy learning the aulos melodies to which the enemy's *horses* responded.

With regard to this custom, Plutarch adds,

> If one studies the poetry of Sparta, of which some specimens were still extant in my time, and makes himself familiar with the marching songs which they used, to the accompaniment of the aulos, when charging upon their foes, he will conclude that Terpander and Pindar were right in associating valor with music. The former writes thus of the Lacedaemonians:
> > Flourish there both the spear of the brave and the
> > Muse's clear message,
> > Justice, too, walks the broad streets.

And Pindar says:

> There are councils of Elders,
> And young men's conquering spears,
> And dances, the Muse, and joyousness.

The Spartans are thus shown to be at the same time most musical and most warlike;

> In equal poise to match the sword hangs the sweet art of the harpist,

as their poet says.[19] Thucydides also mentions that the Lacedaemonians had specific 'war-songs' by which they generated enthusiasm and courage for the coming battle.[20]

In another place,[21] Thucydides provides us with a description of the use of music in a religious-cult ceremony involving the blessing of ships before they sail.

> When the ships were manned, and every thing was put on board which was to be taken with them, silence was ordered by the sound of the trumpet, and the usual prayers directed by law were recited, not by each ship separately, but all together, the whole multitude responding to the voice of the heralds; cups of wine, too, were mixed throughout the whole armament, and the officers and soldiers made libations out of golden and silver goblets … And after the singing the Paean, and completing the libations, they put to sea.

Xenophon mentions on two occasions the military troops singing 'the paean' just before the commencement of battle.[22]

Finally, Herodotus writes of representatives of the Ionians and Aeolians who went to Sardis to plea with the Persian leader Cyrus for reasonable terms after their defeat during the Persian conquest of Lydia. Cyrus, by way of telling them they were too late to make such a request, told a nice story.

> An aulos player who saw some fish in the sea played his instrument in the hope that they would come ashore. When they refused to do so, the aulos player took a net, netted a large catch and hauled them in. Seeing the fish jumping about he said to them, 'It is too late to dance now; you might have danced to my music but you would not.'[23]

19   Plutarch, *Lives*, 'Lycurgus,' xxi.

20   Thucydides, bk 5, xvii, 69

21   Thucydides, bk 6, xxxii.

22   'The Anabasis of Cyrus,' in Xenophon, *Anabasis*, bk 4.16 and bk 5.14.

23   Herodotus, bk 1.142.

ENTERTAINMENT MUSIC

The description of a private banquet by Xenophon above, also includes music of a purely entertainment nature performed by the infamous single-pipe girl who is frequently associated with these kinds of affairs.

> When the tables had been removed and the guests had poured a libation and sung a hymn, there entered a man from Syracuse, to give them an evening's merriment. He had with him a fine single-pipe girl, a dancing girl—one of those skilled in acrobatic tricks,—and a very handsome boy, who was expert at playing the lyre and at dancing; the Syracusan made money by exhibiting their performances as a spectacle. They now played for the assemblage, the single-pipe girl on the single-pipe, the boy on the lyre; and it was agreed that both furnished capital amusement. Thereupon Socrates remarked: 'On my word, Callias, you are giving us a perfect dinner; for not only have you set before us a feast that is above criticism, but you are also offering us very delightful sights and sounds.'

Next the dancing girl performed while juggling twelve hoops, followed by turning somersaults around upright swords, all to the accompaniment of the single-pipe girl. Then one of the guest joined in dancing, asking the single-pipe girl to 'hit up the time faster.' Finally the boy sang while playing his lyre, again accompanied by the single-pipe.

After these performances, which one guest praised, Socrates makes one of those remarks which reveals that, talented or not, the performers were looked down upon.

> CHARMIDES. It seems to me, gentlemen, that, as Socrates said of the wine, so this blending of the young people's beauty and of the notes of the music lulls one's griefs to sleep and awakens the goddess of Love.
> SOCRATES. These people, gentlemen, show their competence to give us pleasure; and yet I, I am sure, think ourselves considerably superior to them. [24]

24   Ibid., 2.

Herodotus also describes a private banquet during which one of the guests 'ordered the single-pipe player to strike up a tune for him' and began dancing on the table. [25] This dancer, Hippocleides, was one of several men who were competing for the hand in marriage of the daughter of Cleisthenes. Hippocleides, who had been drinking, proceeded to dance several Laconian and Attic dances,

25   Herodotus, bk 6.129.

which the father of the bride was not amused by, loathing the thought of having such a son-in-law. When Hippocleides then stood on his head and beat time to the music with his legs, the father of the bride announced, 'Son of Tisander, you have danced away your marriage.'

Xenophon, in another work,[26] gives a very valuable account of more formal and traditional dances, the type of dance which acts out a story. It is this type of dance that we assume was taught in school as part of physical education.

26 'The Anabasis of Cyrus,' in Xenophon, *Anabasis*, 6.

> After they had made libations and sung the paean, two Thracians rose up first and began a dance in full armor to the music of an aulos, leaping high and lightly and using their sabers; finally, one struck the other, as everybody thought, and the second man fell, in a rather skillful way. And the Paphlagonians set up a cry. Then the first man despoiled the other of his arms and marched out singing the Sitalcas, while other Thracians carried off the fallen dancer, as though he were dead; in fact, he had not been hurt at all.
>
> After this some Aenianians and Magnesians arose and danced under arms the so-called carpaea. The manner of the dance was this: a man is sowing and driving a yoke of oxen, his arms laid at one side, and he turns about frequently as one in fear; a robber approaches; as soon as the sower sees him coming, he snatches up his arms, goes to meet him, and fights with him to save his oxen. The two men do all this in rhythm to the music of the aulos. Finally, the robber binds the man and drives off the oxen; or sometimes the master of the oxen binds the robber, and then he yokes him alongside the oxen, his hands tied behind him, and drives off.
>
> After this a Mysian came in carrying a light shield in each hand, and at one moment in the dance he would go through a pantomime as though two men were arrayed against him, again he would use his shields as though against one antagonist, and again he would whirl and throw somersaults while holding the shields in his hands, so that the spectacle was a fine one. Lastly, he danced the Persian dance, clashing his shields together and crouching down and then rising up again; and all this he did, keeping time to the music of the aulos.
>
> After him the Mantineans and some of the other Arcadians arose, arrayed in the finest arms and accouterments they could command, and marched in time to the accompaniment of an aulos playing the martial rhythm and sang the paean and danced, just as the Arcadians do in their festal processions in honor of the gods.

Finally, Thucydides, in his only reference to entertainment, quotes a speech by Pericles in which the latter gives what we regard as perhaps the highest definition of public entertainment.

> We, moreover, provide the greatest variety of recreation for the public mind, by the exhibition of games and sacrifices throughout the whole year, and by the use of those private and handsomely furnished entertainments and spectacles, the daily delight of which dispels all weariness. [27]

27   Thucydides, bk 2.xxxviii.

In summary, the evidence left by these historians suggests that art music continued the momentum and high level reached during the sixth century. Again we read of quiet audiences and listeners being moved to tears by the music. We are told that, while older compositions were performed, newly composed music was especially praised. We also note Thucydides' phrase, 'music's magic,' a reference to Music's unseen power over the spirit, a characteristic not easily defined in words, but which has always been one of its hallmarks. We see this in the ancients' association of music with the divine; we read in the Middle Ages of the 'science and mystery' of the art of the minstrel; and in our generation a music educator spoke of 'some mysterious alchemy' that music evokes in the listener.

These historians provide us with interesting additional detail regarding the large choral ensembles which were so important in early Greek music. Xenophon tells us that the best choirs were characterized by a high degree of discipline, long periods of training and expert conductors. He also contends that it was the contest system which was the catalyst for their high level of achievement. Plutarch, in his biography of Pericles, a great Greek leader who was trained and was active in music, suggests that these contests were held in concert halls, were carefully organized and adjudicated, and that the choirs remained in the hall to hear the other participants.

Considering the apparent high level of this musical activity, it is no surprise to also find a rising level of criticism of the musicians and their performances. Xenophon quotes Socrates as frowning on the aura of the famous instrumentalist, who dressed extravagantly, maintained his own servants as well as a paid claque to applaud. In another work, Socrates identifies the Rhapsodists as musicians who give public performances, but did not convey the deeper, inner meaning of their repertoire.

The music used in cult-religious celebrations is little discussed by these historians, but Herodotus does mention a newly composed work and gives the composer's name—which we believe reflects a higher recognition of such music.

Since the focus of these histories is political and military struggles, the role of the aulos by the military is mentioned with interesting details including its contribution to affect the character of the soldier, to provide valor. We also find interesting the several references to the singing by the common soldiers, which reflects some form of music education not found in our own era.

Finally, the references to Entertainment Music by these historians reflect a very high aesthetic level for such music. Thucydides defines the purpose of entertainment music to be 'recreation for the mind' and to 'dispel weariness.' Xenophon speaks of banquet music he heard as being 'capital amusement' and he also quotes Socrates as acknowledging having received 'pleasure' from the music he heard at a banquet, in spite of his contempt for the lower quality of people who perform such music.

10 FIFTH CENTURY PHILOSOPHY BEFORE PLATO

The fragments of Greek philosophy which have survived from the period before Plato are characterized by an intellectual attempt to understand the material world. Of what elements is the universe composed? How did man and animal life evolve? What happens after death? These are the kinds of questions discussed in the fragmentary remains of their work.

As a natural extension of this line of inquiry, we find the fifth-century philosophers beginning to wonder how the mind is organized and how the information of our senses, and what we call 'experience,' is related to 'reason.' These kinds of questions are, of course, a necessary and logical philosophical prerequisite for any study of aesthetics.

Democritus,[1] for example, clearly understood there were separate forms of knowledge, but like most early philosophers it was impossible for him to accept the nature of information derived from the senses as being as important as information dwelt with by 'reason.'

> There are two forms of knowledge, one legitimate, one obscure; and the following all belong to the obscure form, sight, hearing, smell, taste, and touch.[2]

Archytas believed that 'sensation occurs in the body, reason in the soul.'[3] Metopus used the modern terms rational and irrational, but he also associated these properties with the 'soul' instead of the brain.[4] Theages also assigned reasoning to the soul, but his ideas hold additional interest for us as he includes in his discussion the concept of pleasure, which represents another necessary step toward any theory of the aesthetic.

> The soul is divided into reasoning power, anger and desire. Reasoning power rules knowledge, anger deals with impulse, and desire bravely rules the soul's affections. When these three parts unite into one action, exhibiting a composite energy, then in the soul results concord and virtue. When sedition divides them, then discord and vice appear. Virtue therefore contains three elements: reason, power, and deliberate choice. The soul's reasoning power's virtue is wisdom, which is a habit of contemplating and judging.

1 The exact dates of Democritus are not known, but we understand him to be earlier than Plato as Aristoxenus, in *Historical Notes*, tells us that Plato wanted to burn the entire works of Democritus.

2 Quoted in Milton C. Nahm, *Selections from Early Greek Philosophy* (New York: Appleton-Century-Crofts, 1964), 197.

3 Quoted in Kenneth Guthrie, *The Pythagorean Sourcebook and Library* (Grand Rapids: Phanes Press, 1987), 180. In a famous anecdote, Archytas, who was also a musician, upon being reproached for not advertising himself more, said, 'It is my instrument which speaks for me.'

4 Quoted in ibid., 249.

The irascible part's virtue is courage, which is a habit of enduring dreadful things, and resisting them. The appetitive part's virtue is temperance, which is a moderation and detention of the pleasures which arise from the body. The whole soul's virtue is justice, for men indeed become bad either through vice, or through incontinence, or through a natural ferocity. They injure each other either through gain, pleasure or ambition. More appropriately therefore does vice belong to the soul's reasoning part. While prudence is similar to good art, vice resembles bad art, inventing contrivances to act unjustly. Incontinence pertains to the soul's appetitive part, as continence consists in subduing, and incontinence in failure to subdue, pleasures.

...

Now the virtues subsist in and about the passions, so we may call the latter the matter of the former. Of the passions, one is voluntary, and the other involuntary, pleasure being the voluntary, and pain the involuntary.

...

Since however the virtue of manners consists in dealing with the passions, over which pleasure and pain are supreme, virtue evidently does not consist in extirpating the passions of the soul, pleasure and pain, but in regulating them. So too health, which is an adjustment of the bodily powers, does not consist in expelling the cold and the hot, the moist and the dry, but in adjusting them suitably and symmetrically. Likewise in music, concord does not consist in expelling the sharp and the flat, but in exterminating dissonance by concord arising from their adjustment.

...

For the reasoning power of the soul induces health, while the irrational induces disease. So far as anger and desire are governed and led by the soul's rational part, continence and endurance become virtues; but in so far as this is affected by violence, involuntarily, thus become vices. For virtue must carry out what is proper not with pain but pleasure.

...

We should then, in virtue, see passion as shadow and outline in a picture which depends on animation and delicacy, imitating the truth, in conjunction with goodness of coloring. The soul's passions are animated by the natural incitation of enthusiasm of virtue, which is generated from the passions, and subsisting with them. Similarly, harmony includes the sharp and the flat, and mixtures consist of heat and cold, and equilibrium results from weight and lightness. Therefore, neither would it be necessary nor profitable to remove the passions of the soul; but they must be mutually adjusted to the rational part, under the direction of propriety and moderation.[5]

5   Quoted in ibid., 225–228.

Photius almost arrived at the correct understanding of all the senses being characteristics of the brain itself, and not the 'soul.'

While the four main senses are confined to their special senses in the head, touch is diffused throughout the head and the whole body, and is common to all the senses, but is specialized in the hands.[6]

6   Quoted in ibid., 138.

In Parmenides, second half of the sixth to first half of the fifth century BC, founder of the Eleatic school of philosophy, we find the general line of thought which will continue through Plato: The senses, and experience, are real, but it is Reason, and not they, that is to be trusted.

You must debar your thought from this way of search, nor let ordinary experience in its variety force you along this way, allowing the eye, sightless as it is, and the ear, full of sound, and the tongue, to rule.[7]

7   Fragment seven, quoted in Giovanni Reale, *A History of Ancient Philosophy* (Albany: State University of New York Press, 1985), 88.

Only in Gorgias, who flourished ca. 425 BC, do we find a philosopher who has recognized this entire question as being more complicated. How, he asks, can language even express what we perceive through our senses?

For how could any one communicate by word of mouth that he has seen? And how could that which has been seen be indicated to a listener if he has not seen it? For just as the sight does not recognize sounds, so the hearing does not hear colors but sounds; and he who speaks, speaks, but does not speak a color or a thing. When, therefore, one has not a thing in the mind, how will he get it there from another person by word or any other token of the thing except by seeing it, if it is a color, or hearing it, if it is a noise? For he who speaks does not speak a noise at all, or a color, but a word; and so it is impossible to conceive a color, but only see it, nor a noise, but only to hear it.[8]

8   Quoted in ibid, 167.

This question regarding what the word can communicate must have been very bothersome to Gorgias, because in another place he admits that, in the case of the theater, he has seen the ability of words to convey emotions with great power.

All poetry can be called speech in meter. Its hearers shudder with terror, shed tears of pity, and yearn with sad longing; the soul, affected by the words, feels as its own an emotion aroused by the good and ill fortunes of other people's actions and lives.[9]

9   Ibid., 171.

Plutarch, in a discussion of theater, quotes a seemingly enigmatic statement by Gorgias.

10   Ibid.

But tragedy blossomed forth and won great acclaim, becoming a wondrous entertainment for the ears and eyes of the men of that age and, by the mythological character of its plots and vicissitudes which its characters undergo, it effected a deception wherein, as Gorgias remarks,

he who deceives is more honest than he who does not deceive and he who is deceived is wiser than he who is not.[10]

The meaning of this is found in the fact that on stage before the public non-fiction can be dangerous, whereas in faction one can be honest and not be punished.

References to music by these earliest extant philosophers are very rare, with the exception of the Pythagoreans whom we shall mention below. From Thales (640–546 BC) we have only a single aphorism, 'A lack of culture is a serious thing.'[11] When hymns are mentioned, they are mentioned with reference to their functional, rather than musical, role. Gorgias, for example, writes,

11   Quoted in Ibid., 143.

Victories over the barbarians require hymns of celebration, over the Greeks laments.[12]

12   Quoted in Rosamond Kent Sprague, *The Older Sophists* (Columbia: University of South Carolina Press, 1972). 48.

and similarly in Xenophanes (576–480 BC),

Men making merry should first hymn the god with propitious stanzas and pure words.[13]

13   Fragment, quoted in Nahm, *Selections from Early Greek Philosophy*, 82. Xenophanes in another fragment seems to criticize the epic poets, Homer and Hesiod, saying they have, 'attributed to the gods all things which are disreputable and worthy of blame when done by men.' And in yet another incomplete fragment he seems to call the lyric poet Simonides a 'skinflint.'

Only in a fragment by Heraclitus (fl. ca. 513 BC) do we find a philosopher passing judgment on any aspect of the use of hymns.

14   Fragment quoted in Geoffrey S. Kirk, *The Presocratic Philosophers* (Cambridge: Cambridge University Press, 1983), 209.

For if it were not to Dionysus that they made the procession and sung the hymn to the shameful parts, the deed would be most shameless; but Hades and Dionysus, for whom they rave and celebrate Lenaean rites, are the same.[14]

Another fragment of Heraclitus, which we especially wish we possessed in entirety, seems to be cautioning the musician not to make the response of the audience his aim.

> What discernment or intelligence do they possess? They place their trust in popular bards, and take the throng for their teacher, not realizing that 'the majority are bad, and only few are good.[15]

Plato, in a charming description of the philosopher Hippias (fl. ca. 450 BC),[16] tells us that he was also a composer. We know he gave an elegy on the loss of a Messenian boys' chorus who died crossing a river, but this is not extant.[17]

Finally, the extant speeches of Antiphon, a famous fifth century speaker, and early interpreter of dreams, include some interesting references to the famous choral contests. In a fragment of a speech[18] discussing the fact that pleasure often follows pain, he mentions contests in general and observes,

> For honors, prizes, the baits which God has given to mankind, bring them to the necessity of great toil and sweat.

Of particular interest is a speech, known as 'On the Chorus Boy,' which Antiphon wrote for an unknown defendant who was in charge of the chorus[19] at Thargelia in 412 BC. This speech provides valuable details regarding the establishment and provisions of a boy's chorus.

> When I was appointed in charge of the chorus [choregus] at Thargelia … , I performed the office as well and conscientiously as I could. In the first place, I provided a room for training in the most convenient part of my house, where I used to train when I was choregus at the Dionysia. Secondly, I enrolled a chorus in the best way I could, not penalizing anyone nor forcibly exacting security nor making an enemy of anyone; but, as was most agreeable and convenient to both parties, I made my requests and demands, while the parents sent their sons with good grace and willingly …
>
> I appointed Phanostratus to look after the chorus in case they needed anything. Phanostratus is a fellow demesman of the prosecutors and a kinsman of mine, in fact, my son-in-law, and I expected him to look after them well. I appointed two other men too, Ameinias of the tribe Erechtheis, whom the tribesmen themselves regularly elected to enroll and look after the tribe, a man with a good reputation; and the second man from the Cecropid tribe, who regularly convened that tribe. Then I appointed a fourth, Philippus, who

15   Fragment 104, quoted in Heraclitus, *Fragments*, trans. Thomas M. Robinson (Toronto: University of Toronto Press, 1987), 61–63.

16   Plato, *Hippias Minor*, 368b.

17   Plato, in ibid., says that he regarded the powers of memorization to be Hippias' most brilliant achievement. An early writer, Ammianus Marcellinus, says that Hippias obtained these great powers of memory 'by drinking certain potions.' (Sprague, *The Older Sophists*, 100).

18   Quoted in Sprague, *The Older Sophists*, 228.

19   Athenaeus, *Deipnosophistae*, 14.633, says *choregus* originally was used to mean the conductor of the chorus, not, as later, the administrator, or 'provider.'

was commissioned to buy and spend any money necessary on the authority of the poet or of an other of the officials, so that the boys should enjoy the best possible *choregia* and should go in want of nothing because of my inability to give them my attention.

THE PYTHAGOREANS

Pythagoras ... one of the most outstanding mathematicians of all times [and] an eminent idealistic philosopher.
    Walther Kirchner, 1960[20]

20   Walther Kirchner, *Western Civilization to 1500* (New York: Barnes & Noble, 1960), 40.

Pythagoras is the chief captain of swindlers.
    Heraclitus, ca. 500 BC[21]

21   Fragment 81a, quoted in Heraclitus, *Fragments*.

These two dissimilar assessments of Pythagoras (580–500 BC) reflect the fact that even today it is not possible to evaluate the contribution of this man with complete confidence. The first problem is that we possess not a single word actually written by him. What we have, primarily the accounts of his followers, picture him as being somewhat a cross between an eccentric genius and a cult figure. For example, Plutarch maintained that Pythagoras imposed a term of five years' silence upon new students who came to study with him[22] and Porphyry adds that 'none was allowed to become his friend or associate without being examined in facial expression and disposition.'[23] His followers maintained that he had the ability to be seen in different cities at the same time, that he gave predictions of earthquakes, chased away a pestilence, suppressed violent winds and hail and calmed storms on the seas, for the comfort and safe passage of his friends.[24]

22   Plutarch, 'Of Inquisitiveness into Things Impertinent.'

23   Porphyry (ca. 233–305 AD), 'Life of Pythagoras,' in *The Pythagorean Sourcebook and Library*, trans. Kenneth S. Guthrie.

24   Ibid.

Regarding the teaching of Pythagoras, Porphyry writes,

He taught the following. A cultivated and fruit-bearing plant, harmless to man and beast, should neither be injured nor destroyed. A deposit of money or of teachings should be faithfully preserved by the trustee.

There are three kinds of things that deserve to be pursued and acquired: honorable and virtuous things, those that conduce to the use of life, and those that bring pleasures of the blameless, secure and solemn kind, and not the vulgar intoxicating kinds. Of pleasures three are two kinds: one that indulges the stomach and lusts by a profusion of wealth, which he compared to the murderous songs of the Sirens; the other kind consists of things honest, just, and necessary to life, which are just as sweet as the first, without being followed by repentance, and these pleasures he compared to the harmony of the Muses.

…

His utterances were of two kinds, plain or symbolical. His teaching was twofold: of his disciples some were called Students (*mathematikoi*), and other Hearers (*akousmatikoi*). The Students learned the fuller and more exactly elaborate reasons of science, while the Hearers heard only the summarized instructions of learning, without more detailed explanations.

Examples of his symbolic utterances (and one scholar's deduction of their presumed meaning[25]) are:

25   Guthrie, *The Pythagorean Sourcebook and Library*, pp. 159–161.

Do not poke the fire with a sword.
   (Do not further inflame the quarrelsome).

Suffer no swallows around your house.
   (Associate not with those who chatter vainly).

Wear not a narrow ring.
   (Seek freedom, avoid slavery).

Abstain from beans.
   (Avoid democratic voting).

Abstain from eating animals.
   (Have no conversation with unreasonable men).

Never break the bread.
   (When giving charity, do not pare too closely).

Do not urinate against the sun.
   (Be modest).

Never sing without lyre accompaniment.
   (Make of life a whole).

Pick not up what is fallen from the table.
   (Always leave something for charity).

Place not the candle against the wall.
   (Persist not in enlightening the stupid).

26   Iamblichus (ca. 250–325 AD), 'The Life of Pythagoras,' in *The Pythagorean Sourcebook and Library*.

Porphyry tells us that Pythagoras' first study was with a lyre player, a gymnast and a painter. Another biographer tells us he spent twelve years in Egypt where he studied 'arithmetic, music and all the other sciences.'[26] Porphyry suggests that as an adult, Pythagoras continued his activity as a musician on a daily basis.

He himself held morning conferences at his residence, composing his soul with the music of the lyre, and singing certain ancient paeans of Thales. He also sang verses of Homer and Hesiod, which seemed to soothe the mind. He danced certain dances which he thought conferred on the body agility and health.

Regarding this reference to 'composing his soul' with music, Iamblichus gives us a very interesting, and more detailed, account of Pythagoras' use of music in relationship to health. It is no doubt this passage which has caused some more recent scholars to regard Pythagoras as 'the Father of Music Therapy.'

Pythagoras conceived the first attention that should be given to men should be addressed to the senses, as when one perceives beautiful figures and forms, or hears beautiful rhythms and melodies. Consequently he laid down that the first erudition was that which subsists through music's melodies and rhythms, and from these he obtained remedies of human manners and passions, and restored the pristine harmony of the faculties of the soul. Moreover, he devised medicines calculated to repress and cure the diseases of both bodies and souls. Here is also, by Zeus, something which deserves to be mentioned above all: namely, that for his disciples he arranged and adjusted what might be called 'preparations' and 'touchings,' divinely contriving mingling of certain diatonic, chromatic and enharmonic melodies, through which he easily switched and circulated the passions of the soul in a contrary direction, whenever they had accumulated recently, irrationally, or clandestinely—such as sorrow, rage, pity, over-emulation, fear, manifold desires, angers, appetites, pride, collapse or spasms. Each of these he corrected by the rule of virtue, attempering them through appropriate melodies, as through some salutary medicine.

In the evening, likewise, when his disciples were retiring to sleep, he would thus liberate them from the day's perturbations and tumults, purifying their intellective powers from the influxive and effluxive waves of corporeal nature, quieting their sleep, and rendering their dreams pleasing and prophetic. But when they arose again in the morning, he would free them from the night's heaviness, coma and torpor through certain peculiar chords and modulations, produced by either simply striking the lyre, or adapting the voice.[27]

One of Pythagoras' followers, Euryphamus, continued the association of music and health by making an analogy with the lyre.

> Human life resembles a properly tuned and cared for lyre. Every lyre requires three things: apparatus, tuning, and musical skill of the player. By apparatus we mean preparation of all the appropriate parts: the strings, the plectrum and other instruments cooperating in the tuning of the instrument. By tuning we mean the adaptation of the sounds to each other. The musical skill is the motion of the player in consideration of the tuning. Human life requires the same three things. Apparatus is the preparation of the physical basis of life, riches, renown, and friends. Tuning is the organizing of these according to virtue and the laws. Musical skill is the mingling of these according to virtue and the laws, virtue sailing with a prosperous wind and no external resistance.[28]

Another disciple of Pythagoras, Diotogenes, in a fragment entitled, 'Concerning a Kingdom,' gives the same analogy, but on a larger scale.

> The king should therefore organize the well-legislated city like a lyre, first in himself establishing the justest boundary and order of law, knowing that the people's proper arrangement should be organized according to this interior boundary, the divinity having given him dominion over them.[29]

Pythagoras, as well, believed that since music was an important key to maintaining the balance of health in the individual, so must the same idea must be valid for the larger society. When consulted by Crotonian civic leaders, Iamblichus relates that Pythagoras responded as follows:

> His first advice was to build a temple to the Muses, which would preserve the already existing concord. He observed to them that all of these divinities were grouped together by their common names, that they subsisted only in conjunction with each other, that they specially rejoiced in social honors, and that the choir of the Muses subsisted always one and the same. They comprehended symphony, harmony, rhythm, and all things breeding concord. Not only to beautiful theorems does their power extend, but to the general symphonious harmony.[30]

27 Ibid.

28 Quoted in Guthrie, *The Pythagorean Sourcebook and Library*, 245.

29 Ibid., 223.

30 Iambilichus, in *The Pythagorean Sourcebook and Library*.

Among musicians today, of course, Pythagoras is remembered as the person who is credited with working out the numerical ratios of the overtone series. But here again, since we do not have an account in his own words, we are deprived of everything we would like to know about his historic discovery. The story that has been passed down to us, by one of his disciples, however, is a story which appears to be based on a misunderstanding of the principle involved in the physics of sound.

Once as he was intently considering music, and reasoning with himself whether it would be possible to devise some instrumental assistance to the sense of hearing, so as to systematize it, as sight is made precise by the compass, rule, and telescope, or touch is made reckonable by balance and measures—so thinking of these things Pythagoras happened to pass by a brazier's shop where he heard the hammers beating out a piece of iron on an anvil, producing sounds that harmonized, except one. But he recognized in these sounds the concord of the octave, the fifth, and the fourth. He saw that the sound between the fourth and the fifth, taken by itself, was a dissonance, and yet completed the greater sound [the octave] among them.

Delighted, therefore, to find that the thing he was anxious to discover had by divine assistance succeeded, he went into the smithy [blacksmith's shop], and by various experiments discovered that the difference of sound arose from the magnitude of the hammers, but not from the force of the strokes, nor from the shape of the hammers, nor from the change of position of the beaten iron. Having then accurately examined the weights and the swing of the hammers, he returned home, and fixed one stake diagonally to the walls, lest some difference should arise from there being several of them, or from some difference in the material of the stakes.

From this stake he then suspended four gut-strings, of similar materials, size, thickness, and twist. A weight was suspended from the bottom of each. When the strings were equal in length, he struck two of them simultaneously, he reproduced the former intervals, forming different pairs. He discovered that the string stretched by the greatest weight, when compared with that stretched by the smallest weight, had the interval of an octave. The weight of the first was twelve pounds, and that of the latter, six. Being therefore in a double ratio, it formed the octave, which was made plain by the weights themselves. Then he found that the string from which the greatest weight was suspended compared with that from which was suspended the weight next to the smallest, and which weight was eight pounds, produced the interval known as the fifth. Hence he discovered that this interval is in a ratio of one and a half to one, or three to two, in which ratio the weights also were to each other.

In spite of the explanations given in early accounts, the discovery itself is so frequently mentioned that there is little reason to doubt that Pythagoras in fact did arrive at the numerical ratios of at least the lower part of the overtone series. Ironically, his great contribution to science was not in this discovery itself, but in the realization which followed. That is, that numbers could represent abstract thought. This might be called, in fact, the beginning of all higher mathematics.

Aristotle, in making reference to this, explains how, for Pythagoras, the idea of the 'music of the spheres' followed rather automatically.

> The so-called Pythagoreans, who were the first to take up mathematics, not only advanced this study, but also having been brought up in it they thought that its principles were the principles of all things. And since of these principles *numbers* are by nature the first, and in numbers they seemed to see many resemblances to the things that exist and come into being—more than in fire and earth and water ... since again, they saw that the modifications and the ratios of the musical scales were expressible in numbers—since, then, all other things seemed in their whole nature modeled on numbers, and numbers seemed to be the first things in the whole of nature, *they supposed the elements of numbers to be the elements of all things, and the whole heaven to be a musical scale and a number.*[31]

31   Aristotle, *Metaphysics*, quoted in Reale, *A History of Ancient Philosophy*, 61.

According to Porphyry, Pythagoras claimed the sole ability to hear this 'music of the spheres,' his students not being developed enough to be able to do so.

> He himself could hear the Harmony of the Universe, and understood the universal music of the spheres, and of the stars which move in concert with them, and which we cannot hear because of the limitations of our weak nature ...
>
> Pythagoras affirmed that the Nine Muses were constituted by the sounds made by the seven planets, the sphere of the fixed stars, and that which is opposed to our earth, called the 'counter-earth.' He called Mnemosyne, or Memory, the composition, symphony and connection of them all, which is eternal and unbegotton as being composed of all of them.[32]

32   Porphyry, 'Life of Pythagoras,' in *The Pythagorean Sourcebook and Library*.

Aristotle, again, provides us with the thought process of this Pythagorean view of the universe.

33 Aristotle, *de Caelo*, 2, quoted in Nahm, *Selections from Early Greek Philosophy*, 58. Athenaeus, in *Deipnosophistae*, 3.103, provides a satire on the Pythagoreans' tendency to find music as the organizational principle of nearly everything.

A: For myself, I never enter the kitchen.
B: Why, what do you do?
A: I sit near by and watch, while others do the work; to them I explain the principles and the result. 'Softly! the mincemeat is seasoned sharp enough.'
B: You must be a musician, not a cook!
A: 'Play fortissimo with the fire. Make the tempo even. The first dish is not simmering in tune with the others next to it.'
B: Save us!
A: It's beginning to look like an art to you, what? You see, I serve no course without study mingle all in a harmonious scale.
B: What does that mean?
A: Some things are related to each other by fourths, by fifths, or by octaves. These I join their own proper intervals, and weave them into a series of appropriate courses.

Some think it necessary that noise should arise when so great bodies are in motion, since sound does arise from bodies among us which are not so large and do not move so swiftly; and from the sun and moon and from the stars in so great number, and of so great size, moving so swiftly, there must necessarily arise a sound inconceivably great. Assuming these things and that the swiftness has the principle of harmony by reason of the intervals, they say that the sound of the stars moving on in a circle becomes musical. And since it seems unreasonable that we also do not hear this sound, they say that the reason for this is that the noise exists in the very nature of things, so as not to be distinguishable from the opposite silence; for the distinction of sound and silence lies in their contrast with each other, so that as blacksmiths think there is no difference between them because they are accustomed to the sound, so the same things happen to men. What occasions the difficulty and makes the Pythagoreans say that there is a harmony of the bodies as they move, is a proof. For whatever things move themselves make a sound and noise; but whatever things are fastened in what moves or exist in it as the parts in a ship, cannot make a noise, nor yet does the ship if it moves in a river.[33]

Plutarch provides us with the development of this concept among some of the followers of Pythagoras.

For some there are who seek these proportions in the swift motions of the spheres of the planets; others rather in the distances, others in the magnitude of the stars; others, more accurate and nice in their inquiry, seek for the same proportions in the diameters of the epicycles; as if the Supreme Architect, for the sake of these, had adapted the soul, divided into seven parts, to the celestial bodies. Many also there are, who hither transfer the inventions of the Pythagoreans, tripling the distances of bodies from the middle. This is done by placing the unit next the fire; three next the Antichthon, or earth which is opposite to our earth; nine next the Earth; 27 next the Moon; 81 next to Mercury; 243 upon Venus; and 729 upon the Sun. The last (729) is both a tetragonal and cubical number, whence it is, that they also call the sun a tetragon and a cube.

…

Others there are, who fancy the earth to be in the lowest string of the harp, called proslambanomenos; and so proceeding, they place the moon in hypate, Mercury and Venus in the diatoni and lichani; the sun they likewise place in mese, as in the midst of the diapason, a fifth above the earth and a fourth from the sphere of the fixed stars.

But neither doth this pleasant conceit of the latter come near the truth, neither do the former attain perfect accuracy. However, they who will not allow the latter to depend upon Plato's sentiments will yet grant the former to partake of musical proportions; so that there being five tetrachords, and in these five distances they place all the planets; making the first tetrachord from the Moon to the Sun and the planets which move with the Sun, that is, Mercury and Venus; the next from the Sun to the fiery planet of Mars; the third between this and Jupiter; the fourth from thence to Saturn; and the fifth from Saturn to the sphere of the fixed stars. So that the sounds and notes which bound the five tetrachords bear the same proportion with the intervals of the planets.

…

So it is most probable that the bodies of the stars, the distances of spheres, and the swiftness of the motions and revolutions, have their sundry proportions, as well one to another as to the whole fabric, like instruments of music well set and tuned, though the measure of the quantity be unknown to us.[34]

One of the members of the Pythagorean School, Archytas, correctly (if circuitously) arrived at the observation that higher frequencies travel with more energy.

Of the sounds that fall within the range of our senses, some—those that come quickly from the bodies struck—seem shrill; those that arrive slowly and feebly, seem of low pitch. In fact, when one agitates some object slowly and feebly, the shock produces a low pitch; if the waving is done quickly, and with energy, the sound is shrill. This is not the only proof of the fact, which we can prove when we speak or sing; when we wish to speak loud and high, we use a great force of breath. So also with something thrown; if you throw them hard, they go far; if you throw them without energy, they fall near, for the air yields more to bodies moved with much force, than to those thrown with little. This phenomenon is also reproduced in the sound of the voice, for the sounds produced by an energetic breath are shrill, while those produced by a feeble breath are weak and low in pitch. This same observation can be seen in the force of a signal given from any place: if you pronounce it loud, it can be heard far; if you pronounce the same signal low, we do not hear it even when near. So also in the aulos, the breath emitted by the mouth and which presents itself to the holes nearest the mouthpiece, produces a shriller sound, because the impulsive force is greater; farther down, they are of lower pitch. It is therefore evident that the swiftness of the movement produces shrillness, and slowness, lower pitch.[35]

34 'Of the Procreation of the Soul'. Plutarch, himself, in 'Conjugal Precepts,' carried the logic of the overtone series into the domestic environment.

As in musical concords, when the upper strings are so tuned as exactly to accord, the base always gives the tone; so in well-regulated and well-ordered families, all things are carried on with the harmonious consent and agreement of both parties, but the conduct and contrivance chiefly redounds to the reputation and management of the husband.

35 Fragment 15, quoted in Guthrie, *The Pythagorean Sourcebook and Library*, 184.

Finally, this same philosopher provides a brief attempt at defining the constituent parts of a work of art. It is the first of a type of logical dissection of the nature of art which will be continued in great detail by Aristotle.

All kinds of arts deal with five things: the matter, the instrument, the part, the definition, the end.[36]

36   Fragment 29, quoted in Ibid., 193.

In summary, it is during this period that philosophers moved beyond offering explanations of the natural world to the contemplation of man. We may assume that they all understood, by intuition or from common observation, that man has the capacity for reason, a faculty which represents everything they understood by 'knowledge.' But they were equally aware that man is under the influence of an entirely different sphere: emotions (passions, as they called them), direct experiences, and the input of the senses.

Due to brain research, we know today that reason and experience are dwelt with separately in the left and right hemispheres of the brain, respectively, and that sensory input is received in both hemispheres. The ancient philosophers, with no knowledge of the mute right hemisphere, had great difficulty in accounting for the non-rational. One must guess that it was their realization, on some level, that it is the experiential side of ourselves, and not reason, that is the *real* us, which led them to center so much of their thought in the concept of the 'soul.' But no matter how much effort they expended in trying to divide the soul into regions to contain the emotions, the senses, and reason, they made no progress toward the real truth of how the brain is organized. One feels their frustration in dealing with emotion and the senses in their constant falling back to the position that whatever these are, reason must rule and control them. Theages, as probably most of them, equated Wisdom as the end of reason. Today we would say *knowledge* is the end of reason; Wisdom is the end of *experience*.

There was some discussion among these philosophers of the concepts of pleasure and pain, but we do not find them enlightening. In Antiphon's contention that pleasure follows pain, we are attracted, however, to his demonstration that the pleasure of performance follows the pain of rehearsal.

We also find interesting the fragment by Heraclitus in which he questions the collective judgment of large audiences.

The best known of all these philosophers today, Pythagoras, is certainly the most enigmatic. He was an eccentric and perhaps that was one of the attractions to those who have preserved his name.

We find many of the statements attributed to Pythagoras to be expressed parables which make little sense to the modern reader, but here and there is a lovely idea—such as the idea that one should preserve what one has learned from a teacher with the same sense of value that one saves a gift of money.

There seems to be no question that he was educated in music and a practicing musician all his life. Of his various observations on music, it is those associated with health which are most worthy of contemplation today.

Of all of Pythagoras' ideas, the one which had the most impact on following philosophers, has been most frequently discussed, and led to his only real impact on later intellectual processes was his theory of the 'harmony of the spheres.' Ironically, with respect to music and astrology this idea was nonsense,[37] but from this seed grew an unexpected and mighty tree of knowledge— higher mathematics!

37 Maybe. In 2002, NASA's Chandra X-ray Observatory found that a black hole in the Perseus cluster produces a B♭, 57 octaves below middle C!

We have always thought that any general discussion of the great dramatists of the fifth century BC, should begin by at least mentioning in passing the nearly six hundred fables of Aesop (620–560 BC), for each is truly a little drama. One of these in particular attracts our attention.

'The Lyre Player'

A lyre player of very little talent practiced constantly in a room with plastered walls, and from the echo he began to think that his playing sounded very well. So, in his vanity, he decided that he should go on the stage, but when he made his appearance and played very badly, he was run off with stones.[1]

Reading this, one can not help but wonder if the audiences in the era of the rhapsodists and lyric poets were really so critical as to stone some performers![2]

The only other fable which includes a musician concerns,

'The Kid and the Aulos Playing Wolf'

A kid had lagged behind the flock and was set upon by a wolf. The kid turned around and said to the wolf, 'I'm sure that I'm to be your dinner, but just so that I won't die ignominiously, play a tune on our aulos for me to dance to.' While the wolf played and the kid danced, the dogs heard and chased the wolf away. The wolf turned back and said to the kid, 'This is what I deserve. A butcher like me oughtn't to try to be an aulos player.'[3]

This fable may remind the reader of the Greek myth concerning death and the advisability of having aulos players on hand to play. The accepted 'moral' of this fable, however, has something to do with neglecting the business at hand, therefore we turn to the principal subject.

We shall now look for clues to aesthetics in music practice in the dramatic works of the three great tragedians, Aeschylus (525–456 BC),[4] Sophocles (495–406 BC) and Euripides (480–408 BC), together with the first great master of comedy, Aristophanes (448–380 BC).

1　Nr. 121, in Aesop, *Aesop Without Morals: The Famous Fables, and a Life of Aesop*, trans. Lloyd W. Daly (New York: Yoseloff, 1961). We might remind the reader that in the age before recordings, singers used echos as a means of hearing their practice.

2　Euripides once gave encouragement to a younger playwright who had been *hissed* by the audience, according to Plutarch, quoted in Sir Arthur Wallace Pickard-Cambridge, *The Dramatic Festivals of Athens* (Oxford: Clarendon Press, 1953), 266.

3　Nr. 97, in Aesop, *Aesop Without Morals*.

4　Chamaeleon, quoted by Athenaeus, in *Deipnosophistae*, 1.22, says 'Aeschylus wrote his tragedies when drunk.' Athenaeus adds, 'Sophocles, anyway, reproached Aeschylus with the remark that even if he wrote as he should, he did it unconsciously.'

The beginning of the period of the great Greek tragedies overlaps the period of the last of the lyric poets. In his play, *The Poet and the Women*, we clearly see Aristophanes not only recalling some of the early poet–singers by name but he also confirms that their poetry was sung: they were musicians. The poet, Agathon, comments,

> Anyway, it's terribly uncultured for a poet to go round looking all wild and hairy. Look at Ibycus, and Anacreon of Teos, and Alcaeus, with those exquisitely tempered harmonies of theirs—they all wore the proper minstrel's sash, and their movements were graceful, like mine.[5]

When Aeschylus died, in 456 BC, Pindar had at least ten years of activity left and Bacchylides was still in middle life. To some degree it was the narrative dithyramb[6] of the lyric poets which expanded and became fifth century tragedy. The choral odes of the older poets, those works sung in public festivals and choral competitions, become the 'choruses' of the fifth century dramatists and their stage directions indicate, contrary to productions today, that they were still *sung* choruses. An example of this proof can be seen in *The Wasps* by Aristophanes when the leader of the chorus speaks just before the chorus sings:

> Not like him to shirk his duties when there's a trial on—he's usually first in the line leading the singing: he's a great one for the old songs. Let's stop and sing to him now, shall we?[7]

This play is a comedy and so the idea of beginning a trial with a choral ode was no doubt a comment on so many important occasions in ancient Greece having choral odes in their ceremonies. The plays of the fifth century BC dramatists often include the lyrics of these odes and one which we find to be very much in the style of the old choral odes is one found in *Alcestis* by Euripides.

Chorus (singing)

O house of a bountiful lord,
Even open to many guests,
The God of Pytho,
Apollo of the beautiful lyre,
Designed to dwell in you
And to live a shepherd in your lands!
On the slope of the hillsides
He played melodies of mating
On the Pipes of Pan to his herds.

5   Aristophanes, *The Poet and the Women* (New York: Penguin Classics, 1964), 105.

6   Nagy, *Pindar's Homer*, 105, fn. 118, notes, 'By the time that Aristotle was composing his *Poetics*, about 330 BC, the dithyramb seems to have been the only kind of choral lyric that was still alive enough to deserve his notice in that work.'

7   Aristophanes, *The Wasps* (New York: Penguin Classics, 1964), 48. Later, ibid., 70, is another reference to beginning the trial with an ode.

And the dappled lynxes fed with them
In joy at your singing;
From the wooded vale of Orthrys
Came a yellow troop of lions;
To the sound of your lyre, O Phoebus,
Danced the dappled fawn
Moving on light feet
Beyond the high-crested pines,
Charmed by your sweet singing.[8]

A Chorus in Aristophanes also mentions Phoebus, as well as the above mentioned choral competitions.

To thee, oh Phoebus, I dedicate my most beauteous songs; to thee, the sacred victor in the poetical contests.[9]

Moreover, the choruses in these plays may have continued to dance, as well as sing, again in the tradition of the older choral odes. Athenaeus quotes Chamaeleon as saying,

Aeschylus was the first to give poses to his choruses, employing no dancing masters, but devising for himself the figures of the dance, and in general taking upon himself the entire management of the piece.[10]

Athenaeus also tells us that Sophocles, himself, was expert in both music and dancing.

Sophocles, besides being handsome in his youth, became proficient in dancing and music, while still a lad, under the instruction of Lamprus. After the battle of Salamis, at any rate, he danced to the accompaniment of his lyre around the trophy, naked and anointed with oil. Others say he danced with his cloak on. And when he brought out the *Thamyris* he played the lyre himself.[11]

One important difference between the fifth-century stage works and the earlier performances of the lyric poets is that while the lyre is still mentioned in these plays, it does seem that the aulos begins to be the preferred instrument for accompaniment in the fifth century. Sir Arthur Pickard-Cambridge provides the reasoning of the time.

The instrument by which both the singing and recitative were normally accompanied in tragedy and comedy was the aulos. In the

8 Euripides, *Alcestis*, 568. Unless otherwise indicated, all translations for these four dramatists are quoted from Whitney J. Oates, ed., *The Complete Greek Drama: All the Extant Tragedies of Aeschylus, Sophocles and Euripides* (New York: Random House, 1938).

9 Aristophanes, *The Themophoriazusae*, 108.

10 Athenaeus, *Deipnosophistae*, 1.22. Athenaeus also lists Thespis, Pratinas, Cratinus, and Phrynichus among older playwrights who 'not only relied upon the dancing of the chorus for the interpretation of their plays, but, quite apart from their own compositions, they taught dancing to all who wanted instruction.

11 Athenaeus, *Deipnosophistae*, 1.20.

12 Sir Arthur Pickard-Cambridge, *The Dramatic Festivals of Athens*, 163. This author, as was the case with almost all earlier English authors, incorrectly translates the aulos as 'flute,' whereas it was in fact a reed, and probably a double-reed, instrument. Sir Arthur goes into considerable detail regarding his belief that the aulos was used in specific relationships with the metrics of the text. An example (p. 162):

It has been made plain that the anapaests of the parabasis were accompanied by the flute, as also, in all probability, were any tetrameter speeches delivered by an actor while the chorus or a semi-chorus was dancing, and in particular the epirrhema and antepirrhema of the parabasis, which were commonly in trochaic or iambic tetrameters.

13 Pickard-Cambridge, 164, 218, 300ff.

14 Euripides, *Electra*, 425. Also in Aristophanes, *The Frogs*, 1314:

Where many a songful dolphin trips To lead the dark blue beaked ships, …

Athenaeus, *Deipnosophistae*, 7.328, mentions the trichis as another sea creature which delights in music. Strabo, *The Geography of Strabo*, 15.2.12, on the other hand describes the use of trumpets to scare off whales.

15 'The Banquet of the Seven Wise Men.'

16 Sophocles, *Antigone*, 310.

Problems of Aristotle, xix, 43, it is argued that the aulos gives a better accompaniment to the human voice than the lyre, because both aulos and voice are wind instruments and so blend better … It appears probable that the lyre was used in the drama mainly for special effects, as when the young Sophocles played it in his *Thamyris*.[12]

We know that by the fourth century the aulos player was a regular contract member of the drama company; we know he wore costumes; and we have considerable documentation for at least one famous player, Kraton of Chalkedon.[13]

The value of this body of dramatic literature, with respect to our study, is that it is the very nature of drama to reflect, at least to some degree, life as it is known to the observer. Therefore, we might expect to find clues which are more reflective of genuine musical practice, not to mention the concerns of the ordinary people, than we might find in other literature. To give a rather charming example, there are references in both Euripides and Aristophanes to the musical inclination of dolphins, an animal which much fascinated the Greeks. In Electra, the Chorus sings,

Ye famous ships, that on a day were brought to land at Troy by those countless oars, what time ye led the Nereids' dance, where the music loving dolphin rolled and gamboled round your dusky prows.[14]

Plutarch also mentions this popular idea that the gentle dolphin was a lover of music.

And this we know undoubtedly, that these creatures delight infinitely in music; they love it, and if any man sings or plays as he sails along in fair weather, they will quietly swim by the side of the ship, and listen till the music is ended.[15]

On the other hand, one finds virtually no reference in these plays to the great questions the philosophers were struggling with, which may again only reflect the fact that the ordinary person was not concerned with these questions. For example, the philosophers were much concerned with the senses. Do we hear in the ear, the brain, or the soul? The only reference to this inquiry, found in Sophocles, does, however, neatly epitomize this debate.

CREON: Knowest thou not that even now thy voice offends?
GUARD: Is thy smart in the ears, or in the soul?
CREON: And why wouldst thou define the seat of my pain?[16]

The actual descriptions of musical style found in these dramatic works only once again intrigue and frustrate us. As mentioned in the Preface, above, because only a small handful of specimens of actual early Greek music are known to us today, we can not know, for example, what is meant when the early writers associate the various modes with the theater. Sir Arthur Pickard-Cambridge summarizes these views as follows:

> Aristoxenus (who as a pupil of Aristotle may be assumed to be trustworthy in regard to tragedy) recorded that the modes proper to tragedy were the pathetic Mixolydian and the stately and majestic Dorian; but that these were not exclusively used is shown by Aristoxenus' own statement recorded in the *Life of Sophocles* that Sophocles had introduced the Phrygian mode (which was the special mode of dithyramb), and by a passage in the Aristotelian *Problems* which justifies the use of the Hypodorian and Hypophrygian modes for the lyrics sung by actors, when realistic action was called for, but not for those of the chorus ...
>
> A writer of perhaps a century later than Aristotle rejects somewhat violently the view that different types of music influenced character ... and it is possible that such influence had grown less in the course of time; but it cannot be seriously doubted that Plato and Aristotle and Arixtoxenus knew what they were talking about, and that the music employed helped to give a certain emotional color to the performances with which it was associated, though it is impossible to trace the effects in detail.[17]

We must point out that only a very small proportion of the works of Aristoxenus survive and on that basis we are hesitant to base any conclusions on this writer. Modern writers do, however, simply because Aristoxenus, a pupil of Aristotle, is the only literature which is extant from his generation. In any case, these 'modes' which we know today only as tuning relationships on the lyre, should be thought of as 'styles' of music of a particular people, a subject of which we know nothing today due to having insufficient extant specimens. Moreover, there must have been great a variety of musical styles and types within these larger denominations, as there is today within music which we call 'French' or 'German.' All understanding of this, save the superficial, is lost to us today and we can not know what was meant by Aristophanes' expression, a 'soft Ionian Love song,'[18] not to mention Aeschylus',

Through me too sorrow runs
Like a strange Ionian Song ...[19]

17 Pickard-Cambridge, *The Dramatic Festivals of Athens*, 263, 265.

18 Aristophanes, *The Ecclesiazusae*, 881.

19 Aeschylus, *The Supplices*, 69, trans. Gilbert Murray, *The Complete Plays of Aeschylus* (London: George Allen, 1952).

What can 'a *strange* Ionian Song' mean? This adjective occurs twice in Euripides and once again causes us to wish we had the music and not the description.

> O Muse, be near me now, and make
> A strange song for Ilion's sake.[20]
>
> ...
>
> A lad alone on Ida,
> Playing tunes on his pipe, strange melodies,
> Like the melodies Olympus sang.[21]

There are specific geographical references in Aristophanes, including a specific call for the music of a 'Persian' dance[22] and in another place the interesting observation by the chorus that Asia is 'the Mother of our songs and dances.'[23] Neither can we know what is meant by 'songs of mystic melody,'[24] nor 'the harmony of auloi.'[25]

And even more intriguing are the occasional subjective references to the music. How we would love to hear once again the touching music which inspired Euripides, in *The Trojan Women*, to use three times the phrase 'a tune of tears.'

> My body rocketh, and would fain
> Move to the tune of tears that flow:
> For tears are music too, and keep
> A song unheard in hearts that weep.[26]

Art Music

Several times in lines given to the chorus by Sophocles we hear praise of the beautiful in music, in language that reminds us of similar praise by the lyric poets.

> Music of aulos, soothing and sweet ... [27]
>
> Let the maidens raise a joyous strain ...
> My spirit soars; I will not reject the wooing of the aulos.[28]
>
> Soon shall the glorious voice of the aulos go up for you again ...
> with such music as the lyre maketh to the gods![29]

And Aristophanes describes the joy of a listener in hearing a performance at a competition.

20   Euripides, *The Trojan Women*, 510.

21   Euripides, *Iphigenia in Aulis*, 574.

22   Aristophanes, *The Poet and the Women*, 2.1176.

23   Ibid., 1.127.

24   Euripides, *The Bacchae*, 1056.

25   Aristophanes, *Peace*, 531.

26   118, 512, and 602:
Even as the sound of a song
Left by the way, but long
Remembered, a tune of tears
Falling where no man hears

27   Sophocles, *Ajax*, 1204.

28   Sophocles, *The Trachiniae*, 204, 210.

29   Ibid., 637.

But the day when I was impatiently awaiting a piece by Aeschylus, what tragic despair it caused me when the herald called, 'Theognis, introduce your Chorus!' Just imagine how this blow struck straight at my heart! On the other hand, what joy Dexitheus caused me at the musical competition, when right after Moschus he played a Boeotian melody on the lyre![30]

30 Aristophanes, *The Archarnians*, 7.

On the other hand, in this the more realistic form of drama, we also find some who do not respond to the music they hear, such as the choral comment, in *The Acharnians* of Aristophanes, which complains about,

this musician, who plagues us with his silly improvisations …[31]

31 Ibid., 844.

or the character in *The Wasps* who never allowed himself to be *moved*.

He was the hardest of us all; he alone *never* allowed himself to be moved. If anyone tried to move him, he would lower his head, saying, 'You might just as well try to boil a stone.'[32]

32 Aristophanes, *The Wasps*, 274.

Given the close relationship between the dramatic choruses and earlier choral odes, together with the frequent mention as late as Aristophanes of actual lyric poets, we have every reason to suppose that older choral repertoire works were still known and performed during the fifth century. A line in Euripides confirms that this was the case.

For I sing this day to Dionysus
The song that is appointed from of old.[33]

33 Euripides, *The Bacchae*, 70.

However, by the time this particular play was produced (ca. 407 BC) it is clear that some no longer appreciated the works of the older lyric poets. Athenaeus quotes a play called *The Helots*, in which a character says,

To sing the songs of Stesichorus, of Alkman, and Simonides is out of date. Rather, Gnesippus is the one to hear, for he has invented serenades for adulterers, with iambuca and triangle in hand, to sing and lure their ladies with.[34]

34 Athenaeus, *Deipnosophistae*, 14.638.

We see this viewpoint again in Aristophanes, in an interesting account of one of the typical indoor 'concerts' performed at the conclusion of a dinner party. As was characteristic of such performances of art music during earlier centuries, the musician refuses to play while people are still eating or drinking. In this instance, the host requests a work by one of the lyric poets, Simonides, which the musician refuses, insulting not only this poet, but the more recent ones.

> LEADER OF THE CHORUS: But how did the fight begin? tell the Chorus; you cannot help doing that much.
> STREPSIADES: I will tell you what was the start of the quarrel. At the end of the meal, as you know, I bade him take his lyre and sing me the song of Simonides, which tells of the fleece of the ram. He replied bluntly, that it was stupid, while drinking, to play the lyre and sing, like a woman when she is grinding barley.
> PHIDIPPIDES: Why, by rights I ought to have beaten and kicked you the very moment you told me to sing!
> STREPSIADES: This is just how he spoke to me in the house, furthermore he added, that Simonides was a detestable poet. However, I mastered myself and for a while said nothing. Then I said to him, 'At least, take a myrtle branch and recite a passage from Aeschylus to me.'—'For my own part,' he at once replied, 'I look upon Aeschylus as the first of poets, for his verses roll superbly; they're nothing but incoherence, bombast and turgidity.' Yet still I smothered my wrath and said, 'Then recite one of the famous pieces from the modern poets.' Then he commenced a piece in which Euripides shows, oh! horror! a brother, who violates his own uterine sister.[43]

35 Aristophanes, *The Clouds*, 1352ff.

In the same spirit, there is a comic scene in *The Frogs* where Aristophanes presents Euripides attempting to prove how bad the choral music of Aeschylus was—to which the Chorus wonders how he can find fault in such a 'master of inspiration.'

> EURIPIDES:
>   Songs?: Yes, I have materials to show
>   How bad his are, and always all alike.
> CHORUS (SINGING):
>   What in the world shall we look for next?
>   Aeschylus' music! I feel perplexed
>   How he can want it mended.
>   I have always held that never a man
>   Had written or sung since the world began
>   Melodies half so splendid!
>   (Can he really find a mistake
>   In the master of Inspiration?

I feel some consternation
For our Bacchic prince's sake!)
EURIPIDES:
Wonderful songs they are! You'll see directly;
I'll run them all together into one.
DIONYSUS:
I'll take some pebbles, then, and count for you.
EURIPIDES (SINGING):
'O Phthian Achilles, canst hark to the battle's man-slaying shock,
Yea, shock, and not to succor come?
Lo, we of the mere give worship to Hermes, the fount of our stock,
Yea, shock, and not to succor come!'
DIONYSUS:
Two shocks to you, Aeschylus, there!
EURIPIDES (SINGING):
'Thou choice of Achaea, wide-ruling Atrides, give heed to
my schooling!
Yea, shock, and not to succor come.'
DIONYSUS:
A third shock that, I declare!
EURIPIDES (SINGING):
'Ah peace, and give ear! For the Bee-Maids be near to ope wide
Artemis' portals.
Yea, shock-a-nock a-succor come!
Behold it is mine to sing of the sign of the way fate-laden
to mortals;
Yah, shocker-knocker succucum!'
DIONYSUS:
O Zeus Almighty, what a chain of shocks!
I think I'll go away and take a bath;
The shocks are too much for my nerves and kidneys!
EURIPIDES:
Not till you've heard another little set
Compounded from his various cithara-songs.
DIONYSUS:
Well then, proceed; but don't put any shocks in!
EURIPIDES (SINGING):
'How the might twin-throned of Achaea for Hellene chiv-
alry bringeth
Flattothrat toflattothrat!
The prince of the posers of storm, the Sphinx thereover
he wingeth
Flattothrat toflattothrat!
With deedful hand and lance the furious fowl of the air
Flattothrat toflattothrat!

That the wild wind-walking hounds unhindered tear
    Flattothrat toflattothrat!
And War toward Ajax leaned his weight,
    Flattothrat toflattothrat!!'

Dionysus:
  What's Flattothrat? Was it from Marathon
  You gathered this wool-gatherer's stuff, or where?

Aeschylus:
  Clean was the place I found them, clean the place
  I brought them, loath to glean with Phrynichus
  The same enchanted meadow of the Muse.
  But any place will do for *him* to poach,
  Drink-ditties of Meletus, Carian pipings,
  And wakes, and dancing songs—Here, let me show you!
  Ho, some one bring my lyre! But no; what need
  Of lyres for this stuff? Where's the wench that plays
  The bones?—Approach, Euripidean Muse,
  These songs are meet for your accompaniment![36]

36 Aristophanes, *The Frogs*, 1249ff.

Similarly, the tradition of singing of the glories of men and battles of the past is satirized by Aristophanes. In the following scene,[37] a boy has come to sing after a banquet. Every time he begins one of these historical songs he is interrupted by a guest who is impatient with this old style of song.

37 Aristophanes, *Peace*, 1268ff.

Trygaeus: Hi! child! what do you reckon to sing? Stand there and give me the opening line.

Boy: 'Glory to the young warriors … '

Trygaeus: Oh! leave off about your young warriors, you little wretch; we are at peace and you are an idiot and a rascal.

Boy: 'The skirmish begins, the hollow bucklers clash against each other.'

Trygaeus: Bucklers! Leave me in peace with your bucklers.

Boy: 'And then there came groanings and shouts of victory.'

Trygaeus: Groanings! ah! by Bacchus! look out for yourself, you cursed squaller, if you start wearying us again with your groanings and hollow bucklers.

Boy: Then what should I sing? Tell me what pleases you.

Trygaeus: 'Tis thus they feasted on the flesh of oxen,' or something similar, as, for instance, 'Everything that could tickle the palate was placed on the table.'

Boy: 'Tis thus they feasted on the flesh of oxen and, tired of warfare, unharnessed their foaming steeds.'

Trygaeus: That's splendid; tired of warfare, they seat themselves at table; sing to us how they still go on eating after they are satiated.

BOY: 'The meal over, they girded themselves ... '

TRYGAEUS: With good wine, no doubt?

BOY: ' ... with armor and rushed forth from the towers, and a terrible shout arose.'

TRYGAEUS: Get you gone, you little scapegrace, you and your battles! You sing of nothing but warfare.

In a similar scene, in Aristophanes' *The Wasps*, Bdelycleon is trying to teach Philocleon how to behave at a banquet. He must recline, 'in an elegant style,' then the meal, libations to the gods, and finally participate in an imaginary after dinner concert performed by the guests themselves.

BDELYCLEON: The aulos player has finished the prelude. The guests are Theorus, Aeschines, Phanus, Cleon, Acestor; and beside this last, I don't know who else. You are with them. Shall you know exactly how to take up the songs that are started?

PHILOCLEON: Quite well.

BDELYCLEON: Really?

PHILOCLEON: Better than any born mountaineer of Attica.

BDELYCLEON: That we shall see. Suppose me to be Cleon. I am the first to begin the song of Harmodius, and you take it up: 'There never yet was seen in Athens ...

PHILOCLEON: ... such a rogue or such a thief.'

BDELYCLEON: Why, you wretched man, it will be the end of you if you sing that. He will vow your ruin, your destruction, to chase you out of the country.

PHILOCLEON: Well! then I shall answer his threats with another song: 'With your madness for supreme power, you will end by overthrowing the city, which even now totters towards ruin.'

BDELYCLEON: And when Theorus, prone at Cleon's feet, takes his hand and sings, 'Like Admetus, love those who are brave,' what reply will you make him?

PHILOCLEON: I shall sing, 'I know not how to play the fox, nor call myself the friend of both parties.'

BDELYCLEON: Then comes the turn of Aeschines, the son of Sellus, and a well-trained and clever musician, who will sing, 'Good things and riches for Clitagora and me and eke for the Thessalians!'

PHILOCLEON: 'The two of us have squandered a great deal between us.'

BDELYCLEON: At this game you seem at home.[38]

Finally, in a lost play called *The Harper*, by Menander, a character speaks of someone playing a musical instrument, 'He is very fond of music, and always practicing tunes in luxurious ease.'[39]

38 Aristophanes, *The Wasps*, 1218ff.

39 Quoted in Athenaeus, *Deipnosophistae*, 12.510.

EDUCATIONAL MUSIC

Of these dramatists, only Aristophanes makes any reference to the use of music in education. He makes up for the others, however, in a breadth of comments which suggest that he was a keen observer of this aspect of society. He mentions the 'teacher of choirs who forgets his position'[40] and the student who refused to learn any but the Dorian style.

40   Aristophanes, *The Frogs*, in Oates, *The Complete Greek Drama*, 360.

> You also know what a pig's education he has had; his school-fellows can recall that he only liked the Dorian style and would study no other; his music master in displeasure sent him away saying; 'This youth, in matters of harmony, will only learn the Dorian style because it is akin to bribery.'[41]

In *The Clouds*, Aristophanes, through the mouth of a character called, Just Discourse, provides us with a stark vision of the nature of discipline in music education 'in the old days'—days when music education meant singing of the glories of one's elders and in music of the old style (none of this modern music!).

41   Aristophanes, *The Knights*, 990. Note the reference here to Dorian as a *style*, not a scale, etc., exactly the case we have been making above with respect to the modes. Also the reference to bribery (*dorodokos*, 'taker of bribes') involves a play on words with the term *Doristi* ('in the Dorian style'). A French translator captured it best in referring to it as the 'Louis d'or-ian mode.'

> Very well, I will tell you what was the old education, when I used to teach justice with so much success and when modesty was held in veneration. Firstly, it was required of a child, that it should not utter a word. In the street, when they went to the music school, all the youths of the same district marched lightly clad and ranged in good order, even when the snow was falling in great flakes. At the master's house they had to stand with their legs apart and they were taught to sing either, 'Pallas, the Terrible, who overturneth cities,' or 'A noise resounded from afar' in the solemn tones of the ancient harmony. If anyone indulged in buffoonery or lent his voice any of the soft inflections, like those which today the disciples of Phrynis take so much pains to form, he was treated as an enemy of the Muses and belabored with blows … At table, they would not have dared, before those older than themselves, to have taken a radish, an aniseed or a leaf of parsley, and much less eat fish or thrushes or cross their legs.

The product of this kind of education is praised by the Leader of the Chorus in *The Frogs*,

> So with men we know for upright, blameless lives and noble names,
> Trained in music and palaestra, freemen's choirs and freemen's games,[42]

42   Aristophanes, *The Frogs*, 728.

and by a character in *The Thesmophoriazusae*, who tells us that one's choice of music reveals one's character.

> Answer me. But you keep silent. Oh! just as you choose; your songs display your character quite sufficiently.[43]

43   Aristophanes, *The Thesmophoriazusae* 143.

This we presume is a reflection on the long held concept of the relationship between music and character, which is discussed at length by Plato and others. Euripides makes an interesting observation on composers which is related to this, here relative to the character of the composer and his art. He says, the composer who does not enjoy his own music cannot expect others to enjoy his music.

> He who maketh songs should take a pleasure in their making; for if it be not so with him, he will in no wise avail to gladden others, if himself have sorrow in his home; nay, 'tis not even right to expect it.[44]

44   Euripides, *The Suppliants*, 174.

FUNCTIONAL MUSIC

The highest form of functional music in the fifth century was that which was involved in the cult, or quasi-religious, celebrations. Euripides gives us two vivid descriptions of such celebrations, in which we are witness not only to the general frenzy of the celebrants, but also the broad use of music. The first, from *Helen*, is set in the time of the gods.

> Loudly rattled the Bacchic castanets in shrill accord, what time those maidens, swift as whirlwinds, sped forth with the goddess on her chariot yoked to wild creatures, in quest of her that was ravished from the circling choir of virgins ...
>
> But when for gods and tribes of men alike she made an end to festal cheer, Zeus spoke out, seeking to soothe the mother's moody soul, 'Ye stately Graces, go banish from Demeter's angry heart the grief her wanderings bring upon her for her child, and go, ye Muses too, with tuneful choir.' Thereon did Cypris, fairest of the blessed gods, first catch up the crashing cymbals, native to that land, and the drum with tight-stretched skin, and then Demeter smiled, and in her hand did take the deep-toned flute, well pleased with its loud note ...
>
> Oh! mighty is the virtue in a dress of dappled fawn-skin, in ivy green that twineth round a sacred thyrsus, in whirling tambourines struck as they revolve in the air, in tresses wildly streaming for the revelry.[45]

45   Euripides, *Helen*, 1302ff.

And in *The Bacchae* we are given a similar description set in the present time.

> Uplift the dark divine wand,
> The oak-wand and the pine-wand,
> And don thy fawn-skin, fringed in purity
> With fleecy white, like ours …
>
> For thee of old some crested Corybant
> First woke in Cretan air
> The wild orb of our orgies,
> Our Timbrel; and thy gorges
> Rang with this strain; and blended Phrygian song
> And sweet keen auloi were there.
>
> But the Timbrel, the Timbrel was another's,
> And away to Mother Rhea it must wend;
> And to our holy singing from the Mother's
> The mad Satyrs carried it, to blend
> In the dancing and the cheer
> Of our third and perfect Year;
> And it serves Dionysus in the end! …
>
> Hither, O fragrant of Tmolus the Golden,
> Come with the voice of timbrel and drum;
> Let the cry of your joyance uplift and embolden
> The God of the joy-cry; O Bacchanals, come!
> With pealing of auloi and with Phrygian clamor,
> On where the vision of holiness thrills,
> And the music climbs and the maddening glamor.[46]

The sense we have here of the power of the music is emphasized in a Chorus from *The Eumenides* by Aeschylus, where music is described as completely possessing the participant.

> But our sacrifice to bind,
> Lo, the music that we wind,
> How it dazeth and amazeth
> And the will it maketh blind,
> As it moves without a lyre
> To the throb of my desire;
> 'Tis a chain about the brain,
> 'Tis a wasting of mankind.[47]

46   Euripides, *The Bacchae*, 109ff. In *The Poet and the Women*, by Aristophanes (New York: Penguin Classics, 1964), 1.2.328, we find the chorus singing with a lyre at a religious event.

47   Aeschylus, *The Complete Plays of Aeschylus*, ln. 326ff.

One passage in Euripides mentions regular cult celebrations which were held at night.

> For thy worship is aye performed with many a sacrifice, and never art thou forgotten as each month draweth to its close, when young voices sing and dancers' music is heard abroad, while on our wind-swept hill goes up the cry of joy to the beat of the maidens' feet by night.[48]

48 Euripides, *The Heracleidae*, 777ff.

The dancing was not always sedate, and hence a reflection of the character of the accompanying music, as we see in another comment by Euripides, 'lift high the nimble foot.'[49] In yet another place, Euripides also mentions that dancing was also done around the altar.[50]

49 Euripides, *Electra*, 868.

50 Euripides, *Iphigenia in Aulis*, 675.

Closely related to the quasi-religious cult ceremonies were the celebrations of marriage. Euripides again gives us an idealized picture recalling such a celebration among the gods.

> Who knows the marriage-song that once so proudly rang
> To the flute and the pipe and the dancer's lyre,
> The song the Muses sang?
> Up Pelion's glades they danced,
> The bright Pierian choir:
> Their golden sandals glanced,
> Their tresses gleamed as they made their way,
> Chanting the names, the names of bride and bridegroom,
> Through woods where Centaurs lay
> To the god-given feast
> For Thetis and her lover.
> Page Ganymede, the Phrygian boy,
> Darling of Zeus, his luxury's toy,
> Poured wine in golden beakers.
> Far down on white-lit sand
> Beside Aegaean waters
> Danced, circling hand-in-hand,
> The Nereid maids,
> The Sea-king's fifty daughters.[59]

51 Ibid., 1041ff.

And again Euripides gives us an example in a contemporary setting,

> Come, greet ye Hymen, greet
> Hymen with songs of pride:
> Sing to him loud and long,
> Cry, cry, when the song
> Faileth, for joy of the bride![52]

52 Euripides, *The Trojan Women*, 365ff.

In other references to marriage celebrations, Euripides mentions, 'the glad music of lutes at her wedding,'[53] and 'the sound of aulos and dancing feet.'[54]

We might also mention that the later playwright, Menander, a representative of so-called 'New Comedy,' provides an interesting account of the preparations necessary for a wedding procession—which also seems to have been at night.

> All that remains is to fetch the ritual water. Chrysis, send out the women, the water-carrier and the musician. And someone bring us out a torch and garlands, so that we can form a proper procession.[55]

Music is also usually mentioned by the dramatists in references to the dirge. An interesting example, musically, is sung by the Chorus in *Iphigenia in Tauris* by Euripides.

> To thee thy faithful train
> The Asiatic hymn will raise,
> A doleful, a barbaric melody,
> Responsive to thy lays,
> And steep in tears the mournful song,—
> Notes, which to the dead belong;
> Dismal notes, attuned to woe.[56]

In an equally dark passage in *Helen*, Euripides includes a very rare mention of a flute-type instrument which is neither the panpipes, nor is it a mistranslation for aulos.

> Ah me! what piteous dirge shall I strive to utter, now that I am beginning my melody of bitter lamentation? What Muse shall I approach with tears or songs of death or woe? Ah me! ye Sirens, Earth's virgin daughters, winged maids, come, oh! come to aid my mourning, bringing with you the Libyan flute or pipe, to waft to Persephone's ear a tearful plaint, the echo of my sorrow, with grief for grief, and mournful chant for chant, with songs of death and doom to match my lamentation.[57]

There are two quite unusual passages in Euripides which fall in the context of the dirge. One is a reference to dancing as part of the mourning ceremony[58] and the other is a curious appeal to a bird to accompany the dirge.

> Thee let me invoke, tearful Philomel, lurking 'neath the leafy covert in thy place of song, most tuneful of all feathered songsters, oh!

53 Euripides, *Heracles*, 8.

54 Euripides, *Iphigenia in Aulis*, 432.

55 Menander, *The Girl from Samos*, 729ff., trans. Norma Miller, *Menander Plays and Fragments* (London: Penguin Books, 1987).

56 Euripides, *Iphigenia in Aulis*, 178.

57 Euripides, *Helen*, 219.

58 Euripides, *The Suppliants*, 77.

come to aid me in my dirge, trilling through thy tawny throat, as I
sing the piteous woes of Helen.[59]

59 Euripides, *Helen*, 1113ff.

Finally in Aeschylus the dirge is mentioned as a symbol for a
similar emotion, when the Chorus in *The Supplices* sings,

As I speak there comes a crying
From within that checks my breath:
Tis a music full of tears
For some terror that it hears,
As a dirge over the dying;
For this life I count as death.[60]

60 Aeschylus, *The Supplices*, 112ff.

Functional music for the military is, of course, usually limited
to references to the trumpet,[61] either as a giver of signals or as a
symbol of the noise and anxiety of the battle. An example of the
latter is Aeschylus',

61 Aeschylus in *The Supplices*, 684, complains that the warrior 'knows not dance or lyre.' In this playwright's *Peace*, a stage note refers to the arrival of a trumpet maker seeking to make a sale.

Wild brazen bells make music of affright.[62]

62 Aeschylus, *The Seven Against Thebes*, 386.

In this same passage, by the way, we find a reference similar to those
found in ancient Hebrew and Roman literature, of the change in
the character of the horse when he hears the battle trumpet.

As some wild war-horse when the trumpets sound
Stiffens and champs the curb and paws the ground.

Among these plays there are two references to a new kind of
trumpet, which Euripides calls 'the Tuscan trumpet,'[63] and Sophocles the 'bronze-mouthed Tyrrhene trumpet.'[64] These are references
to a new instrument developed by the Etruscans (Greek: *Tyrrhe-
nians*) and which is known in Roman literature as the cornu, a great
hoop-shaped instrument of bronze or iron, with transverse grip,
looking somewhat like a capital letter *G*.

63 Euripides, *The Phoenissae*, 1379.
64 Sophocles, *Ajax*, 16.

We know also that the aulos was a basic instrument of the Greek
army and there are two passages which document its presence in
battle. In Aeschylus', *The Seven Against Thebes*,

His fiery coursers eager to attack
And die; but ever more he wheels them back,
Their frontlets tossing, while the pipes beneath
In barbarous music whistle to their breath.[65]

65 Aeschylus, *The Seven Against Thebes*, ln. 460ff.

and in Euripides', *The Trojan Women*.

66   Euripides, *The Trojan Women*, 130.

And the noise of your music flew,
Clarion and aulos did shriek.[66]

Another category of functional music is that associated with occupations. In Aristophanes' *The Acharnians*, for example, the character, Dicaeopolis, says,

67   Aristophanes, *The Acharnians*, 555.

We hear nothing but the sound of whistles, of flutes [aulos] and fifes to encourage the workers.[67]

In *The Frogs*, the same playwright speaks of music used to provide the beat for rowers.

68   Aristophanes, *The Frogs*, 204.

You'll row all right; as soon as you fall to,
You'll hear a first-rate tune that *makes* you row.[68]

Finally, the occupation of the shepherd is mentioned twice and both times, of course, he appears with his traditional panpipe instrument. First, in Sophocles' *Philoctetes*,

69   Sophocles, *Philoctetes*, 239.

Like the shepherd with his rural pipe
And cheerful song[69]

and in Euripides' *Electra*,

70   Euripides, *Electra*, 703.

How on a day Pan, the steward of husbandry, came breathing dulcet music on his jointed pipe.[70]

Entertainment Music

There is one interesting description of entertainment music by Euripides in which, it seems to us, he had in mind the following lines from book 10 of *The Iliad*, by Homer.

So often as [Agamemnon] gazed toward the Trojan plain, he marveled at the many fires that burned before the face of Ilios, and at the sound of aulos and pipes, and the din of men.

In his account of the same battle, Euripides includes the following description:

A very weariness of joy
Fell with the evening over Troy:
And lutes of Afric mingled there
With Phrygian songs: and many a maiden,
With white feet glancing light as air,
Made happy music through the gloom:
And fires on many an inward room
All night broad-flashing, flung their glare
On laughing eyes and slumber-laden.[71]

71   Euripides, *The Trojan Women*, 543.

Aside from this passage, the only descriptions of entertainment music are Aristophanes' several references to the single-pipe girl. While it is presumed this girl also served as a prostitute, in Aristophanes there is no doubt. A single example,[72] from The Wasps, will suffice.

72   Aristophanes, *The Wasps*, 1366ff. Other references to the single-pipe girl by Aristophanes are found in *The Thesmophoriazusae*, 1187, *The Frogs*, 513, in *The Ecclesiazusae*, 887 and in *The Wasps*, 2.2200 and 1335.

BDELYCLEON: Only a rascal would steal the flute-girl away from the other guests.

PHILOCLEON: What flute-girl? Are you distraught, as if you had just returned from Pluto?

BDELYCLEON: By Zeus! But here is the Dardanian wench in person.

PHILOCLEON: Nonsense. This is a torch that I have lit in the public square in honor of the gods.

BDELYCLEON: Is this a torch?

PHILOCLEON: A torch? Certainly. Do you not see it is of several different colors?

BDELYCLEON: And what is that black part in the middle?

PHILOCLEON: That's the pitch running out while it burns.

BDELYCLEON: And there, on the other side, surely that is a girl's bottom?

PHILOCLEON: No. That's just a small bit of the torch, that projects.

BDELYCLEON: What do you mean? what bit? Hi! you woman! come here!

PHILOCLEON: Oh! What do you want to do?

BDELYCLEON: To take her away from you and lead her off. You are too much worn out and can do nothing. (He takes the girl into the house.)

The reader will observe that in the course of Greek performances from Homer until the Christian Era there is a gradual degradation, from performances which make the listener cry to those which only desire to appeal to the crowd. It is interesting, therefore, that we find clues that these playwrights were beginning to question the entire range of entertainment music. Plutarch, in retrospect, noticed, for example, in Aeschylus,

> And Aeschylus also makes it a point of wisdom not to be blown up with pride when a man is honored, nor to be moved or elevated with the acclamations of a multitude.[73]

73 Plutarch, 'How a Young Man Ought to Hear Poems.'

As an example, he points to the following passage from *The Seven Against Thebes*.

> So spake the prophet, while his brazen shield
> Hung calmly swinging. No design it held;
> Not to seem great he seeketh, but to be.[74]

74 Aeschylus, *The Seven Against Thebes*, trans. Murray, ln. 589ff.

In *Agamemnon*, Aeschylus directly criticizes entertainment music.

> For this roof, there clings
> Music about it, like a choir which sings
> One-voices, but not well-sounding, for not good
> The words are. Drunken, drunken, and with blood.[75]

75 Aeschylus, *Agamemnon*, 1183.

Euripides, in *Iphigenia in Aulis*, seems to disapprove of the singer who specializes in satire.

> Not only the idle song
> Of a singer laughing at truth.[76]

76 Euripides, *Iphigenia in Aulis*, 793.

In a most enlightening passage, Euripides mentions 'idle music' again, now critical of the entertaining singer of both former and present times. Here he seems to wonder why, when musicians have the potential for doing so much good ('to heal men's wounds by music's spell'), do they waste their talents on entertaining at a banquet, when the banquet itself is sufficient entertainment?

> Wert thou to call the men of old time rude uncultured boors thou wouldst not err, seeing that they devised their hymns for festive occasions, for banquets, and to grace the board, a pleasure to catch the ear, shed o'er our life, but no man hath found a way to allay hated grief by music and the minstrel's varied strain, whence arise slaughters and fell strokes of fate to o'erthrow the homes of men. And yet these were surely a gain, to heal men's wounds by music's spell, but why tune they their idle song where rich banquets are spread? For of itself doth the rich banquet, set before them, afford to men delight.[77]

77 Euripides, *Medea*, 179.

In summary, because the dramatic art works of these play-wrights are among the highest achievements in ancient literature, we are not surprised to find that most of their references to music are to art music and not functional or entertainment music. What specific aesthetic values can we deduce from these plays?

First, we believe inspiration was still an important association with the most highly regarded music. Aristophanes names Aeschylus one of the greatest musicians of history and calls him a 'master of Inspiration.' And surely the kinds of music which produced tears in the listener must have also been inspired music. The description of a listener by Euripides is a touching testimonial to such music.

My body rocketh, and would fain
Move to the tune of tears that flow:
For tears are music too, and keep
A song unheard in hearts that weep.

The deep impact on the listener, which is implied here, is perhaps another characteristic which these playwrights would have associated with the highest art music. Aeschylus describes music which completely possesses the listener, 'How it dazeth and amazeth.' Such music, he says, robs one of one's own will and calls it, 'a chain about the brain.' In *The Wasps*, he specifically complains about a listener who never allowed himself to be *moved* by music. Perhaps it is in distinction to music which moves the listener that Aristophanes states his objection to a musician who merely exhibits technical display, 'who plagues us with his silly improvisations.'

In Sophocles perhaps we find the expectation that art music must above all be beautiful. The music he praises, he calls 'soothing and sweet' and 'glorious.' Upon hearing 'a joyous melody,' he exclaims, 'my spirit soars.'

From these descriptions we may assume that art music was listened to, and not background music. Indeed, Aristophanes mentions a musician who refused to play at a banquet until the guests were finished eating and drinking.

There is an important new dimension to the relationship of music and listener which is introduced by these playwrights, the idea that music can affect, or even change, the character of the listener. The references we find here clearly suggest that this topic was one of discussion in the decades before it reaches its strongest endorsement in the writings of Plato. Aristophanes maintains that the listener's choice of music reveals his character and that a composer's music will reflect the character of the composer. It is for this reason that specific styles of music [*modes*] were introduced in appropriate situations in these plays.

Closely related to this, is the use of music to influence action, as we see in the example of the character who speaks of specific music performed before galley rowers. 'You will hear music,' he says, 'that *makes* you row.' No doubt this was also the purpose of military trumpet music, which in this literature is called 'barbarous' and 'shrieking.'

It is evident that there was a repertoire of older music still known and recognized, as is implied in Euripides' phrase 'a song long remembered.' We have the specific testimony of Athenaeus, who tells us that Aeschylus not only kept alive the tradition of choral dancing, but choreographed the Choral sections of his own plays.

On the other hand, we can see in this literature the beginnings of the decay of Greek art music in the instances of characters who ridicule the older 'classics.' A character in Aristophanes calls Simonides, one of the earlier lyric poets, 'detestable.' Athenaeus also mentions that the lyric poetry of Simonides, and others, was by this time out of date and was being replaced by 'serenades for adulterers,' accompanied by the iambuca and triangle!

Aristophanes also demonstrates that the epic poets, those who sang of the glories of the past, were being ridiculed. The latter had apparently begun to be replaced by singers who satirized the great, a practice which Euripides specifically objects to in *Iphigenia in Aulis*.

Finally, regarding entertainment music, we must mention the interesting questions raised by Euripides. Why he asks, when musicians have the talent to do so much good, do they waste their talents on 'idle song' for banquets? Why do we even need music for entertainment at banquets, he wonders, when a banquet is itself entertainment? A question we might ask in today's world: with five hundred channels of television, together with sporting events, etc., does the school system need to provide the public with more entertainment?

12 PLATO (427–347 BC)

After the Persian wars of 490–470 BC, when Sparta and Athens combined to defeat the efforts of Darius and Xerxes to colonize Greece, there follows a century of remarkable intellectual growth in science, mathematics, philosophy and the arts. In philosophy we have one of the great contributions to the literature of Western Europe in the writings of Plato together with his representation of Socrates.

Plato was born in comfort, was an experienced soldier, and had won prizes for physical feats in the Isthmian games. His coming into contact with Socrates changed his life and he would later observe, 'Thank God I was born Greek and not barbarian, freeman and not slave, man and not woman; but above all, that I was born in the age of Socrates.'[1]

After the death of Socrates, Plato, a young man of twenty-eight, began a period of travel, first to Egypt for a period of study at Heliopolis, then to Sicily, Italy and finally returning to Greece where he visited the members of the school founded by Pythagoras. He returned to Athens in 387 BC, a man of forty years of age and fully prepared to begin his historic writing.

As everyone knows, most of the extant Dialogues are composed as if the author were Socrates and we can not be sure when Plato himself is speaking through the various participants and when he is quoting what he learned from Socrates. We shall, therefore, quote the speakers as Plato has given them, but refer to the thoughts as being those of Plato. This identification, after all, is not so important from our perspective as the recognition that these philosophical thoughts all represent this particular time and place.

THE PHYSIOLOGY OF AESTHETICS

In the same way we wonder what Einstein might have achieved had he lived in the age of computers, so we wonder at the impact Plato would have had on later philosophy if he could have known of the results of modern clinical research in brain function. Failing this, he and most early philosophers could understand the concept

1 Quoted in Durant, *The Story of Philosophy*, 13.

of Reason but were greatly confused by anything non-rational, in particular, how to deal with the senses, emotions and music.

But even within the realm of Reason there were obvious things he could not adequately explain. One of these was what we would call today genetic knowledge, the collected wisdom we possess which is derived from our evolution. Plato, as with nearly all early philosophers who lived before medicine established a real, but non-rational, form of knowledge in the right hemisphere of our brain, placed nearly everything he could not explain as Reason in the domain of the 'soul.' In one passage he seems to clearly suggest that he believed some of our knowledge represents a recollection of past existence which is carried in our soul. After securing a series of correct answers from Meno's uneducated slave boy, Socrates first questions Meno to make sure the boy had not been previously taught these things, and then observes,

> SOCRATES. But if he did not acquire them in this life, then he must have had and learned them at some other time?
> MENO. Clearly he must.
> SOCRATES. Which must have been the time when he was not a man?
> MENO. Yes.
> SOCRATES. And if there are always to be true notions in him, both while he is and while he is not a man, which only need to be awakened into knowledge by putting questions to him, his soul must remain always possessed of this knowledge; for he must always either be or not be a man.
> MENO. Obviously.
> SOCRATES. And if the truth of all things always exists in the soul, then the soul is immortal. Wherefore be of good cheer, and try to discover by recollection what you do not now know, or rather what you do not remember.[2]

2   *Meno*, 85e. This and all following quotations from Plato are taken from *The Dialogues of Plato*, ed. Benjamin Jowett (Oxford: Clarendon Press, 1953).

Plato therefore appears to accept the idea that some form of knowledge dwells in the soul. And while he does not quite think of this, as we do, as genetic, he nevertheless assumes that this special knowledge, whatever it is, cannot be taught.

> But then, certain professors of education must be wrong when they say that they can put knowledge into the soul which was not there before, like sight into blind eyes.[3]

3   Ibid., 518c.

One form of non-rational knowledge which Plato could accept is that which he believed is given man by the gods, in particular the Muses. This idea came up during a discussion Socrates had with the 'rhapsodist,' Ion of Ephesus, a specialist in Homer. The rhapsodists were a type of orator who gave public presentations of the epic poets in a kind of sung speech. While our normal speech today still has melodic inflection, this rhapsodizing nearly three thousand years ago may have offered the last trace of the kind of sung vowel speech which many philologists believe to have been man's first form of speech.

Here Plato mentions a form of knowledge which is not learned but comes from some other source, in this case the 'Muse.' The great value of this discussion is found in the fact that while explaining this to Ion Socrates creates a brilliant analogy of how a work of art, a composition for example, is able to communicate with the performer and in turn with the audience.

> SOCRATES. The gift which you possess of speaking excellently about Homer is not an art, but, an inspiration; there is a divinity moving you, like that contained in the stone which Euripides calls a magnet, but which is commonly known as the stone of Heraclea. This stone not only attracts iron rings, but also imparts to them a similar power of attracting other rings; and sometimes you may see a number of pieces of iron and rings suspended from one another so as to form quite a long chain: and all of them derive their power of suspension from the original stone. In like manner the Muse first of all inspires men herself; and from these inspired persons a chain of other persons is suspended, who take the inspiration.
>
> ...
>
> Do you know that the spectator is the last of the rings which, as I am saying, receive the power of the original magnet from one another? Yourself, and the actor, are intermediate links, and the poet himself is the first of them.[4]

4 *Ion*, 533d, 535e.

Another kind of genetic knowledge which Plato was aware of was what he called the 'animal nature' that appears from time to time in men. In the *Republic* we find an especially vivid example.

> I mean those which awake when the rest of the soul—the reasoning and human and ruling power—is asleep; then the wild beast within us, gorged with meat or drink, starts up and having shaken off sleep goes forth to satisfy his desires; and you know that there is no action which at such a time, when he has parted company with all shame and sense, a man may not be ready to commit; for he does not, in

his imagination, shrink from incest with his mother, or from any unnatural union with man, or god, or beast, or from parricide, or the eating of forbidden food. And in a word, no action is too irrational or indecent for him.[5]

5   *Republic*, 9.571c; also see 3.411e..

Plato's reference here to the 'reasoning' side of ourselves 'going to sleep' is again an indication that he was fully aware that man is more than the Rational even if he could not explain it. Lacking our modern knowledge of the separate but valid kinds of knowledge housed in the separate hemispheres of our brain, he struggled mightily to understand this aspect of man and the reader cannot help but sympathize with his struggle.

Sometimes his writing suggests that he had intuitively come to understand the twin natures of our personality. In one passage in particular, Plato seems to have arrived at precisely the correct intuition and he begins with the correct answer. It soon becomes clear, however, that he is really struggling to discern how the various emotions, together with reason, can be explained within *one* mind. Interestingly enough, he quotes Homer, who clearly seems to have understood correctly, but Plato fails to grasp the point.

> Then we may fairly assume that they are two, and they differ from one another; the one with which a man reasons, we may call the rational principle of the soul, the other, with which he loves and hungers and thirsts and feels the flutterings of any other desire, may be termed the irrational or appetitive, the ally of sundry pleasures and satisfactions?
>
> Yes, he said, we may fairly assume them to be different.
>
> So much, then, for the definition of two of the principles existing in the soul. And what now of passion, or spirit? Is it a third, or akin to one of the preceding?
>
> …
>
> And are there not many other cases in which we observe that when a man's desires violently prevail over his reason, he reviles himself, and is angry at the violence within him, and that in this struggle, which is like the struggle of factions in a State, his spirit is on the side of his reason … ?
>
> …
>
> But a further question arises: Is passion different from reason also, or only a kind of reason; in which the latter case, instead of three principles in the soul, there will only be two, the rational and the concupiscent? … .
>
> Yes, he said, there must be a third.

Yes, I replied, if passion, which has already been shown to be different from desire, turns out also to be different from reason.

But that is easily proved:—We may observe even in young children that they are full of spirit almost as soon as they are born, whereas some of them never seem to attain to the use of reason, and most of them late enough.

Excellent, I said, and you may see passion equally in brute animals, which is a further proof of the truth of what you are saying. And we may once more appeal to the words of Homer, which have been already quoted by us,

He smote his breast, and thus rebuked his heart;

for in this verse Homer has clearly supposed the power which reasons about the better and worse to be different from the unreasoning anger which is rebuked by it.[6]

6 Ibid, 4.439d and following.

In another passage, Plato again appears about to make the case of reason versus feeling, but once again turns in another direction, never quite coming to the real point.

And as there are two principles of human nature, one the spirited and the other the philosophical, some god, as I should say, has given mankind two arts answering to them (and only indirectly to the soul and body), in order that these two principles (like the strings of an instrument) may be relaxed or drawn tighter until they are duly harmonized.[7]

7 Ibid., 3.412.

Similarly, in his *Laws*, speaking of the right handedness of most people, he begins with precisely the correct idea, but then fails to follow this idea, attributing the whole question to bad training instead.

AN ATHENIAN STRANGER. In that the right and left hand are supposed to be by nature differently suited for our various uses of them; whereas no difference is found in the use of the feet and lower limbs; but in the use of the hands we are, as it were, maimed by the folly of nurses and mothers; for although our several limbs are by nature balanced, we create a difference in them by bad habit.[8]

8 *Laws*, 7.794e.

Because Plato was unaware of the reality of the separate kinds of knowing in our twin brain hemispheres, and could not therefore understand that experiential knowledge is both real and valid, one can understand his clear bias toward the knowledge of the left hemisphere. He expresses this over and over:

It is proper for the rational principle, which is wise, and has the care of the whole soul, to rule.[9]

9 *Republic*, 4.441e.

Unless the person is able to abstract from all else and define rationally the Idea of good, and unless he can run the gauntlet of all objections, and is keen to disprove them by appeals not to opinion but to absolute truth, never faltering at any step of the argument—unless he can do all this ... he knows neither the Idea of good nor any other good.[10]

10 Ibid., 7.534e.

Another aspect of non-rational knowledge which Plato and other early philosophers struggled with was how to explain the apparent validity of the perception which comes from the senses. He explores this problem at length in his *Theaetetus*, where he first admits that we can not always really *know* without the benefit of experience. Speaking of the fact that only women who have had child bearing experience should act as midwives, he says,

> SOCRATES. It is said that Artemis was responsible for this, because though she is the goddess of childbirth, she is not herself a mother. She could not, indeed, allow the barren to be midwives, because human nature cannot know the mystery of an art without experience.[11]

11 *Theaetetus*, 149c.

Perhaps, he decides, perception must be a form of knowledge.

> THEAETETUS. Now he who knows anything perceives what he knows, and, as far as I can see at present, knowledge is simply perception.[12]

12 Ibid., 151e.

The problem with this argument, for Plato, is—can perception be true knowledge, if everyone's perception is an individual reality?

> SOCRATES. There can be no such thing as perceiving and perceiving nothing; and that the object, whether it become sweet, bitter, or of any other quality, must have relation to a percipient; nothing can be sweet which is sweet to no one ... Then, if that which acts upon me has relation to me and to no other, I and no other am the percipient of it?
>
> THEAETETUS. Of course.
>
> SOCRATES. Then my perception is true to me, being inseparable from my own 'being'; and, as Protagoras says, to myself I am judge of what is and what is not to me.[13]

13 Ibid., 160b.

Surely, therefore, perception is not the same thing as the knowledge of something, but rather something entirely different.

> SOCRATES. Shall we admit that we at once know whatever we perceive by sight or hearing? For example, shall we say that not having learned, we do not *hear* the language of foreigners when they speak to us? Or shall we say that we hear and therefore know what they are saying? Or again, in looking at letters which we do not understand, shall we say that we do not *see* them? Or shall we aver that, seeing them, we must know them?
>
> THEAETETUS. We shall say, Socrates, that we know what we actually see and hear of them—that is to say, we see, and hence know, the figure and color of the letters, and we hear and know the elevation or depression of the sound; but we do not perceive by sight or hearing, and hence do not know, that which grammarians and interpreters teach about them.[14]

14 Ibid., 163b.

To Plato this is nonsense.

> SOCRATES. Can the same man know and also not know that which he knows?[15]

15 Ibid., 165b.

We know today that it *is* possible for one to know on the basis of his own experience, through perception, and that this form of knowledge is real and valid even though another person may have an entirely *different* perception. This much Plato recognized, as he illustrates in the example of two men having different perceptions of the same food.

> SOCRATES. To the sick man his food appears to be and is bitter, and to the man in health it is and appears the opposite. Now I cannot conceive that one of these men can be or ought to be made wiser than the other: nor can you call the sick man foolish because he has one impression, and say that the healthy man because he has another is wise.[16]

16 Ibid., 166e.

But in the end, he could not understand this in the terms we know to be true. He concludes that while perception exists, real knowledge is still something apart.

> SOCRATES. Then knowledge does not consist in impressions of sense, but in reasoning about them; in that only, and not in the mere impression, truth and being can be attained.[17]

17 Ibid., 186d.

The problem which follows his inability to accept the reality of the truths presented by the senses, is that he can never quite accept music, in its experiential sense, as being a genuine form of knowledge. This was not only because music is clearly non-rational for the listener, but you cannot even see music. It is these problems which result in the final line of the following.

> Music, as you will remember, was the counterpart of gymnastic, and trained the guardians by the influences of habit, by harmony making them harmonious, by rhythm rhythmical, but not giving them science; and the words, whether fabulous or closer to the truth, were meant to impress upon them habits similar to these. But in music there was nothing which tended to that good which you are now seeking.[18]

18   *Republic*, 7.522.

THE PSYCHOLOGY OF AESTHETICS

ON PLEASURE

> SOCRATES. The soul and body being two, have two arts corresponding to them: there is the art of politics attending on the soul; and another art attending on the body, of which I know no single name, but which may be described as having two divisions, one of them gymnastic, and the other medicine.[19]

19   *Gorgias*, 464b.

This curious passage from *Gorgias* immediately strikes the modern reader as being incomplete: Plato has left out all mention of the arts as being among those things which 'attend to the soul.' It seems very odd to us that he can appreciate the components of high art, that he can understand the process of the performer, and that he can see the reaction of the audience, but he seemingly can not see (or perhaps not quite believe) the deep inner impression which the arts make on the experiential, or spiritual, nature of the person. We must wait for Aristotle to address this. On the other hand there is something about the language of the above quotation which prepares the reader for the difficulties which Plato experienced in his attempt to define the nature of Pleasure.

20   *Republic*, 583c also *Phaedo*, 60b.

In the *Republic*,[20] Plato says pleasure and pain are opposites. But there is a neutral state, which is neither—as for example when one is in pain, the mere relief seems like pleasure even though it is not an actual form of pleasure. This is only the 'appearance' of pleasure.

But to suggest that the absence of pain is pleasure and the absence of pleasure is pain seems incorrect to Plato. Furthermore, there are pleasures, such as smell, which have no antecedent in pain. Therefore, he concludes we can not say pure pleasure is merely the cessation of pain, and vice versa.

Another irony, Plato notes, is that most pleasures are bad.[21] That is, such pleasures as over eating and drinking end in pain and therefore rob us of other pleasures.[22] On the other hand, such things as gymnastic exercises and military service are painful, but good! This leads the discussion to the question: Should we first speak of good and evil, rather than pleasure and pain? Plato's initial conclusion is that life consists of weighing choices, choosing the lesser pain for the greater pleasure, etc.[23]

But, if pleasure is good, is there any danger inherent in some form of too much good, or too much pleasure? Yes, says Plato, as in the example above, over eating only leads to bad results. However, Plato also provides an argument to the contrary, through the character of Callicles in *Gorgias*. Callicles says man's desires for pleasure should have no limits.

> CALLICLES. I plainly assert that he who would truly live ought to allow his desires to wax to the uttermost, and not to chastise them; but when they have grown to their greatest he should have courage and intelligence to minister to them and to satisfy all his longings. And this I affirm to be natural justice and nobility. To this, however, the many cannot attain; and they blame the strong man because they are ashamed of their own weakness, which they desire to conceal, and hence they say that intemperance is base. As I have remarked already, they enslave the nobler natures, and being unable to attain full satisfaction of their pleasures, they praise temperance and justice out of their own cowardice …
>
> Nay, Socrates, you profess to be a votary of the truth, and the truth is this:—that luxury and intemperance and license, if they be provided with means, are virtue and happiness—all the rest is a mere bauble, agreements contrary to nature, foolish talk of men, nothing more.[24]

Socrates agrees this is what most people think, but are afraid to say.

Plato returns to the association of pleasure and the good in his *Laws*, where he contrasts at length the life styles of the temperate, rational, courageous and healthful with their opposite the intemperate, foolish, cowardly and diseased.[25] He finally concludes that it is the noblest life which appears to give the most pleasure and

21 *Philebus*, 13b.

22 *Protagaoras*, 353e.

23 Ibid., 356.

24 *Gorgias*, 492.

25 *Laws*, 732e and following.

that, for him, wisdom is better than pleasure (although he admits no-one wants a life devoid of pleasure).

> SOCRATES. Philebus was saying that enjoyment and pleasure and delight, and the class of feelings akin to them, are a good to every living being, whereas I contend, that not these, but wisdom and intelligence and memory, and their kindred, right opinion and true reasoning, are better and more desirable than pleasure.[26]

26   *Philebus*, 11b.

At the end of his life, waiting in prison, Socrates is described as again taking up the topic of pleasure and pain. At this time he confides a reoccurring dream that he should 'Set to work and make music.' But while he apparently did compose at least one hymn in prison, he curiously interpreted his dream in a way that is not clear today.

> I had imagined that this was only intended to exhort and encourage me in the study of philosophy, which has been the pursuit of my life, and is the noblest and best of music.[27]

27   *Phaedo*, 60e.

It is difficult to see the connection here, but it does remind us of a judgment by Beethoven, who said, 'Music is a more lofty revelation than all wisdom and philosophy!'

ON BEAUTY

Plato recognized this to be an important topic and usually discusses it as an intellectual idea, that of 'absolute beauty.' Because of his strong bias toward rational analysis, Beauty was something he thought should be defined by reason, and not the senses.

> Well, but there is another thing, Simmias: Is there or is there not an absolute justice?
>   Assuredly there is.
>   And an absolute beauty and absolute good?
>   Of course.
>   But did you ever behold any of them with your eyes?
>   Certainly not.
>   Or did you ever reach them with any other bodily sense?—and I speak not of these alone, but of absolute greatness, and health, and strength, and, in short, of the reality or true nature of everything. Is the truth of them ever perceived through the bodily organs? Or rather, is not the nearest approach to the knowledge of their several

natures made by him who so orders his intellectual vision as to have the most exact conception of the essence of each thing which he considers?

Certainly.

And he attains to the purest knowledge of them who goes to each with the intellect alone, not introducing or intruding in the act of thought sight or any other sense together with reason, but with the intellect in its own purity searches into the truth of each thing in its purity; he who has got rid, as far as he can, of eyes and ears and, so to speak, of the whole body, these being in his opinion distracting elements which when they associate with the soul hinder him from acquiring truth and knowledge.[28]

28 Ibid., 65d.

One of the troubling aspects of this question Plato found in the familiar instance of painters who, 'give up the truth in their images and make only the proportions which appear to be beautiful, disregarding the real ones.'[29]

29 *Sophist*, 236.

In any case, Plato says, only a true philosopher can understand the idea of absolute beauty, by which he means a rational definition of beauty. Although Plato was unaware of the fact that the right hemisphere of the brain does in fact house a genuine form of understanding, he seems to recognize some form of non-rational understanding but calls it only an 'imitation' of the real thing. In this passage Socrates is the narrator and Glaucon begins,

Musical amateurs, too, are a folk strangely out of place among philosophers, for they are the last persons in the world who would come to anything like a philosophical discussion if they could help it; while they run about at the Dionysiac festivals as if they had let out their ears for the season to hear every chorus, and miss no performance either in town or country. Now are we to maintain that all these and any who have similar tastes, as well as the professors of quite minor arts, are philosophers?

Certainly not, I replied; they are only an imitation.

. . .

And this is the distinction which I draw between the sight-loving, art-loving, practical class which you have mentioned, and those of whom I am speaking, and who are alone worthy of the name of philosophers.

How do you distinguish them? he said.

The lovers of sounds and sights, I replied, are, as I conceive it, fond of fine tones and colors and forms and all the artificial products that are made out of them, but their mind is incapable of seeing or loving absolute beauty.

The fact is plain, he replied.

Few are they who are able to attain to this ideal beauty and contemplate it.

Very true.

And he who, having a sense of beautiful things, has no sense of absolute beauty, or who, if another lead him to a knowledge of that beauty, is unable to follow—of such a one I ask, Is he awake or in a dream only? Reflect: is not the dreamer, sleeping or waking, one who likens dissimilar things, who puts the copy in the place of the real object?

I should certainly say that such a one was dreaming.

But he who, on the contrary, recognizes the existence of absolute beauty and is able to contemplate both the Idea and the objects which participate in it, neither putting the objects in the place of the Idea nor the Idea in the place of the objects—is he a dreamer, or is he awake?

He is wide awake.

And since he knows, it would be right to describe his state of mind as knowledge, and the state of mind of the other, who opines only, as opinion?

30 *Republic*, 476c.   Certainly.[30]

In the discussion we have been following, taken primarily from *Phaedo*, Plato never really comes to a clear definition of Beauty. In fact, in the following comments, which Socrates directs to a character named Cebes, Plato appears to avoid the question by simply declaring, in effect, that beauty is the cause of beauty, as greatness is the cause of the great, smallness of the small, etc. The whole passage may strike the reader as nonsense, and even Plato admits it is all 'perhaps foolish.' We believe his point is that the real question is simply whether something is beautiful or not to the observer and that there is no guarantee that any specific details will always result in Beauty.

I shall have to go back to those familiar theories which are in the mouth of everyone, and first of all assume that there is an absolute beauty and goodness and greatness, and the like; grant me these and admit that they exist, and I hope to be able to show you the nature of cause, and to prove the immortality of the soul.

Cebes said: You may proceed at once with the proof, for I grant you this.

Well, he said, then I should like to know whether you agree with me in the next step; for I cannot help thinking that if there be anything beautiful other than absolute beauty it is beautiful only in so far as it partakes of absolute beauty—and I should say the same of everything. Do you agree in this notion of the cause?

Yes, he said, I agree.

He proceeded: I no longer look for, nor can I understand, those other ingenious causes which are alleged; and if a person says to me that the bloom of color, or form, or any such thing is a source of beauty, I dismiss all that, which is only confusing to me, and simply and singly, and perhaps foolishly, hold and am assured in my own mind that nothing makes a thing beautiful but the presence or participation of beauty in whatever way or manner obtained; for as to the manner I am uncertain, but I stoutly contend that by beauty all beautiful things become beautiful. This appears to me to be the safest answer which I can give, either to myself or to another, and to this I cling, in the persuasion that this principle will never be overthrown, and that to myself or to anyone who asks the question, I may safely reply, That by beauty beautiful things become beautiful. Do you not agree with me?

I do.

And that by greatness great things become great and greater, and by smallness the less become less?

True.[31]

There is one of the Dialogues of Plato which is entirely devoted to the question, What is Beauty? This is a relatively brief work known as *Greater Hippias* and it is one in which we can finally deduce some more specific criteria for Beauty. In this Dialogue, Socrates, as he sometimes does, pretends he himself knows nothing and is only asking questions of Hippias for the purpose of later answering some third party. Socrates puts forth a number of possible contentions which Hippias readily agrees with, only to have Socrates then reverse himself and argue against them. As is often the case in discussions with Socrates, poor Hippias is turned around and around until he is totally confused.

First Socrates reminds his student that there is an element of personal opinion which complicates the definition of Beauty. He leads Hippias to admit the possibility of a woman being beautiful, but that a horse may also be beautiful and even a pot. After Hippias reluctantly agrees, Socrates adds a complication by observing that the most beautiful ape is ugly when compared to a man and the most beautiful pot is ugly when compared to a maiden. How then, asks Socrates, can something be both ugly and beautiful?

Hippias mentions that everyone considers gold beautiful. Socrates points out that a certain artist must have erred by not

31 *Phaedo*, 100b. The comment that smallness becomes less and less reminds one of Bruno Walter's famous explanation that a poor composition only becomes poorer in rehearsal, as the rehearsal brings into sharper focus the elements which make it poor in the first place.

32 *Greater Hippias*, 290d.

giving his marble statue golden eyes, or even ivory eyes. From this Socrates concludes, 'Do not ivory and gold cause a thing to appear beautiful when they are appropriate, and ugly when they are not?'[32] When Hippias agrees, Socrates changes his mind again and wonders if the presence of something appropriate causes a thing to *be* beautiful, or only makes it *appear* to be so.

Further discussion leads to the conclusion that achieving good is not the same thing as beauty, therefore utility is not a definition of Beauty.

Finally Socrates introduces the role of the senses and gets Hippias to admit that Beauty is that in which we find delight through hearing and sight. But this cannot be the complete definition of Beauty because this leaves out the senses of touch and smell.

In the end, the poor confused Hippias tells Socrates that these 'pettifogging arguments of yours … [are] trumpery nonsense.' He believes he has learned nothing. But Socrates points out that he has indeed learned something, the true meaning of the proverb, 'All that is beautiful is difficult.'

In summary, here we find a rather helpful definition of Beauty and it will perhaps be more clear if we summarize as follows:

1. The concept of Beauty cannot be separated from its medium.
2. The quality of Beauty cannot be separated from its parts.
3. Beauty is perceived by the individual.
4. Beauty needs no purpose.
5. Beauty can be perceived by any of the senses.

THE AESTHETICS OF MUSIC

Plato's comments that might be associated with a theory of aesthetics in music are centered on the lyric poet–musician.

He begins with a discussion of the nature of perception, a topic which he questioned in spite of the fact, as we have seen above, he did value the idea of experience. In a lengthy discussion in the

33 Ibid., 10.595b–602b

Republic,[33] Plato considers the aspect of imitation in art, a topic which is not only fundamental to an understanding of his view of the arts, but one which will be discussed by every writer on aesthetics ever after. Here we find the conclusion that painting and poetry—even that of the greatest Greek poet of them all, Homer—will not be allowed in the utopia which much of the *Republic* describes. They are rejected because they are imitations and not

Truth. It is significant that Plato does not include music together with art and painting, a fact which indicates that he understood that music is the real thing and not a representation of something else. This is why, as we shall see below, he says art music is 'Truth,'[34] and also why he notes that experienced singers can immediately know if a composition is a 'good or bad imitation' of a good or bad soul.[35]

The theater, even tragedy, is also only an imitation of something else, and thus will not be allowed in the ideal state.

34 *Laws*, 668b.

35 Ibid., 812b ff.

> SOCRATES. Of the many excellences which I perceive in the order of our State, there is none which upon reflection pleases me better than the rule about poetry.
> GLAUCON. To what do you refer?
> SOCRATES. To our refusal to admit the imitative kind of poetry, for it certainly ought not to be received ...
> GLAUCON. What do you mean?
> SOCRATES. Speaking in confidence, for you will not denounce me to the tragedians and the rest of the imitative tribe, all poetical imitations are ruinous to the understanding of the hearers, unless as an antidote they possess the knowledge of the true nature of the originals.
> GLAUCON. Explain the purport of your remark.

Socrates then explains using a common table as an illustration. The table, he says, is an idea. The maker of a table makes not the idea, but an imitation of the idea. The painter is yet another degree removed from truth, because he only paints a picture of an imitation of an idea.

He continues with his surprisingly strong lack of appreciation of the playwright. In the course of this discussion he mentions the use of music in tragedy. This is a topic for which all drama critics wish there were more information. It is clear in Aristotle's careful analysis of the parts of tragedy that music was included, but even he let the topic stand without explanation of its role.

> SOCRATES. Then the imitator is a long way off the truth, and can reproduce all things because he lightly touches on a small part of them, and that part an image. For example, a painter will paint a cobbler, carpenter, or any other artisan, though he knows nothing of their arts; and, if he is a good painter, he may deceive children or simple persons when he shows them his picture of a carpenter from a distance, and they will fancy that they are looking at a real carpenter ...

Next, we have to consider tragedy and its leader, Homer; for we hear some persons saying that these poets know all the arts; and all things human; where virtue and vice are concerned, and indeed all divine things too; because the good poet cannot compose well unless he knows his subject, and he who has not this knowledge can never be a poet. We ought to consider whether here also there may not be a similar illusion ...

Now do you suppose that if a person were able to make the original as well as the image, he would seriously devote himself to the image-making branch? Would he allow imitation to be the ruling principle of his life, as if he had nothing higher in him? ...

We have a right to know respecting warfare, strategy, the administration of States and the education of man, which are the chief and noblest subjects of his poems, and we may fairly ask him about them. 'Friend Homer,' then we say to him, 'if you are only in the second remove from truth in what you say of virtue, and not in the third—not an image maker, that is, by our definition, an imitator—and if you are able to discern what pursuits make men better or worse in private or public life, tell us what State was ever better governed by your help? ...

Then must we not infer that all these poetical individuals, beginning with Homer, are only imitators, who copy images of virtue and the other themes of their poetry, but have no contact with the truth? The poet is like a painter who, as we have already observed, will make a likeness of a cobbler though he understands nothing of cobbling; and his picture is good enough for those who know no more than he does, and judge only by colors and figures.

GLAUCON. Quite so.

SOCRATES. In like manner the poet with his words and phrases may be said to lay on the colors of the several arts, himself understanding their nature only enough to imitate them; and other people, who are as ignorant as he is, and judge only from his words, imagine that if he speaks of cobbling, or of military tactics, or of anything else, in meter and harmony and rhythm, he speaks very well—such is the sweet influence which melody and rhythm by nature have. For I am sure that you know what a poor appearance the works of poets make when stripped of the colors which art puts upon them, and recited in simple prose ...

There are [then] three arts which are concerned with all things: one which uses, another which makes, and a third which imitates them ... And the excellence and beauty and rightness of every structure, animate or inanimate, and of every action of man, is relative solely to the use for which nature or the artist has intended them.

GLAUCON. True.

SOCRATES. Then beyond doubt it is the user who has the greatest experience of them, and he must report to the maker the good or bad qualities which develop themselves in use; for example, the flute player will tell the flute maker which of his flutes is satisfactory to the performer; he will tell him how he ought to make them, and the other will attend to his instruction.

GLAUCON. Of course.

SOCRATES. So the one pronounces with knowledge about the goodness and badness of flutes, while the other, confiding in him, will make them accordingly?

GLAUCON. True.

SOCRATES. The instrument is the same, but about the excellence or badness of it the maker will possess a correct belief, since he associates with one who knows, and is compelled to hear what he has to say; whereas the user will have knowledge.

GLAUCON. True.

SOCRATES. But will the imitator have either? Will he know from use whether or not that which he paints is correct or beautiful? Or will he have the right opinion from being compelled to associate with another who knows and gives him instructions about what he should paint?

GLAUCON. Neither …

SOCRATES. Thus far then we are pretty well agreed that the imitator has no knowledge worth mentioning of what he imitates. Imitation is only a kind of play or sport, and the tragic poets, whether they write in iambic or in heroic verse, are imitators in the highest degree.

In another treatise, the *Symposium*, Plato again mentions the poets who employ music but here it appears he is thinking more of the lyric poets and not the playwrights.

They are not all called poets, but have other names; only that one portion of creative activity which is separated off from the rest, and is concerned with music and meter, is called by the name of the whole and is termed poetry, and they who possess poetry in this sense of the word are called poets.[36]

And again,

SOCRATES. Well now, suppose that we strip all poetry of melody and rhythm and meter, there will remain [only] speech?

CALLICLES. To be sure.[37]

36 *Symposium*, 205c. In 196e Plato quotes from a fragment of *Sthenoboea* by Euripides, which mentions one Eryximachus who could by his touch create poets of someone, 'even though he had no music in him before.'

37 *Gorgias*, 502c.

In general it appears to us that Plato, himself, placed a higher value on the poets than did his teacher, Scorates, with respect to the representation of Truth. We find in the *Laws*,

> An Athenian Stranger. For poets are a divine race, and often in their strains, by the aid of the Muses and the Graces, they attain truth.[38]

38   *Laws*, 682.

Plato pays the usual tribute to the Gods for the genetic gift of music:

> An Athenian Stranger. And did we not say that the sense of harmony and rhythm spring from this beginning among men, and that Apollo and the Muses and Dionysus were the Gods whom we had to thank for them?
>
> Cleinias. Certainly.

Beyond his discussion of the relationship of music and poetry, Plato wrote in considerable detail about music itself. We know that he was fully aware that the Greek traditions of music practice came from Egypt from a passage in the *Laws*,[39] not to mention his own study in that country, and he was also acutely aware that this inherited tradition had experienced a loss of discipline over the centuries in Greece. He saw an evolution from the noble old purposes to one of merely trying to please the crowd, resulting, he says, in licentiousness. Indeed, his discussion of the audience in the following passage is quite interesting and is near the heart of his views regarding the importance of the moral values which music should communicate to the listener.

39   Ibid., 656d.

> An Athenian Stranger. Let us speak of the laws about music,— that is to say, such music as then existed,—in order that we may trace the growth of the excess of freedom from the beginning. Now music was early divided among us into certain kinds and manners. One sort consisted of prayers to the Gods, which were called hymns; and there was another and opposite sort called lamentations, and another termed paeans, and another, celebrating (I believe) the birth of Dionysus, called 'dithyrambs.' And they used the actual word 'laws' for another kind of song; and to this they added the term 'citharoedic.' All these and others were duly distinguished, nor were the performers allowed to confuse one style of music with another. And the authority which determined and give judgment, and punished the disobedient, was not expressed in a hiss, nor in the most unmusical shouts

of the multitude, as in our days, nor in applause and clapping of hands. But the directors of public instruction insisted that the spectators should listen in silence to the end; and boys and their tutors, and the multitude in general, were kept quiet by a hint from a stick. Such was the good order which the multitude were willing to observe; they would never have dared to give judgment by noisy cries. And then, as time went on, the poets themselves introduced the reign of vulgar and lawless innovation. They were men of genius, but they had no perception of what is just and lawful in music; raging like bacchanals and possessed with inordinate delights—mingling lamentations with hymns, and paeans with dithyrambs; imitating the sounds of the aulos on the lyre, and making one general confusion; ignorantly affirming that music has no Truth, and, whether good or bad, can only be judged of rightly by the pleasure of the hearer. And by composing such licentious works, and adding to them words as licentious, they have inspired the multitude with lawlessness and boldness, and made the audience fancy that they can judge for themselves about melody and song. And in this way the theaters from being silent have become vocal, as though they had understanding of good and bad in music and poetry; and instead of an aristocracy, an evil sort of theatrocracy has grown up. For if there had been a democracy in music alone, consisting of free men, no fatal harm would have been done; but in music there first arose the universal conceit of omniscience and general lawlessness;—freedom came following afterwards, and men, fancying that they knew what they did not know, had no longer any fear, and the absence of fear begets shamelessness. For what is this shamelessness, which is so evil a thing, but the insolent refusal to regard the opinion of the better by reason of an over-daring sort of liberty?[40]

40 Ibid., 700ff.

Plato, in a most charming way, warns that this lack of appreciation for music and the arts will not go unnoticed by the gods

SOCRATES. A lover of music like yourself ought surely to have heard the story of the grasshoppers, who are said to have been human beings in an age before the Muses. And when the Muses came and song appeared the grasshoppers were ravished with delight; and singing always, never thought of eating and drinking, until at last in their forgetfulness they died. And now they live again in the grasshoppers, who, as a special gift from the Muses, require no nourishment, but from the hour of their birth are always singing, and ever eating and drinking; and when they die they go and inform the Muses in heaven which of us honors one or other of the Muses. They win the love of Terpsichore for the dancers by their report of them; of Erato for the lovers, and of the other Muses for those who do them honor, according to the several ways of honoring them;—and to Calliope the eldest Muse and Urania who is next to her, they make a report of those who honor music of their kind, and spend their time in philosophy; for these are the Muses who are chiefly concerned with the heavens and with reasoning, divine as well as human, and they have the sweetest utterance.[41]

41 *Phaedrus*, 259c.

Another passage in the *Symposium* presents Plato's attempt in explaining how the lower intervals of the overtone series are to be considered from an aesthetic perspective.

Anyone who pays the least attention to the subject will also perceive that in music there is the same reconciliation of opposites; and I suppose that this must have been the meaning of Heracleitus, although his words are not accurate; for he says the One is united by disunion, like the harmony[42] of the bow and the lyre. Now it is the height of absurdity to say that harmony is discord or it is composed of elements which are still in a state of discord. But what he probably meant was, that harmony is attained through the art of music by the reconciliation of differing notes of higher and lower pitch which once disagreed; for if the higher and lower notes still disagreed, there could be no harmony,—clearly not. For harmony is a symphony, and symphony is a kind of agreement; but an agreement of disagreements while they disagree there cannot be; you cannot, I repeat, harmonize that which disagrees. In like manner rhythm is compounded of elements short and long, once differing and now in accord; which accordance, as in the former instance medicine, so in all these other cases music implants, making love and concord to grow up among them; and thus music, too, is a science of the phenomena of love in their application to harmony and rhythm. Again, in the constitution of a harmony as of a rhythm there is no difficulty in discerning love, and as yet there is no sign of its duality. But when you want to use them in actual life, either in the kind of composition to which the term 'lyrical' is applied or in the correct employment of melodies and meters already composed, which latter is called education,[43] then indeed the difficulty begins, and the good artist is needed. Then the old tale has to be repeated of fair and heavenly love—the love that comes from Urania the fair and heavenly muse—and of the duty of gratifying the temperate,[44] and those who are as yet intemperate only that they may become temperate, and of preserving their love; and again, of the common love that comes from Polyhymnia, that must be used with circumspection in order that the pleasure be enjoyed, but may not generate licentiousness.[45]

42 The Greeks used the word 'harmony' in a larger sense, the whole rather than one of the parts; indeed, it is often used as we might use today the word 'music' itself. The term 'symphony' was sometimes used to express what we mean by 'harmony.'

43 More modern translations render this passage as follows,

But when you want to use them in actual life, either in the composition of songs or in the correct performance of melodies or meters composed already, which latter is called education.

44 By temperance Plato means something like self-discipline.

45 *Symposium*, 187b.

As Plato so often equates the value of music with inculcating virtue, so he also devotes considerable discussion to the qualities and education which the artist must have. In the following he mentions having a good ear, knowledge of the physics of music, knowing how emotions are communicated in the dancing which accompanies music (a topic, unfortunately, he never elaborates on) and the importance of rational classification of this information. It is most important here how he carefully separates the grammar of music from music itself. It is one of the curious ironies in higher education in music today that there is little critical discussion of any part of music other than the grammar.

SOCRATES. And yet not by knowing either that sound is one or that sound is infinite are we perfect in the art of speech, but the knowledge of the number and nature of sounds is what makes a man a grammarian.

PROTARCHUS. Very true.

SOCRATES. And the knowledge which makes a man a musician is of the same kind.

PROTARCHUS. How so?

SOCRATES. Sound is one in music as well as in grammar?

PROTARCHUS. Certainly.

SOCRATES. And there is a higher note and a lower note, and a note of equal pitch:—may we affirm so much?

PROTARCHUS. Yes.

SOCRATES. But you would not be a real musician if this was all that you knew; though if you did not know this you would know almost nothing of music.

PROTARCHUS. Nothing.

SOCRATES. But when you have learned what sounds are high and what low, and the number and nature of the intervals and their limits or proportions, and the systems compounded out of them, which our fathers discovered, and have handed down to us who are their descendants under the name of harmonies; when you have learned also how similar affections appear and come to be in the movements of bodies, which when measured by numbers ought, as they say, to be called rhythms and measures; and they tell us that the same principles should be applied to every one and many; when, I say, you have learned all this, then, my dear friend, you have technical skill; and you may be said to understand any other subject, when you have a similar grasp of it. But the infinity of kinds and the infinity of individuals which there is in each of them, when not classified, creates in every one of us a state of infinite ignorance; and he who never looks for number

46 *Philebus*, 17c.

in anything, will not himself be looked for in the number of famous men.[46]

In another place, Plato mentions that the ability to tune an instrument is not the same thing as knowledge of harmony. It is also nice to read here that all musicians then only spoke in gentle voices!

> SOCRATES. Happening to meet such a man who thinks that he is a musician because he knows how to pitch the highest and lowest note; happening to meet such an one he would not say to him savagely, 'Fool, you are mad!' But like a musician, in a gentle and harmonious tone of voice, he would answer: 'My good friend, he who would be a musician must certainly know this, and yet one who has not got beyond your stage of knowledge may understand nothing of harmony, for you only know the necessary prelimi-naries of harmony and not harmony itself.'[47]

47 *Phaedrus*, 268e.

It is also comforting to read that the successful musician was char-acterized by a love for his teacher!

> And as to the artists, do we not know that he only who has love for his instructor emerges into the light of fame?—he whom Love touches not walks in darkness.[48]

48 *Symposium*, 197.

Unfortunately, we have more descriptions regarding the educa-tion of musicians than we do accounts of what musicians were like as performers. The most precise hints we get are found in the discussion between Socrates and Ion, who was a 'rhapsodist,' one who specialized in public recitation in a kind of sung speech. Here Plato begins with an observation with which every fine modern musician would agree—that to be a fine artist one must not just reproduce the words the poet left, but one must try to see behind the words to the original idea of the poet. It is the proper goal of every musician today!

> SOCRATES. I have often envied the profession of a rhapsodist, Ion; for it is a part of your art to wear fine clothes and to look as beautiful as you can, while at the same time you are obliged to be continually in the company of many good poets, and espe-cially of Homer, who is the best and most divine of them, and to understand his mind, and not merely learn his words by rote; all this is a thing greatly to be envied. I am sure that no man can become a good rhapsodist who does not understand the meaning

of the poet. For the rhapsodist ought to interpret the mind of the poet to his hearers, but how can he interpret him well unless he knows what he means?[49]

49 _Ion_, 530c

We get a rather vivid description of this kind of performer before the public, and although the rhapsodist is at best only what we might call a near-musician, the description is familiar enough to suggest that the nature of performance in general may not have changed too much. Plato begins by telling us that a good performance must be inspired, as opposed to a mere demonstration of the rules of the art (technique). It is also particularly interesting here to read of his description of the emotional involvement of the audience.

> SOCRATES. Many are the noble words in which poets speak concerning the actions of men; but like yourself when speaking about Homer, they do not speak of them by any rules of art: they are simply inspired to utter that to which the Muse impels them, and that only; and when inspired, one of them will make dithyrambs, another hymns of praise, another choral strains, another epic or iambic verses, but not one of them is of any account in the other kinds. For not by art does the poet sing, but by power divine; had he learned by rules of art, he would have known how to speak not of one theme only, but of all; and therefore God takes away reason from poets, and uses them as his ministers, as he also uses the pronouncers of oracles and holy prophets, in order that we who hear them may know them to be speaking not of themselves, who utter these priceless words while bereft of reason, but that God himself is the speaker, and that through them he is addressing us.
>
> ...
>
> I wish you would frankly tell me, Ion, what I am going to ask you: When you produce the greatest effect upon the audience in the recitation of some striking passage, such as the apparition of Odysseus leaping forth on the floor, recognized by the suitors and shaking out his arrows at his feet, or the description of Achilles springing upon Hector, or the sorrows of Andromache, Hecuba, or Priam,—are you in your right mind? Are you not carried out of yourself, and does not your soul in an ecstasy seem to be among the persons or places of which you are speaking ... ?
>
> ION. That proof strikes home to me, Socrates. For I must frankly confess that at the tale of pity my eyes are filled with tears, and when I speak of horrors, my hair stands on end and my heart throbs.

SOCRATES. Well, Ion, and what are we to say of a man who at a sacrifice or festival, when he is dressed in an embroidered robe, and
has golden crowns upon his head, of which nobody has robbed
him, appears weeping and panic-stricken in the presence of
more than twenty thousand friendly faces, when there is no one
despoiling or wronging him;—is he in his right mind or is he not?

ION. No indeed, Socrates, I must say that, strictly speaking, he is
not in his right mind.

SOCRATES. And are you aware that you produce similar effects on
most of the spectators?

ION. Only too well; for I look down upon them from the stage, and
behold the various emotions of pity, wonder, sternness, stamped
upon their faces when I am performing: and I am obliged to give
my very best attention to them; for if I make them cry I myself
shall laugh, and if I make them laugh I myself shall cry, when
the time of payment arrives.[50]

50   *Ion*, 534c–535e.

ART MUSIC

We believe the idea of art music has several mandatory parts which
must be present at all times. The first is that aesthetic music has
no secondary purpose. Second, this music must be conscientiously
performed; the original idea of the composer must be faithfully
represented. Finally, the music must be listened to; there must be a
contemplative listener. This does not require concert halls, although
references to such halls can be found in ancient Greek literature.[51]
Our purpose here is to consider if such conditions for art music
existed at the time Plato describes and if it is possible to determine
what might have been some of the characteristics of an art music
for which we no longer have extant examples.

51   *Laws*, 765b, Jowett actually uses
the word 'concert,' but does not
supply the original Greek.

We have seen above Plato's lament for 'the good old days,' when
audiences of musical performances stayed to the end and listened
in silence.[52] There is no question that in his view music had begun
to fall from its former high ideals to goals of mere entertainment.
We can see this in a survey he provides in *Gorgias*.

52   Ibid., 700.

SOCRATES. Can you tell me the pursuits which delight mankind—
or rather ... which of them belong to the pleasurable class, and
which of them not? In the first place, what say you of aulos playing? Does not that appear to be an art which seeks only pleasure,
Callicles, and thinks of nothing else?

CALLICLES. I assent.

SOCRATES. And is not the same true of all similar arts, as, for example, the art of playing the lyre at festivals?

CALLICLES. Yes.

SOCRATES. And what do you say of the choral art and of dithyrambic poetry?—are not they of the same nature? Do you imagine that Cinesias the son of Meles cares about what will tend to the moral improvement of his hearers, or about what will give pleasure to the multitude?

CALLICLES. There can be no mistake about Cinesias, Socrates.

SOCRATES. And what do you say of his father, Meles the harp-player? When he sang to the harp, did you suppose that he had his eye on the highest good? Perhaps he indeed could scarcely be said to regard even the greatest pleasure, since his singing was an infliction to his audience? In fact, would you not say that all music of the harp and dithyrambic poetry in general have been invented for the sake of pleasure?

CALLICLES. I should.

According to Plato, Socrates held the view that there was a similar decline in serious dramatic productions.

SOCRATES. And as for the Muse of Tragedy, that solemn and august personage—what are her aspirations? Is all her aim and desire only to give pleasure to the spectators, or does she strive to refrain her tongue from all that pleases and charms them but is vicious? To proclaim, in speech and song, truth that is salutary but unpleasant, whether they welcome it or not?—which in your judgment is of the nature of tragic poetry?

CALLICLES. There can be no doubt, Socrates, that Tragedy has her face turned towards pleasure and the gratification of the audience.

SOCRATES. And is not that the sort of thing, Callicles, which we were just now describing as flattery?

Apart from such views, one can find references in Plato which suggest that there were still serious performances and careful listeners. For example, regarding the quality of performance, he tells us in *Alcibiades I* that the word, 'Musically,' is the very 'name for correctness in the art of music.'[53] And when Plato writes of 'musical instruments used to charm the souls of men,'[54] we know the performer must still have attentive listeners.

53 *Alcibiades I*, 108d.

54 *Symposium*, 215c.

One type of music which must have had the full potential for being art music was the instrumental prelude, a form which Plato tells us was composed with 'wonderful care.'

> AN ATHENIAN STRANGER. Because all discourses and vocal exercises have preludes and overtures, which are a sort of artistic beginnings intended to help the music which is to be performed; lyric measures and music of every other kind have preludes framed with wonderful care.[55]

55   *Laws*, 722d.

This reminds us of a passage in *Laws*, where Plato describes this same kind of 'wonderful care' in the example of the painter.

> You know the endless labor which painters expend upon their pictures—they are always putting in or taking out colors, or whatever be the term which artists employ; they seem as if they would never cease touching up their works, which are always being made brighter and more beautiful.[56]

56   Ibid., 769b.

It seems clear that the conditions for true art music were available. But can we determine what Plato's own definition of art music might have been? First, we can be confident that one characteristic which Plato would insist upon is that the music must be inspired. In *Ion*, he writes,

> All good poets, epic as well as lyric, compose their beautiful poems not by art, but because they are inspired and possessed.[57]

57   *Ion*, 534.

In the *Apology*, he makes the point again.

> I learnt that not by wisdom do poets write poetry, but by a sort of genius and inspiration.[58]

58   *Apology*, 22c.

Another characteristic of pure art music must be the contemplative listener. We believe this is implied in Plato's definition of the purpose of art music

59   *Republic*, 3.403c.

> For what should be the end of music if not the love of beauty?[59]

It is clear here that Plato valued the idea of beauty for its own sake, but his ability to carry such discussion further was limited, as it was for all early philosophers, by the problem of where to place this in man's mind. Most of the early philosophers seemed to understand that beauty in general, and beautiful music in particular, were perceived by the senses but they also seemed to understand that these perceptions are not rational. Since the brain was the seat of only the rational for them, where do you assign the location of these kinds of things. Plato, in the following, avoids this question by simply concluding that these artistic perceptions have a certain parallel association with the rational.

> We would not have our guardians grow up amid images of moral deformity, as in some noxious pasture, and there browse and feed upon many a baneful herb and flower day by day, little by little, until they silently gather a festering mass of corruption in their own soul. Let us rather search for artists who are gifted to discern the true nature of the beautiful and graceful; then will our youth dwell in a land of health, amid fair sights and sounds, and receive the good in everything; and beauty, the effluence of fair works, shall flow into the eye and ear, like a health-giving breeze from a purer region, and insensibly draw the soul from the earliest years into likeness and sympathy with the beauty of reason.[60]

60 _Ibid, 401b.

Plato goes to some care to establish the point that the contemplation of the beautiful is not the same thing as experiencing mere 'pleasure' in music.

> An Athenian Stranger. When anyone says that music is to be judged by pleasure, his doctrine cannot be admitted; and if there be any music of which pleasure is the criterion, such music is not to be sought out or deemed to have any real excellence, but only that other kind of music which is an imitation of the good, and bears a resemblance to its original.
> Cleinias. Very true.
> An Athenian Stranger. And those who seek for the best kind of song and music ought not to seek for that which is pleasant, but for that which is True.[61]

61 *Laws*, 668b.

There is a striking similarity between this passage and a statement given in Los Angeles by the famous Conductor, Sergiu Celibadache.

> Anyone who still hasn't got past the stage of the beauty of music still knows nothing about music. Music is not beautiful. It has beauty as well, but the beauty is only the bait. Music is True.[62]

62 Quoted in *Los Angeles Philharmonic Notes*, April, 1989.

What do they mean by this? What does to be *True* mean in music? Plato's definition is based on the relationship of music to the soul. The most important music is that in which the emotions and meaning of the music corresponds to the highest virtue of the soul. This kind of music he calls 'the good,' or for us, aesthetic music. Plato, in the following discussion gives considerable care in distinguishing this kind of music from that which is merely 'pleasant,' music to entertain or amuse.

> SOCRATES. I would have you consider ... whether there are not other similar activities which have to do with the soul—some of them activities of art, making a provision for the soul's highest interest; others despising the interest, and as in the parallel case considering only the pleasure, of the soul, and how this may be acquired, but not considering what pleasures are good or bad, and having no other aim but to afford gratification, whether good or bad. In my opinion, Callicles, there are such activities, and this is the sort of thing which I term flattery, whether concerned with the body or the soul or anything else on which it is employed with a view to pleasure and without any consideration of good and evil. And now I wish that you would tell me whether you agree with us in this notion, or whether you differ.
> CALLICLES. I do not differ ...
> SOCRATES. And is the notion true of one soul, or two or more?
> CALLICLES. Equally true of two or more.
> SOCRATES. Then a man may delight a whole assembly, and yet have no regard for their highest interests?
> CALLICLES. Yes.[63]

63　*Gorgias*, 501b.

In his summary for this discussion Plato offers another distinction between aesthetic music (the 'good') and that intended merely for pleasure. Good music, he says, is the result of 'order and Truth.' 'Pleasant' music is clearly the opposite of that but we have no idea of knowing what kind of music that was for Plato. It is difficult to suppose 'disordered music' was improvised music at a time when no music was notated. But Plato clearly heard some music as being ordered and presumably some as being disordered and perhaps we can only assume that he was hearing a distinction between an educated musician and one whom he considered uneducated.

> SOCRATES. Listen to me, then, while I recapitulate the argument: Is the pleasant the same as the good? Not the same. Callicles and I are agreed about that. And is the pleasant to be pursued for the sake of the good, or the good for the sake of the pleasant? The pleasant is to be pursued for the sake of the good. And that is pleasant at the presence of which we are pleased, and that is good by the presence of which we are good? To be sure. And we are

good, and all good things whatever are good, when some virtue is present in us or them? That, Callicles, is my conviction. But the virtue of each thing, whether body or soul, instrument or creature, when given to them in the best way comes to them not by chance but as the result of the order and truth and art which are imparted to them: am I not right? I maintain that I am. And is not the virtue of each thing dependent on order or arrangement? Yes I say. And that which makes a thing good is its appropriate order inhering in each thing? Such is my view.[64]

64 Ibid., 506d.

For Plato, then, art music is inspired and carefully composed, both of which suggests a contemplative listener. It is music which is well ordered, or perhaps well constructed, which aims at the highest values of the soul (the 'good') and not mere pleasure.

EDUCATIONAL MUSIC

Before we begin Plato's discussion of music in the schools, we should remind the reader that in the above pages under The Aesthetics of Music he will find that Plato has given us a rather detailed list of the qualities one should find in a good musician. And since we normally assume that becoming a good musician entails education, Plato's list of the qualities of a good musician are at the same time a list of the goals for the education of the musician. We might call it a list of the skills needed by the music major. They are:

1. A good ear
2. Knowledge of the physics of music
3. Knowledge of harmony
4. Love for one's teacher
5. Musical insight, not mere technical ability on an instrument
6. The ability to inspire through music. In performance, Plato says, the performer is 'not in his right mind,' his soul is in ecstasy.

Assuming love for one's teacher is still to be expected today (!), one can nevertheless only wonder how our university studio instruction would change if the juries at the end of each semester graded not on the basis of technique, but on the final two requirements in Plato's list! Does the student inspire the listener?! Does the student communicate to the listener his musical insights?!

Although Plato's discussion on the use of music for the education of children is the earliest substantial one, he tells us that the
basic ideas were in place 10,000 years earlier. Athenaeus provides
a brief discussion which may serve as an introduction to this topic,
especially as he mentions Damon of Athens, who was the teacher
of Socrates.

> Music contributes also to the exercise and the sharpening of the
> mind; hence all Greeks as well as those barbarians [those who do
> not speak Greek well!] with whom we are acquainted make use
> of it. With good reason Damon of Athens and his school say that
> songs and dances are the result of the soul's being in a kind of
> motion; those songs which are noble and beautiful produce noble
> and beautiful souls, whereas the contrary kind produce the con-
> trary. Whence also came that witty remark of Cleosthenes, the ruler
> of Sicyon, which reveals his cultivated mind. For, as they say, after
> seeing one of his daughter's suitors dancing in vulgar posture he
> declared that he had 'danced away' his marriage, probably believing
> that the young man's soul was also vulgar. For, whether in danc-
> ing or in walking, decency and dignity of bearing are beautiful,
> whereas immodesty and vulgarity are ugly. For this reason, in fact,
> from the very beginning, the poets arranged dances for freemen,
> and they used the dance figures only to illustrate the theme of the
> songs, always preserving nobility and manliness in them ... But
> if any one arranged his figures with undue exaggeration, or when
> he came to his songs said anything that did not correspond to the
> dance, he was discredited.[65]

65   Athenaeus,
Deipnosophistae, 14.628.

The most frequently quoted definition by Plato regarding the
early Greek educational system is this sentence.

> Education has two branches,—one of gymnastic, which is con-
> cerned with the body, and the other of music, which is designed
> for the improvement of the soul.[66]

66   *Laws*, 795d.

From Plato's perspective, indeed from the perspective of all
early Greek philosophy as we have seen above, the key word is the
'soul.' Music, according to Plato, was given to man by the gods for
its positive influence on the soul and not for mere entertainment.

> Harmony, which has motions akin to the revolutions of our souls, is
> not regarded by the intelligent votary of the Muses as given by them
> with a view to irrational pleasure, which is deemed to be the pur-
> pose of it in our day, but as meant to correct any discord which may

have arisen in the courses of the soul, and to be our ally in bringing her into harmony and agreement with herself; and rhythm too was given by them for the same reason, on account of the irregular and graceless ways which prevail among mankind generally, and to help us against them.[67]

67   *Timaeus*, 47d.

The goals of music education, for Plato, were associated with these positive influences on the soul but also those of a moral nature, the development of character. The broad range of these goals are spelled out in a discussion between Socrates, the narrator, and Glaucon, a brother to Plato.

Therefore, I said, Glaucon, musical training is a more potent instrument than any other, because rhythm and harmony find their way into the inward places of the soul, on which they mightily fasten, imparting grace, and making the soul of him who is rightly educated graceful, or of him who is ill-educated ungraceful; and also because he who has received this true education of the inner being will most shrewdly perceive omissions or faults in art and nature, and with a true taste, while he praises and rejoices over and receives into his soul the good, and becomes noble and good, he will justly blame and hate the bad, now in the days of his youth, even before he is able to know the reason why; and when reason comes he will recognize and salute the friend with whom his education has made him long familiar.

   Yes, he said, I quite agree with you in thinking that it is for such reasons that they should be trained in music.

. . .

   Even so, as I maintain, neither we nor the guardians, whom we say that we have to educate, can ever become musical until we and they know the essential forms of temperance [self-discipline], courage, liberality, magnanimity, and their kindred, as well as the contrary forms, in all their combinations, and can recognize them and their images wherever they are found, not slighting them either in small things or great, but believing them all to be within the sphere of one art and study.[68]

68   *Republic*, 401d.

The aim of this education was, of course, to produce Plato's ideal adult, or guardian, for this utopia, as we read in a continuation of this discussion.

The blending of music and gymnastic will bring them into accord, nerving and sustaining the reason with noble words and lessons, and moderating and soothing and civilizing the wildness of passion by harmony and rhythm?

Quite true, he said.

And these two, thus nurtured and educated, and having learned truly to know their own functions, will rule over the concupiscent, which in each of us is the largest part of the soul and by nature most insatiable of gain; over this they will keep guard, lest, waxing great and strong with the fullness of bodily pleasure, as they are termed, the concupiscent soul, no longer confined to her own sphere, should attempt to enslave and rule those who are not her natural-born subjects, and overturn the whole life of man?

Very true, he said.

Both together will they not be the best defenders of the whole soul and the whole body against attacks from without; the one counseling, and the other going out to fight as the leader directs, and courageously executing his commands and counsels?

True.

Likewise it is by reference to spirit that an individual man is deemed courageous, because his spirit retains in pleasure and in pain the commands of reason about what he ought or ought not to fear?

Right, he replied.[69]

69   Ibid., 442. Regarding the 'blending of music and gymnastic,' which Plato mentions here, Athenaeus, *Deipnosophistae*, 14.629ff, gives an extensive catalog of specific dances used for exercise with music. Through these, he says, the students acquired courage.

70   *Laws*, 804e and *Republic*, 5.452.

In this same discussion, Plato, because he had observed the power which music seemed to have over some listeners, understood the experiential impact of music. He was therefore quick to point out that, for all its utilitarian value in his educational scheme, it was important that the students (male *and* female![70]) did not have *too much* music!

When a man allows music to play upon him and to pour into his soul through the funnel of his ears those sweet and soft and melancholy melodies of which we were just now speaking, and his whole life is passed in warbling and the delights of song; in the first stage of the process the passion or spirit which is in him is tempered like iron, and made useful instead of brittle and useless. But if he carries on the softening and soothing process, in the next stage he begins to melt and waste his spirit, until he has wasted it away and cut out the sinews of his soul; and he becomes a feeble warrior.

Very true.

If the element of spirit is naturally weak in him the change is speedily accomplished, but if he have a good deal, then the power of music weakening the spirit renders him excitable;—on the least provocation he flames up at once, and is speedily extinguished; instead of having the spirit he grows irritable and passionate and peevish.[71]

71   *Republic*, 411b.

Plato returns to this point in another place, where he adds that too much gymnastics is also undesirable.

> Did you never observe, I said, the effect on the mind itself of exclusive devotion to gymnastic, or the opposite effect of an exclusive devotion to music?
>
> In what way shown?, he said.
>
> The one producing a temper of hardness and ferocity, the other of softness and effeminacy, I replied.
>
> Yes, he said, I am quite aware that the mere athlete becomes too much of a savage, and that the mere musician is melted and softened beyond what is good for him.[72]

72   *Republic*, 3.410c.

And, needless to say, Plato was not interested in creating professional musicians through this music education—only that music education which a well-educated person should know. Socrates warns a student to learn,

> the same way you learned the arts of the grammarian, or musician, or trainer, not with the view of making any of them a profession, but only as a part of education, and because a private gentleman and freeman ought to know them.[73]

73   *Protagoras*, 312b.

Although, as we shall see below, the children were instructed in some instrumental music, the principal medium for music education in Plato's utopia was singing. The final line here suggests that by music education he means the voice educating the soul.

> AN ATHENIAN STRANGER. The whole choral art is also in our view the whole of education; and of this art, rhythms and harmonies form the part which has to do with the voice.
>
> CLEINIAS. Yes.
>
> AN ATHENIAN STRANGER. The movement of the body has rhythm in common with the movement of the voice, but gesture is peculiar to it, whereas song is simply the movement of the voice.
>
> CLEINIAS. Most true.
>
> AN ATHENIAN STRANGER. And the sound of the voice which reaches and educates the soul, we have ventured to term music.[74]

74   *Laws*, 672e.

Earlier in this discussion, Plato carefully defines accountability in music and dance education, as he returns to the good and bad influences on the soul. It is this moral choice which Plato always places at the heart of the shaping of the character of the student. We have seen earlier that by 'good music' he means what we would call art music or educational music and by 'bad music' he means music simply for pleasure. And to stress the relationship with accountability he has Cleinias conclude, 'There is a great difference in the two kinds of education.'

> AN ATHENIAN STRANGER. And the uneducated is he who has not been trained in the chorus, and the educated is he who has been well trained?
> CLEINIAS. Certainly.
> AN ATHENIAN STRANGER. And the chorus is made up of two parts, dance and song?
> CLEINIAS. True.
> AN ATHENIAN STRANGER. Then he who is well educated will be able to sing and dance well?
> CLEINIAS. I suppose that he will.
> AN ATHENIAN STRANGER. Let us see; what are we saying?
> CLEINIAS. What?
> AN ATHENIAN STRANGER. He sings well and dances well; now must we add that he sings what is good and dances what is good?
> CLEINIAS. Let us make that addition.
> AN ATHENIAN STRANGER. We will suppose that he knows the good to be good, and the bad to be bad, and makes use of them accordingly: which now is the better trained in dancing and music—he who is able to move his body and use his voice in what he understands to be the right manner, but has no delight in good or hatred of evil; or he who is scarcely correct in gesture and voice and in understanding, but is right in his sense of pleasure and pain, and welcomes what is good, and is offended at what is evil?
> CLEINIAS. There is a great difference, stranger, in the two kinds of education.
> AN ATHENIAN STRANGER. If we know what is good in song and dance, then we truly know also who is educated and who is uneducated; but if not, then we certainly shall not know wherein lies the safeguard of education, and whether there is any or not.[75]

75 _Ibid., 654b.

The dance, which was apparently accompanied by the aulos, was in Plato's view especially valuable in the relief of certain powerful emotions. It is what Aristotle will later name catharsis.

> The affection both of the Bacchantes and of the children is an emotion of fear, which springs out of an evil habit of the soul. And when someone applies external agitation to affections of this sort, the motion coming from without gets the better of the terrible and violent internal one, and produces a peace and calm in the soul, and quiets the restless palpitation of the heart, which is a thing

much to be desired, sending the children to sleep, and making the
Bacchantes, although they remain awake, to dance to the pipe with
the help of those gods to whom they offer acceptable sacrifices, and
producing in them a sound mind, which takes the place of their
frenzy.[76]

76 Ibid., 791.

Before we examine the actual music education process, we might
mention that Plato recommends the music teachers be elected[77] and
he also provides a few additional details regarding them.

77 Ibid., 813.

In these several schools let there be dwellings for teachers, who
shall be brought from foreign parts by pay, and let them teach them
who attend the schools the art of war and the art of music, and the
children shall come not only if their parents please, but if they do
not please.[78]

78 Ibid., 804d.

In *Protagoras*, Plato again discusses music education and now
provides very interesting insights into the actual curriculum,
beginning once more with a reference to the moral foundation of
music education, here the influence of good and the bad emotions
in music. The music teacher must be proficient on the lyre and it
appears that instruction begins with this instrument, 'the teacher
and the learner ought to use the sounds of the lyre,' because they
are 'pure,' which we presume is a reference to the teacher who may
not have a reliable voice. The instruction begins with the student
playing in unison with the teacher and later in two parts. Rhythm,
it appears here, included complex figures, all in correspondence
with the notes of the lyre. Finally, this basic course in music education should last three years.

AN ATHENIAN STRANGER. And now that we have done with the
teacher of letters, the teacher of the lyre has to receive orders
from us.

CLEINIAS. Certainly.

AN ATHENIAN STRANGER. I think that we have only to recollect
our previous discussions, and we shall be able to give suitable
regulations touching all this part of instruction and education
to the teachers of the lyre.

CLEINIAS. To what do you refer?

AN ATHENIAN STRANGER. We were saying, if I remember rightly,
that the sixty years old choristers of Dionysus were to be specially
quick in their perceptions of rhythm and musical composition,
that they might be able to distinguish good and bad imitation,
that is to say, the imitation of the good or bad soul when under

the influence of passion, rejecting the one and displaying the other in hymns and songs, charming the souls of youth, and inviting them to follow and attain virtue by the way of imitation.

CLEINIAS. Very true.

AN ATHENIAN STRANGER. And with this view the teacher and the learner ought to use the sounds of the lyre, because its notes are pure, the player who teaches and his pupil rendering note for note in unison; but complexity, and variation of notes, when the strings give one sound and the poet or composer of the melody gives another,—also when they make concords and harmonies in which lesser and greater intervals, slow and quick, or high and low notes, are combined—or, again, when they make complex variations of rhythms, which they adapt to the notes of the lyre,—all that sort of thing is not suited to those who have to acquire a speedy and useful knowledge of music in three years; for opposite principles are confusing, and create a difficulty in learning, and our young men should learn quickly, and their mere necessary acquirements are not few or trifling, as will be shown in due course. Let the director of education attend to the principles concerning music which we are laying down.[79]

79   *Laws*, 812b.

Next, Plato tells us the music which the lyre teacher uses must also be appropriate to children.

The teachers of the lyre take similar care that their young disciple is temperate and gets into no mischief; and when they have taught him the use of the lyre, they introduce him to the poems of other excellent poets, who are the lyric poets; and these they set to music, and make their harmonies and rhythms quite familiar to the children's souls, in order that they may learn to be more gentle, and harmonious, and rhythmical, and so more fitted for speech and action; for the life of man in every part has need of harmony and rhythm. Then they send them to the master of gymnastic.[80]

80   *Protagoras*, 326b.

What kind of music is Plato describing here as being appropriate? For this period, chronologically, it is a rather detailed answer, although for the modern reader the lack of musical examples makes it difficult to say with confidence what Plato meant by the various styles he mentions. The reader will notice that once again Plato mentions the moral value of the repertoire, the 'good' as opposed to entertainment music, and he freely admits that the latter was more popular with both children and the general public.

You would agree with me in saying that one [style] is simple and has but slight changes; and that if an author expresses this style in fitting harmony and rhythm, he will find himself, if he does his work well, keeping pretty much within the limits of a single harmony (for the changes are not great), and in like manner he will make a similar choice of rhythm?

That is quite true, he said.

Whereas the other requires all sorts of harmonies and all sorts of rhythms if the music and the style are to correspond, because the style has all sorts of changes.

That is also perfectly true, he replied.

And do not the two styles, or the mixture of the two, comprehend all poetry and every form of expression in words? No one can say anything except in one or other of them or in both together.

They include all, he said.

And shall we receive into our State all the three styles, the one only of the two unmixed styles? Or would you include the mixed?

I should prefer only to admit the pure imitator of virtue.

Yes, I said, Adeimantus; and yet the mixed style is also charming: and indeed the opposite style to that chosen by you is by far the most popular with children and their attendants, and with the masses.

I do not deny it.[81]

81   *Republic*, 3.397c.

Second, in the most frequently quoted passage regarding Plato's views on music education, we are told the choice of 'modes' are to be strictly limited. We know, as we have pointed out in our introductory chapter on ancient Greek music, that these 'modes' were originally references to styles of music representing separate and distinct populations. Because music was not yet notated, and therefore no examples survive, no one today can say what these styles were other than by quoting brief references to them, such as here that Lydian was 'relaxed.' What that meant to Plato, we can never know.

The harmonies which you mean are the mixed or tenor Lydian, and the full-toned or bass Lydian, and such-like.

These then, I said, must be banished; even to women who have a character to maintain they are of no use, and much less to men.

Certainly.

In the next place, drunkenness and softness and indolence are utterly unbecoming the character of our guardians.

Utterly unbecoming.

And which are the soft and convivial harmonies?

The Ionian, he replied, and some of the Lydian which are termed 'relaxed.'

Well, and are these of any use for warlike men?

Quite the reverse, he replied; and if so the Dorian and the Phrygian are the only ones which you have left …

If these and only these are to be used in our songs and melodies, we shall not want multiplicity of strings or a panharmonic scale?

I suppose not.[82]

82   Ibid., 3.398e. In *Laches*, 188d, Plato remarks that the Dorian is the true Hellenic mode.

For the same reasons, we can never know what Plato meant when he complains about the 'composite use of harmony' which he heard in performance by aulos players. A reasonable guess was that he was referring to having heard more complex improvisation by aulos players in the streets playing music for entertainment purposes.

But what do you say to aulos-makers and aulos-players? Would you admit them into our State when you reflect that in this composite use of harmony the aulos is worse than any stringed instrument; even the panharmonic music is only an imitation of the aulos?

Clearly not.

There remain then only the lyre and the harp for use in the city, and the shepherds in the country may have some kind of pipe.[83]

83   Ibid., 399d.

Fourth, the rhythmic structure of music, like the harmonic structure, must be simple. Here Plato appears to concentrate on dance with music and it appears once again that he does not seem to have an authentic personal background in music. He admits this and says he will consult another teacher named Damon. He begins again with a strong concentration on the moral values inherent in music and movement.

Plato also extends his definition of 'good' music here by adding two new definitions: good music must have grace and simplicity. He is probably reflecting his own taste as a listener here and these judgments could be just appropriately made by any other listener who is not educated in music.

Next in order to harmonies, rhythms will naturally follow, and they should be subject to the same rules, for we ought not to seek out complex systems of meter, and a variety of feet, but rather to discover what rhythms are the expressions of a courageous and harmonious life; and when we have found them, we shall adapt the foot and the melody to words having a like spirit, not the words to the foot and melody. To say what these rhythms are will be your duty—you must teach me them, as you have already taught me the harmonies.

But, indeed, he replied, I cannot tell you. I know from observation that there are some three principles of rhythm out of which metrical systems are framed, just in sounds there are four notes [strings on the lyre] out of which all the harmonies are composed. But of what sort of lives they are severally the imitations I am unable to say.

Then, I said, we must take Damon into our counsels; and he will tell us what rhythms are expressive of meanness, or insolence, or fury, or other unworthiness, and what are to be reserved for the expression of opposed feelings. And I think that I have an indistinct recollection of his mentioning a complex Cretic rhythm; also a dactylic or heroic, and he arranged them in some manner which I do not quite understand, making the rhythms equal in the rise and fall of the foot, long and short alternating; and, unless I am mistaken, he spoke of an iambic as well as of a trochaic rhythm, and assigned to them short and long quantities. Also in some cases he appeared to praise or censure the movement of the foot quite as much as the rhythm; or perhaps a combination of the two; for I am not certain what he meant. These matters, however, as I was saying, had better be referred to Damon himself, for the analysis of the subject would be difficult, you know?

Rather so, I should say.

But it does not require much analysis to see that grace or the absence of grace accompanies good or bad rhythm.

None at all.

And also that good and bad rhythm naturally assimilate to a good and bad style; and that harmony and discord in like manner follow style; for our principle is that rhythm and harmony are regulated by the words, and not the words by them …

Then beauty of style and harmony and grace and good rhythm depend on simplicity,—I mean the true simplicity of a rightly and nobly ordered mind and character, not that other simplicity which is only a euphemism for folly.[84]

84 _Ibid., 400.

Now Plato considers the nature of the lyrics which are contained in the songs used in music education. First, children need Truth. While he admits that the very young are told fictitious tales, these, he says, are not suitable for school age children.

Shall we just carelessly allow children to hear any casual tales which may be devised by casual persons, and to receive into their minds ideas for the most part the very opposite of those which we shall wish them to have when they are grown up?[85]

85 Ibid., 377b.

Even the classic tales of Homer are unsuitable, because he observes that the young can not distinguish whether they are supposed to have an allegorical meaning or not.[86]

Once again the fundamental issue here is a moral one, music teachers must not be allowed to give the students merely whatever they desire, because the quality of the music will have a direct impact on the development of the character of the child.

Several other interesting observations are contained here. First, he tells us that it is experience which determines whether music is 'good' or not. He mentions again the importance of molding and improving the emotional development of the child and he seems to suggest that compositions were commissioned for this purpose.

> An Athenian Stranger. And is any harm done to the lover of vicious dances or songs, or any good done to the approver of the opposite sort of pleasure?
>
> Cleinias. I think that there is.
>
> An Athenian Stranger. 'I think' is not the word, but I would say, rather, 'I am certain.' For must they not have the same effect as when a man associates with bad characters, whom he likes and approves rather than dislikes, and only censures playfully because he has but a suspicion of their badness? In that case, he who takes pleasure in them will surely become like those in whom he takes pleasure, even though he be ashamed to praise them. This result is quite certain; and what greater good or evil can a human being undergo?
>
> Cleinias. I know of none.
>
> An Athenian Stranger. Then in a city which has good laws, or in future ages is to have them, bearing in mind the instruction and amusement which are given by music, can we suppose that the poets are to be allowed to teach in the dance anything which they themselves like, in the way of rhythm, or melody, or words, to the young children of any well-conditioned parents? Is the poet to train his choruses as he pleases, without reference to virtue or vice?
>
> Cleinias. That is surely quite unreasonable, and is not to be thought of.
>
> ...
>
> An Athenian Stranger. The inference at which we arrive is that education is the constraining and directing of youth toward that right reason, which the law affirms, and which the experience of the eldest and best has agreed to be truly right. In order, then, that the soul of the child may not be habituated to feel joy and sorrow in a manner at variance with the law, and those who

obey the law, but may rather follow the law and rejoice and sorrow at the same things as the aged—in order, I say, to produce this effect, chants appear to have been invented, which really enchant, and are designed to implant that harmony of which we speak. And, because the mind of the child is incapable of enduring serious training, they are called plays and songs, and are performed in play; just as when men are sick and ailing in their bodies, their attendants give them wholesome diet in pleasant meats and drinks, but unwholesome diet in disagreeable things, in order that they may learn, as they ought, to like the one, and to dislike the other. And similarly the true legislator will persuade, and, if he cannot persuade, will compel the poet to express, as he ought, by fair and noble words, in his rhythms, the figures, and in his melodies, the music of temperate and brave and in every way good men.[87]

87 *Laws*, 656f and 659d.

Finally, there were apparently also contests held in the realm of music education, in both instrumental and choral music. Plato provides an interesting discussion on the goals and organization of such contests. The discussion includes details of both the adjudication and the qualifications of conductors.

It will be proper to appoint directors of music and gymnastic, two kinds of each—of the one kind the business will be education, of the other, the superintendence of contests … In speaking of contests, the law refers to the judges of gymnastics and of music; these again are divided into two classes, the one having to do with music, the other with gymnastics; and the same who judge of the gymnastic contests of men, shall judge of horses; but in music there shall be one set of judges of solo singing, and of imitation—I mean of rhapsodists, players on the harp, the aulos and the like, and another who shall judge of choral songs. First of all, we must choose directors for the choruses of boys, and men, and maidens, whom they shall follow in the amusement of the dance, and for our other musical arrangements;—one director will be enough for the choruses, and he should be not less than forty years of age. One director will also be enough to introduce the solo singers, and to give judgment on the competitors, and he ought to be less than thirty years of age. The director and manager of the choruses shall be elected after the following manner:—Let any persons who commonly take an interest in such matters go to the meeting, and be fined if they do not go, but those who have no interest shall not be compelled. Any elector may propose as director someone who understands music, and he in the scrutiny may be challenged on the one part by those who say he has no skill, and defended on the other hand by those who say that he has. Ten are to be elected by vote, and he of the ten who is chosen by lot shall undergo a scrutiny, and lead the choruses for a year according to law. And in like manner the competitor who wins the lot shall be leader of the solo and concert music for that year; and he who is thus elected shall deliver the award to the judges.[88]

88   Ibid., 764d.

FUNCTIONAL MUSIC

The most important use of functional music in Greek society was that used in the religious and cult festivals. Although Plato tells us that the traditions in Greece which these celebrations observed came originally from Egypt,[89] in his view the real origin was with the gods, who gave them an ideal purpose. It is curious that for Plato just having the music accompany the religious festivals does not seem quite enough to justify having music in the first place. Therefore, in a kind of gesture to music therapy, he says the music must also promote rest for the worker–listeners.

89   Ibid., 799.

> The Gods, pitying the toils which our race is born to undergo, have appointed holy festivals, wherein men alternate rest with labor; and have given them the Muses and Apollo, the leader of the Muses, and Dionysus, to be companions in their revels, that these may be saved from degeneration, and men partake in spiritual nourishment in company with the Gods.[90]

90   Ibid., 653d.

Plato adds that these festivals were held very frequently and included contests for choirs.

> AN ATHENIAN STRANGER. Next, with the help of the Delphian oracle, we have to institute festivals and make laws about them, and to determine what sacrifices will be for the good of the city, and to what gods they shall be offered; but when they shall be offered, and how often, may be partly regulated by us.
> CLEINIAS. The number—yes.
> AN ATHENIAN STRANGER. Then we must first determine the number; and let the whole number be 365—one for every day,—so that one magistrate at least will sacrifice daily to some god or demigod on behalf of the city, and the citizens, and their possessions ... The law will say that there are twelve feasts dedicated to the twelve gods, after whom the several tribes are named; and that to each of them they shall sacrifice every month, and appoint choruses, and musical and gymnastic contests, assigning them

so as to suit the gods and seasons of the year. And they shall have festivals for women, distinguishing those which ought to be separated from the men's festivals, and those which ought not.[91]

91 Ibid., 828.

The reader has seen above Plato's observation that there had been a general decay in the traditions of musical practice which had been taken from Egypt. Here it is evident that Plato was alarmed by hearing music which he found inappropriate for these religious ceremonies. Of course we cannot know what kind of music he heard as 'horribly blasphemes,' but given his frequently expressed concern regarding how music can affect man we are not surprised here to find him worrying that the listeners will be the recipients of 'evil omens.'

We find here the suggestion that many choral groups participated in these rites including some from foreign places.

AN ATHENIAN STRANGER. No one in singing or dancing shall offend against public and consecrated models, and the general fashion among the youth, any more then he would offend against any other law. And he who observes this law shall be blameless; but he who is disobedient shall be punished by the guardians of the laws, and by the priests and priestesses. Suppose that we imagine this to be our law.

CLEINIAS. Very good.

AN ATHENIAN STRANGER. Can anyone who makes such laws escape ridicule? Let us see. I think that our only safety will be in first framing certain models for composer. One of these models shall be as follows:—If a sacrifice has been offered, and the victims burnt according to law,—if, I say, anyone who may be a son or brother, standing by another at the altar and over the victims, horribly blasphemes, will not his words inspire despondency and evil omens and foreboding in the mind of his father and of his other kinsmen?

CLEINIAS. Of course.

AN ATHENIAN STRANGER. And this is just what takes place in almost all our cities. A magistrate offers a public sacrifice, and there come in not one but many choruses, who take up a position a little way from the altar, and from time to time pour forth all sorts of horrible blasphemies on the sacred rites, exciting the souls of the audience with words and rhythms and melodies most sorrowful to hear; and he who at the moment when the city has offered sacrifice makes the citizens weep most, carries away the palm of victory. Now, ought we not to forbid such strains as these? And if ever our citizens must hear such lamentations, then on some unblest and inauspicious day let there be choruses of foreign and hired musicians with barbarous Carian chants. That is the sort of thing which will be appropriate if we have such strains at all; and let the apparel of the singers of the funeral dirge be, not circlets and ornaments of gold, but the reverse.

Enough of all this. I will simply ask once more whether we shall lay down as one of our principles of song —

Cleinias. What?

An Athenian Stranger. That we should avoid every word of evil omen; let that kind of song which is of good omen be heard everywhere and always in our state. I need hardly ask again, but shall assume that you agree with me …

And our third law will be to the effect that our poets, understanding prayers to be requests which we make to the Gods, will take special heed that they do not by mistake ask for evil instead of good. To make such a prayer would surely be too ridiculous …

Shall we make a law that the poet shall compose nothing contrary to the ideas of the lawful, or just, or beautiful, or good, which are allowed in the state? …

It will be proper to have hymns and praises of the Gods, intermingled with prayers; and after the Gods prayers and praises should be offered in like manner to demigods and heroes, suitable to their several characters.

Cleinias. Certainly.

An Athenian Stranger. In the next place there will be no objection to a law, that citizens who are departed and have done good and energetic deeds, either with their souls or with their bodies, and have been obedient to the laws, should receive eulogies; this will be very fitting.

Cleinias. Quite true.

An Athenian Stranger. But to honor with hymns and panegyrics those who are still alive is not safe; a man should run his course, and make a fair ending, and then we will praise him; and let praise be given equally to women as well as men who have been distinguished in virtue.[92]

92 Ibid., 800.

In order to make certain these goals of composition are observed, Plato recommends the necessity of censors.

Nor shall the composer be permitted to communicate his compositions to any private individuals, until he shall have shown them to the appointed judges and the guardians of the law, and they are satisfied with them.[93]

93 Ibid., 801d.

…

O ye sons and scions of the softer Muses, first of all show your
songs to the magistrates, and let them compare them with our own,
and if they are the same or better we will give you a chorus; but if
not, my friends, we cannot.[94]

94 Ibid., 817d.

After the discussion of the laws which the composers must not
break, Plato once again considers the moral implications of the
lyrics of the choral repertoire and here he attempts to describe by
example how the nature of the music can affect the character of
the listener.

There are many ancient musical compositions and dances which
are excellent, and from these it is fair to select what is proper and
suitable to the newly-founded city; and they shall choose judges of
not less than fifty years of age, who shall make the selection, and any
of the old poems which they deem sufficient they shall include; any
that are deficient or altogether unsuitable, they shall either utterly
throw aside, or examine and amend, taking into their counsel
poets and musicians, and making use of their poetical genius; but
explaining to them the wishes of the legislator in order that they
may regulate dancing, music and all choral strains, according to
the mind of the judges; and not allowing them to indulge, except in
some few matters, their individual pleasures and fancies. Now the
irregular strain of music is always made ten thousand times better
by attaining to law and order, and rejecting the honeyed Muse—not
however that we mean wholly to exclude pleasure, which is characteristic of all music. And if a man be brought up from childhood
to the age of discretion and maturity in the use of the orderly and
severe music, when he hears the opposite he detests it, and calls it
illiberal; but if trained in the sweet and vulgar music, he deems the
severer kind cold and displeasing. So that while he who hears them
gains no more pleasure from the one than from the other, the one
has the advantage of making those who are trained in it better men,
whereas the other makes them worse …

We must distinguish and determine on some general principle
what songs are suitable to women, and what to men, and must
assign to them their proper melodies and rhythms. It is shocking
for a whole composition to be inharmonical, or for a rhythm to be
unrhythmical, and this will happen when the melody is inappropriate to them. And therefore the legislator must assign to these also
their forms. Now both sexes have melodies and rhythms which of
necessity belong to them; and those of women are clearly enough
indicated by their natural difference. The grand, and that which
tends to courage, may be fairly called manly; but that which inclines

to moderation and temperance, may be declared both in law and in ordinary speech to be the more womanly quality.[95]

Plato provides us with some interesting information on the musical contests associated with the religious festivals. He never seemed very interested in this sort of thing and here only concludes that they are not difficult to organize and do neither much good nor much harm to the public.

> As to rhapsodists and the like, and the contests of choruses which are to perform at feasts, all this shall be arranged when the months and days and years have been appointed for gods and demigods, whether every third year, or again every fifth year, or in whatever way or manner the gods may put into men's minds the distribution and order of them. At the same time, we may expect that the musical contests will be celebrated in their turn by the command of the judges and the director of education and the guardians of the law meeting together for this purpose, and themselves becoming legislators of the times and nature and conditions of the choral contests and of dancing in general. What they ought severally to be in language and song, and in the admixture of harmony with rhythm and the dance, has been often declared by the original legislator; and his successors ought to follow him, making the games and sacrifices duly to correspond at fitting times, and appointing public festivals. It is not difficult to determine how these and the like matters may have a regular order; nor, again, will the alteration of them do any great good or harm to the state.[96]

Plato mentions a special category of festival associated with the gods, one which helps prepare the peaceful citizens for possible future battles. Following his frequent emphasis on Virtue, here Plato returns to the question of the moral influence on the listener. For this reason he suggests that perhaps the poets who supply the words for the music must be older persons with experience. This is so important, Plato says, that the work may be chosen for performance on the basis of the words even if it is a poor composition.

> Let poets celebrate the victors,—not however every poet, but only one who in the first place is not less than fifty years of age; nor should he be one who, although he may have musical and poetical gifts, has never in his life done any noble or illustrious action; but those who are themselves good and also honorable in the state, creators of noble actions—let their poems be sung, even though they are not very musical. And let the judgment of them rest with

the instructor of youth and the other guardians of the laws, who
shall give them this privilege, and they alone shall be free to sing;
but the rest of the world shall not have this liberty. Nor shall anyone
dare to sing a song which has not been approved by the judgment
of the guardians of the laws, not even if his strain be sweeter than
the songs of Thamyras and Orpheus; but only such poems as have
been judged sacred and dedicated to the Gods, and such as are the
works of good men.[97]

97   Ibid., 829c.

In another place Plato mentions without discussion various
kinds of popular functional music, such as hymns sung to the gods
at the beginning of a banquet[98] and music for weddings.[99]

98   *Symposium*, 176.

99   *Laws*, 775b.

ENTERTAINMENT MUSIC

Most persons say that the excellence of music is to give pleasure to
our souls. But this is intolerable and blasphemous.[100]

100   Ibid., 655d.

Only a person with Plato's moral perspective of music could
make such a statement. By 'excellence' of music, he means that of
the highest value and since he believes the highest value of music is
in promoting the highest virtue, therefore he regards any reference
to mere pleasure as 'intolerable' and lacking in Truth. Indeed, the
most positive recognition which he could give to entertainment in
general is that it is amusing and provides neither harm nor good.

AN ATHENIAN STRANGER. That only can be rightly judged by the
standard of pleasure, which makes or furnishes no utility or
Truth or likeness, nor on the other hand is productive of any
hurtful quality, but exists solely for the sake of the accompanying
charm; and the term 'pleasure' is most appropriately applied to
it when these other qualities are absent.
CLEINIAS. You are speaking of harmless pleasure, are you not?
AN ATHENIAN STRANGER. Yes; and this I term amusement, when
doing neither harm nor good in any degree worth speaking of.[101]

101   Ibid., 667e.

Plato's principal concern was that amusement in any form, aside
from the immediate pleasure, had a potential for harming the soul.

SOCRATES. I would have you consider ... whether there are not other
similar activities which have to do with the soul—some of them
activities of art, making a provision for the soul's highest interest;

others despising the interest, and as in the parallel case considering only the pleasure, of the soul, and how this may be acquired, but not considering what pleasures are good or bad, and having no other aim but to afford gratification, whether good or bad. In my opinion, Callicles, there are such activities, and this is the sort of thing which I term flattery, whether concerned with the body or the soul or anything else on which it is employed with a view to pleasure and without any consideration of good and evil.[102]

102   *Gorgias*, 501b.

Another concern of Plato was that in sampling entertainment one tends to become like the gourmand who, 'snatches a taste of every dish which is successively brought to the table, without having allowed himself time to enjoy the one before.'[103] The question is inseparable from his concerns for moral values and, of course, he was especially concerned over the potential for harm of entertainment within the educational environment.

103   *Republic*, 1.354b.

> Then, I said, our guardians must lay the foundations of their fortress in music?
>
> Yes, he said; the lawlessness of which you speak too easily steals in.
>
> Yes, I replied, in the form of amusement, and as though it were harmless.
>
> Why, yes, he said, and harmless it would be; were it not that little by little this spirit of license, finding a home, imperceptibly penetrates into manners and customs; whence issuing with greater force it invades contracts between man and man, and from contracts goes on to laws and constitutions, in utter recklessness, ending at last, Socrates, by an overthrow of all rights, private as well as public.
>
> Is that true? I said.
>
> That is my belief, he replied.
>
> Then, as I was saying, our boys should be trained from the first in a stricter system, for if childish amusement becomes lawless, it will produce lawless children, who can never grow up into well-conducted and virtuous citizens.[104]

104   Ibid., 4.424d.

Plato correctly recognized that the artist makes a Faustian compromise when he decides to create or perform according to dictates of the masses. How, he wondered, can the artist 'allow himself to be dazzled by the foolish applause of the world, and heap up riches to his own infinite harm?'[105]

105   Ibid., 9.591d.

And in what way does he who thinks that wisdom is the discernment of the tempers and tastes of the motley multitude, whether in painting or music, or, finally, in politics, differ from him whom I have been describing? For when a man consorts with the many, and exhibits to them his poem or other work of art or the service which he has done the State, making them his judges when he is not obliged, the so-called necessity of Diomede will oblige him to produce whatever they praise. And yet the reasons are utterly ludicrous which they give in confirmation of their own notions about the honorable and good.[106]

Plato also makes a passing reference to the lowest forms of the use of music in entertainment, drinking songs[107] and the infamous prostitute 'single-pipe girl,' who played for male banquets.[108] Regarding the latter, he could not understand why a group of cultivated men would not find greater pleasure merely in intelligent discussion among themselves.

To talk about poetry would make our gathering like the symposia of common and vulgar men. For being unable, through lack of cultivation, to amuse one another in company at a symposium, by their own resources or through their own voices and conversation, they raise high the market-price of single-pipe girls, hiring for a large sum an alien voice—that of the single-pipe girls—and for this they come together. But wherever men of gentle breeding and culture are gathered at a symposium, you will see neither single-pipe girls nor dancing-girls nor harp-girls; on the contrary, they are quite capable of entertaining themselves without such nonsense and child's play, but with their own voices, talking and listening in their turn, and always decently, even when they have drunk much wine.[109]

On the subject of entertainment, Plato reserves his most lengthy discussion for the popular contests and festivals of music and dance. In describing these, he returns to the subject of that art which is addressed to the masses. He also makes interesting comments on the qualification of the judges, recommendations which are still worthy of note today: the judge must be highly qualified, he must have the courage not to be influenced by the audience, he must be honest and maintain the highest standards of performance.

He also provides a rather lofty definition of the best entertainment music—that which pleases the most highly educated listener. To leave this judgment to the masses results in the elimination of good entertainment music.

106 Ibid., 6.493d.

107 *Gorgias*, 451e.

108 *Symposium*, 176e. Socrates said, 'Send her away so we can have a good conversation!'

109 'Protagoras,' 347c, here as quoted by Athenaeus, *Deipnosophistae*, 3.97.

AN ATHENIAN STRANGER. Our young men break forth into dancing and singing, and we who are their elders deem that we are fulfilling our part in life when we look on at them. Having lost our agility, we delight in their sports and merry-making, because we love to think of our former selves; and gladly institute contests for those who are able to awaken in us the memory of our youth.

CLEINIAS. Very true.

AN ATHENIAN STRANGER. Is it altogether unmeaning to say, as the common people do about festivals, that he should be adjudged the wisest of men, and the winner of the palm, who gives us the greatest amount of pleasure and mirth? For on such occasions, and when mirth is the order of the day, ought not he to be honored most, and, as I was saying, bear the palm, who gives most mirth to the greatest number? Now is this a true way of speaking or of acting?

CLEINIAS. Possibly.

AN ATHENIAN STRANGER. But, my dear friend, let us distinguish between different cases, and not be hasty in forming a judgment: One way of considering the question will be to imagine a festival at which there are entertainments of all sorts, including gymnastic, musical, and equestrian contests: the citizens assembled; prizes are offered, and proclamation is made that anyone who likes may enter the lists, and that he is to bear the palm who gives the most pleasure to the spectators—there is to be no regulation about the manner how; but he who is most successful in giving pleasure is to be crowned victor, and deemed to be the pleasantest of the candidates. What is likely to be the result of such a proclamation?

CLEINIAS. In what respect?

AN ATHENIAN STRANGER. There would be various exhibitions: one man, like Homer, will exhibit a rhapsody, another a performance on the lute; one will have a tragedy, and another a comedy. Nor would there be anything astonishing in someone imagining that he could gain the prize by exhibiting a puppet-show. Suppose these competitors to meet, and not these only, but innumerable others as well—can you tell me who ought to be the victor?

CLEINIAS. I do not see how anyone can answer you, or pretend to know, unless he has heard with his own ears the several competitors; the question is absurd.

AN ATHENIAN STRANGER. Well, then, if neither of you can answer, shall I answer this question which you deem so absurd?

CLEINIAS. By all means.

AN ATHENIAN STRANGER. If very small children are to determine the question, they will decide for the puppet-show.

CLEINIAS. Of course.

AN ATHENIAN STRANGER. The older children will be advocates of comedy; educated women, and young men, and people in general, will favor tragedy.

CLEINIAS. Very likely.

AN ATHENIAN STRANGER. And I believe that we old men would have the greatest pleasure in hearing a rhapsodist recite well the Iliad and Odyssey, or one of the Hesiodic poems, and would award an overwhelming victory to him. But, who would really be the victor?—that is the question.

CLEINIAS. Yes.

AN ATHENIAN STRANGER. Clearly you and I will have to declare that those whom we old men adjudge victors ought to win; for our ways are far and away better than any which at present exist anywhere in the world.

CLEINIAS. Certainly.

AN ATHENIAN STRANGER. Thus far I too should agree with the many, that the excellence of music is to be measured by pleasure. But the pleasure must not be that of chance persons; the fairest music is that which delights the best and best educated, and especially that which delights the one man who is preeminent in virtue and education. And therefore the judges must be men of character, for they will require wisdom and have still greater need of courage; the true judge must not draw his inspiration from the theatre, nor ought he to be unnerved by the clamor of the many and his own incapacity; nor again, knowing the truth, ought he through cowardice and unmanliness carelessly to deliver a lying judgment, with the very same lips which have just appealed to the gods before he judged. He is sitting not as the disciple of the theatre, but, in his proper place, as their instructor, and he ought to be the enemy of all pandering to the pleasure of the spectators. The ancient and common custom of Hellas was the reverse of that which now prevails in Italy and Sicily, where the judgment is left to the body of spectators, who determine the victor by show of hands. But this custom has been the destruction of the poets themselves; for they are now in the habit of composing with a view to please the bad taste of their judges, and the result is that the spectators instruct themselves;—and also it has been the ruin of the theater; they ought to be receiving a higher pleasure, but now by their own act the opposite result follows.[110]

110   *Laws*, 657d.

Plato continues his discussion on the prerequisites of the judges: they must be capable of distinguishing the good from the bad and have a wide span of knowledge.

AN ATHENIAN STRANGER. Surely then he who would judge correctly must know what each composition is; for if he does not know what is the character and meaning of the piece, and what it actually represents, he will never discern whether the intention is correct or mistaken.

CLEINIAS. Certainly not.

AN ATHENIAN STRANGER. And will he who does not know what is True be able to distinguish what is good and bad? My statement is not very clear; but perhaps you will understand me better if I put the matter in another way.

CLEINIAS. How?

AN ATHENIAN STRANGER. There are ten thousand likenesses which we apprehend by sight?

CLEINIAS. Yes.

AN ATHENIAN STRANGER. Even in their case, can he who does not know what the exact object is which is imitated, ever know whether the resemblance is truthfully executed? I mean, for example, whether a statue has the proportions of a body, and the true situation of the parts; what those proportions are, and how the parts fit into one another in due order; also their colors and conformations, or whether this is all confused in the execution: do you think that anyone can know about this, who does not know what the animal is which has been imitated?

CLEINIAS. Impossible.

AN ATHENIAN STRANGER. But even if we know that the thing pictured or sculptured is a man, who has received at the hand of the artist all his proper parts and colors and shapes, shall we therefore know at once, and of necessity, whether the work is beautiful or in any respect deficient in beauty?

CLEINIAS. If this were true, stranger, we should almost all of us be judges of beauty.

AN ATHENIAN STRANGER. Very true; and may we not say that in everything imitated, whether in drawing, music, or any other art, he who is to be a competent judge must possess three things;—he must know, in the first place, of what the imitation is; secondly, he must know that it is True; and thirdly, that it has been well executed in words and melodies and rhythms?

CLEINIAS. Certainly.

AN ATHENIAN STRANGER. Then let us not faint in discussing the peculiar difficulty of music. Music is more celebrated than any other kind of imitation, and therefore requires the greatest care of them all. For if a man makes a mistake here, he may do himself the greatest injury by welcoming evil dispositions, and the mistake may be very difficult to discern, because the poets are artists very inferior in character to the Muses themselves, who would never fall into the monstrous error of assigning to the words of men the intonation and song of women; nor after combining the melodies with the gestures of freemen would they add on the rhythms of slaves and men of the baser sort; nor, beginning with the rhythms and gestures of freemen, would they assign to them a melody or words which are of an opposite character; nor would they mix up the voices and sounds of animals and of men and instruments, and every other sort of noise, as if they were all one. But human poets are fond of introducing this sort of inconsistent mixture, and so make themselves ridiculous in the eyes of those who, as Orpheus says, 'are ripe for true pleasure.' The experienced see all this confusion, and yet the poets go on and make still further havoc by separating the rhythm and the figure of the dance from the melody, setting bare words to meter, and also separating the melody and the rhythm from the words, using the lyre or the aulos alone. For when there are no words, it is very difficult to recognize the meaning of the harmony and rhythm, or to see that any worthy object is imitated by them. And we must acknowledge that all this sort of thing, which aims at only swiftness and smoothness and a brutish noise, and uses the aulos and the lyre not as the mere accompaniments of the dance and song, is exceedingly coarse and tasteless. The use of either instrument, when unaccompanied, leads to every sort of irregularity and trickery. This is all rational enough. But we are considering now how our choristers, who are from thirty to fifty years of age, and may be over fifty, are not to use the Muses, but how they are to use them. And the considerations which we have urged seem to show that these fifty-years-old choristers who are to sing, will require something better than a mere choral training. For they need have a quick perception and knowledge of harmonies and rhythms; otherwise, how can they ever know whether a melody would be rightly sung to the Dorian mode, or the the rhythm which the poet has assigned to it?

CLEINIAS. Clearly they cannot.

AN ATHENIAN STRANGER. The many are ridiculous in imagining that they know what is proper harmony and rhythm, and what is not, when they can only be made by force to sing to the aulos and step in rhythm; it never occurs to them that they are ignorant of what they are doing. Now every melody is right when it has suitable harmony and rhythm, and wrong when unsuitable.

CLEINIAS. That is most certain.

AN ATHENIAN STRANGER. But can a man who does not know a thing, as we were saying, know that the thing is right?

CLEINIAS. Impossible.

AN ATHENIAN STRANGER. Then as now, as would appear, we are making the discovery that our newly appointed choristers, whom we hereby invite and, although they are their own masters, compel to sing, must be educated to such an extent as to be able to follow the steps of the rhythm and the notes of the song, that they may review the harmonies and rhythms, and be able to select what are suitable for men of their age and character to sing; and may sing them, and have innocent pleasure from their own performance, and also lead younger men to receive the virtues of character with the welcome which they deserve. Having such training, they will attain a more accurate knowledge than falls to the lot of the common people, or even of the poets themselves. For the poet need not know the third point, viz. whether the imitation is good or not, though he can hardly help knowing the laws of melody and rhythm. But our critics must know all the three, that they may choose the best, and that which is nearest to the best; for otherwise they will never be able to charm the souls of young men in the way of virtue.[111]

111   Ibid., 668c.

After this wide ranging discussion of these public festivals, Plato finally rewards us with an extended picture of the ideal festival, as he might plan it. While he begins, once again, by emphasizing the educational purpose of such a festival, Plato shows us his pragmatic side through his scheme for gaining the participation of the older generation by way of an invitation for the god Dionysus to attend!

AN ATHENIAN STRANGER. Our choruses shall sing to the young and tender souls of children, reciting in their strains all the noble thoughts of which we have already spoken … the sum of them shall be, that the life which is by the Gods deemed to be the happiest is also the best;—thus we shall both affirm what is most certainly true, and the mind of our young disciples will be more likely to receive these words of ours than any others which we might address to them.

CLEINIAS. I assent to what you say.

AN ATHENIAN STRANGER. First will enter in their natural order the choir of the Muses, composed of children, which is to sing lustily the heaven-taught lay to the whole city. Next will follow the choir of young men under the age of thirty, who will call upon the God Paean to testify to the truth of their words, and will pray him to be gracious to the youth and to turn their hearts. Thirdly, the choir of elder men, who are from thirty to sixty years of age, will also sing. There remain those who are too old to sing and they will tell stories, illustrating the same virtues, as with the voice of an oracle.

CLEINIAS. Who are those who compose the third choir, stranger? I do not clearly understand what you mean to say about them.

AN ATHENIAN STRANGER. And yet almost all that I have been saying has been said with a view to them.

CLEINIAS. Will you try to be a little plainer?

AN ATHENIAN STRANGER. I was speaking at the commencement of our discourse, as you will remember, of the fiery nature of young creatures: I said that they were unable to keep quiet either in limb or voice, and they they called out and jumped about in a disorderly manner; and that no other animal attained to any perception of order in these two things, but man only. Now the order of motion is called rhythm, and the order of voice, in which high and low are duly mingled, is called harmony; and both together are termed choric song. And I said that the Gods had pity on us, and gave us Apollo and the Muses to be our playfellows and leaders in the dance; and Dionysus, as I dare say that you will remember, was the third.

CLEINIAS. I quite remember.

AN ATHENIAN STRANGER. Thus far have I spoken of the chorus of Apollo and the Muses; the third and remaining chorus must be called that of Dionysus.

CLEINIAS. How is that? There is something strange, at any rate on first hearing, in a Dionysiac chorus of old men, if you really mean that those who are above thirty, and may be fifty, or from fifty to sixty years of age, are to dance in his honor.

AN ATHENIAN STRANGER. Very true; and therefore it must be shown that there is good reason for the proposal.

CLEINIAS. Certainly.

AN ATHENIAN STRANGER. Are we agreed thus far?

CLEINIAS. About what?

AN ATHENIAN STRANGER. That every man and boy, slave and free, both sexes, and the whole city, should never cease charming themselves with the strains of which we have spoken; and that there should be every sort of change and variation of them in order to take away the effect of sameness, so that the singers may always receive pleasure from their hymns, and may never weary of them?

CLEINIAS. Everyone will agree.

AN ATHENIAN STRANGER. Where, then, will that best part of our city which, by reason of age and intelligence, has the greatest influence, sing these fairest of strains in such a way as to do most good. Shall we be so foolish as to neglect this regulation, which may have a decisive effect in making the songs most beautiful and useful?

CLEINIAS. But, says the argument, we cannot neglect it.

An Athenian Stranger. Then how can we carry out our purpose with decorum? Will this be the way?

Cleinias. What?

An Athenian Stranger. When a man is advancing in years, he is afraid and reluctant to sing;—he has no pleasure in his own performances; and if compulsion is used, he will be more and more ashamed, the older and more discreet he grows;—is not this true?

Cleinias. Certainly.

An Athenian Stranger. Well, and will he not be yet more ashamed if he has to stand up and sing in the theater to a mixed audience?—and if moreover when he is required to do so, like the other choirs who contend for prizes, and have been trained under a singing master, he is pinched and hungry, he will certainly have a feeling of shame and discomfort which will make him very unwilling to perform.

Cleinias. No doubt.

An Athenian Stranger. How, then, shall we reassure him, and get him to sing? Shall we begin by enacting that boys shall not taste wine at all until they are eighteen years of age; we will tell them that fire must not be poured upon fire, whether in the body or in the soul, until they begin to go to work—this is a precaution which has to be taken against the excitableness of youth;—afterwards they may taste wine in moderation up to the age of thirty, but while a man is young he should abstain altogether from intoxication and from excess of wine; when, at length, he has reached forty years, after dinner at a public mess, he may invite not only the other gods, but Dionysus above all, to the mystery and festivity of the elder men, making use of the wine which he has given men to lighten the sourness of old age; that in age we may renew our youth, and forget our sorrows; and also in order that the nature of the soul, like iron melted in the fire, may become softer and so more impressible. In the first place, will not anyone who is thus mellowed be more ready and less ashamed to sing,—I do not say before a large audience, but before a moderate company; nor yet among strangers, but among his familiars, and, as we have often said, to chant, and to enchant?

Cleinias. He will be far more ready.

An Athenian Stranger. There will be no impropriety in our using such a method of persuading them to join with us in song.

Cleinias. None at all.

An Athenian Stranger. And what strain will they sing, and what muse will they hymn? The music should clearly be of some kind suitable to them.

Cleinias. Certainly.

AN ATHENIAN STRANGER. And what strain is suitable for heroes? Shall they sing a choric strain?

CLEINIAS. Truly, stranger, we of Crete and Lacedaemon know no strain other than that which we have learnt and been accustomed to sing in our chorus.

AN ATHENIAN STRANGER. I dare say; for you have never acquired the knowledge of the most beautiful kind of song, in your military way of life, which is modeled after the camp, and is not like that of dwellers in cities; and you have your young men herding and feeding together like young colts. No one takes his own individual colt and drags him away from his fellows against his will, raging and foaming, and gives him a groom to attend to him alone, and soothes and rubs him down, and sees that nothing is missing in his education which will make him not only a good soldier, but also a governor of a state and of cities. Such a one, as we said at first, would be a greater warrior than he of whom Tyrtaeus sings; and he would honor courage everywhere, but always as the fourth, and not the first part of virtue, either in individuals or states.

13 ARISTOTLE

Aristotle! What an impact that word still has after more than two thousand years! He, like Newton, Kant, and Einstein, belongs to that select circle of 'one name' people whose accomplishments were so far reaching as to convey a sense of awe even to those who have never read their works. Those who *have* read Aristotle's works know that just a few of the topics covered in his *extant* writings include politics, every branch of science known at the time, the arts, government, the art of public speaking, philosophy and ethics. And we must not fail to mention that he invented the philosophical branch of study we call Aesthetics. As Will Durant so aptly put it, Aristotle was a one-man 'Encyclopedia Britannica of Greece.'[1]

Fortunately, Aristotle was born (in 384 BC) into circumstances which made possible the fulfillment of his genius. His father was a physician to the King of Macedonia, the grandfather to Alexander the Great, whom Aristotle would tutor. At age fifty-three, Aristotle founded in Athens his own school, known as the Lyceum. It is assumed that the many students who were drawn to this school shared in the burden of his work, collecting data, carrying out observations and experiments, and perhaps even in the actual writing. This must have been the case if some ancient writers were correct in attributing to him between four hundred and a thousand books.

In subjects such as logic or rhetoric, where Aristotle needed only his native intelligence and his love for step-by-step rational analysis, his writings must still impress every modern reader. In the field of science, our perspective after two thousand years of discoveries makes it more difficult to appreciate his pronouncements. Even if we keep in mind that the man had none of the modern tools for scientific measurement and that many basic concepts, including gravitation, the nature of chemical and electrical phenomena, etc., were as yet unknown, still we are startled at some of the 'weird science' we find in his pages.

We can understand how someone of his epoch could believe the earth was stationary and did not move (how else would we see the same stars tomorrow night that we see tonight?). But, considering he knew the basics of anatomy, how could he have concluded that the brain is cold, bloodless, and *fluid* in nature, or that the delay in

1 Durant, *The Story of Philosophy*, 46.

the closure of the cranial bone in infants has to do with the need for 'evaporation?'[2] And how could he have not guessed that it is in the brain that we experience the senses, concluding instead that it is in the heart?

> For the passages of all the sense-organs … run to the heart.[3]
>
> …
>
> Because the source of the sensations is in the heart, therefore this is the part first formed in the whole animal.[4]

Sometimes he seems to have believed, and passes on, observations which he must have received second-hand, such as, 'More males are born if copulation takes place when north rather than south winds are blowing.' In this case, he tells us that shepherds confirm that the direction of the wind influences the production of males and females in animals if an animal even *looks* in one direction or the other while copulating![5]

In the field of music, Aristotle concluded correctly that Pythagoras and his 'music of the spheres' was nonsense.

> It is clear that the theory that the movement of the stars produces a harmony, i.e., that the sounds they make are concordant, in spite of the grace and originality with which it has been stated, is nevertheless untrue.[6]

He could not entirely free himself, however, of this attractive imagery—he once referred to the heavens as a 'choral dance'[7] and another time as a 'chorus' with God being the 'chorus master.'[8]

On the other hand, his lack of understanding of the true nature of frequency of vibration vs. dynamics, the general role of air in the production of the singing voice or playing an instrument, and really the whole of the physics of music, result in some odd conclusions. A typical example:

> In the case of oboes and other instruments of the same class, the sounds produced are clear when the breath emitted from them is concentrated and intense. For the impacts on the external air must be of that kind, and it is in this way that they will best travel to the ear in a solid mass.
>
> …
>
> The reeds of oboes must be solid and smooth and even, so that the breath may pass through smoothly and evenly, without being dispersed. Therefore mouthpieces which have been well steeped and

2 *De Partibus Animalium*, 2.6. Unless otherwise noted, all translations are from William Ogle, *The Works of Aristotle* (London: Oxford University Press, 1911).

3 *De Generatione Animalium*, 5.2.

4 Ibid., 2.6.

5 Ibid., 4.2.

6 *De Caelo*, 290b.13.

7 *On the Cosmos*, 391b.15.

8 Ibid., 399a.15.

soaked in grease give a pleasant sound, while those which are dry produce less agreeable notes.[9]

9 *De Audibilibus*, 802a.9, and 802b.19.

He also did not seem to quite understand the overtone series, which makes us also wonder if we have not given too much credit to Pythagoras and his school for their true understanding. Aristotle, for example, expressed wonder why a lower tone contains an upper octave within it, but an upper tone does not contain a lower octave within it.[10]

10 *Problemata*, 918a.19.

Aristotle was, nevertheless, a keen observer of music and musicians. He recognized the difference between the musical and the unmusical performance[11] and he noticed that quality of birth or wealth was not the factor that resulted in a good player.[12] In various places, Aristotle mentions the institution of the chorus, how it is supported,[13] that the conductors should be elected,[14] and the modes in which their music was composed.[15] The breadth of observations which he lists in his *Problemata*, in a chapter devoted to music, is very impressive. Among them are,

11 *Coming-to-be and Passing-away*, 2.6.

12 *Politica*, 1283a.

13 *Atheniensium Respublica*, 56.2.

14 *Politica*, 1299a.17.

15 *Problemata*, 922b.10. He says they do not use Hypodorian or Hypophrygian, but like everyone else in ancient Greece, he assumes the reader knows what these terms mean. He only reminds us that the first was 'magnificent and steadfast,' and that the second had 'the character of action.'

A sound made by a chorus travels farther than that of a solo singer.
Most people prefer hearing music they already know.
Most people prefer to hear an accompanied singer, rather than a solo singer.
Low notes which are out of tune are more noticable than high notes which are out of tune.
A large chorus keeps better time than a smaller one.

Finally, the ever thorough Aristotle even reports that he has heard that on the Ionian island of Lipara, there is a tomb where at night one can distinctly hear, 'the sound of drums and cymbals, and laughter, along with uproar and the rattle of castanets.'[16]

16 *De Mirabilibus*, 839a.

The interesting thing is, while we have numerous observations of, and references to, music throughout his writings, and while he once specifically mentions the concert hall in Athens,[17] he never once mentions a specific musical performance nor does he ever speak of music in personal terms.[18] We believe the reason for this is that, like his teacher Plato, the world of *reason* was where he felt most comfortable and that he sensed correctly that music could not be explained by rational thinking.

17 *Metaphysica*, 1010b.12.

18 While it is assumed that many of Aristotle's books are lost, we believe that given the many opportunities where he could have discussed these things in the extant books and did not, suggests that even given another hundred books, he would not have altered his reticence on this subject.

THE PHYSIOLOGY OF AESTHETICS

To understand Aristotle's general perspective of music one must first understand that like Plato, he assigned the place of music to the 'soul' for he knew it could not easily be explained by Reason and he had no clue that the brain also consists of genuine non-rational knowing in the right hemisphere. In view of this, it is curious and remarkable that Aristotle imagined the soul to consist of both rational and non-rational understanding.

> Now the soul of man is divided into two parts, one of which has a rational principle in itself, and the other, not having a rational principle in itself, is able to obey such a principle. And we call a man in any way good because he has the virtues of these two parts. In which of them the end is more likely to be found is no matter of doubt to those who adopt our division; for in the world both of nature and of art the inferior always exists for the sake of the better or superior, and the better or superior is that which has a rational principle.[19]

19   *Politica*, 1333a.17.

In spite of his thinking being constrained by this complicated, and false, physiological map, Aristotle managed to intuit some very important, and accurate, principles. For example, he very clearly understood that all rational 'knowing' is based not on our own experience, but on that which we have been told, or that which we have read. He states this in the very first sentence of his *Posterior Analytics*.

20   Aristotle, *Posterior Analytics*, trans. Hugh Tredennick (Cambridge, MA: Harvard University Press, 1960).

> All teaching and learning that involves the use of reason proceeds from pre-existent knowledge.[20]

21   'Ethica Nicomachea,' 1138b.35.

In another place[21] where he discusses the division of the soul, Aristotle suggests that the rational includes the intellect, while the non-rational includes 'character.' Character has to do with 'virtue' and while Aristotle does not use the word, it is clear that he believed that this kind of learning is largely *experiential* and non-rational in nature. It is all the more curious, therefore, that his references to music here suggest that he recognized primarily the mechanical aspects of music and not the more important aspects of feeling and Truth derived from personal experience. In the same way, he recognizes that teachers are indispensable in the field of music, but it is not clear that he understands the reason why.

Of all the things that come to us by nature we first acquire the potentiality and later exhibit the activity (this is plain in the case of the senses; for it was not by often seeing or often hearing that we got these senses, but on the contrary we had them before we used them, and did not come to have them by using them); but the virtues we get by first exercising them, as also happens in the case of the arts as well. For the things we have to learn before we can do them, we learn by doing them, e.g. men become builders by building and lyre players by playing the lyre; so too we become just by doing just acts, temperate by doing temperate acts, brave by doing brave acts …

It is from the same causes and by the same means that every virtue is both produced and destroyed, and similarly every art; for it is from playing the lyre that both good and bad lyre players are produced … For if this were not so, there would have been no need of a teacher, but all men would have been born good or bad at their craft. This, then, is the case with the virtues also … Thus, in one word, *states of character arise out of like activities*. This is why the activities we exhibit must be of a certain kind; it is because the states of character correspond to the differences between these. It makes no small difference, then, whether we form habits of one kind or another from our very youth; it makes a very great difference, or rather *all* the difference.[22]

22   Ibid., 1103a.25 and following.

Aristotle, like Plato, appears comfortable only with the rational and is inclined to distrust information derived directly from the senses because it is clearly not rational in nature.

Now there are three things in the soul which control action and truth—sensation, reason, desire.
Of these sensation originates no action; this is plain from the fact that the lower animals have sensation but no share in action.[23]

23   Ibid., 1139a.18.

And in another place,

For whenever, if A is, B necessarily is, men also fancy that, if B is, A necessarily is. It is from this source that deceptions connected with opinion based on sense-perception arise.[24]

24   Aristotle, *On Sophistical Refutations*, 5, trans., Edward Seymour Forster (Cambridge, MA: Harvard University Press, 1955).
25   *De Anima*, 424a.18.

By the 'senses' Aristotle means, 'the power of receiving into itself the sensible forms of things *without matter*.'[25] 'Perception' has a broader meaning, for perception is a necessary part of thinking (one has to perceive something in order to think about it).[26] But, he says, it follows,

26   Ibid., 427a.17.

> That perceiving and practical thinking are not identical is therefore obvious …
>
> Thinking is different from perceiving and is held to be in part imagination, in part judgment.[27]

27   Ibid., 427b.7 and 27.

But now Aristotle makes an error in his logic, again largely due to his lack of our modern understanding of the two hemispheres of the brain and how they specialize. What is more correct in the second of these sentences is to say, 'Perception is the knowledge which is perceived by perception.'

> Knowledge is thus *of* the knowable; the knowable is knowable *by* knowledge. Perception is *of* the perceptible, which is perceived *by* perception.[28]

28   Aristotle, *The Categories*, 7, trans. Harold P. Cook (Cambridge, MA: Harvard University Press, 1962).

Next, Aristotle considers the voice, which he recognizes is in some way also the voice of the soul.

> Voice is a kind of sound characteristic of what has soul in it; nothing that is without soul utters voice, it being only by a metaphor that we speak of the voice of the aulos or the lyre or generally of what (being without soul) possesses the power of producing a succession of notes which differ in length and pitch and timbre. The metaphor is based on the fact that all these differences are found also in voice.[29]

29   *De Anima*, 420b.5.

From this thought process Aristotle arrives at one of his most important revelations: that the words we speak are only symbols of something else and that therefore written words are symbols of symbols of the real thing. The voice is also one representation of the emotions of the soul, something which Aristotle finds universal in character. Equally important is his realization that while the names of emotions vary from language to language, the emotions themselves are universal.

> Words spoken are symbols or signs of emotions or impressions of the soul; written words are the symbols of words spoken. As writing, so also is speech not same for all races of men. But the emotions themselves, of which these words are primarily signs, are the same for the whole of mankind.[30]

30   Aristotle, *On Interpretation*, 1, trans. Harold P. Cook (Cambridge, MA: Harvard University Press, 1962).

With this background we can understand how Aristotle wanted to associate the language of words and the language of music as being somehow similar since in both cases the words represent something else.

Knowledge, the genus, we define by a reference to something beyond it, for knowledge is knowledge *of* something. Particular branches, however, of knowledge are not thus explained. For example, we do not define by a reference to something external a knowledge of grammar or music. For these, if in some sense relations, can only be taken for such in respect of their genus or knowledge. That is to say, we call grammar the knowledge, *not* grammar, of something, and music we call, in like manner, the knowledge, *not* music, of something.[31]

Here, because of his lack of understanding of the right hemisphere of the brain and subsequently of the true nature of music, Aristotle is not quite correct. Music is not a symbol of anything else, it is a direct communication between composer and listener. It would have been more to the point if he had concluded the above by calling grammar the *knowledge* of music, meaning that grammar is the knowable, rational way we describe music. But you cannot say the grammar of music is music.

Aristotle refers to grammar and music once again in a passage where he contends that the 'harmony' of a community derives from the mixture of opposites.

Some people have wondered how the cosmos, if it is composed of the 'opposite' principles (I mean dry and wet, cold and hot), has not long ago been destroyed and perished; it is as if men should wonder how a city survives, composed as it is of the most opposite classes (I mean poor and rich, young and old, weak and strong, bad and good). They do not recognize that the most wonderful thing of all about the harmonious working of a city-community is this: that out of plurality and diversity it achieves a homogeneous unity capable of admitting every variation of nature and degree. But perhaps nature actually has a liking for opposites; perhaps it is from them that she creates harmony, and not from similar things, in just the same way as she has joined male and female ... Music mixes high and low notes, and longs and shorts, and makes a single melody of different sounds; by making a mixture of vowels and consonants, grammar composes out of them the whole of its art.[32]

31 *The Categories*, 8. In *Topica*, 1.10, Aristotle again says that grammar and music 'seem to be similar and akin.'

32 Aristotle, *On the Cosmos*, 5, trans. David J. Furley (Cambridge, MA: Harvard University Press, 1965).

THE PSYCHOLOGY OF AESTHETICS

As Aristotle found emotions to be universal, it should be no surprise that he found music to also be universal. Why, he asks, do all men love music? Aristotle, always seeking the rational rather than the experiential explanation, seemed to find his answer partly in nature and partly as an expression of his theory of 'Opposites.' Perhaps the most important thought here is that we take pleasure in listening to some kinds of melodies for their moral character.

> Is it because we naturally rejoice in natural movements? This is shown by the fact that children rejoice in [rhythm and melody] as soon as they are born. Now we delight in the various types of melody for their moral character, but we delight in rhythm because it contains a familiar and ordered number and moves in a regular manner; for ordered movement is naturally more akin to us than disordered, and is therefore more in accordance with nature ... We delight in concord because it is the mingling of contraries which stand in porportion to one another. Porportion, then, is order, which, as we have said, is naturally pleasant.[33]

33 *Problemata*, 920b.28.

Because he associated music with the soul, and because he did not know how to deal with the physical aspects of music affecting the soul, he was perplexed at how changes in the soul could take place.

> How [can] 'alterations' in the soul take place? How, for example, could the change from being musical to being unmusical occur, or could memory or forgetfulness occur?[34]

34 *Coming-to-be and Passing-away*, 6.

The answer to this, he says, is the task for another investigation—which, unfortunately, is lost.

Before leaving the general subject of aesthetics, we must mention Aristotle's views on pleasure and pain, a subject to which he devotes an extended discussion. For Aristotle, the distinction between pleasure and pain is a matter of moral choice, but unfortunately for our study his discussion is primarily concerned with bodily pleasure and pain and the subsequent relationship with virtue and character. He does not think of this subject as an aesthetic one, therefore, but rather a study which 'belongs to the province of the *political* philosopher.' He begins as follows:

We must take as a sign of states of character the pleasure or pain that
ensues on acts; for the man who abstains from bodily pleasures and
delights in this very fact is temperate, while the man who is annoyed
at it is self-indulgent, and he who stands his ground against things
that are terrible and delights in this or at least is not pained is brave,
while the man who is pained is a coward. For moral excellence is
concerned with pleasures and pains; it is on account of the pleasure
that we do bad things, and on account of the pain that we abstain
from noble ones.[35]

35 *Ethica Nicomachea*, the
discussion occupying most of
the material between 1104b.4
through 1206a.35.

In his methodical manner, Aristotle first surveys the views of
others ('This is what people say'), finding some people who say all
pleasure is bad. An example of their reasons for this belief is that
'pleasures are a hindrance to thought,' illustrated in the example
of sexual pleasures—'for no one could think of anything while
absorbed in this.'[36] Others say that *not all* pleasures are good, and
Aristotle admits that there are some pleasures that are indeed 'actually base and objects of reproach.'

36 Ibid., 1152b.18.

Aristotle disposes of most of these arguments on the basis that
they are all too general and not specific and thus he says, 'What
pleasure is, or what kind of thing it is, will become plainer if we
take up the question again from the beginning.' When he 'starts
at the beginning,' he now begins to phrase his comments in terms
which are more appropriate to art. His first definition is particularly
characteristic of music: pleasure must be defined as something
complete in the present tense.

Seeing seems to be at any moment complete, for it does not lack
anything which coming into being later will complete its form;
and pleasure also seems to be of this nature. For it is a whole, and
at no time can one find a pleasure whose form will be completed
if the pleasure lasts longer. For this reason, too, it is not a movement ... It is complete, therefore, only in the whole time or at that
final moment.[37]

37 Ibid., 1174a.14.

Second, since pleasure must be associated with one of the senses,
the highest form of pleasure must therefore be the finest and most
complete object of the sense in question.

Since every sense is active in relation to its object ... it follows
that in the case of each sense the best activity is that of the best-
conditioned organ in relation to the finest of its objects. For, while
there is pleasure in respect to any sense, and in respect to thought
and contemplation no less, the most complete is the pleasantest.[38]

38 Ibid., 1174b.15.

Third, pleasure is always associated with some activity, from which follows several observations. Since no one is capable of continuous activity, there can be no such thing as continuous pleasure. Next, every man is most active about 'those things and with those faculties that he loves most, thus the musician is active with his hearing in reference to melodies, etc.'[39] Thus it also follows that when we are enjoying pleasure we love, our concentration with that sense can prevent pleasures of the other senses.

39 Ibid., 1175a.10.

> This will be even more apparent from the fact that activities are hindered by pleasures arising from other sources. For people who are fond of playing the aulos are incapable of attending to arguments if they overhear some one playing the aulos, since they enjoy aulos playing more than the activity in hand; so the pleasure connected with aulos playing destroys the activity concerned with argument.[40]

40 Ibid., 1175b. Aristotle, rather unwittingly, here hits upon the fundamental problem of music for the voice: the listener simply can not concentrate on the 'music' (right hemisphere) and the words (left hemisphere) at the same time equally with both hemispheres. The whole era of the recitative and aria was one solution, or perhaps we should say avoidance, for the 'solution' was to merely take turns.

Fourth, those activities are most desirable which are desirable in themselves and from which nothing is sought beyond the activity.[41] Pleasant amusements are of this nature; we choose them not for the sake of other things.

Finally, he returns to the moral aspect of pleasure and contends that the best pleasures are those which contribute to the virtuous life and not those which consist of mere amusement.

41 Ibid., 1176b.5.

> The happy life is thought to be virtuous; now a virtuous life requires exertion, and does not consist in amusement. And we say that serious things are better than laughable things and those connected with amusement, and that the activity of the better of any two things ... is the more serious.[42]

42 Ibid., 1177a.

ART MUSIC

This is a subject which, unfortunately, Aristotle does not address at length. We wish he had devoted the same careful attention to the definition of aesthetic music that he gave to drama, or perhaps he did and the book has been lost. More likely is the evident fact that he was only comfortable in discussing the mechanical aspects of music and not the experiential aspects. In any case, we must look elsewhere for corresponding comments which perhaps reveal his thinking on this subject.

The ancient question regarding the definition of art is, does that word describe what is in the artist's mind, for his act of creating (as in 'the art of painting') or in the finished art object itself? Aristotle thought of the first two of these being of one and the same thing, although his discussion centers on the second of the three. It is also quite interesting to read that he believed a certain unpredictability is inherent in the process of creation.

> All art is concerned with coming into being, i.e., with contriving and considering how something may come into being which is capable of either being or not being, and whose origin is in the maker and not in the thing made; for art is concerned neither with things that are, or come into being, by necessity, nor with things that do so in accordance with nature (since these have their origin in themselves). Making and acting being different, art must be a matter of making, not of acting. And in a sense chance and art are concerned with the same objects; as Agathon says, 'art loves chance and chance loves art.' Art, then, as has been said, is a state concerned with making, involving a true course of reasoning, and lack of art on the contrary is a state concerned with making, involving a false course of reasoning; both are concerned with the variable.[43]

43 Ibid., 1140a.

One definition of *good art*, he offers, is that art in which 'it is not possible either to take away or to add anything.'[44] But this may perhaps be thought of as another way of considering universality, if he meant most people can't imagine changes. Clearly he believed in the principle of universality, that great art has such an epitomized form of expression that it communicates very broadly. For this reason he once pointed out that many people are a better judge of music than a single man.[45]

44 Ibid., 1106b.8.

45 *Politica*, 3.2.1281b, 8.

Another standard by which Aristotle must have judged music with respect to aesthetics was its moral value. Good art is that it must be 'good' in the sense of virtue.

> We must see that every science and art has an end, and that too a good one; for no science or art exists for the sake of evil. Since then in all the arts the end is good, it is plain that the end of the best art will be the best good.[46]

46 *Magna Moralia*, 1182a.33.

In another place Aristotle actually makes the term 'musical' and the morally good man synonymous.

A good man is one that delights in virtuous actions and is vexed at vicious ones, as a musical man enjoys beautiful melodies but is pained at bad ones.[47]

47   *Ethica Nicomachea*, 1170a.9.

In one discussion Aristotle addresses the good, or the virtuous, in art, and separates the *art* from the *end*, observing that in some cases the end may be good (high in character), but not the art that creates it ('the activity').

Every art and every inquiry, and similarly every action and pursuit, is thought to aim at some good; and for this reason the good has rightly been declared to be that at which all things aim. But a certain difference is found among ends; some are activities, others are products apart from the activities that produce them. Where there are ends apart from the actions, it is the nature of the products to be better than the activities.[48]

48   Ibid., 1094a.

What he means here, in the case of music, is that while music is a 'good,' the musician himself is of a lower order (often he was a slave). This is a reflection of the way many people at the top of Greek society thought at this time. Plutarch states this view very vividly in his biography of Pericles.

Many times ... when we are pleased with the work, we slight and set little by the workman or artist himself, as, for instance, in perfumes and purple dyes, we are taken with the things themselves well enough, but do not think dyers and perfumers otherwise than low and sordid people. It was not said amis by Antisthenes, when people told him that one Ismenias was an excellent aulos player, 'It may be so,' said he, 'but he is but a wretched human being, otherwise he would not have been an excellent aulos player.'[49]

49   Plutarch, *Lives*, 'Pericles.'

There is no question that Aristotle shared this view and it is very likely that this attitude tempered his entire thinking about music.

Why is it that some men spend their time in pursuits which they have chosen, though these are sometimes mean, rather than in more honorable professions? Why, for example, should a man who chooses to be a conjurer or an actor or an aulos player prefer these callings to that of an astronomer or an orator?[50]

50   *Problemata*, 917a.5.

With regard to what might have been Aristotle's criteria of aesthetic musical literature, in his *Problemata* he offers a few hints. The first is his observation that we get the most pleasure in hearing music which is 'expressive of meaning.'[51] The second is his judgment that 'a woeful and quiet character and type of music' is 'more human.'[52] And he also observes that most people prefer hearing music they already know, which we might take as the principle of familiarity.[53]

By far the most important contribution to a definition of Art Music is found in his famous book, the *Poetics*. While this discussion concentrates on the difference between Tragedy and Epic Theater, it is here that he creates the definitions of the aesthetic experience which will be the starting point for all later discussion of this subject during the succeeding two thousand years. Needless to say, some of these basic definitions have equal significance for aesthetics in music.

Aristotle begins by stating that Epic Poetry, Tragedy, Comedy, Dithyrambic Poetry and Music must be viewed as having in common the fact that they are forms of imitation.[54] They differ with one another in how this imitation is carried out, their medium and their objects (which refers to the type of characters in the theatrical works).

The origin for all of them he finds in human nature. First, imitation is natural to man from childhood and is one of his advantages over lower animal forms. Second, we delight in imitation, even, to viewing the most realistic representations of objects we should not wish to see in real life, such as dead bodies.

Now comes what is probably the single most remembered sentence by Aristotle, his definition of Tragedy, which he considers the highest form of theater art. It is this single sentence, with its new concept of catharsis, which begins the study of aesthetics as a separate branch of philosophy.

> A tragedy is the imitation of an action that is serious and also, as having magnitude, complete in itself; in language with pleasurable accessories, each kind brought in separately in the parts of the work; in a dramatic, not in a narrative form; with incidents arousing pity and fear, wherewith to accomplish its catharsis of such emotions.[55]

While performances of Greek tragedy do not include music today, he reminds us how important music was to the performances he knew, when he says,

> by 'language with pleasurable accessories' I mean that with rhythm and harmony or song superadded; and by 'the kinds separately' I mean that some portions are worked out with verse only, and others in turn with song.

51 Ibid., 918a.33.

52 Ibid., 922b.20.

53 Ibid., 922b.10ff.

54 Here, of course, he is wrong. Music alone among the arts is not an imitation of anything. It is the real thing, the real feelings communicated from composer to listener.

55 *Poetics*, 1449b.24.

There are several other elements of his definition of tragedy which one could easily associate with the highest art in music: that it is serious, that it has a certain magnitude, and that it is complete in itself. But with regard to aesthetics, it is of course the famous heart of this definition, 'arousing pity and fear, wherewith to accomplish its catharsis of such emotions,' which interests us most and which is most directly applicable to the performance of music.

By 'pity,' he means empathy. He makes this clear when he defines this word in his book on rhetoric.

> Pity may be defined as a feeling of pain caused by the sight of some evil, destructive or painful, which befalls one who does not deserve it, and which we might expect to befall ourselves or some friend of ours, and moreover to befall us soon.

'Fear' goes beyond empathy with the action on the stage and becomes *personal*—what we see happening to the character on the stage might happen to us as well, if we make the same mistake. The play (or musical performance) which produces these effects reaches us in a deeper level than those arts we call entertainment. Entertainment we enjoy fully, but it never gets inside us, never reaches us at this deeper level. It is in the aesthetic work, when we experience 'pity and fear' that 'catharsis' follows.

What did Aristotle mean by *catharsis*? Gerald F. Else, in his extensive study[56] of the *Poetics*, points out that while Aristotle did not use this word again in this book, critics and philologists ('men not to be daunted by lack of evidence') have created an enormous literature upon it. Regarding the definition of this key word, catharsis, he summarizes for us what he calls, 'the presuppositions that are shared by all or most of the writers on the subject.'

1. Almost all agree that Aristotle is talking about a change of feeling (an emotional reaction), or even of [one's] character, which tragedy brings about, or effectuates, in the spectator.
2. They all assume (implicitly) that this effect is automatic and is produced by all 'tragedies.'
3. They almost all presuppose that the change regards feelings.
4. Most of them take 'pity and fear' as denoting the spectator's emotions (not pitiful or fearful actions on the stage); pity and fear are aroused in him and subsequently purified or purged.

56   Gerald Frank Else, *Aristotle's Poetics: The Argument* (Cambridge, MA: Harvard University Press, 1967), 225ff.

In future centuries, philosophers of aesthetics would carry this idea somewhat further, to mean that the spectator is to some degree actually a changed person as a result of the catharsis experience.

We sometimes explain this concept of catharsis to our students in an analogy with the cinema. We have all had the experience of going to the cinema with a group of friends and seeing a film in which, while it is running, we are totally involved—we laugh, we cry, etc. But, when it is over, it is over. We leave the theater talking about other subjects, friends, events in our lives, etc.

On the other hand, we have all had the experience of going to the cinema with a group of friends and seeing a film, but when it is over we leave the theater and no one talks! The impact of the film can stay with us for days or more.

The first is an entertainment experience. The second is an aesthetic experience—we have been reached on a deeper level.

A similar analogy could be made with musical performances and Aristotle's concept of catharsis is just as appropriate to this experience. Some performances we applaud the accomplishments of the performers, or worse are merely amused, and go about our business, in other cases we are reached on a deeper level and something of the experience stays with us. This is the fundamental distinction between the aesthetic and the entertainment in music.

Aristotle makes some additional observations in this book which perhaps may also be appropriate to the musical experience. He disdains the poets who think first of the audience, 'merely following their public, writing as its wishes dictate.'[57] Closely related to this, he admits that just the fascination with the stage action, the 'spectacle,' can arouse pity and fear, but that it is better if they are aroused by the structure and incidents of the play. As an analogy with music we might think of the impact of the performance as opposed to the impact of the music itself.[58] He says the story should be simplified to a universal form; certainly universality is a characteristic of great music. But then, Aristotle makes an observation which seems to contradict the concept of universality.

> It may be argued that the less vulgar is the higher and the less vulgar is always that which addresses the better public, an art addressing any and every one is of a very vulgar order.[59]

He is using the word, vulgar, of course in the sense of *vulgus*, meaning the common people. He seems to suggest that great art cannot be understood by the masses. With respect to music and

57 *Poetics*, 1453a.34.

58 Of course the performance can detract from the aesthetic experience. In this regard, Aristotle complains about bad stage business, citing aulos players 'rolling about … pulling at the chorus leader. But this censure may have to do with the interpreter; it is quite possible to overdo gesturing.'

59 *Poetics*, 1461b.27.

theater he is wrong for here one can easily find the true meaning of universality. It might be appropriate to mention here a nice story Aristotle tells about a mad man who used to visit the theater on days when it was empty.

> It is said that a certain man in Abydos being deranged in mind, and coming into the theater during many days looked on (as though actors were performing a play), and applauded; and, when he was restored to his senses, he declared that that was the happiest time he had ever spent.[60]

60 *De Mirabilibus*, 832b.18.

Educational Music

In Aristotle we find a surprisingly long discussion of music education. Unlike his treatment of most other subjects, where he usually has a very clear idea to present, here[61] we find him struggling with the idea itself. In retrospect this most rational man no doubt struggled personally as he tried to find a way to bring music under rational discussion. It seems clear he knew it was non-rational in character, but what do you do with it? It is as if we are observing him in the act of talking to himself, trying out arguments, testing his deductions, and in general seeking a logical explanation for several rather clear beliefs which he seems to have had in the first place.

61 The discussion is found in the *Politics*, 8.2, beginning with line 1337.

He begins by stating that education is too important to be left to the parents. Since the effectiveness of the education of the young affects the entire community in the end, it should be available to everyone and it should be public and not private ('not as at present, when everyone looks after his own children separately, and gives them separate instruction of the sort which he thinks best.').

The next problem, with education in general, is that people do not agree on what the object of education itself should be. Is it to make someone useful in life? Is it to teach virtue? Is it to provide higher knowledge for its own sake? Of these three viewpoints, the first seems to him most questionable.

> There can be no doubt that children should be taught those useful things which are really necessary, but not all useful things; for occupations are divided into liberal and illiberal; and to young children should be imparted only such kinds of knowledge as will be useful to them without vulgarizing them. And any occupation, art, or science, which makes the body or soul or mind of the freeman less

fit for the practice or exercise of virtue, is vulgar; wherefore we call those arts vulgar which tend to deform the body, and likewise all paid employments, for they absorb and degrade the mind.[62]

62 Ibid., 1337b.3.

One additional conclusion seems clear to Aristotle at the outset: If one learns anything for the sake of his own improvement he will be applauded, but he learns for the sake of others [like learning a trade] he will be viewed menial and servile.

Aristotle reports the customary branches of education as being: [1] reading and writing, [2] gymnastic exercises, [3] music, and sometimes [4] drawing. Of these he finds reading and writing are the most useful for daily life; gymnastic exercises are thought to infuse courage; but concerning music 'a doubt may be raised.'

The doubt which Aristotle has about music being in the curriculum has to do with his concern regarding the role of music in society, its role after the period of education. First, he observes that at the present time 'men cultivate music for the sake of pleasure.'[63] But this does not seem right,

63 Ibid., 1337b, 29.

> Clearly we ought not to be amusing ourselves, for then amusement would be the end of life.

That is inconceivable to Aristotle and yet he understands that man needs 'relaxation and amusement' following serious occupations. The emotions they create in the soul are a relaxation and from this pleasure we obtain rest. He continues this line of thought observing that happiness is an end and should be accompanied by pleasure and not pain, that pleasure is regarded differently by different persons and that pleasure of the best man is the best. It is amusing to read this most prolific man conclude,

> The first principle of all action is leisure. Both are required, but leisure is better than occupation.[64]

64 Ibid., 1337b, 33.

The purpose of this entire discussion is to set the stage, and circuitously substantiate, his first conclusion, that music must have been first introduced into education for the purpose of training man to make the most positive use of his leisure time.

> And therefore our fathers admitted music into education, not on the ground either of its necessity or utility, for it is not necessary, nor indeed useful in the same manner as reading and writing, which are useful in moneymaking, in the management of a household, in

the acquisition of knowledge and in political life, nor like drawing, useful for a more correct judgment of the works of artists, nor again like gymnastic, which gives health and strength; for neither of these is to be gained from music. There remains, then, the use of music for intellectual enjoyment in leisure; which is in fact evidently the reason of its introduction.[65]

65   Ibid., 1338a.9 and 14.

But Aristotle must have known that was inadequate the minute he said it, for he must have known full well that things like managing the household and making money are not exactly lofty educational goals themselves. So he immediately follows this conclusion by adding a second one, that parents should train their sons in music not because it is useful or necessary, but because it is liberal and noble.[66]

66   Ibid., 1338a, 30.

He concludes this introduction to the justification of having music in the curriculum by two final observations, first that music has long been accepted.

The ancients are a witness to us, for their opinion may be gathered from the fact that music is one of the received and traditional branches of education.[67]

67   Ibid., 1338a, 35.

Second, that the essence of music education is performance and not lectures.

Now it is clear that in education practice must be used before theory, and the body be trained before the mind.[68]

68   Ibid., 1338b, 5.

Now Aristotle turns for a while to the subject of the use of gymnastic exercises in education where he felt on more comfortable ground for the effects of that branch of education are obvious to the observer. But he must return to his subject and he sighs, 'It is not easy to determine the nature of music, or why anyone should have a knowledge of it.'[69]

69   Ibid., 1339a, 15.

Is it for the sake of amusement and relaxation, like sleep and drinking?
Or shall we argue that music conduces to virtue, on the ground that it can form our minds and habituate us to true pleasures?
Or does it contribute to the enjoyment of leisure and mental cultivation?

After some discussion of the first and third of these possible reasons for having music in the school, he raises a new objection,

Even granting that music may form the character, the objection still holds: why should we learn ourselves?[70]

By this he means, can one not obtain the values of music by just being a listener rather than having to learn how to actually play an instrument? He points to the Lacedaemonians, whom he says followed this model and adds that we notice the gods, such as Zeus, do not sing or play the lyre. And furthermore 'we call professional performers vulgar; no freeman would play or sing unless he were intoxicated or in jest.'[71]

Once more Aristotle realizes he has wandered off the track and so he reminds us that the question is whether music is or is not to be part of education. Now he goes over the same ground, considering the value of music for relaxation and for 'innocent pleasures,' etc. When he returns again to the question of music developing the character of the student, Aristotle now mentions one of the most important reasons of all for having music in the schools. Failing the knowledge of modern clinical studies regarding the non-rational importance of our emotions, Aristotle does not quite realize the true importance of what he is saying but he is right on the mark. Music can help the student come to know himself with respect to his individual emotional template. He also recognizes in passing that some aspects of music are genetic.

> In addition to this common pleasure, felt and shared by all (for the pleasure given by music is natural, and therefore adapted to all ages and characters), may it not have also some influence over the character and the soul? It must have such an influence if characters are affected by it. And that they are so affected is proved in many ways, and not least by the power which the songs of Olympus exercise; for beyond question they inspire enthusiasm, and enthusiasm is an emotion of the ethical part of the soul.
>
> Besides, when men hear imitations, even apart from the rhythms and melodies themselves, their feelings move in sympathy. Since then music is a pleasure, and virtue consists in rejoicing and loving and hating aright, there is clearly nothing which we are so much concerned to acquire and to cultivate as the power of forming right judgments, and of taking delight in good dispositions and noble actions. Rhythm and melody supply imitations of anger and gentleness, and also of courage and temperance, and of all the qualities contrary to these, and of the other qualities of character, which hardly fall short of the real emotions, as we know from our

72 Ibid., 1340a. Also here a very rare reference by Aristotle to his listening to music.

own experience, for in listening to such compositions our souls undergo a change.[72]

Aristotle attributes the ability of music to thus move the emotions primarily to the ancient modes. Even though he describes them in relative detail, for example that some make men sad and grave and that others enfeeble the mind, we have no idea today what he is talking about. These early modes, Dorian, Phrygian, and Lydian were styles of the music of particular cities and not a single example has survived as the music was never notated.[73] He also gives rhythm credit for participating in this role of the emotions affecting character, but again we have no examples from which to understand what he was thinking of.

73 There are a few examples of so-called ancient Greek notation but these come from several hundred years after Aristotle, from the period known as the Roman Period of ancient Greece.

In another place, Aristotle makes the interesting observation that of everything perceived by all our senses, only that perceived by hearing, specifically music, influences character.

> Why is it that of all things which are perceived by the senses that which is heard alone possesses moral character? For music, even if it is unaccompanied by words, yet has character; whereas a color and an odor and a savor have not.[74]

74 *Problemata*, 919b.26.

In his *Prior Analytics,* in discussing facial expressions, Aristotle once again makes reference to his firm belief that the study of music influences character.

> It is possible to judge men's character from their physical appearance, if one grants that body and soul change together in all natural affections. No doubt after a man has learned music his soul has undergone a certain change.[75]

75 *Prior Analytics*, 2.27.

In summary, we can see Aristotle clearly took the subject seriously.

> The whole subject has been well treated by philosophical writers on this branch of education, and they confirm their arguments by facts.
>
> …
>
> There seems to be in us a sort of affinity to musical modes and rhythms, which makes some philosophers say that the soul is a tuning, others, that it possesses tuning.[76]

76 Ibid., 1340b, 17.

Now Aristotle begins to focus on the actual curriculum of music in the schools. He begins by answering a previous rhetorical question, Do you have to be a performer or can you not just be a listener?

Clearly there is a considerable difference made in the character by the actual practice of the music. It is difficult, if not impossible, for those who do not perform to be good judges of the performance of others … We conclude then that they should be taught music in such a way as to become not only critics but performers.[77]

77 Ibid., 8.6.1340b, 22ff.

The next question is, 'what [kind of music] is or is not suitable for different ages?' Aristotle suggests that those who are to answer this question, and we believe he means the music teachers,

must also be performers, and that they should begin to practice early, although when they are older they may be spared this execution; they must have learned to appreciate what is good and to delight in it, thanks to the knowledge which they acquired in their youth.[78]

78 Ibid., 1340b, 35.

In other words, they must not only have experience in teaching materials but they must be performers themselves in order to demonstrate before the class ('this execution').

Another question which had been raised was whether the study of music had a 'vulgarizing effect,' probably a reference to popular music ('vulgate'). For Aristotle this question entailed two considerations, the first being the actual music. He admits that 'it is quite possible that certain methods of teaching and learning music do really have a degrading effect.'[79] Here he makes two distinctions,[80] first that the level of student performance,

79 Ibid., 1341a, 4.
80 Ibid., 1341a, 10

should not aspire to reach the levels of 'those fantastic marvels of execution' which are now the fashion in professional contests and have now passed into education,

and second a question of the musical literature,

Let the young practice such music as we have prescribed until they are able to feel delight in noble melodies and rhythms, and not merely in that common part of music in which every slave or child and even some animals find pleasure.

The second question which centered on the possible 'vulgarizing effect' had to do, in Aristotle's mind, with the actual instruments used in class. Here his primary concern was that the aulos, an early proto-type oboe, was to be excluded.[81] This instrument he found was too exciting and not expressive of moral character. The proper time to use this instrument was not in instruction, but 'for

81 Ibid., 1341a, 18ff.

the relief of the passions.' The ancients were right, he concludes, in not allowing this instrument in the schools and it is also too difficult to play, citing the old myth of the goddess who destroyed her aulos when she noticed in a mirror how playing it made her face ugly. Other instruments which were also not recommended included the harp (too difficult) and those used in popular music, the heptagon, triangle and sambuca.

Aristotle also bans the 'professional mode of music education,' that used by performers whose goal is to give pleasure, 'that of a vulgar sort,' to the listeners and not for the sake of his own improvement.[82] It follows that 'the vulgarity of the spectator tends to lower the character of the music and therefore the performers.'

82 Ibid., 1341b, 10.

The topic in which we find Aristotle most interested in of all is the kinds of musical literature used in education.[83] First, he accepts the division of music proposed by 'certain philosophers' into ethical melodies (music), melodies of action and passionate or inspiring melodies, with each having 'as they say' a specific mode corresponding to it. He maintains further that music should be studied not for the sake of one of the above, but for many benefits, with a view to (1) education, (2) catharsis and (3) for the intellectual enjoyment, for relaxation and for recreation after exertion.

83 Ibid.,1341b, 33.

It is clear, he says, that all the modes must be used but not all in the same manner. And here once again Aristotle places the focus directly on the development of the emotions of the child.

> In education the most ethical modes are to be preferred, but in listening to the performances of others we may admit the modes of action and passions also. For feelings such as pity and fear, or, again, enthusiasm, exist very strongly in some souls, and have more or less influence over all. Some persons fall into a religious frenzy, whom we see as a result of the sacred melodies—when they have used the melodies that excite the soul to mystic frenzy—restored as though they had found healing and purgation. Those who are influenced by pity and fear, and every emotional nature, must have a like experience, and others in so far as each is susceptible to such emotions, and all are in a manner purged and their souls lightened and delighted. The purgative melodies likewise give an innocent pleasure to mankind.[84]

84 Ibid, 1342a. Some of these modes were apparently so associated with particular forms, that Aristotle cites [1342b, 10] an instance of a performer who attempted to perform a dithyramb, 'acknowledged to be Phrygian,' in the Dorian and could not do it.

After a brief mention of the emotional needs of the different classes of listeners, Aristotle returns to a discussion of the modes used in education. For ethical music the Dorian is recommended, 'though we may include any others which are approved by philoso-phers who have had a musical education.'[85]

> All men agree that the Dorian music is the gravest and manliest. And whereas we say that the extremes should be avoided and the mean followed, and whereas the Dorian is a mean between the other modes, it is evident that our youth should be taught the Dorian music.[86]

86 Here Aristotle criticizes Socrates as having been wrong to admit the Phrygian in education, because it was associated with the aulos— too exciting.

Finally, Aristotle, in observing that there is music appropriate to every age, makes a brief reference to the elderly, those who have lost their powers and cannot sing very well. Nature herself seems to suggest that their songs should be of the more relaxed kind.

> And so, with a view also to the time of life when men begin to grow old, they ought to practice the gentler modes and melodies as well as the others, and, further any mode, such as the Lydian above all others appears to be, which is suited to children of tender age, and possesses the elements both of order and of education.[87]

87 Ibid., 1342b, 28.

Thus it is clear, Aristotle concludes, that education should be based upon three principles,

> the mean (literature of neither extreme), the possible (not using inappropriate instruments) and the becoming (referring to the emotional development of the child), these three.

Before leaving the subject of education, we might mention that in his book, *Ethica Nicomachea*, Aristotle briefly mentions the question of the monetary value of education. Should the value of the education be established by the teacher or the student? While he indicates this should probably be a fixed fee, he mentions an anecdote about Protagoras.

> Whenever he taught anything whatsoever, he bade the learner assess the value of the knowledge, and accepted the amount.[88]

88 Ibid. 1164a.22.

A practice some music educators today might find risky!

Aristotle, in his extant books, does not discuss functional music. His remarks on entertainment music are limited to his above dis-cussion of amusement, with respect to the styles appropriate to music education.

14 THE ALEXANDRIAN PERIOD OF ANCIENT GREECE (323–146 BC)

The period which begins with the defeat of the Greeks by Philip of Macedonia, in 338 BC, and includes the reign of his son, Alexander the Great, was the beginning of the end of the glory of ancient Greece. Indeed, one might date the rapid decline of the Greek culture from the year 323–322 BC, which saw the death of both Alexander and Aristotle.[1] Chief among the generals who divided up the empire of Alexander was Ptolemy, who became king of Egypt, made Alexandria his capital and built his famous library there. Because he invited important scholars and artists to join him, many of the writers who document the decline of Greece were residents of Alexandria. Athenaeus quotes from the Chronicles of one of these writers, Andron of Alexandria, regarding this critical period.

> The Alexandrians were the teachers of all Greeks and barbarians [meaning Macedonians] at a time when the entire system of general education had broken down by reason of the continually recurring disturbances which took place in the period of Alexander's successors. I say, then, a rejuvenation of all culture was again brought about in the reign of the seventh Ptolemy who ruled over Egypt, the king who received from the Alexandrians appropriately the name of Malefactor. For he murdered many of the Alexandrians; not a few he sent into exile, and filled the islands and towns with men who had grown up with his brother—philologians, philosophers, mathematicians, musicians, painters, athletic trainers, physicians, and many other men of skill in their profession.[2]

The great central themes of Greek thought now began to disintegrate into a number of schools of philosophy, from the Cynics, who spoke of virtue and abstinence, to the Epicurians, who said pleasure was the highest good. Music, of course, was not immune to these disturbances. While music was a topic discussed by nearly all important earlier Greek philosophers, it is notable that the philosophers of the Alexandrian Period (with the exception of Aristotle's student, Aristoxenus) rarely mention it at all.

We can best witness the general decline of musical practice in the writings of the writers who followed the Alexandrian Period, chiefly in the work of Athenaeus.

1 The decline may have begun somewhat earlier, as Athenaeus, in *Deipnosophistae*, 1.3, cites the comic poet Eupolis (d. 411 BC) as having mentioned that the works of Pindar were already a 'sealed book, because of the decay of popular taste.'

2 Atheanaeus, *Deipnosophistae*, 4.184.

ART MUSIC

Athenaeus epitomizes the decline of Art Music during this period as a movement from an aim for the noble and beautiful to an aim of merely pleasing the crowd.

In olden times the feeling for nobility was always maintained in the art of music, and all its elements skillfully retained the orderly beauty appropriate to them. Hence there were flutes[3] peculiarly adapted to every mode, and every player had flutes suited to every mode used in the public contests. But Pronomus of Thebes began the practice of playing all the modes on the same auloi. Today, however, people take up music in a haphazard and irrational manner. In early times popularity with the masses was a sign of bad art; hence, when a certain aulos player once received loud applause, Asopodorus of Phlius, who was himself still waiting in the wings, said, 'What's this? Something awful must have happened!' The player evidently could not have won approval with the crowd otherwise. And yet the musicians of our day set as the goal of their art success with their audiences.[4]

3   The aulos.

4   Athenaeus, *Deipnosophistae.*, 14.631.

Athenaeus also quotes from a lost book, *Drinking Miscellany*, by Aristoxenus, a student of Aristotle and eyewitness to this period of decline. Aristoxenus had been speaking of the people of Poseidonia, 'who were originally Greeks, but had been completely barbarized, becoming Tuscans or Romans; changing their speech and other practices,' and then adds,

In like manner we also, now that our theaters have become utterly barbarized and prostituted and music has moved on into a state of grave corruption, will get together by ourselves, few though we be, and recall what the art of music used to be.[5]

5   Ibid., 14.632. The Greeks used the term 'barbarized' to refer to one who did not speak Greek well.

Some playwrights themselves commented on how music was being misused in the theater. The writer of comedies, Pherecrates, for example, introduces a character called Music, all bruised and battered and dressed in woman's clothes. Justice asks what is wrong and Music replies,

Music
'Tis mine to speak, thy part to hear,
And therefore lend a willing ear;
Much have I suffered, long opprest
By Meanlippides, that beast;

He haled me from Parnassus' springs,
And plagued me with a dozen strings.
His rage however sufficed not yet,
To make my miseries complete.
Cinesias, that cursed Attic,
A mere poetical pragmatic,
Such horrid strophes in mangled verse
Made the unharmonious stage rehearse,
That I, tormented with the pains
Of cruel dithyrambic strains,
Distorted song, that you would swear
The right side now the left side were.
Nor did my miseries end here;
For Phrynis with his whirlwind brains,
Wringing and racking all my veins,
Ruined me quite, while nine small wires
With harmonies twice six he tires.
Yet might not he so much be blamed,
From all his errors soon reclaimed;
But then Timotheus with his freaks
Furrowed my face, and ploughed my cheeks.

Justice
Say which of them so vile could be?

Music
Milesian Pyrrhias, that was he,
Whose fury tortured me much more
Than all that I have named before;
Where'er I walk the streets alone,
If met by him, the angry clown,
With his twelve cat-guts strongly bound,
He leaves me helpless on the ground.[6]

According to Plutarch[7] this decline began early in the fourth century BC, for he quotes a passage from a lost work by Aristophanes which complains of the poet Philoxenus introducing lyric verses in the middle of the choruses. Again, a character called Music speaks.

He filled me with discordant measures airy,
Wicked Hyperbolaei and Niglari;
And to uphold the follies of his play,
Like a lank radish bowed me every [which] way.

6 Quoted by Plutarch, in *Concerning Music*. The sixteenth line must be a figure of speech and not a reference to the bicameral brain.

7 Ibid.

8   In ibid., 8.352, Athenaeus says Stratonicus was 'the first to introduce multiplicity of notes in simple harp playing; he was also the first to receive pupils in harmony, and to compile a table of musical intervals.'

Athenaeus introduces us to a witty harp player of the Alexandrian Period, Stratonicus of Athens,[8] whose comments on the other artists he heard give us an eyewitness view of the decline in Art Music.

In Byzantium a harp singer sang his prelude beautifully, but made a mess of the songs that followed. Stratonicus got up and made the proclamation: 'Whoever will reveal the hiding place of the harp singer who sang the prelude will receive a thousand drachmas.'

...

Giving a recital in Rhodes and receiving no applause, he left the theater remaking, 'If you won't give that which costs you nothing, how can I expect to receive a *fee* from you?'

...

When King Ptolemy was discussing with him, rather too contentiously, the art of harp playing, he said, 'O King, a scepter is one thing, a plectrum is another.'

...

Having been invited on one occasion to hear a harp singer, after the recital he said, 'And the Father granted one part to him, but denied him the other.' When someone asked, 'Which part?' he answered: 'He granted the power to play badly, but denied the power to sing beautifully.'

...

After winning a contest in Sicyon, he dedicated in the Temple of Asclepius a memorial with the inscription: 'Dedicated by Stratonicus from the spoils of bad harp players.'[9]

9   Ibid., 8.350 and following. Speaking once of 'art' in more general terms, he observed that 'a poor doctor could send his patients to Hades in a single day.'

We should add that his habit of making these kinds of remarks cost Stratonicus his life, for after making fun of the son of Nicocles, King of Cyprus, he was forced to drink poison!

Athenaeus also mentions an equally strong willed aulos player of the Alexandrian Period, named Dorion, who is discussed by several early writers.[10] Once when dining in the house of a nobleman in Cyprus he praised a cup. When the nobleman offered to have another made for him by the same craftsman, Dorion answered, 'No, he can make one for you; I'll take this one.' Athenaeus explained this improper response to a nobleman by a musician in an old saying, 'In an aulos player the gods implanted no sense; no, for with his blowing his sense takes wing and flies from him.' Athenaeus quotes another, more touching, story about this musician by the writer, Aristodemus.

10   Ibid., 8.337ff.

Dorion the music master, who was club-footed, once lost the shoe
of his lame foot at a dinner party. He said: 'I shall utter no heavier
curse upon the thief than the wish that that sandal may fit him.'

Educational Music

Athenaeus writes that Stratonicus, as a teacher, had only two students but in his studio he had statues of the nine Muses as well as
one of Apollo. Thus, when someone asked him how many pupils
he had, he would answer, 'With the assistance of the gods, around
a dozen.'[11] We are also told he had a tablet on the wall of his studio
which read, 'In protest against all bad harpists.'

    Once when he heard a recital by the students of another harp
teacher, who himself was not a very good player, Stratonicus told
those present, 'The man who cannot teach himself to play because
he is so bad, is seen at his worst when he tries to teach others.'

    Two more views of Stratonicus as a teacher are provided
by Athenaeus:

> While giving a harp lesson to a Helvetian pupil, he became enraged
> at the pupil's failure to do as he was told and cried out, 'To hell-veta
> with you!'
>
> …
>
>   To a student of music who had formerly been a gardener and who
> got into an argument with him on a question of music, he quoted,
> 'Every man should tend the art he knows.'

Functional Music

Athenaeus includes a description, taken from a lost book by Chares,
of a lavish wedding given by Alexander after his defeat of Darius.
While the account does not describe the actual wedding music, it
is valuable for its rare listing of names of aulos and harp players
who performed, as well as singers, dancers, and poets.[12]

    Stratonicus is mentioned again by Athenaeus, now in the midst
of a cult-religious ceremony.

> When a poor aulos player was on the point of playing his instrument
> at a sacrifice, Stratonicus said, 'Hush, until we've poured a libation
> and prayed to the gods!'[13]

11   Ibid., 8.348 and following.

12   Ibid., 12.538ff.

13   Ibid., 8.349.

Entertainment Music

With the general decay of the Greek culture, one class of musicians apparently prospered. These were the prostitute single-pipe girls, some of whom now became wealthy. Athenaeus gives a lengthy account of such a girl, named Lamia (third century BC), who even gave a dinner for the king of Macedonia![14]

As mentioned above, the general decay in music was one that moved from art to entertainment. This change in attitude can be seen in a lost play by Sotion, called *The Teacher of Profligacy*, of which Athenaeus preserves for us a portion of dialog which mentions the 'concert hall' of Athens, the Odeum. A character says,

> What's this nonsense you are talking, forever babbling, this way and that, of the Lyceum, the Academy, and the Odeum gates—mere sophists' rubbish? There's no good in them. Let's drink, and drink our fill, Let's have a good time while we may still keep the life in our bodies. Whoop it up, Men! There's nothing nicer than the belly.[15]

Athenaeus attributes much of this kind of attitude to Epicurus (who indeed said, 'The beginning and the root of all good is the pleasure of the stomach.'[16]) and his followers, 'those who walk with eyebrows uplifted,' whom he says believed that 'pleasure is the highest Good.'[17] Certainly we may take as an illustration of the Alexandrian Epicurean, Athenaeus' account of one, Caranus of Macedonia, and the banquet he gave for twenty of his friends to celebrate his marriage.[18]

We are told that as the guests arrived they received as gifts gold tiaras and silver cups. The first course included duck, ringdove, chicken, and a goose; the second course featured rabbit, more geese, young goats, pigeons, turtle-doves, partridge, and other fowl. The custom was for the guest to merely sample this and then pass the rest back to their servants behind a curtain. More gifts followed and then drinks.

Now the single-pipe girls entered, together with other entertainers. 'To me,' goes the account, 'these girls looked quite naked, but some said that they had on tunics. After a prelude they withdrew.' Another round of gifts followed: jars of gold and silver, perfume, and a great silver platter with a roast pig, filled with a variety of small fowl. Again gifts were distributed: more perfume, more gold and silver, and breadbaskets made of ivory.

14   Ibid., 3.101 and 13.577ff.

15   Ibid., 8.336. In Book 8, 339, Athenaeus also mentions a profligate harp player.

16   Epicurus, *Epicurus: The Extant Remains*, trans. Cyril Bailey (Oxford: Clarendon Press, 1926), 135.

17   Ibid., 7.279.

18   Ibid., 4.128ff.

Next more entertainers appeared, including naked female jugglers who performed tumbling acts among swords and blew fire from their mouths. This was followed by more gifts: a large gold cup for each guest, a large silver platter filled with baked fish, a double jar of perfume and gold tiaras twice the size of the first ones.

After a round of drinking a chorus of one hundred men entered, 'singing tunefully a wedding hymn; then came in dancing girls, some attired as Nereids, others as Nymphs.' Now a curtain was drawn back revealing statues of Cupids, Dianas, Pans, and Hermae holding torches in silver brackets. While they were admiring this, 'veritable Erymanthian boars' were served to each guest, on square platters rimmed with gold and skewered with silver spears.

The sounding of a trumpet announced the end of the banquet and the enriched guests all went out to look for real estate agents!

15 THE ALEXANDRIAN PHILOSOPHERS

It is with the generation after Aristotle that we come to the one person who should have answered all our questions about Greek music of the fourth and fifth centuries BC. His name is Aristoxenus (b. ca. 379 BC), he was a student of Aristotle's and he specialized in writing books on music. Unfortunately, most of his books are lost, among them *On Aulos Players*, *On The Aulos and Musical Instruments*,[1] *On Aulos Boring*,[2] *On Music*, and *Brief Notes*, whose titles are mentioned by Athenaeus.

Because no actual music from the fifth and sixth centuries, the period of Socrates through Aristotle, has survived and because the extant information pertains to how music was used in society and not in detailed description of the actual music, scholars tend to treat Aristoxenus as a fundamental authority. We have known professors whose entire understanding of the music of the ancient Greek period is drawn from this one writer. We regret having to disappoint those who have taken notes in such classes, but the fact is there is very little useful information to be found in Aristoxenus. All that has come down to us is one chapter of one book, *Elements of Rhythm*, and three chapters of another, *Elements of Harmony*. In the case of the latter book, the three chapters seem to come from the beginning of the book and much of the material deals with definitions of terms and an outline of what he will be discussing in the greater portion of the book which is now lost. He takes great care in this as he seems to sense a difficulty in what he is trying to do. Upon defining a 'scale' as 'the compound of two or more intervals,' for example, he begs the reader to remember that music is not easy to define.

> Here we would ask our hearers to receive these definitions in the right spirit, not with the jealous scrutiny of the degree of their exactness. We would ask him to aid us with his intelligent sympathy, and to consider our definition sufficiently instructive when it puts him in the way of understanding the thing defined. To supply a definition which affords an unexceptionable and exhaustive analysis is a difficult task.[3]

1 Athenaeus, in *Deipnosophistae*, 4.174, quotes Aristoxenus, probably from this book, as saying he preferred string instruments to winds, as the winds were too easy—as, for example, people like shepherds can learn to play panpipes without even being taught! In 4.183, Athenaeus quotes from an unnamed book of Aristoxenus regarding string instruments.

2 Athenaeus, *Deipnosophistae*, 14.634, quotes from this book that Aristoxenus knew five kinds of aulos, which he named: the virginal, child-pipes, harp-pipes, complete, and super-complete.

3 Aristoxenus, *The Elements of Harmony*, 16, trans. Henry Stewart Macran (Hildesheim: Georg Olms Verlag, 1974).

We regret all the more the loss of the bulk of this book, for he also seems to have the intent to present a very complete discussion, something he found missing in former books on music. In his preface to the discussion of scales, for instance, he mentions,

> Our forerunners simply ignored the distinction between 'melodious' and 'unmelodious'; as to the second, they either made no attempt at all at enumeration of scale-distinctions ... or if they made the attempt, they fell very short of completeness, like the school of Pythagoras of Zacynthus, and Agenor of Mitylene. The order that distinguishes the melodious from the unmelodious resembles that which we find in the collocation of letters in language. For it is not every collocation but only certain collocations of any given letters that will produce a syllable.

His 'complete' discussion of what this all means is, again, lost.

We do possess enough of this book to see that 'mode' by this time has come to mean something similar to a system of scales, but they are so different from what we think of as scales today that the reader can read this material and still have little confidence that he really understands the full meaning of what Aristoxenus has written. As the English translator, Henry Macran, concludes, 'it is impossible for us now to recover the meaning of this dead music of ancient Greece.'[4] This is particularly evident with respect to the question of the 'character' of these modes, which was so often mentioned by earlier Greek writers. Even now that these modes resemble scales, it is clear that there is more to what they mean, as Aristoxenus points out.

4   Ibid., p. 3.

> [Just because] a man notes down the Phrygian scale it does not follow that he must know the *essence* of the Phrygian scale. Plainly then notation is not the ultimate limit of our science.[5]

5   Ibid., 39.

And once again, his more complete explanation is lost.

From the book on rhythm we have only one chapter, but it is a chapter of considerable detail. His discussion concentrates on what we might call the mathematical description of rhythm, but he seemed to be aware that this does not fully explain how we use and hear rhythm in an aesthetic sense.

> It hardly needs argument to convince us that not every arrangement of time-lengths is rhythmical. But we must pay attention to the analogies and try to understand what they reveal, until proof is provided by actual observation and experience.

We are familiar with what happens in combinations of letters of the alphabet and combinations of musical intervals. We know that we cannot combine letters at random in speech or musical intervals in singing. There are only a few combinations that we actually use, and numerous ones that the voice cannot reproduce in pronunciation and our sense of hearing refuses to accept and rejects.[6]

It is especially interesting that in discussing the division of Time, in two places he seems to suggest the existence of something like the modern conductor, once saying 'signals' are necessary to make the division and in another place, 'Rhythm cannot exist without … someone to divide the time.'[7]

We have only enough of these books to give us a full sense of our loss that the rest is not extant.

THE PHYSIOLOGY OF AESTHETICS

We have seen above how earlier philosophers struggled with trying to explain the distinction between understanding through reason and understanding through the senses. Now, one philosopher of the Alexandrian Period of Greece, Pyrrho (360–270 BC), a representative of the Sceptic School, points out that one can not really completely trust either one, for 'the senses can deceive, and reason says different [conflicting] things.'[8] It is a good point and certainly one that is reflected in all the incorrect explanations of natural science arrived at by 'reason' among some of these early philosophers. Epicurus (342–270 BC), founder of the Epicurean School of philosophy, for example, gave four possible, but incorrect, explanations for what causes thunder.

Thunder may be produced by the rushing about of wind in the hollows of the clouds, as happens in vessels on earth; or by the reverberation of fire filled with wind inside them; or by the rending and tearing of clouds; or by the friction and bursting of clouds when they have been congealed into a form like ice.[9]

Of particular interest for our subject, is the continuing attempt to explain the various kinds of knowledge which today we understand through the separate natures of the left and right hemispheres of our bicameral brain. Zeno (333–261 BC), founder of the Stoic School of philosophy divided man's being into three parts, the physical, the ethical, and the logical, which he explained in the simile of an

6   Aristoxenus, *Elementa Rhythmica*, trans. Lionel Pearson (Oxford: Clarendon Press, 1990), 8.

7   Michael Psellus, *Introduction to the Study of Rhythm*, quoted in Aristoxenus, ibid , 23, 25. Psellus is a later author who seems to have copied his material from portions of the Aristoxenus books which are now lost.

8   Quoted in Diogenes Laertius, *Lives of the Eminent Philosophers*, trans., Robert Drew Hicks (Cambridge, MA: Harvard University Press, 1950), 2.507. Pyrrho, in ibid., 2.511, arrives at the conclusion that there is no such thing as motion. Another Diogenes (ca. 404–323 BC), founder of the Cynic School of philosophy, on hearing a similar statement, answered by simply getting up and walking around the room!

9   'Letter to Pythoclea,' in Epicurus, *Epicurus: The Extant Remains*, trans. Cyril Bailey (Oxford: Clarendon Press, 1926), 69.

egg: the shell is Logic, the white is Ethics, and the yolk, the center, is Physics.[10] Ariston (320–250 BC), a student of Zeno, spoke of the same three characteristics, but discarded Physics, as beyond our reach, and Logic, which does not concern us, concluding that only Ethics should matter.[11]

Zeno recognized both the rational and the non-rational, the former being processes of thought and the latter 'having no name.'[12] In the category of the 'irrational,' Zeno includes passion and emotion, of which he finds four classes: grief, fear, desire or craving, and pleasure.[13]

Zeno applied the term 'sense' to three things: the 'current' passing from the principal part of the soul to the senses; apprehension by means of the senses; and the apparatus of the sense organs, in which some persons are deficient. Interestingly enough, he points out that our 'impressions' may be either scientific or unscientific, which he illustrates in the example of a statue, which is seen differently by the trained eye of a sculptor and by an ordinary man— but he makes no reference here to art. Indeed, in the end, Zeno, like Plato and Aristotle before him, places his faith primarily in the rational.

> Of the three kinds of life, the contemplative, the practical, and the rational, we ought to choose the last, for that a rational being is expressly produced by nature for contemplation and for action.[14]

Epicurus, on the other hand, was one of the first philosophers who understood that 'reason' is not enough. We have an expression today, 'Seeing is believing,' which we have heard corrected thus, 'No, seeing is understanding; *feeling* is believing.' This, too, is what Epicurus meant when he argued that by 'feelings and the senses you will obtain the most trustworthy ground of belief.'[15] Sensations, he thought, must be spread throughout the body, because a person who has lost a limb still experiences sensation.[16] Further, he observed that language developed from natural sounds, caused by feelings and impressions, thus proving that nature had to come first and reason later.[17]

Theophrastus (372–287 BC), also a student of Aristotle, was another who was not prepared to trust everything to reason. In his *Metaphysics*, he begins by asking, is there not some 'connection and, as it were, a mutual partnership between objects of reason and the things of nature.'[18] He wished to explore this question because it was obvious to him that,

10   Diogenes Laertius, *Lives of the Eminent Philosophers*, 2.149ff.

11   Ibid., 2.265.

12   Ibid., 2.161ff.

13   Ibid., 2.217.

14   Ibid., 2.235.

15   Epicurus, *Epicurus*, 39 and 21.

16   Ibid., 41.

17   Ibid., 47ff.

18   Theophrastus, *Metaphysics*, trans. William David Ross and Francis Howard Fobes (Hildesheim: Georg Olms Verlag, 1967), 2.

If the objects of reason are found in mathematical objects only, as some say, [then] neither is their connection with the objects of sense very conspicuous, nor do they appear, in general equal to their whole task.[19]

He believed there must be 'ruling principles' which were superior to, and governed, both mathematics and nature. For even in the arts, 'which imitate nature, both the instruments and everything else depend on the ruling principles.'[20]

Next he makes the interesting statement that 'in general we must understand matter by virtue of an analogy with the arts.'[21] By this he was no doubt thinking of an observation which many early philosophers had made, that both music and nature consist of contrasts, and which he phrases in the form of a question:

Why is it that nature, and indeed the whole substance of the universe, consists of contraries?

This is also true with respect to 'knowledge,' which he says also, 'does not exist without some difference[s of opinion].' This is why he was not prepared to trust everything to reason.

With respect to music, Aristoxenus, alone among these philosophers, seems to have understood the mind in terms that seem familiar today. Although he could not have understood the true natures of the left and right hemispheres of the brain, he nevertheless uses the right synonyms for them, the intellect vs. the form of the music the ear hears.

It is plain that the apprehension of a melody consists in noting with both ear and intellect every distinction as it arises in the successive sounds—successive, for melody, like all branches of music, consists in a successive production. For the apprehension of music depends on these two faculties, sense-perception and memory; for we must perceive the sound that is present, and remember that which is past. In no other way can we follow the phenomena of music.[22]

With regard to hearing music, he also makes a statement which we think could only have been made by a philosopher who was also a musician.

The truth is that of all the objects to which the five senses apply, not one other is characterized by an orderliness so extensive and so perfect.[23]

19 Ibid., 3.

20 Ibid., 14.

21 Ibid., 17 and following.

22 Aristoxenus, *The Elements of Harmony*, 41.

23 Ibid., 5.

The Philosophy of Aesthetics

For Epicurus, pleasure is the primary object of life.

> We have need of pleasure, when we feel pain owing to the absence of pleasure … And for this cause we call pleasure the beginning and end of the blessed life. For we recognize pleasure as the first good innate in us, and from pleasure we begin every act of choice and avoidance, and to pleasure we return again, using the feeling as the standard by which we judge every good.[24]

In applying this principle to art, Epicurus added that 'the beautiful' has no value if it does not produce pleasure.[25]

One might imagine that a philosophy based on pleasure must have been attractive to many. Indeed, when someone observed that pupils from other schools went over to Epicurus, but converts were never made from the Epicureans, Arcesilaus (318–242 BC), a member of the Skeptic School, answered, 'Because men may become eunuchs, but a eunuch never becomes a man!'[26]

Diogenes pointed out that in some cases the opposite of pleasure can be pleasure to some men, as for example in the rigorous training of the athlete or in the 'incessant toil' necessary to be a musician. 'Yet,' he says, 'such is their madness that they choose to be miserable.'[27]

The Stoic School considered art as being more related to virtue, much as did Plato and Aristotle earlier, associating 'the beautiful' with 'the good.'[28] Zeno added, as characteristics of the beautiful, that which has 'perfect proportion' and that which 'lends new grace to anything.'[29] He also observed that 'pleasure is an irrational elation' and 'to be in transports of delight is the melting away of virtue.'[30] We doubt that he was thinking of music in making this statement, for when someone once commended Theophrastus for having more students than any other philosopher, Zeno replied, 'His chorus is indeed larger than mine, but mine has the sweeter voices.'[31]

Pleasure, he seemed to associate not with art as we understand it today, but with the more utilitarian aspects of life, pointing to the work of the craftsman as an example of how 'Nature aims at both utility and at pleasure.'[32]

Finally, Pyrrho believed that nothing was good or bad by nature, for if this were true something would have to be good or bad for all

24   Epicurus, *Epicurus*, 87.

25   Ibid., 139.

26   Diogenes Laertius, *Lives of the Eminent Philosophers*, 2.421.

27   Ibid., 2.73. One of the most memorable statements of Diogenes was in response to someone who asked why it was that people give to beggars but not to philosophers? He answered, 'Because they think they may one day be lame or blind, but never expect that they will turn to philosophy.' He also once called Plato's lectures, 'a waste of time.'

28   Ibid., 2.207ff.

29   Ibid.

30   Ibid., 2.219ff.

31   Quoted by Plutarch in 'Of Man's Progress in Virtue.'

32   Ibid., 2.253.

persons alike, 'just as snow is cold to all.' This concept he would no doubt apply to art, for he concludes by observing,

> But there is no good or bad which is such to all persons in common; therefore there is no such thing as good or bad by nature. For either all that is thought good by anyone whatever must be called good, or not at all … But if we say that not all that anyone thinks good is good, we shall have to judge the different opinions; and this is impossible because of the equal validity of opposing arguments. Therefore the good by nature is unknowable.[33]

33 Ibid., 2.513.

As mentioned above, these Alexandrian philosophers rarely mention music. We know from occasional references, for example, that the concert hall, the Odeum,[34] still existed in Athens, but performance itself is not discussed. There is certainly no mention of the importance of music, as an art or in education, comparable to what we have read in the writings of Plato and Aristotle. Nevertheless, there are a few oblique references from which we might draw information.

34 In one such reference we are told that the Stoic philosopher, Chrysippus (282–206 BC) died just after taking his students to a performance at the Odeum.

ART MUSIC

While in the literature of the fifth and sixth centuries BC, one never reads of a *poor* performance, during the Alexandrian Period we begin to see such references. There was a musician who always saw his audiences get up and leave early, whom Diogenes named 'Rooster.' When the musician asked why he called him this, Diogenes answered, 'Because your song makes every one get up.'[35] There is reason to suppose that Diogenes may have heard a number of unsuccessful performers, because after an observation regarding the 'incessant toil' required to be a musician, he adds that if instead they had 'transferred their efforts to the training of the mind, certainly their labors would not have been [so] unprofitable or ineffective.'[36]

35 Diogenes Laertius, *Lives of the Eminent Philosophers*, 2.49.

36 Ibid., 2.73.

The famous orator of this period, Demosthenes (385–322 BC), suggests in one of his speeches that he too was not hearing performances of lasting impression. He regrets the large amount of money spent on choral performances 'which affords those of us who are in the theater gratification for a fraction of a day.'[37] On the other hand, in another place he indicates that the annual Spring Festivals were still being given on a lavish scale.

37 Demosthenes, *Against Leptines*, trans. James Herbert Vince (Cambridge, MA: Harvard University Press, 1954), 509.

38   'The First Philippic,' ibid., 89.

Larger sums are lavished upon them than upon any one of your [military] expeditions [and] they are celebrated with bigger crowds and greater splendor than anything else of the kind in the world.[38]

But perhaps these 'bigger crowds' only reflect the shift toward entertainment music which philosophers of this period speak of. We note, for example, that an aulos player whom Zeno complimented,

39   Diogenes Laertius, Lives of the Eminent Philosophers, 2.229.

> The wise man does all things well, just as we say that Ismenias plays all melodies on the aulos well,[39]

40   Ibid., 1.399.

is mentioned rather disrespectfully by another aulos player, Dionysodorus, who comments that no one will ever hear him play, like Ismenias, on ships or at the fountain in the town square![40]

There is one description of an actual repertoire work played at the contests of this period, and we even know the name of the composer, one Timosthenes (fl. ca. 270 BC). This work, performed by rhapsodists with either aulos or lyre accompanying, told the story of a contest between Apollo and a dragon. It consisted of a prelude, the battle, the triumph following the victory, and the expiration of the dragon—with the aulos player imitating the last hissings of the dragon.[41]

41   Strabo, The Geography of Strabo, 9.3.10.

Educational Music

We have spoken, above, of the fact that several early Greek writers have referred to an aesthetic decline in music away from the ideals of the early Greeks toward a goal of mere entertainment. It follows that there must have also been some weakening in the traditional beliefs regarding music and the development of character. We can see evidence of this in a writer of the following period, Strabo, who attacks the philosophy of the Alexandrian writer Eratosthenes (276–194 BC).

> Eratosthenes contends that the aim of every poet is to entertain, not to instruct. The ancients assert, on the contrary, that poetry is a kind of elementary philosophy, which, taking us in our very boyhood, introduces us to the art of life and instructs us, with pleasure to ourselves, in character, emotions, and actions … Why, even the musicians, when they give instruction in singing, in lyre playing, or in aulos playing … maintain that these studies tend to discipline and correct the character.[42]

42   Strabo, ibid., 1.2.3.

Strabo goes on to say that Aristoxenus was one of those who 'declares the same thing.' Plutarch, who knew the now lost books on music by Aristoxenus, also mentions that the latter spoke on the value of music in forming character. Indeed, Plutarch quotes from one of these lost books a story by which Aristoxenus meant to demonstrate that proper lessons once learned become part of the character and cannot be easily changed.

> Now that the right molding or ruin of ingenuous manners and civil conduct lies in a well-grounded musical education, Aristoxenus has made apparent. For, of those that were contemporary with him, he gives an account of Telesias the Theban, who in his youth was bred up in the noblest excellences of music, and moreover studied the works of the most famous lyric poets, Pindar, Dionysius the Theban, Lamprus, Pratinas, and all the rest who were accounted most eminent; who played also to perfection upon the aulos, and was not a little industrious to furnish himself with all those other accomplishments of learning; but being past the prime of his age, he was so bewitched with the theater's new fangles and the innovations of multiplied notes, that despising those noble precepts and that solid practice to which he had been educated, he betook himself to Philoxenus and Timotheus, and among those delighted chiefly in such as were most depraved with diversity of notes and baneful innovation. And yet, when he made it his business to make verses and labor both ways, as well in that of Pindar as that of Philoxenus, he could have no success in the latter. And the reason proceeded from the truth and exactness of his first education.[43]

43   Quoted by Plutarch in 'Concerning Music.'

In the only surviving specimens of Aristoxenus' writing which mentions this point, he is a bit more guarded with respect to music and education.

> Some consider Harmonie a sublime science, and expect a course of it to make them musicians; nay some even conceive it will exalt their moral nature. This mistake is due to their having run away with such phrases in our preamble as ... 'one class of musical art is hurtful to the moral character, another improves it'; while they missed completely our qualification of this statement, 'in so far as musical art can improve the moral character.'[44]

44   Aristoxenus, *The Elements of Harmony*, 31.

No early writer addresses this topic with more heartfelt passion than the historian Polybius. He departs from his description of the internal wars of the period 220–216 BC to give a fervent testimonial to the role music plays in shaping the character of entire peoples and a plea that the Cynaetheans return to this use of music to save themselves. In the course of his argument he gives us one of the most extraordinary pictures of the educational use of music ('I mean *real* music,' he says) in ancient Greece.

It is worth while to give a moment's consideration to the question of the savagery of the Cynaetheans, and ask ourselves why, though unquestionably of Arcadian stock, they so far surpassed all other Greeks at this period in cruelty and wickedness. I think the reason was they were the first and indeed the only people in Arcadia to abandon an admirable institution, introduced by their forefathers with a nice regard for the natural conditions under which all the inhabitants of that country live.

For the practice of music, I mean real music, is beneficial to all men, but to Arcadians it is a necessity. For we must not suppose, as Ephorus, in his Preface to his History, making a hasty assertion quite unworthy of him, says, that music was introduced by men for the purpose of deception and delusion; we should not think that the ancient Cretans and Lacedaemonians acted at haphazard in substituting the aulos and rhythmic movement for the trumpet in war, or that the early Arcadians had no good reason for incorporating music in their whole public life to such an extent that not only boys, but young men up to the age of thirty were compelled to study it constantly, although in other matters their lives were most austere.

For it is a well-known fact, familiar to all, that it is hardly known except in Arcadia, that in the first place the boys from their earliest childhood are trained to sing in measure the hymns and paeans in which by traditional usage they celebrate the heroes and gods of each particular place; later they learn the measures of Philoxenus and Timotheus, and every year in the theater they compete keenly in choral singing to the accompaniment of professional aulos players, the boys in the contest proper to them and the young men in what is called the men's contest. And not only this, but through their whole life they entertain themselves at banquets not by listening to hired musicians but by their own efforts, calling for a song from each in turn. Whereas they are not ashamed of denying acquaintance with other studies, in the case of singing it is neither possible for them to deny a knowledge of it because they all are compelled to learn it, nor, if they confess to such knowledge can they excuse themselves, so great a disgrace is this considered in that country. Besides this the young men practice military parades to the music of the aulos and perfect themselves in dances and give annual performances in the theaters, all under state supervision and at public expense.

Now all these practices I believe to have been introduced by the men of old time, not as luxuries and superfluities but because they had before their eyes the universal practice of personal manual labor in Arcadia, and in general the toilsomeness and hardship of the men's lives, as well as the harshness of character resulting from the cold and gloomy atmospheric conditions usually prevailing in these parts—conditions to which all men by their very nature must perforce assimilate themselves; there being no other cause than this why separate nations and peoples dwelling widely apart differ so much from each other in character, feature, and color as well as in the most of their pursuits. The primitive Arcadians, therefore, with the view of softening and tempering the stubbornness and harshness of nature, introduced all the practices I mentioned, and in addition accustomed the people, both men and women, to frequent festivals and general sacrifices, and dances of young men and maidens, and in fact resorted to every contrivance to render more gentle and mild, by the influence of the customs they instituted, the extreme hardness of the national character.

The Cynaetheans, by entirely neglecting these institutions, though in special need of such influences, as their country is the most rugged and their climate the most inclement in Arcadia, and by devoting themselves exclusively to their local affairs and political rivalries, finally became so savage that in no city of Greece were greater and more constant crimes committed …

I have said so much on this subject firstly in order that the character of the Arcadian nation should not suffer for the crimes of one city, and secondly to deter any other Arcadians from beginning to neglect music under the impression that its extensive practice in Arcadia serves no necessary purpose. I also spoke for the sake of the Cynaetheans themselves, in order that, if Heaven ever grant them better fortune, they may humanize themselves by turning their attention to education and especially to music; for by no other means can they hope to free themselves from that savagery which overtook them at this time.[45]

Athenaeus confirms the point Polyibus is making.

But the people of Cynaetha came at the end to neglect these customs [the use of music in education], although they occupied by far the rudest part of Arcadia in point of topography as well as climate; when they plunged right into friction and rivalry with one another they finally became so brutalized that among them alone occurred the gravest acts of sacrilege.[46]

45 Polybius, *The Histories*, 4.20.5ff, trans. William Roger Paton (Cambridge, MA: Harvard University Press, 1954).

46 Athenaeus, *Deipnosophistae*, 14.626.

There is one philosopher of the Alexandrian Period, Crates of Thebes (fl. 326 BC), a member of the Cynic School of Diogenes, who appreciated the musical education he had received, for he reflected that he valued not his money, which 'is prey to vanity,' but rather that which he has learned and thinks, 'The noble lessons taught me by the Muses.'[47]

Finally, there are two passages from the philosophers of this period which offer us brief glimpses of actual educational practices in music. First, Diogenes mentions one of the techniques of choral conductors:

> He used to say that he followed the example of the trainers of choruses; for they too set the note a little high, to ensure that the rest should hit the right note.[48]

Second, Zeno tells an anecdote about the educational philosophy of an aulos teacher named Caphisius. When one of his students began playing too loudly, the teacher gave him a slap and said, 'Good playing consists not in bigness, but bigness depends upon good playing.'[49]

FUNCTIONAL MUSIC

Diogenes Laertius tells an anecdote about Arcesilaus which mentions work songs sung by brick makers.

> A certain dialectic, a follower of Alexinus, was unable to repeat properly some argument of his teacher, whereupon Arcesilaus reminded him of the story of Philoxenus and the brickmakers. He found them singing some of his melodies out of tune; and so he retaliated by trampling on the bricks they were making, saying, 'If you spoil my work, I'll spoil yours.'[50]

ENTERTAINMENT MUSIC

Finally, Diogenes Laertius quotes a poem by a different Athenaeus, which he says represents the views of all the Stoic philosophers. In it are two lines which suggest that at least some people of this period still understood the difference between art music and entertainment music.

> Those who place their happiness in pleasure
> Are led by the least worthy of the Muses.[51]

47   Diogenes Laertius, *Lives of the Eminent Philosophers*, 2.89.

48   Ibid., 2.37.

49   Ibid., 2.133. This is retold in Athenaeus, *Deipnosophistae*, 14.629.

50   Diogenes Laertius, *Lives of the Eminent Philosophers*, 1.413.

51   Ibid., 2.143.

16 ALEXANDRIAN POETS

One of the modern collections of the poetry of the Alexandrian Period of Ancient Greece is called, *Last Flowers*.[1] It is an appropriate title, for among the Greeks, these poets, Theocritus (ca. 315–264 BC), Hermesianax (ca. early third century BC), Bion (fl. 105 BC) and Moschus (fl. 100 BC), are the last link with the style of the old lyric poets who sang their poetry to the accompaniment of lyre or aulos. They are also the last link with the 'old Greece' of the period of Homer, with rural characters playing their panpipes[2] in an environment of pastoral tranquility.

The repertoire of the original lyric poets had begun to be attacked as 'old fashioned' in the works of the fifth-century playwrights and according to Athenaeus[3] this style was now reduced to parody by comedians. It is therefore noteworthy that the repertoire of the present poets is filled with praise for the old masters. It is as if they felt a burden to restore the memory of those original, and remarkable, poet-musicians. Notably, Theocritus has left two epigrams which seem as if they were intended as inscriptions for statues of these old poets. The first, pleading with us not to forget, calls out to us,

> Stop and admire Archilochus, the ancient maker of
> Iambic verse, his fame of such extent
> It stretched from occident to orient.
> Him did the Muses and Delian Apollo dearly love,
> So musical and clever to invent
> Lyrics he sang to the lyre's accompaniment.

And another, more insistent, reads,

> Stranger, on this statue gaze with care
> Then, when you get home again, declare,
> 'I saw the likeness of Anacreon
> At Teos, excellent among bye-gone Bards.'[4]

Theocritus, in his 'Idyll Nr. XVI,' makes reference to Simonides, 'the poet of Ceos,' whom he credits for keeping alive the memory of even earlier Greeks.

1 Henry Harmon Chamberlin, *Last Flowers* (Cambridge, MA: Harvard University Press, 1937).

2 Theocritus even wrote one poem in the *shape* of a panpipe, consisting of twenty lines, each shorter than the last.

3 Athenaeus, *The Deipnosophists*, 1.19, trans., Charles Burton Gulick, (Cambridge, MA: Harvard University Press, 1951).

4 All Theocritus translations are from Daryl Hine, *Theocritus: Idylls and Epigrams* (New York: Atheneum, 1982). Indeed, Athenaeus, *The Deipnosophists*, 1.19, mentions such a statue of Archilochus erected by the Milesians. He adds that while there were no such statues of Pindar at Thebes, there was one of the singer Cleon, which had an inscription reading, 'Behold here the son of Pytheas, Cleon, bard of Thebes, who hath placed upon his brow more laurels than any other mortal, and his fame hath reached the skies.' Athenaeus quotes Polemon, who noted that this statue was destroyed when Alexander the Great razed Thebes, but the local respect for the statue was such that a refugee placed some money in the remaining portion of the statue and returned to find it untouched thirty years later.

Having abandoned their all and the wealth that was theirs, unremembered
During long ages they might have been lying among the unhappy
Dead, had the heavenly poet of Ceos, atuning his brilliant
Strains to the many-stringed instrument not made them famous
among the
Men who came later.

Hermesianax, whom we know only through a fragment of his 'Prologue of the Leontium,' mentions in this fragment three of the older lyric poets.

And Lesbian Alcaeus, well you know
For Sappho's sake would smite upon the lyre;
To many a revel, with a song he'd go,
Yearning for her with passionate desire.

The bard, the lover of that nightingale,
A Teian grieved with eloquence of song,
Honeyed Anacreon, who would fain prevail
On her, supreme the Lesbian girls among.[5]

5 Chamberlin, *Last Flowers*, 79.

In this period of the 'Last Flowers' of the poet-musicians of lyric poetry, a line by Theocritus suggests that perhaps this generation of lyric poets were no longer the widely respected artists but now worked in an environment of harder won recognition, for he observes that, 'Poverty's the only thing that wakens the arts and crafts; it is want that instructs human beings to toil.'[6] But if poverty is the mother of the arts, Bion, at least, felt the child had a high value.

6 Theocritus, 'Idyll Nr. 21.'

Leave me not bare; for hire will Phoebus sing.
Goods are worth more if they a premium bring.[7]

7 Bion, 'Fragment V,' quoted in Chamberlin, *Last Flowers*, 44.

Perhaps Theocritus shared this sense of worth, for in his 'Idyll Nr. 9,' he cries,

Pastoral Muses, all hail and farewell! Do publish the song that
I unaccompanied sang in the company once of these herdsmen.

This plea to remember his song perhaps carries with it a hint that the art of the lyric poet is coming to an end, that these are indeed the 'Last Flowers.' Is this not the message, also, of the beautiful poem of this period, 'Elegy on the Death of Bion,' which proclaims that Dorian music itself has died? We do not know the poet who wrote this, although he says he was a student of Bion. He treasures the fact that, while others will be the beneficiaries of Bion's estate, he has received the greater gift of his music, 'To me the larger heritage will go.'

> Ravines and Dorian waters, sigh with me;
> And rivers, mourn for Bion … He is dead;
> The lovely singer lies within the tomb …
>
> No more the pastoral song may Bion sing;
> With him, alas, has died the lyric strain;
> And all the Dorian music has been slain …
>
> He who the herds once charmed will sing no more,
> Sitting in solitude the oaks among
> To make his music. Now he sings before
> Pluto; forgetfulness is all his song …
>
> Bion, your fate Apollo's self bemoans;
> Full many a Satyr and Priapus weeps
> In sable raiment. Pans with sobs and groans
> Bewail your music. From the watery deeps
> Full many a nymph her tearful visage rears;
> The woodland springs are fountains of their tears …
>
> Who now will play your pipes, O thrice bewailed?
> Who on the reedy vents his mouth would place?
> Thus overbold, he little had availed,
> Where still your lips and breath have living grace,
> Where Echo on the reeds your song maintains.
> To Pan I bring your pipes; with little zest
> For him, who fears to emulate your strains
> Lest he himself should come off second best,
> Lest far beyond him would your music go …
>
> Dear master, long before I learned from you
> The Dorian mode; to others may belong
> Your wealth; but your sweet music is my due;
> To me the larger heritage will go.[8]

8 Ibid., 67 ff.

Art Music

Foremost among these poets is a constant reference to the beauty of music and nearly always an eager listener. In Bion, for example, we find,

> Now pray you, Lycidas, a melody
> Sing sweetly, a Sicilian song for me,
> An amorous tune charming every heart.[9]

9   Bion, 'The Couch of Deidameia,' in Chamberlin, *Last Flowers*, 38.

10   Theocritus, 'Idylls I, XV, and XX.'

Theocritus speaks of 'delectable song,'[10] as well mentioning two singers with sweet voices, one with an analogy often used of the original lyric poets themselves, 'sweeter than a honey comb dripping with honey.' Moschus mentions the power of music to 'lull my sorrow to sleep,'[11] and notes that it is 'sweet soft music' the shepherd loves, not that which sounds like 'wild noise.'

11   Moschus, 'Idyll IX,' in Andrew Lang, trans., *Theocritus, Bion and Moschus* (London: Macmillan, 1920), 210.

> The sweet soft music of a bubbling spring
> In sheltered forest glade, I love to hear;
> Forever drowsy with that murmuring
> I hearken to a tune that still comes near:
> And pleasant to the rustic is a voice
> That never will harass him with wild noise.[12]

12   Moschus, 'Sea and Woodland,' in Chamberlin, *Last Flowers*, 20.

Theocritus also reveals an acute awareness of the qualities of fine musicianship. In 'Idyll VII,' he has a singer confess,

> Everyone says, the best singer, although I am slow to believe them
> Truly, for in my opinion I cannot begin to compete with
> Noble Sicelidas, who is from Samos, or even Philetas,
> Not in Musicianship! Sooner a bullfrog might rival a cricket.

Another epigram suited for a statue, now in the form of a memorial to the Muses by a lyric poet named Xenacles, also emphasizes musicianship.

> Goddesses, on pleasing all nine of you intent,
> Xenacles erected this marble monument.
> The title of musician nobody refuses
> Him. Respected for his wit, he thanks the Muses.[13]

13   Theocritus, 'Epigram X.' The poets referred to in this and the previous Idyll are of the generation before Theocritus and whose works do not survive.

A similar memorial, now to Dionysus, by a choral conductor, suggests that the choral contests were, at least on some occasions, still musical contests.

Damomenes the choirmaster put us this tripod,
Dionysus, and your image, blest and blythest god.
Measured in all things, he won the victory
With his male choir, observing beauty and degree.[14]

Speaking of contests, there is a remarkable testimonial to the old lyric poets found in three separate Idylls[15] of Theocritus, each of which stages a musical contest similar to those in which the original poets participated. Now, in keeping with the subjects of these Idylls, the participating musicians are rural tenders of animals. In 'Idyll Nr. VIII,' for example, we find the shepherd, Menalcas, challenging the cattle boy, Daphnis, to a musical duel. Daphnis responds,

Herdsman of wool-bearing sheep and performer on Panpipes, Menalcas,
You'll never beat me, although you may injure yourself in the effort.

They both agree to the contest and Daphnis proposes they wager an animal from each of their flock. Menalcas says he cannot wager a lamb, but instead will put at risk his instrument.

I have a pipe that I fashioned myself,[16] it's a fine one of nine notes,
Fastened together with white wax, even on top and on bottom,
That I am willing to wager, but what is my father's I will not.

Daphnis responds that he, too, has a panpipe he made himself, although he injured himself in the process!

Well, as it happens, I too have a beautiful panpipe of nine notes
Fastened together with white wax, even on top and on bottom,
Which I confected the day before yesterday—and even yet my
Finger is terribly sore from a reed I was splitting which cut me.

Every contest must have an adjudicator and in this case they saw a goatherd whom they enlisted for this purpose. The contest itself consisted of each poet-musician singing alternate stanzas. They began as follows.

Both of the children then shouted; the goatherd approached when
    he heard them.
Since they were willing to sing, he was equally willing to judge them.
First, and according to lot, the soprano Menalcas began to
Sing, and then Daphnis in answer resumed the responsive bucolic
Song. It is thus that Menalcas as senior began the performance.

---

14   Theocritus, 'Epigram XII.'

15   'Idylls Nr. V, VI, and VIII.' In the second of these, the contest ended in a tie.

16   A relatively easy instrument to construct, Bion, in an extant fragment, tells a young person not to depend on expert craftsmen for everything, but to make the instrument himself.

Dear child, it is not right that you
    should bring
Orders to specialists for everything;
Nor give away what work you have
    to do.
Make your own pipes—an easy
    task for you.

Menalcas
Valleys and rivers, divine generation, if ever Menalcas
Played on his panpipe or sang melody pleasing to you,
Pasture my flocks with sincere generosity; if ever Daphnis
Come to this place with his cows, may he obtain nothing less.

Daphnis
Fountains and pasturage, sweet vegetation, if ever your Daphnis
Made any music that might rival the nightingales', please
Fatten his flock; if Menalcas bring anything, may he discover
Everything generous here, grazing and welcome as well.

The contest continued in this manner until the end, when the
judge decided on Daphnis.

Daphnis, your diction is pleasant, your voice is extremely attractive.
I'd sooner listen to you making music than sup upon honey.
Take as your guerdon the panpipe, for you are the victor in singing.

Daphnis, we are told, celebrated by 'clapping his hands and
jumping for joy, as a fawn might have jumped all around its own
mother.' But, since one of the problems of all musical contests is
that there must of necessity be a 'loser,' Menalcas, 'smoldered and
worried his heart with his sorrow.'

As might be expected, another common theme of these pastoral
poems is love, although Bion says music is sweeter even than love![17]
One of the most remarkable of the love poems is the fragment
by Hermesianax. In addition to the love of the poet-musicians
Alcaeus and Anacreon for Sappho, he mentions 'a very faithful
warden of the aulos, Philoxenus,' who loved Galatea, 'who loved
him not again.'

Two playwrights are included, Euripides, whom we are told spent
his retirement years chasing a slave girl, and the more fortunate
Sophocles, whom the God Zeus rewarded with 'the fair Erigone,'
even though he had been so critical of women in his plays.

Now of a prudent man I'd have my say;
Against all women would his raillery go;
He won the hate of all upon his way.

Even philosophers, for whom our poet has poor regard, cannot
escape love, in spite of their academic prowess.

17 'Fragment XVIII,' in
Chamberlin, *Last Flowers*, 61.

And they to whom the arid lives belong
Of men who walk in Learning's devious ways,
Whose every speech was throttled by their skill
When awful Truth their counsels held in sway;
From wind and lovers' turmoil could but ill
Escape when these occurred upon the way.
Under that chariot driver all went down.

Here the poet mentions also Pythagoras.

And madness for Theano strongly bound
Pythagoras of Samian renown,
Who subtle spirals measured on the ground,
Who sharply etched upon a little ball
The current of the ether in the vast
Of Heaven.

The last in his catalog of lovers is a teacher, Aristippus, who left his school and job to chase his love, Lais, 'whose loveliness has never been described.'

To her he fled; and so he left behind
The lecture hall and audience as well;
Unto his love he clung with heart and mind.

Finally, we must mention that this same poem reveals to us that Zeus guards all who serve the Muse!

Another lovely poem, by Bion, asks one of these rustic musicians to take Love to school to teach him pastoral music. Here is the complete poem.

Before me mighty Cypris took her stand;
And silly Eros hanging of his head
She guided onward with a shapely hand,
And in my dream these words the goddess said:

'Master of rustic song, take Love to school;
Teach him the pastoral music.' So she spake,
And so departed. I, like any fool,
Taught him as though he cared these songs to make;

How Pan the pipes invented, fair and well;
How by Athena first the aulos was made;
How Hermes wrought the lyre from tortoise shell;
How sweetly Apollo on the harp played.

To all my words he gave but little heed;
Instead the amorous tunes of light love
He taught to me, his mother's every deed,
And passion shared by men and gods above.

All I have taught to Eros slipped my mind;
But everything that Eros taught to me,
Of lyric love I evermore shall find
Reverberating in my memory.[18]

18   Chamberlin, *Last Flowers*, 50.

FUNCTIONAL MUSIC

The only reference to functional music in these poems is found
in one by Bion, called 'The Dirge for Adonis.' This, according to
Chamberlin, was an annual Spring festival commemorating a marriage which did not take place, due to the death of Adonis. Thus
the usual marriage hymns turn to dirges.

Now Hymen all the torches round the door
Quenches; on earth he scatters all the flowers
The bride and groom for bridal garlands wore;
No longer he sings 'Hymen' to the hours.

No longer Hymen sings his wonted song;
But 'Out! alas, Adonis!' now he cries;
His lamentation rises loud and long;
No bridal, but a dirge for one who dies.[19]

19   Ibid., 35.

ENTERTAINMENT MUSIC

The only two references to entertainment music in this body of
poetry both speak of the single-pipe girl prostitutes who entertain
at banquets. Theocritus, in 'Idyll II,' mentions 'the mother of her
who performs on the aulos at parties.' A more interesting reference, again by Theocritus, tells of a farm worker, a reaper, who has
been unable to work because he cannot take his mind off one of
these girls.

MILON. Which of the local young ladies distresses you so?
BUCAEUS. Polybotas, she who was playing the aulos at Hippokion's
    yesterday for us.

MILON. Heaven discovers the sinner! You've got what you prayed
for this long while:
Namely a girl like a grasshopper willing to cuddle you all night.
BUCAEUS. Now you're beginning to tease me, but money is not the
unique blind
God; there's indifferent Love. So you'd better not talk highfalutin.
MILON. I do not talk highfalutin! However, abandon your reaping
Now, and take up an affectionate tune for your girl.
You will work more happily then.
And you used in the past to be quite a musician.[20]

20 Theocritus, 'Idyll X.'

17 THE ROMAN PERIOD OF ANCIENT GREECE (146 BC – 529 AD)

Following some of the most famous wars of history, the Punic Wars and the Macedonian Wars, Greece under the Roman Empire became the era of the *Pax Romana*, a time of relative peace and security which permitted an economical and cultural progress, especially in the cities such as Athens, Corinth, Alexandria, Miletus, Thessaloniki, and Smyrna. The Romans welcomed the Greek culture and Latin and Greek became the dominant languages of the Empire.

During this period a few important Greek writers remained and they represent and describe the final chapter of ancient Greece philosophy and music.

THE PHYSIOLOGY OF AESTHETICS

With Plotinus (204–270 AD) we come to the last great philosopher of antiquity, a man whose writings are still important to philosophy, theology, and mysticism. According to his student, Porphyry, Plotinus had a 'thorough theoretical knowledge' of music, although he did not actually practice it.

Plotinus begins his major work, *The Enneads*, with a discussion of the emotions. He first observes that the emotions must be sensations, or at least do not occur apart from sensation. Like his famous predecessors who were unaware of the nature and workings of the twin hemispheres of our brain, he concludes that all experiences and all emotions have their seat in the soul.[1] And like his predecessors, once the soul is introduced into the discussion, things become very difficult to explain physiologically.

> Now the Soul uses the body as an instrument, [but] it does not follow that the Soul must share the body's experiences: a man does not himself feel all the experiences of the tools with which he is working.
>
> It may be objected that the Soul must, however, have Sense-Perception since its use of its instrument must acquaint it with the external conditions, and such knowledge comes by way of sense. Thus, it will be argued, the eyes are the instrument of seeing, and seeing may bring distress to the Soul …
>
> But, we ask, how, possibly, can these affections pass from body to Soul?[2]

1 Plotinus, *The Enneads*, trans. Stephen MacKenna (London: Faber and Faber, 1962), 21. He reserves just the slightest doubt, saying we can agree on this 'if only reason allows.'

2 Ibid., 22.

In discussing further the nature of the soul, Plotinus turns to Pythagoras' analogy with the lyre, which he rejects due to its philosophical difficulties.

> Soul belongs, then, to another nature. What is this? Is it something which, while distinct from body, still belongs to it, for example a harmony or accord?
>
> This view, which the Pythagorean school holds with some difference, envisages the Soul as comparable to the accord in the strings of a lyre. When the lyre is strung a certain condition is produced upon the strings, and this is known as accord: in the same way our body is formed of distinct constituents brought together, and the blend produces at once life and that soul which is the condition existing upon the bodily total.
>
> That this opinion is untenable has already been shown at length. The Soul is a prior (to body), the accord is a secondary to the lyre. Soul rules, guides, and often combats the body; as an accord of body it could not do these things. Soul is a real being, accord is not. That due blending (or accord) of the corporeal materials which constitute our frame would be simply health. Each separate part of the body, entering as a distinct entity into the total, would require a distinct (its own accord or note), so that there would be many souls to each person. Weightiest of all: before this soul there would have to be another soul to bring about the accord as, in the case of the musical instrument, there is the musician who produces the accord upon the strings by his own possession of the principle on which he tunes them: neither musical strings nor human bodies could put themselves in tune.[3]

As for the intellect itself, Plotinus proposes three stages of growth: the 'lower life'; the second, where one has made 'as it were a footprint but must still advance within the realm [of the Intelligibles]'; and third, 'the topmost peak of the Intellectual realm.'[4] He discusses this in terms of three types: the metaphysician (who makes this progression by instinct), the musician, and the 'born lover,' the latter two of which 'need outside guidance.' He then gives his analysis of the temperamental makeup of the musician.

> We must begin by distinguishing the three types. Let us take the musician first and indicate his temperamental equipment for the task.
>
> The musician we may think of as being exceedingly quick to beauty, drawn in a very rapture to it: somewhat slow to stir of his own impulse, he answers at once to the outer stimulus: as the timid

3 Ibid., 351.

4 Ibid., 36ff.

are sensitive to noise so he to tones and the beauty they convey; all that offends against unison or harmony in melodies or rhythms repels him; he longs for measure and shapely pattern.

This natural tendency must be made the starting-point to such a man; he must be drawn by the tone, rhythm, and design in things of sense: he must learn to distinguish the material forms from the Authentic-Existent which is the source of all these correspondences and of the entire reasoned scheme in the work of art: he must be led to the Beauty that manifests itself through these forms; he must be shown that what ravished him was no other than the Harmony of the Intellectual world and the Beauty in that sphere, not some one shape of beauty but the All-Beauty, the Absolute Beauty; and the truths of philosophy must be implanted in him to lead him to faith in that which, unknowing it, he possesses within himself.

The last part of this means, basically, that Beauty is more than the sum of its parts, a topic to which we shall return below.

In the end, while Plotinus, again like his predecessors, can accept that the senses contribute to knowledge, he cannot accept that this information itself is a form of, or constitutes true knowledge.

> Knowledge in the reasoning soul is on the one side concerned with objects of sense, though indeed this can scarcely be called knowledge and is better indicated as opinion or surface-knowing.[5]

5 Ibid., 438.

One wonders, and he does not reveal, how he reconciled this thought with a statement he makes in another place, that 'All human beings from birth onward live in the realm of sense more than in the Intellectual.'[6]

6 Ibid., 434.

Another philosopher of this period, Epictetus (55–135 AD), in the opening sentence of his *Discourses*, makes the same point: only the rational truly exists in a form by which one can comprehend its nature. In explaining this, it is interesting that he makes an association we have seen before in ancient Greek philosophy, the association of the character of music and grammar.

> Of our faculties in general you will find that none can take cognizance of itself; none therefore has the power to approve or disapprove its own action. Our grammatical faculty for instance: how far can that take cognizance? Only so far as to distinguish expression. Our musical faculty? Only so far as to distinguish tune. Does any one of these then take cognizance of itself? By no means. If you are writing to your friend, when you want to know what words to write grammar will tell you; but whether you should write to your friend

or should not write grammar will not tell you. And in the same way music will tell you about tunes, but whether at this precise moment you should sing and play the lyre or should not sing nor play the lyre it will not tell you. What will tell you then? That faculty which takes cognizance of itself and of all things else. What is this? The reasoning faculty: for this alone of the faculties we have received is created to comprehend even its own nature; that is to say, what it is and what it can do, and with what precious qualities it has come to us, and to comprehend all other faculties as well.[7]

7 Epictetus, *The Discourses of Epictetus*, trans. Percy Ewing Matheson (New York: Random House, 1957), 224. In another place, p. 372, he says, 'for it is being a child to be unmusical in musical things, ungrammatical in grammar ...'

Today, of course, we understand that an analogy can be made between the *notated* form of music and grammar. But this notated form is the *least* important aspect of music, while the *most* important aspect of grammar.

Epictetus, as many philosophers before him, recognizes the existence of both the rational and the irrational. But by no means does he consider these equal, indeed he begins by saying, 'by nothing is the rational creature so distressed as by the irrational.' While such a statement suggests that the rational is somehow the more dependable, his following comments carry with them the implication that *neither* the rational or the irrational is dependable, as they vary from person to person.

> But rational and irrational mean different things to different persons, just as good and evil, expedient and inexpedient, are different for different persons. That is the chief reason why we need education, that we may learn so to adjust our preconceptions of rational and irrational to particular conditions as to be in harmony with nature. But to decide what is rational and irrational we may not only estimate the value of things external, but each one of us considers what is in keeping with his character.[8]

8 Ibid., 226ff.

Of the philosophers of this period, Plutarch (46–120 AD) alone seems to understand the necessary *coordination* of the rational and 'irrational' in the way we understand it today. He arrived at this purely by deduction, not knowing anything, of course, of the true nature of our left and right brain hemispheres.

First, however, he mentions the fact that the earlier philosophers were concerned primarily with the rational. His reference to Pythagoras in this regard is particularly interesting, as this information survives in no other source.

Pythagoras, that grave philosopher, rejected the judging of music by the senses, affirming that the virtue of music could be appreciated only by the intellect. And therefore he did not judge of music by the ear, but by the harmonical proportion.[9]

9   Plutarch, 'Concerning Music.'

Having acknowledged this, Plutarch now attempts to demonstrate the necessity of *both* kinds of knowing. He begins by explaining how the intellect (left hemisphere) created 'reason' out of mere sounds.

Now then, as voice, merely voice, is only an insignificant and brutish noise, but speech is the expression of the mind as significant utterance; as harmony consists of sounds and intervals,—a sound being always one and the same, and an interval being the difference and diversity of sounds, while both being mixed together produce melody;—thus the passive nature of the soul was without limits and unstable, but afterwards became determinate, when limits were set and a certain form was given to the divisible and manifold variety of motion. Thus having comprised the Same and the Other, by the similitudes and dissimilitudes of numbers which produce concord out of disagreement, it becomes the life of the world, sober and prudent, harmony itself, and reason overruling necessity mixed with persuasion.[10]

10   Plutarch, 'Of the Procreation of the Soul.'

But, on the other hand, he observes, correctly, that it is the emotions (right hemisphere) which provide *meaning* to 'reason.'

These are the powers and virtues of the soul of the universe. And when they once enter into the organs of corruptible bodies, being themselves incorruptible, there the form of the binary and boundless principle shows itself most briskly, while that of the unmixed and purer principle lies as it were dormant in obscurity. And thus it happens, that a man shall rarely observe any human passion or motion of the understanding, void of reason, where there shall not something appear either of desire or emulation, joy or grief. Several philosophers therefore will have the passions to be so many sorts of reasonings, seeing that desire, grief, and anger are all the effects of judgment. Others allege that virtues themselves to be derived from passions; fortitude depending on fear, temperance on voluptuousness, and justice on love of gain. Now the soul being both speculative and practical, contemplating as well generals as particulars, and seeming to comprehend the one by the assistance of the intellect and the other by the aid of sense, common reason, which encounters the Same in the Other and the Other in the Same, endeavors by certain limits and distinctions to separate one from many and the divis-

11   Plutarch, 'On the Procreation of the Soul.'

ible from the indivisible; but she cannot accomplish her design nor be purely in one or the other, in regard the principles are so oddly interwoven and intermixed and confusedly huddled together.[11]

Thus, the normally functioning person needs *both* the intellect, or the rational, *and* the emotional, or the experiential, or as we would say today, both the left and right hemispheres. Plutarch clearly understood this on some level, for he gives us two examples of how this works in practice. To demonstrate how the right hemisphere contributes to the left hemisphere, or in his words that it was 'his personal *experience* which gives meaning to *words*,' he provides an example from his own life.[12]

12   Plutarch, 'Life of Demosthenes.'

> But if any man undertake to write a history, that has to be collected from materials gathered by observation and the reading of works not easy to be got in all places, nor written always in his own language, but many of them foreign and dispersed in other hands, for him, undoubtedly, it is in the first place and above all things most necessary, to reside in some city of good note, addicted to liberal arts, and populace; where he may have plenty of all sorts of books, and upon inquiry may hear and inform himself of such particulars as, having escaped the pens of writers, are more faithfully preserved in the memories of men, lest his work be deficient in many things, even those which it can least dispense with.
>
> But for me, I live in a little town, where I am willing to continue, lest it should grow less; and having had no leisure, while I was in Rome or other parts of Italy, to exercise myself in the Roman language, on account of public business and of those who came to be instructed by me in philosophy, it was very late, and in the decline of my age, before I applied myself to the reading of Latin authors. Upon which that which happened to me, may seem strange, though it be true; for it was not so much by the knowledge of words, that I came to understanding of things, as by my experience of things I was enabled to follow the meaning of words.

On the other hand to demonstrate that this relationship can also flow in the opposite direction, he provides an example of how the intellect can play on the emotions, here from his 'Life of Pericles,' where he observes,

13   One is reminded of a contemporary of Rousseau, who said of him at the time of the French Revolution, 'He made madmen of people who would otherwise only have been fools.'

> Rhetoric, or the art of speaking, is … the government of the souls of men, and that her chief business is to address the affections and passions,[13] which are as it were the strings and keys to the soul, and require a skillful and careful touch to be played on as they should be.

THE PSYCHOLOGY OF AESTHETICS

PLEASURE AND PAIN

Although this topic was the subject of much discussion by earlier Greek philosophers, in this period the whole topic seems to have been laid aside. Perhaps the period of decay and collapse of institutions after Alexander the Great simply made Pleasure a topic which was taken for granted for all but slaves.

One writer who does bring up this old question again is Athenaeus (late second to early third centuries AD), but his is unfortunately a discussion which lacks both depth and detail. His first observation is the most interesting, which is that Pleasure had been discussed not so much as an emotion as an ethical problem. Probably assuming that his readers were familiar with this topic from the works of Plato and Aristotle, he does not elaborate and elects instead to merely point to an ancient example of failure from this ethical perspective.

> Some people say that pleasure is ordained by nature, because all living things are slaves to it, as if cowardice and fear and other feelings as well did not exist in all alike, though *they* are discountenanced by those who follow reason. And so to pursue pleasures recklessly is to hunt pain. This is why Homer, desiring to represent pleasure as reprehensible, declares that even the highest gods are in no wise protected by their own power, but receive the greatest injuries if they are misled by pleasure. For all the plans that Zeus made for the Trojans as he lay awake were upset when day came because he was over-mastered by pleasure.[14]

14 Athenaeus, *Deipnosophistae*, 12.511. He refers to the *Iliad*, 14.159.

When speaking of his own time, suddenly Pleasure becomes a positive, indeed a necessity. Now he is no longer speaking of an ethical point of view, but rather from the perspective of 'the finer things of life.'

> Indeed, to have pleasure and luxury is a mark of the freeborn; it eases their minds and exalts them; but to live laborious lives is the mark of slaves and of men of low birth; hence their very natures also become contracted. And so the city of Athens, as long as it enjoyed luxury, was very great and reared men who were very lordly and proud. For they wrapped themselves in cloaks dyed in purple, they put on embroidered tunics, they bound up their hair in topknots and wore golden cicadas on their forehead and temples; their slaves carried folding stools for them so that they should not sit as chance

might have it. Such, then, were the men who won the battle of Marathon, the only people who overcame the power of all Asia. Even the wisest men, Heracleides says, they who enjoy the highest reputation for wisdom, recognize pleasure as the highest good, Simonides, for example, saying: 'What life among mortals is desirable without pleasure, or what lordly power? Without this not even the life of the gods is enviable.'[15]

15 Ibid., 12.512.

The second century satirist, Lucian (125–180 AD), made fun of the above mentioned style of dress in a dialogue in which Eros is speaking to Zeus.

If you wish to be fascinating … make yourself as charming as possible, let your hair flow loosely down in curls on both sides of your face and tie them up with a head-band; wear a purple garment, put on gold-embroidered shoes and walk, keeping time to the music of aulos and drums—and you'll see more women following after you.[16]

16 Lucian, 'Dialogues of the Gods,' in *A Second Century Satirist*, trans. Winthrop Dudley Sheldon (Philadelplhia: Drexel Biddle, 1901), 59.

ON BEAUTY

Plotinus is the only philosopher of this period to discuss at length Beauty as an abstract idea. While his interest was more in the spiritual aspects of Beauty, as pertaining to the soul and religious theory, nevertheless his thoughts contain interesting concepts which are germane to artistic beauty as well.

He begins by stating that the perception of Beauty exists on two levels, a lower aesthetic of the senses and a higher one of the intellect.

Beauty addresses itself chiefly to sight; but there is a beauty for the hearing too, as in certain combinations of words and in all kinds of music, for melodies and cadences are beautiful; and minds that lift themselves above the realm of sense to a higher order are aware of beauty in the conduct of life, in actions, in character, in the pursuits of the intellect; and there is the beauty of the virtues.[17]

17 Plotinus, *The Enneads*, 56.

Next, Plotinus makes a contention which is central to his general definition of Beauty: Beauty is found in the sum of the parts, yet each part must also contain beauty.

Almost everyone declares that the symmetry of parts towards each other and towards a whole, with, besides, a certain charm of color, constitutes the beauty recognized by the eye, that in visible things, as indeed in all else, universally, the beautiful thing is essentially symmetrical, patterned.

But think what this means.

Only a compound can be beautiful, never anything devoid of parts; and only a whole; the several parts will have beauty, not in themselves, but only as working together to give a comely total. Yet beauty in an aggregate demands beauty in details: it cannot be constructed out of ugliness; its law must run throughout.[18]

18 Ibid.

The artist achieves beauty in these details, says Plotinus, not by working with details first, but rather by having a vision of the beauty of the whole from which the details emerge.

All that comes to be, work of nature or of craft, some wisdom has made: everywhere a wisdom presides at a making.

No doubt the wisdom of the artist may be the guide of the work; it is sufficient explanation of the wisdom exhibited in the arts; but the artist himself goes back, after all, to that wisdom in Nature which is embodied in himself; and this is not a wisdom built of theorems but of one totality, not a wisdom consisting of manifold detail coordinated into a unity but rather a unity working out into detail.[19]

19 Ibid., 426.

That the artist can only work from the vision of the whole proceeding to the parts is made comprehensible by another important definition of art: 'Art' is not in the finished object at all. 'Art' is that *within* the artist himself. Plotinus saw this entire relationship as one centered on the role of the soul.

And the Soul includes a faculty peculiarly addressed to Beauty—one incomparably sure in the appreciation of its own, when Soul entire is enlisted to support its judgment.

Or perhaps the Soul itself acts immediately, affirming the Beautiful where it finds something accordant with the Ideal-Form within itself, using this Idea as a canon of accuracy in its decision.

But what accordance is there between the material and that which antedates all Matter?

On what principle does the architect, when he finds the house standing before him correspondent with his inner ideal of a house, pronounce it beautiful? Is it not that the house before him, the stones apart, is the inner idea stamped upon the mass of exterior matter, the indivisible exhibited in diversity?[20]

20 Ibid., 58.

In another place, Plotinus expands on this idea and adds an important additional observation: the finished work of art can never be as beautiful as the original vision within the artist himself.

Suppose two blocks of stone lying side by side: one is unpatterned, quite untouched by art; the other has been minutely wrought by the craftsman's hands into some statue of god or man, A Grace or a Muse, or if a human being, not a portrait but a creation in which the sculptor's art has concentrated all loveliness.

Now it must be seen that the stone thus brought under the artist's hand to the beauty of form is beautiful not as stone—for so the crude block would be as pleasant—but in virtue of the Form or Idea introduced by the art. This form is not in the material; it is in the designer before ever it enters the stone; and the artificer holds it not by his equipment of eyes and hands but by his participation in his art. The beauty, therefore, exists in a far higher state in the art; for it does not come over integrally into the work; that original beauty is not transferred; what comes over is a derivative and a minor: and even that shows itself upon the statue not integrally and with entire realization of intention but only in so far as it has subdued the resistance of the material ...

Every prime cause must be, within itself, more powerful than its effect can be: the musical does not derive from an unmusical source but from music; and so the art exhibited in the material work derives from an art yet higher.[21]

21 Ibid., 422.

With regard to the observer of art, Plotinus now gives us a new contention, that the soul itself is capable of sense perception. First, he says the soul can hear what the traditional senses cannot and he gives an example which, for the first time, suggests that the ancients had come to finally understand the overtone series as it truly exists.

Harmonies unheard in sound create the harmonies we hear and wake the Soul to the consciousness of beauty.[22]

22 Ibid., 59.

Also, Plotinus says, the soul can see what the eyes cannot. In his last sentence here, we believe he creates a remarkable definition which captures the unsettling effect which can sometimes occur from encountering the 'spirit of Beauty' in a work of art.

But there are earlier and loftier beauties than these. In the sense-bound life we are no longer granted to know them, but the Soul, taking no help from the organs [of sense], sees and proclaims them. To the vision of these we must mount, leaving sense to its own low place.

As it is not for those to speak of the graceful forms of the material world who have never seen them or known their grace—men born blind, let us suppose—in the same way those must be silent upon the beauty of noble conduct and of learning and all that order who have never cared for such things, nor may those tell of the splendor of virtue who have never known the face of Justice and of Moral-Wisdom beautiful beyond the beauty of Evening and Dawn.

Such vision is for those only who see with the Soul's sight—and at the vision, they will rejoice, and awe will fall upon them and a trouble deeper than all the rest could ever stir, for now they are moving in the realm of Truth.

This is the spirit that Beauty must ever induce, wonderment and a delicious trouble, longing and love and a trembling that is all delight.[23]

23 Ibid.

The ultimate beauty for Plotinus, then, is intellectual beauty in the soul. Moreover a soul possessed of this kind of beauty, one 'cleansed' of the 'lower order' of beauty which is the object of the senses, achieves a kind of purification making possible appreciation of 'the Good,' in a divine sense.

For, as the ancient teaching was, moral-discipline and courage and every virtue, not even excepting Wisdom itself, all is purification …

The Soul thus cleansed is all Idea and Reason, wholly free of body, intellective, entirely of that divine order from which the wellspring of Beauty rises and all the race of Beauty.

Hence the Soul heightened to the Intellectual-Principle is beautiful to all its power. For Intellection and all that proceeds from Intellection are the Soul's beauty, a graciousness native to it and not foreign, for only with these is it truly Soul. And it is just to say that in the Soul's becoming a good and beautiful thing is its becoming like to God, for from the Divine comes all the Beauty and all the Good in beings.[24]

24 Ibid., 61.

Perhaps Plotinus thought that the role he assigned to the soul in the perception of art might sound a bit too easy, for after all the artist and musician must also, their inner vision notwithstanding, expend much effort in perfecting their craft. Therefore he adds the qualification that one must also train the soul in its function.

You must close the eyes and call instead upon another vision which is to be waked within you, a vision, the birth-right of all, which few turn to use …

Newly-awakened it is all too feeble to bear the ultimate splendor. Therefore the Soul must be trained—to the habit of remarking, first, all noble pursuits, then the works of beauty produced not by the labor of the arts but by the virtue of men known for their goodness.[25]

25 Ibid., 63.

This ultimate beauty, the intellectual beauty in the soul, of which Plotinus speaks, he says finds its highest manifestation in those arts which communicate with some aspect of the universality of the Intellectual Cosmos. For varying reasons, music, geometry, oratory and generalship belong to this select club. The rest of the arts, as they are more 'earth-based,' are of a lower order. The crafts too, a category in which medicine is included together with carpentry and agriculture, are 'not wholly in the Intellectual' realm.[26]

26 Ibid., 440.

Finally, to clarify this long discussion by Plotinus we might summarize his definition of Beauty as follows:

1. Beauty exists on two levels, a lower aesthetic of the senses and a higher aesthetic of the intellect.
2. Beauty is found both in the sum of an object's parts, but also necessarily in its parts individually.
3. The artist achieves Beauty not through the accumulation of detail, but from the vision of the whole from which the details emerge. It is this vision within the artist which is 'art,' not the finished object. The finished object can never be as beautiful as the original vision of the artist.
4. The complete perception of Beauty in art is the perception which takes place in the soul, which can perceive more completely than the senses themselves. Since what the soul perceives is of the 'realm of Truth,' when the soul absorbs the spirit of beauty the result is often 'wonderment and a delicious trouble, longing and love and a trembling that is all delight.'

The Aesthetics of Music

Before considering the views on the aesthetics of music by the Greek philosophers of this last period of ancient Greece, we might first consider a few reflections on the state of music in general from their perspective. Some modern writers make the assumption in reading the fragments left by Aristoxenus that the original modes, 'Dorian,' 'Lydian,' etc., had evolved from systems of tuning into something more like scales, even though Aristoxenus himself was quick to point out that such a description of them did not capture the real *essence* of them. But it is possible that we would be jumping too far ahead in thinking of a worked out theory of scales, for these final philosophers of ancient Greece, writing five hundred years later than Aristoxenus, are still talking about the *character* of the modes and not the grammar of the modes.

Athenaeus begins by agreeing with an argument, in a now lost book by Heracleides of Pontus, that really one should only speak of three Greek modes, the Dorian, Aeolian, and Ionian, as these represent the three main tribes of the Greeks.[27] Phrygian and Lydian, he says originated with the 'barbarians' (meaning those who do not speak Greek well) and were learned by the Greeks from them. He then attempts to portray the character of these three tribes, with the obvious suggestion that the music of these modes somehow is of the same character. Since the actual music is virtually extinct, we cannot, of course, study this further, but it remains a fascinating clue that what these terms meant to the ancient Greeks is nowhere revealed by the 'scales' we write on university blackboards today when discussing the later medieval modes by the same names.

27 Athenaeus, *Deipnosophistae*, 14.624–626.

> Now the Dorian mode exhibits the quality of manly vigor, of magnificent bearing, not relaxed or merry, but sober and intense, neither varied nor complicated. But the Aeolian character contains the elements of ostentation and turgidity, and even conceit; these qualities are in keeping with their horse-breeding and their way of meeting strangers; yet this does not mean malice, but is, rather, lofty and confident. Hence also their fondness for drinking is something appropriate to them, also their love affairs, and the entirely relaxed nature of their daily life.

The suggestion that the character of the mode is something apart from the theoretical description of the mode, he seems to emphasize in an example of a song he gives which is sung to the *Hypodorian scale*, but is described as being in the *Aeolian mode*! The third main mode, the Ionian, he describes as follows.

> Next in order let us examine the Milesians' character, which the Ionians illustrate. Because of their excellent physical condition they bear themselves haughtily, they are full of irate spirit, hard to placate, fond of contention, never condescending to kindliness nor cheerfulness, displaying a lack of affection and a hardness in their character. Hence also the kind of music known as the Ionian mode is neither bright nor cheerful, but austere and hard, having a seri-

ousness which is not ignoble; and so their mode is well-adapted to tragedy. But the character of the Ionians today is more voluptuous, and the character of their mode is much altered.

Aside from the fact that we lack sufficient specimens of actual ancient Greek music to study how all of this was expressed by these musicians themselves, according to Plutarch whatever was meant to these people by modes, either with respect to character or more technical classifications, were in this period now beginning to be disregarded.

> But our musicians nowadays have so utterly exploded the most noble of all the modes, which the ancients greatly admired for its majesty, that hardly any among them make the least account of enharmonic distances. And so negligent and lazy are they grown, as to believe the enharmonic diesis to be too contemptible to fall under the apprehension of sense, and they therefore exterminate it out of their compositions, deeming those to be triflers that have any esteem for it or make use of the mode itself. For proof of which they think they bring a most powerful argument, which rather appears to be the dullness of their own senses; as if whatever fled their apprehensions were to be rejected as useless and of no value.[28]

28   Plutarch, 'Concerning Music.'

We might also point out that Plutarch, whom it is obvious was an acute listener and observer of music, in his essay, 'According to Epicurus,' poses a series of interesting questions about music including rare comments by this time on acoustics. The last of his questions, referring to the modes, demonstrates his critical awareness of the impact of music on the listener, which is one of the hallmarks of true aesthetic music.

> Why should the slenderer of two flutes of the same longitude speak flatter?—Why, if you raise the aulos, will all its notes be sharp, and flat again, if you lower it?—Why, when clapped to another, will it sound flatter; and sharper again, when taken from it?—Why also, if you scatter chaff or dust about the orchestra of a theater, will the sound be softened?—Why, when one would have set up a bronze statue of Alexander for a frontispiece to a stage at Pella, did the architect advise to the contrary, because it would spoil the actors' voices?—And why, of the several kinds of music, will the chromatic diffuse and the harmonic compose the mind?

As long as music was considered an exact science, as maintained by Pythagoras and others,[29] the entire concept of aesthetics had little urgency. But music is not an exact science and this idea could not be sustained. Certainly after the detailed elaboration of the aesthetic details in Tragedy by Aristotle, it is reasonable to assume that the tenor of philosophical discussion changed with regard to all the arts. While most of the books which focused specifically on music are lost, the commentary which survives clearly suggests that by the beginning of the Christian Era, at least, some basic definitions regarding the aesthetics of music were beginning to emerge.

The same basic distinction which Aristotle found in drama, that of Tragedy which involved empathy and reaches the observer on a deeper level resulting in catharsis, as opposed to the more superficial enjoyment of the Spectacle, now begins to be seen in descriptions of music. One kind of music offers 'delight,' and we might imagine the occasion after a banquet where one heard and 'delighted' in a remarkable performance. But another kind of performance is different, it is a performance which compels one to lift his thoughts above the surroundings to a higher level of reflection and contemplation. The metaphor which these philosophers used for this reaching above one's self was the Divine, as we can see in the following by Strabo (63 BC to 14 AD). It is also important to notice here that Strabo was one who was aware of these two kinds of music, as is evident in his choice of the terms 'delight' and 'artistic beauty.'

> Music, which includes dancing as well as rhythm and melody, at the same time, by the delight it affords and by its artistic beauty brings us in touch with the divine, and this for the following reason; for although it has been well said that human beings then act most like the gods when they are doing good to others, yet one might better say, when they are happy; and such happiness consists of rejoicing, celebrating festivals, pursuing philosophy, and engaging in music.[30]

Athenaeus was also aware of these two kinds of music. He tells of a performance he heard which was a perfect example of the highest kind of music, or performance, which affords 'delight':

> He entered, and after drinking he took up his lyre and delighted us to such an extent that all were amazed at his playing, fluency being combined with correct technique, as well as at the tunefulness of his voice.

29 There are indications that Epictetus, *The Discourses of Epictetus*, 319, still associated music with the same category as geometry as late as the first century AD.

30 Strabo, *The Geography of Strabo*, 10.3.9. To look at this from the other side of the coin, we might add that Plutarch said, in 'The Banquet of the Seven Wise Men,' that 'the Gods are better pleased with the sounds of panpipes and the aulos than with the voice of men.' This, in turn, was perhaps because he also pointed out, in 'Concerning Music,' that 'Some have thought that the God himself played upon the aulos.'

But Athenaeus describes another kind of music in quite different language. In one place he concludes, 'It is plain to me also that music should be the subject of philosophic reflection.'[31] In another place he quotes a remark by Eupolis, 'Music is a matter deep and intricate,' adding his own observation that music is always supplying something new for those who can perceive.[32] This, in a word, is aesthetic music.

For the Greeks, however, aesthetic music still had an additional burden. In addition to 'artistic beauty,' it also had to offer the listener, as part of the process of contemplation, an educational dimension. Even in the case of the better banquet entertainers this aspect was present. They were, Athenaeus says, required,

> to offer a beautiful song for the common enjoyment. They believed that the beautiful song was the one which seemed to contain advice and counsel useful for the conduct of life.[33]

To Plutarch, this meant music should also be 'useful.'

> Therefore, if it be the aim of any person to practice music with skill and judgment, let him imitate the ancient manner; let him also adorn it with those other sciences, and make philosophy his tutor, which is sufficient to judge what is in music decent and useful.[34]

For the education of the musician, it followed that there were also two levels: a more practical education in performance, which would be all that would be required for creating 'delight,' and an aesthetic education which went beyond the 'details' of music. This detailed practical knowledge is one thing, Plutarch says, but understanding *how to use* this knowledge is something quite different. This represents a higher expectation of the practical requirements of the player than we have seen in the past for this kind of musician. One should also point out that in several places Plutarch uses the term 'elegancy' in his attempt to find a subjective, non-technical term characteristic of aesthetic music.

> He then that has both judgment as well as skill is to be accounted the most complete musician. For he that understands the Dorian mode, not being able withal to discern by his judgment what is proper to it and when it is fit to be made use of, shall never know what he does; nay, he shall quite mistake the nature and custom of the mode. Indeed it is much questioned among the Dorians themselves, whether the enharmonic composers be competent judges of

31 Athenaeus, *Deipnosophistae*, 14.632.

32 Ibid, 14.623.

33 Ibid., 15.694.

34 Plutarch, 'Concerning Music.'

the Dorian songs. The same is to be said concerning the knowledge of rhythm. For he that understands a paean may not understand the proper use of it, though he know the measure of which it consists. Because it is much doubted among those that make use of paeans, whether the bare knowledge make a man capable to determine concerning the proper use of those rhythms; or, as others say, whether it aspire to presume so far. Therefore it behooves that person to have two sorts of knowledge, who will undertake to judge of what is proper and what improper; first, of the aesthetics [custom] and manner of elegancy for which such a composition was intended, and next of those things of which the composition consists. And thus, that neither the bare knowledge of harmony, nor of rhythm, nor of any other things that singly by themselves are but a part of the whole body of music, is sufficient to judge and determine either of the one or the other, what has been already said may suffice to prove.[35]

35 Ibid.

Therefore Plutarch concludes that musicians trained only in the details of music are not even capable of judging Music itself. He is absolutely correct and we make the same mistake in the twenty-first century: we train musicians in skills and concepts, but not in aesthetic ideals or philosophical aspects of music itself.

We are next to consider whether the masters of music are sufficiently capable of being judges of it. Now I aver the negative. For it is impossible to be a perfect musician and a good judge of music by the knowledge of those things that seem to be but parts of the whole body, as by excellency of hand upon the instrument, or singing readily at first sight, or exquisiteness of the ear, so far as this extends to the understanding of harmony and time. Neither does the knowledge of time and harmony, pulsation or elocution, or whatever else falls under the same consideration, perfect their judgment. Now for the reasons why a musician cannot gain a perfect judgment from any of these, we must endeavor to make them clear. First then it must be granted that, of things about which judgment is to be made, some are perfect and others imperfect. Those things which are perfect are the compositions in general, whether sung or played, and the expression of those, whether upon the instruments or by the voice, with the rest of the same nature. The imperfect are the things to these appertaining, and for whose sake they are made use of. Such are the parts of expression. A second reason may be found in poetry, with which the case is the same. For a man that hears a consort of voices and instruments can judge whether they sing or play in tune, and whether the language be plain or not. But every one of these are only parts of instrumental and vocal expression; not the aesthetic end itself, but for the sake of the end. For by these things of the same nature shall the elegancy of elocution be judged, whether it be proper to the poem which the performer undertakes to sing. The same is to be said of the several passions expressed in the poetry.[36]

One finds in the late Greek literature a tendency among the Greek aristocracy to love music but have little desire to associate with the musician himself, he being often a slave. Epictetus reminds us, however, that aesthetic art still requires hard work.

Every art, when it is being taught, is tiresome to one who is unskilled and untried in it. The products of the arts indeed show at once the use they are made for, and most of them have an attraction and charm of their own; for though it is no pleasure to be present and follow the process by which a shoemaker learns his art, the shoe itself is useful and a pleasant thing to look at as well. So too the process by which a carpenter learns is very tiresome to the unskilled person who happens to be by, but his work shows the use of his art. This you will see still more in the case of music, for if you are by when a man is being taught you will think the process of all things the most unpleasant, yet the effects of music are pleasant and delightful for unmusical persons to hear.[37]

Finally, Strabo raises an interesting question related to aesthetics: is there a relationship between the character of the artist and the character of his art? He had apparently made the observation that the best lyric poets he heard were also men with outstanding personal qualities.

Of course we do not speak of the excellence of a poet in the same sense as we speak of that of a carpenter or a blacksmith; for their excellence depends upon no inherent nobility and dignity, whereas the excellence of a poet is inseparably associated with the excellence of the man himself, and it is impossible for one to become a good poet unless he has previously become a good man.[38]

On the Performance of Aesthetic Music

The decline in Art Music in ancient Greece, which began in the Alexandrian Period, is everywhere evidenced as continuing during this period. Athenaeus, for one, summarizes the current state of this decline.

36 Plutarch, 'Concerning Music.'

37 Epictetus, *The Discourses of Epictetus*, 308.

38 Strabo, *The Geography of Strabo*, 1.2.5.

It happened that in ancient times the Greeks were music lovers; but later, with the breakdown of order when practically all the ancient customs fell into decay, this devotion to principle ceased, and debased fashions in music came to light, wherein every one who practiced them substituted effeminacy for gentleness, and license and looseness for moderation. What is more, this fashion will doubtless be carried further if some one does not bring the music of our forebears once more to open practice.[39]

It is interesting that Plutarch uses the same word, 'effeminate,' to describe the decay in the theater.

The ancients made use of music for its worth, as they did all other beneficial sciences. But our men of art, condemning its ancient majesty, instead of that manly, grave, heaven-born music, so acceptable to the Gods, have brought into the theaters a sort of effeminate musical tattling, mere sound without substance.[40]

Athenaeus finds only the Spartans have preserved the old values.

Of all the Greeks the Spartans have most faithfully preserved the art of music, employing it most extensively, and many composers of lyrics have arisen among them. Even to this day they carefully retain the ancient songs, and are very well taught in them and strict in holding to them … For people [are] glad to turn from the soberness and austerity of life to the solace of music, because the art has the power to charm.[41]

One of the most noble of the old traditions were the choral odes of the sixth century BC. Now we also see a rather dismal stage of their evolution.

Pratinas of Phlius, when hired aulos players and dancers usurped the dancing places, became indignant at the way in which the aulos players failed to accompany the choruses in the traditional fashion, and choruses now sang a mere accompaniment to the aulos players; … 'What uproar is this? What dances are these? What outrage hath assailed the alter of Dionysus with its loud clatter? … 'Tis the song that is queen, established by the Pierian Muse; but the aulos must be second in the dance, for he is even a servant; let him be content to be leader in the revel only, in the fist-fights of tipsy youngsters raging at the front door. Beat back him who has the breath of a mottled toad, burn up in flames that spit-wasting, babbling raucous reed, spoiling melody and rhythm in its march, that hireling whose body is fashioned by an auger!'[42]

39 Athenaeus, *Deipnosophistae*, 14.633.

40 Plutarch, 'Concerning Music.'

41 Athenaeus, *Deipnosophistae*, 14.632.

42 Ibid., 14.617. It should also be mentioned, for those who are interested, that Athenaeus devotes considerable discussion to the aulos of this period. He gives a list of terms 'applied to aulos playing,' some of which must be repertoire names: comus, pastoral, gingras, tetracomus, epiphallus, choir-dance, triumph-song, battle-song, gentle comus, Satyr's whirl, door-knock, tickle-tune, and Helot-lad [14.618]; speaks of famous players and schools of aulos instruction [4.184]; famous treatises on aulos playing [14.634]; and reveals that by this time there was a large number of instruments, of differing size, name and construction (including one that plays two different pitches at the same time), which all under the name of 'aulos.' [4.176] Extensive surveys of other instruments known to Athenaeus can be found under 4.174ff and 14.633ff.

The second century AD satirist, Lucian also offers us a glimpse of an undisciplined chorus.

> For not only the sounds they make are out of tune, but also their attitudes are unlike, and their movements contradictory, and in their purposes they are utterly at variance, until the conductor of the chorus drives every one of them off the stage, declaring that he has no further use for them.[43]

Lucian also makes a brief reference[44] to the tradition of the lyric poet, the poet–musician–philosopher who in ancient times was admired for his wisdom. The scene is an 'Auction of Philosophers' and Pythagoras, who remained an object of interest and curiosity among all the later Greeks, is put on the block first. One will note here the suggestion that Pythagoras was aware of at least some of the genetic properties of music when he says, 'I shall merely rub up your memory.'

> HERMES. Gentlemen! I have here for sale a live philosopher, the best of the lot, and with the most imposing presence. Who'll buy? Who wants to be more than a man? Who wants to understand the music of the spheres and return to life again?
> A CUSTOMER. He's not a mean looking fellow. But what does he know best?
> HERMES. Oh—arithmetic, astronomy, jugglery, geometry, music and witchcraft …
>
> …
>
> CUSTOMER. Well, if I purchase you, what will you teach me?
> PYTHAGORAS. I shall teach you nothing. I shall merely rub up your memory.
> CUSTOMER. Why, how will you do that?
> PYTHAGORAS. By first cleansing your soul and washing off the filth there is on it.
> CUSTOMER. Well, suppose now that I am already cleansed—what is your method of refreshing the memory?
> PYTHAGORAS. In the first place, one must lead a quiet life for a long time and observe silence—not uttering a word for five entire years … Then you shall practice music and geometry.
> CUSTOMER. That's a clever suggestion of yours—that I must first learn to play the harp before I can be wise.

Athenaeus also reports that the ancient tradition of the rhapsodist, he who specialized in reciting the Epic Poets in a style part speech and part music still existed.[45] Now, however, this too

43   Lucian, *A Second Century Satirist*, 361.

44   Ibid., 399.

45   Ibid., 14.620ff.

had broadened to include new specialists, including *hilarodists*, 'joy-singers whom some today call *simodists*,' and *magodists*, who specialized in bisexual roles, and *Ionicologos* or *kinaidologos*, who recite poems. Athenaeus relates the sad fate of one of the latter, one Apollonius, who in his performances insulted several kings. Finally, one of these, Ptolemy, arrested him and 'thrusting him into a leaden jar he carried him out to sea and sank him in the deep.'

Strabo found a much more distinguished rhapsodist in the person of Anaxenor, who was not only honored by the public in the theater but by Mark Anthony as well. The latter, we are told,

> even appointed him exactor of tribute from four cities, giving him a body-guard of soldiers. Further, his native land greatly increased his honors, having clad him in purple as consecrated to Zeus, as is plainly indicated in his painted image in the market-place. And there is also a bronze statue of him in the theater, with the inscription, 'Surely this is a beautiful thing, to listen to a singer such as this man is, like unto the gods in voice.'[46]

46 Ibid., 14.1.41.

On Music Education

We begin this discussion with Athenaeus who offers a broad perspective of the subject, beginning with his personal observation that 'indeed music trains character, and tames the hot-tempered and those whose opinions clash.'[47] In another place he provides us with an interesting summary of the current use of music for educational purposes among the Arcadians.

47 Ibid., 14.623.

> It was not by chance that the earliest Arcadians carried the art of music into their entire social organization, so that they made it obligatory and habitual not only for boys but also for young men up to thirty years of age, although in all other respects they were most austere in their habits of life. It is only among the Arcadians, at any rate, that the boys, from infancy up, are by law practiced in singing hymns and paeans, in which, according to ancestral custom, they celebrate their national heroes and gods. After these they learn the tunes of Timotheus and Philoxenus and dance them annually in the theaters with Dionysiac aulos players, the boys competing in the boys contests, the young men in the contests of adult males. And throughout their whole lives, in their social gatherings they do not pursue methods and practices so much with the aid of imported

entertainments as with their own talents, requiring one another to sing each in his turn. As for other branches of training, it is no disgrace to confess that one knows nothing, but it is deemed a disgrace among them to decline to sing. What is more, they practice marching-songs with aulos accompaniment in regular order, and further, they drill themselves in dances, and display them annually in the theaters with elaborate care and at public expense.

All this, therefore, the men of old taught them, not to gratify luxury and wealth, but because they observed the hardness in every one's life and the austerity of their character, which are the natural accompaniment of the coldness of their environment and the gloominess prevailing for the most part in their abodes; for all of us human beings naturally become assimilated to the character of our abode; hence it is also differences in our national position that cause us to differ very greatly from one another in character, in build, and in complexion. In addition to the training just described, their ancestors taught the Arcadian men and women the practice of public assembly and sacrifice, also at the same time choruses of girls and boys, eager as they were to civilize and soften the toughness of their natures by customs regularly organized.[48]

48 Ibid., 14.626ff.

In general, however, Plutarch finds a general decline in the values of music education during the first century AD, in particular that interest in music for the theater has replaced concern for music education.

Among the more ancient Greeks, music in theaters was never known, for they employed their whole musical skill in the worship of the Gods and the education of youth … But in our age is such another face of new inventions, that there is not the least remembrance or care of that use of music which is related to education; for all our musicians make it their business to court the theater Muses, and study nothing but compositions for the stage.[49]

49 Plutarch, 'Concerning Music.'

Where he finds music education, he finds it is being done more by chance than by a well thought out system.

First therefore we are to consider that all musical learning is a sort of habituation, which does not teach the reason of her precepts at one and the same time to the learner. Moreover, we are to understand that to such an education there is not requisite an enumeration of its several divisions, but every one learns by chance what either the master or scholar, according to the authority of the one and the liberty of the other, has most affection for. But the more prudent sort reject this chance-medley way of learning, as the Lacedaemo-

nians of old, the Mantineans, and Pallenians, who, making choice
either of one single method or else but very few styles, used only
that sort of music which they deemed most proper to regulate the
inclinations of youths.[50]

50 Ibid.

Plutarch warns his readers not to blame music itself for the current failures in music education, but rather one should blame the
teachers for how they use it.

> In brief therefore, a rational person will not blame the sciences
> themselves, if any one make use of them amiss, but will adjudge
> such a failing to be the error of those that abuse them. So that who-
> ever he be that shall give his mind to the study of music in his youth,
> if he meet with a musical education, proper for the forming and
> regulating his inclinations, he will be sure to applaud and embrace
> that which is noble and generous, and to rebuke and blame the
> contrary, as well in other things as in what belongs to music. And
> by that means he will become clear from all reproachful actions, for
> now having reaped the noblest fruit of music, he may be of great use,
> not only to himself but to the commonwealth; while music teaches
> him to abstain from every thing indecent both in word and deed,
> and to observe decorum, temperance, and regularity.[51]

51 Ibid.

Strabo agreed with this viewpoint, observing,

> If music is perverted when musicians turn their art to sensual
> delights at symposiums and in orchestric and scenic performances
> and the like, we should not lay the blame upon music itself, but
> should rather examine the nature of our system of education, since
> this is based on music.[52]

52 Strabo, *The Geography of
Strabo*, 10.3.9.

For Plutarch, the fundamental reason why music was so powerful a tool in education lay in what he perceived to be the unique,
direct link with the soul of hearing itself.

> Of this Theophrastus affirms, that [hearing] is the most sensitive
> of all the senses. For the several objects of sight, tasting and feel-
> ing do not excite in us so great disturbances and alterations as the
> sudden and frightful noises which assault us only at the ears. Yet
> in reality this sense is more rational than sensitive. For there are
> many organs and other parts of the body which serve as avenues
> and inlets to the soul to give admission to vice; there is but one pas-
> sage of virtue into young minds, and that is by the ears, provided
> they be preserved all along free from the corruptions of flattery and
> untainted with lewd discourses. For this reason Xenocrates was of

the opinion that children ought to have a defense fitted to their ears rather than fencers or prize-fighters, because the ears only of the latter suffered by the blows, but the morals of the former were hurt and maimed by words.[53]

In spite of this rather dim perspective of music education in the first century A D, two centuries later we find the most important discussion of music education since Aristotle. It is by a writer known as Aristides Quintilianus (late third century to the early fourth century A D) and is found in his larger treatise, *De Musica*.[54] It is a valuable discussion not only for filling in philosophical detail, but because of its very existence it seems to suggest that these ideas may have been continuously held by Greek society for six or seven centuries.

Aristides begins with the following prospective:

> We ought to investigate whether it is possible to educate by means of music or not; whether such education is useful or not; whether it can be given to all or only to some; and whether it can be given through just one kind of composition or through several. We must inquire whether the kinds thought unsuitable for education have no use at all, or whether even these can sometimes be found beneficial.

But first, he says, 'we must give some account of the soul.' Aristides then makes a few comments relative to the soul's relationship with the body. It is a brief discussion, because he assumes the reader is familiar with these ideas which had been discussed at length by many Greek philosophers, as the present reader has seen in the course of this book. Like earlier philosophers, because Aristides lacked the knowledge we have from the modern clinical study of our bicameral brain, he becomes a bit confusing in his attempt to account for his awareness of the rational and irrational aspects of our nature, which he relates to the soul as follows. 'He who orders the universe' gave the soul two basic parts. One, Reason, is associated with the divine and was given to the soul for the purpose of bringing order to the world. The other, the irrational, is attached to desire and through this the soul seeks 'after things in this world.' 'God' gave the soul memory, so the soul would not forget the beauties of 'the other world' and become interested in things less worthy than itself. As an antidote against irrationality, he sent the sciences to be 'its companion in its downward journey.'

These, then, are its two aspects, the rational, through which it accomplishes the works of wisdom, and the irrational, through which it engages in the business of the body.

Now it follows that there are two different kinds of branches of learning. This we recognize today as the left and right hemisphere of the brain. Although this is knowledge after his time, it is nevertheless quite interesting how he proposes the control of each side, or branch as he calls it, first the left and then the right. One branch he believes deals with the rational part, it keeps this part pure by 'gifts of wisdom.' The other branch deals with the irrational part, 'as though it were some savage beast that is moved without order,' taming it, allowing it neither 'excesses nor to be wholly subdued.' The 'leader and high priest' of the first branch of learning is philosophy, the 'ruler' of the second is music.

This second branch of education, he says, is especially important for children, for they would reject mere words, as they contain no pleasure, and it permits education 'which does not stir up the rational part before its time.' Everyone understands that children are by nature attracted to music, therefore he finds,

> Song always comes readily to all children, as we can see, and so do patterns of joyful movement: nor would anyone in his senses forbid them the pleasure they get from such things …
>
> Since all this is so, we have a reply to those who doubt whether everyone is moved by melody. To begin with, they have failed to realize that learning is for children, all of whom, as we can see, are naturally overcome by this kind of delight. Secondly, they have not noticed that even if it does not at once capture those whose way of life makes them less amenable to it, nevertheless it enslaves them before long. Just as one and the same drug applied to the same kind of complaint in several bodies does not always work in the same way, depending on the slightness or severity of the condition, but cures some more quickly, others more slowly, so music too arouses those more open to its influence immediately, but takes longer to capture the less susceptible.

Aristides gives two reasons why music 'captures' children so successfully, as he has just described, and in doing so he very accurately defines the true nature of music. First, unlike painting which appeals first only to the eye, music appeals to several senses. Second, while the other arts cannot *quickly* bring us to a conception of the actions they represent, music does so immediately. This is because music is not a representation of the 'characters and emotions of the soul,' but is rather *synonymous* with those characters and emotions.

> Music persuades most directly and effectively, since the means by which it makes its imitation [*mimesis*] are of just the same kind as those by which the actions themselves are accomplished in reality.

It is this character of music, Aristides says, which makes it so valuable in achieving the general aim of education, as was so clearly understood by the 'ancients.'

> Hence education of this sort should attend most especially upon children, so that through the imitations and likenesses they encounter when they are young they may come, through familiarity and practice, to recognize and to desire the things which are accomplished in earnest in adult life.
>
> Why then are we surprised to find that it was mostly through music that people in ancient times produced moral correction?—for they saw how powerful a thing it is, and how effective its nature makes it. Just as they applied their intelligence to such other human attributes as health and bodily well-being, seeking to preserve one thing, working to increase another, limiting to what is beneficial anything that tended towards excess, so also with the songs and dances to which all children are naturally attracted. It was impossible to prohibit them without destroying the children's own nature: instead, by cultivating them, little by little and imperceptibly, they devised an [educational] activity both decorous and delightful, and out of something useless made something useful.

Aristides next observes that music is especially valuable in dealing with the emotions, something which the rational part of us is noticeably unsuccessful at.

> No cure could be found in Reason alone for those who were burdened by these emotions; for pleasure is a very powerful temptation, captivating even the animals that lack reason, and grief which remains unsolaced casts many people into incurable illnesses; while inspired ecstasies, if not kept in moderation ... bring on superstition and irrational fears.

The practical importance of this is for the restoration of the soul, which, he adds, has a relationship with age and sex. Children sing of pleasure, women of grief and old men of divine possession.

Thus the ancients made everyone cultivate music from childhood throughout their lives in order that the proper kind of music would have a positive impact on the soul. The effectiveness of music in doing this he compares to the 'diverting of a stream, which was rushing through impassable crags or dispersing itself in marshy places, into an easily trodden and fertile plain.'

Once again we find an ancient Greek philosopher making an association between music and character, for Aristides reports that the ancients who had anxieties about the use of music were concerned with two kinds of people. First,

> those who neglected music, melody and unaccompanied poetry alike, were utterly crude and foolish; [and second] those who had involved themselves in it in the wrong way fell into serious errors, and through their passion for worthless melodies and poetry stamped upon themselves ugly idiosyncrasies of character.

It was for these concerns that the ancients so carefully controlled the kinds of music used in education. Therefore, he notes, they 'assigned educational music to as many as a hundred days, and the relaxing kind [of music] to no more than thirty.' Unfortunately we do not know for sure what he was referring to by this statement. Most likely it was a reference to the great tradition of spring festivals, for he adds,

> Through the serious songs and dances they educated persons of the better sort—audiences and performers alike—while through the pleasurable kind they gave recreation to the common people.

With this observation, he pauses to consider for a moment the question of entertainment music in general. He notes, with disapproval, that some people dismiss entertainment music in entirety.

> Some of them have treated melodies that are conducive to pleasure as completely worthless, without distinguishing the people for whom they are suitable and the manner in which they are used.

But this is wrong, he says, and 'I say this without condoning those melodies which are altogether discreditable.' Rather the point is, as in everything else, to 'separate out the best from the worst,' while keeping in mind the true purpose of music.

> We should not avoid song altogether just because it gives pleasure. Not all delight is to be condemned, but neither is delight itself the

objective of music. Amusement may come as it will, but the aim set for music is to help us toward virtue.

By 'the aim of music to help us toward virtue,' Aristides specifically means the use of music to form the character. 'Music,' he says, 'is the most powerful agent of education, rivaled by no other, [and it can be shown] that our characters commonly deteriorate if they are left undisciplined, lapsing into base or brutal passions.' Here he points to the success of the Greeks in using music for forming character. Other cultures, in failing to do this have arrived, in his view, at a rather alarming condition.

So far as education is concerned, there are two undesirable conditions, lack of culture and corruption of culture. The first comes from absence of education, the second from poor teaching. Now the soul is found to contain two generic varieties of emotion, spirit and appetite. Hence of the races that have never tasted the beauties of music at all, those that truckle to their appetites are insensitive and bovine, as are the peoples of Opicia and Leucania, while those that encourage their spirited side are savage, like wild beasts, as are the peoples of Garamantis and Iberia. Of those among whom music has been perverted against its nature into depravity and cultural corruption, the peoples that cultivate the appetites have souls that are too slack, and improper bodily affectations, like those who live in Phoenicia and their descendants in Africa; while those that are ruled by the spirited part lack all mental discipline—they are drunkards, addicted to weapon-dances no matter whether the occasion is right, excessive in anger and manic in war, like the Thracian peoples and the entire Celtic race. But the races that have embraced the learning of music and dexterity in its use, by which I mean the Greeks and any there may be who have emulated them, are blessed with virtue and knowledge of every kind, and their humanity is outstanding. If music can delight and mold whole cities and races, can it be incapable of educating individuals? I think not.

It is surprising to the modern reader to find how much importance Aristides assigns to this larger civic role of music. 'No other activity,' he says, 'has so great a capacity both for establishing a community and for sustaining it once it is established.' It was his understanding that music performed this role even in the prehistoric period of Greece.

Thus it was that in the earliest times, when political institutions were nowhere firmly established, the cultivation of music in association with virtue corrected civil discord and put an end to hostilities with neighboring cities and races. It specified set times for communal assemblies, and through the celebrations and revels customary at such occasions it restrained their aggressiveness towards one another, replacing it with kindliness.

'Now,' Aristides says, 'it is time to explain what kinds of melody and rhythm will discipline the natural emotions.' Here he promises to not only set forth the principles written down by the great philosophers, but to reveal to us some of the things they did not write about—those 'esoteric secrets' they reserved 'for their discussions with one another.' He must do this, he says, because now,

> indifference to music (to put it politely) is so widespread, we cannot expect people with only a mild interest in the subject to tolerate being faced with a book in which not everything is explicitly spelled out.

Like all earlier Greek philosophers, Aristides assigns the emotions to the soul, but now he adds something new as he divides the emotions into male and female qualities. This same duality he finds in nature as well, in plants, minerals, and spices, expressed through their qualities of color or texture and their opposites.

> Passions arise in the soul out of its affinity with the male or the female or with both. Thus the female is seriously lacking in restraint, and with it the appetitive part [of the soul] is in accord, while the male is violent and energetic, and the spirited part [of the soul] resembles it. In the female—both the female type of soul and the female branch of humanity—griefs and pleasures are rife, anger and recklessness in the male. Couplings of these passions arise too: of griefs with pleasures and of anger with recklessness, of recklessness with pleasure and grief, of anger with both, and indeed of each with any one or more of the others. One could find a thousand different varieties of these emotions if one studied them in all their complexity.

Aristides acknowledges that each person has his own unique emotional makeup and that this affects perception. Also the objects of our perception have their own emotional characteristics. Thus when the soul encounters an object, through perception, it 'obtains an impression' of the object and compares it to the emotions of itself. By this he means first comparing it to the male and female natures.

> We distinguish as belonging to the female those colors and shapes that are vivid and decorative, and to the male those that are subdued and conducive to mental reflection. Secondly, among the objects of hearing, we associate sounds that are smooth and gentle with the female, rougher ones with its opposite. To avoid mentioning everything individually, one may assert that it is quite generally true, in all cases, that those objects of perception which naturally invite us to pleasure and to the gentle relaxation of the mind are to be adjudged female, those that stimulate us to thought and arouse activity are to be assigned to the province of the male.

This duality Aristides finds in the simplest elements of music, even in single notes, or sounds. 'Some of them are hard and male, others relaxed and female.' It is because of this that some melodies are suitable for the harp which would be inappropriate on the aulos, as he will explain below.

To demonstrate how character is found in melody, Aristides provides a lengthy discussion of the male and female qualities of vowels, diphthongs, consonants, etc., which reveals little to the modern reader. Although he says these same principles apply to melody with respect to instruments, he does not explain this.

It is the identification of these emotional characters in a melody which is the first step in affecting character through music education. Unfortunately he does not explain this process beyond indicating that one selects a melody of a desired character in order to introduce this character into children, 'and older people too,' in which this character is missing. We lose some confidence in his own understanding of this specific educational process when he concludes,

> If it is obscure and hard to diagnose, you should begin by applying whatever melody comes to hand. If this is effective in influencing the soul, you should persist with it, but if the patient remains unaltered you should introduce a modulation; for it is likely that someone who is resistant to one sort of melody will be attracted by its opposite.

Aristides next turns to rhythm, which he also considers in terms of emotion and character. Like all ancient Greeks, he associates the beginning of rhythm with the rise and fall of marching feet: those rhythms associated with the *arsis* are restless and those associated with the *thesis* are more peaceful. Rhythms composed of short syllables are faster and 'more passionate,' those composed only of long syllables are slower and calm and mixtures have the qualities of both. Compound rhythms are more emotional and 'the impression they give is tempestuous, because the number from which they are constructed does not keep the same order of its parts in each position.' Running rhythms inspire us to action, other are supine and flabby.

Since Aristides finds that rhythm is so closely associated with character, it follows, he believed, that one can judge a person by his manner of walking.

> We find that people whose steps are of good length and equal, in the manner of the spondee, are stable and manly in character: those whose steps are long but unequal, in the manner of trochees or paions, are excessively passionate: those whose steps are equal but too short, in the manner of the pyrrhic, are spineless and lack nobility: while those whose steps are short and unequal, and approach rhythmical irrationality, are utterly dissipated. As to those who employ all the gaits in no particular order, you will realize that their minds are unstable and erratic.

Here too, rhythm is an important aspect of education, to the degree that it is an element which can be imitated. Thus, he says, noble people should not listen at all to the music of the common people.

> Concerning the art of delivery the following must be said. Of the bodily movements in which delivery consists, those which imitate ideas, diction, melodies and rhythms of a reverent and male character, and which incite us to manliness, should be seen and copied by everyone. Those whose nature is the opposite may be watched and imitated by the common people—but not all of them, and not by everyone. At any rate, people of noble nature and sound character should refrain from imitating and watching them altogether.

Musical instruments also have character, which explains why a particular listener will 'love and admire the instruments that are suited to them.' Thus he finds the trumpet to be male, because of its vehemence, and the aulos female, 'since it has a mournful and dirge-like sound.' Similarly, among the strings, he finds the lyra to be male, because of its extreme deepness and roughness and the *sambyke* to be female, 'since it lacks nobility and incites people to abandonment because of its very high pitch.'

> Are not those who have heard all these things filled more than ever with a desire to discover why it is so, and to find out what it is that makes the soul so easily captivated by the melody of instruments? The account I shall give is an ancient one, but its exponents were wise men, and it is to be trusted. Even if other considerations might lead us to doubt it, its truth is indisputably attested by experience; for the fact that the soul is naturally stirred by the music of instruments is one that everybody knows.

This ancient explanation which he promises to give us turns out to be the same point he made with respect to perceptions. Here, since each individual instrument has its own inherent character, and so does our soul, it follows that we are attracted to, or are influenced by, those instruments whose character conforms with that of our soul. Before continuing his argument, Aristides reminds us,

> There are two useful forms of music-making, one valuable for the benefit it brings to the best of men, the other for the harmless relaxation it gives to the common run of mankind, and to anyone there may be still less exalted than they.

Putting these two ideas together, he takes the example of the aulos, which he tells us the goddess threw away, 'on the grounds that the pleasure the instrument gave was unsuitable for those who desire wisdom,'[55] although he says it might have some value for those 'worn out by the exertions of constant physical labor.' In this regard, Aristides quotes something of Pythagoras which is not found elsewhere.

This was also the sense of the advice Pythagoras is said to have given his disciples: that if they heard the aulos they should wash out their ears because the breath had defiled them,[56] but that they should use well-omened melodies sung to the lyra to cleanse their souls of irrational impulses. The aulos, he said, serves the thing that is master of our worse part, while the lyra is loved and enjoyed by that which cares for our rational nature.

55 In the form of this myth which has come down to us today, the goddess threw the aulos away when she discovered, by looking into a pond while she was playing, that the exertion of playing disfigured her face.

56 Many philosophers at the time of Pythagoras considered the player himself to be of the lower class, 'sordid persons,' as Plutarch called them. The suggestion here is that it is the breath of the aulos player, rather than sound waves, which travels through space to the ear of the listener, hence 'defiling them.'

Aristides concludes this idea, and his essay on music education, by projecting this idea to cosmic proportions.

> Learned men of all nations also bear witness for me that it is not our souls alone that are constituted in this way, but also the soul of the whole universe. Some of them worship the region below the moon, which is full of breaths and has a moist constitution, and yet derives its activity from the life of the region of aether: these people make propitiation to it with both kinds of instruments, wind and stringed. Others worship the pure and aetherial region: they reject all wind instruments as defiling the soul and tempting it towards earthly things, and sing their hymns and praises with the kithara and lyra alone, because these are purer. Wise men imitate and emulate the aetherial region.

In summary, Aristides Quintilianus has left a fascinating discussion of music education, which begins with a few observations on music in earlier Greek society. The ancients, he said, were especially concerned with [1] those who neglected music, and were therefore 'utterly crude and foolish,' and [2] those who use music incorrectly, stamping upon themselves 'ugly idiosyncrasies of character.' It was for these two reasons that the ancients so carefully controlled the kinds of music used in music education.

Regarding his own views, he contends the following:

1. There are two branches of learning, those of the rational and the non-rational. The 'high priest' of the former is philosophy and the 'ruler' of the latter is music.

2. Music is especially valuable for children as it is a form of education which does not 'stir up the rational part before its time.' Also, music captures the interest of children because, [1] it appeals to more then one of the senses, and [2] the emotions in music are synonymous with their own emotions. Music is clearly more valuable than the rational part for dealing with the emotions.

3. The purpose of music education is to develop the character, 'to help us toward virtue.'

4. This is accomplished in the relationship of music and the soul. Each soul has an individual emotional nature which affects perception. When the soul encounters something, it obtains an impression of the object and then compares it to its own nature.

5. Character is developed in music education in part by the inherent character of the materials themselves. Among these:

a. All the elements of music, even single notes, have male and female qualities.
b. Rhythm, too, expresses emotions and character, so accurately that you can judge a person's character by how he walks!
c. Musical instruments are also either male [trumpet] or female [aulos].

Functional Music

Although Plutarch suggests that it was still rare at this time for 'sacrifices to be performed without the aulos and dances,'[57] Athenaeus suggests once again that a general decline had taken place in the religious-cult festivals.

> But the men of today, who pretend to sacrifice to the gods and call together their friends and intimates, curse their children, quarrel with their wives, drive their slaves to tears, threaten the crowd …[58]

Athenaeus also documents a general decline in the observance of wedding celebrations.

> Today we are serving a wedding feast; the animal to be slaughtered is an ox. The father of the bride is distinguished, distinguished too is the groom. The women of this company are priestesses to goddess and to god; there will be drunken revelers, aulos playing, all-night vigils, a riot.[59]

He even mentions in one place the performance by a prostitute 'single-pipe girl' at a wedding celebration![60]

Athenaeus also mentions that the military still depended on music[61] and that it was still used for funerals.[62] He also gives an extensive list of kinds of music employed by workers, with specific kinds of music sung by those grinding grain, working the loom, the wool-spinners and wool-carders, nurses, reapers, farmers, bath-tenders, shepherds, millers, etc.[63]

Perhaps most surprising of the kinds of functional music mentioned by Athenaeus is that used for diplomacy!

> Many of the barbarians [those who do not speak Greek well] also conduct diplomatic negotiations to the accompaniment of aulos and harp to soften the hearts of their opponents.[64]

57 Plutarch, 'How a Young Man Ought to Hear Poems.'

58 Athenaeus, *Deipnosophistae*, 8.364.

59 Ibid., 9.377.

60 Ibid., 4.175.

61 Ibid., 12.516.

62 Ibid., 14.619.

63 Ibid., 14.618.

64 Ibid., 14.627. In 14.631, Athenaeus gives the form name of this kind of music as 'apostolic (also called parthenioi).'

ENTERTAINMENT MUSIC

Theodorus, an actor of tragedies, supposedly said to Satyrus, a comedian, that it takes greater art to move an audience to tears than to make it laugh. Plutarch, who mentions this, answers for the comedian that perhaps it is a more noble aim to free them from their sorrows[65] Entertainment with so high an aim is rarely mentioned in the literature of the period. There are interesting references to songs which *all* the guests sung during banquets[66] and a very interesting reference to the women of Corcyra who, 'to this very day sing as they play ball.'[67]

The most common references to entertainment music are those relative to the prostitute 'single-pipe girls.' This was no doubt what Plutarch was thinking of when he mentions 'light music and wanton songs and discourses which suggest to men obscene fancies, debauch their manners and incline them to an unmanly way of living in luxury and wantonness.'[68] Such was the case with the Lydians at this time, according to Athenaeus.

> So dissolute did they become in unseasonable carousing that some of them never saw the sun either rising or setting. And so they passed a law, which was still in force in our day, that the single-pipe girls and harp-girls and all such entertainers should receive wages from early in the morning until midday, and from then until lamplight; and from this time on they were immersed in drinking for the rest of the night.[69]

The satirist, Lucian, describes the philosopher Aristippus of Cyrene as one who enjoyed single-pipe girls in the spirit of the previous description.

> Well, in brief, he's handy to have as a constant companion, and good to crack a bottle with and sing and dance with the single-pipe girl—in fact, just the fellow for a master who is fond of favorites and given to riotous living. As for the rest, he knows how to make pastry, and is skilled in fine cookery—in short, an expert in the art of luxurious living. At all events, he got his education at Athens, and was also at one time in the service of the tyrants of Sicily, and held in high esteem among them. His course of life may be summed up as follows—to think slightly of everything, make use of everything, and lay every form of pleasure under contribution.[70]

65   Plutarch, 'How a Man may Praise Himself without being Envied.'

66   Athenaeus, *Deipnosophistae*, 15.694.

67   Ibid., 1.24.

68   Plutarch, 'How a Young Man Ought to hear Poems.'

69   Athenaeus, *Deipnosophistae*, 12.526. In 13.571, Athenaeus suggests that some of these girls were quite young, 'just beginning to ripe.'

70   Lucian, 'The Auction of Philosophers.'

On the other hand, some single-pipe girls are mentioned as being part of the highest society, one being named after a religious festival and others having houses named for them.[71] The level of their popularity was such among the wealthy that one such girl, named Bromias, we are told,

> would even have played the single-pipe accompaniment to the Pythian Games had she not been prevented from doing so by the populace.[72]

71 Ibid., 13.587 and 576.

72 Ibid., 13.605.

PART 4

Aesthetics in the Musical Practice of Ancient Rome

THE MUSIC OF THE ETRUSCANS

The Etruscans [Latin: *tusci*; Greek: *Tyrrhenoi*] inhabited the western region of Italy, known today as Tuscany. These peoples, of Eastern Mediterranean origin, migrated to the Italian Peninsula in the ninth or tenth century BC and formed a strong cultural entity until their eventual absorption into the Roman Empire in 27 BC. Because the Etruscans traded with the Greeks, their musical culture was based on Grecian models and it was the Etruscans who seem to have played a major role in passing these traditions on to the Roman Empire. Our knowledge of the Etruscans' role in the transfer of culture from Greece to Rome is limited primarily to observations we can make in iconography, especially paintings in tombs.[1] We also gain insight from a few Greek and Roman references, which are all the more valuable since the language of the Etruscans themselves cannot yet be deciphered.

We can, for example, see a clear example of this link between Greece and Rome in the case of a new kind of trumpet invented by the Etruscans. Although the Greek trumpet [*salpinx*] was a familiar instrument, beginning with the sixth century BC Greek writers occasionally mention a different instrument which they associate with the Etruscans.

SOPHOCLES
I hear thy call and seize it in my soul, as when a Tyrrhenian bell speaks from mouth of bronze![2]

EURIPIDES
Then the Tyrrhenian trumpet blast burst forth, like fire.[3]

AESCHYLUS
Let the piercing Tyrrene trumpet, filled with human breath, send forth its shrill blare to the folk![4]

This new instrument with which the Greeks were familiar was probably the *cornu*, which becomes a basic instrument of the Roman army.[5] Another new kind of trumpet, which the Etruscans passed on to the Romans, was the *lituus*, recognizable by its bell bent backward.[6]

1 Like the Egyptians, the Etruscans believed that in the life after death the deceased would continue his same activities.

2 Sophocles, Ajax, 16–17.

3 Euripides, *The Phoenician Woman*, 1377–1378.

4 Aeschylus, *Eumenides*, 567.

5 The instrument looks somewhat like a capital 'G.' This instrument can be seen already in the seventh century BC in an Etruscan wall painting of the tomb of Castel Rubello, Orvieto.

6 The instrument looks somewhat like an horizontal letter 'J.' Two early lituus survive: one Etruscan (Rome, Villa Giulia Museum, Nr. 51216) and one Roman (Rome, Museo Etrusco-Gregoriano, Room III).

The Etruscans also seem to have experimented with the Greek aulos, adding a bell to it, which, again, we find later in Rome.[7] They may have also renamed it, for Varro (Roman, first century BC) finds in a fragment of poetry by Ennius (236–169 BC) that the Etruscan aulos players were called *Subulo*.[8]

Once a subulo was standing by the stretches of the sea.[9]

Ovid also mentions these Etruscan aulos players and their 'homely' music, which suggests perhaps that he associated them with folk music, rather than as artists.[10]

ART MUSIC

Since we lack literature from the Etruscans, it is very difficult to establish the role of art music, although we can assume that the musical performances in the theater were of the nature of art music. In addition, one comment by Livy seems to suggest that the Etruscans had developed recognizable national styles in the theater arts.[11]

Probably there were the performances of art music after the tables were cleared at banquets, as one found in Greece. Such a performance may be represented in a third century BC tomb painting in Scudi, Tarquinia, in which an aulos player, wearing a toga, is seen playing for a banquet.

Another possible reference to art music may be the music and plays offered the general public by the Etruscan leaders, Tyrrhenus and Lydus, to appease public opinion during a famine.[12]

FUNCTIONAL MUSIC

The wide range of functional music employed by the Etruscans, can be seen in the statement of an early writer, who observed that they 'knead bread, practice boxing, and flog their slaves to the accompaniment of the aulos.'[13]

A stone sarcophagus from Nefro, from the fourth century BC, shows a wedding procession in which the bride and groom are followed by musicians playing the harp, cornu, and aulos.[14]

Cornu and lituus players can also be seen in funeral processions in the tombs of Bruschi and Tifone, near Tarquinia. Professional

7   A fifth century BC fresco in the tomb of Leopardi, near Tarquinia, shows a bell on each body similar to that of the modern oboe.

8   Varro, *On the Latin Language*, 7.35.

9   Ibid.

10   Ovid, *The Art of Love*, 1.111.

11   Livy, *History of Rome*, 7.2.

12   Cited by Sendrey, *Music in the Social and Religious Life of Antiquity*, 377.

13   Alcimus, quoted in Athenaeus, *The Deipnosophists*, 12.518. The British Museum has a beautiful pot [B 64] from the sixth century BC, which shows two boxing figures and a man playing the aulos. In a wall painting on the tomb of Golini I, Orvieto one can see a fourth century BC aulos player playing in the kitchen while servants work.

14   A fifth century urn (Chiusi, Museo Civico, Nr. 2260) shows an aulos player leading a wedding procession.

aulos players also performed during the lying-in-state, sacrificial rites and magic lamentations for the dead.[15]

There is an extraordinary tale involving hunting and an Etruscan aulos player who must have been very charismatic!

> There is an Etruscan story current which says that the wild boars and the stags in that country are caught by using nets and hounds, as is the usual manner of hunting, but that music plays a part, and even the larger part, in the struggle. And how this happens I will now relate. They set the nets and other hunting gear that ensnare the animals in a circle, and a man proficient on the aulos stands there and tries his utmost to play a rather soft tune, avoiding any shriller note, but playing the sweetest melodies possible. The quiet and stillness easily carry [the sound] abroad; and the music streams up to the heights and into ravines and thickets—in a word into every lair and resting place of these animals. Now at first when the sound penetrates to their ears it strikes them with terror and fills them with dread, and then an unalloyed and irresistible delight in the music takes hold of them, and they are so beguiled as to forget about their offspring and their homes. And yet wild beasts do not care to wander away from their native haunts. But little by little these creatures in Etruria are attracted as though by some persuasive spell, and beneath the wizardry of the music they come and fall into the snares, overpowered by the melody.[16]

15 Grove, *New Grove Dictionary of Music and Musicians*, vol. 6, p. 289. An excellent example of an aulos player performing for the lying-in-state can be seen in the fragment of a tomb stone from Chiusi, now in Rome, Barracco.

16 Claudius Aelianus (second century A D), *Of the Characteristics of Animals*, 12.46.

THE MUSIC OF THE EARLY ROMANS

For the period before the Republic Period of Rome (before 240 BC) our knowledge comes primarily from the extant portions of the *History of Rome* by Titus Livius, known as Livy. Writing in the first century BC, Livy was concerned mostly with political events and only rarely does he mention music.

The first reference to music in Livy's work is quite revealing. The King Servius Tullius (ca. sixth century BC) created a formal organization of society, based on wealth, which would be used for the assessment of taxes and military obligation. In this social order we can see that the only represented musicians, trumpeters, were valued rather low, in the fifth of six classes. What this meant, at least in human terms, can be seen in how the various levels were equipped for defense. The first class was equipped with helmet, round shield, greaves, breast-plate and armed with sword and spear. The fourth class had only spear and javelin and the fifth class, which included the musicians, had only slings and stones.[17]

17 Livy, *A History of Rome*, 1.43.

ART MUSIC

Livy provides a remarkable and logical summary of the birth of art song and theater, which he dates from the middle of the fourth century BC, as part of ceremonies meant to reconcile the people to the gods following a plague. There are some modern scholars who wonder if the ancient Greek plays were all sung, and not just the choruses. For those inclined to this view, the second paragraph invites a possible explanation of how sung stage works developed into spoken drama.

> Amongst their other ceremonies intended to placate divine wrath, they are said to have introduced scenic entertainments, something quite novel for a warlike people whose only previous public spectacle had been that of the circus. These began only in a modest way, as most things do, and were in fact imported from abroad. Players were brought from Etruria to dance to the strains of the aulos without any singing or miming of song, and made quite graceful movements in the Etruscan style. Then the young Romans began to copy them, exchanging jokes at the same time in crude improvised verse, with gestures to fit the words. Thus the entertainment was adopted and became established by frequent repetition. The native actors were called *histriones*, because the Etruscan word for an actor is *ister*; they stopped bandying ribald improvised lines, like Fescennine verses, and began to perform *saturae* or medleys amplified with music, the singing properly arranged to fit the aulos and movement in harmony with it.
>
> Some years later, Livius first ventured to give up the *satura* and compose a play with a plot. Like everyone else at the time, he also acted in his own dramas; and the tale is told that when he lost his voice after repeated recalls, he was given permission to place a boy in front of the aulos player to sing the songs while he acted them himself, and did so with a good deal more vigor when not hampered by having to use his voice. From then on began the actors' practice of employing singers while they confined themselves to gesture and used their voices only for dialog. This style of performance began to detach the play from impromptu joking to raise a laugh, and drama gradually developed into an art.[18]

18   Ibid., 7.2.

FUNCTIONAL MUSIC

The origin of the use of music in the religious-cult celebrations in Rome is assigned, by tradition, to the time of Numa Pompilius (seventh to eighth centuries BC) when singers and dancers performed rites in honor of the god Mars. During the earliest years it appears to have been the brass instruments from the Etruscans and the aulos which participated in these kinds of ceremonies. Something of the spirit of these primitive celebrations can be seen in a description of the worship of the Idaean Mother by Lucretius (99–55 BC).

> Their open palms slap the taut drums
> To Terrible thunder, the hollow cymbals clash,
> The horns blare raucous, and the auloi shrill
> With sharp insistence.[19]

19   Lucretius, *The Way Things Are*, Book 2, p. 619ff.

On one famous occasion in the fourth century BC, the aulos players who performed for the religious festivals went on strike when the city could not pay their full wages for participating in the Feast of Jupiter. The aulos players actually left town and took up residence in Tibur, leaving Rome without the whole range of services usually rendered by these players, as noted by Ovid.

> The aulos was missed in the theater, missed at the altars; no dirge accompanied the bier on the last march.[20]

20   Ovid, *Fasti*, 6.666ff.

After negotiations failed to secure the return of these players, citizens of Tibur proposed to trick them into returning. They threw a great party for them and when they were 'reeling with heady wine' they arranged to take them to their lodgings by wagon. The wagons instead took the sleeping aulos players to Rome, where, in order to help them save face, they were disguised in masks and long gowns. For some time this was commemorated in an annual festival, during which musicians would parade in long gowns and masks.

There are two early accounts of this incident which provide interesting detail. The earliest is by Livy, who not only characterizes these aulos players in an unfavorable light, but reveals his general disinterest in music itself by noting that this story 'would scarcely be worth mentioning, were it not connected to religion.'

The aulos players were angry at having been forbidden by the last censors to hold their feast in the temple of Jupiter, according to ancient custom, and marched off to Tibur in a body, with the result that there was no one in the City to play the auloi at sacrifices. The Senate was seized with pious misgivings about the incident, and sent delegates to Tibur to request the citizens to do their best to return the men to Rome. The Tiburtines courteously promised to do so, and first summoned the aulos players to their senate house and urged them to go back to Rome. Then, when they found that persuasion achieved nothing, they dealt with the men by a ruse nicely in tune with their nature. On a public holiday various citizens invited parties of aulos players to their homes on the pretext of celebrating the feast with music, and sent them to sleep by plying them with wine, for which men of their kind are generally greedy. In that condition they dumped them, heavily asleep, in carts and carried them off to Rome. The carts were left in the Forum and the aulos players knew nothing until daylight surprised them there, still very drunk. The people quickly gathered round them and prevailed on them to stay. They were given permission on three days a year to roam the City in fancy dress, making music and enjoying the license which is now customary, and those of them who played auloi at sacrifices had their right to hold a feast in the temple restored.[21]

21 Livy, *A History of Rome*, 9.30.

It is evident this festival was still celebrated in the first century AD, as it is mentioned by Plutarch.

QUESTION. Why are the minstrels allowed to go about the city on the Ides of January, wearing women's apparel?

SOLUTION. This sort of men (as it seems) had great privileges accruing to them from the grant of King Numa, by reason of his godly devotion; which things afterward being taken from them when the Decemviri managed the government, they forsook the city. Whereupon there was a search made for them, and one of the priests, offering sacrifice without music, made a superstitious scruple of so doing. And when they returned not upon invitation, but led their lives in Tibur, a certain freedman told the magistrates privately that he would undertake to bring them. And providing a plentiful feast, as if he had sacrificed to the Gods, he invited the minstrels; women-kind was present also, with whom they reveled all night, sporting and dancing. There on a sudden the man began a speech, and being surprised with a fright, as if his patron had come in upon him, persuaded the auloi to ascend the caravans that were covered all over with skins, saying he would carry them back to Tibur. But this whole business was but a trepan; for he wheeling about the caravan, and

they perceiving nothing by reason of wine and darkness, he very
cunningly brought them all into Rome by the morning. Most of
them, by reason of the night-revel and the drink that they were
in, happened to be clothed in flowered women's robes; whereupon, being prevailed upon by the magistrates and reconciled,
it was decreed that they should go up and down the city on that
day, habited after this manner.[22]

22 Plutarch, 'The
Roman Questions.'

Among his discussions of military events of the fourth century
BC, Livy on three occasions mentions the songs of soldiers. His
descriptions, however, always seem to carry an uncomplimentary
tone, as in the case of the 'rough soldiers' songs,' sung by the troops
who entered Rome in a procession with Quintus Fabius.[23]

23 Livy, *A History of Rome*, 10.30.

His most colorful descriptions are of the songs of the enemy, the
Gauls. A very intriguing reference, for ca. 403–390 BC, only makes
us wish we could hear the music itself.

All too soon cries like the howling of wolves and barbaric songs
could be heard, as the Gallic squadrons rode hither and thither
close outside the walls.[24]

24 Ibid., 5.39.

Perhaps his choice of language here only reflects his feelings for the
enemy, whom in another place he pictures in one of their moments
of victory.

Some Gallic horsemen came in sight, carrying heads hanging from
their horses' breasts and fixed on their spears, singing their customary song of triumph.[25]

25 Ibid., 10.26.

Livy mentions only one instance each of the use of the trumpet
for civic or military signal duty,[26] although it must have been a
common occurrence. The latter instance, 'the continuous noise of
trumpets,' suggests that the instruments may have been plentiful.[27]

26 Ibid., 8.32.

27 Ibid., 1.65.

19 THE REPUBLIC (240–27 BC)

Some historians paint a rather dismal picture of musical practice during the Roman Empire, beginning with those who suggest that the Romans really had no culture of their *own* to begin with.

> Roman music was really Greek, transformed to Roman soil and adapted to Roman condition.[1]

Others assign to the Romans a 'rather uncouth and vulgar' taste in music.[2] Sendrey, on the other hand, suggests a vigorous musical practice throughout all levels of Roman society.

> In general, contemporary records indicate that the tendency to practice music prevailed, at least in public life, in gigantic proportions. Music teachers and music schools furnished dilettantes *en masse*; it belonged to the *bon ton* of every bourgeois family to give their daughters instruction in lyre playing. Rich people employed multitudes of slaves, who made music day and night, to the despair of their neighbors. At banquets there was no longer any conversation, since music drowned out every attempt at it. A veritable invasion of virtuosi of all kinds flooded the theaters and concert halls, bringing with them all their idiosyncrasies, vanities, and intrigues.[3]

This same writer characterizes the aim of Roman musical practice during this early period as 'practical usefulness.'[4] He mentions as an illustration of this aesthetic the satirical poem, 'The Donkey as a lyre-player,' by Marcus Varro (116–26 BC), in which there is a debate on the usefulness of music. One group believed music to be effeminate and unnecessary, while the other group saw a particular value in the use of music to alleviate the drudgery of workers.[5]

In part this view of music reflected the fact that in the earliest Roman years it was slaves who provided the music. Thus, Cicero in his defense of Milo mentions, in an aside, that the latter 'happened on this occasion to have with him some singing boys of his wife, and a bevy of waiting maids.'[6] Cicero himself had a musical slave, who, as he mentions in a letter to Atticus, helped stack a jury.

> You know who I mean by Baldhead, my trumpet-blower, whose complimentary speech about me I mentioned to you. Well, he fixed up the whole job in a couple of days with the help of a slave, and a

1 Albert Trevor, *History of Ancient Civilization* (New York: Harcourt Brace, 1939), 2:590.

2 Paul Henry Lang, *Music in Western Civilization* (New York: Norton, 1941), 31.

3 Sendrey, *Music in the Social and Religious Life of Antiquity*, 379.

4 Ibid., 380.

5 Ibid., 380. Unfortunately, Varro's more significant discussion, 'De musica,' a chapter in the treatise *Disciplinae*, is lost.

6 Cicero, *Pro Milone* [In Defense of Titus Annius Milo], 55.

gladiator at that. He sent for people, gave promises, sureties, cash down. He even went so far—God, what a scandal!—as to enhance the bribe to some members of the jury by offering nights with certain ladies and introductions to young men of good family.[7]

7 Cicero, *Letters of Cicero*, trans. L.P. Wilkinson (New York: Norton, 1966), 34.

It was for this reason that the historian Nepos (100–22 BC) wrote that the practice of music and singing was not appropriate to a man of distinction.[8] The vast number of these slaves made possible some very large performing forces. A procession in the time of Ptolemaeus Philadelphus (283–246 BC), for example, included no fewer than six hundred singers and three hundred kithara players.[9] A similar report by Horace reports numerous aulos and lyres accompanying songs in the temple of Venus.[10] Many of these musicians were Greeks who fled to Rome after the conquest of Macedonia in 167 BC and the destruction of Corinth in 144 BC.[11]

8 Sendrey, *Music in the Social and Religious Life of Antiquity*, 407.

9 Ibid., 411.
10 Horace, *Carmina*, 4.1.22.

But there must be another point of view. To begin with, the relegation of music to the sphere of the utilitarian would not explain the fervent practice of it by some members of the highest level of society. For example, Sulla, though a harsh ruler, was a good singer. The consul Lucius Flaccus (fl. ca. 19 AD) was a diligent trumpet player, practicing daily it would appear.[12] And while we know nothing specific of Julius Caesar's interest in music, perhaps his sympathy for it is reflected in the fact that upon his death and ritual cremation, the musicians of Rome threw their professional clothes onto the fire as an expression of grief.[13]

11 Their instruments went with them, but changed names. Marcus Varro, in *On the Latin Language*, 6.75 and 8.61, gives *tuba* for trumpet and *tubicines* for the players (*liticines* and *bucinator* for the other types of trumpet); *cornicines* for 'horn blowers'; *tibiae* for auloi and *tibicines* for the players; and *cithara* for lute.

12 Sendrey, *Music in the Social and Religious Life of Antiquity*, 391.

Cicero tells us of one member of the aristocracy, Chrysogonos, whom he felt supported too much music.

13 Suetonius, *Lives of the Caesars*, Book 1, lxxxiv.

But what am I to say about his vast household of slaves and the variety of their technical skill? I say nothing about such common trades, such as those of cooks, bakers, litter-bearers: to charm his mind and ears, he has so many artists, that the whole neighborhood rings daily with the sound of vocal music, stringed instruments, and auloi, and with the noise of banquets by night. When a man leads such a life ... can you imagine his daily expenses, his lavish displays, his banquets? Quite respectable, I suppose, in such a house, if that can be called a house rather than a manufactory of wickedness and a lodging house of every sort of crime.[14]

14 Cicero, *Pro Roscio Amerino* [In Defense of Sextus Roscius of Ameria], 46.134.

He also mentions a distinguished citizen who walked around with an aulos player following him, as a kind of status symbol. This too, Cicero disapproved of.

Gaius Duellius, the first Roman to win a naval victory over the Carthaginians, was often seen by me in my childhood, when he was an old man, returning home from dining out, attended, as was his delight, by a torch-bearer and aulos player—an ostentation which as a private citizen he had assumed, though without precedent: but that much license did his glory give him.[15]

15 Cicero, *Cato Maior de Senectute* [Cato the Elder on Old Age], 8.44.

Perhaps it was more difficult for women to display their skills as singers, since the singing prostitute was such an institution in antiquity. It is in this perspective that the historian Sallust (86–34 BC) mentioned of a court lady that she sang more artfully than was suitable for an honorable woman.

Among their number was Sempronia, a woman who had committed many crimes that showed her to have the reckless daring of a man. Fortune had favored her abundantly, not only with birth and beauty, but with a good husband and children. Well educated in Greek and Latin literature, she had greater skill in lyre playing and dancing than there is any need for a respectable woman to acquire.[16]

16 Sallust, *The Conspiracy of Catiline*, 25,5.

ART MUSIC

The earliest specific references to art music in Rome are with respect to the theater. We read of Etruscan actors who performed with music as early as 389 BC.[17] There is a vase from this period (fourth century BC), now in the Hermitage, Moscow, which pictures an aulos player playing in the theater. An early actor and producer of theatrical works, Livius Andronicus (fl. ca. 240 BC), performed plays after the Greek models, including the use of the aulos as an accompanying instrument. On one occasion, when his voice failed, he had another singer perform with the aulos while he underscored the singing with mimical gestures—an event which is considered the beginning of pantomime.[18] A relief (Inv. Nr. 6687, Museo, Nazionale, Naples) from the second century BC also shows an aulos player in the theater.

17 Sendrey, *Music in the Social and Religious Life of Antiquity*, 424.

18 Ibid., 424.

In the plays of Terence there is extant information which actually gives us the name of the composer of the music for the play. In *The Girl from Andros*, for example, we read, 'Scored for equal auloi by Flaccus, freedman of Claudius.' This same composer composed the music for *The Brothers*, but here specified Etruscan ('Tyrian') auloi.

19 For example, Plautus, *The Twin Menaechmi*, act 5, scene 2.

20 Plautus, *The Rope*, act 2, scene 1, where three fishermen 'chant their chorus in unison.'

21 Cicero, *Academica*, 2.7.20.

22 Cicero, *De Finibus Bonorum et Malorum* [About the Ends of Goods and Evils], 1.21.72.

The music of the theater included an instrumental prelude, as well as music to underscore the drama and accompany the dancers. Often the production was preceded by a procession of cornu and lituus players. In the plays of Plautus there is an occasional song sung by an actor[19] and in one case even a chorus in the Greek tradition, although here only three singers.[20]

Among the observers there seem to have been connoisseurs who on hearing the first notes of a composition used in the theater could identify the play—something which surprised Cicero.[21] This kind of music must have been changing, however, for Cicero complains of the loss of the 'austere sweetness' of music as it was heard in olden times on the stage. What he heard at present, he described as *delectatio puerilis* [childish amusement].[22]

Sometimes things did not go as planned in theatrical performances and the audiences were rather entertained than moved. An extraordinary case in point is related by the historian, Polybius (second century BC). He tells of a special performance in the arena [Circus] organized by the Roman General, Lucius Anicius, to celebrate his defeat and capture of King Genthius of the Illyrians.

> Having summoned the most distinguished artists of Greece and constructed a very large stage in the Circus, he first brought on the aulos players; there were Theodorus of Boeotia, Theopompus, Hermippus, Lysimachus, all of them the most distinguished. Posting them, then, at the front of the stage with the chorus, he directed them to play all together. As they started to perform their music to accompany the dance motions which corresponded to it, he sent word to them that they were not playing in the right way, and ordered them to whoop up the contest against one another. Since they were puzzled at this, one of the officials indicated that they should turn and advance upon one another and act as if they were fighting. Quickly the players caught the idea, and taking on motions in keeping with their own licentious characters they caused great confusion. For the aulos players by a concerted movement turned the middle choruses against those at the ends, while they blew on their auloi unintelligible notes, and all differing, and then they drew away in turn upon each other; and at the same time the members of the choruses clashed noisily against the players as they shook their gear at them and rushed upon their antagonists, to turn again and retreat. And so in one case a member of the chorus girded himself, and stepping out of the ranks he turned and raised his fists as if to box against the aulos player who plunged against him; and then, if not before, the applause and shouts that arose from the specta-

tors knew no bounds. Furthermore, while these were contending in a pitched battle, two dancers entered with castanets, and four boxers mounted upon the stage accompanied by trumpeters and horn players. All these contests went on together, and the result was indescribable.[23]

23   Ploybius, *The Histories*, 30.

Beginning with the second century BC, the tradition of the art song made its way from Greece to Rome. We know the poet Catullus mentions the lyric poet Simonides,[24] and in another poem he notes,

24   Poem 38.

> Nor can the Muses give you any peace
>   With all the sweetest poetry of Greece.[25]

25   Poem 68.

Sendrey summarizes this activity in Rome.

> Female kithara players and virtuosi from Greece, Egypt, and Asia Minor, accompanying their singing on stringed instruments, were welcome in the public as well as private homes of the Romans. The public singing of lyric poems accompanied by instruments became so popular that lovers of music, mainly amateurs, from all classes of society, devoted themselves with ardor to this art form, and sometimes even entered contests with professional singers.[26]

26   Sendrey, *Music in the Social and Religious Life of Antiquity*, 407.

This art form continued for some time for we know that Ovid expressed the desire that his *Heroides* should be sung with musical accompaniment. We also know that the poems of Pliny the Younger (first century AD) were sung to lyres and kitharas.

Another form of art song sung at banquets were those praising great men and events, although Cicero seems to suggest that this form was no longer practiced at this time.

> … would there were still extant those songs, of which Cato in his *Origines* has recorded, that long before his time the several guests at banquets used to sing in turn the praise of famous men![27]

27   Cicero, *Epistulae ad Brutum* [Letters to Brutus], 19.75.

EDUCATIONAL MUSIC

Music education seems to have been available, but not required, in the schools of Rome from a very early period. We know that in the late third century BC, for example, the music teachers were more highly paid than those of reading or gymnastics. This education consisted of instruction in music theory and performance on the kithara, with examinations at the end of the school term.[28]

28 Sendry, *Music in the Social and Religious Life of Antiquity*, 404.

Music education on a private basis was also highly organized, as we know from a papyrus dating from 206 BC. This document is a contract between a music teacher and a young slave named Narcissus and details specific amount of repertoire to be learned, as well as specifying study on two kinds of aulos, panpipes, and kithara.[29]

29 Ibid., 404.

In the second century BC there were also private academies specializing in singing and dance instruction, which were attended by the aristocracy. A reference to the study of music in *The Eunuch*, by Terence, suggests that such study was a social expectation.

> *Parmeno*
> Inspect him, please.
> Examine his Literature. Music. Athletics.
> Guaranteed performance in all the pursuits deemed fit and proper
> For a well-brought-up young gentleman.

In the writings of Cicero, we find little to suggest that he found value in the study of music. Rather, he seemed to believe it was merely something which might cause one to neglect the more important studies, like philosophy. Speaking of Epicurus, he contends,

> You are pleased to think him uneducated. The reason is that he refused to consider any education worth the name that did not help to school us in happiness. Was he to spend his time in perusing poets, who give us nothing solid and useful, but merely childish amusement? Was he to occupy himself like Plato with music and geometry, arithmetic and astronomy, which starting from false premises cannot be true, and which moreover if they were true would contribute nothing to make our lives pleasanter and therefore better? Was he to study arts like these, and neglect the master art, so difficult and correspondingly so fruitful, the art of living?[30]

30 Cicero, *De Finibus*, 1.21.72.

Curiously, he nevertheless admits that Nature has left man unfinished[31] and that one should aspire to develop life to its full perfection.[32] And indeed, in one place, Cicero does mention a conversation in which he heard of a knight who had studied music as a boy and was still practicing his singing.[33]

31 Ibid., 4.8.35.

32 Ibid., 5.9.27.

33 Cicero, *De oratore ad Quintum fratrem libri tres* [On the Orator, three books for his brother Quintus], 3.23.87.

Cicero's idea of education was probably something much more severe, like that of the Spartans.

The laws of the Cretans, in accordance with Jupiter's wishes, as the poets tell, and those of Lycurgus too, train the young men by making them toil, hunting and running, going hungry and thirsty, feeling cold and heat. At Sparta, in fact, boys are received at the altar with such blows that,

much blood flows from the flesh,

sometimes even, as I heard when I was there, to the death. Not only did none of them ever cry out, none even groaned.[34]

34   Cicero, *Tusculan Disputations*, 2.34.

FUNCTIONAL MUSIC

We possess today some extraordinary accounts of the celebration of religious-cults in ancient Rome which included the use of music. The accounts of the more important of these must be seen in the perspective of a society which had numerous gods for every aspect of public and private life. So many gods that Varro estimated their number at 30,000 and Petronius (7–66 AD) said some towns had more gods than inhabitants.[35] Lucretius offers a lovely explanation for the people's need for gods as he discusses the origin of Pan.

35   Quoted in Sendrey, *Music in the Social and Religious Life of Antiquity*, 383ff.

I have sometimes heard
As many as six or seven echoes cry
In answer to one voice. So hills to hills
Redound and bounce reiteration back
Each to the other till the nearby folk
Invent the presences of goatfoot gods,
Satyrs and nymphs and fauns, night-wandering,
Whose rumpuses and rowdy pranks, they swear
To the last man, disturb the peace at night;
And they go on to talk about the sound
Of music, sweet and sad, the twang of strings
The pipes, the singing voices. Far away,
If you believe their stories, farmer-folk
Listen while Pan, nodding his shaggy head
with the pine needles hanging over his ears,
Keeps time, lips up and down the open reeds
So that the woodland melodies pour out
With never a silence. No man likes to think
His home is some forgotten wilderness
Abandoned even by gods, and this is why
They toss around these marvels in their talk,
These stories of the weird and wonderful.[36]

36   Lucretius, *The Way Things Are*, Bk 4, 577.

Another important religious-cult festival was held in honor of Cybele and dates from the defeat of the Romans by Hannibal in 216 BC. The Romans were advised that Hannibal would depart if this Phrygian goddess were brought to Rome. When this was done, in the form of a black stone said to personify the goddess, Hannibal left Rome. A poem of Catullus (84–54 BC) describes this festival.

> To the Phrygian forests, to the fame of Cybele,
> Where the cymbals sing loud and the smitten drums
> Resound and on rounded reed and the double-pipe
> Breathe out a booming bass, where the maenads,
> Ivy-wreathed and wanded and wagging their heads,
> Shriek shrilly and shake the emblems;
> Take the way of the wandering worshipers thither
> Devotion directs us to dance and adore.[37]

37   Catullus, Poem 63.

The cult of Isis had its origin in Greece and began to be celebrated in Rome in the second century BC. These festivals also included music and the accompanying shrines dedicated to this god were built by the Romans in places as distant as London.

Another festival transported from Greece was that of Ceres, and in some comments by Cicero to the Senate we can see the extent of the Greek influence.

> It was the wish of our fathers, gentlemen, that the rites of Ceres should be performed with the strictest reverence and ceremonial; and since they were introduced from Greece, they were always performed through Greek priestesses and all the terms in use are Greek. But, although they chose from Greece a woman who should expound and perform that Greek rite, yet they saw fit that she should be a citizen when she performed rites on behalf of Roman citizens, so that she might offer prayers to the immortal gods with knowledge that was foreign and from abroad, but in a spirit that was of our own home and citizenship.[38]

38   Cicero, Pro Balbo, 24.55.

Varro quotes two fragments of poetry from the second century BC which speak of music in the worship of religious cults. First, from Ennius (236–169 BC),

39   Varro, On the Latin Language, 7.20.

> Muses, ye who with dancing feet beat mighty Olympus.[39]

And from the 'Hymn of the Salians,'

40   Ibid., 7.27.

> Sing ye to the Father of the Gods, entreat the God of Gods.[40]

A particularly interesting reference to music in the Temple of Minerva was made by Julius Caesar.

> At Pergamum in the secret and concealed parts of the temple, whither no one but the priests is allowed to approach … there was a sound of drums.[41]

41 Julius Caesar, *Civil Wars*, Bk 3, 105.

The most notorious cult celebration was that in honor of the Greek god Dionysus, or *Bacchanalia* for the Roman god Bacchus. Characterized by music, drinking, and sexual depravity, representatives from all levels of Roman society seem to have participated eagerly in this celebration. A poem of Catullus describes this strange festival.

> And, all around, the maenads pranced in a frenzy,
> Crying the ritual cry, 'Euhoe! Euhoe!,'
> Tossing their heads; some of them brandishing
> The sacred vine-wreathed rod, some bandying
> Gobbets of mangled bullock, others twining
> Their waists with belts of writhing snakes, and others
> Reverently bearing, deep in caskets,
> Arcane things which the uninitiated
> Long, but in vain, to see, while others stretched
> Fingertips to play the drum,
> Struck a shrill clang from the semicircular cymbals,
> With raucous playing on the horn or made
> the double-pipe scream.[42]

42 Catullus, Poem 64.

The historian Livy pictures a much more depraved celebration, apparently representing these activities just before the actions of the government to outlaw them. The purpose of the music seems to have been in part to drown out the cries of the victims.

> There were initiatory rites which at first were imparted to a few, then began to be generally known among men and women. To the religious element in them were added the delights of wine and feasts, that the minds of a larger number might be attracted. When wine had inflamed their minds, and night and the mingling of males with females, youth with age, had destroyed every sentiment of modesty, all varieties of corruption first began to be practiced, since each one had at hand the pleasure answering to that to which his nature was more inclined. There was not one form of vice alone, the promiscuous matings of free men and women, but perjured witnesses, forged seals and wills and evidence, all issued from this same workshop;

likewise poisonings and secret murders, so that at times not even the bodies were found for burial. Much was ventured by craft, more by violence. This violence was concealed because amid the howlings and the crash of drums and cymbals no cry of the sufferers could be heard as the debauchery and murders proceeded.[43]

According to Livy the nature of this ancient celebration began with the arrival of an unnamed Greek in Etruria who began to introduce 'sacrifices and soothsaying.'[44] 'This evil,' writes Livy, 'with all its disastrous influence, spread from Etruria to Rome like an epidemic.'

In 186 BC the testimony of a woman came to the attention of one of the consuls and led to an investigation of this cult. Her testimony conforms to the picture drawn by Livy, but adds that a choir participated.

> It was common knowledge that for the past two years no one had been initiated who was over the age of twenty. As each one was introduced, he became a kind of sacrificial victim for the priests. They led the initiate to a place which resounded with shrieks, with the chanting of a choir, the clashing of cymbals and the beating of drums, so that the victim's cries for help, when violence was offered to his chastity, might not be heard.

Her understanding was that until recent years it has been a three-day festival for women only, with matrons chosen in rotation as priestesses. She identified the priestess Paculla Annia as the one who altered this tradition, ostensibly on the advice of the gods. She changed from three days per year to five days per month held at night.

> From this time when the rites were held promiscuously, with men and women mixed together, and when the license offered by darkness had been added, no sort of crime, no kind of immorality, was left unattempted. There were more obscenities practiced between men than between men and women. Anyone refusing to submit to outrage or reluctant to commit crimes was slaughtered as a sacrificial victim … Men, apparently out of their wits, would utter prophecies with frenzied bodily convulsions; matrons, attired as Bacchantes, with their hair disheveled and carrying blazing torches, would run down to the Tiber, plunge their torches into the water and bring them out still alight—because they contained a mixture of live sulfur and calcium. Men were said to have been carried off

by the gods—because they had been attached to a machine and whisked away out of sight to hidden caves.

She indicated that many people were involved in these rites, including members of the aristocracy. Indeed, when the larger government investigation began there was such a flight of people from Rome that legal proceedings became temporarily impossible.

The government, naturally, feared that any covert society of this size might have the potential to become a political threat to the state itself. In time the Senate arranged for one of its members to speak to the public to help mitigate the general sense of fear and panic caused by the wide-ranging investigations. He placed the blame on the women.

> The Bacchic rites have for a long time been performed all over Italy, and recently they have been celebrated even in many places in Rome itself; I am quite sure that you have been made aware of this not only by rumors but also by the bangings and howlings heard in the night, which echo throughout the city …
>
> As for their number, if I tell you that there are many thousands of them, you are bound to be scared out of your wits, unless I go on to describe who they are and what kind of people they are. In the first place, then, a great part of them are women, and they are the source of this evil thing; next, there are males, scarcely distinguishable from females.

The government eventually determined that more than seven thousand persons were involved in these rites, and Livy tells us that many committed suicide and that the number condemned to death and executed outnumbered those who were thrown into prison.

In addition to these kinds of cult celebrations, there were special rites held for a wide variety of special occasions. For example, Livy, mentions a special nine-day rite to bless troops preparing to leave Rome, ca. 210–207 BC. On this occasion twenty-seven virgins marched through the city singing a hymn composed for the occasion by Livius.

> In the forum the procession stopped, and the virgins, linked together by a cord passed through their hands, moved on, beating time with their feet to the music of their voice. They then proceeded … to the Temple of Juno Regina; where two victims were immolated.[45]

45 Livy, *History of Rome*, 27.37.

Similarly, for the sailing of a ship, ca. 205 BC, Livy quotes the official prayer, which reads in part,

> Ye gods and goddesses who preside over the seas and lands, I pray and entreat you, that whatever things have been, are now, or shall be performed during my command, may turn out prosperously to myself, the state, and the commons of Rome … That you would bring these and me again to our homes, safe and unhurt; victorious over our vanquished enemies, decorated with spoils, loaded with booty, and triumphant, etc.

After this prayer, Livy tells us, the commander-in-chief,

> threw the raw entrails of a victim into the sea, according to custom, and, with the sound of a trumpet, gave the signal for sailing.[46]

Also, whenever bad omens seemed to occur, a special rite was held to appease the apparent displeasure of the gods. Livy assures us that during a period of days in 201 BC the sun appeared red for an entire day, a lamb was born with a pig's head, a pig was born with a human head, and several children were born whose 'sex was doubtful.' During the subsequent panic this caused, the infants in question were 'immediately thrown into the sea' and a rite was organized in which the twenty-seven virgins again marched through the streets of Rome singing a hymn, composed on this occasion by Publius Licinius Tegula.[47]

Finally we should mention that among these many festivals there were some held in honor of musical instruments. There was a festival day in honor of the aulos, held each June 13, and called 'lesser Quinquatrus,' during which,

> the aulos players take a holiday, and after roaming through the City, assemble at the Temple of Minerva.[48]

Another festival, held March 23 and May 23, called 'Tibulus-trium' [*lustrum*, 'purificatory offering'[49]] celebrated the trumpet. Ovid says the ceremony involved a blessing of the instruments, 'to purify the melodious trumpets,'[50] a ceremony Varro said took place in the Shoemaker's Hall.[51]

In Rome there seems to have been traditional wedding music from an early period. In Plautus's *Casina*,[52] Olympio says to a musician on the stage,

46 Ibid., 29.27.

47 Ibid., 31.12.

48 Varro, *On the Latin Language*, 6.17.

49 Ibid., 5.153.

50 Ovid, *Fasti*, 10, Kal. 23rd.

51 Varro, *On the Latin Language*, 6.14.

52 Plautus, *Casina*, act 4, scene 3. In *Curculio*, lines 145, a character sings a serenade outside a lady's door.

Come, piper, make the entire street resound with a sweet wedding
song, as they bring out the new bride.

Lysidamus and Olympio (singing)
Hymen hymenaee o hymen![53]

In *The Brothers*, by Terence, there is a reference to the musicians
who sing the wedding hymn, as well as 'Guests, torches, music,
hymn singing.'[54] On some occasions such music must have been
sung by professional singers, for in Poem 62 of Catullus we find,

Worthy of these rites, which none will mar
Who sing the sacred marriage hymn before your eyes.
Companions listen: how their voices rise
In practiced song.

We can assume the use of music for funerals was common in
early Rome, as everywhere else. Here the aulos must have become a
status symbol for important funeral processions, for the city issued
an edict in the fifth century BC limiting such processions to only
five players.[55] There were also professional mourners, called *Praefica*
('praise-leader') who were hired to sing the praises of the deceased
in front of his house. In mentioning this, Varro also quotes a fragment from Claudius.

A woman who *praeficeretur* 'was to be put in charge' of the maids
as to how they should perform their lamentations, was called a
praefica.[56]

In the Roman literature of this period there is an occasional reference to the use of the trumpet for playing military signals.[57] In the
confusion of battle perhaps one heard trumpets from all sides, as
in a conflict of 190 BC described Livy in which, 'a hubbub of indistinguishable shouts, almost drowned by the blare of trumpets.[58]
Cicero seems to have known of and admired the discipline supplied by music among the Greeks.

As for military affairs—I mean ours, not the Spartans', whose line
advances to a musical measure and the aulos, and every cry of
encouragement is expressed in the anapaestic meter.[59]

One reference to these military musicians, during the Jugurthine
War, suggests that these men may have enjoyed a respect above
that of the normal soldier. When Marius needed a small group to

53 This phrase, 'Hymen, god
of marriage,' must have been a
traditional one for it also appears as a
refrain in Poem 61 of Catullus.

54 Terence, *The Brothers*, act 5,
scene 7.

55 Sendrey, *Music in the Social and
Religious Life of Antiquity*, 410.

56 Varro, *On the Latin
Language*, 7.70.

57 For example, Livy, *History of
Rome*, 33.9.

58 Ibid., 37.29.

59 Cicero, *Tusculan
Disputations*, 2.37.

climb a rock wall to spy on an enemy fortress, he turned to 'five of the most agile men he could find among his trumpeters and horn blowers, and four centurions.'[60]

Suetonius mentions the fact that soldiers sang songs while marching and also relates an extraordinary tale of a ghost trumpeter.

> On a sudden there appeared hard by a being of wondrous stature and beauty, who sat and played upon a reed; and when not only the shepherds flocked to hear him, but many of the soldiers left their posts, and among them some of the trumpeters, the apparition snatched a trumpet from one of them, rushed to the river, and sounding a war-note with mighty blast, strode to the opposite bank.[61]

Varro quotes from a document which describes the trumpet being used for civic signal duty.

> Likewise in what pertains to those who have received from the censors the contract for the trumpeter who gives the summons to the centuriate assembly, they shall see to it that on that day, on which the assembly shall take place, the trumpeter shall sound the trumpet on the Citadel and around the walls.[62]

Livy mentions an instance of the trumpet being used together with the civic announcer, exactly as would become the custom in medieval Europe.

> The people took their seats for the show; and the herald advanced, in the customary fashion, with his trumpeter. He came into the middle of the arena where, according to usage, the festival is opened with a traditional formula. The trumpet call imposed silence; and then the herald made this pronouncement.[63]

Finally, in Poem 64 by Catullus, we find an unusual instance of the use of music for prophesy. Here we are told that elder ladies ('their snow white heads') sang a song of prophesy while working spindles and making thread from wool.

> Then as they worked, their song
> Of fate arose in voices, clear and strong,
> And all of time will never prove it wrong.

Perhaps music was more directly associated with early Roman prophesy than we realize, for Cicero also mentions the 'sing-song

60 Sallust, *The Jugurthine War*, 94, 1ff.

61 Suetonius, *Lives of the Caesars*, 1.49 and 32.

62 Varro, *On the Latin Language*, 6.92.

63 Livy, *History of Rome*, 33.32.

ritual of augury,'[64] a description which sounds similar to the style of the Greek rhapsodist.

Finally, a curious use of music for oratorical purposes is mentioned by Plutarch.

> Wherefore Caius Gracchus, the orator, being of a rugged disposition and a passionate kind of speaker, had a pipe made for him, such as musicians use to vary their voice higher or lower by degrees; and with this pipe his servant [Licinius] stood behind him while he pronounced, and give him a mild and gentle note, whereby he took him down from his loudness, and took off the harshness and angriness of his voice.[65]

Cicero also mentions this 'pitchpipe' and supplies some interesting additional insights.

> Gracchus made a practice of having a skilled attendant to stand behind him out of sight with a little ivory pipe when he was making a speech, in order promptly to blow a note to rouse him when he was getting slack or to check him from overstraining his voice ...
>
> In every voice there is a mean pitch, but each voice has it own; and for the voice to rise gradually from the mean is not only agreeable (because it is a boorish trick to shout loudly at the beginning) but also beneficial for giving it strength; then there is an extreme point of elevation, which nevertheless falls short of the shrillest possible screech, and from this point the pipe will not allow one to go further, and will begin to call one back from the actual top note; and on the other side there is similarly an extreme point in the lowering of the pitch, the point reached in a sort of descending scale of sounds. This variation and this passage of the voice through all the notes will both safeguard itself and add charm to the delivery. But you will leave the piper at home, and only take with you down to the house the perception that his training gives you.[66]

Quintilian mentions this orator in his discussion of the importance of the study of music for preparation for oratory. He adds that Gracchus observed this practice even in speeches under the most stressful circumstances and also provides us with the name of the pitchpipe.

> [I] will content myself by citing the example of Gaius Gracchus, the leading orator of his age, who during his speeches had a musician standing behind him with a pitchpipe, or *tonarion* as the Greeks call it, whose duty it was to give him the tones in which his voice

64 Cicero, *De Divinatione*, 1.47.

65 Plutarch, 'Concerning the Cure of Anger.'

66 Cicero, *De Oratore*, 3.60.225ff.

was to be pitched. Such was the attention which he paid to this point even in the midst of his most turbulent speeches, when he was terrifying the patrician party and even when he had begun to fear their power.[67]

67 Quintilian, *The Education of an Orator*, 1.10.27.

ENTERTAINMENT MUSIC

It would be no surprise to find in Rome the young musician–prostitutes who entertained at banquets, as one finds throughout the Near East and in Greece four or five centuries BC. Livy, however, gives a specific date for the importation of this custom to Rome, a celebration to honor the victory of Gnaeus Manlius Volso over the Gauls, in 187 BC.

> It was at this time that female lutenists and harpists and other purveyors of convivial entertainment became adjuncts to dinner parties; the banquets themselves also began to be laid on with greater elaboration and at greater expense.[68]

68 Livy, *History of Rome*, 39.6.

The single-pipe girl prostitute who is so frequently described as entertaining at Greek banquets also has a counterpart found in Roman literature. Plautus, in particular, mentions this entertainer several times in his plays. In *The Haunted House* there are both single-pipe and lute girl entertainers.[69]

69 Terence's *The Brothers* has a character, Ctesipho, who is a lute girl.

> PHANISCUS. There haven't been three days here without a party— eating and drinking, bringing in strumpets and single-pipe girls and lute girls, and fast living.[70]

70 Plautus, *The Haunted House*, lines 960ff.

In another play Plautus mentions that these girls were purchased at a market along with the other supplies for a banquet.

> STROBILUS.
> After my master had laid in his stores,
> And hired his cooks and single-pipe players at the market ...[71]

71 Plautus, *The Pot of Gold*, act 2, scene 4. In *Epidicus*, act 1, scene 1, Plautus indicates that these girls were sometimes acquired from the army.

Terence's play, *The Eunuch*, also refers to selling these girls, in this case by auction.

> THAIS
> Her brother, who tends, where money's concerned,
> To greed, took one look at the girl and saw

Her beauty and musical talent as potential profit.
He listed her right on the spot and sold her at auction.[72]

72 Terence, *The Eunuch*, line 130.

In Epidicus we learn that some of these girls were owned as slaves by individuals. One such girl who had been given her freedom actually has a brief speaking part in this play.

PERIPHANES (*To the Music Girl*). Did Apoecides buy you from the pimp today?

MUSIC GIRL. I've never heard the man mentioned before today, and besides, no one could buy me at any price. I've been a free woman for more than five years.

PERIPHANES. What business do you have in my house, then?

MUSIC GIRL. I'll tell you. I was hired to come and sing to the lute for an old man while he offered sacrifice.

PERIPHANES (*aside*). I'm the most worthless old idiot in all Attic Athens, I realize it. (*To the Music Girl*) Look here, you, do you know the music girl Acropolistis?

MUSIC GIRL. As well as I know myself.

PERIPHANES. Where does she live?

MUSIC GIRL. I can't really say where she does live, now that she's free.

PERIPHANES. What's that? She's free? Who freed her, I want to know, in case you know.

MUSIC GIRL. I'll tell you what I've heard. They say that Stratip-pocles, the son of Periphanes, arranged to have her freed during his absence.

PERIPHANES (*aside*). Jupiter! I'm royally ruined, if this is true. Epidicus has eviscerated that purse of mine, no doubt about it.

MUSIC GIRL. That's what I've heard. (*Sweetly*) There isn't anything else you wish, is there?

PERIPHANES (*shouting*). Yes, that you die a horrible death and get out of here at once.

MUSIC GIRL. Won't you give me back my lute?

PERIPHANES. Neither lutes nor single-pipes! Hurry up and get out of here, if the gods love you!

In addition to entertainment music at banquets, there were apparently parties devoted to music. Cicero mentions these in a reference which associates these with other rather unsavory entertainments.

The accusers are dinning into our ears the words debauchery, amours, misconduct, trips to Baiae, beach parties, feasts, revels, concerts, musical parties, pleasure boats ...[73]

73 Cicero, *Pro Caelio* [In Defense of Marcus Caelius Rufus], 15.36.

It is interesting to note that Caesar was apparently rather bored by the games of the Circus and indeed was criticized for using this time 'for reading or answering letters and petitions.'[74]

Toward the end of the Republic the use of musical entertainment at banquets became widespread. Caesar himself liked to have music with his meals.[75] The ability to host such banquets may have been a mark of refinement, for Sallust quotes a speech of the consul, Marius, in which he said,

> They call me vulgar and unpolished, because I do not know how to put on an elegant dinner and do not have actors at my table.[76]

74 Suetonius, *Lives of the Caesars*, 2.45.

75 Sendrey, *Music in the Social and Religious Life of Antiquity*, 389.

76 Sallust, *The Jugurthine War*, 85, 47.

20 REPUBLICAN PHILOSOPHY

The first substantial body of Roman philosophical commentary comes from four writers: the philologist, Varro, (116–27 BC), the orator and philosopher, Cicero (106–43 BC), the poet–philosopher, Lucretius (99–55 BC), and the historian, Sallust (86–34 BC). One of the interesting aspects of their writing is its relationship to Greece. While the Greek heritage was very much part of their thought, of the four only Lucretius freely acknowledged their debt to Greece.

> O glory of the Greeks, the first to raise
> The shining light out of tremendous dark
> Illumining the blessings of our life,
> You are the one I follow; in your steps
> I tread, not as a rival, but for love
> Of your example. Does the swallow vie
> With swans? Do wobbly-legged little goats
> Compete in strength and speed with thoroughbreds?[1]

But,

> I am well aware how very hard it is
> To bring to light by means of Latin verse
> The dark discoveries of the Greeks. I know
> New terms must be invented, since our tongue
> Is poor, and this material is new.[2]

Cicero, on the other hand, emphasized the need for Roman philosophy to be independent.

> It would redound to the fame and glory of the Roman people to be made independent of Greek writers in the study of philosophy, and this result I shall certainly bring about if my present plans are accomplished.[3]

He was also quite sure that philosophy was the most reputable of the disciplines of study.

> For philosophy does not resemble the other sciences—for what good will a man be in geometry if he has not studied it? Or in music? He will either have to hold his tongue or be set down as a

1 Lucretius, *The Way Things Are*, 3.

2 Ibid., 1.135.

3 Cicero, *De Divinatione*, 2.2.5.

positive lunatic; whereas the contents of philosophy are discovered by intellects of the keenest acumen in eliciting the probable answer to every problem.[4]

4   Cicero, *De Oratore*, 3.20.79.

Of these early Roman writers only Sallust failed to acknowledge any debt to Greek philosophy, suggesting that the fame of Greece was only attributable to the fact that they had better historians.

There can be no question that Fortune is supreme in all human affairs. It is a capricious power, which makes men's actions famous or leaves them in obscurity without regard to their true worth. I do not doubt, for instance, that the exploits of the Athenians were splendid and impressive; but I think they are much overrated. It is because she produced historians of genius that the achievement of Athens is so renowned all the world over; for the merit of successful men is rated according to the brilliance of the authors who extol it. The Romans never had this advantage, because at Rome the cleverest men were also the busiest.[5]

5   Sallust, *The Conspiracy of Catiline*, 8.

Among these philosophers we find the least known, but most interesting, to be Lucretius. He had the clear sense that he was breaking new ground.

Exploring ways where none have gone before,
Across the Muses' realms I make my way,
Happy to come to virgin springs, to drink
Their freshness, to discover all the flowers
No man has ever seen, and of them twine
Myself a garland, which no poet yet
Has had from any Muse. This I deserve
Because I teach great things, because I strive
To free the spirit, give the mind release
From the constrictions of religious fear,
Because I write clear verse about dark things,
Enduing what I touch with grace and charm.[6]

6   Lucretius, *The Way Things Are*, 4.

By 'grace and charm,' he is referring to the fact that he is writing in poetry, rather than prose. Several times he mentions this as 'honey sweet,' very much in the language of the Greek lyric poets.

I've meant
To explain the system in a sweeter music,
To rim the lesson, as it were, with honey,
Hoping, this way, to hold your mind with verses
While you are learning all that form, that pattern
Of the way things are.[7]

7   Ibid., 1.946.

Of these four philosophers, Lucretius is the only one to speak much of science. His perspective was one of admiration for nature and he doubted that anyone would ever be able to explain all its wonders.

> Whose genius has the power to utter song
> For the grandeur of the way things are,
> For these discoveries? Who has the strength
> In words to fashion any adequate praise
> For what that man deserves, whose intellect
> Found and bequeathed us such a store of wealth?
> No one of us, no son of mortal stock,
> Will ever, I'd guess, rise to the majesty
> Required to praise such greatness.[8]

8   Ibid., 5.

From his reflections on science, it was clear to him that there is a fixed organization to nature.

> Why could nature not bring forth
> Men huge enough to wade the deepest oceans,
> Split mountains with their hands, and outlive time?
> The answer is, that limits have been set
> Fixing the bounds of all material.[9]

9   Ibid., 1.202.

His understanding of some natural laws seems strange to us today. On one hand, for example, he did not believe in gravity,[10] yet at the same time he understood the principle that differing weights fall at the same time in a vacuum.[11]

10   Ibid., 1.1051.

11   Ibid., 2.236.

THE PHYSIOLOGY OF AESTHETICS

THE SENSES

Cicero begins his discussion of the senses by admiring the distribution and design of the senses, relative to the body, and for the 'lavishness and splendor of [these] gifts bestowed by the gods on men.'

> The senses, posted in the citadel of the head as the reporters and messengers of the outer world, both in structure and position are marvelously adapted to their necessary services. The eyes as the watchmen have the highest station, to give them the widest outlook for the performance of their function. The ears also, having the duty of perceiving sound, the nature of which is to rise, are rightly placed in the upper part of the body. The nostrils likewise are rightly

placed high inasmuch as all smells travel upwards, but also, because they have much to do with discriminating food and drink, they have with good reason been brought into the neighborhood of the mouth. Taste, which as the function of distinguishing the flavors of our various viands, is situated in that part of the face where nature has made an aperture for the passage of food and drink. The sense of touch is evenly diffused over all the body, to enable us to perceive all sorts of contacts and even the minutest impacts of both cold and heat. And just as architects relegate the drains of houses to the rear, away from the eyes and nose of the masters, since otherwise they would inevitably be somewhat offensive, so nature has banished the corresponding organs of the body far away from the neighborhood of the senses.

Again what artificer but nature, who is unsurpassed in her cunning, could have attained such skillfulness in the construction of the senses? ... The organ of hearing ... is always open, since we require this sense even when asleep, and when it receives a sound, we are aroused even from sleep. The auditory passage is winding, to prevent anything from being able to enter, as it might if the passage were clear and straight; it has further been provided that even the tiniest insect that may attempt to intrude may be caught in the sticky wax of the ears. On the outside project the organs which we call ears, which are constructed both to cover and protect the sense-organ and to prevent the sounds that reach them from sliding past and being lost before they strike the sense. The apertures of the ears are hard and gristly, and much convoluted, because things with these qualities reflect and amplify sound; this is why tortoise-shell or horn gives resonance to a lyre, and also why winding passages and enclosures have an echo which is louder than the original sound.[12]

12 Cicero, *De Natura Deorum*, 2.56.140ff.

Cicero concludes this discussion by remarking on how these senses excel those of the lower animals. With respect to hearing, he observes,

The ears are likewise marvelously skillful organs of discrimination; they judge differences of tone, of pitch and of key in the music of the voice and of wind and stringed instruments, and many different qualities of voice, sonorous and dull, smooth and rough, bass and treble, flexible and hard, distinctions discriminated by the human ear alone.[13]

13 Ibid., 58.

In another treatise, Cicero seems amazed, yet at a loss to explain, how we absorb such a wide range of information through our senses.

Among natural objects, as it seems to me, there is none which does not comprise in its own kind a multiplicity of things that are different from one another and yet are esteemed as having a similar value: for instance, our ears convey to us a number of perceptions which, while consisting in sounds that give us pleasure, are nevertheless frequently so different from one another that you think the one you hear last the most agreeable; also our eyes collect for us an almost countless number of pleasures, whose charm consists in their delighting a single sense in a variety of different ways; and the rest of the senses enjoy gratifications of various kinds, making it difficult to decide which is the most agreeable. Moreover this observation in the sphere of natural objects can also be transferred to the arts as well, There is a single art of sculpture, in which eminence was attained by Myron, Polyclitus and Lysippus, all of whom were different from one another, yet without the consequence of our desiring any one of them to be different from what he was. There is a single art and method of painting, and nevertheless there is an extreme dissimilarity between Zeuxis, Aglaophon and Apelles, while at the same time there is not one among them who can be thought to lack any factor in his art.[14]

14 Cicero, *De Oratore*, 3.7.

The philosopher, Lucretius, noticed the curious characteristic of the feeling sense that we call today 'phantom limb.' But because none of the early philosophers understood the primary relationship of the senses with the brain, he could do little more than acknowledge this curiosity in rather gory detail.

It is said scythe-bearing battle chariots,
Red-steaming from their killing course, can cut
Limbs off so quickly you can see them tremble
Or quiver on the ground, before their soldier
Has any inkling what has happened to him.
His fighting spirit pushes his attack
With what equipment he still has; he'll charge
And never know his left arm and his shield
Are swept off with marauding chariot-wheels
And scythes and horses, while near by, a comrade
Lifts his right arm to scale a wall, and sees
His right arm isn't there, or attempts to rise
While his leg is kicking at him from the ground.[15]

15 Lucretius, *The Way Things Are*, 3.641.

Lucretius is the only philosopher among these four who mentions the fundamental relationship between our senses and the experiential part of ourselves. He asks,

> Can anyone
> Explain what bodily sensation is
> Unless he trusts his own experience of it?[16]

16 Ibid., 3.351.

The most important conclusion which the Roman philosophers were beginning to understand was that there is a clear relationship between the senses and all other kinds of knowledge, including 'reason.' The Greek philosophers tended to separate all of these functions as unique characteristics of the soul. Now Cicero saw clearly an association between these two kinds of 'knowing.'

> Every mental presentation has its origin in sensation: so that no certain knowledge will be possible, unless all sensations are true.[17]

17 Cicero, *De Finibus*, 1.19.64.

And in another treatise,

> From this class of perception [the senses] are imprinted upon us our notions of things, without which all understanding and all investigation and discussion are impossible.[18]

18 Cicero, *Academica*, 2.7.21.

For Cicero, the truth of this lay in simple observation. By way of demonstration, he quotes a syllogism of Zeno, reasoning that something devoid of sensation can have no parts which have sensation and since the world has parts which have sensation, therefore the world is not devoid of sensation. Zeno offered the following musical demonstrations:

> If auloi playing musical tunes grew on an olive-tree, surely you would not question that the olive-tree possessed some knowledge of the art of aulos playing; or if plane-trees bore well-tuned lutes, doubtless you would likewise infer that the plane-trees possessed the art of music.[19]

19 Cicero, *De Natura Deorum*, 2.8.22.

Cicero believed that it was the greater development of these faculties which best explained the artist.

> How remarkable are the faculties which you Academics invalidate and abolish, our sensory and intellectual perception and comprehension of external objects; it is by collating and comparing

our percepts that we also create the arts that serve either practical necessities or the purpose of amusement.[20]

20   Ibid., 2.59.148.

In another place Cicero also conveys his astonishment with the nature of the perception of the senses and here makes a remark very rare for his pen, and very reflective of ancient Greek thought, that it was the senses and not Reason which could sometimes discover Truth.

> Let us begin therefore from the senses, whose verdicts are so clear and certain that if human nature were given the choice, and were interrogated by some god as to whether it was content with its own senses in a sound and undamaged state or demanded something better, I cannot see what more it could ask for … In my judgment the senses contain the highest truth, given that they are sound and healthy and also that all obstacles and hindrances are removed. That is why we often desire a change of the light and of the position of the objects that we are observing, and diminish or enlarge their distances from us, and take various measures, until mere looking makes us trust the judgment that it forms. The same is done in the case of sounds and smell and taste, so that among us there is nobody who desiderates keener powers of judgment in the senses, each in its class. But when we add practice and artistic training, to make our eyes sensitive to painting and our ears to music, who is there who can fail to remark the power that the senses possess? How many things painters see in shadows and in the foreground which we do not see! How many things in music that escape us are caught by the hearing of persons trained in that department of art, who when the aulos player blows his first note say, 'That is *Antiope*' or '*Andromache*,' when we have not even a suspicion of it![21]

21   Cicero, *Academica*, 2.7.

In the end, however, in answer to the statement by Epicurus that 'the senses themselves decide pleasure to be good and pain evil,' Cicero could not agree. 'A just decision,' he believed, 'can only be delivered by Reason.'[22]

22   Cicero, *De Finibus*, 2.7.35–37.

THE EMOTIONS

It seems rather curious to the modern reader that while Cicero could understand that the senses were a natural part of man he failed to see that the same could be said of the emotions. It would almost seem as if to him the emotions were some kind of behavior problem operating outside the man himself. They are something to be avoided, he says, as one might avoid certain food or drink. If it can be said that his concept of the emotions was based on ancient Greek philosophy, then one would have to qualify the idea by saying that the concern for the role of the emotions in man by the Greeks becomes in Cicero an idea greatly amplified. One wonders if the ideas expressed below were more general in ancient Rome, for certainly one can easily draw a straight line to the philosophy of the leaders of the early Christian Church in Rome who abhorred emotions to the same degree.

> The emotions of the mind, which harass and embitter the life of the foolish (the Greek term for these is *pathos*, and I might have rendered this literally and styled them 'diseases,' but the word 'disease' would not suit all instances; for example, no one speaks of pity, nor yet anger, as a disease though the Greeks term these pathos. Let us then accept the term 'emotion,' the very sound of which seems to denote something vicious, and these emotions are not excited by any natural influence. The list of the emotions is divided into four classes, with numerous subdivisions, namely sorrow, fear, lust, and that mental emotion which the Stoics call by a name that also denotes a bodily feeling, *hedone*, 'pleasure,' but which I prefer to style 'delight,' meaning the sensuous elation of the mind when in a state of exultation), these emotions, I say, are not excited by any influence of nature; they are all of them mere fancies and frivolous opinions. Therefore the Wise Man will always be free from them.[23]

23 Ibid., 3.10.35.

And again, in his treatise *On Duties*, sounding like a Puritan, he emphasizes that any display of emotions suggests that we are not in control of ourselves. The more highly developed person, he with a 'greater soul,' must especially observe this warning. Although, of course, Cicero had no understanding of the bicameral nature of man's brain, he does inadvertently here come very close to the mark when he contrasts passion with thought.

> We must be careful that the movements of our soul do not diverge from nature, and the care must be all the greater as the soul is greater. We shall achieve this if we are careful not to reach states of extreme excitement or alarm and if we keep our minds intent on the preservation of *decorum*. The movements of our souls are of two kinds: some involve thought, others involve passion. Thought is mostly expended in seeking out the truth, passion urges men to action. Therefore we must take care to expend thought on the best objects and to make clear that our passions are obedient to our intellect …

Throughout a man's life the most correct advice is to avoid agitations, by which I mean excessive commotions in the soul that do not obey intelligence … Whenever passionate feelings disturb our activities, we are, of course, not acting with self-control and those around us cannot approve what we do.[24]

24 Cicero, *De Officiis*, 131ff.

In another place Cicero expresses himself even more strongly, picturing the life of the man who falls victim to his emotions and does not maintain his self-control.

Disorderly movements and agitations of souls stirred up and carried away in a thoughtless rush drive away all reason and leave no part of the happy life …

The man whom we see on fire and raging with lusts frantically pursuing everything with insatiable desire, and the more lavishly he swallows down pleasure from all quarters, the worse and more burning his thirst—would you not be entitled to call him most unhappy? The man who is carried away with frivolity and empty euphoria and uncontrolled desires, is he not the more wretched the happier he *thinks* he is? So just as these people are wretched, so are those happy whom no fears alarm, no distresses gnaw, no lusts arouse, no pointless euphoria dissolves in languorous pleasure. Just as the sea is recognized as calm when not even the slightest breeze ruffles the waves, so a state of mind can be accounted calm and peaceful, when there is no disturbance by which it can be agitated.[25]

25 Cicero, *Tusculan Disputations*, 5.15ff.

While Cicero then apparently cannot understand the emotions as being a natural part of man, much less that they are universal and genetic, curiously enough he has correctly noticed that the emotions are sufficiently universal as to be read by the observer.

Just as in lyre playing the ears of musicians perceive even the smallest details, so we should acquire the habit of making important deductions from trivial details if we want to become sharp and untiring critics. From the stare, from the raising or lowering of the eyebrows, from sadness, from joviality, from a laugh, from a spoken phrase, from a significant silence, from a raised voice, from its lowering, from other similar indications we shall begin to judge quickly which of these actions is in tune, which of them clashes with moral duty and nature.[26]

26 Ibid., 1.146.

Clinical psychologists today have proven it is the face which primarily communicates emotions, while Cicero, as many persons today, incorrectly believed it was the eyes alone.

But everything depends on the face, while the face itself is entirely dominated by the eyes; hence our older generation were better critics, who used not to applaud even Roscius very much when he wore a mask. For delivery is wholly the concern of the feelings, and these are mirrored by the face and expressed by the eyes; for this is the only part of the body capable of producing as many indications and variations as there are emotions, and there is nobody who can produce the same effect with the eyes shut.[27]

27 Cicero, *De Oratore*, 3.59.221.

Finally, of these four philosophers, only Lucretius makes a point of mentioning that animals also have some form of emotion.

Even the dumb beasts,
The inarticulate animals, make sounds
That indicate emotions, fear, or pain,
Or even happiness. This is obvious.[28]

28 Lucretius, *The Way Things Are*, 5.1059.

MIND, BODY AND SOUL

The Roman philosophers, as the Greeks before them, struggled to understand and explain how emotions, the senses, and the intellect were contained and organized within man. Cicero, in one place, uses the old Greek idea of the happy life being one in which everything is in 'harmony.'

In lyre playing or in aulos playing the instruments may be only slightly out of tune, but musical experts can usually notice the fact. In the same way one must conduct one's life so that there is no accidental discord, or even more importantly, so that the harmony of one's activities is greater and more pleasing than that of music.[29]

29 Cicero, *De Officiis*, 1.145.

The philosopher, Lucretius, objected to this metaphor of 'harmony' to represent the well-adjusted man as a simplification. Whatever this term is, he says, 'give it back to the musicians!' He makes a point of saying that the individual nature of the various organs, bones, arteries and breath make any sort of 'harmony' impossible.

The reader will also be amazed, no doubt, to find here that at this time that the 'mind' and the intellect were not yet associated with the brain.

First,
The mind—the intellect, we sometimes call it—
The force that gives direction to a life
As well as understanding, is a part
Of a man's make-up, every bit as much
As are his hands and feet and seeing eyes.
Some say the sentient mind is not located
In any one fixed area, but pervades
The body as a vital force; the Greeks
Called this a *harmony*, a relationship
Which gives us intellect, though mind itself
Lacks any fixed location. Just as health
Inheres in bodily structure, but no man
Has any part he can identify
As being the organ where his health resides,
So these philosophers give no fixed part
As the abode of mind. In this, I think,
They are very wrong indeed. Sometimes we see
Part of a body sicken before our eyes,
While what we do not see enjoys good health;
And it can be the other way around:
You can be sick in mind and well in body,
Your foot can hurt while you are free of headache.
When all our limbs relax in easy slumber
And our body lies insensible, unconscious,
There is something in us, wakeful even then,
Susceptible to anxiety or joy.
Look at what happens if some bodily parts,
More than a few, are lost, life still keeps on
Within the limbs; from this you can be sure
Sensation, sentience, dwells within the limbs
Without the need of common *harmony*
To be their source of consciousness. Again,
When a few particles of heat disperse
And breath is forced out of the mouth, the spirit
With that same breath leaves artery and bone.
Not all the organs, you must realize,
Are equally important nor does health
Depend on all alike, but there are some—
The seeds of breathing, warm vitality—
Whereby we are kept alive; when these are gone
Life leaves our dying members. So, since mind
And spirit are by nature part of man,
Let the musicians keep that term brought down
To them from lofty Helicon—or maybe

They found it somewhere else, made it apply
To something hitherto nameless in their craft—
I speak of harmony. Whatever it is,
Give it back to the musicians.[30]

30 Lucretius, *The Way Things Are*, 3.97ff.

We see this lack of association between the mind and the brain again when he concludes it must be located somewhere near the heart.

I maintain
That mind and spirit are held close together,
Compose one unity, but the lord and master
Holding dominion over all the body
Is purpose, understanding - in our terms
Mind or intelligence, and this resides
In the region of the heart.[31]

31 Ibid., 3.133.

In one place, in a survey of where the mind might be located, he almost says the right thing—that the mind is in the head.

Mind must derive from body, mind can never
Be far from blood and sinew. But if mind
(And this would be more likely) could exist
In one location only, say the head,
Or shoulders, or the bottom of the heels,
Even so, its residence would have to be
In the same man, that is to say, the same
Containing vessel.[32]

32 Ibid., 5.131.

If Lucretius cannot manage to physically locate the mind he does correctly associate it with the nature of the man himself, a quality which he calls the spirit.

So, first of all, if I say *mind*, or *spirit*,
Consider them as one; they truly are,
Combined together, one mortal entity.[33]

33 Ibid., 3.423.

And again, while he cannot speak with any authority and the physical nature of the mind (brain), it is very interesting that he imagines its activity as being something similar to what we call molecules today.

And so the spirit must
Consist throughout of very tiny seeds,
All sown minutely in sinew, flesh, and veins -

So tenuous that when it leaves the body
There seems no difference, no diminution
Of outward contour nor of inward weight.
The same thing happens when the scent of wine,
Or nard's aroma, or any effluence,
Vanishes into air, and still its source
Appears no less substantial to our eyes,
Especially since nothing of its weight
is lost—so many and such tiny seeds
Imparting scent and flavor in all things.[34]

34 Ibid., 3.215.

Most early philosophers, not understanding the role of the brain, used the 'soul' as the agency which contains and controls everything. Lucretius, too, uses this term, but his imagination carries him far beyond the ancient Greeks in wondering about the physical nature of the soul.

We do not know
The nature of the soul: is it something born
By, of, and for itself? Does it find its way
Into ourselves when we are being born,
To die when we do? Or does it, after our death,
Tour Hell's tremendous emptiness and shadow?[35]

35 Ibid., 1.112.

On the other hand, Varro, as his work was devoted mostly to brief definitions and does not go into philosophical details regarding the workings of the mind, under a discussion of 'Regularity,' outlines the mental process as consisting of the senses, reason, instinct, and speech, all located within a rather complicated 'soul.' With all this 'weird science' the modern reader can have nothing but sympathy for the struggle of these early philosophers in their attempt to explain man's faculties. It would be another thousand years before philosophers began to guess correctly at the bicameral nature of the brain and another six hundred years after that before medical research confirmed their intuitions.

As [man and woman] are made up of soul and body, are not also the parts of soul and body alike with the same regularity?
    What then of the fact that the souls of men are divided into eight parts—are these parts not mutually alike with regularity? Five [parts] with which we perceive, the sixth with which we think, the seventh with which we procreate, the eighth with which we utter articulate words?[36]

36 Varro, *On the Latin Language*, 9.23.29ff.

Sallust, the historian, took a moral, rather than a philosophical, view of the pursuits of man and his soul.

> As man consists of body and soul, all our possessions and pursuits partake of the nature of one or the other. Thus personal beauty and great wealth, bodily strength, and all similar things, soon pass away; the noble achievements of the intellect are immortal like the soul itself. Physical advantages, and the material gifts of fortune, begin and end; all that comes into existence, perishes; all that grows, must one day decay. But the soul, incorruptible and eternal, is the ruler of mankind; it guides and controls everything, subject itself to no control. Wherefore we can but marvel the more at the unnatural conduct of those who abandon themselves to bodily pleasures and pass their time in riotous living and idleness, neglecting their intelligence—the best and noblest element in man's nature—and letting it become dull through lack of effort; and that, too, when the mind is capable of so many different accomplishments that can win the highest distinction.[37]

In another place, Sallust returns to this idea, now stressing that it is the mind which separates man from the lower animals.

> Every man who wishes to rise superior to the lower animals should strive his hardest to avoid living all his days in silent obscurity, like the beasts of the field, creatures which go with their faces to the ground and are the slaves of their bellies. We human beings have mental as well as physical powers; the mind, which we share with gods, is the ruling element in us, while the chief function of the body, which we have in common with the beasts, is to obey. Surely, therefore, it is our intellectual rather than our physical powers that we should use in the pursuit of fame ... Wealth and beauty can give only a fleeting and perishable fame, but intellectual excellence is a glorious and everlasting possession.[38]

Cicero approaches a little closer to the concept of the bicameral brain when he speaks of the soul as being in two parts, one of which is Reason and the other nameless. It is man's responsibility, he says, to make sure that Reason controls. His degradation of the 'nameless' side, the right hemisphere, is characteristic of the left hemisphere, the source of language, and its distrust for what it cannot know.

> The soul is divided into two parts, one of which partakes of reason, the other does not. So when the instruction that we should rule over ourselves is given, the instruction is that reason should restrain impulsiveness. There is in practically everybody's souls by nature

37 Sallust, *The Jugurthine War*, 2. Sallust here also observes that among the intellectual pursuits, one of the most useful is History—which he elects not to speak of, for fear 'someone might think that vanity was making me sing the praises of my own favorite occupation.'

38 Sallust, *The Conspiracy of Catiline*, 1.

something soft, lowly, abject, nerveless so to speak, and feeble. If there were nothing else, a human being would be the ugliest thing that exists. But at hand is the mistress and queen of all, Reason, which through its own strivings advances forward and becomes perfected virtue. It is man's responsibility to ensure that it rules over that part of the soul which ought to obey.[39]

39 Cicero, *Tusculan Disputations*, 2.47.

In another treatise, Cicero writes of the mind containing both knowledge and the senses (but Reason must rule!) but he still does not think of this as being in the brain, he only distinguishes it as being of a higher order than the body.

Now it is manifest that man consists of body and mind, although the mind plays the more important part and the body the less. Next we further observed both that man's body is of a structure surpassing that of other animals, and that his mind is so constituted as not only to be equipped with senses but also to possess the dominant factor of intellect, which commands the obedience of the whole of man's nature, being endowed with the marvelous faculties of reason, of cognition, of knowledge and of all the virtues. In fact the faculties of the body are not comparable in importance with the parts of the mind.[40]

40 Cicero, *De Finibus*, 5.7.34.

While Cicero admits that he has no idea where the mind is actually located,[41] nevertheless he contends that the man who governs himself through reason also achieves a life of virtue, the greatest good.

41 Cicero, *Academica*, 2.39.124.

That greatest good which you are seeking must be placed in what is the best part of a human being. But what is better in a human being than an intelligent and good mind? So we must enjoy the benefit of the good of the mind, if we want to be happy. But the good of the mind is Virtue. Therefore the happy life consists in Virtue.[42]

42 Cicero, *Tusculan Disputations*, 5.67.

Thus he concludes by providing us a portrait of such a man.

Let us assume a man excelling in the finest qualities, and let us spend a little time forming a mental picture of him. First, he must be of outstanding intelligence: Virtue does not readily accompany slow wits; and secondly, have passionate enthusiasm for finding out the truth. Hence that triple offspring of the soul will emerge, one consisting in the knowledge of the Universe and the unraveling of nature, the second in distinguishing things to be sought and things to be avoided and in the theory of living, the third in judging what follows each proposition and what conflicts with it: in this there is both precision of argument and truth of judgment.[43]

43 Ibid., 5.68.

The Psychology of Aesthetics

On Pleasure and Pain

Cicero devotes an extensive study of this topic in his treatise on ethics, *de Finibus Bonarum et Malorum*. The primary reason for this treatise seems to have been a compulsion to attack the three most popular schools of ethical philosophy of his time, the Epicurean, the Stoic and the Academy under Antiochus.

He begins by stating the fundamental position of Epicurus on this topic, that Nature dictates that pleasure and pain lie at the root of every act of choice and avoidance, which he rejects immediately.

> It is in my judgment a doctrine in the last degree unworthy of the dignity of man. Nature, in my opinion at all events, has created and endowed us for higher ends.[44]

44 Cicero, *De Finibus*, 1.7.23.

Cicero believes, rather, that man is somewhat more practical in his choices, for example:

> But in certain emergencies and owing to the claims of duty or the obligations of business it will frequently occur that pleasures have to be repudiated and annoyances accepted. The wise man therefore always holds these matters to this principle of selection: he rejects pleasures to secure other greater pleasures, or else he endures pains to avoid worse pains.[45]

45 Ibid., 1.10.3.

While Cicero assumes that a life of pleasure is good, he believes that a life of pleasure depends more on having the wisdom to discern good and evil.

> The great disturbing factor in man's life is ignorance of good and evil; mistaken ideas about these frequently rob us of our greatest pleasures, and torment us with the most cruel pain of mind. Hence we need the aid of Wisdom, to rid us of our fears and appetites, to root out all our errors and prejudices, and to serve as our infallible guide to the attainment of pleasure. Wisdom alone can banish sorrow from our hearts and protect us from alarm and apprehension; put yourself to school with her, and you may live in peace, and quench the glowing flames of desire. For the desires are incapable of satisfaction; they ruin not individuals only but whole families, nay often shake the very foundations of the state. It is they that are the source of hatred, quarreling and strife, of sedition and of war. Nor do they only flaunt themselves abroad, or turn their blind onslaughts solely against others; even when prisoned within the

heart they quarrel and fall out among themselves; and this cannot but render the whole of life embittered. Hence only the Wise Man, who prunes away all the rank growth of vanity and error, can possibly live untroubled by sorrow and by fear, content within the bounds that nature has set.[46]

In any case, Cicero observes, there are things worse than pain. Disgrace, for example.

Disgrace is a worse thing than pain, pain is simply nothing at all. So long as you think it disgraceful and unmanly to groan, wail, lament, be shattered and broken down by pain, so long, that is, as honor, nobility, good reputation are present, and contemplating them, you control yourself, surely pain will give ground to virtue, and grow feeble through the application of your mind.[47]

Cicero summarizes his own principles regarding good and evil and their relationship to pleasure and pain as follows.[48] First, we never mistake pleasure and pain; where we go wrong is in knowing what produces one or the other. Second, both pleasure and pain arise from bodily sensations. Third, mental pleasures and pains, however, are much more intense, because while the body only knows the present, the mind knows the past and future as well. Fourth, he rejects the Epicurean idea that the mere absence of pain results in pleasure, or that the absence of pleasure results in pain.

But it is the ability of the mind to dwell on the future and the past that is, for Cicero, the chief source of pain in the foolish man.

Why, if the pleasantness of life is diminished by the more serious bodily diseases, how much more must it be diminished by the diseases of the mind! But extravagant and imaginary desires, for riches, fame, power, and also for licentious pleasures, are nothing but mental diseases. Then, too, there are grief, trouble and sorrow, which gnaw the heart and consume it with anxiety, if men fail to realize that the mind need feel no pain unconnected with some pain of body, present or to come. Yet there is no foolish man but is afflicted by some one of these diseases; therefore there is no foolish man that is not unhappy … Besides, they do not recollect their past nor enjoy their present blessings; they merely look forward to those of the future, and as these are of necessity uncertain, they are consumed with agony and terror; and the climax of their torment is when they perceive too late that all their dreams of wealth or station, power or fame, have come to nothing. For they never attain any of the pleasures, the hope of which inspired them to undergo all their

46 Ibid., 1.8.43ff.

47 Cicero, *Tusculan Disputations*, 2.31.

48 Cicero, *De Finibus*, 1.17ff.

arduous toils. Or look again at others, petty, narrow-minded men, or confirmed pessimists, or spiteful, envious, ill-tempered creatures, unsociable, abusive, brutal; others again enslaved to the follies of love, impudent or reckless, wanton, headstrong and yet irresolute, always changing their minds. Such failings render their lives one unbroken round of misery. The conclusion is that no foolish man can be happy, nor any wise man fail to be happy.[49]

49   Ibid., 1.18.59ff.

Cicero also rejects the Epicurean ideas that there is no intermediate state between pleasure and pain[50] and that instinct seeks pleasure. Instinct, says, Cicero, seeks rather self-preservation.[51]

50   Ibid., 2.3 and 2.5.
51   Ibid., 2.11.

Rather than base a philosophy of life on pleasure and pain, Cicero maintains that it is Virtue which must be the end of life.[52] Indeed, if pleasure is the chief Good, the chief value of life, then the lower animals must be superior to ourselves.

52   Ibid., 2.8 and 2.14.

The Earth of herself without labor of theirs lavishes on them food from her stores in great variety and abundance; whereas we with the most laborious efforts can scarcely if at all supply our needs. Yet I cannot think that the Chief Good can possibly be the same for a brute beast and for a man. What is the use of all our vast machinery of culture, of the great company of liberal studies, of the goodly fellowship of the virtues, of all these things are sought after solely for the sake of pleasure?[53]

53   Ibid., 2.34.

On Imitation

With regard to this important dimension of aesthetics, Cicero understood correctly that the goal of the artist is not merely to imitate, but through his imitation to suggest to the observer something even more beautiful.

I am firmly of the opinion that nothing of any kind is so beautiful as not to be excelled in beauty by that of which it is a copy, as a mask is a copy of a face. This ideal cannot be perceived by the eye or ear, nor by any of the senses, but we can nevertheless grasp it by the mind and the imagination. For example, in the case of the statues of Phidias, the most perfect of their kind that we have ever seen, and in the case of painting ..., we can, in spite of their beauty, imagine something more beautiful. Surely that great sculptor, while making the image of Jupiter or Minerva, did not look at any person whom he was using as a model, but in his own mind there dwelt a surpassing vision of beauty; at this he gazed and all intent on this he guided his artist's hand to produce the likeness of the god. Accordingly, as there is something perfect and surpassing in the case of sculpture and painting—an intellectual ideal by reference to which the artist represents those objects which do not themselves appear to the eye, so [in the case of oratory] with our minds we conceive the ideal of perfect eloquence, but with our ears we catch only the copy.[54]

54 Cicero, *De Oratore*, 2.8.

Cicero, ever thinking as an orator himself, is quick to add that his art is the exception. While actors deal in imitation, orators are the *real thing* and always *better* than their imitation! His point notwithstanding, this passage does seem to contradict his previous statements. Speaking on the art of delivery, he notes,

> My reason for dwelling on these points is because the whole of this department has been abandoned by the orators, who are the players that act real life, and has been taken over by the actors, who only mimic reality. And there can be no doubt that reality beats imitation in everything; and if reality unaided were sufficiently effective in presentation, we should have no need at all for art.[55]

55 Cicero, *De Oratore*, 3.56.214.

ON THE ARTS

While Cicero seems, in his comments above, to have understood the purpose of art to *represent* something more beautiful than the art object itself, on other occasions he seems to have missed the point entirely, as we see in the following passage where he sees painting as consisting only of the skill of drawing. In the end we believe he really did not appreciate art as art, or as a form of Truth. Probably he saw art as simply a kind of decoration, to make drab walls more interesting. It is a view which can be found well into the middle ages.

> Just as in the other arts, when the hardest portions of each have been taught, the rest, through being either easier or just like the former, call for no teaching; as in painting, for instance, he who has thoroughly learned how to paint the semblance of a man, can without further lessons paint one of any figure or time of life, nor is there any danger that he, who would paint to admiration a lion or bull, will be unable to do the like with many other four-footed animals (there being no art whatever wherein all its possibilities require professorial teaching, since those who have rightly learned

56 Ibid., 2.16.69.

the general principles of fundamental and established things attain the rest without difficulty and unaided).[56]

Of course Cicero is wrong in this view, it is not learning how to draw which is difficult in art but imagining what to draw. The arts, he finds, can accomplish their function 'unaided by eloquence,'[57] however, he agrees with a famous actor, Roscius, that the chief thing in the arts is to observe 'good taste,' although this cannot be taught.

57 Ibid., 2.9.38.

Even for the great Roscius himself; whom I often hear affirming that the chief thing in art is to observe good taste, though how to do this is the one thing that cannot be taught by art.[58]

58 Ibid., 1.29.132.

As the reader can see, Cicero did not really understand art at all and he found genuine respect only for the poets.

Rightly, then, did our great Ennius call poets 'holy,' for they seem recommended to us by the benign bestowal of God. Holy then, gentlemen, in your enlightened eyes let the name of poet be.[59]

59 Cicero, *Pro Archia Poeta*, 8.18. Ennius (b. 239 BC) was considered the father of Roman poetry. In this same treatise, 8.20, Cicero recognizes a more practical value to poetry, in saying,

There is no man to whom the Muses are so distasteful that he will not be glad to entrust to poetry the eternal emblazonment of his achievements.

In another place he continued this theme, suggesting that poetic inspiration is proof of the divine connection with our souls.

The human soul is in some degree derived and drawn from a source exterior to itself. Hence we understand that outside the human soul there is a divine soul from which the human soul is sprung …
    And poetic inspiration also proves that there is a divine power within the human soul.[60]

60 Cicero, *De Divinatione*, 32.70 and 37.

Whereas Cicero considered music to be associated with the lower class, it is interesting that he feared the effect of poetry on this class.

But do you see what harm the poets inflict? They introduce great heroes wailing, they enfeeble our souls, and on top of that are so agreeable that they are not only read but actually learned by heart. So when to bad home upbringing and a sheltered and dainty way of life the poets are added as well, they crush all the sinews of virtue. So Plato was right to expel them from the society which he framed in his search for the best character and the best political constitution.[61]

61 Cicero, *Tusculan Disputations*, 2.27.

When Isocrates was quoted as saying that 'people listen to orators with solemn attention, but to poets with pleasure,'[62] Cicero countered,

62 Cicero, *De Oratore*, 51.174.

I recognize that [poets] have a greater freedom in the formation and arrangement of words that we orators have, and also that, with the approval of some critics, they pay more attention to sound than to sense.[63]

63 Ibid., 19.68.

With regard to the theater, Cicero seemed to have a certain respect for actors, due in part to the very high standard that was expected by the public.

If an actor makes a movement that is a little out of time with the music, or recites a verse that is one syllable too short or too long, he is hissed and hooted off the stage.[64]

And again,

But whereas [the public] does not forgive a poet, it makes allowances for us [the orators].[65]

64 Cicero, *Paradoxa Stoicorum*, 26. We have very little detailed information about the movements which apparently were used by the Greek choruses. The hint found in this statement by Cicero may suggest that the movements were of a nature so illustrative of the words that even the audience were familiar with the movements.

65 Cicero, *De Oratore*, 3.51.198.

On Communication with the Audience

In an interesting discussion on the goals of the orator, Cicero, although he does not specifically mention music, lists goals which would be identical with the performing musician: to instruct, give pleasure, and stir the emotions of the listener. He also mentions here the very important aesthetic topic of Universality. Cicero takes the position that if the fine speaker accomplishes the goals he has listed above, it will always be the masses, and not the experts, who identify the excellent speaker.[66]

66 Debussy noted that an artist is most complimented when he is complimented by the real experts in his field; however, '*fame* is a gift of the masses who know nothing.'

This discussion about the reasons for esteeming an orator good or bad I much prefer should win the approval of you and of Brutus, but as for my oratory I should wish it rather to win the approval of the public. The truth is that the orator who is approved by the multitude must inevitably be approved by the expert …

Now there are three things in my opinion which the orator should effect: instruct his listener, give him pleasure, stir his emotions. By what virtues in the orator each one of these is effected, or from what faults the orator fails to attain the desired effect, or in trying even slips and falls, a master of the art will be able to judge. But whether or not the orator succeeds in conveying to his listeners the emotions which he wishes to convey, can only be judged by the assent of the multitude and the approbation of the people. For that reason, as to the question whether an orator is good or bad, there has never been disagreement between experts and the common people …

When one hears a real orator he believes what is said, thinks it true, assents and approves; the orator's words win conviction. You, sir, critic and expert, what more do you ask? The listening throng is delighted, is carried along by his words, is in a sense bathed deep in delight. What have you here to cavil with? They feel now joy now sorrow, are moved now to laughter now to tears; they show approbation detestation, scorn aversion; they are drawn to pity to shame to regret; are stirred to anger, wonder, hope fear; and all these come to pass just as the hearers' minds are played upon by word and thought and action. Again, what need to wait for the verdict of some critic? It is plain that what the multitude approves must win the approval of experts … There have been orators in great number with many varied styles of speaking, but was there ever among them all one who was adjudged preeminent by the verdict of the masses who did not likewise win the approval of the experts?[67]

67   Cicero, *Brutus*, 49.184ff.

In particular, Cicero identified emotion as the universal element which captures the appreciation of the large audience, something which he found similar in both music and oratory.

For just as from the sound of the strings on the harp the skill with which they are struck is readily recognized, so what skill the orator has in playing on the minds of his audience is recognized by the emotion produced.[68]

68   Ibid., 54.199.

But universality is not the same thing as popularity. Cicero understood this and in his *Tusculan Disputations* he makes it very clear that to actually program at the level of the masses is something quite different and something which the artist does not do.

It must be realized that neither is popular fame to be sought for itself, nor obscurity to be dreaded. 'I came to Athens,' said Democritus, 'and nobody there recognized me.' A steadfast and serious man, to glory in his lack of glory! Or can it be that while the aulos players and those who play the lyre use their own judgment, not that of the crowd, to tune their songs and melodies, the wise man, endowed with a far greater skill, searches out not what is most true, but what the crowd wants? Or is anything more foolish than to think that those whom as individuals one despises as mere hacks and hooligans amount to something when taken all together? He will despise our ambitions and frivolities and spurn the people's honors, even when offered without his seeking them. But we don't know how to despise them until we come to regret our error.[69]

69 Cicero, *Tusculan Disputations*, 5.104.

On the other hand, Cicero realized that with regard to public speakers the above distinction between what we call universality and popularity are only poles of aesthetic communication. In actual practice other factors make this question somewhat more complicated. First, sometimes the material itself is too complex for the masses to appreciate. He quotes an anecdote in which Demosthenes was reading a long poem and in the midst of his reading all the audience walked out except for Plato. Demosthenes is reported to have said, 'I shall go on reading just the same; for me Plato alone is as good as a hundred thousand.' Quite right, says Cicero,

> for a poem full of obscure allusions can from its nature only win the approbation of the few; an oration meant for a general public must aim to win the assent of the throng.[70]

70 Cicero, *Brutus*, 51.191.

Second, he had apparently observed that a particularly smooth speaker could win the admiration of the audience even though the speech itself was devoid of content.

> Thus, for example, if the wind instrument when blown upon does not respond with sound, the musician knows that the instrument must be discarded, and so in like manner the popular ear is for the orator a kind of instrument; if it refuses to accept the breath blown into it, or if, as a horse [refuses to move] to the rein, the listener does not respond, there is no use of urging him. There is however this difference, that the crowd sometimes gives its approval to an orator who does not deserve it, but it approves without comparison. When it is pleased by a mediocre or even bad speaker it is content with him; it does not apprehend that there is something better; it approves what is offered, whatever its quality; for even a mediocre orator will hold its attention, if only he amounts to anything at all, since there is nothing that has so potent an effect upon human emotions as well-ordered and embellished speech.[71]

71 Ibid., 51.192.

It was perhaps for these mediocre speakers that one heard 'hired' applause, a practice which, needless to say, Cicero objected to.

> Expressions of public opinion at Assemblies and at meetings are sometimes the voice of truth, but sometimes they are falsified and corrupt: at theatrical and gladiatorial shows it is said to be common for some feeble and scanty applause to be started by a hired

and unprincipled claque, and yet, when that happens, it is easy to see how and by whom it is started and what the honest part of the audience does.[72]

72   Cicero, *Pro Sestio*, 54.115.

Finally, however, we must believe that Cicero did not object in principle to the idea that the orator, or artist, might aspire to be successful with his audience.

Ambition is a universal factor in life, and the nobler a man is, the more susceptible is he to the sweets of fame. We should not disclaim this human weakness, which indeed is patent to all; we should rather admit it unabashed. Why, upon the very books in which they bid us scorn ambition philosophers inscribe their names![73]

73   Cicero, *Pro Archia Poeta*, 10.26.

THE AESTHETICS OF MUSIC

Lucretius, in his classic *The Way Things Are*, gives a miniature history of music which includes some interesting aesthetic purposes of music, such as 'to please the ear,' 'to ease the spirit,' and 'have more joy.'

As for music,
Men started first by imitating birdsong.
That came before they made up little tunes
With words to please the ear; and the stir of a breeze
Through reedy hollows whispering conveyed
Hints of Pan-Pipe. Pretty soon they tried
The sweet but sadder melodies they could make
With fingers on the flute, the native reed
Found in the pathless woods or upland groves
Where shepherds dwell, almost in idleness,
Almost in solitude, with music's charm
After a good square meal[74] (for that's the time
Music gives most delight) to ease the spirit.
Often they sprawled on the soft meadow grass
Beside a stream, under a lofty tree,
And things went well at very little cost,
Especially when the season smiled, and spring
Stippled the greenery with colored flowers.
Then there were jokes, good talk, and laughter; then
The rustic Muse was at her liveliest
And fun and foolishness bade people twine

74   From the most ancient times one finds the phrase, 'after the tables were cleared' before the description of the time to listen to music. It reflects the need for the contemplative listener necessary to art music.

Wreaths around heads and shoulders, and step out
Stiff-legged, hayfoot, strawfoot in a march
Or maybe it was a dance—it made them laugh,
Titter and giggle at this brave new world
So strange and wonderful. Who needed sleep
When they could blend their voices in the song
Or curve the lip around the reed-pipes's tops?
Even today men who must keep awake
Continue this tradition; they have learned
A stricter sense of time, but even so
I doubt they have more joy in song and dance
Than those old woodland aborigines.[75]

75 Lucretius, *The Way Things Are*, 5.1378.

Varro was frustrated that subjects like music seemed to elude the normal intellectual processes of reason and logic and in the fact that the writings he knew on music did not correspond with each other. Even in those cases where the writers do agree, the reader must be vigilant to the fact that they may be wrong.

> You will have to reject all the arts, because in medicine and in music and in many other arts the writers do not agree; you must take the same attitude in the matters in which they agree in their writings, if none the less nature rejects their conclusions. For in this way, as is often said, it is not the art but the artist that is to be found fault with, who, it must be said, has in his writing failed to see the correct view; we should not for this reason say that the correct view cannot be formulated in writing.[76]

76 Varro, *On the Latin Language*, 9.64.111.

Cicero made a similar observation, suggesting that it was nearly impossible to define aesthetics when every artist thought his work was the best. Speaking of the legendary musician, Dionysius, Cicero observes,

> A most enthusiastic musician, a tragic poet too, we are told—how good a one is irrelevant. In this area, for some reason more than in others, every one admires his own work. I have never yet known a poet who did not think himself the best. That's how it is. 'You like your work I like mine.'[77]

77 Cicero, *Tusculan Disputations*, 5.63.

We have mentioned above our impression that Cicero did not really understand art in general. In the case of music we believe it is clear that one can go further. There are some people, and Aristotle was one, who seem to be born left-hemisphere men. They seem to operate only on the level of data, language and mathemat-

78   My father was such a man. When he was over the age of eighty the police insisted on his being tested before continuing to allow him to drive. A test was given in which he scored so high in the left hemisphere that he was found to be far above men thirty years younger (there was no existing data to compare him with men his age). On the other hand, his right hemisphere was found to be nearly dormant.

79   Cicero, *De Oratore*, 1.49.

80   Ibid., 1.50.217.

81   Cicero, *Academica*, 2.27.

82   Ibid., 3.10.35. It was a view the early Roman Church would strictly observe.

83   Cicero, *De Oratore*, 3.57.216.

ics.[78] We believe Cicero was such a man and it accounts for how he could include music, poetry, and philology among 'the more trivial arts.'[79] Poetry he admits as a part of 'natural philosophy,' but music and geometry belong to neither the 'natural' nor the 'moral' branches of philosophy.

> Even the moral philosophers themselves, who would have all things for their own, in right of dominion and in fact of possession as well, do not venture to claim that either geometry or the pursuit of music belongs to the moral philosopher.[80]

In a number of places, one might conclude from his comments that Cicero simply had no ear for music, as in the following example.

> But you call in the aid of art to plead in defense even of the senses. A painter sees things that we do not, and a musical expert recognizes a tune as soon as the aulos player has blown a note. Well, does not this seem to argue against you, if without great artistic acquirements, to which few people, of our race indeed very few, attain, we are unable either to see or to hear?[81]

It also seems possible that it may have been Cicero's strong belief that one should not display emotions that prevented him from appreciating the essence of music. As we have quoted above, he said, 'emotions, the very sound of which seems to denote something vicious ... the Wise Man will always be free from them.'[82] Even though he recognized there was something universally human about emotions, and even though in the following it is music itself which he uses as a metaphor to discuss the display of emotions, yet he mentions only acting and painting as arts for which they are appropriate.

> For nature has assigned to every emotion a particular look and tone of voice and bearing of its own; and the whole of a person's frame and every look on his face and utterance of his voice are like the strings of a harp, and sound according as they are struck by each successive emotion. For the tones of the voice are keyed up like the strings of an instrument, so as to answer to every touch, high, low, quick, slow, forte, piano, while between all of these in their several kinds there is a medium note; and there are also the various modifications derived from these, smooth or rough, limited or full in volume, tenuto or staccato, faint or harsh, diminuendo or crescendo. For there are none of these varieties that cannot be regulated by the control of art; they are the colors available for the actor, as for the painter, to secure variety.[83]

It is evident, in any case, that Cicero had observed carefully the practice of music and he gives himself away in his most revealing and interesting comments where he uses the model of music to explain some point he wishes to make with regard to oratory. For example, he notes that the orator, like the actor, poet and musician, must have a variety of pitch and volume.

> For both poets and composers employ a definite fall in tone and then a rise, a sinking and a swell, variations, pauses.[84]

84 Cicero, *De Oratore*, 3.26.102.

In particular, Cicero pointed to rhythm as the element which made the orator an 'artist.' The development of this style, he points out, has its origin in music.

> Who then is the man who gives people a thrill? Whom do they stare at in amazement when he speaks? Who is interrupted by applause? Who is thought to be so to say a god among men? It is those whose speeches are clear, explicit and full, perspicuous in matter and in language, and who in the actual delivery achieve a sort of rhythm and cadence—that is, those whose style is what I call artistic.[85]
>
> ...
>
> After attention to [syntax] comes also the consideration to the rhythm and shape of the words, a point which I am afraid Catulus here may consider childish; for the old Greek masters held the view that in this prose style it is proper for us to use something almost amounting to versification, that is, certain definite rhythms. For they thought that in speeches the close of the period ought to come not when we are tired out but where we may take breath ... It is said that Isocrates first introduced the practice ... by means of an element of rhythm, designed to give pleasure to the ear. For two contrivances to give pleasure were devised by the musicians, who in the old days were also the poets, verse and melody, with the intention of overcoming satiety in the hearer by delighting the ear with the rhythm of the words and the mode[86] of the notes ...
>
> In this matter an extremely important point is, that although it is a fault in oratory if the connection of the words produces verse, nevertheless we at the same time desire the word-order to resemble verse in having a rhythmical cadence ... [Nothing] more distinguishes him from an inexperienced and ignorant speaker.[87]

85 Ibid., 3.14.53.

86 This refers to the fact that the early poets were also singers.

87 Cicero, *De Oratore*, 3.44.173ff.

Of particular interest, in another place Cicero speaks of the aesthetic contribution of rhythm.

There are, speaking generally, two things which lend flavor to prose, pleasing words and agreeable rhythms. Words furnish a certain raw material which it is the business of rhythm to polish …

Wherefore if the question be asked, which rhythms are used in prose, the answer is, 'all, but one is better suited to one part and one to another.' The place? In all parts of a phrase. What is its origin? In the pleasure of the ear … For what purpose is it used? To give pleasure. When? Always. In what place? Throughout the whole period. What produces pleasure? The same phenomena as in verse; theory sets down the exact measure of these, but without theory the ear marks their limits with unconscious intuition.[88]

Finally, Cicero, mentions rhythm with respect to the accommodations the public performer must make for age; he again cites the actor Roscius.

As we are taking from a single artist a number of details for our likeness of an orator, that same Roscius is fond of saying, that, the older he grows, the slower he will make the aulos player's rhythms and the lighter the music. Now if he, fettered as he is by a definite system of measures and meters, is none the less thinking out some relief for his old age, how much more easily can we not merely slacken our methods, but change them altogether![89]

Cicero also discusses in some detail the use of pitch as an important aspect of vocal delivery, once observing 'that nature herself modulates the voice to gratify the ear of mankind.'[90] In another place he discusses this in more detail, the role of movement and music with respect to the orator.

Manner of speech falls into two sections, delivery and use of language. For delivery is a sort of language of the body, since it consists of movement or gesture as well as of voice or speech. There are as many variations in the tones of the voice as there are in feelings, which are especially aroused by the voice. Accordingly the perfect orator … will use certain tones according as he wishes to seem himself to be moved and to sway the minds of his audience … I might also speak about gestures, which include facial expression. The way in which the orator uses these makes a difference which can scarcely be described …

Demosthenes was right, therefore, in considering delivery to be in the first, second and third in importance … Therefore the one who seeks supremacy in eloquence will strive to speak intensely with a vehement tone, and gently with lowered voice, and to show dignity in a deep voice, and wretchedness by a plaintive tone. For

88   Cicero, *De Oratore*, 55.185 and 60.203. Also in this treatise, 23.78, Cicero, in speaking of the sentence construction observes there is such a thing as 'careful negligence,' and, by way of example, he points to some women who 'are said to be handsomer when unadorned— this very lack of ornament becomes them.'

89   Cicero, *De Oratore*, 1.60.254.

90   Ibid., 3.48.185.

the voice possesses a marvelous quality, so that from merely three registers, high, low and intermediate, it produces such a rich and pleasing variety in song. There is, moreover, even in speech, a sort of singing ... which Demosthenes and Aeschines mean when they accuse each other of vocal modulations ... Here I ought to emphasize a point which is of importance in attaining an agreeable voice: nature herself, as if to modulate human speech, has placed an accent, and only one, on every word ... Therefore let art follow the leadership of nature in pleasing the ear ... The superior orator will therefore vary and modulate his voice; now raising and now lowering it, he will run through the whole scale of tones.[91]

91 Ibid., 17.55ff.

For all this comparison with music, Cicero, makes it clear that in his view music can never compare to oratory. 'Can any music be composed,' he asks, 'that is sweeter than a well-balanced speech?'[92]

92 Cicero, *De Oratore*, 2.8.33.

Rarely do we find any tribute by Cicero to the power of music. In a notable exception, he writes,

The very rocks of the wilderness give back a sympathetic echo to the voice; savage beasts have sometimes been charmed into stillness by song; and shall we, who are nurtured upon all that is highest, be deaf to the appeal of poetry?[93]

93 Cicero, *Pro Archia Poeta*, 8.19.

For the most part, Cicero seems to have missed the essence of music as an art. He seems to have only seen the functional side of music, which in his time was often performed by slaves. Thus in a discussion of the professions, in which he found medicine, architecture, and the teaching of 'respectable subjects'[94] to be respectable, he displays considerable prejudice toward many jobs—and music ranks at the very bottom!

94 Cicero, *De Officiis*, 1.155, Cicero adds the autobiographical observation, 'What ever useful services I personally rendered to my country, if I performed any worth mentioning, I undertook them after receiving intellectual and literary training for them from the lessons of my teachers. It is not only living contemporaries who instruct and teach those eager to learn, but teachers fulfill the same task after death by their literary records.'

Now the following is the gist of my understanding about professions and trades, those that free men can think of entering and those that are contemptible. First, no one can approve professions that arouse people's dislike, for example, collectors of harbor duties or usurers. Similarly, the work of all hired men who sell their labor and not their talents is servile and contemptible. The reason is that in their case wages actually constitute a payment for slavery. Another disreputable class includes those who buy whole lots from wholesalers to retail immediately. They would not make a profit unless they indulged in misrepresentation, and nothing is more criminal than fraud. All mechanics work in contemptible professions because no one born of free parents would have anything to do with a workshop. The employments lest worthy of approval are those that pander to pleasure: 'Fishmongers, butchers, cooks, sausage-makers, fishermen,' as Terrence says. Add to this list, if you like, perfume makers, stage dancers, and the whole musical stage.[95]

95 Ibid., 1.151.

Only once does Cicero acknowledge that members of the upper class were interested in music, and then he characterizes it as an innocent amusement as a form of rest from more important duties or when they have nothing else to do.

But just as persons usually engaged in constant daily employment, when debarred from work because of the weather, betake themselves to tennis or gambling or dicing or even devise for themselves some novel game to occupy their leisure, so when the persons in question have been debarred from their work of politics by the circumstances of the time or have chosen to take a vacation, some of them have devoted themselves entirely to poetry, others to mathematics, and others to music.[96]

96 Cicero, *De Oratore*, 3.15.58.

Likewise, in Cicero, we find no descriptions of concerts or of audiences attending concerts.[97] The sole such reference is to an aulos recital, which Cicero is quick to point out the audience did *not* like. The incident is worthy of mention for the comment made by the teacher of this unhappy player, 'Play for me and for the Muses.'[98]

97 A possible reason for this may lie in the fact that his own taste was so low that he was embarrassed to mention the subject. In a letter to Atticus, for example, we find a reference to 'low-grade music halls.' Cicero, *Letters to Atticus* (New York: Penguin Classics, 1978), 54.

We know much public performance of poetry at this time was still accompanied by the lyre or the aulos, but again, while Cicero often speaks with great praise of poets, he never mentions the music. Only one passing comment, where he quotes a passage of Latin poetry and observes, 'the rest of the passage, unless accompanied by the aulos, is exactly like prose,'[99] reveals any knowledge by Cicero of this tradition.

98 Cicero, *Brutus*, 49.187.

Likewise, when he mentions the theatrical festivals, the music which was so much a part of them is never described by Cicero. In a letter to Marcus Marius, Cicero speaks of great theatrical performances which must have had considerable musical participation, but to him whatever he heard was only part of the 'elaboration of the spectacle.'

99 Cicero, *De Oratore*, 55.184.

Need I tell you more? You know what else happens at festivals. This did not even have the charm that less pretentious ones have, since all the fun was lost in the elaboration of the spectacle, with which you, I know, would have been only too willing to dispense. For what pleasure can there be in six hundred mules in the *Clytemnestra* or three thousand wine bowls in the *Trojan Horse*, or variegated cavalry and infantry equipment in some battle scene or other? These excited the admiration of the groundlings, but would have added nothing to your enjoyment.[100]

100 Letter to Marcus Marius, 55 BC.

These were obviously Greek plays and therefore we may have a description here which reflects Cicero's general dislike for Greek productions, for we know from an earlier letter,

There was some breath of rumor that the opening of the Greek performances had been badly attended, which didn't surprise me at all. You know what I think of Greek shows.'[101]

101 Letter to Atticus, 44 BC.

Where Cicero does mention music it is usually accompanying some, often rather low, form of entertainment. In one case, for example, he joins in the same category, debauch, love affairs, nocturnal revels with music, lechery, and ruinous spending.'[102] Even in Homer's remarkable story about the Sirens, Cicero refused to believe it was the *music* that captured the sailors—it was, he prefers to believe, their left-hemisphere language which halted the boat of the sailors!

102 Cicero, *In Defense of Murena*, 6.

For my part I believe Homer had something of this sort [delight in knowledge] in view in his imaginary account of the songs of the Sirens. Apparently it was not the sweetness of their voices or the novelty and diversity of their songs, but their professions of knowledge that used to attract the passing voyagers; it was the passion for learning that kept men rooted to the Sirens' rocky shores ... Homer was aware that his story would not sound plausible if the magic that held his hero immeshed was merely an idle song! It is knowledge that the Sirens offer, and it was no marvel if a lover of wisdom held this dearer than his home.[103]

103 Cicero, *De Finibus*, 5.18.49.

Given the associations above of debauchery, lechery, and revels with music, not to mention his moral approach to everything, it will come as no surprise that Cicero had a very poor view of the entire range of amusement. As he considered amusement to be something primarily 'for the untutored masses,'[104] he particularly objected to the money wasted on amusements. Here he was not only thinking of economy of money, but of the fact that amusements are so fleeting in nature.

104 Cicero, *In Defense of Murena*, 19.

In the case of the enormous expenditures and limitless outlays on shows, we do not feel any great amazement. Yet they do not relieve any need, they do not increase anyone's importance, the crowd itself gets amusement only for a brief and limited time, only the most thoughtless elements feel amused, and what is more, their memory of being amused starts fading the moment they have had enough of it.[105]

105 Cicero, *De Officiis*, 2.56. This is the case with all amusements.

Better to spend public money on city walls, dockyards, port facilities, and aqueducts, not theaters.[106]

106 Ibid., 2.60.

Charity belongs to men of dignity and greatness; but public spectacles seem to be the mark of those who fawn on the people, those, it seems, who use pleasure to encourage the frivolity of the crowd.[107]

107 Ibid., 2.63.

As for himself, 'I did not devote myself to trivial amusements unworthy of an educated man.[108] But, 'If we must have amusement,' Cicero asks, 'why not the study of philosophy?'

108 Ibid., 2.2.

If you want intellectual amusement and relaxation from cares, what can be compared with the studies of men who are always trying to find a relevant and effective way to live well and happily?[109]

109 Ibid., 2.6.

It was one of the distinct advantages of old age, thought Cicero, that one is relieved from the need for entertainment, from lust

O glorious boon of age, if it does indeed free us from youth's most vicious fault![110]

110 Cicero, *De Senectute*, 12.

and the over indulgence of the banquet!

Old age lacks the heavy banquet, the loaded table, and the oft-filled cup; therefore it also lacks drunkenness, indigestion, and loss of sleep.[111]

111 Ibid., 13.

We are fortunate to have extant from this period a number of works by Horace (66–8 BC), one of the greatest philosophers of early Rome. While the size of his output is neither as large nor far reaching as that of Plato and Aristotle, he certainly belongs in their company as an astute observer of the arts. While he sometimes pretends modesty, we know from one of his letters that he believed that he was the first to introduce much of the early Greek poetry to Rome.[1]

In the field of aesthetics he is especially valuable as the only early Roman philosopher who made an important contribution. Unlike Cicero, who almost ignored music entirely, Horace composed, sung and played the lyre.[2] We know he was well read and that among the Roman writers he especially appreciated Virgil and Varius.[3]

There is a remarkable passage in one of his extant letters in which he considers the influence of Greek culture on Rome. These lines give us a fascinating first-century view of the decay of Greek culture, its spread to Rome, and the sense of cultural insecurity the Romans apparently felt at this time.

> From the day she stopped her wars, Greece took to trifling, and amid fairer fortunes drifted into folly: she was all aglow with passion, now for athletes, now for horses; she raved over workers in marble or ivory or bronze; with eyes and soul she hung enraptured on the painted panel; her joy was now in the aulos players, and now in actors of tragedy. Like a baby girl playing at its nurse's feet, what she wanted in impatience, she soon, when satisfied, cast off …
>
> Greece, the captive, made her savage victor captive, and brought the arts into rustic Latium. Thus the stream of that rude Saturnian measure ran dry and good taste banished the offensive poison; yet for many a year lived on, and still live on, traces of our rustic past. For not till late did the Roman turn his wit to Greek writings, and in the peaceful days after the Punic wars he began to ask what service Sophocles could render, and Thespis and Aeschylus. He also made essay, whether he could reproduce in worthy style, and took pride in his success, being gifted with spirit and vigor; for he has some tragic inspiration, and is happy in his ventures, but in ignorance, deeming it disgraceful, hesitates to blot.[4]

1   Horace, *Epistles*, 1.19.21.

2   Horace, *Odes*, 1.22 and 31.

3   Horace, *Satires*, 1.10.43 and *Epistles*, 2.1.245.

4   Horace, *Epistles*, 2.1.93 and 156.

The Philosophy of Aesthetics

Horace was the only philosopher of importance from this brief period whose works addressed this subject. However, in the large body of extant poetry we can find additional clues regarding the understanding of aesthetics in this period.

The Purpose of Art

The fundamental purpose of art, according to Horace, is a basic one shared by almost every epoch: Art is 'for the soul's delight.'[5] 'Go now,' he says, 'and gaze with rapture on silver plate, antique marbles, bronzes and works of art.'[6]

It is this same purpose which Virgil had in mind when he spoke of the 'arts which enrich man's life.'

> He looked at the others
> To right and to left on the grass as they feasted and sang
> A joyful paean in chorus, there in the fragrant
> Laurel grove where the great river Eridanus rolls
> Through the woods to the upper world.
> Here was a band
> Of men who had suffered wounds while fighting for country;
> Some who were priests and chaste while their life remained,
> And others loyal seers who spoke things worthy of Phoebus,
> Some creative in arts which enrich man's life,
> And others whose merit had made men remember them.[7]

Closely related is the purpose of art to relieve us from our daily concerns and worries, as Horace reminds us.

> I shall not feel ardor again for any
> Woman, learn the harmonies I will teach your
> Loving voice to sing: by a song our dreary
> Troubles are lightened.[8]

An important purpose of art which we recognize today is illumination, the raising of the awareness of the observer through exposure to higher ideas, or greater minds. This purpose of art is often expressed in illusions to the poets being 'divine,' or 'holy,' referring to the poet's connection with higher ideas. Ovid repeatedly credits the divine as the source of the poet's inspiration.

5 Horace, *Ars Poetica*, trans. H. Rushton Fairclough (Cambridge, MA: Harvard University Press, 1955), 481.

6 Horace, *Epistle*, 1.6.17.

7 Virgil, *Aeneid*, 6.656.

8 Horace, *Odes*, 4.11.

Now, since a god inspires my lips, I will dutifully follow the inspiring god; I'll open Delphi and the heavens themselves and unlock the oracles of the sublime mind. Great matters, never traced out by the minds of former men, things that have long been hidden, I will sing.[9]

9   Ovid, *Metamorphoses*, 15.143.

...

Be kind, ye fair, to the poetic choir.
Whom Muses love and deities inspire.
God's in us and with heaven we discourse,
In springs divine our instinct has its source.[10]

10   Ovid, *Amores* [The Loves], 3.547.

For the modest Horace it was the lack of this genius to convey lofty thoughts, rather than the mundane things of which he wrote, which prevented him from thinking of himself as a *real* poet.

First, I exclude my own name from the roster of genuine poets.
Merely composing a metrical unit is not, you would say, what
Qualifies someone; you would not consider a 'poet' a man who
Wrote about matters belonging in mere conversation, as I do.
Only on genius commanding the mind and the lips to deliver
Utterance fit for a god would you ever bestow that distinction.[11]

11   Horace, *Satires*, 1.4.39.

Another purpose of art is to commemorate for posterity the deeds of the artist's contemporaries. Horace writes that while he can not give gifts like paintings and sculpture, he can give the gift of immortality through his poetry.

Gifts of ritual bowls I would bestow, and bronze
Vases suiting each friend's taste, Censorinus, yes,
Tripods such as the Greek victors received, and your
Gift would not be the least precious of all the lot,
If, that is, I but owned works of the different arts
Such as Scopas produced or as Parrhasius,
One creating from stone, one from his liquid paints,
Experts both at the shaped likeness of man and god.
No such power is mine, nor, with your wealth and taste,
Have you needed to go hankering for such toys.
You find poems a joy, poems I *can* bestow,
And, what's more, can explain poetry's value too.
Marble likeness and name carved at the state's behest
Bring no leader's achieved fame or his spirit back
Once he passes to death; nor do retreat and rout,
Threats of Hannibal hurled backwards upon himself,
Devastation that burned impious Carthage down,

Give that man, who from tamed Africa won a name
But no other reward, glory to equal what
Fair Calabria's Muse won for him later; nor
Will you profit at all from an accomplishment
If no book tells the tale.[12]

12 Horace, *Odes*, 4.8.

Thus, Horace wonders, how many heroes are forgotten because they had no poet to commemorate them?

Before great Agamemnon there lived a host
Of heroes, now submerged in the endless night
Without our tears and nameless all, for
Lack of a consecrate poet's praises.[13]

13 Ibid., 4.9.

Horace makes one new and historic comment relative to the aim of art. Horace now for the first time adds the possibility that the didactic, pragmatic educational goals, may be part of the aim of art. Hereafter, it will become an independent view of aesthetics, that art has the obligation to educate. His reference to this idea is the earliest which has come down to us in this meaning.

Poets aim either to benefit, or to amuse, or to utter words at once both pleasing and helpful to life. Whenever you instruct, be brief, so that what is quickly said the mind may readily grasp and faithfully hold: every word in excess flows away from the full mind.[14]

14 Horace, *Ars Poetica*, 479.

Finally, in another place, Horace surveys the entire range of the purposes of art, including the new purpose to educate, 'he molds the heart by kindly precepts.'

The poet fashions the tender, lisping lips of childhood; even then he turns the ear from unseemly words; presently, too, he molds the heart by kindly precepts, correcting roughness and envy and anger. He tells of noble deeds, equips the rising age with famous examples, and to the helpless and sick at heart brings comfort. Whence, in company with chaste boys, would the unwedded maid learn the suppliant hymn, had the Muse not given them a bard? Their chorus asks for aid and feels the presence of the gods, calls for showers from heaven, winning favor with the prayer he has taught, averts disease, drives away dreaded dangers, gains peace and a season rich in fruits. Song wins grace with the gods above, song wins it with the gods below.[15]

15 Horace, *Epistles*, 2.1.127.

Such noble purposes of art we know are not universally appreciated today. A comment by Ovid suggests the same may be said of the Augustan period. He has a character say,

'Quit fooling people,'
They said, 'Quit fooling silly ignorant people
With your pretense of music!'[16]

16 Ovid, *Metamorphoses*, 5.307.

This is a shocking comment by so great a poet. However, in another place Ovid expresses his own doubt of the value of art and even on his having pursued it.

What verse is worth, I doubt. It's always harmed me,
And my success has made men envious.
Though there was Thebes and Troy and Caesar's exploits,
Only Corinna fired my genius.

I wish the Muse had balked at my beginnings
And Phoebus left me stranded at the start.
Yet poets aren't on oath, you know; I'd rather
Less weight were given to my wordy art.[17]

17 Ovid, *Amores*, 3.12.

On the Characteristics of Art

Of the various aspects of aesthetics discussed by Horace, he devotes the most attention to verisimilitude, examining a number of facets of this aspect of art. First, he says that the poet's purpose must be the artistic presentation of verisimilitude, that Truth and the artistic representation of Truth may be two different things.

Most of us poets … deceive ourselves by the semblance of Truth. Striving to be brief, I become obscure. Aiming at smoothness, I fail in force and fire. One promising grandeur, is bombastic; another, overcautious and fearful of the gale, creeps along the ground. The man who tries to vary a single subject in monstrous fashion, is like a painter adding a dolphin to the woods, a boar to the waves. Shunning a fault may lead to error, if there be lack of art.[18]

18 Horace, *Ars Poetica*, 453.

With this Ovid agrees.

Yes, there's no limit to poetic license,
And it's not tied to truths of history.[19]

19 Ovid, *Amores*, 3.12, lines 26–27.

Second, the poet must be knowledgeable of both the history of his art and the traditional styles associated with the different forms of his art. Ignorance, Horace says, is no excuse.

> In what measure the exploits of kings and captains and the sorrows of war may be written, Homer has shown. Verses yoked unequally first embraced lamentation, later also the sentiment of granted prayer: yet who first put forth humble elegiacs, scholars dispute, and the case is still before the court. Rage armed Archilochus with his own *iambus*: this foot comic sock and high buskins alike adopted, as suited to alternate speech, able to drown the clamors of the pit, and by nature fit for action. To the lyre the Muse granted tales of gods and children of gods, of the victor in boxing, of the horse first in the race, of the loves of swains, and of freedom over wine. If I fail to keep and do not understand these well-marked shifts and shades of poetic forms, why am I hailed as poet? Why through false shame do I prefer to be ignorant rather than to learn?[20]

20 Horace, *Ars Poetica*, 457.

Third, the characters must be consistent, whether one treats an historical character or invents something new. With regard to historical characters, again the aim is not literal quotation, but the artistic representation of the character.

> Either follow tradition or invent what is self-consistent. If haply, when you write, you bring back to the stage the honoring of Achilles, let him be impatient, passionate, ruthless, fierce; let him claim that laws are not for him, let him ever make appeal to the sword. Let Medea be fierce and unyielding, Ino tearful, Ixion forsworn, Io a wanderer, Orestes sorrowful. If it is an untried theme you entrust to the stage, and if you boldly fashion a fresh character, have it kept to the end even as it came forth at the first, and have it self-consistent …
>
> In ground open to all you will win private rights, if you do not linger along the easy and open pathway, if you do not seek to render word for word as a slavish translator.[21]

21 Ibid., 461.

Fourth, verisimilitude includes the faithful characterization of the ages of man.

> Now hear what I, and with me the public, expect. If you want an approving hearer, one who waits for the curtain, and will stay in his seat till the singer cries 'Give your applause,' you must note the manners of each age, and give a befitting tone to shifting natures and their years. The child, who by now can utter words and set firm step upon the ground, delights to play with his mates, flies into a

passion and as lightly puts it aside, and changes every hour. The beardless youth, freed at last from his tutor, finds joy in horses and hounds and the grass of the sunny Campus, soft as wax for molding to evil, peevish with his counselors, slow to make needful provision, lavish of money, spirited, of strong desires, but swift to change his fancies. With altered aims, the age of spirit of the man seeks wealth and friends, becomes a slave to ambition, and is fearful of having done what soon it will be eager to change. Many ills encompass an old man, whether because he seeks gain, and then miserably holds aloof from his store and fears to use it, or because, in all that he does, he lacks fire and courage, is dilatory and slow to form hopes, is sluggish and greedy of a longer life, peevish, surly, given to praising the days he spent as a boy, and to reproving and condemning the youth. Many blessings do the advancing years bring with them: many, as they retire, they take away. So, lest haply we assign a youth the part of age, or a boy that of manhood, we shall ever linger over traits that are joined and fitted to the age.[22]

22 Ibid., 463.

Finally, he contends that for the theater it is the eye, rather than the ear, which convinces the observer of verisimilitude.

Either an event is acted on the stage, or the action is narrated. Less vividly is the mind stirred by what finds entrance through the ears than by what is brought before the trusty eyes, and what the spectator can see for himself.[23]

23 Ibid., 465.

Ovid, writing in his last years, lists some of the important characteristics of great art by way of reflecting that he no longer could produce them.

Supply what I lack—details, the fire,
    grace, elegance, everything. Even the mood
    of rejoicing is hard for me now. My lyre is shabby, cracked,
    and doesn't do well anymore in the major modes.[24]

24 Ovid., *Poetry of Exile*, 3.4.

Is Art Native or Learned?

Horace addresses a question still asked in our own era: Is the great artist a product of his education or the product of native genius? Earlier in this treatise Horace seems to take a rather firm position: true art cannot be taught; native talent is more important than 'wretched art,' that is, the learned craft.[25] Later, however, he

25 Horace, *Ars Poetica*, 475.

returns to this question and now softens his position. In the end, however, he concludes that he cannot attribute his own art to his education in that field.

> Often it is asked whether a praiseworthy poem is due to Nature or to art. For my part, I do not see of what avail is either study, when not enriched by Nature's vein, or native wit, if untrained; so truly does each claim the other's aid, and make it a friendly league. He who in the race-course craves to reach the longed-for goal, has borne much and done much as a boy, has sweated and shivered, has kept aloof from wine and women. The aulos player who plays at the Pythian games, has first learned his lessons and been in awe of a master. Today this is enough to say: 'I fashion wondrous poems: the devil take the rest! 'Tis unseemly for me to be left behind, and to confess that I really do not know what I have never learned.'[26]

26 Ibid., 485.

But, if Horace would not attribute the quality of his art to education, he was willing to acknowledge the role of simple hard work.

> I am merely
> Bee-like and busy,
> Culling honeyed thyme with prodigious effort
> Through the groves and well-watered glens of Tibur,
> Working up my poems from little substance
> Crafted with labor.[27]

27 Horace, *Odes*, 4.2.

Given this work ethic, one can understand why Horace complained of the poet, Cassius, who delighted himself in writing two hundred lines before breakfast and another two hundred after dinner! Sniffed Horace,

> Of him they say that his books and their cases supplied all the fuel
> Needed to cremate him after his death.[28]

28 Horace, *Satires*, 1.10.61. There were two poets of this name and it is not known which Horace referred to. One of them, by the way, was one of the slayers of Caesar.

Regarding the craft involved in the production of any art, however, Horace is mindful that humans, even artists, are not free of error and he uses music as a metaphor to make this point. However, just make sure you don't make the same mistake twice!

> Yet faults there are which we can gladly pardon; for the string does not always yield the sound which hand and heart intend, but when you call for a flat often returns you a sharp; nor will the bow always hit the mark it threatens. But when the beauties in a poem are more in number, I shall not take offense at a few blots which a careless

hand has let drop, or human frailty has failed to avert. What, then, is the truth? As a copying always makes the same mistake, and a harpist is laughed at who always blunders on the same string: so the poet who often defaults.[29]

29   Horace, *Ars Poetica*, 479.

To avoid error the poet must have the courage to examine his work objectively and make changes accordingly.

But the man whose aim is to have wrought a poem true to Art's rules, when he takes his tablets, will take also the spirit of an honest censor. He will have the courage, if words fall short in dignity, lack weight, or be deemed unworthy of rank, to remove them from their place, albeit they are loth to withdraw.[30]

30   Horace, *Epistles*, 2.2.109.

Failing this, he advises that if one writes something, and your father or a friend criticizes it in a private reading, better to 'put it in the closet for nine years'—for once you release it to the world you can never take it back.[31]

Horace's own fears, with regard to his craft, were simply that he might not be able to do justice to the occasion.

31   Horace, *Ars Poetica*, 483. Which reminds one of Brahms who waited for so long to release his first symphony.

> Being feeble at grand themes, and while modesty
> And the Muse of this mild lyre bid us not to mar
> Praise of you—and thereby eminent Caesar's self—
> With a talent that shows a flaw.[32]

32   Horace, *Odes*, 1.6.

MUSIC IN THE THEATER

Horace also provides some interesting comments regarding the role of music in the theater. First, as with the subject and characterization, his concern seems to be that the music be genuine, suited to and contributing to the stage action.

Let the Chorus sustain the part and strenuous duty of an actor, and sing nothing between acts which does not advance and fitly blend into the plot. It should side with the good and give friendly counsel; sway the angry and cherish the righteous. It should praise the fare of a modest board, praise wholesome justice, law and peace with her open gates; should keep secrets, and pray and beseech the gods that fortune may return to the unhappy, and depart from the proud.[33]

33   Horace, *Ars Poetica*, 467.

With regard to instrumental music in the theater, Horace reminds the reader of the history of this art. While it began with the role of amplifying the stage action, the popularity of the music itself soon led to its usurping the attention of the audience.

> The aulos—not, as now, bound with brass and a rival of the trumpet, but slight and simple, with few stops—was once of use to lead and aid the chorus and to fill with its breath benches not yet too crowded, where, to be sure, folk gathered, easy to count, because few—sober folk, too, and chaste and modest. But when a conquering race began to widen its domain, and an ampler wall embraced its cities, and when, on festal days, appeasing the Genius by daylight drinking brought no penalty, then both time and tune won greater license. For what taste could you expect of an unlettered throng just freed from toil, rustic mixed up with city folk, vulgar with nobly born? So to the early art the aulos player added movement and display, and, strutting over the stage, trailed a robe in train. So, too, to the sober lyre new tones were given, and an impetuous style brought in an unwonted diction; and the thought, full of wise saws and prophetic of the future, was attuned to the oracles of Delphi.[34]

34 Ibid.

THE PUBLIC

There is a famous remark by Mozart regarding the reception of his music by the public at large.

> These passages are written in such a way that the less learned cannot fail to be pleased, though without knowing why.[35]

35 Letter to his father, December 28, 1782.

Horace made his aim in the theater the same.

> My aim shall be poetry, so molded from the familiar that anybody may hope for the same success, may sweat much and yet toil in vain when attempting the same: such is the power of order and connection, such the beauty that may crown the commonplace.[36]

36 Horace, *Ars Poetica*, 471.

But if this was his aim, in practice Horace seems to have found the public incapable of accuracy in the ability to judge quality in art. He seems especially sensitive to having to compete with the reputation of the poets of old.

> At times the public sees straight; sometimes they make mistakes. If they admire the ancient poets and cry them up so as to put nothing above them, nothing on their level, they are wrong.[37]

37 Horace, *Epistles*, 2.1.63.

But then, he admits, it is natural that men should disagree.

> After all, men have not all the same tastes and likes. Lyric song is your delight, our neighbor here takes pleasure in iambics, the one yonder in Bion's satires, with their caustic wit.[38]

In general, Horace saw the public of his day as being interested only in entertainment. He probably felt the noisy public had little interest in his art.

> I loathe the mob impure and forbid its place.
> Let tongues be silent! Songs hitherto unheard,
> As priestly spokesman of the Muses
> I shall now sing for our youths and maidens.[39]

Horace was well aware of the decline of the theater arts since the time of the Greek lyric poets and how the writers of his day too often succumbed to the entertainment demands of the audience. In the following we glimpse the feeling of futility he felt in writing for such audiences.

> Often even the bold poet is frightened and put to rout, when those who are stronger in number, but weaker in worth and rank, unlearned and stupid and ready to fight it out if the knights dispute with them, call in the middle of a play for a bear or for boxers: 'tis in such things the rabble delights. But nowadays all the pleasure even of the knights has passed from the ear to the vain delights of the wandering eye. For four hours or more the curtains are kept down, while troops of horse and files of foot [soldiers] sweep by: anon are dragged in kings, once fortune's favorites, their hands bound behind them: with hurry and scurry come chariots, carriages, wains, and ships; and borne in triumph are spoils of ivory, spoils of Corinthian bronze. Were Democritus still on earth, he would laugh; whether it were some hybrid monster—a panther crossed with a camel—or a white elephant, that drew the eyes of the crowd—he would gaze more intently on the audience than on the play itself, as giving him more by far worth looking at. But for the authors—he would suppose that they were telling their tale to a deaf ass. For what voices have ever prevailed to drown the din with which our theaters resound? One might think it was the roaring of the Garganian forest or of the Tuscan Sea: amid such clamor is the entertainment viewed, the works of art, and the foreign finery, and when, overlaid with this, the actor steps upon the stage, [and the applause is instantly heard]. 'Has he yet said anything' Not a word. 'Then what [excites the audience] so?' 'Tis the woolen robe that view

38   Ibid., 2.2.58.

39   Horace, *Odes*, 3.1.

with the violet in its Tarentine dye. And lest, perchance, you may think that I begrudge praise when others are handling well what I decline to try myself, methinks that poet is able to walk a tight rope, who with airy nothings wrings my heart, inflames, soothes, fills it with vain alarms like a magician, and sets me down now at Thebes, now at Athens.[40]

As he says, Horace could not write for this kind of public. When he reflected on those writers who took this path of following the crowd, a path from which there was no turning back, he was reminded of a fable about a fox.

If the people of Rome should ask me why I do not have the same judgments as they, why I do not follow or eschew what they love or hate, I should reply as once upon a time the prudent fox made answer to the sick lion: 'Because those footprints frighten me; they all lead toward your den, and none lead back!'[41]

The reason to follow the public's taste was, of course, for financial success. Even the famous Plautus, Horace disrespected for writing for this reason.

Yes, he is eager to drop a coin into his pocket and, that done, he cares not whether his play fall or stand square on its own feet.[42]

For the true poet, says Horace, money does not matter at all!

Seldom is the poet's heart set on gain: verses he loves; this is his one passion. Money losses, runaway slaves, fires—he laughs at all.[43]

ART MUSIC

For the festival in honor of Saturn, described below, we have a remarkable example of art music. Augustus commissioned Horace to compose a *carmen saeculare*, which was performed by a chorus of twenty-seven boys and girls on 3 June 3 BC, on the front steps of the temple of Apollo Palatinus.[44] Horace was selected for this commission not only because he was a famous poet, but also because he was a skilled musician. In fact, for this performance he both conducted and accompanied the children on a lyre.

Augustus also sponsored theatrical plays in all languages, although he preferred those in the Greek language, which must

40   Horace, *Epistles*, 2.1.183ff.

41   Ibid., 1.1.70.

42   Ibid., 2.1.174.

43   Ibid., 2.1.119.

44   Horace, *Odes*, 2.12.17, also makes a passing reference to the fact that the choral dance tradition still existed.

have included music. His attention to this art form can be judged by the fact that on several occasions he punished, and even banished, actors who misbehaved.[45]

We are indebted to Horace for a brief portrait of the leading art singer in the court of Augustus. It is evident that Horace, himself, was not fond of this character, as we can see in the first reference, a reference to the death of this singer being mourned by only the lowest level of society.

> Guilds of our single-pipe-playing ladies, retailers of nos-
> trums, performing
> Mime artists, street entertainers, and mendicant priests,—all that
> class of
> People are mightily mourning the death of Tigellius the singer
> 'Always so free with his money!'[46]

Above all it was the independence of this artist which amazed Horace, in particular that he, and not his masters, determined when he sang. Sometimes he would sing throughout an entire banquet, from beginning to end ('from egg-course to apples'). Yet on other occasions he would refuse to sing at all and even Caesar himself could not prevail upon him to do so.

> Singers have one sorry habit in common: when asked among
> friends to
> Sing for the company, nothing on earth will induce them to do so;
> If *unasked*, there's no way to stop them. Sardinian Tigellius was
> like that.
> Caesar, who could have invoked his authority if he had wished to,
> Either by citing the friendship of Julius or citing his own, could
> Never get anywhere with him at all. When the mood was upon him
> He would intone the 'Hail, Bacchus!' from egg-course to apples,
> now playing
> High in the treble, now deep in the bass, on all four of the lyre strings.
> Nothing consistent about the man: sometimes he went at a run as
> If he were fleeing from foes, then again at a pace such as Juno's
> Cult-object bearers observe in processionals. Two hundred
> slaves might
> Serve him at times, than again only ten. He might sometimes talk
> kings and
> Tetrarchs and grandeurs; or else it was: 'Give me a three-legged table,
> Unscented salt in a sea shell container, and any old coarse-weave
> Toga to keep out the cold.' Yet this man who contented with little
> Would, if you gave him a million, discover his money chest empty

45 Suetonius, *Lives of the Caesars*, bk 2, 43, 45, and 89.

46 Horace, *Satires*, 1.2. It is also interesting here that we learn the single-pipe prostitute-musicians had now organized themselves into the guilds, or colleges, as did the other professional musicians in Rome.

Five days thereafter. At night you would find him awake till the
  dawn, then
All day long he would snore. There was never a man that was quite
  so fickle.[47]

47 Ibid., 1.3.

Horace also mentions this 'prima donna' attitude once regarding
instrumental musicians.

Why at this moment must
Berecynthian auloi lack breath?
Why do reed-pipes and lyre hang on the wall, untouched?
Skimping hands are a thing I hate.[48]

48 Horace, *Odes*, 3.19.18.

Ovid makes two references to women artists, a topic we rarely
read about. First, he tells of his attraction to a singer who accompanied herself on the lyre.

She's a fine singer, quite a virtuoso;
I'm longing, as she sings, to snatch a kiss.
She sweeps the plaintive strings with clever fingers;
Who could not fall in love with hands like this?[49]

49 Ovid, *Amores*, 2.4.

In another place he says that the woman's education is not complete without the study of music.

The Sirens were sea fairies, who by force
Of song could stay the swiftest vessel's course.
Ulysses nigh broke loose upon the sound,
His comrades' ears, we're told, in wax were bound.
Learn singing, fair ones. Song's a thing of grace;
Voice oft's a better procuress than face.
Melodies from the marble theater repeat,
Or tunes danced with light Egyptian beat.
No woman trained according to my will
Should lack the art to handle lyre and quill.[50]

50 Ibid., 3, lines 311ff.

EDUCATIONAL MUSIC

The writers of this period do not speak much of the use of music for educational purposes, although we know from the reference of Horace mentioned above that something of this nature existed.

There are references to the tradition of singing of the great deeds of former great men, which often had a distinct educational purpose associated with it. Horace mentions that this was an ancient custom in Rome.

> As I considered making a song of war
> And conquered cities, Phoebus with sounded lyre
> Gave warning not to hoist my little
> Sails on Tyrrhenian seas …
> Let us by ancient custom recall great men
> In song sustained by Lydian auloi: let us
> Of Troy and Anchises sing, and
> Bountiful Venus's high descendants.[51]

Virgil also mentions the age of this tradition, dating it from the earliest period of Roman history.

> Then the Salian priests sang songs
> Round the burning altars, their brows twined with poplar branches.
> On this side the chorus of youths, on that side the old men
> Sang praises of Hercules and of his deeds.[52]

In another place Horace mentions that such performances were sometimes heard outdoors by large crowds.[53]

We might also presume that songs relating great battles were accompanied by the aulos, which had become a stronger and coarse instrument in Rome, for Horace mentions that such topics are ill-suited 'for the tender lyre.'[54] Virgil, faced with the desire to craft such a song, calls on one of the Muses for support.

> O you, Calliope, breathe grace upon
> The singer, and you, Muses, tell what slaughter,
> What deaths were wrought by Turnus' sword, which man
> Each fighter sent to Orcus, and unroll
> With me the lengthy tale of this great war:
> For you recall and you can tell the story.[55]

51 Horace, *Odes*, 4.15, 1 and 29.

52 Virgil, *Aeneid*, 8.305.

53 Horace, *Odes*, 2.13.30.

54 Ibid., 2.12.4.

55 Virgil, *Aeneid*, 9.541.

FUNCTIONAL MUSIC

In 17 BC, Augustus instituted a three-day festival in honor of Saturn, called *Saturnalia*, featuring theatrical plays, called *ludi*, and competitions. This name had an ancient connection with Rome, for according to Varro, the hill on which the Capitoline stood was in remote times called Saturian Hill, after an old town named Saturnia.[56]

56 Marcus Varro, *On the Latin Language*, 5.42.

Percussion instruments were a feature of this festival, reflecting an ancient myth about the god Saturn. An oracle having told that he would be deposed by his son, Saturn sought to prevent this by eating all of his offspring. Finally his wife, Rhea, tricked him after giving birth by concealing a stone in infant garments, which Saturn swallowed. To keep the baby secret, Rhea's servants beat on helmets and shields to create noise to cover its cries. An account of this festival by Ovid also mentions a parade and the fact that even the law courts closed in its observance.

57 We believe this is a reference to the bent-bell which the Etruscans added to the Greek aulos.

Let the sky revolve thrice on its never-resting axis; let Titan thrice yoke and thrice unyoke his steeds, straightaway the Berecyntian aulos will blow a blast on its bent horn,[57] and the festival of the Idaean Mother will have come. Eunuchs will march and thump their hollow drums, and cymbals clashed on cymbals will give out their tinkling notes; seated on the unmanly necks of her attendants, the goddess herself will be borne with howls through the streets in the city's midst. The stage is clattering, the games are calling. To your places, Quirites! and in the empty law courts let the war of suitors cease![58]

58 Ovid, *Fasti*, 4.179ff.

The Idaean Mother was the mythical mother of the founders of Rome and she is mentioned again by Virgil.

To speak truly, not men, rush out on the heights of Mount Dindymus,
Where the aulos gives out a tune to its devotees.
The kettle-drum calls you, the Berecyntian flute of the Mother
Of Ida; yield arms to he-men and give up your swords.[59]

59 Virgil, *Aeneid*, trans., L.R. Lind (Bloomington: Indiana University Press, 1958), 9.642.

Ovid's description of two religious cult celebrations, taken from among his poetry written in exile, are particularly interesting for their suggestion of large choruses of singers participating. The first of these also contains a plea to Augustus to lift his sentence of exile.

My books praise your name—those you dislike,
   but the *Metamorphoses* too. Not that you need praise,
   but even Jupiter's pleased to be celebrated
   and figure in the songs of men, the great chorus
   or the single voice, quavering. Caesar, I pray you,
   listen, accept my tribute, as Jupiter also accepts
   as well the blood of a hundred flawless bulls
   this little sprig of incense offered up sincerely.[60]

      60 Ovid, *Tristia*, 2.

The second refers to the Egyptian god, Ibis, and offers a description of a religious rite which is unusually rich in detail.

I pray
   that whatever spirits attend me may hear and approve and will fly,
   as only spirits can, to wait on Ibis,
   return to Rome in the wink of an eye and mark how the tears
   pour down his face. Greet him in evil omen
   with the left foot forward and clad in funereal black.
The procession is ready? Good! Let it begin.
The priest does not delay but turns to face the assembled congregation, bows three times to the altar,
   signals the chorus master for the pious hymn to commence,
   takes a breath, and intones: 'Offer thy throat,
   O terrified victim, freely to me.' He raises
   the shining knife and holds it high, as the rite,
   awesome, dreadful, but beautiful too, is re-enacted.[61]

      61 Ovid, ibid., 94ff.

One of the poems of Horace describes a private celebration of a great naval battle, of 2 September 31 BC. No doubt these kinds of civic celebrations, in addition to the religious ones, were common.

When shall the two of us, Maecenas, lucky man
By Caesar's victory made glad,
Drink up the Caecuban reserved for festive times
In your high house,—as pleases Jove,
With flutes and lyres both sounding, lyres in Doric hymns
And flutes in Asian revelry,
The way we did when 'Neptune's son' was driven from
The Straits with all his ships on fire.[62]

      62 Horace, *Epodes*, 9.

Funeral processions continued to depend on music as a symbol of the status of the deceased. We obtain some idea of the impor- tance of this status symbol when Ovid mentions that a government regulation at this time limited the number of aulos players for such

63   Ovid, *Fasti*, 6.663–664.

occasions at ten.[63] The principal funeral song was the *Nenia*, which praised the deceased in song with aulos accompaniment.

Propertius mentions two uses of the trumpet which are not found elsewhere in this early Roman literature. First, the use of the trumpet in the funeral ceremony.

> What dreams would my aulos sing to you then,
>   aulos sadder than funeral trumpet [tuba]?[64]

64   Propertius, *The Poems*, 2.7. The funeral trumpet is mentioned again in Poem, 2.13a.

The second reference is to the night watchman, who, with his instrument, served as a surrogate clock. This is a common feature in descriptions of medieval civic life, but only in this single reference can we see that the tradition is much older. In this instance it is the instrumental signal given to announce impending dawn, which in the Middle Ages became the type of music known as the *aubade*.

> Now the fourth horn sings coming light,
>   & the stars glide down seaward,
>   I will search for sleep,
>   search for you in dreams.[65]

65   Ibid., 4.4.

Another well-known medieval tradition which appears to be older than generally thought is the use of the trumpet player as a form of passport to accompany diplomats, as is implied in Horace's brief mention of 'trumpeting envoys.'[66]

Regarding the military trumpet, Horace mentions this type only twice, in the first instance acknowledging a certain popularity for the entire environment of this sort of music.

66   Horace, *Odes*, 4.4.69.

> Many people enjoy camps and the din of curved
> Trumpets in signal calls, warfare itself, indeed,
> By all mothers abhorred.[67]

67   Horace, *Odes*, 1.1.23.

For him, however, this kind of music was clearly too noisy. Let's not forget, he says, the softer arts.

> At times you deafen ears with the din and threat
> Of trumpet blasts, the bugles at times shrill forth ...
> And yet, pert Muse, you must not abandon jest
> And love song for the grief of a Cean dirge:
> Together in Dione's grotto
> Let us seek music of lighter poems.[68]

68   Ibid., 2.1.

Virgil mentions the military trumpet three times in his Aeneid, one of which is a curious reference to a 'hollow' trumpet.[69] More interesting is his attempt to describe the most ancient form of such trumpet signals. We feel, in this passage, a sense of the terror that primitive people must have felt in hearing the blast of the 'war horn,' as is sometimes described.

> But the terrible goddess
> Had spied out the moment for further harm from her lofty
> Look-out and flew to the top of the stable and from that
> Summit she sang out the shepherd's signal: she blew
> A blast out of Tartarus on her curved horn. The deep woodlands
> And groves re-echoed and trembled. The lake of Diana
> Heard from afar; and Nar River, its stream white with sulfur,
> Heard it, and the springs of Velinus; and shuddering
> Mothers pressed children close to their breasts. Then swiftly
> Men ran when they heard the sound of the frightening horn.[70]

A poem by Propertius conveys a similar image as the 'frightening horn,' above, when we read, 'trumpeter, put away that wild music.'[71]

It is not surprising that the Augustan lyric poets, who wrote mostly of love, were hostile to the whole idea of war and war music. Propertius sang,

> O I hope oblivion was that man's fate
>   who first raised a palisade
>   hewn from harmless trees,
>   & contrived the shrill-boned war fife.[72]

Tibullus expressed nearly identical thoughts.

> What man, what devil, first conceived the sword?
>   shaper of iron, himself an iron heart,
>   begetter of battles on a innocent world,
>   marking new routes to death on mankind's chart! ...
> If I could choose an age, I would live in that one,
>   with no trumpet-call, no war's alarms and shocks.[73]

A final reference to types of military music is found in Virgil, who mentions the songs of soldiers.

> They marched to even rhythms and they sang
> To praise their king.[74]

69 Virgil, *Aeneid*, 3.272. Probably the new 'cornu' trumpet. Also see 6.246 and 7.658, 664.

70 Ibid., 7.511.

71 Ibid., 4.4.

72 Propertius, *The Poems*, 4.3. He mentions the military trumpets associated with guard duty in Poem, 4.4.

73 Tibullus, *The Poems*, 1.10.

74 Virgil, *Aeneid*, 7.731.

Regarding music specific to various occupations, here, as in Greek literature, the most frequently mentioned is the music of the shepherd. Horace mentions the shepherd with his traditional panpipe, together with a rarely mentioned instance of singing with this instrument.

> Shepherds lie in the young grass as they tend their plump
> Sheep and sing to the reed pipes that delight the god.[75]

75   Ibid., 4.12.9. See also, Ovid, *Remedia Amoris* [The Cures for Love], 181.

In another place he mentions the goat-herd together with the familiar idea of 'music calming the savage beast.'

> Nor do my kidlets have cause for fearing
> Green vipers or the warrior clan of wolves,
> My Tyndaris, as long as his dulcet pipes
> Are heard along the smooth-worn rocks on
> Ustica's slope and along the valleys.[76]

76   Ibid., 1.17.8. In the *Ode*, 2.13.33, Horace makes a similar, but allegorical, illusion.

Ovid also mentions the shepherd and his music, together with an extensive additional list of occupational music.

> Remember I'm in exile,
>   writing not for fame but solace, to work
>   my woe into an artifact, that change in its nature
>   a kind of distraction better even than comfort.
> So does the shackled slave, digging his ditch, sing
>   as he swings his pick: the task remains the same,
>   but he is free and becomes his song, as the bargee does
>   performing a mule's work on the cindered towpath,
>   tugging and singing. And galley oarsmen contrive to float
>   on the purl of the very flute that sets their rhythm.
> The shepherd perched on his rock passes the boring hours
>   with this pipes of Pan. The household slave girl spins
>   singing along with her wheel. The art is anodyne,
>   as Achilles discovered, playing upon his lyre
>   after Briseis was gone. And Orpheus sang his dirges
>   to which rocks and rivers rang in chorus
>   after he'd lost Eurydice to Hades a second time.
> The same mercy the Muse has shown to me,
>   penitent here in the Pontus. She has been my friend,
>   undeterred by Sintians, undismayed
>   by raging seas, howling winds, or the leaden skies
>   of this vast waste.[77]

77   Ovid, *Tristia*, 4.1.

To this list Virgil adds the music of the housewife.

> One farmer stays awake and splits up wood
> For torches with his knife. And all the while
> His wife relieves her lengthy task with song.[78]

78 Virgil, *Georgics*, 291.

Among the poems of the lyric poets there are two references to farmer's singing. Tibullus has the farmer singing as he is walking.

> Diana would blush as she met him moving through fields and farms
>   like any mortal farmer, a stray lamb in his arms;
>   and when his music sounded from valleys he walked along,
>   the bellow of the oxen would break on his song.[79]

79 Tibullus, *The Poems*, 2.3.

Propertius mentions farmer songs in connection with a strange, primitive and unnamed cult ceremony in which 'a pale virgin descends to lurid rites.'

> If she be chaste, she returns to her parents' arms
>   & the farmers sing that it will be a prosperous year.[80]

80 Propertius, *The Poems*, 4.8.

Tibullus, while reflecting on the impact the goddess of love, Venus, has on the behavior of men, expresses astonishment how through the hope of love she keeps 'the spark alive in men,' even the most abject of men, the slave.

> Why does she keep that spark alive in men?—
>   spurring them on to plant hard-fisted earth,
>   to net the fowl, to bait the hook for fish,
>   and comforting the slave, despite the chains
>   that clamp his legs—she bids him sing at his task.[81]

81 Tibullus, *The Poems*, 2.6.

Finally there is only one reference to music and prophesy among mortals in the literature of this period (prophesy of the gods will be mentioned in the following chapter). In Virgil we read,

> The prophets sang that she would have a glorious
> Fame and fate, but bring great war upon
> Her people.[82]

82 Virgil, *Georgics*, 7.83.

ENTERTAINMENT MUSIC

Suetonius tells us of the banquets of Augustus.

> He served a dinner of three courses or of six when he was most lavish, without needless extravagance but with the greatest good fellowship. For he drew into the general conversation those who were silent or chatted under their breath, and introduced music and actors, or even strolling players from the circus, and especially story tellers.[83]

83 Suetonius, *Lives of the Caesars*, 2.74.

We have mentioned above the fact that the single-pipe prostitutes had now formed their own guilds. Presumably these guilds welcomed their string player associates, such as the one requested by Horace.

> Won't someone go fetch Lyde, the easy wench
> From down the path? And tell her to hurry up,
> And bring her ivory lyre, and wear her
> Hair in a bun like a Spartan woman.[84]

84 Horace, *Odes*, 2.11.21.

The fickle public has changed its taste and is fired throughout with a scribbling craze; sons and grave sires sup crowned with leaves and dictate their lines. I myself, who declare that I write no verses, prove to be more of a liar than the Parthians: before sunrise I wake, and call for pen, paper, and writing-case. A man who knows nothing of a ship fears to handle one; no one dares to give southernwood to the sick unless he has learnt its use; doctors undertake a doctor's work; carpenters handle carpenters' tools; but, skilled or unskilled, we scribble poetry, all alike.[1]

1 Horace, *Epistles*, 2.1.117.

There was indeed at this time an outpouring of poetry, poetry in the style of the lyric poets of Greece. Moreover, like the Greek repertoire, this poetry was sung, as we know for example from Propertius' comment that he 'took to the lyre & sang.'[2] Horace is even more specific.

2 Propertius, *The Poems*, 1.3.

You have no cause to think that *the words which I,*
By far-resounding Aufidus born, *compose*
For singing to the lyre, in meters
All but unknown before mine, will perish.

Some of the greatest of the early Roman writers contributed to this body of lyric poetry, including Virgil (70–19 BC), Horace (66–8 BC), Tibullus (54–18 BC), Propertius (50–16 BC), and Ovid (43 BC – 17 AD). Probably all of these poets were also performing musicians. In addition to Horace, by their own words we know that Ovid once sang at a wedding,[3] Propertius played the lyre and sang,[4] and Virgil in his youth played and sang shepherd songs.[5]

3 Ovid, *Letters in Exile*, 1.2.

4 Propertius, *The Poems*.

5 Virgil, *Georgics*, 4.564.

It is apparent that the Roman lyric poetry was inspired by the earlier Greek lyric poets and indeed Horace observes that of all the Greek writers, it were these older lyric poets who were the best.[6] The extent to which these Roman lyric poets knew the Greek poets and their literature is documented by repeated references to it. Horace, for example, mentions both Sappho, 'in her Aeolian strains complaining about the girls that lived in her native land,'[7] and Anacreon.

6 Horace, *Epistles*, 2.1.28. He also adds here that one should not attempt to compare the Greek and Roman lyric poets, as that would be like comparing apples and oranges, as we would say today (he said 'olives and nuts'). In any case, says Horace, we, the Romans, 'have much more skill than the well-oiled Greeks.'

7 Horace, *Odes*, 2.13.

I am in love, as Anacreon, poet of Teos, is said to

Have been with his Bathyllus once,
He who lamented his love to his lyre in the simplest of meters
And unelaborated forms.[8]

8 Horace, *Epodes*, 14.

In another place, Horace mentions most of the rest of the important Greek lyric poets and reserves for himself the credit for introducing this literature to the Roman audience.

I was the first to plant free footsteps on a virgin soil; I walked not where others trod. Who trusts himself will lead and rule the swarm. I was the first to show to Latium the iambics of Paros, following the rhythms and spirit of Archilochus, not the themes or the words that hounded Lycambes. And lest you should crown me with a scantier wreath because I feared to change the measures and form of verse, see how manlike Sappho molds her Muse by the rhythm of Archilochus; how Alcaeus molds his, though in his themes and arrangement he differs, looking for no father-in-law to besmear with deadly verses, and weaving no halter for his bride with defaming rhyme. Him, never before sung by other lips, I, the lyrist of Latium, have made known. It is my joy that I bring things untold before, and am read by the eyes and held in the hands of the gently born.[9]

9 Horace, *Epistles*, 1.19.34.

Like those poets of ancient Greece, these later poets of Rome, no doubt as a manifestation of the spirit of lyric poetry itself, also looked to the muses and gods as the source of their ability and inspiration. Horace, for instance, provides a perfect illustration of this heart-felt association.

By the race of the Roman's, earth's
Greatest, I have been deemed worthy of rank among
Noble choirs of its singing bards;
Thus I now am the less hounded by Envy's fang.
O my Muse of the golden shell,
You who modulate sweet sounding of harmonies,
Who could grant even toneless fish
Gifts of song like the swan's, were you so willed to do,
All of this is a gift from you:
Having passers-by point fingers at me as Rome's
Lyric singer; if what I write
Pleases, yours were the thoughts, yours was the pleasure's source.[10]

10 Horace, *Odes*, 4.3.

And in another place,

Phoebus has inspired me, and Phoebus gave me
Technical skill in song and the name of poet.[11]

11 Ibid., 4.6.

Because of the power of music, something every listener can feel yet cannot see, and because of the well-known association of various mythical gods with music, the Roman poets, as the Greeks before them, sometimes speak of their special relationship with the gods or of the divine nature of the poet's profession. Thus, a poem of Tibullus warns the ladies to have respect for the poets who are favored by the gods.

> But you, my girl, watch out; the gods love poets;
> I warn you, have respect for a sacred bard
> singing of Messalinus, who drives before him
> whole conquered cities—the victor, battle-scarred
> and crowned with bay, while round him his bay-wreathed soldiers
> deafen the crown with their wild triumphal song.[12]

Ovid tells of one poet who was *not* protected by the gods, in fact he was murdered in the act of performance!

> And poor Lampetides—he had been summoned
> To no such revels, only to play the lute,
> To grace the feast with song, and so he stood there
> Holding the ivory quill, surely no fighter,
> And Pettalus mocked him: 'Sing that song in Hell,
> The rest of it, at least!' and pierced his temple,
> And as he fell, the dying fingers struggled,
> To play once more, and made only a discord.[13]

Perhaps this contributed to Ovid finally indicating he had lost faith in the gods. He reveals this in an interesting passage, while nevertheless mentioning again that the poets are favored by the gods.

> We bards are classed as holy, heaven's care;
> Divinity, they say, flows in our veins.
> But every holy thing brash death profanes;
> There's nothing that his murky clutches spare.
>
> Orpheus' great parents—what did they avail?
> Or song whose magic power the beasts subdued?
> To sad reluctant lyre in the wild wood
> 'Ah, Linus, Linus' went his father's wail.
>
> And Homer too, whose founts of song inspire
> The Muses' streams on poets' lips for ay,
> Sank to Avernus' depths on his last day:
> Verse, verse alone escapes the insatiate pyre.

12 Tibullus, *The Poems*, 2.5. In the Poem 3.4, Apollo says 'Gods love all poets.' In the actual experience of love, like Ovid, Tibullus reveals, in Poem 1.4, a lack of confidence.

> Spare me, I beg you; let me not be railed at
> as one who tried to teach an art he failed at!

13 Ovid, *Metamorphoses*, 5.111ff.

In poetry the toils of Troy live on,
And that slow web night's cunning would unwind.
So Nemesis and Delia fame will find,
Who last and first their poet's worship won.

What use is that Egyptian ritual,
Those timbrels, these long nights of chastity?
When evil fate dooms good men, may I be
forgiven if I've no faith in gods at all![14]

14   Ovid, *Amores*, 3.9.

Ovid's complaint notwithstanding, because of the special relationship these lyric poets felt with the gods and muses, we sometimes find them addressing pleas to their gods for inspiration—even as centuries later Bach would sometimes pen a note at the top of his manuscripts asking for God's help. Here Horace addresses a plea for subject matter to the Muse Clio.

Come, what man or demigod shall you choose to
Hymn with lyre or high-shrilling pipe, Muse Clio,
Or what god? Whose name shall be lifted up and
Sportively echoed

Down the shaded glens of Mount Helicon or
On the slopes of Pindus or snow-capped Haemus?
There the forests crowded to follow singing
Orpheus, whose music

(Taught him by his mother) made rushing rivers
Cease their flow and blustering winds be silent,
All so sweetly sounding to strings of lyre that
Ears grew on oak trees.[15]

15   Horace, *Odes*, 1.12.

To Mercury, Horace addresses a plea for musical inspiration.

Grant me music, Mercury, as you did when
Stones moved into place for Amphion singing;
Bear my song, O tortoise-shell deftly strung with
Seven strings sounding,

Once a lifeless object unpleasing, welcome
Now at rich men's tables as in the temples:
Sing such strains that even the stubborn ears of
Lyde will listen.[16]

16   Ibid., 3.11.

A similar plea for inspiration is addressed to the Muse, Calliope ('beautiful voiced').

Calliope, descend from the skies, O queen,
And sing your flute a lingering melody,
Or lift your lovely voice alone, or
Sing to the lyre or the harp of Phoebus.

Hark! Is illusion sweetly deceiving me?
I seem to hear those strains, as I seem myself
A stroller in the scared groves where
Waters and breezes are softly stirring.[17]

17 Ibid., 3.4.

In another Ode, to commemorate the death of his friend Quintil-
ius, Horace appeals to another of the Muses, Melpomene, for help.

Could shy reticence set limits to grief for so
Fondly cherished a head? Teach me your saddest strains,
Muse Melpomene,[18] whom All-father blessed with pure
Voice along with the lyre he gave ...

18 Melpomene, 'Songstress,' from the Greek *melos*, or melody.

Say you drew from the lyre lovelier tones than did
Thracian Orpheus when trees harkened to hear him play.[19]

19 Horace, *Odes*, 1.24.

Ovid describes a professional singer who begins his song with
an appeal to Jove for inspiration. Before this, however, he gives us a
rare reference to the musician tuning up, with a specific indication
of some kind of harmony.

And when he had tried the chords by touching them with his thumb,
and his ears told him that the notes were in harmony although they
were of different pitch, he raised his voice in this song: 'From Jove, O
Muse, my mother—for all things yield to the sway of Jove—inspire
my song! Oft have I sung the power of Jove before; I have sung the
giants in a heavier strain, and the victorious bolts hurled on the
Phlegraean plains. But now I need the gentler touch, for I would
sing of boys beloved by gods, and maidens inflamed by unnatural
love and paying the penalty of their lust.[20]

20 Ovid, *Metamorphoses*, 10.143.

Finally, traditional testimony to the power of music is also
found here expressed in mythical symbolism. An Ode of Horace,
for example, in a variation of the adage 'Music calms the savage
beast,' writes,

No wonder, then, that, hearing those songs, the beast
Lays back the swarthy ears on his hundred heads
And in the Furies' hair the coiling
Snakes come to rest from their ceaseless writhing.[21]

21 Horace, *Odes*, 2.13.

And similarly,

> Trees and tigers walk in your train, O lyre, and
> You can halt the currents of rapid rivers;
> At the gate of Horror the very watchdog,
> Cerberus, yielded
>
> Once before your ravishment, though a hundred
> Snakes bedeck his hideous head and though his
> Triple gullet reeks with a fetid breath and
> Blood-dripping slaver …[22]

22   Horace, ibid., 3.11.

It might be interesting to the reader to read a sampling of the frequent references to music found in the poetry which this group of poets addressed to the traditional Greek gods.

APOLLO

Tibullus attributes to Apollo not only the usual association with music, but also emphasizes his powers of prophesy.

> His long robes hid the hallowed form from sight,
>   and the hem seemed to ripple round his feet.
> At his left side a lyre hung, worked with skill
>   that made it gleam with gold and tortoise-shell,
>   and while he sang, he plucked it with a quill.
> But O the warning sung at that song's end!
>   'Gods love all poets,' he said, 'and such men find
>   Bacchus, Apollo, and each Muse a friend.
> Yet those wise sisters and the god of wine—
>   they lack the power to see the future plain.
> Jove's gift of foresight is not theirs but mine.
>   To me, inevitable fate is clear.[23]

23   Tibullus, *The Poems*, 3.4.

Tibullus mentions prophesy in association with Apollo in another poem, although here the alternative name for Apollo, Phoebus, is used.

> Your blessing, Phoebus; a new priest enters your temple.
>   Be gracious, greet his coming with voice and lyre,
>   and when your fingers set the strings to sounding,
>   let it be loyalty that they inspire.

Come, be among us while we heap the altars,
　　your brow encircled with a wreath of bay—
　　comb your long hair, put on your treasured raiment,
　　O come, god bright and beautiful as the day!
Be as you were when you sang of Jove's triumph
　　with Saturn finally driven from the throne.
Prophet, the priest who serves you learns the meaning
　　of the notes of that bard to which the future is known.
You guide the lots as they fall; you show the augur
　　what marks of the god to read in the entrails;
　　with you as master, the Sibyl's six-metered strophes
　　have given us counsel whose wisdom never fails.[24]

According to Greek mythology, Apollo killed Cyclops, forger of the thunderbolts of Zeus, to avenge the death of his son at the hands of Zeus. In return, Zeus forced Apollo to serve for a time as a herder for the mortal king, Admetus. It is in this role that we see Apollo, in Ovid's *Metamorphoses*, living the life of a shepherd and playing on panpipes.

　　… for Apollo
Could never change the will of Jove: moreover,
Even if he could, he was not there, but living
In Elis at the time, where he had taken
A shepherd's cloak, a pipe of seven reeds,
A forest wand for staff, and all his thinking
Of love and playing music, so his cattle
Went wandering off and Mercury saw them, stole them,
Drove them into a forest where he hid them.[25]

Tibullus also mentions this aspect of the Apollo myth, with interesting musical references. Here Apollo himself speaks:

It is not told in mockery that I
　　served as Admetus' shepherd, long ago,
　　and lost the will to play the lyre, or try
　　new harmonies for voice and strings to share—
　　but used an unstopped pipe, in my despair.[26]

In another place, Tibullus also attributes to Apollo the power to heal the sick.

Come near, Apollo, come and make me well—
　　heal me, Apollo of the flowing hair …
Be near me, holy presence; bring your songs
　　and all your delicacies that soothe the sick.[27]

24 Tibullus, *The Poems*, 2.5. Propertius, in Poem 2.31, tells of visiting a temple built to honor Apollo by Caesar Augustus. He describes seeing a marble statue of Apollo, posed as singing with his lyre.

25 Ovid, *Metamorphoses*, 2.677ff.

26 Tibullus, *The Poems*, 3.4.

27 Ibid., 3.10.

DIANA

Diana was a twin sister to Apollo, and daughter to Zeus and Latona. We have a hymn to Diana by Horace which begins,

> Raise your hymn, tender girls, sing of Diana now,
> Hymn the Cynthian,[28] lads, god of the unshorn locks,
> Sing Latona as well, most
> Deeply loved by the heart of Jove.[29]

28 This refers to Apollo, who according to tradition was born on Mount Cynthus.
29 Horace, *Odes*, 1.21.

MERCURY

Mercury, known as Hermes to the Greeks, according to mythical history was a son to Zeus and Maia, the daughter of Atlas. Here we have an example of how myths may reflect historical events from long before any form of written history. In this instance, Mercury is said to have invented, a few hours after birth, the lyre by stretching sheep-gut strings over the hollow of a tortoise shell. He was also the god of athletics and a 'master' of language, all of which are mentioned by Horace.

> Nimble-spoken Mercury, Atlas' grandson,
> Who by speech astutely advanced mankind from
> Brute and worked a comeliness into him by
> Grace of gymnastics,
>
> You I sing, great Jupiter's herald bearing
> Words of gods, first founder of song and lyre-shell.[30]

30 Ibid., 1.10.

NEPTUNE

Horace begins a poem in praise of Neptune and then progresses to several other deities as well.

> I shall start with a song about
> Neptune's might and his nymphs green-haired within the sea;
> You shall then take the lyre and sing
> Of Latona and swift Cynthia's whetted darts;
> Hers my song who with swan-yoked car
> Visits Paphus and rules Cnidus and all the isles
> Of the glittering Cyclades;
> Lastly, we will salute Night with a lullaby.[31]

31 Ibid., 3.28.

ORPHEUS

In the traditional myth of Orpheus, the most famous of mythical musicians, he goes to Hades to look for Eurydice, who has been killed by a snake. Orpheus is killed there, but his ghost remains with his beloved Eurydice.

Ovid, in his *Metamorphoses*, has Orpheus killed on earth. This passage, while extraordinarily violent, has numerous and interesting references to music. It begins with the origin of the phrase 'music calms the savage beast,' and the bard he refers to is Orpheus.

While with such songs the bard of Thrace drew the trees, held beasts enthralled and constrained stones to follow him, behold, the crazed women of the Cicones, with skins flung over their breasts, saw Orpheus from a hill top, fitting songs to the music of his lyre. Then one of these, her tresses streaming in the gentle breeze, cried out: 'See, see the man who scorns us!' and hurled her spear straight at the tuneful mouth of Apollo's bard; but this, wreathed in leaves, marked without harming him. Another threw a stone, which, even as it flew through the air, was overcome by the sweet sound of voice and lyre, and fell at his feet as if it would ask forgiveness for its mad attempt. But still the assault waxed reckless: their passion knew no bounds; mad fury reigned. And all their weapons would have been harmless under the spell of song; but the huge noise of the Berecyntian flutes, mixed with discordant horns, the drums, and the breast-beatings and howlings of the Bacchanals, drowned the lyre's sound; and then at last the stone's were reddened with the blood of the bard whose voice they could not hear. First away went the multitudinous birds still spellbound by the singer's voice, with the snakes and the train of beasts, the glory of Orpheus' audience, harried by the Maenads; then these turned bloody hands against Orpheus and flocked around like birds when in the day they see the bird of night wandering in the daylight; and as when in the amphitheater in the early morning of the spectacle the doomed stag in the arena is the prey of dogs. They rushed upon the bard and hurled at him their wands wreathed with green vines, not made for such use as this. Some threw clods, some branches torn from trees, and some threw stones. And, that real weapons might not be wanting to their madness, it chanced that oxen, toiling beneath the yoke, were plowing up the soil; and not far from these, stout peasants were digging the hard earth and sweating at their work. When these beheld the advancing horde, they fled away and left behind the implements of their toil. Scattered through the deserted fields lay hoes, long mattocks and heavy grubbing tools. These the savage women caught up and, first tearing in pieces the oxen who threatened them with their horns, they rushed back to slay the bard; and, as he stretched out his suppliant hands, uttering words then, but never before, unheeded, and moving them not a whit by his voice, the impious women struck him down. And (oh, the pity of it!) through those lips, to which rocks listened, and to which the hearts of savage beasts responded, the soul, breathed out, went faring forth in air.

The mourning birds wept for thee, Orpheus, the throng of beasts, the flinty rocks, and the trees which had so often gathered to thy songs; yes, the trees shed their leaves as if so tearing their hair in grief for thee. They say that the rivers also were swollen with their own tears, and the naiads and dryads alike mourned with disheveled hair and with dark bordered garments. The poet's limbs lay scattered all around; but his head and lyre, O Hebrus, thou didst receive, and (a marvel!) while they floated in mid-stream the lyre gave forth some mournful notes, mournfully the lifeless tongue murmured, mournfully the banks replied. And now, borne onward to the sea, they left their native stream and gained the shore of Lesbos near the city of Methymna. Here, as the head lay exposed upon a foreign strand, a savage serpent attacked it and its streaming locks still dripping with the spray. But Phoebus at last appeared, drove off the snake just in the act to bite, and hardened and froze to stone, just as they were, the serpent's widespread, yawning jaws.

The poet's shade fled beneath the earth, and recognized all the places he had seen before; and, seeking through the blessed fields, found Eurydice and caught her in his eager arms.[32]

32 Ovid, *Metamorphoses*, 11.1ff.

PAN

Of all the gods, Pan is the one most associated with rural life, in particular with the shepherd. In Virgil's *Georgics*, a commemoration of the country life he knew as a youth, we sense his attraction for this god.

> Now we shall sing the shepherds' rural gods,
> Recall Apollo's role in guarding herds,
> And sing the woods and rivulets of Pan.
> All other themes are stale, diverting tunes
> To while the time away.[33]

33 Virgil, *Georgics*, 3.1ff.

Ovid, in his *Metamorphoses*, has the god Mercury tell the story
of the invention of the panpipe, the instrument always associated
with Pan and known to the ancients as the *Syrinx*.

And Mercury came flying
On winged sandals, wearing the magic helmet,
Bearing the sleep-producing wand, and lighted
On earth, and put aside the wings and helmet
Keeping the wand. With this he plays the shepherd
Across the pathless countryside, a driver
Of goats, collected somewhere, and he goes
Playing a little tune on a pipe of reeds,
And this new sound is wonderful to Argus.
'Whoever you are, come here and sit beside me,'
He says, 'This rock is in the shade; the grass
Is nowhere any better.' And Mercury joins him,
Whiling the time away with conversation
And soothing little melodies, and Argus
Has a hard fight with drowsiness; his eyes,
Some of them, close, but some of them stay open.
To keep himself awake by listening,
He asks about the pipe of reeds, how was it
This new invention came about?
  The god
Began the story: 'On the mountain slopes
Of cool Arcadia, a woodland nymph
Once lived, with many suitors, and her name
Was Syrinx. More than once the satyrs chased her,
And so did other gods of field or woodland,
But always she escaped them, virgin always
As she aspired to be, one like Diana,
Like her in dress and calling, though her bow
Was made of horn, not gold, but even so,
She might, sometimes, be taken for the goddess.
Pan, with a wreath of pine around his temples,
Once saw her coming back from Mount Lycaeus,
And said—' and Mercury broke off the story
And then went on to tell what Pan had told her,
How she said *No*, and fled, through pathless places,
Until she came to Ladon's river, flowing
Peaceful along the sandy banks, whose water
Halted her flight, and she implored her sisters
To change her form, and so, when Pan had caught her
And thought he held a nymph, it was only reeds
That yielded in his arms, and while he sighed,

The soft air stirring in the reeds made also
The echo of a sigh. Touched by this marvel,
Charmed by the sweetness of the tone, he murmured
This much I have! and took the reeds, and bound them
With wax, a tall and shorter one together,
And called them Syrinx, still.[34]

34 Ovid, *Metamorphoses*, 1.671ff.

A poem by Tibullus confirms, by its description, that the pan-pipe known by the ancient Romans was shaped as the one we know today.

A milk-drenched Pan stood in the ash-tree's shelter,
    and Pales graced a rough-carved wooden shrine;
a pipe, its thin voice stilled, from a branch might dangle,
    the shepherd's pledge for favors a god would show—
with its range of reeds from the largest to the lesser,
    joined by way in an ever-dwindling row.[35]

35 Tibullus, *The Poems*, 2.5.

One of the more frequently told myths of Greece involved a musical contest between Pan with his panpipes and Apollo with his lyre. Apollo, as a god of music, of course wins in every retelling. The adjudicator, in this version by Ovid, is a mountain god, Tmolus. Midas is the famous king who came to hate gold by having too much of it.

But Midas, hating wealth, haunted the woods and fields, worshiping Pan, who has his dwelling in the mountain caves. But stupid his wits still remained, and his foolish mind was destined again as once before to harm its master. For Tmolus, looking far out upon the sea, stands stiff and high, with steep sides extending with one slope to Sardis, and on the other reaches down to little Hypaepae. There, while Pan was singing his songs to the soft nymphs and playing airy interludes upon his reeds close joined with wax, he dared speak slightingly of Apollo's music in comparison with his own, and came into an ill-matched contest with Tmolus as the judge.

The old judge took his seat upon his own mountain-top, and shook his ears free from the trees. His dark locks were encircled by an oak-wreath only, and acorns hung around his hollow temples. He, looking at the shepherd-god, exclaimed: 'There is no delay on the judge's part.' Then Pan made music on his rustic pipes, and with his rude notes quite charmed King Midas, for he chanced to hear the strains. After Pan was done, venerable Tmolus turned his face toward Phoebus [Apollo]; and his forest turned with his face. Phoebus' golden head was wreathed with laurel of Parnasus, and his mantle, dipped in Tyrian dye, swept the ground. His lyre, inlaid with gems and Indian ivory, he held in his left hand, while his right hand held the plectrum. His very pose was that of an artist. Then with trained thumb he plucked the strings and, charmed by those sweet strains, Tmolus ordered Pan to lower his reeds before the lyre.[36]

36 Ibid., 11.147ff. In 13.780, Ovid introduces the giant, Cyclops, playing a great panpipes consisting of one hundred pipes. The sound it made was proportionally large:

> All the mountains felt the sound
> of his rustic pipings; the waves
> felt it too.

VENUS

The fourth book of Odes by Horace begins with a kind of love song to Venus, the god of love. Although he is now too old for the 'warfare' of love, he imagines in this poem a temple to Venus, to be constructed by an aristocrat, Paulus Maximus, a friend of Ovid and confidant of the emperor.

> He will set you in marble shape
> Under a cedarwood roof out by the Alban lakes.
> There your nostrils will breathe the sweet
> Wafted incense in clouds, there Berecynthian
> Aouli and lyres will afford delight
> Intermingled with hymns, not without reedy pipes;
> There twice daily your goddess-self
> Shall in dances be praised, dances of lads and girls
> Treading three-quarter meters like
> Those of Salian priests, nimbly on gleaming feet.[37]

37 Horace, Odes, IV, 1.

ART MUSIC

By Art Music we mean descriptions of performances which were not functional or entertainment in character and which seem to be performances which were really listened to as music. There are few descriptions of actual performances in the Roman literature, but when Ovid describes a musician singing and accompanying himself on a lyre and relates of the listeners, 'the cheeks of the Eumenides were wet with tears,'[38] one can see evidence of true art music.

38 Ovid, *Metamorphoses*, 10.45.

As in their Greek models, the most common topics were the Muses, the gods, and love. We find all of these in a passage by Ovid in which, after making the interesting observation that poets are more susceptible to love because of the emotions that have invested in their love poetry, he reminds the ladies (prostitutes) that poets have associations with the gods and for this reason it is really not appropriate to ask for money from a poet!

> Guile too in poet's nature hath no part;
> Our characters are molded by our art.
> No lust of place or riches weighs us down,
> We love our shady couch and spurn the town.
> But quickly caught, by passions strong we're burnt,
> Too well the lesson of true love we've learnt.
> Our hearts are softened by our gentle trade,
> And by our calling is our conduct swayed.
> Be kind, ye fair, to the poetic choir
> Whom Muses love and deities inspire.
> God's in us and with heaven we discourse,
> In springs divine our instinct has its source.
> It's sin to look for payment from the bard,
> A sin, alas, that women ne'er regard.[39]

Tibullus also comments on his susceptibility to love. He tries to think of other things, but he cannot escape its power.

> Venus farewell; farewell, my loves!
> I'm strong, I love the piercing trumpet-call.
> My words sound well—but my bravado fails;
>   the slamming of a door can strike me dumb—
>   that door I took an oath never to seek.
> No use; my feet return of their own will.
> I'd break your weapons if I could, fierce Love;
>   would, if I could, even put out your torch.
> You stretch me on the rack; I curse myself
>   and all the gods; you leave me wild and spent.
> I would have killed myself long since, but Hope
>   tempts me, and I believe her promises.[40]

Most of the poems which were sung and which have come down to us are poems of love. From the pen of Horace we have a love song addressed not to his lover but to the mistress of Caesar. This poem is one of several which contain hints that the Greek choral tradition [with dance] was also continued by the Romans.

> My sweet Muse bids me sing lady Licymnia's
> Praise, describing the fair light of her lustrous eyes

39   Ovid, *Ars Amatoria*, 3.539. As it turned out, it was not love, but the love poems which got Ovid in trouble. He wrote, in *Remedia Amoris*, 361,

For lately people have attacked my poems;
They blame my Muse as bawdy and immoral.
So long as I give fun and I'm world famous,
If one or two decry me, I shan't quarrel.
Unfortunately it only took one, Augustus, to decry him and he was sent off in exile!

40   Tibullus, *The Poems*, 2.6.

And the mutual trust holding her heart and yours
In the bonds of devoted love.

Stiff constraint does not keep her from the choral dance,
Nor from the light repartee, nor from entwining arms
With the maidens attired grandly before the throngs
On Diana's most holy day.[41]

41 Horace, *Odes*, 2.12.

For the most part, however, the love songs are more personal,
songs of the woes of the lover. First, Propertius offers advice to the
young man captured by love to turn to music to win the girl: You
might as well put aside your serious studies and sing the song she
wants to hear!

I told you your time would come, love-mocker,
 & now you are no longer at liberty
 to bestow fine words so freely,
 & you lie supplicating and pliant in her hands.
This new-bought concubine exercises now
 a queenly dominion.
The priestess-oracles of Zeus
 cannot speak with more authority than I can
 as to which girl will snare which bachelor.
I have some skill, some experience, in these matters;
 I have felt the ache,
 looked through the tear-shadowed eyes.
Would to god I was still a stiff & clumsy novice,
 my burden of love laid down;
 what comfort is your solemn anthem
 your lamentation at the lyre-raised walls
 of Thebes brought down?
Mimnermus is better than Homer
 in matters of the heart.
Soft love demands a polished tune,
 so go and put aside your somber books
 & sing the song she wants to hear.[42]

42 Propertius, *The Poems*, 1.9.

In making this advice, Propertius reminds his listener that he
speaks from experience. He may not be rich or famous, but he is
successful with the ladies! Again, he says, it is songs of love that
the ladies are interested in, not philosophy, astronomy or physics.

But no bull plows without apprenticeship on a noose,
 nor can you undergo grim love just yet;
 but let my song be your beginning.

No girl asks reasons
   for the way of the world
   or the course of the moon,
   or if a judge sits enthroned
   beyond the waters of hell,
   or if it is a god crackles the lightening.
Consider my condition: a small fortune,
   no generals among my forbearers;
   yet I reign at the table
   in the company of young women,
   this being the product of those skills
   you take so lightly.[43]

This is one of the great values of music, says Propertius, to aid one in capturing the heart of the girl. In fact, he says, the fame of his music with the public means nothing compared to his success in love.

Eros orders me
   to walk under the oriflamme
   of the slender Muses
   & live in Hesiod's sacred grove;
Not so I might sing wild creatures
   down mountain valleys in Thrace,
   or float my lyrics among the oaks of Helicon;
But so I might astonish a girl,
   take her with my song.
Thereat I should be more famous
   with my art than Linus,
   lyre teacher of Orpheus.
I admire more than her beauty,
   nor is it enough
   for a woman to be of a pure & proud descent.
Let it be my joy to have sung my verses
   reclining with a brilliant girl
   & for my meters to have found esteem
   in her hearing.
These things fulfilled,
   the public in its wordy confusion
   no longer concerns me
For I will be content with Love for a judge.[44]

43 Ibid., 2.34.

44 Ibid., 2.13.

Tibullus goes even further. If music fails him now in his pursuit
of the girl, then he has no further use for it!

> She waits, and with her, bondage;
>   my fathers' freedom, farewell!
> Slavery, chains, are my fate now,
>   the tight-bound shackles of love
>   to chafe me, all unjustly.
> My cruel girl holds the torch
>   to my flesh—I would turn to stone
>   on the cold hills to escape,
>   or turn to a wind-vexed cliff
>   for waves to hurl ships against.
> Bleak days and bleaker nights,
>   no moment without new gall;
>   no help in song, or its god—
>   her hand is outstretched for gold.
> Be off, Muse, aidless to lovers,
>   I would not make war-chants
>   nor sing of the sun, or the night-route
>   of the horses of the moon.
> My song must open one door;
>   if it fails, then, Muse, be gone![45]

45   Tibullus, *The Poems*, 2.4.

PROPERTIUS AND CYNTHIA

The most extraordinary body of love songs of this period are the
poems written by Propertius for Cynthia, a musical prostitute.
These love poems, which are filled with references to music, cover
the entire course of their relationship.

First he seems proud to tell us that it was music itself, and not
money or gifts which won Cynthia.

> Not by gold
>   did I twist her into this orbit,
>   nor by Indian pearl,
>   but with the offering of alluring song.

> The Muses rule over love,
>   & Phoebus is never far from love,
>   & I rely on these gods
>   in my affair
>   & rare Cynthia is mine.[46]

46   Propertius, *The Poems*, 1.8a5.

The genuine feelings of Propertius for this girl are expressed over and over in some of the most beautiful poetry of the ancient world.

> Have I seemed too little sanguine,
>   love unseen on my face?
>
> The oak tree & the pine tree here
>   sacred to Pan
>   witness my love. They have heard the melody
>   in the shadow of their leaves
>   & Cynthia's name
>   is engraved in bark.[47]

In another poem he states he would not write of great historical events, neither is he inspired by the Muses. Rather, it is Cynthia who inspires his lyric poetry. In this same poem he tells us that she also plays the lyre.

> You would know the source
>   of these many engravings,
>   these words of love,
>   this book of supple words,
>   words from the lips softly.
>
> Neither Apollo nor Calliope
>   sings in my ear,
>   but Cynthia's genius presides
>   & shapes my songs …
>
> If her hair falls in her eyes,
>   I say her hair is splendid
>   & she walks exalted
>   & delights in my praises;
>
> Or if her ivory fingers
>   strike a song through the lyre
>   I display suitable wonder
>   at her artful touch on the strings.[48]

He sings of the depth of his love for her, of his inability to get her out of his mind, of the impossibility to go about his usual studies. It is not her beauty, nor her dress, but her singing and lyre playing which has so firmly drawn him to her.

47 Ibid., 1.18.

48 Ibid., 2.1.

You, Propertius, bragging yourself invincible,
   have now tumbled into her pit,
   your proud spirit captured,
   trussed to your own desire.
Every month some new alarm,
   and now another book of disgraces.

A fish might come out & stroll on the sand,
   or a boar take to the sea,
   if I were able to pass the night
   in the propriety of study.
Love may be put aside
   for a little time,
   but not cured.

It is not her fine ivory beauty
   that seizes me
   (Although no lily compares with her,
   & her complexion is like rose petals
   floating in milk,
   like snow & Spanish cinnabar)
   nor is it her hair
   flowing light over her neck,
   nor her bright eyes
   which sparkle in my soul,
   nor the Arab silks she walks lit by;
   I am not so frivolous as that;

But with the cups thrown down
   she dances like lovely Ariadne
   leading the bacchanalian chorus,
   and when she strikes up a tune
   with Aeolian plectrum,
   her lyre equals a goddess's, a muse by her fountain;

Her graven verses rival those
   of antique Corinna,
   & if she reckons her songs as fine
   as Erinna's were,
   can she be far wrong?[49]

49 Ibid., 2.3.

Another poem, while it does not mention Cynthia by name, is clearly inspired by his love for her. His love, he says, expressed in his songs, will outlast even the pyramids. This poem, filled with associations with music, is one of the most beautiful in the literature.

Let us meanwhile
    return to the ring of song,
      let its usual pleasure touch her.

Orpheus allured feral beasts
    with the Thracian lyre
    and bewitched the rivers;

The singing lute strung mountain rocks
    into a Theban wall
    and Polyphemus' song
    wheeled about the foam-speckled horses
    of the sea-goddess Galetea
    beneath the fires of Aetna.

Should we then stand amazed
    that a crowd of maidens cherish our words,
    we who are favored by Apollo
    & beloved of Bacchus?

My dwelling is simple,
    its roof without gold
    without ivory vaults;
    no black-marbled colonnade graces the porch,
I have no fields of fruit trees
    nor fountains watered
    by the Marcian aqueduct.

But I go
    a companion of the Muses,
    my verses are favored by those who read,
    & Calliope does not tire
    of my dancing tune;

My book celebrates
    a fortunate woman,
My songs will be a monument to her beauty,
    for neither the rich pyramids
    lifted high beneath the stars
    nor Zeus's great sanctuary
    on the mountain of heaven
    nor the golden crypt of Mausolus
    is spared death's final ravages.

Fire and rain erode their greatness
   & they will be ruined & broken in,
But the name of genius is hewn
    in timeless glory,
    the grace of genius eludes destruction.[50]

50 Ibid., 3.2.

One night she does not come to his house and, tormented, he turns to wine for help in sleeping. He promises to sing the praises of the god of wine, if only he can get some sleep!

O drown this pain in my soul,
    for only wine or death
    will numb the torment,
    a slow fire licked in my bones.

A sober night is always agony
    for lonely lovers,
    hope and fear alternately shearing their souls,
    but if Bacchus brings sleep to my bones
    through his gift,
    the hot flush of wine,
    then I will plant vines;
    cleat rows of vines to the hills
    & by vigilance assure
    that they are not ravaged by wild beasts …

Dircean Thebes will beat the quiet timbrels,
    and goat-footed satyrs will play the reed pipe,
    the cymbals will beat out the harsh Idaean dance
    close by great Cybele,
    turret-crowned goddess.

Before the temple
    with the wine bowl
    the high priest will decant the wine
    in a gold goblet
    over the offering.

I will repeat these things,
    sing of them
    not abjectly
    but with Pindaric cadence,
    only free me from these iron chains
    & break through my mind's turmoil with sleep.[51]

51 Ibid., 3.17.

In truth, Cynthia has been unfaithful to him and in several poems we read of his pain. At first his reaction is one of anger.

> Damn you,
>   may you lead the sort of night
>   that I am forced to,
>   you debauched drunkard.
>   I led sleep astray
>   weaving a rhythm
>   at the loom
>   & tiring of that
>   took to the lyre & sang
>   my abandonment and your lingering
>   with a strange lover,
>   until
>   soft winged sleep
>   darkened my cares
>   among tears.[52]

52 Ibid., 1.3.

Anger leads to spite, and here Propertius tells her that he, being a poet, will not return the pain as other men, but rather by confirming her infidelity for all time through the immortality his poems.

> Twist free from your unjust yoke
>   while you can, Propertius;
>   the first night is the hardest,
>   after which love's pain
>   begins to abate a little …
>
> I would not rip the clothes from your deceiving beauty,
>   nor will break through the door now shut
>   or lay hold of your pulled-back hair in anger
>   nor would I trace the marks of my knuckles on you;
> I leave that to louts undeserving
>   of ivy wreaths in their hair.
>
> But I may pen a verse or two,
>   & they are hard to erase,
>   'Cynthia of radiant looks & light words,'
>   and although you dismiss your murmuring detractors
>   in contempt
>   perhaps my art will bring a paleness into your face at last,
>   perhaps a song will return you the pain.[53]

53 Ibid., 2.5.

Next he begins to feel sorry for himself.

> What gifts I gave, & what great songs I spun;
>> but this brazen girl never spoke,
>> never said 'I love you.'[54]

54 Ibid., 2.86.

And now he appeals to both the girl and Eros, the god of love: who, but he, can praise her through such art as his lyric poetry?

> And if you bring me
>> to absolute ruin,
>> who then will lift up your song?

> This light Muse within me,
>> is your greatest glory, Eros,
>> and after me what melody
>> will celebrate her face,
>> who will sing her hands,
>> & what canticle
>> will light the sloe eyes,
>> & set forth the slow footfall,
>> of Cynthia, my beloved?[55]

55 Ibid., 2.12.

Having lost her love, Propertius now is embarrassed at the songs he has dedicated to her. It was all because he was in the grasp of Aphrodite and even his friends could not talk him out of it. Enough of love, now he will devote himself to Reason!

> You worship a faltering flame,
>> your beauty is illusion, woman,
>> my eyes have made you vain.

> Love praised you excessively, Cynthia,
>> & now my face burns
>> that my verses glorified your liveliness.

> I often sang
>> your manifold attractions
>> so well put together;
>> Love considered it true beauty,
>> not mere appearance.

> I often rhapsodized on the radiance of your looks,
>> an excellent counterfeit
>> of the pale red light

of the morning star;
but it was the glow of artifice,
sheen of paint and cosmetic …

But as with a garlanded ship
anchored safely in port
seething riptides & Syrtes' shoals crossed,
so now I am safe
having found my wits
with my wounds healing up.

O Right Reason,
if there is such a goddess,
I dedicate myself to your shrine
since Father Jupiter stood silent in heaven
when I lifted up my prayers
for his ear.[56]

56   Ibid., 3.24.

Finally, Ovid, in his *Metamorphoses*, recreates for the Roman audience an allegorical version of the ancient Greek art song contests.[57] The contest ensues as the result of nine daughters of Pierus, 'a rich lord in Pella,' who challenge the nine Muses to a musical contest. The daughters issue their challenge and propose both recommendations for adjudicators and the prize.

57   Ovid, *Metamorphoses*, 5.307ff.

'Quit fooling people,'
They said, 'Quit fooling silly ignorant people
With your pretense of music! Hear our challenge!
We are as many as you are, and our voices,
Our skill at least as great. If you are beaten,
Give us Medussa's spring, and Aganippe:
Or, if we lose, we will cede you all Emathia
From plains to snow-line; the nymphs shall be the judges.'

The Muses are forced to accept.

If it was shameful to accept their challenge,
It would have been more shameful to ignore it.

A representative of the nine daughters is the first to sing, an epic song of battle between gods and giants. Ovid indicates there was little point to the story, nor any more compelling was the music—'if you can call it music.'

Whoever it was who first proposed the singing
Never so much as bothered to draw lots,
Giving herself the first chance; a song of battles
She sang, that raged between the gods and giants.
The giants got none the worst of it, the gods,
As she went warbling on, got none the better …

…

That was the gist of it, with voice and harp
attuned together, if you could call it tuneful.

Now it was the Muses' turn and they were represented by Calliope, the goddess who was the mother of the famous mythical
musician, Orpheus.

Our sister, with her flowing hair arrayed
In ivy wreaths. She tried the plaintive chords,
Running her thumb across the strings, then, sweeping
The music soft and low, she sang this song,
The praise of Ceres:

The song itself is a lengthy (three hundred and twenty lines) narra-
tion of the myth of Ceres, for which the nymphs awarded the Muses
the victory. As for the nine daughters, 'they were bad losers,' and
protested the decision. For this, the gods turned them all into birds.

Magpies, the chatterboxes of the woodland,
Still loving, as they always did, the sound
Of their own voices, the appetite for gabble.

EDUCATIONAL MUSIC

Among the repertoire of the lyric poets one finds relatively few
examples of works which have the secondary purpose of educating
the listener through the praise of contemporary or former political leaders and historical myths, although, of course, works like
The Aeneid by Virgil and Ovid's *Metamorphoses* are significant
exceptions. Perhaps it was because they lacked the rich literature of
earlier Roman times comparable to that which the Greeks enjoyed
and, although they took much inspiration from the Greek lyric
poets, they probably had little compulsion to praise Greek history.

It is also likely that the Roman lyric poets encountered the same pressures which artists experience in any era, to use their art for more practical, public purposes. That there is a small extant repertoire of such works may indicate these artists, again like artists of every era, resisted this pressure. One senses this in a poem by Propertius where Apollo, who in addition to being a god of music was also the god of the bow, urges the poet to abandon his love poetry as something of little value. The Muse, Calliope, however, comes to his support, telling him to continue on the path he is on.

> Apollo watched from the trees before a cave
>   leaning on his golden lyre & said:
>   Lunatic, who asked you to muddy the fountain?
> Your glory lies elsewhere,
>   so roll your small wheels on softer terrain.
> Your book will be the lonely reading
>   of a nervous girl awaiting her lover
>   & will be put down at his arrival.
> Propertius, why do your tunes
>   revolve in wrong orbits?
> Your skiff is fast and light,
>   let your oars flash close to shore;
>   avoid the trackless sea.'
> So spoke Phoebus Apollo, & with ivory plectrum
>   he pointed out a footpath
>   moss-grown on the forest floor
>   and a sea-green cave
>   studded with chrysoprase,
>   tambourines hanging from the walls,
>   from soft stone concavities.
> And the mysteries of the Muses
>   floated among the rocks,
>   & a clay idol of father Silenus stood there,
>   & Cytherean pigeons crowded their red beaks
>   into the Hippocrene cistern
>   & the nine delicate-fingered deities
>   were about their work,
>   winding ivy on the staff,
>   measuring song to the lyre,
>   lacing roses into wreaths,
>   whereupon Calliope, the fiery beauty,
>   touched me, & spoke:

'Be content to follow the path
  of the bright swan always;
  shun the road of the rattling cavalry,
  shiver no airs with brass-throated war note;
Keep the stain of war from the leaves of Helicon.
  The standards of Marius stand without your help,
  & you need not celebrate
Teutonic wars reddening the dismal Rhine,
  clotting its waters with corpses.
You will sing instead of the lover in laurel
  waiting before his true love's lintel,
  you will sing the passwords
  of drunken night flights,
  and through your artful incantations
  guarded girls may be sung loose
  from their suspicious proprietors.'[58]

58 Propertius, *The Poems*, 3.3.

Propertius admits that Virgil is much better at praising those historical figures and events and he will cede this area to him. However, he notes, Virgil also has been known to pen love poetry.

But Virgil, you also sing
  beneath the shadowing pines of Galaesus,
  & your reed flute polishes Daphnis' tune
  & the tune of ten apples
  & an unweaned goat given
to break a girl's resistance.[59]

59 Ibid., 2.34.

In another poem, Propertius seems to imply that love poetry, such as that which he excels in, is not as highly esteemed as the work of the epic poets. But, he counters, writing love poetry is a special art, it does not come by itself. When one finds oneself in need of this ability he has, then one will have respect for him. So, he says to the epic poet, don't look down on love poetry!

And you will wish to bind down more supple verses
  without much luck, love being insufficient
  to lift up its own canticles;
  and you will then take great notice,
  & I will seem no mean versemaker then;
  indeed you may have me at the head
  of that whole not ungifted pack,
  and I do not think the young will stand mute
  at my graveside, but they will call me
  the poet of their flame who lies there.
Beware of hauteur, epic poet; despise no love songs;
  Love coming late is dearly bought.[60]

60 Ibid., 1.7.

But, as it turns out, Propertius does employ his pen in this kind of poetry, in the praise of Caesar Augustus. In the following poem he suggests this is a new experience for him and that perhaps this kind of poetry should be done by older men, the younger poets specializing in love poetry. This, he says, is more serious, requiring a 'graven frown,' and he leaves the implication that this kind of epic poetry was accompanied by a type of lute new to him as well. He concludes with an apology that if his work is not lofty enough, it is because his art is still inspired by the goddess of love.

> The time comes for a new dance on the mountain,
>   a new rite on Helicon;
> The time comes to chant horsemen under the hill,
>   and I will now sing of battle,
>   and squads of heroes, & Caesar's Roman camp;
> And if my strength fails, still, a laudable essay
>   To try the great song brings its own commendation.
> In a man's early years, his tune is a love tune;
>   let age sing of swordplay;
>   War will be my canticle
>   when Cynthia's beauty is well inscribed in my books.
> I would now wear a graven frown & learn a new lute,
>   my spirit rising from the low song
>   taking strength out of heaven,
>   for the work needs a booming voice.
> Now the Euphrates rolls unguarded by Parthians,
>   & Persia grieves to have cut down the Crassi;
>   India kneels before Caesar,
>   & virgin Arabia trembles in her tent;
> For Caesar's hand will soon menace the rims of the wide earth,
>   & I will follow along tall among camp poets;
>   may fate reserve me that honor.
> But when we cannot reach a great statue's pinnacle
>   we lay our wreaths at the foot;
>   and so now, without means to lift up a crown of song
>   I put my myrrh in the fire with the simple ceremony of poverty,
>   for my verses are not yet baptized in the fountain of Hesiod,
>   but their tune still flows
>   from the bright stream holy to Aphrodite.[61]

61 Ibid., 2.10.

In a similar vein, he again points out that this type of poetry is a 'new path' for him. But he notes his poetry is nevertheless inspired, therefore he adds the demand for silence that his efforts might be heard.

Let there be silence, that the sacrifice fall well;
   the heifer is struck down now
   before the fire of my altar,
   with properly inspired consecration.
Let the Roman wreath contend with the ivy berries of Philetas,
   let the jar splash me with Cyrenian water, give me
   mild myrrh & alluring olibanum,
   & wind the wool disk 3 times round the fire;
   pour the ablution down,
   let the ivory flute ring a tuneful song here by the new altar;
Deception, depart; let evil float in another air.
   Smooth the singer's new path with laurel.
Muse, we will bring anew
   the story of Palatine Apollo's shrine; Calliope,
   the work deserves your favor.
I sing these songs in Caesar's name,
   & while Caesar is sung, I pray even Zeus be silent.[62]

There are three poems which sing the praises not of political leaders, but of patrons of the arts. Tibullus has written a poem in honor of his patron, Messalla, mentioning that he will join those competing to praise this man in hopes of winning first prize.[63] In another poem referring to his service to Messalla, Tibullus includes his view of the music to be heard in heaven.

I have no cause to fear as they do who blaspheme,
   but if my days are done, the span that the gods allot me,
   set over my bones a stone, engraved in a clear hand:
HERE TIBULLUS LIES, WHOM DEATH SEIZED AS
   HE FOLLOWED,
OVER THE LAND AND OVER THE SEA, MESSALLA,
   HIS FRIEND.
It will be Venus herself (she has always found me faithful)
   who will lead me along the way to the Elysian fields
   where song and dancing go on forever, and overhead, curving
   and fluting and falling, song from the delicate throats of birds.[64]

Similarly, Propertius, in honor of Maecenas, a friend of Augustus and a patron of Virgil, Horace, and Propertius, sings,

I will attend your chariots singing hallelujahs
   from one rim of the world to the other.[65]

62 Ibid., 4.6.

63 Tibullus, *The Poems*, 3.7.

64 Ibid., 1.3. Propertius, in Poem 1.2, cites as one of the wonders of nature the fact that 'birds sing without any instruction.'

65 Propertius, *The Poems*, 3.9.

There is also a touching elegy by Propertius in honor of one, Marcellus, who drowned at Baiae, a resort on the Bay of Naples. As part of an interesting description of this town, Propertius writes,

> Where Misenus, Trojan trumpet player, lies sand-buried,
>   & Hercules' causeway booms in the ocean,
>   & where the cymbals rang for the Theban god
>   When he went auspiciously searching
>   through mortal cities.[66]

Finally, there is a poem by Propertius which describes the area of Rome before the city was built.[67] Of particular interest is a very rare hint of the nature of the music played by the signal-horn players of old.

> What was Rome then, when Cures' hornblower
>   broke his long notes on godly cliffs hard by ...

Also, the area where now the Senate building sits was once,

> a fruitful grove secret in an ivied cleft
> where the trees sounded against native springs,
> branch & reed pipe, Sylvanian home,
> the sheep went to the music to a shadowed well ...

FUNCTIONAL MUSIC

The cult-religious festivals of ancient Rome must have had their origin in still more ancient rituals based on the cycles of agriculture, consisting of prayers to the gods for planting and harvesting. In Virgil's Georgics, a celebration of country life, we find the suggestion that these rural celebrations still continued among the peasants. He praises the land, olives, berries, and of course grapes.

> All hail, Saturnian Land, our honored Mother!
> For thee I broach these themes of ancient art
> And dare disclose the sacred springs of verse,
> Singing Hesiod's song through Roman towns ...
> This soil is good for grapes, and for the juice
> We offer to the gods in cups of gold,
> As the sleek Etruscan plays his ivory pipe
> Beside the alters where we sacrifice
> With steaming entrails loaded high on plates.[68]

66 Ibid., 3.18.

67 Ibid., 4.4.

68 Virgil, *Georgics*, 2.174ff. Earlier in Book 2, Virgil praises the various types of wines produced by specific grapes.

Tibullus has also composed a hymn to these ancient country celebrations which would develop in time into the more familiar festival of Bacchus.

> This is a hymn for them alone, the country gods … .
> The sweaty farmer, tired of plowing in hot noon sun,
>   would rest in the shade and make words that fitted a tune,
>   or, his belly full, would finger the stop on an oaten pipe
>   to win the ear of a god whose image he tried to shape.
> It was such a man, great Bacchus, his face vermilion-dyed,
>   who beat a rustic measure for rustic feet to tread …
> Come, bless our country feast, most holy—but leave behind
>   your arrows; as for your torch, do not let it fire this land!
> Hark when we sing you songs to pray for our flocks' increase
>   and beg you blessings, aloud, for them; in a whisper, for us—
>   or aloud for ourselves as well; no man will be able to hear
>   in that noisy crowd where the curved pipes play a Phrygian air.[69]

69 Tibullus, *The Poems*, 2.1.

Tibullus, in another poem, suggests that the origin of festivals, as well as song itself, centered on the celebration of grapes and wine was not in Greece but in Egypt with the worship of Osiris.

> The river-god and Osiris—theirs is a double altar
>   where hymns to the ox make a wild barbaric strain.
> It was Osiris in truth who was the plow's inventor,
>   turning the virgin earth with an iron share;
>   he was the first to drop seed in the furrow, and gather
>   from nameless trees the fruit they began to bear.
> He learned, and taught to men, how the vine is tied to the pole,
>   and how the hook must lop the leaves from the vine.
> Out of the grape clusters that heavy feet had trampled,
>   none before him had ever brought forth wine—
>   and men, having drunk it, were moved to what would someday
>   be singing,
>   once they had smoothed it out, and to rustic dance …
> Osiris, yours was never a province of misfortune;
>   in your land love and mirth and song are law.[70]

70 Ibid., 1.7.

The festival of Bacchus is the one which these Roman lyric poets focused on most frequently in their poetry, no doubt due to the romantic associations of love and wine. Virgil's references to Bacchus are still framed in the older rural setting.

Now, Bacchus, I shall sing
Of you and of the woodlands, of the shrubs,
Of the slowly growing olive's progeny.
Approach, Lenaean Father: here all things
Are brimming with your gifts, for you the farmlands
Flourish, large with Autumn's trailing vine,
The vintage foams in swelling vats.

…

To Bacchus at each shrine, and tragedies
Of old came on the stage, and Theseus' sons
Gave prizes out for local wit in towns
And crossroads, and they danced in mellow fields
On well-oiled goatskins, tipsy; and Ausonians,
A people sent from Troy to settle here,
Sport their disheveled verses, crude guffaws,
And don their grisly masks of hollow cork
And sing to you, O Bacchus, happy songs,
And hang your swaying mask on lofty pines,
That as the god inclines his noble head
In each direction, ripening vineyards grow,
Hollow vales and deepened glades fill out.
We shall, then, sing, in native songs, our debut
Of praise to Bacchus, bring on cakes and plates
And lead in by the horns a sacred goat
To stand beside the altar, and proceed
To roast his fertile flesh on hazel spits.[71]

71   Virgil, *Georgics*, 1ff and 380ff.

Some of the poetic descriptions emphasize the mythical aspect of
Bacchus, as in this example by Horace. The music of the reed-pipes
he says was as sweet as honey.

I did see Bacchus, high in a mountain glen—
Believe me, future hearers!—instructing nymphs
In dithyrambs of his, and goat-foot
Satyrs all cocking their ears to learn them.

Evoe! My mind still reels from that recent dread
And in my heart, by Bacchus possessed, I fell
Wild joy. Evoe. But spare me, Liber,
Spare me the goad of your painful thyrsus!

I feel a strong compulsion to sing in praise
Of dancers dancing tirelessly, fountain jets
Of wine and milk, abounding brooks, and
Honey that drips from the hollow reed-wands;

I feel compelled to sing of the blessed spouse
Immortalized in stars,[72] and the palace hall
Of Pentheus toppled to a ruin,
And of the Thracian Lycurgus's downfall.[73]

Often the emphasis seems to be on the power of wine and its impact on the actions of men. We find this in the only other description of the Bacchus celebration by Horace, as well as his suggestion that wine lifts the quality of his work to new heights of creativity.

Whither, Bacchus, am I swept on,
Thus possessed by your wine? What are the groves and caves
This new self of mine must behold?
By what grottoes shall I, singing, be heard to tell
Caesar's eminent glory set
High in Jupiter's hall up with eternal stars?
Fame conferring, unheard of song,
New and strange, shall be mine …
Nothing common shall I compose,
Nothing destined to die. Sweet is the peril braved,
Wine-press god, in your footsteps' wake,
While with tendrils of green grapevine my brows are crowned.

A poem by Propertius deals with the same themes.

Wine imperils glamor & gets the better of manhood,
    & a woman in the heat of wine may forget her proper lover.
But … I speak too harshly, I don't mean it.
Bacchus cannot change you, so imbibe and look lovely;
    the fruit of the vine becomes you.
Your trailing laurel hangs over the cup
    & my music lifts your soft voice.[74]

The references to the festival of Bacchus by Ovid seem to point not to the rural character but to the later secret ceremonies of women. Ovid gives us a vivid picture of the ritual dress of the women in this episode when Procne invades this female ceremony looking for her sister.

It was the time when all the Thracian mothers
Held festival for Bacchus, and the night
Shared in their secrets; Rhodope by night
Resounded as the brazen cymbals clashed,

72 Bacchus/Dionysus found Ariadne on the island of Naxos and upon marrying her turned her bridal crown into a constellation [see also the finale of *Ariadne auf Naxos* by Strauss].

73 Horace, *Odes*, 2.19.

74 Propertius, *The Poems*, 2.33.

> And so by night the queen went from her palace,
> Armed for the rites of Bacchus, in all the dress
> Of frenzy, trailing vines for head-dress, deer-skin
> Down the left side, and a spear over the shoulder.
> So, swiftly through the forest with attendants,
> Comrades and worshipers in throngs, and driven
> By madness, terrible in rage and anger,
> Went Procne, went the Bacchanal, and came
> At last to the hidden cottage, came there shrieking,
> 'Hail, Bacchus!' broke the doors in, found her sister,
> Dressed her like all the others, hid her face
> With ivy-leaves, and dragged her out, and brought her
> Home to the palace.[75]

75   Ovid, *Metamorphoses*, 6.585ff.

In other references to this festival, Ovid speaks of this hidden ritual continuing for ten days[76] and with a larger participation of musical instruments.

76   Ibid., 11.96.

> When suddenly timbrels sounded, unseen timbrels
> Harsh in their ears, auloi piped, and horns resounded
> And cymbals clashed, and all the air was full
> Of the smell of myrrh and saffron, and their weaving
> Turned green, and the hanging cloth resembled ivy
> Or grape-vines, and the threads were tendrils clinging.[77]

77   Ibid., 4.391ff.

Virgil's references to the Bacchus festival in his epic poem, *The Aeneid*, seems to describe the more recent period. No longer do we read of a simple rural celebration, but now something wild and out of control.

> When she saw Latinus was stubborn, and deep in her heart
> The maddening serpent's venom had sunk and spread over
> Her entire body, then truly the unhappy woman,
> Disturbed by gigantic horrors, ran out of control
> And raged through the wide-sprawling city …
> Even into the forests she ran, pretending the power
> Of Bacchus controlled her, to commit a greater sin
> Against heaven, a greater madness. She hid her daughter
> In leafy mountains, to snatch her from Trojan marriage
> And delay its torches. 'Euhoe, Bacchus,' she shouted,
> Calling you worthy alone of the girl; for you
> She was seizing the pliant thyrsus, for you she was dancing
> In chorus, growing a sacred hair-lock for you.
> The news of Amata flew far. Each mother was fired
> With madness to seek in like fashion new homes. They deserted

Their old ones and, baring their necks and hair to the winds,
They filled the air with a tremulous howling. Their dresses
Were animal-skins, they carried vine-stalks as spears.
In their midst Amata brandished a flaming pine-torch
And chanted a wedding-song for her daughter.

…

But you are not sluggish
For love and its nightly combat nor when the curved pipe
Announces the Bacchic dance. Be eager for feasts
And wine on a groaning board—this is love, this you long for …[78]

78 Virgil, *Aeneid*, 7.375ff
and 11.736ff.

Another festival associated with agricultural life was the festival
in honor of Ceres, the goddess of agriculture. Again, we especially find the genuine rural picture of this celebration in Virgil's *Georgics*.

See that your country folk adore the goddess:
For her let milk and honey flow, and wine,
And lead the sacrificial victims round the crops
Three times, to bring good fortune, let a chorus
Follow the procession, singing hymns
To Ceres, ask her blessing on their homes;
Let no one lay his sickle to the grain
Until, with festive oak wreath on his brow,
He honors Ceres' name in dance and song.[79]

79 Virgil, *Georgics*, 1.344ff.

Ovid in a poem celebrating the festival of Ceres mentions a great
variety of wildlife and crops. We quote the beginning and ending
of this poem.

Now comes the yearly festival of Ceres,
And my love lies alone in bed at night.
O golden goddess, garlanded with wheatears,
Why must your feast inhibit our delight?

…

A feast day calls for song and wine and women;
Those are the gifts the lordly gods should gain.[80]

80 Ovid, *Amores*, 3.10.

Ovid provides more musical information relative to the festival
of Juno, who was the mythical daughter to Saturn and wife to Jupiter. The poem is also interesting for the details of the procession
and the references to its Greek origin.

The orchard town Camillus took, Falerii,
Was my wife's birthplace; we came there one day.
Juno's chaste feast was being celebrated,
With games and sacrifice the place was gay;
A feast well worth the visit, though the journey
Is difficult, a steep and toilsome way.

A grove stands there, ancient and dense and gloomy;
The place must be a god's, one can be sure.
The faithful offer incense at an altar,
An artless altar reared in days of yore.

Here, to the sound of auloi and solemn chanting,
The long procession passes every year
Through streets bedecked, with white Falerian heifers
From their own fields, while all the people cheer ... .

...

Young men and shy girls go before the goddess,
Their trailing vestments sweeping the wide street.
The girls' hair is adorned with gold and jewels,
And stately gowns half-hide their gilded feet.

High on their heads they bear the holy vessels,
White-robed according to the old Greek rites.
The crowd is hushed as June in her golden
Procession comes behind her acolytes.

The form of the procession comes from Argos.
On Agamemnon's death Halaesus fled
The murder and his father's wealth and wandered
Long over land and sea as exile led.[81]

81 Ibid., 3.13.

23   THE EMPIRE (14–476 AD)

There were significant numbers of the aristocracy who had a serious interest in music during the reign of the emperors. Among the members of the Senate, for example, we know of Caius Calpurnius Piso, one of the conspirators against Nero in 65 AD, who was an accomplished lyre player.[1]

The musical accomplishments of many of the emperors is surprising.[2] Caligula (12–41 AD) received an education which included both vocal and instrumental music and used to perform in private concerts before the aristocracy. Caligula once asked a famous singer, Apelles, whether he considered he or Jupiter the greater. When the singer unfortunately hesitated in his answer, Caligula had him scourged, but complimented his voice as being attractive even in his cries of pain! We are also told that 'if anyone made even the slightest sound while his favorite was dancing, he had the person dragged from his seat and scourged him with his own hand.'[3]

Nero (37–68 AD), the most debauched and cruel of the emperors (he murdered his mother when age twenty-two!), loved music, poetry and the theater. He studied the lyre with the foremost teacher of his time, Terpnos, as is described by Suetonius.

> Having gained some knowledge of music in addition to the rest of his early education, as soon as he became emperor he sent for Terpnus, the greatest master of the lyre in those days, and after listening to him sing after dinner for many successive days until late at night, he little by little began to practice himself, neglecting none of the exercises which artists of that kind are in the habit of following, to preserve or strengthen their voices. For he used to lie upon his back and hold a leaden plate on his chest,[4] purge himself by the syringe and by vomiting, and deny himself fruits and all foods injurious to the voice. Finally encouraged by his progress, although his voice was weak and husky, he began to long to appear on the stage, and every now and then in the presence of his intimate friends he would quote a Greek proverb meaning, 'Hidden music counts for nothing.' And he made his debut at Naples, where he did not cease singing until he had finished the number which he had begun, even though the theatre was shaken by a sudden earthquake shock. In the same city he sang frequently and for several successive days. Even when he took a short time to rest his voice, he could not

1 Sendrey, *Music in the Social and Religious Life of Antiquity*, 391.

2 Ibid., 392ff.

3 Suetonius, *Lives of the Caesars*, Book 4, 55.

4 This information comes from Pliny the Elder, *Natural History*, 34.44.167, who says,

> Nero, whom heaven was pleased to make emperor, used to have a plate of lead on his chest when singing songs *fortissimo*, thus showing a method for preserving the voice.

keep out of sight but went to the theater after bathing and dined in the orchestra with the people all about him, promising them in Greek, that when he had wetted his whistle a bit, he would ring out something good and loud …

Returning from Greece, since it was at Naples that he had made his first appearance, he entered that city with white horses through a part of the wall which had been thrown down, as is customary with victors in the sacred games. In like manner he entered Antium, then Albanum, and finally Rome; but at Rome he rode in the chariot which Augustus had used in his triumphs in days gone by, and wore a purple robe and a Greek cloak adorned with stars of gold, bearing on his head the Olympic crown … while the rest were carried before him with inscriptions telling where he had won them and against what competitors, and giving the titles of the songs … His car was followed by his claque … All along the route victims were slain, the streets were sprinkled from time to time with perfume, while birds, ribbons, and sweetmeats were showered upon him. He placed the sacred crowns in his bed chambers around his couches, as well as statues representing him in the guise of a lyre player; and he had a coin too struck with the same device. So far from neglecting or relaxing his practice of the art after this, he never addressed the soldiers except by letter or in a speech delivered by another, to save his voice; and he never did anything for amusement or in earnest without an elocutionist by his side, to warn him to spare his vocal organs and hold a handkerchief to his mouth. To many men he offered his friendship or announced his hostility, according as they had applauded him lavishly or grudgingly.[5]

5   Suetonius, *Lives of the Caesars*, bk 6, 20ff.

Nero's musical activities after he returned to Rome are covered extensively by Tacitus. It seems apparent that Tacitus considered the performance of music to be something done by slaves. Therefore, in all his accounts of Nero's performances he points over and over to the disgrace associated with an emperor engaging in such public performances.

He had long had a fancy for driving a four-horse chariot, and a no less degrading taste for singing to the harp, in a theatrical fashion, when he was at dinner. This he would remind people was a royal custom, and had been the practice of ancient chiefs; it was celebrated too in the praises of poets and was meant to show honor to the gods. Songs indeed, he said, were sacred to Apollo, and it was in the dress of a singer that that great and prophetic deity was seen in Roman temples as well as in Greek cities …

Still, not yet wishing to disgrace himself on a public stage, he instituted some games under the title of 'juvenile sports,' for which people of every class gave in their names. Neither rank nor age nor previous high promotion hindered any one from practicing the art of a Greek or Latin actor and even stooping to gestures and songs unfit for a man. Noble ladies too actually played disgusting parts, and in the grove, with which Augustus had surrounded the lake for the naval fight, there were erected places for meeting and refreshment, and every incentive to excess was offered for sale. Money too was distributed, which the respectable had to spend under sheer compulsion and which the profligate gloried in squandering. Hence a rank growth of abominations and of all infamy. Never did a more filthy rabble add a worse licentiousness to our long corrupted morals ... Last of all, the emperor himself came on the stage, tuning his lute with elaborate care and trying his voice with his attendants. There were also present, to complete the show, a guard of soldiers with centurions and tribunes, and Burrus, who grieved and yet applauded ...

In the year of the consulship of Caius Laecanius and Marcus Licinius a yet keener impulse urged Nero to show himself frequently on the public stage. Hitherto he had sung in private houses or gardens, during the Juvenile games, but these he now despised, as being but little frequented, and on too small a scale for so fine a voice.[6]

6 Tacitus, *Annals*, 9.14ff and 15.33.

In another place, Tacitus explains how the Senate, in an attempt to keep Nero off the stage, voted to award him first prize in a singing contest in advance of the contest itself.

The Senate, as they were now on the eve of the quinquennial contest, wishing to avert scandal, offered the emperor the 'victory in song,' and added the 'crown of eloquence,' that thus a veil might be thrown over a shameful exposure on the stage. Nero, however, repeatedly declared that he wanted neither favor nor the Senate's influence, as he was a match for his rivals, and was certain, in the conscientious opinion of the judges, to win the honor by merit. First, he recited a poem on the stage; then, at the importunate request of the rabble that he would make public property of all his accomplishments (these were their words), he entered the theater, and conformed to all the laws of harp playing, not sitting down when tired, nor wiping off the perspiration with anything but the garment he wore, or letting himself be seen to spit or clear his nostrils. Last of all, on bended knee he saluted the assembly with motion of the hand, and awaited the verdict of the judges with pretended anxiety. And then the city populace, who were wont to encourage every gesture even of actors, made the place ring with measured strains of elaborate applause. One would have thought they were rejoicing, and perhaps they did rejoice, in their indifference to the public disgrace.

All, however, who were present from remote towns, and still retained the Italy of strict morals and primitive ways; all too who had come on embassies or on private business from distant provinces, where they had been unused to such wantonness, were unable to endure the spectacle or sustain the degrading fatigue, which wearied their unpracticed hands, while they disturbed those who knew their part, and were often struck by soldiers, stationed in the seats, to see that not a moment of time passed with less vigorous applause or in the silence of indifference. It was a known fact that several knights, in struggling through the narrow approaches and the pressure of the crowd, were trampled to death, and that others while keeping their seats day and night were seized with some fatal malady. For it was still worse danger to be absent from the show, as many openly and many more secretly made it their business to scrutinize names and faces, and to note the delight or the disgust of the company. Hence came cruel severities, immediately exercised on the humble, and resentments, concealed for the moment, but subsequently paid off, towards men of distinction.[7]

Nero is also recorded as having invited leading members of the Senate to his palace and performing for them on the water organ.[8] He also played the kitharode, giving concerts on the Tiber and in Naples. During the great fire in Rome in 64 A D, a fire which Tacitus infers Nero may have had set in order to create a new city named for himself, Nero,

8 The origin of this, the first true organ, is not known. However, it is clear its design was inspired by the panpipe.

at the very time when the city was in flames, appeared on a private stage and sang of the destruction of Troy, comparing present misfortunes with the calamities of antiquity.

Near the end of his reign, when there was talk of replacing him, he made a public vow that if he retained his power he would celebrate his victory with a great music festival in which he would perform on the water organ, aulos, and bagpipe, as well as dance. At this time he also had murdered a popular actor, Paris, whom he thought might receive too much of the applause at this planned festival.

According to Suetonius, Titus (79–81 A D) was also educated in music and 'sang and played harp agreeably and skillfully.'[9] Domitian (81–96 A D) installed the Capitolinian Plays in 86 A D, which included musical contests, including 'those of the lyre players, between choruses of such players and in the lyre alone, without singing.'[10] For these he built a large concert hall on the Campus

9 Suetonius, *Lives of the Caesars*, 8.3.

10 Ibid., 8.4.

Martius. Trajan (52–117 AD) also constructed a music hall on the Forum. His successor, Hadrian (76–138 AD), was educated in music, sang and played harp. Marcus Aurelius (121–180 AD) suffered from one of the best teacher–student ratios in history. His personal teachers included a lawyer, four grammarians, four rhetoricians, and eight philosophers. His music teachers were the best available: Andronius and the lyre-singing specialist, Geminus. Caracalla (188–217 AD) played the kithara and on the death of his kithara teacher, Mesomedes, built a magnificent cenotaph for him.

Elagabalus (205–222 AD) is recorded as having been a performer of the aulos and panpipes in religious-cult services honoring Baal and again during the ceremonies relative to his coronation. He also performed on the trumpet, lute, water organ and sang. Severus Alexander (208–235 AD) sang, played the aulos, lyre, and organ, but performed only for the members of his family. He also legalized the guild system, which included various musical guilds [*collegia*],[11] and allowed them to elect spokesmen. Maximian (286–305 AD) also built a concert hall.

Even during the period of the emperor Theodoric (489–526 AD), when the political greatness of Rome had come to an end, the musical culture of Rome retained, according to Sendrey, its ancient vitality.[12]

ART MUSIC

By the beginning of the Empire there were still some who failed to appreciate music as an art, but generally, according to Sendrey,

> by around 50 AD music in Rome was recognized as an art form valued for itself. From then on, it became an essential element in the education of every distinguished Roman, male or female; women especially passed entire days practicing music, singing, and even composing new songs. Even the emperors were affected by the music mania …
>
> Lyric poems had to be performed with musical accompaniment—art music was composed mainly for this purpose.[13]

Choral performance become more popular during this period and in addition to performances for plays,[14] weddings, and religious celebrations, there were also public concerts of both choral and solo performances. Juvenal, while commenting on the fact that deaf

11   Each instrument had its own guild. The aulos guild, *Collegium tibicinum* enjoyed being fed at public expense in the temple of Jupiter. There was also a guild of concert artists, called *Synodus magna psaltum*. According to Plutarch these guilds began in the seventh century BC and the aulos guild was one of the oldest professional organizations in Rome [*Grove*, 16:147].

12   Sendrey, *Music in the Social and Religious Life of Antiquity*, 391.

13   Sendrey, *Music in the Social and Religious Life of Antiquity*, 387.

14   The *Trojan Women* by Seneca includes a chorus in the Greek tradition, which mentions both lamentations (1.77) and a wedding hymn (2.202).

people cannot appreciate music, mentions the robes these choirs wore as well as references to concert halls and famous soloists.

> How can the deaf appreciate music? The standard
> Of the performance eludes them: a top-line soloist,
> Massed choirs in their golden robes, all mean less than nothing.
> What does it matter to them where they sit in the concert hall
> When a wind band blowing its guts out is barely audible?[15]

Perhaps some choral performances were less disciplined than others. Lucian, in one of his satires, describes what the earth might look like from heaven above and compares it to the chaos of a poor choral performance. While this description is not intended to be of a real chorus, the fact that he employs this analogy suggests he must have seen such things.

> MENIPPUS. You must try to conceive what a queer jumble it all made. It was as if a man were to collect a number of choristers, or rather of choruses, and then tell each individual to disregard the others and start a melody of his own; if each did his best, went his own way, and tried to drown his neighbor, can you imagine what the musical effect would be?
> A FRIEND. A very ridiculous confusion.
> MENIPPUS. Well, friend, such are the earthly dancers; the life of man is just such a discordant performance; not only are the voices jangled, but the steps are not uniform, the motions not concerted, the objects not agreed upon—until the impresario dismisses them one by one from the stage, with a 'not wanted.' Then they are all alike, and quiet enough, confounding no longer their undisciplined rival melodies. But as long as the show lasts in its marvelous diversity, there is plenty of food for laughter in its vagaries.[16]

The reference here to each chorus member going his own way reminds us that, like the Greek choirs, these ensembles both sang and danced. Thus, Pliny the Elder's reference, while discussing geography, of a curious promontory in Illyria.

> There are also small islands at Nymphaeum called the Dancing Islands, because they move to the foot-beats of persons keeping time with the singing of a choral song.[17]

15 Juvenal, *Satire X*, 211.

16 Lucian, *Icaromenippus*. Tacitus, *Annals*, 11.31, also mentions a 'lascivious chorus' in connection with a wine festival.

17 Pliny the Elder, *Natural History*, 2.96.209. In 8.70.185, he mentions a festival in Egypt which includes a chorus of boys singing praises of the Ox.

Sendrey summarizes the wide spectrum of Art Music during the Empire Period.

In the pantomimes, *symphoniae* were inserted, which meant that a choir sang and danced to the accompaniment of a group of instrumentalists. Sometimes an actor sang a solo aria; in other instances a professional singer sang the lyrics, while a mime interpreted the words with gestures and appropriate dances. The pantomimes were frequently presented in gigantic proportions; sometimes 3000 singers and 3000 dancers participated in them.

There were numerous instrumental virtuosi, and the number of good average artists was legion. From all parts of the empire musicians converged on Rome, attracted by the gold of the capital of the world. The huge number of musically educated slaves made it possible for their masters to maintain large choirs and orchestras with almost no expense ...[18]

Many wealthy persons had their own permanent music groups. Some had their especially gifted musicians sent to famous teachers for further education.

Professional virtuosi were in great demand and undertook extended concert tours in all parts of the empire. They were highly paid and often became the idols of the audiences. For several of them monuments or statues were erected ... Women of high society adored them and paid large sums for their love; other female admirers fought for the possession of a plectrum the admired artist had used in the concerts; others offered sacrifices to the gods to insure victory for their favorites in the festival contests ... The victors in poetical and musical contests received the coveted oak wreath from the hands of the emperor ...

The honoraria of some of the traveling virtuosi bordered on the fantastic ...

In a fresco of Herculaneum (now in the Naples Museum) a concert is depicted in the home of a wealthy man. It shows a female aulos player ... and accompanied by a kithara player. That it is a real house concert and not merely a private musical entertainment is evident from the large audience depicted in this fresco.[19]

One cannot know how common home concerts, such as seen in the last named fresco, were in Rome of this period, but we should acknowledge that Pliny the Younger mentioned a regular practice of such music.

At supper, if I have only my wife or a few friends with me, some author is read to us; and after supper we are entertained either with music or an interlude.[20]

18 Painting, however, was reserved for those of noble birth. Pliny the Elder, in *Natural History*, 35.36.78, says slaves were forbidden to be instructed in it and he observes that in both painting and sculpture there were no famous works executed by a slave.

19 Sendrey, *Music in the Social and Religious Life of Antiquity*, 387ff.

20 Letter 108, to Fuscus.

The mention, above, of three thousand singers, while extraordinary, only reflects the great number of practicing musicians in Rome. In 284 AD, Carinus presented a series of plays in which he used, among other things, one hundred trumpeters and one hundred horn players.[21] Seneca mentioned that sometimes it seemed that there were more people on the stage than there used to be in the audience.[22]

21 Sendrey, *Music in the Social and Religious Life of Antiquity*, 412.

22 Seneca, *Epistolae*, 84.10.

> Do you not see how many voices there are in a chorus? Yet out of the many only one voice results. In that chorus one voice takes the tenor, another the bass, another the baritone. There are women, too, as well as men, and the aulos is mingled with them. In that chorus the voices of the individual singers are hidden; what we hear is the voices of all together. To be sure, I am referring to the chorus which the old-time philosophers knew; in our present day exhibitions we have a larger number of singers than there used to be spectators in the theaters of old. All the aisles are filled with rows of singers; brass instruments surround the auditorium; the stage resounds with auloi and instruments of every description; and yet from the discordant sounds a harmony is produced.

The Greek tradition of singing Art Music at banquets, after the tables were cleared, seems to have been practiced in Rome as well. There is an account of Aulus Gellius (ca. 117 – ca. 180 AD) in which he describes such a concert consisting of choral groups singing poems of Anacreon and Sappho, as well as contemporary love-elegies.[23] Another account tells of a famous singer of Alexandria who performed in Rome during the late second century AD whose music was so popular that many 'music lovers knew the songs performed by him by heart.'[24]

23 Sendrey, *Music in the Social and Religious Life of Antiquity*, 408.

24 Ibid., 409.

The poet, Persius (35–62 AD) satirizes such an after dinner concert, but in his description of 'making the listeners cry' we may believe he had actually heard such songs.

> Look: here's a banquet. Well fed, Romulus'
> posterity is busy drinking. They ask:
> 'And what has the divine poet to tell us?'
> Somebody in a hyacinthine stole
> utters hesitantly, down his nose,
> something that's been kept around a bit long—
> a 'Phyllis,' an 'Hypsipyle,' Tales to Make
> You Cry from the Earlier Roman Poets.
> He tries to let them flow clear, but the words catch
> and stumble on his tender little palate.[25]

25 Persius, *Satire I*, 30ff.

During the third century A D a report by the astronomer Fir-
micus Maternus mentions 'public musicians' who compose music
for theatrical plays.[26] It is possible that some of these productions in
the theater were of a very elevated artistic character, for Quintilian
refers to the theater as 'a kind of temple for the solemnization of a
sacred feast.'[27] Music contests were also introduced on the occasion
of public theatrical plays.[28]

There were also famous instrumentalists, including Nero's
teacher, Terpnos, the kithara player. Nero also rewarded the kitharode player, Menecrates, with a palace and estate. The emperor Vespasian (69–79 A D) gave huge cash gifts to the lyre players Terpnus
and Diodorus.[29] Another kitharode player, Anaxeron, was not only
honored by a monument erected in a public square in his birthplace, but was given the tax income of four cities by Mark Anthony.

Canus, the most famous aulos player of the first century A D
made the interesting statement that if the audiences only knew how
much pleasure he received from playing, instead of paying him, he
would be required to pay them.[30] The rhetorician and biographer,
Flavius Philostratus,[31] recounts a visit by a traveler named Apollonius to this aulos player. In describing to him the kinds of music
he played, Canus provides a list of types of music which would seem
familiar today: music for those who are sad; music for celebration;
music for lovers; and music for religious usage.

> [The purpose of my music is] that the mourner may have his sor-
> row lulled to sleep by the pipe, and that they that rejoice may have
> their cheerfulness enhanced, and the lover may wax warmer in his
> passion, and that the lover of sacrifice may become more inspired
> and full of sacred song.[32]

Upon further questioning, Canus admits it is the music itself
which accomplishes these ends, not the aulos 'constructed of gold
or brass and the skin of a stag, or perhaps the shin of a donkey.'
Finally, Canus provides a very rare glimpse into the basic technique
of playing the aulos.

> … namely reserves of breath … and facility with the lips consisting
> in their taking in the reed of the pipe and playing without blowing
> out the cheeks; and manual skill I consider very important, for the
> wrist must not weary from being bent, nor must the fingers be slow
> in fluttering over the notes.

26 Sendrey, *Music in the Social
and Religious Life of Antiquity*, 391.
The poet, Calpurnius Siculus, in
Eclogue VII, 23ff., gives an interesting
first-hand description of one of the
outdoor theaters.

27 Quintilian, *The Education of an
Orator*, 3.8.30.

28 Sendrey, *Music in the Social and
Religious Life of Antiquity*, 387.

29 Suetonius, *Lives of the
Caesars*, 8.19.

30 Sendrey, *Music in the Social and
Religious Life of Antiquity*, 411.

31 Philostratus, *The Life of
Apollonius of Tyana*, 5.21.

32 Aelianus, in *On the
Characteristics of Animals*, 12.44,
mentions another use of the aulos in
Libya: 'This is the aulos music which
throws mares into an amorous frenzy
and makes horses mad with desire to
couple. This in fact is how the mating
of horses is brought about.'

We are fortunate to have a few insights into the nature of artistic contests of this period in Suetonius' account of Nero's participation in them.

Nero was greatly taken too with the rhythmic applause of some Alexandrians, who had flocked to Naples from a fleet that had lately arrived, and summoned more men from Alexandria. Not content with that, he selected some young men of the order of knights and more than five thousand sturdy young commoners, to be divided into groups and learn the Alexandrian styles of applause (they called them 'the bees,' 'the roof-tiles,' and 'the bricks'), and to ply them vigorously whenever he sang …

Considering it of great importance to appear in Rome as well, he repeated the contest of the Neronia before the appointed time, and when there was a general call for his 'divine voice,' he replied that if any wished to hear him, he would favor them in the gardens; but when the guard of soldiers which was then on duty seconded the entreaties of the people, he gladly agreed to appear at once. So without delay he had his name added to the list of the lyre players who entered the contest, and casting his own lot into the urn with the rest, he came forward in his turn, attended by the prefects of the Guard carrying his lyre, and followed by the tribunes of the soldiers and his intimate friends. Having taken his place and finished his preliminary speech, he announced through the ex-consul Cluvius Rufus that 'he would sing Niobe'; and he kept at it until late in the afternoon, putting off the award of the prize for that event and postponing the rest of the contest to the next year, to have an excuse for singing oftener …

Not content with showing his proficiency in these arts at Rome, he went to Achaia, as I have said, influenced by the following consideration. The cities in which it was the custom to hold contests in music had adopted the rule of sending all the lyric prizes to him.[33] These he received with the greatest delight, not only giving audience before all others to the envoys who brought them, but even inviting them to his private table. When some of them begged him to sing during dinner and greeted his performance with extravagant applause, he declared that 'the Greeks were the only ones who had an ear for music and that they alone were worthy of his efforts.' So he took ship without delay and immediately on arriving at Cassiope made a preliminary appearance as a singer at the altar of Jupiter Cassius, and then went the round of all the contests.

To make this possible, he gave orders that even those which were widely separated in time should be brought together in a single year, so that some had even to be given twice, and he introduced a musical competition at Olympia also, contrary to custom. To avoid being

33 Suetonius, *Lives of the Caesars*, 6.12, relates, unfortunately without explaining the significance, that on one such occasion Nero, when the prize for lyre playing was offered him, knelt before it and ordered that it be laid at the feet of Augustus's statue.

distracted or hindered in any way while busy with these contests, he replied to his freedman Helius, who reminded him that the affairs of the city required his presence, in these words: 'However much it may be your advice and your wish that I should return speedily, yet you ought rather to counsel me and to hope that I may return worthy of Nero.'

While he was singing no one was allowed to leave the theatre even for the most urgent reasons. And so it is said that some women gave birth to children there, while many who were worn out with listening and applauding, secretly leaped from the wall, since the gates at the entrance were closed, or feigned death and were carried out as if for burial. The trepidation and anxiety with which he took part in the contests, his keen rivalry of his opponents and his awe of the judges, can hardly be credited. As if his rivals were of quite the same station as himself, he used to show respect to them and try to gain their favor, while he slandered them behind their backs, sometimes assailed them with abuse when he met them, and even bribed those who were especially proficient.

Before beginning, he would address the judges in the most deferential terms, saying that he had done all that could be done, but the issue was in the hands of Fortune; they however, being men of wisdom and experience, ought to exclude what was fortuitous. When they bade him take heart, he withdrew with greater confidence, but not even then without anxiety, interpreting the silence and modesty of some as sullenness and ill-nature, and declaring that he had his suspicions of them.

In competition he observed the rules most scrupulously, never daring to clear his throat and even wiping the sweat from his brow with his arm. Once indeed, during the performance of a tragedy, when he had dropped his scepter but quickly recovered it, he was terribly afraid that he might be excluded from the competition because of his slip, and his confidence was restored only when his accompanist swore that it had passed unnoticed amid the delight and applause of the people. When the victory was won, he made the announcement himself; and for that reason he always took part in the contests of the heralds. To obliterate the memory of all other victors in the games and leave no trace of them, their statues and busts were all thrown down by his order, dragged off with hooks, and cast into privies.[34]

Tacitus mentions other examples of Nero behavior toward his rival artists. He tried to prevent the publication of the poems of Lucanus.[35] An aristocrat who sang at some games instituted at Nero's birthplace was actually murdered by Nero.[36]

34 Ibid., 6.20.

35 Tacitus, *Annals*, 15.49.
36 Ibid., 16.21.

As the reader can see, Nero's native cruelty was never absent for long. Once, after giving the order that only he could wear a special dye of purple, he saw a lady in the audience of one of his recitals dressed in this material, pointed her out to his agents, who dragged her out and stripped her on the spot.[37]

37 Suetonius, *Lives of the Caesars*, 6.32.

Nero's successor, Tacitus describes as follows:

> Vitellius used to make a display of his admiration for Nero, and had constantly followed him when he sang, not from the compulsion to which the noblest had to yield, but because he was the slave and chattel of profligacy and gluttony.[38]

38 Tacitus, *The History*, 2.71.

But perhaps the love of music was more sincere than Tacitus wanted to admit, for there is an interesting reference to art music performed at a banquet during the brief reign of Vitellius (69 AD). When an aulos player received applause from the guests, Vitellius urged him to perform 'something from the Master's Book.' Thus, we are told, when the aulos player began to play some of the 'songs of Nero, Vitellius was the first to applaud him and even jumped for joy.'[39]

39 Suetonius, *Lives of the Caesars*, 7.11.

Some of the more austere philosophers failed to appreciate all this music, especially Seneca the Elder (first century AD) who complained that the noble sciences were being neglected and that the mentality of the masses was being governed by ignoble occupations, such as singing and dancing, which exerted an effeminate influence on youth. Thus he observes,

> I am always ashamed of humanity, when I enter the school of the philosophers; the Neapolitans are interested in the theater and are eager to find a good bagpiper ... but where a man should receive a good education, there is nobody, there is no interest for such a purpose.[40]

40 Seneca the Elder, *Controversiae*, 1, poem, quoted in Sendrey, *Music in the Social and Religious Life of Antiquity*, 390.

We must assume his complaint was not singular for we find a similar objection in the fourth century AD. Ammianus Marcellinus reports that,

> the Roman palaces, formerly famous for disseminating sciences, now resound with the singing and playing of instruments. Where formerly the philosophers were welcome, there are now singers and music teachers in their place; everywhere one could hear music, but the libraries, the depositories of knowledge, were silent as the graves.[41]

41 Ibid., 391.

Seneca the Younger complained that lovers of music spend their entire day in singing and composing songs, forcing their voices by artificial means to attain a different character from the natural sound.[42]

42 Seneca the Younger, *De brevitate vitae*, 12, 4, quoted in Sendrey, *Music in the Social and Religious Life of Antiquity*, 390.

EDUCATIONAL MUSIC

There was apparently in Rome some continuation of the Greek usage of music for the purpose of educating the young through formal performances at banquets which sang of the great deeds of past heroes. The historian Valerius Maximus (first century AD) mentions that during banquets the elders would compose, to the accompaniment of the aulos, their ancestors' outstanding deeds in song, so that by this they might make the younger men more eager to imitate them.[43]

43 Valerius Maximus, *Factorvm et Dictorvm Memorabilivm*, 2.1.10ff.

FUNCTIONAL MUSIC

We must assume that music continued to play an important role in the celebration of the religious-cult ceremonies. An excellent example of three trumpets participating in an offering procession can be seen in the first century altarpiece in the Museo del Vaticano, Belvedere, Rome.[44] In another extant icon, we see an aulos playing during a sacrifice (an axe is poised over a cow) in a sarcophagus carving from the second century AD in the Museo del Palazzo Ducale, Mantua.

44 Juvenal mentions trumpets in a civic procession in *Satire X*, 44.

The common people were never far from the primitive and superstitious origins of these quasi religious cults. Tacitus, for example, tells of an occasion when, upon the occurrence of a lunar eclipse, the soldiers in the field became frightened and immediately lapsed into a cult ceremony directed at the god in question.

Suddenly in a clear sky the moon's radiance seemed to die away. This the soldiers in their ignorance of the cause regarded as an omen of their condition, comparing the failure of her light to their own efforts, and imagining that their attempts would end prosperously should her brightness and splendor be restored to the goddess. And so they raised a din with brazen instruments and the combined notes of trumpets and horns, with joy or sorrow, as she brightened or grew dark. When clouds arose and obstructed their sight, and

45 Tacitus, *Annals*, 1.28. Tacitus, in *The History*, 5.5, mentions that some thought the religious music of the Jews was based on secular cult traditions:

From the fact, however, that their priests used to chant to the music of auloi and cymbals, and to wear garlands of ivy, and that a golden vine was found in the temple, some have thought that they worshiped Father Liber ... though their institutions do not by any means harmonize with the theory; for Liber established a festive and cheerful worship, while the Jewish religion is tasteless and mean.

46 Sendrey, *Music in the Social and Religious Life of Antiquity*, 421.

47 Ibid., 405.

48 Josephus, *The Jewish Wars*, 3.89ff.

49 *De Musica*, quoted in Andrew Barker, *Greek Musical Writings* (Cambridge: Cambridge University Press, 1989), 2.466. References to the military trumpet of this period can also be found in Seneca's *Thyestes*, 189; Pliny the Younger, Letter 20, to Macrinus; Tacitus, *Annals*, 4.25 and 15, 30; and in Valerius Flaccus (d. ca. 94 AD), *Argonautica*, 7.629.

50 Georges Kastner, *Manuel général de musique militaire* (Paris, 1848), 35.

it was thought she was buried in the gloom, with that proneness to superstition which steals over minds once thoroughly cowed, they lamented that this was a portent of neverending hardship, and that heaven frowned on their deeds.[45]

Military trumpet signals were fundamental to the success of the Roman army. Trumpets were also used in the navy, sometimes for the purpose of establishing rhythm for the oarsmen. The musicians of the army were noncommissioned officers, while the musicians of the navy were slaves.[46]

Pollux mentions specific signals for attack, for encouragement during the battle, for retreat and for setting up camp.[47] Josephus writes that in camp the Roman trumpets gave the signal to wake, a second to prepare to march, and a third for departure.[48] There are accounts of having some trumpet players placed far behind the troops for the purpose of misleading the enemy regarding the location of the Roman armies.

The Greek writer, Aristides Quintilianus, mentions the effectiveness of these musical signals.

As to war, in which Rome was and is outstandingly glorious (and, let me add, may it so remain), the fact that drill exercises 'in pyrrhic style' are done to music hardly needs mentioning, since everyone knows it quite well. What most people do not know is that in the perils of battle itself they often avoid the use of verbal commands, since damage would be done if they were understood by those of the enemy who speak the same language. Instead they signal by musical means, using that martial and rousing instrument the *salpinx* [trumpet], and each command is assigned a specific tune. Thus frontal attacks and flanking advances, for instance, have each been given their own particular melodies; another sounds the retreat; there are special calls for wheeling to left or to right. Thus they can go through all these maneuvers one after another, using signals which are incomprehensible to the enemy but perfectly clear to their own side, and which are understood the moment they are given. The signals are not heard first by one section, then the next; the whole army acts at a single sound.[49]

Aristides' suggestion here that every soldier knew these signals seems to be confirmed by an occasion when Hannibal attempted to confuse the Roman soldiers by having his trumpeters play false signals, but was unable to confuse them.[50] Also, this system of signals being so vital to the progress of the battle, it was important, of course, that the correct signals be played at the correct time. In one famous instance when this failed to happen, Hirtius, in his *History of the War of Africa*, reported hearing the cornus pass on the order for attack, while Julius Caesar was still making up his mind to attack or not![51]

There is not sufficient extant information to know how many trumpet and cornu players were used with an army of a particular size. There is one extant listing of players in the third Augustan Legion in Lambaesis (Numidia) which gives a surprisingly large contingent of thirty-nine trumpet players and thirty-six cornu players.[52] Plutarch, speaking of the sounds of the trumpets, 'coming from every direction,' also seems to confirm such large numbers of players.

> Moving stealthily over the ground between, they charged the camp about midnight, and with loud shouts and blasts of trumpets from every direction, by their din threw the Gauls … into complete confusion.[53]

Polybius, as well, in his account of a battle between the Romans and the Celts, speaks of 'the dreadful din, for there were innumerable cornu blowers and trumpeters.'[54]

Less frequently mentioned are the lituus, which were apparently assigned to the cavalry, and the *buccina*. This last instrument, made from an animal horn, was used for giving signals during the night, when the louder trumpet might prevent sleep entirely.[55]

Regarding occupational music, Quintilian points to the ability of music to lighten labor as one of its important characteristics.

> Indeed nature itself seems to have given music as a boon to men to lighten the strain of labor: even the rower in the galleys is cheered to effort by song. Nor is this function of music confined to cases where the efforts of a number are given union by the sound of some sweet voice that sets the tune, but even solitary workers find solace at their toil in artless song.[56]

One of the poems of Seneca mentions the use of music not only to make the work of loom workers more pleasant, but to make them work faster.

> Now plucking the strings, now happily passing the wool.
> He keeps them to work with his song, beguiling their labor,
> No praise too much for his lyre, his brotherly songs.
> Their hands spin more than they used; and the work he salutes
> Surpasses the lot of man.[57]

51 Quoted in ibid., 34.

52 G. Wilmanns, ed., *Corpus inscriptionum latinarum* (Berlin, 1881), 8, Nr. 2557, 295.

53 Plutarch, *Lives*, 'Camillus,' 23.

54 Polybius, *Histories*, 2.29, 6–7.

55 Kastner, *Manuel général de musique militaire*, 33.

56 Quintilian, *The Education of an Orator*, 1.10.16.

57 Seneca, *Apocolocyntosis divi Claudii* [The Pumpkinification of the Divine Claudius], 4.2.15. Tacitus, *Annals*, 14.52, says Seneca 'composed poetry more assiduously, [only] as soon as a passion for it had seized Nero.'

ENTERTAINMENT MUSIC

Aristocratic entertainment designed for larger numbers of participants must have been quite extravagant during the Empire Period. One given by Nero, as described by Tacitus, is particularly interesting as it reveals many of the characteristics of the allegoric entertainments of the later middle ages.

> Nero, to win credit for himself of enjoying nothing so much as the capital, prepared banquets in the public places, and used the whole city, so to say, as his private house. Of these entertainments the most famous for their notorious profligacy were those furnished by Tigellinus, which I will describe as an illustration, that I may not have again and again to narrate similar extravagance. He had a raft constructed on Agrippa's lake, put the guests on board and set it in motion by other vessels towing it. These vessels glittered with gold and ivory; the crews were arranged according to age and experience in vice. Birds and beasts had been procured from remote countries, and sea monsters from the ocean. On the edge of the lake were set up brothels crowded with noble ladies, and on the opposite bank were seen naked prostitutes with obscene gestures and movements. As darkness approached, all the adjacent grove and surrounding buildings resounded with song, and shone brilliantly with lights.[58]

58 Tacitus, *Annals*, 15.37.

We might expect that music was rather continuous during such large-scale entertainment occasions. This kind of continuous banquet music so annoyed the writer, Martial, that he said the best way to arrange a good banquet was to eliminate the singing of the choir and its accompaniment![59] Judging by Quintilian, perhaps part of Martial's objection lay in the low quality of the music as well. Quintilian, speaking of the bad influence of their environment on the education of children, observes,

59 Sendrey, *Music in the Social and Religious Life of Antiquity* 409.

> We have no right to be surprised. It was we that taught them: they hear us use [profane] words, they see our mistresses and minions; every dinner party is loud with foul songs, and things are presented to their eyes of which we should blush to speak.[60]

60 Quintilian, *The Education of an Orator*, 1.2.8.

Even private banquets might have such non-stop music, as is perhaps the point of a satire, 'The Banquet of Trimalchio,' by Petronius, which describes the use of music for bringing in the food, carving it, and even to provide rhythm for the cleaning of the tables. He felt he was in a theater, not a private home!

Some private entertainments at the aristocratic level were no doubt more elegant. One of the extant letters of Pliny the Younger is written to a friend who failed to appear for a private dinner. After gently scolding his friend, Pliny tells him what he missed that evening and in so doing provides us with a brief view of a more refined private entertainment.

> I had prepared, you must know, a lettuce apiece, three snails, two eggs, and a barley cake, with some sweet wine and snow (the snow most certainly I shall charge to your account, as a rarity that will not keep). Olives, beet-root, gourds, onions, and a thousand other dainties equally sumptuous. You should likewise have been entertained either with an interlude, the rehearsal of a poem, or a piece of music, whichever you preferred; or (such was my liberality) with all three.[61]

61 Letter 11, to Septitius Clarus.

The Emperor Theodosius, in 385 AD banned the sale of harp girls, as well as their use in performing for banquets.[62] One famous Greek harp girl of this time, named Leaena, which also means lioness, was a prostitute employed by the tyrants Harmodius and Aristogeiton. She was tortured to death, but refused to betray a plot to assassinate these tyrants. Consequently the Athenians honored her by commissioning Amphicrates to sculpt a statue of a lioness without a tongue.[63]

62 Sendrey, *Music in the Social and Religious Life of Antiquity*, 388. Pliny the Elder, in *Natural History*, 10.26, mentions Glauce, harp girl to King Ptolemy of Egypt, whom he says both a goose and a ram fell in love with.

There was also music used for entertainment in the games in the arena. A first-century mosaic in the amphitheater at Zliten shows a trumpet player and two cornu players performing while two gladiators engage in combat.

Horse shows were also a popular form of entertainment in the arena and these productions developed into the horse ballets of later European tradition. Pliny the Elder remarks with astonishment,

> [The horses] docility is so great that we learn that the entire cavalry of the army of Sybaris used to perform a sort of ballet to instrumental music [*symphoniae*].[64]

63 Plinty the Elder, *Natural History*, 34.19.72. In the course of his discussion of art, he also mentions a famous statue of the time called 'Tipsy Girl playing the Aulos,' by Lysippus [34.19.63], a 'Trumpet player' by Epigonus [34.19.88.] and 'Murmuring Athene,' by Ctesilaus, designed so that the dragons on her Gorgon's head reverberated to the sound of a harp [39.19.76]. Tacitus, *Annals*, 14.60, also tells of slave girls being tortured in an attempt to gain information about a slave single-pipe player implicated in a love affair.

64 Pliny the Elder, *Natural History*, 8.64.157.

Finally we have an interesting description of some sort of mechanical trumpet which played during an entertainment featuring a 'sea battle,' given by the emperor Claudius (41–54 AD). Claudius, who according to Suetonius would 'foam at the mouth and trickle at the nose; he stammered besides and his head was very shaky at all times, but especially when he made the least exertion,'[65] is further described as,

65 Suetonius, *Lives of the Caesars*, 5.30.

leaping from his throne and running along the edge of the lake with his ridiculous tottering gait, he induced them to fight, partly by threats and partly by promises. At this performance a Sicilian and a Rhodian fleet engaged, each numbering twelve triremes, and the signal was sounded on a horn by a silver Triton, which was raised from the middle of the lake by a mechanical device.[66]

66 Ibid., 5.21.

We begin our survey of the comments by philosophers of the Empire with Pliny the Elder who revived the old idea of Pythagoras of the 'music of the spheres.' He first observed that if there is such music, caused by the motion of the heavenly bodies, man cannot hear it.

> The world thus shaped then is not at rest but eternally revolves with indescribable velocity, each revolution occupying the space of 24 hours: the rising and setting of the sun have left this not doubtful. Whether the sound of this vast mass whirling in unceasing rotation is of enormous volume and consequently beyond the capacity of our ears to perceive, for my own part I cannot easily say—any more in fact than whether this is true of the tinkling of the stars that travel round with it, revolving in their own orbits; or whether it emits a sweet harmonious music that is beyond belief charming. To us who live within it the world glides silently alike by day and night.[1]

1 Pliny the Elder, *Natural History*, 2.3.

The precise theory of Pythagoras, Pliny found more entertaining than believable.

> But occasionally Pythagoras draws on the theory of music, and designates the distance between the earth and the moon as a whole tone, between Mercury and Venus the same, between her and the sun a tone and a half, between the sun and Mars a tone, between Mars and Jupiter half a tone, between Jupiter and Saturn half a tone, between Saturn and the zodiac a tone and a half; the seven tones thus producing the so-called diapason, i.e. a universal harmony; in this Saturn moves in the Dorian mode, Jupiter in the Phrygian, and similarly with the other planets—a refinement more entertaining than convincing.[2]

2 Ibid., 2.20. There are no extant writings of Pythagoras which contain this idea.

Quintilian (30–96 AD) passes on the same idea and states he is 'ready to accept the verdict of antiquity.'

> Pythagoras and his followers popularized the belief, which they no doubt had received from earlier teachers, that the universe is constructed on the same principles which were afterwards imitated in the construction of the lyre, and not content merely with emphasizing that concord of discordant elements which they style harmony, attributed a sound to the motions of the celestial bodies.[3]

3 Quintilian, *Institutio Oratoria* [The Education of an Orator], trans. H.E. Butler (London: Heinemann, 1938), 1.10.12.

After the 'music of the spheres,' earlier philosophers often turned their curiosity to the natural music of the earth, especially the music made by animals. Pliny revives a belief put forth by a number of Greek philosophers that the dolphin in particular had a natural fondness for music.

> The dolphin is an animal that is not only friendly to mankind but is also a lover of music, and it can be charmed by singing in harmony, but particularly by the sound of the water-organ.
>
> …
>
> Dolphins are obviously able to hear; for dolphins are charmed even by music, and are caught while bewildered by the sound.[4]

From the world of song birds, Pliny focuses on the nightingale for a fascinating discussion of the repertoire, technique and musical education of this bird. We believe most readers will be astonished at the vocal variety suggested here.

> Nightingales pour out a ceaseless gush of song for fifteen days and nights on end when the buds of the leaves are swelling—a bird not in the lowest rank remarkable. In the first place there is so loud a voice and so persistent a supply of breath in such a tiny little body; then there is the consummate knowledge of music in a single bird: the sound is given out with modulations, and now is drawn out into a long note with one continuous breath, now varied by managing the breath, now made staccato by checking it, or linked together by prolonging it, or carried on by holding it back; or it is suddenly lowered, and at times sinks into a mere murmur, loud, low, bass, treble, with trills, with long notes, modulated when this seems good—soprano, mezzo, baritone; and briefly all the devices in that tiny throat which human science has devised with all the elaborate mechanism of the aulos … And that no one may doubt its being a matter of science, the birds have several songs each, and not all the same but every bird songs of its own. They compete with one another, and there is clearly an animated rivalry between them; the loser often ends her life by dying, her breath giving out before her song. Other younger birds practice their music, and are given verses to imitate; the pupil listens with close attention and repeats the phrase, and the two keep silence by turns: we notice improvement in the one under instruction and a sort of criticism on the part of the instructress … Frequent cases have been seen before now of nightingales that have begun to sing when ordered, and have sung in answer to an organ, as there have been found persons who could reproduce the birds' song with an indistinguishable resemblance by

4   Pliny, *Natural History*, 9.8.25 and 50.137.

putting water into slanting reeds and breathing into the holes, or by applying some slight check with the tongue. But these exceptional and artistic trills after a fortnight gradually cease, though not in such a way that the birds could be said to be tired out or to have had enough singing; and later on when the heat has increased their note becomes entirely different, with no modulations or variations.[5]

5 Ibid., 10.43ff.

Pliny, in his encyclopedic *Natural History*, offers the following miscellaneous information: that 'melodious auloi' are made from the lotus tree;[6] that some auloi, as well as flutes, were made from a type of bamboo;[7] that some auloi were made from reeds grown on the shores of Lake Orchomenus, a type of reed which required an unusual amount of curing. Buried in this dry list of facts suddenly the phrase 'glorious music' leaps out at us, a subject we wish he had described as extensively as the details of the reeds.

6 Ibid., 3.32.106.

7 Ibid., 3.16.

These supplied the instruments for glorious music, though mention must also not be omitted of the further remarkable trouble required to grow them, so that excuse may be made for the present-day preference for musical instruments of silver. Down to the time of the aulos player Antigenides, when a simple style of music was still practiced, the reeds used to be regarded as ready for cutting after the rising of Arcturus. When thus prepared the reeds began to be fit for use a few years later, though even then the actual auloi needed maturing with a great deal of practice, and educating to sing of themselves, with the tongues pressing themselves down, which was more serviceable for the theatrical fashions then prevailing. But after variety came into fashion, and luxury even in music, the reeds began to be cut before midsummer and made ready for use in three years, their tongues being wider open to modulate the sounds, and these continue to the present day. But at that time it was firmly believed that only a tongue cut from the same reed as the pipe in each case would do, and that one taken from just above the root was suitable for a left-hand aulos and one from just below the top for a right-hand aulos; the reeds that had been washed by the waters of Cephisus itself were rated as immeasurably superior. At the present time the flutes used by the Tuscans in religious ritual are made of box-wood, but those for theatrical performances are made of lotus and asses' bones and silver.[8]

8 Ibid., 16.66.170ff.

Finally, Pliny adds the following historical attributions which he has gathered from unnamed sources available to him.

The bronze trumpet [was invented] by Pysaeus son of Tyrrhenus ... Amphion [was responsible for the invention of] music, Pan son of Mercury the flute and single aulos, Midas in Phrygia the slanted flute, Marsyas in the same nation the double aulos, Amphion the Lydian modes, Thracian Thamyras the Dorian, Marsyas of Phrygia the Phrygian, Amphion, or others say Orpheus and others Linus, the harp. Terpander first sang with seven strings, adding three to the original four, Simonides added an eighth, Timotheus a ninth. Thamyris first played the harp without using the voice, Amphion, or according to others Linus, accompanied the harp with singing; Terpander composed songs for harp and voice. Ardalus of Troezen instituted singing to the aulos.[9]

9 Ibid., 7.61.204ff.

THE PHYSIOLOGY OF AESTHETICS

The soul, a topic so widely discussed by the Greeks, is now little mentioned. Marcus Aurelius believed that man consists of,

> body, soul, intelligence: to the body belong sensations, to the soul appetites, to the intelligence principles.[10]

10 Marcus Aurelius, *Meditations*, 3.16.

In spite of the apparent separation here of soul and intelligence, a later comment suggests that both are contained in what we would call 'mind' today.

> These are the properties of the rational soul: it sees itself, analyzes itself, and makes itself such as it chooses.[11]

11 Ibid., 11.1.

Quintilian remarked on the astonishing ability of the human mind to engage in multiple actions at the same time, using the harpist for illustration.

> [Some] critics show an insufficient appreciation of the capacities of the human mind, which is so swift and nimble and versatile, that it cannot be restricted to doing one thing only, but insists on devoting its attention to several different subjects not merely in one day, but actually at one and the same time. Do not harpists simultaneously exert the memory and pay attention to the tone and inflections of the voice, while the right hand runs over certain strings and the left plucks, stops or releases others, and even the foot is employed in beating time, all these actions being performed at the same moment?[12]

12 Quintilian, *Institutio Oratoria*, 1.12.3.

We know today that part of the explanation of the division of duties by the mind, especially with regard to the duties of the separate hands, lies in the unique separate hemispheres of our brain, something unknown to early philosophers of course. But, because the left hemisphere is the rational, speaking part of our brain, and because it does not recognize the existence of the right hemisphere, there runs through nearly all cultures a preference for the right hand. The 'favorite sits on the right hand of the King' and we are not pleased to be paid a 'left-handed compliment.' This is reflected in a discussion of the origin of finger rings by Pliny the Elder, as he is disapproving of the use of gold rings as vanity. He mentions that the first such ring was worn by the mythical king Midas.

> It was the hand and what is more the left hand, that first won for gold such high esteem …

The word Pliny uses for 'left,' *sinistrae*, also suggests 'unlucky' or 'sinister,' properties sometimes associated with the mysterious, mute, right hemisphere!

The subject of the senses was given little discussion by the Roman philosophers of this period, although Pliny the Elder does make some interesting statements. First, he makes the contention that of the senses man surpasses the animals only in the sophistication of touch and taste.[13] He makes the correct assessment that the brain 'is the citadel of sense perception'[14] and contends that the brevity of life which nature has bestowed on man is actually a gift, considering that all the senses deteriorate with aging. With regard to the latter, he observes with astonishment that, 'the musician Xenophilus lived to 105 without any bodily disablement.'[15]

A topic which appears more interesting to these philosophers is emotion. First, while it is actually the face which communicates emotions, Pliny the Elder makes the mistake sometimes made by early writers that it is the eyes.

> No other part of the body supplies greater indications of the mind— this is so with all animals alike, but specially with man—that is, indications of self-restraint, mercy, pity, hatred, love, sorrow, joy. The eyes are also very varied in their look—fierce, stern, sparkling, sedate, leering, askance, downcast, kindly: in fact the eyes are the abode of the mind. They glow, stare, moisten, wink; from them flows the tear of compassion, when we kiss them we seem to reach the mind itself, they are the source of tears and of the stream that bedews the cheek. What is the nature of this moisture that at a

13 Pliny, Natural History, 10.88.

14 Ibid., 11.49.135.

15 Ibid., 7.50.169.

moment of sorrow flows so copiously and so promptly? Or where
is it in the remaining time? In point of fact it is the mind that is
the real instrument of sight and of observation; the eyes act as a
sort of vessel receiving and transmitting the visible portion of the
consciousness. This explains why deep thought blinds the eyes by
withdrawing the vision inward.[16]

16   Ibid., 11.54.146.

We have mentioned in a previous chapter the fact that the Roman
pre-Christian philosophers were uncomfortable with the topic of
the emotions and, as Quintilian points out, many of them regarded
'susceptibility to emotion as a vice.'[17] In remarks directed toward
lawyers, he uses a phrase which probably best reflects the position
of early philosophers, that the emotions 'disturb the mind,' meaning the *rational* mind.

17   Quintilian, *Institutio
Oratoria*, 6.7.

There have been certain writers of no small authority who have held
that the sole duty of the orator was to instruct: in their view appeals
to the emotions were to be excluded for two reasons, first on the
ground that all disturbance of the mind was a fault, and secondly
that it was wrong to distract the judge from the truth by exciting
his pity, bringing influence to bear, and the like.[18]

18   Ibid., Preface to book 5.

Pliny the Younger agrees that it is the duty of the orator to
restrain, rather than excite, the emotions, however he does add
the interesting suggestion that it is through the emotions that one
must appeal to men to become teachers.

The pleasures of the senses are so far from wanting the oratorical
arts to recommend them that we stand in need of all the powers
of eloquence to moderate and restrain rather than stir up their
influence. But the work of getting anybody to cheerfully undertake
the monotony and drudgery of education must be effected not by
pay merely, but by a skillfully worked-up appeal to the emotions
as well.[19]

19   Letter 5, to Pompeius Saturninus.

Quintilian, on the other hand, believed the orator must excite
the emotions of the listener if he is to be successful. He elaborated
his contention in a discussion of the difference between *pathos*
and *ethos*. This is a particularly valuable passage because his discussion of various emotions and his comments on the expression
of emotions also apply to musical performance as well. He begins
by attempting to convey the meaning of these Greek terms to his
Latin readers.

Emotions however, as we learn from ancient authorities, fall into two classes; the one is called *pathos* by the Greeks and is rightly and correctly expressed in Latin by *adfectus* (emotion): the other is called *ethos*, a word for which in my opinion Latin has no equivalent: it is however rendered by *mores* (morals) and consequently the branch of philosophy known as *ethics* is styled *moral* philosophy by us. But close consideration of the nature of the subject leads me to think that in this connection it is not so much *morals* in general that is meant as certain peculiar aspects; for the term *morals* includes every attitude of the mind. The more cautious writers have preferred to give the sense of the term rather than to translate it into Latin. They therefore explain *pathos* as describing the more violent emotions and *ethos* as designating those which are calm and gentle: in the one case the passions are violent, in the other subdued, the former command and disturb, the latter persuade and induce a feeling of goodwill.[20]

20 Quintilian, *Institutio Oratoria*, 6.2.8 through 36.

He agrees with some authors who maintain that while the *ethos* is continuous, *pathos* is more momentary in character. On the other hand, *pathos* and *ethos* are sometimes of the same nature, differing only in degree.

> Love for instance comes under the head of *pathos*, affection of *ethos*; sometimes however they differ, a distinction which is important for the peroration, since *ethos* is generally employed to calm the storm aroused by *pathos*.

Quintilian now goes into greater detail in defining *ethos*, with regard to how it is applied by the orator–lawyer. The first kind of *ethos* is calm, mild, ingratiating and courteous, intended to excite pleasure and affection in the listener. This kind of *ethos* is appropriate where the persons are intimately connected and 'the speaker wishes to display no anger or hatred.'

Another type is represented by cases dealing with father and son, guardian and ward, or husband and wife. Here the *ethos* must convey the seriousness of the wrongdoing, but not indicate dislike or loss of love. But when an old man has been insulted by a youthful stranger, or a man of high rank by his inferior, then the orator should be 'really deeply moved.'

Closely related, though less violent, is the emotion demonstrated when 'we ask pardon for the errors of the young, or apologize for some youthful amour.' Here one may sometimes use 'gentle raillery' or 'the skillful exercise of feigned emotion or the employment of irony' in making apologies. From the same source comes 'a more powerful method of exciting hatred, when by a feigned submission to our opponents we pass silent censure on their violence.'

The emotion of love and longing for our friends, he calls one of an intermediate character, being stronger than *ethos* and weaker than *pathos*. Also, since *ethos* denotes moral character, Quintilian says it must therefore necessarily be employed when addressing 'rustics, misers, cowards and superstitious persons.'

Finally, if the speaker is to make use of *ethos*, it goes without saying that he himself must be a man of good character.

> For the orator who gives the impression of being a bad man while he is speaking, is actually speaking badly, since his words seem to be insincere owing to the absence of *ethos* which would otherwise have revealed itself.

Now Quintilian defines *pathos* in more detail, beginning with an analogy from the theater.

> The *pathos* of the Greeks, which we correctly translate by *emotion*, is of a different character, and I cannot better indicate the nature of the difference than by saying that *ethos* rather resembles comedy and *pathos* tragedy. For *pathos* is almost entirely concerned with anger, dislike, fear, hatred and pity …
>
> I wish to point out that fear is of two kinds, that which we feel and that which we cause in others. Similarly there are two kinds of *invidia* (hatred, envy), to which the two adjectives *invidus* (envious) and *invidiosus* (invidious, hateful) correspond. The first supplies an epithet for persons, the second for things, and it is in this latter connection that the orator's task is even more onerous. For though some things are hateful in themselves such as parricide, murder, poisoning, other things have to be made to seem hateful.

The orator employs *pathos*, or emotion, when he wishes to create empathy in the listener.

> The aim of appeals to the emotion is not merely to show the bitter and grievous nature of ills that actually are so, but also to make ills which are usually regarded as tolerable seem unendurable, as for instance when we represent insulting words as inflicting more grievous injury than an actual blow or represent disgrace as being worse than death.

But how does the orator do this? Quintilian now tells us that he will reveal to us 'secret principles of this art.' What follows is a precursor of Stanislavsky's 'method acting,' through which one learns to re-experience the emotions one has to convey from the stage. Among the performing arts only musicians are spared such processes, for in music the emotions expressed *are* the real ones. Nevertheless, Quintilian's discussion should remind musicians that true emotional communication must be founded on genuine emotions.

> The prime essential for stirring the emotions of others is, in my opinion, first to feel those emotions oneself. It is sometimes positively ridiculous to counterfeit grief, anger and indignation, if we content ourselves with accommodating our words and looks and make no attempt to adapt our own feelings to the emotions to be expressed. What other reason is there for the eloquence with which mourners express their grief, or for the fluency which anger lends even to the uneducated, save the fact that their minds are stirred to power by the depth and sincerity of their feelings? Consequently, if we wish to give our words the appearance of sincerity, we must assimilate ourselves to the emotions of those who are genuinely so affected, and our eloquence must spring from the same feeling that we desire to produce in the mind of the judge. Will he grieve who can find no trace of grief in the words with which I seek to move him to grief? Will he be angry, if the orator who seeks to kindle his anger shows no sign of laboring under the emotion which he demands from his audience? Will he shed tears if the pleader's eyes are dry? It is utterly impossible …
>
> Accordingly, the first essential is that those feelings should prevail with us that we wish to prevail with the judge, and that we should be moved ourselves before we attempt to move others. But how are we to generate these emotions in ourselves, since emotion is not in our own power? I will try to explain as best I may. There are certain experiences which the Greeks call *φαντασίας*, and the Romans *visions*, whereby things absent are presented to our imagination with such extreme vividness that they seem actually to be before our very eyes. It is the man who is really sensitive to such impressions who will have the greatest power over the emotions … It is a power which all may readily acquire if they will.

Finally, Quintilian points to some examples in the theater of those who were skillful in this kind of emotional communication and attributes his own fame to his ability to do this.

Again, when we desire to awaken pity, we must actually believe that the ills of which we complain have befallen our own selves, and must persuade our minds that this is really the case. We must identify ourselves with the persons of whom we complain that they have suffered grievous, unmerited and bitter misfortune, and must plead their case and for a brief period feel their suffering as though it were our own, while our words must be such as we should use if we stood in their shoes. I have often seen actors, both in tragedy and comedy, leave the theater still drowned in tears after concluding the performance of some moving role ...

Suppose we are impersonating an orphan, a shipwrecked man, or one in grave peril. What profit is there in assuming such a role unless we also assume the emotions which it involves? I have thought it necessary not to conceal these considerations from my reader, since they have contributed to the acquisition of such reputation for talent as I possess or once possessed. I have frequently been so much moved while speaking, that I have not merely been wrought upon to tears, but have turned pale and shown all the symptoms of genuine grief.

In another place, Quintilian explains that the ability of the orator to communicate emotions to the audience depends on the use of both the voice and the body. Here he recommends to the orator the study of music for learning how this is done.

Let us discuss the advantages which our future orator may reasonably expect to derive from the study of Music.

Music has two modes of expression in the voice and in the body; for both voice and body require to be controlled by appropriate rules. Aristoxenus divides music, in so far as it concerns the voice, into *rhythm* and *melody*, the one consisting in measure, the latter in sound and song. Now I ask you whether it is not absolutely necessary for the orator to be acquainted with all these methods of expression which are concerned firstly with gesture, secondly with the arrangement of words and thirdly with the inflections of the voice, of which a great variety are required for law practice. Otherwise we must assume that structure and the euphonious combination of sounds are necessary only for poetry, lyric and otherwise, but superfluous in law, or that unlike music, oratory has no interest in the variation of arrangement and sound to suit the demands of the case. But eloquence does vary both tone and rhythm, expressing sublime thoughts with elevation, pleasing thoughts with sweetness, and ordinary with gentle utterance, and in every expression of its art is in sympathy with the emotions of which it is the mouthpiece. It is by the raising, lowering or inflection of the voice that the orator stirs the emotions of his hearers, and the measure, if I may repeat the term, of voice or phrase differs according as we wish to rouse the indignation or the pity of the judge. For, as we know, different emotions are roused even by the various musical instruments, which are incapable of reproducing speech. Further the motion of the body must be suitable and becoming, or as the Greeks call it *eurythmic*, and this can only be secured by the study of music.[21]

21 Ibid., 1.10.22.

Pliny the Younger also mentions the importance of the orator having the ability to both inform and affect the emotions of the listener and cites an orator, Isaeus, in whom he found this ability.

In a word, he teaches, entertains, and affects you; and you are at a loss to decide which of the three he does best.[22]

22 Letter 18, to Nepos.

ON AESTHETICS

None of the philosophers of this period have contributed a substantial discussion to the definition of art. We can extract some isolated principles found embedded in other discussions. Quintilian, in a defense of oratory as an art, states two general properties of art.[23] First, all art must be based on some form of subject matter. Second, since all art is based on direct perception, art can never deal in false ideas.

23 Quintilian, Institutio Oratoria, 2.17.17.

Marcus Aurelius refers to the Greek idea that art should imitate nature, adding that art will always be something less than nature.

There is no nature which is inferior to art, for the arts imitate the natures of things. But if this is so, that nature which is the most perfect and the most comprehensive of all natures, cannot fall short of the skill of art. Now all arts do the inferior things for the sake of the superior; therefore the universal nature does too.[24]

24 Marcus Aurelius, Meditations, 11.10.

With regard to the repertoire heard in artistic performances, two philosophers remark on the importance of variety. Marcus Aurelius, for example, wrote,

As it happens to you in the amphitheater and such places, that the continual sight of the same things and the uniformity makes the spectacle wearisome.[25]

25 Ibid., 6.46.

The poet Juvenal found formal poetry reading on stage to be particularly lacking in variety.

> Must I *always* be stuck in the audience at these poetry-read-
> ings, never
> Up on the platform myself, taking it out on Cordus
> For the times he's bored me to death with ranting speeches ...
> The stale themes are bellowed daily.[26]

26 Juvenal, *Satire I.*

Pliny the Younger also mentions a similar concern regarding the need for variety.

> Nothing, in my opinion, gives a more amiable and becoming grace
> to our studies, as well as manners, than to temper the serious with
> the gay, lest the former should degenerate into melancholy, and
> the latter run up into levity. Upon this plan it is that I diversify my
> graver works with compositions of a lighter nature.[27]

27 Letter 94, to Arrianus.

Marcus Aurelius proposes the contention that every work of art must have its own inherent value, which is neither increased nor diminished by praise or criticism.

> Everything which is in any way beautiful is beautiful in itself, and
> terminates in itself, not having praise as part of itself. Neither worse
> then nor better is a thing made by being praised. I affirm this also
> of the things which are called beautiful by the vulgar; for example,
> material things and works of art. That which is really beautiful has
> no need of anything; not more than law, not more than truth, not
> more than benevolence or modesty. Which of these things is beauti-
> ful because it is praised, or spoiled by being blamed?[28]

28 Marcus Aurelius,
   Meditations, 4.20.

Regarding criticism, Pliny the Elder tells two nice anecdotes. One is of a painter who, weary of criticism, added a line of poetry under one of his paintings to the effect that it is easier to complain about his work than to copy it. The other story is about another painter who made the habit of standing behind his paintings when they were exhibited for the first time, in order to hear the com-ments of the public. He professed to profit from these remarks as he considered the public to be a more observant critic than him-self. On one occasion when he heard a shoemaker object to some minor detail of a shoe he had painted, the artist actually changed the painting. The next day, hiding behind the painting again, the artist heard the same shoemaker taking pride that his criticism had resulted in the improvement of the shoe in the painting and then elevate his criticism to the leg in the painting. The artist now jumped out from behind the painting, indignantly rebuking him, saying a shoemaker's criticism should not go beyond the sandal—a remark which Pliny says became a proverb![29]

An occasional reference betrays some doubt as to the general value of art itself. Marcus Aurelius, for example, on one occasion referred to plays given in the theater as, 'idle business.'[30] Pliny the Elder objected to those who collect, and pay dear prices for, art objects for the home. Why, he asks, do we value these so highly when we can't even see them half the time?

> When we hear of the prices paid for these vessels, when we see the masses of marble that are being conveyed or hauled, we should each of us reflect, and at the same time think how much more happily many people live without them. That men should do such things, or rather endure them, for no purpose or pleasure except to lie amid spotted marbles, just as if these delights were not taken from us by the darkness of night, which is half our life's span![31]

ON PERFORMANCE AND THE AUDIENCE

Quintilian has contributed an interesting division of art, in the most general sense of the word, into three categories.

> Some arts are based on examination, that is to say on the knowledge and proper appreciation of things, as for instance astronomy, which demands no action, but is content to understand the subject of its study: such arts are called *theoretical*. Others again are concerned with action: this is their end, which is realized in action, so that, the action once performed, nothing more remains to do: these arts we style *practical*, and dancing will provide us with an example. Thirdly, there are others which consist in producing a certain result and achieve their purpose in the completion of a visible task: such we style *productive*, and painting may be quoted as an illustration.[32]

In another place he recognizes that the 'practical' arts must have a vehicle of performance, which he calls the artistic 'instrument.' He adds the important observation that it is not 'Art' which requires the instrument, but the artist.[33] He also reveals that for himself it is not the public performances which lead him to 'self-

29 Pliny, *Natural History*, 35.36.63 and 85.

30 Ibid., 7.3.

31 Pliny, *Natural History*, 36.1.3.

32 Quintilian, *Institutio Oratoria*, 2.18.

33 Ibid., 2.21.24.

contemplation,' rather 'the highest of all pleasures is that which we derive from private study.'[34]

34   Ibid., 2.18.4.

Pliny the Younger maintained the opposite view. He believed that reading a poem was understandable only if you did not have the opportunity of *'hearing* eloquence.' To make his point that it is performance which brings a work to life, he quotes a proverb known to his generation:

35   Letter 18, to Nepos.

The living voice is that which sways the soul.[35]

In one letter, Pliny voices his support of public performance in spite of the audience which he describes as being very inattentive.

This year has produced a plentiful crop of poets: during the whole month of April scarcely a day has passed on which we have not been entertained with the recital of some poem. It is a pleasure to me to find that a taste for polite literature still exists, and that men of genius *do* come forward and make themselves known, notwithstanding the lazy attendance they got for their pains. The greater part of the audience sit in the lounging-places, gossip away their time there, and are perpetually sending to inquire whether the author has made his entrance yet, whether he has got through the preface, or whether he has almost finished the piece. Then at length they saunter in with an air of the greatest indifference, nor do they condescend to stay through the recital, but go out before it is over, some slyly and stealthily, others again with perfect freedom and unconcern. And yet our fathers can remember how Claudius Caesar walking one day in the palace, and hearing a great shouting, inquired the cause: and being informed that Nonianus was reciting a composition of his, went immediately to the place, and agreeable surprised the author with his presence. But now, were one to bespeak the attendance of the idlest man living, and remind him of the appointment ever so often, or ever so long beforehand; either he would not come at all, or if he did would grumble about having 'lost a day!' for no other reason but because he had *not* lost it. So much the more do those authors deserve our encouragement and applause who have resolution to persevere in their studies, and to read out their compositions in spite of this apathy or arrogance on the part of their audience.[36]

36   Letter 9, to Socius Senecio.

Aside from the etiquette of the audience which he has objected to, Pliny was nevertheless intrigued by the influence exerted by the large audience, which may in fact consist of so many individuals who may know, individually, very little.

There is something even in a low and vulgar audience that strikes one with awe. And if you suspect you are not well received at the first opening of your speech, do you not find all your energy relaxed, and feel yourself ready to give way? The reason I imagine to be that there is a certain weight of collective opinion in a multitude, and although each individual judgment is, perhaps, of little value, yet when united it becomes considerable. Accordingly, Pomponius Secundus, the famous tragic poet, whenever some very intimate friend and he differed about the retaining or rejecting anything in his writings, used to say, 'I appeal to the people'; and thus, by their silence or applause, adopted either his own or his friend's opinion; such was the deference he paid to the popular judgment![37]

37 Letter 79, to Celer.

Pliny himself preferred to read his poems only in private, believing a select audience would give him more accurate feedback regarding his work.

I am not in the habit of reciting my works publicly, but only to a select circle, whose presence I respect, and whose judgment I value; in a word, whose opinions I attend to as if they were so many individuals I had separately consulted, at the same time that I stand in as much awe before them as I should before the most numerous assembly.[38]

38 Ibid.

In another letter where he discusses these private recitals, Pliny speaks of his ability to read the *real* reactions of his friends.

Although they should not declare their meaning in express terms, yet the expression of the face, the movement of the head, the eyes, the motion of a hand, a whisper, or even silence itself will easily distinguish their real opinion from the language of politeness.[39]

39 Letter 50, to Titius Aristo.

We can gain some insight into how Pliny arrived at his preference for private recital through some additional comments in his correspondence. First, it was his belief that the value of one's work should not require the approval of the audience. Second, it seems to have been his experience that regardless of how well you do before the audience, there will be inevitable criticism.

I am very sensible how much nobler it is to place the reward of virtue in the silent approbation of one's own breast than in the applause of the world. Glory ought to be the consequence, not the motive, of our actions; and although it happens not to attend the worthy deed, yet it is by no means the less fair for having missed the applause it deserved. But the world is apt to suspect that those who celebrate their own beneficent acts performed them for no other motive than to have the pleasure of extolling them. Thus, the splendor of an action which would have been deemed illustrious if related by another is totally extinguished when it becomes the subject of one's own applause. Such is the disposition of mankind, if they cannot blast the action, they will censure its display; and whether you do what does not deserve particular notice, or set forth yourself what does, either way you incur reproach.[40]

40 Letter 5, to Pompeius Saturninus.

His distrust of the large audience was no doubt increased by the existence of the claque, persons hired to applaud. One found the claque in all public performances, but here Pliny focuses on those found even in law courts.

As things are now, since every fence of modesty and decorum is broken down, and all distinctions are leveled and confounded, the present young generation, so far from waiting to be introduced, break in of their own free will. The audience at their heels are fit attendants upon such orators; a low rabble of hired mercenaries, supplied by contract. They get together in the middle of the court, where the dole is dealt round to them as openly as if they were in a dining-room: and at this noble price they run from court to court. The Greeks have an appropriate name in their language for this sort of people, importing that they are applauders by profession, and we stigmatize them with the opprobrious title of table-flatterers: yet the dirty business alluded to increases every day. It was only yesterday two of my domestic officers, mere strippings, were *hired* to cheer somebody or other, at three denarii apiece: that is what the highest eloquence goes for. Upon these terms we fill as many benches as we please, and gather a crowd; this is how those rending shouts are raised, as soon as the individual standing up in the middle of the ring gives the signal. For, you must know, these honest fellows, who understand nothing of what is said, or, if they did, could not hear it, would be at a loss without a signal, how to time their applause: for many of them don't hear a syllable,[41] and are as noisy as any of the rest. If, at any time, you should happen to be passing by when the court is sitting, and feel at all interested to know how any speaker is acquitting himself, you have no occasion to give yourself the trouble of getting up on the judge's platform, no need to listen; it is easy enough to find out, for you may be quite sure that he that gets the most applause deserves it the least.[42]

41 Pliny the Elder, *Natural History,* 11.62.270, briefly mentions acoustics, observing that the voice is absorbed by 'sawdust or sand that is thrown down on the floor of the theater orchestras, and similarly in a place surrounded by rough walls, and it is also deadened by empty casks.'

42 Letter 22, to Maximus.

Finally, Pliny offers an interesting view of stage fright.

What Cicero says of composing will, in my opinion, holds true of the dread we have of the public: 'Fear is the most rigid critic imaginable.' The very thought of reciting, the very entrance into an assembly, and the agitated concern when one is there; each of these circumstances tends to improve and perfect an author's performance.[43]

43 Letter 79, to Celer.

ON ENTERTAINMENT

As the Roman Empire grew in wealth and power there seems to have been a corresponding trend among many of the aristocratic class to look to lower forms of entertainment for amusement rather than the arts. Pliny the Elder outlines this decay and mourns its impact on society.

The fact is that other customs have come into vogue, and the minds of men are occupied about other matters: the only arts cultivated are the arts of avarice. Previously a nation's sovereignty was self-contained, and consequently the people's genius was also circumscribed; and so a certain barrenness of fortune made it a necessity to exercise the gifts of the mind, and kings innumerable received the homage of the arts, and put these riches in the front place when displaying their resources, believing that by the arts they could prolong their immortality. This was the reason why the rewards of life and also its achievements were then so abundant. But later generations have been positively handicapped by the expansion of the world and by our multiplicity of resources. After senators began to be selected and judges appointed on the score of wealth, and wealth became the sole adornment of magistrate and military commander, after lack of children to succeed one began to occupy the place of highest influence and power, and the legacy-hunting ranked as the most profitable profession, and the only delights consisted in ownership, the true prizes of life went to ruin, and all the arts that derived their name 'liberal' from liberty, the supreme good, fell into the opposite class, and servility began to be the sole means of advancement … The consequence is, I protest, that pleasure has begun to live and life itself has ceased.[44]

44 Pliny the Elder, *Natural History*, 14.1.5.

The kinds of public entertainment which had become popular at this time are described by Pliny the Younger in a letter to a correspondent in which he maintains his complete indifference to these amusements.

> I have spent these several days past, in reading and writing, with the most pleasing tranquility imaginable. You will ask, 'How that can possibly be in the midst of Rome?' It was the time of celebrating the Circensian games; an entertainment for which I have not the least taste. They have no novelty, no variety to recommend them, nothing, in short, one would wish to see twice. It does the more surprise me therefore that so many thousand people should be possessed with the childish passion of desiring so often to see a parcel of horses gallop, and men standing upright in their chariots. If, indeed, it were the swiftness of the horses, or the skill of the men that attracted them, there might be some pretense of reason for it. But it is the *dress* they like; it is the dress that takes their fancy. And if, in the midst of the course and contest, the different parties were to change colors, their different partisans would change sides, and instantly desert the very same men and horses whom just before they were eagerly following with their eyes, as far as they could see, and shouting out their names with all their might. Such mighty charms, such wondrous power reside in the color of a paltry tunic! And this not only with the common crowd (more contemptible than the dress they espouse), but even with serious-thinking people. When I observe such men thus insatiably fond of so silly, so low, so uninteresting, so common an entertainment, I congratulate myself on my indifference to these pleasures.[45]

For Pliny, the ideal form of entertainment was something quite different, something much more enlightening. He had in mind short and 'sprightly' poems which he called, 'poetical amusements.'

> It is surprising how much the mind is enlivened and refreshed by these little poetical compositions, as they turn upon love, hatred, satire, tenderness, politeness, and everything, in short, that concerns life and the affairs of the world.[46]

Quintilian also pointed to the theater as a means of 'relaxation from toil.'[47] In this regard, however, it should be mentioned that Marcus Aurelius lamented that the ancient theater was characterized by Tragedy, which instructed men through the depiction of moral failure on the stage. Old Comedy he says also had some educational value, primarily with regard to quality of speech.

45 Letter 97, to Calvisius.

46 Letter 76, to Tuscus.

47 Quintilian, *Institutio Oratoria*, 3.8.29.

But, Middle Comedy, he regrets has 'gradually sunk down into a mere mimic artifice.' He admits there are some good writers among the contemporary playwrights, but, he wonders, 'What is its purpose?'[48]

48   Marcus Aurelius, *Meditations*, 11.6.

ON MUSIC EDUCATION

The only philosopher of this period who devotes significant discussion to music education is Quintilian. It is, however, not only a fascinating discussion, but one which indicates that knowledge of the Greek's emphasis on this area was not unknown to the Romans. It is a review of that tradition which begins his discussion.[49]

49   Quintilian, *Institutio Oratoria*, 1.10.9ff.

> For myself I should be ready to accept the verdict of antiquity. Who is ignorant of the fact that music was in ancient times the object not merely of intense study but of veneration: in fact Orpheus and Linus, to mention no others, were regarded as uniting the roles of musician, poet and philosopher. Both were of divine origin, while the former, because by the marvel of his music he soothed the savage breast, is recorded to have drawn after him not merely beasts of the wild, but rocks and trees. So too Timagenes asserts that music is the oldest of the arts related to literature, a statement which is confirmed by the testimony of the greatest poets in whose songs we read that the praise of heroes and gods were sung to the music of the lyre at the feasts of kings ...
>
> There can in any case be no doubt that some of those men whose wisdom is a household word have been earnest students of music: Pythagoras for instance ...
>
> But why speak only of the philosophers, whose master, Socrates, did not blush to receive instruction in playing the lyre even when far advanced in years? It is recorded that the greatest generals played on the lyre and the aulos, and that the armies of Sparta were fired to martial ardor by the strains of music. And what else is the function of the horns and trumpets attached to our legions? The louder the concert of their notes, the greater is the glorious supremacy of our arms over all the nations of the earth. It was not therefore without reason that Plato regarded the knowledge of music as necessary to his ideal statesman or politician, as he calls him; while the leaders even of that school, which in other respects is the strictest and most severe of all schools of philosophy, held that the wise man might well devote some of his attention to such studies. Lycurgus himself, the founder of the stern laws of Sparta, approved of the training supplied by music.

In this study we have followed the close relationship between literature and music in the ancient Greek rhapsodists and lyric poets of both Greece and Rome. Quintilian now turns to this relationship between music and literature. He also reminds his reader that the most ancient of Romans also emphasized music.

> Archytas and Euenus held that [letters] are subordinate to [music], while we know that the same instructors were employed for the teaching of both from Sophron, a writer of farces, it is true, but so highly esteemed by Plato, that he is believed to have had Sophron's works under his pillow on his deathbed: the same fact is proved by the case of Eupolis, who makes Prodamus teach both music and literature, and whose Maricas, who was none other than Hyperbolus in disguise asserts that he knows nothing of music but letters. Aristophanes again in more than one of his plays shows that boys were trained in music from remote antiquity, while in the *Hypobolimaeus* of Menander an old man, when a father claims his son from him, gives an account of all expenses incurred on behalf of the boy's education and states that he has paid out large sums to musicians and geometricians. From the importance thus given to music also originated the custom of taking a lyre round the company after dinner, and when on such an occasion Themistocles confessed that he could not play, his education was (to quote Cicero) 'regarded as imperfect.' Even at the banquets of our own forefathers it was the custom to introduce the aulos and lyre, and even the hymn of the Salii has its tune. These practices were instituted by King Numa and clearly prove that not even those whom we regard as rude warriors, neglected the study of music, at least in so far as the resources of that age allowed.

He concludes his introduction by suggesting that the importance of music is so universally understood that he is fearful that in saying too much he risks the impression that the idea needs defense. These comments are particularly interesting in their suggestion that music education was much more the norm in Roman education than extant literature suggests.

> If there were anything novel in my insistence on the study of music, I should have to treat the matter at greater length. But in the view of the fact that the study of music has, from those remote times when Chiron taught Achilles down to our own day, continued to be studied by all except those who have a hatred for any regular course of study, it would be a mistake to seem to cast any doubt upon its value by showing an excessive zeal in its defense.

But if music were so fundamental to education as he suggests, Quintilian was nevertheless worried by the implications of the changes in musical style familiar to him. In this passage he also gives several interesting examples of the power of music over behavior.

> I think I ought to be more emphatic than I have been in stating that the music which I desire to see taught is not our modern music, which has been emasculated by the lascivious melodies of our effeminate stage and has to no small extent destroyed such manly vigor as we still possessed. No, I refer to the music of old which was employed to sing the praises of brave men and was sung by the brave themselves. I will have none of your psalteries and viols, that are unfit even for the use of a modest girl. Give me the knowledge of the principles of music, which have power to excite or assuage the emotions of mankind. We are told that Pythagoras on one occasion, when some young men were led astray by their passions to commit an outrage on a respectable family, calmed them by ordering the aulos player to change her strain to a spondaic meter, while Chrysippus selects a special melody to be used by nurses to entice their little charges to sleep. Further I may point out that among the fictitious themes employed in declamation is one, doing no little credit to its author's learning, in which it is supposed that an aulos player is accused of manslaughter because he had played a tune in the Phrygian mode as an accompaniment to a sacrifice, with the result that the person officiating went mad and flung himself over a precipice.

In another place, Quintilian makes the curious statement,

> It is held that schools corrupt the morals. It is true that this is sometimes the case.[50]

50 Ibid., 1.2.4.

It is perhaps in this light that he expresses concern over the types of poetry introduced in school.

> The reading of tragedy also is useful, and lyric poets will provide nourishment for the mind, provided not merely that the authors be carefully selected, but also the passages from their works which are to be read. For the Greek lyric poets are often licentious and even in Horace there are passages which I should be unwilling to explain to a class. Elegiacs, however, more especially erotic elegy, and hendecasyllables, which are merely sections of Sotadean verse, should be entirely banished, if possible; if not absolutely banished, they should be reserved for pupils of a less impressionable age.[51]

51 Ibid., 1.8.6.

While we have only hints of general public education in music for children, one can assume that there was no lack of education for those aspiring to be professional artists. As much is suggested in a comment by Pliny the Elder, who expresses a sense of surprise in mentioning a sculptor named Silanion and the

remarkable fact [that] he became famous without having had any teacher.[52]

52 Pliny the Elder, *Natural History*, 34.19.51.

It appears that some poetry of the last period of ancient Rome was still considered lyric poetry—poetry to be sung to the accompaniment of the lyre. Indeed, Quintilian not only asks, 'Can the lyric poets be read without [knowledge of music],' but even suggests that orators who read other kinds of poetry cannot do so without a knowledge of music.[1] Other Roman writers of this period make the same point. Pliny the Younger (62–113 AD) mentions a favorite performer who 'sings my verses, adapting them to her lyre,'[2] and the lyric poet, Calpurnius Siculus (ca. 50 AD), assigns these lines to a character:

> I've long been practicing a song to disarm Phyllis.
> Perhaps by hearing verses she can be brought round,
> For she has always praised my poetry to the skies.[3]

It is also evident from Pliny's letters that there was a certain repertoire of lyric poetry which was known and circulated. Pliny mentions praise for the contemporary lyric poet, Spurinna, whose work he calls 'so wonderfully soft, sweet, and gay.'[4] In a letter to this same poet, he mentions Calpurnius Piso, whose poems he found, 'tender, sweet, and flowing.'[5]

The works of Virgil, of the previous century, seem to still be widely known and admired at this time. Pliny mentions a lawyer who was so fond of Virgil that he celebrated his birthday on the same scale as his own and visited his tomb as if it were a temple.[6] Pliny's uncle, Pliny the Elder (23–79 AD), in his *Natural History*, which is really a virtual encyclopedia, mentions that Virgil's will called for the burning of all his poems, but the will was overridden by Augustus.[7]

The works of the Greek lyric poets were still known as well. In a list of 'honors class—list of geniuses,' Pliny the Elder places Homer at the top of his list, followed by the lyric poets of Greece, Pindar and Archilochus, among others.[8] Tacitus even mentions a law case in which the Lacedaemonians were attempting to regain property taken by Philip of Macedonia and the repertoire of these poets was given as evidence of prior ownership.[9]

1 Quintilian, *Institutio Oratoria* [The Education of the Orator], 1.10.29.

2 Letter to Calpurnia Hispulla, 4.19, in *The Letters of The Younger Pliny*, trans. Betty Radice (New York: Penguin Books, 1969), 126. There may have also been some trace of the ancient Greek rhapsodist tradition of sung-speech still in evidence. Pliny, in letter 22, objects to some formal speakers, lawyers, who to engage the audience use a 'sing-song' style of speaking, to which Pliny adds you might as well add cymbals and drums!

3 Calpurnius Siculus, *Eclogue III*, 40.

4 Letter 26, to Calvisius.

5 Letter 55, to Spurinna.

6 Letter 29, to Caninius Rafus.

7 Pliny the Elder, *Natural History*, trans. Harris Rackham (Cambridge: Harvard University Press, 1942), 7.30.114. Tacitus, in a *Dialogue on Oratory*, 13, also mentions the preference of Augustus for Virgil, as well as reports of theater audiences who 'rose in a body and did homage to the poet.'

8 Ibid., 7.29. In a list (Ibid., 7.39.129) of 'the highest salary paid to a person who was a former slave,' Pliny unfortunately mentions no musicians, but cites the famous actor, Roscius, who he says made 500,000 sesterces in a year. This, which we take to be a large sum of money, pales in comparison to a eunuch, Paezon, who was purchased for 50,000,000 sesterces. A sum which, Pliny observes, 'was the price of lust and not of beauty.'

9 Tacitus, *The Annals*, 4.43.

A reference by this same Pliny to strange music heard on Mt. Atlas reminds us that the Greek gods and myths, in this case Pan, remained a source of inspiration for the Roman lyric poets. Pliny describes this African mountain as follows:

> It is said that in the day-time none of its inhabitants are seen, and that all is silent with a terrifying silence like that of the desert, so that a speechless awe creeps into the hearts of those who approach it, and also a dread of the peak that soars above the clouds and reaches the neighborhood of the moon's orb; also that at night this peak flashes with frequent fires and swarms with the wanton gambols of Goat-Pans and Satyrs, and echoes with the music of auloi and pan-pipes and the sound of drums and cymbals.[10]

Seneca (3 BC – 65 AD) mentions Phoebus [Apollo] with his 'unequal pipes' [panpipes][11] and the frequently told tale of Orpheus using music to conquer nature.

> Orpheus born of the melodious Muse, whose plectrum evoked chords at which torrents halted and winds fell silent, at whose music the birds left off their song and with the whole woodland attending followed the singer.[12]

Lucian of Samosata (b. ca. 125 AD) creates a fictional banquet of the gods, during which,

> Apollo harped, Silenus danced his wild measures, the Muses uprose and sang to us from Hesiod's Birth of Gods, and the first of Pindar's odes.[13]

It is also evident that artists and their work, then as now, were somewhat on the periphery of the regular society. In a letter of Pliny the Younger, we learn of an occasion when he recited some of his poetry in a private home and was criticized by some present for spending his time, as a public person,[14] on such pursuits. It is revealing, in the extent that he goes to in his response, that he suggests that it is okay to enjoy lighter literature.

> Among the many agreeable and obliging instances I have received of your friendship, your not concealing from me the long conversations which lately took place at your house concerning my verses, and the various judgments passed upon them is by no means the least. There were some, it seems, who did not disapprove of my poems in themselves, but at the same time censured me in a free

10 Ibid., 5.1.5ff.

11 Seneca, *Phaedra* or *Hippolytus*. Phoebus is mentioned again in *Oedipus*, 494.

12 Seneca, *Medea*, 620, also 350.

13 Lucian, *Icaromenippus*.

14 He was a praetor under Domitian and a consul and governor under Trajan.

and friendly way, for employing myself in composing and reciting them. I am so far, however, from desiring to extenuate the charge that I willingly acknowledge myself still more deserving of it, and confess that I sometimes amuse myself with writing verses of the gayer sort. I compose comedies, divert myself with pantomimes, read the lyric poets, and enter into the spirit of the most wanton muse, besides that, I indulge myself sometimes in laughter, mirth, and frolic, and, to sum up very kind of innocent relaxation in one word, *I am a man.*[15]

15 Letter 50, to the Emperor Trajan.

Tacitus, in a discussion in which he hopes to dissuade a young man from choosing a career as an artist, over law, provides us with an interesting first-hand view of the social difficulties of the artist at this time. The poet, he says,

with the labor of a whole year, through entire days and the best part of nights, he has hammered out, with the midnight oil, a single book, he is forced actually to beg and canvass for people who will condescend to be his hearers, and not even this without cost to himself. He gets the loan of a house, fits up a room, hires benches, and scatters programs. Even if his reading is followed by a complete success, all the glory is, so to say, cut short in the bloom and the flower, and does not come to any real and substantial fruit. He carries away with him not a single friendship, not a single client, not an obligation that will abide in anyone's mind, only idle applause, meaningless acclamations and a fleeting delight … Consider too that a poet, if he wishes to work out and accomplish a worthy result, must leave the society of his friends, and the attractions of the capital; he must relinquish every other duty, and must, as poets themselves say, retire to woods and groves, in fact, into solitude.[16]

16 Tacitus, *Annals*, 9.

When a friend suggests that perhaps those orators who do not make successful lawyers should be encouraged to become poets, Tacitus notes that, on the contrary, he himself began as a poet and longs for the quiet solitude of that life.

For myself, though I am perhaps able to accomplish and effect something as a lawyer, yet it was by the public reading of tragedies that I first began to enter the path of fame, when in Nero's time I broke the wicked power of Vatinius by which even the sanctities of culture were profaned, and if at this moment I possess any celebrity and distinction I maintain that it has been acquired more by the renown of my poems than of my speeches …

As to the woods and groves and that retirement which Aper denounced, they bring such delight to me that I count among the chief enjoyments of poetry the fact that it is composed not in the midst of bustle, or with a suitor sitting before one's door, or amid the wretchedness and tears of prisoners, but that the soul withdraws herself to abodes of purity and innocence, and enjoys her holy resting-place. Here eloquence had her earliest beginnings; here is her inmost shrine. In such guise and beauty did she first charm mortals, and steal into those virgin hearts which no vice had contaminated. Oracles spoke under these conditions.[17]

17 Ibid., 11.

While Tacitus points out, above, that lack of wealth is the reward of the poet, another poet, Juvenal (b. ca. 55 AD), points out that it is the corruption which follows wealth which inspires some of his poetry.

Wealth springs from crime:
Landscape-gardens, palaces, furniture, antique silver—
Those cups embossed with prancing boats—all, all are tainted.
Who can sleep easy today? If your greedy daughter-in-law
Is not being seduced for cash, it'll be your bride: mere schoolboys
Are adulterers now. Though talent be wanting, yet
Indignation will drive me to verse, such as I—or any scribbler—
May still command. All human endeavors, men's prayers,
Fears, angers, pleasures, joys and pursuits, these make
The mixed mash of my verse.[18]

18 Juvenal, *Satire I*, 74.

ART MUSIC

Of the imperial lyric poets, Calpurnius Siculus has left some poetry which is completely in the style and mood of the earlier Greek lyric poets. In *Eclogue III*, we have a genuine love song inspired when Lycidas sees a young lady he has rejected begin to 'make a wax-joined pipe' and sing with another lad under a tree.

Both *Eclogues II* and *VI* center on singing contests in imitation of earlier Greek models. The second of these mentions a contest which has just concluded. Two boastful youths challenge each other, but never get around to actually performing in a similar contest.

Astylus
You're too late, Lycidas. Nyctilus and boy Alcon
Have just ended a singing-match beneath these boughs
With me as judge and for a stake. Nyctilus bet
Kids with their mother-goat, Alcon Leaena's puppy
And swore to his pedigree, but swept the board as winner.

Lycidas

That untrained Alcon beat Nyctilus at singing
I'll credit, Astylus, if crows can beat goldfinches
And hooting owls defeat the tuneful nightingale.

Astylus

I'll give up Petale, the one whom now I pine for,
If Nyctilus comes any nearer him in trained
Skill on the pipes or singing than he does in looks …
Oh, Lycidas, if you had any skill in song
You too could recognize that Alcon deserved praise.

Lycidas

Then, as you're no match even for me, you rascal, will you
(Judge though you may have been) take on my pipes with yours?
Will you compete? And if you like Alcon can umpire.

Astylus

Could you beat anyone? Or would anyone deign
To have a match with you, who struggle to blurt out
A meager trickle of vocal melodies and stuttering words? …
I'd sooner, I confess, go off condemned unheard
Than, using half my voice's range, compete with you.

According to Juvenal, professional singers were sometimes
employed by aristocratic wives to come to their homes for private recitals.

    If your wife has musical tastes, she'll make the professional
Singers come when she wants. She's forever handling
Their instruments, her bejeweled fingers sparkle
Over the lute, she practices scales with a vibrant
Quill once employed by some famous virtuoso—
It's her mascot, her solace, she lavishes kisses on it,
The darling object.
    A certain patrician lady,
Whose lutanist protege was due to compete in
The Capitoline Festival, made inquiry of Janus
And Vesta, offering wine and cakes, to find out
If her Pollio could aspire to the oakwreath prize
For the best performance. What more could she have done
If her husband was sick, or the doctors shaking their heads
Over her little son? She stood there at the altar,
Thinking it no disgrace to veil her face on behalf of
This cheapjack twangler. She made the proper responses

In traditional form, and blanched as the lamb was opened.
Tell me now, I beg you, most ancient of deities,
Old Father Janus, do such requests get answered? There must
Be time to spare in heaven. From what I can see
You Gods have nothing on hand to keep you occupied.[19]

19   Juvenal, *Satire VI*, 379ff.

In another place, Juvenal mentions the singer who performs recitals describing and praising the exploits of former leaders and generals. Juvenal starts to tell the story of one of the earlier Greek battles, and then says, 'O well, the rest,'

You can hear when some tame poet, sweating under the armpits,
Gives his wine-flown recital.[20]

20   *Satire X*, 178.

Calpurnius Siculus has left us a lengthy poem, rich in musical detail, which is an example of an ode in honor of, and intended to please, one of the emperors—in this case, Nero.

Meliboeus
Why, Corydon, the silence and that frequent frown?
Why sit in an unusual place, beneath this plane-tree
By which a noisy brook chatters? You like the moist
Bank? And the nearby river's breath freshens the day?

Corydon
For long, O Meliboeus, I have been pondering songs
Not of the woodland note but such as can proclaim
A golden age and celebrate the God [Nero] himself
Who governs nations and cities and toga'd peace.

Meliboeus
Sweet is your music nor does contrary Apollo
Despise you, young man, but great Rome's divinities
Are fit for no such ballad as Menalcas' sheepfold.

Corydon
Such as it is, although it smacks of the backwoods
To sharp ears and is famous only in our village,
Still my uncouthness, if not for the polished art
Of song, at least wins credit for its dedication.
Beneath this same rock which the mighty pine-tree shades
My brother Amyntas practices the same as I,
Whose time of life brings our two birthdays close together.

Meliboeus
Do you no longer stop the boy from joining reeds
And ties of fragrant wax, whom often you've forbidden
With fatherly concern to play on the light hemlock?
Corydon, more than once I've heard you saying this:
'Break your reeds, boy, and turn your back on empty Muses.
Instead go gather beechnuts and red cornel-cherries;
Drive flocks to milking-pails and loudly through the town
Cart milk for sale. Whatever will your pipe bring in
To ward off hunger? Certainly there's no one hums
My songs but windy echoes among yonder crags.'

Corydon
I did say that, Meliboeus, I own, but long ago.
Now times are different and we have a different God.
Hope smiles more …
I'd surely now be lodging cheap at the world's end—
Ah, grief!—and as a hired hand with Iberian flocks
Whistling useless on a pipe of seven reeds,
No one among the thornbrakes there would care at all
For my Muse. Perhaps even God himself would never lend me
A ready ear to hear, I fancy, the far-distant
Lengthy murmur of my prayers at the world's end.
But if no better tune has claim upon your ears
Or other songs than ours perhaps attract you more,
May today's page of verse be polished by your file? …
So, if you can forgive my nervousness, I'll try
Perhaps those reeds which skilled Iollas yesterday
Gave me and said, 'This panpipe can propitiate
Wild bulls and play the sweetest tunes to our Faunus.
Tityrus owned it, who was first among these hills
To sing a modulated tune on Hybla's oat.'

Meliboeus
By striving to be Tityrus you're aiming high,
Corydon. He was a sacred bard who could on oaten
Pipe outsound the lyre, at whose music wild beasts
Would fawn and frisk …

                    …

Then please begin; I'm with you. But be careful that
No high-pitched pipe of frail boxwood blows the notes
It's used to voicing for you when you praise Alexis.
These, rather, are the reeds to go for. Finger now
The tenor pipes that sang woods worthy of a consul.
Begin and don't wait. Look, here comes your brother Amyntas.
He shall sing second, alternating with your verses …

Corydon
With Jove he should begin, whoever sings of heaven,
Whoever shoulders Atlantean Olympus' weight …

Amyntas
There's peace by his permission on my hills, and thanks
To him, look, no one stops me if I like to sing
Or foot the slow grass thrice, and I can play for dances
And I can keep my songs in writing on green bark
And snarling trumpets no more deafen our reed-pipes.[21]

21 Calpurnius Siculus, *Eclogue IV*.

With the expectation for such formal praise imposed on court poets, one can understand that Statius (45–96 AD) wondered if he were up to the task, when invited to perform for the first time at the table of the emperor Domitian.

But I, on whom Caesar has now for the first time bestowed
The joy of a sacred dinner, to mount to my Prince's table,
How can my lyre make known my devotion, discharge
My gratitude?[22]

22 Statius, *Silvae*, 4.4.2.

This same poet has left two rather dark poems, which nevertheless have interesting musical content. First, the grim and pessimistic poem, *Thebaid*, in which evil gods arrange for the murder of sleeping Thebans, including a musician.

Alert Ialmenus, now never to see the dawn,
    had played his lyre to the last stars, singing the paean
    of Thebes. The god pressed his weakened neck to the left,
    and his head lay heedlessly against the lyre.
Agylleus thrust a sword through his chest and impaled
    his right hand, ready-poised on the hollow lyre-shell,
    his fingers quivering on the strings.[23]

23 Statius, *Thebaid*, 10.304.

Another dark, but beautiful, poem, Statius wrote on the occasion of the death of his father.

Father, grant me yourself from Elysian springs
A dour command of grieving song, the beat
Of an ominous lyre. It is not permitted to stir
The Delian caves or initiate Cirrha's accustomed work
Without you. Whatever Apollo lately ordained
In Corycian shade, or Bacchus upon Ismarian hills,
I have unlearned. Parnassus' woolen band has fled
My hair, I have been aghast at defunctive yew

Stealing among the ivy, the bays—unnatural!—parching.
Yet I, inspired, had set myself to extol the deeds
Of great-hearted kings, to equal in singing lofty Mars.
Who makes my barren heart decay? And who, the Apollo
In me quenched, has drawn cold clouds before my lacking mind?
The goddesses stand dismayed about the seer, and sound
No pleasant music with fingers or voice. Their leader leans
Her head on her silent lyre …

                    …

Only Apollo's choir would be there; I would duly
Praise you, father, and bind on you the poet's leafy prize.
I myself, as priest of the shades and of your soul,
With wet eyes would lead a dirge, from which neither Cerberus
With all his mouths nor Orpheus' spells could turn you away.
And there, as I sang your character and deeds, perhaps
You had not rated mine lower than Homer's mighty speech …

                    …

I shall not bring to my father's pyre as tribute
The funeral music the swan transmits when surer of his doom;
Nor that with which the winged Tyrrhenian Sirens tempt
The sailors most sweetly from dismal cliffs; nor Philomela's
Groaning complaint, her lopped murmur, to her cruel sister:
Bards know these things too well. Who, by the grave has not
Recounted all the Heliads' boughs and their wept buds;
And Phrygian flint; and him who ventured against Apollo,
When Passas rejoiced that the boxwood flute deceived his trust?

Let Pity, that has forgotten man, and Justice, recalled
To heaven, and Eloquence in twofold language lament,
And Pallas, and learned Apollo's Pierian escorts;
Those who draw out their epic verse in six-feet meter;
And those who find their toil and renown in the lyre.[24]

24   Statius, *Silvae*, 5.3.

FUNCTIONAL MUSIC

Calpurnius Siculus has also left a poem refering to the rural celebration of Faunus, god of field, flock and tillage, which includes the following lines:

Corydon
Wherever you call I follow, Ornytus; for my
Leuce by saying No to embraces and night's joys

Allows me access to horned Faunus' holy place.
Out with your reeds then and the songs you've stored away.
My panpipe will not fail you, which resourceful Ladon
Lately put together for me of seasoned reed.[25]

Seneca makes reference to more 'sophisticated' festivals, those of the religious cults with their animal sacrifices.

At the altars you'll make no fast and nimble
Step, as the curved horn booms in stirring rhythms,
Honoring barbaric temples with ancient dance.
O form of death more grim than death itself.
Our walls will see a sight more piteous
Than great Hector's murder.[26]

It is in the satirical poetry of Juvenal that we find some hint of the extent of the decay of these ancient pagan festivals. First, in what seems to be a reference to the Bacchus festival, he writes,

Of the Good Goddess, when flute-music stirs the loins,
And frenzied women, devotees of Priapus,
Sweep along in procession, howling, tossing their hair,
Wine-flown, horn-crazy, burning with the desire
To get themselves laid.[27]

And in the same poem, a reference to another important festival, that of Cybele.

And now in comes a procession,
Devotees of the frenzied Bellona, and Cybele, Mother of Gods,
Led by a giant eunuch, the idol of his lesser
Companions in obscenity. Long ago, with a shard,
He sliced off his genitals: now neither the howling rabble
Nor the kettledrums can outshriek him.[28]

Pliny the Younger mentions a special festival celebrated by slaves, called *Saturnalia*,[29] but unfortunately he does not describe the musical participation.

25   Siculus, *Eclogue I*, 13.

26   Seneca, *Trojan Women*, 3.780.

27   Juvenal, *Satire VI*, 313.

28   Ibid., 512.

29   Letter 23, to Gallus.

ENTERTAINMENT MUSIC

In every era, in every land, music seems to be as indispensable to the menu of a banquet as food. In ancient Rome, even small private banquets required at least one musician, as this charming invitation by Valerius Martial illustrates.

> It's a poor sort of dinner; yet, if you deign to grace it,
> You'll neither say nor hear
> One word that's not sincere,
> You can lounge at ease in your place,
> Wearing your own face,
> You won't have to listen while your host reads aloud from some
>   thick book
> Or be forced to look
> At girls from that sink, Cadiz, prancing
> Through the interminable writhings of professional belly-dancing.
> Instead, Condylus, my little slave,
> Will pipe to us—something not too rustic, nor yet too grave.[30]

But since the spectrum of entertainment is a wide one, we also read of private aristocratic entertainment of a much lower order, here that sought by bored house wives.

> The playhouses closed and empty, in those summer
> Dogdays when only the lawcourts go droning on,
> Some women relieve their boredom by taking in
> Low-down vaudeville farces—and their performers.
> Look at that fellow who scored such a hit in the late-night
> Show as Actaeon's mother, camping it up like mad—
> Poor Aelia's crazy about him. There are the women
> Who'll pay out fancy prices for the chance to defibulate
> A counter-tenor, to ruin a concert performer's voice.[31]
> One as a kink for ham actors. Are you surprised? What else
> Do you expect them to do? Go ape on a good book?
> Marry a wife, and she'll make some flute-player
> Or guitarist a father, not you.[32]

30 Valerius Martial, *Epigrams*, Nr. 78.

31 Peter Green, translator of this passage, in *Roman Poets of the Early Empire* (London: Penguin, 1991), 344, provides the follow explanation for this passage:

> To remove the metal wire inserted through the prepuce to inhibit copulation, which was regarded as detrimental to the singing voice.

32 Juvenal, *Satire VI*, 67ff.

EPILOGUE

Nothing makes awareness of the length of the ascent of man quite so vivid as the study of music. When we find, in literature three thousand years old, descriptions of music which in every way seems so like our own, music which is already an international language using the same basic instruments we use today, we are startled to realize that we are musically of the same era as those early societies and that the true origin and development of music occurred far before any form of history or literature known to us. The ancients listened to music, used music for the same kinds of purpose, and needed music for the same reasons as ourselves. This is because, whether music was described by the Greeks as having a 'divine' aspect, in the Middle Ages as 'mystery,' and by ourselves in psychological terms, it is all the same—music deals with the spirit, with the experiential side of ourselves.

The aesthetic purpose of the earliest Art Music is described in language we might use: 'for joy' and 'nourishment for the heart.' Over and over again we read that this kind of music was not only listened to, but silence was demanded of the listener. In the oldest literature of Greece we read of performers deeply involved in their performance and listeners in tears.

Plato says the purpose of music is for the contemplation of the beautiful, but he observes this cannot happen unless the audience is attentive. He also adds new demands: Art Music must be inspired and it must be well performed.

The final philosophers of ancient Greece begin to focus on the state of the listener. Athenaeus observes that a terrific musical performance produces delight, but aesthetic music is different, something 'deep and intricate,' something requiring 'philosophic reflection.'

Aesthetics as a field of philosophical thought begins with consideration of the natures of pleasure and pain and in attempts to define Beauty. The earliest philosophers exhibit much discomfort when venturing away from Reason to the realms of sensation and emotions. It was only when they gradually begin to realize that the emotions have a distinct influence on Reason that the stage was set for Aristotle.

Aristotle, through astonishing intellectual deduction, understood the importance of the experiential in developing character and the universality of emotions. This prepared the way for his *Poetics*, in which he distinguishes Tragedy from Spectacle and thereby lays the foundation for aesthetics as a recognized branch of philosophy.

The Roman philosopher, Quintilian, was the first to write extensively of the emotions and how the musician and the orator uses them in communication. His contemporary, Plutarch, the last important philosopher of ancient Greece, understood correctly that it is by the coordination of the rational and the non-rational that man functions so remarkably. Little further advance would be made on this subject until the twentieth century.

We find evidence of music education from more than three thousand years ago. It is our impression that most scholars believe that the earliest form of music education in Egypt emphasized technical skills, but we think this view may underestimate these early teachers, some of whom we know were not only famous, but highly respected.

By the earliest period of Greek literature we have testimony of the influence of music on character and this becomes the central purpose of music in education for these people. Plato not only discusses this aspect of education in detail, but defines some goals for musicians which exceed the published requirements of any school of music today, namely that a good musician must have musical *insight* and have the ability to *inspire* through his performance.

Aristotle expands the discussion of music education to topics still debated today. Must we, for example, teach the student to *perform* or is it sufficient to merely teach him to *appreciate* music as a listener?

Plutarch says the purpose of music education is to teach a person to be a good judge of music, therefore all the things taught under the name of music, ear training, sight-singing, harmony, etc., are not the end, but exist for the sake of the end.

The first traces of the decline in the aesthetic quality of music in the ancient civilizations are found already in the plays of Aristophanes in the early fifth century BC, where characters ridicule the most beloved art music of the past. Throughout the remaining centuries before the Christian Era numerous writers comment on the general aesthetic decline in music performances of all kinds. The resultant impact on society, is memorialized in Pliny the Elder's sad observation, 'Pleasure has begun to live and life itself has ceased.'

If one takes a broad overview of the nine centuries before the Christian Era, one is struck by the irony of a high aesthetic level of art music gradually decaying while at the same time civilizations become more 'advanced' and wealthy and philosophy moves forward with steady progress. A summarizing observation by Will Durant regarding these civilizations might be said to describe the musical practice as well.

> Sumeria was to Babylonia, and Babylonia to Assyria, what Crete was to Greece, and Greece to Rome: the first created a civilization, the second developed it to its height, the third inherited it … and transmitted it as a dying gift to the encompassing and victorious barbarians.[1]

Having this rich background in music of such high aesthetic quality, why did it apparently take Western Europe so long to revive these achievements? The instrumental music of the Western Church, for example, would require two thousand years before the commands of the Psalms would be honored in the Masses of the fifteenth century. Here, at least, there are identifiable explanations, but what about secular art music? Why are we under the impression that it disappeared until the late Middle Ages? Did art music really disappear during the 'Dark Ages,' or is it that the descriptions of it in literature disappeared?

This will be a subject for the second book in this series.

1 Will Durant, *Our Oriental Heritage* (New York: Simon and Schuster, 1954), 265.

BIBLIOGRAPHY

Aelianus, Claudius. *Of the Characteristics of Animals.*

Aeschylus. *Eumenides.*

———. *The Complete Plays of Aeschylus.* Translated by George Murray. London: George Allen, 1952.

———. *The Supplices.*

Aesop. *Aesop Without Morals: The Famous Fables, and a Life of Aesop.* Translated by Lloyd W. Daly. New York: T. Yoseloff, 1961.

Allman, Willian F. "The Musical Brain." *U.S. News and World Report,* June 11, 1990.

Apel, Willi. *Harvard Dictionary of Music.* 5th ed. Cambridge, MA: Harvard University Press, 1947.

Aristophanes. *The Clouds.*

———. *The Poet and the Women.* New York: Penguin Classics, 1964.

———. *The Wasps.* New York: Penguin Classics, 1964.

Aristotle. *On Interpretation.* Translated by Cook Harold P. Cambridge, MA: Harvard University Press, 1962.

———. *On Sophistical Refutations.* Translated by Edward Seymour Forster. Cambridge: Harvard University Press, 1955.

———. *On the Cosmos.* Translated by David J. Furley. Cambridge, MA: Harvard University Press, 1965.

———. *Politica.*

———. *Posterior Analytics.* Translated by Hugh Tredennick. Cambridge, MA: Harvard University Press, 1960.

———. *Problemata.*

———. *The Categories.* Translated by Harold P. Cook. Cambridge, MA: Harvard University Press, 1962.

———. *The Works of Aristotle.* Translated by William Ogle. London: Oxford University Press, 1911.

Aristoxenus. *Elementa Rhythmica.* Translated by Lionel Pearson. Oxford: Clarendon Press, 1990.

———. *The Elements of Harmony.* Translated by Henry Stewart Macran. Hildesheim: Georg Olms Verlag, 1974.

Athenaeus. *Deipnosophistae.*

———. *The Deipnosophists.* Translated by Charles Burton Gulick. Cambridge, MA: Harvard University Press, 1951.

Aurelius, Marcus. *Meditations.*

Bacchylides, R. *The Poems and Fragments.* Translated by Richard Claverhouse Jebb. Hildesheim: Georg Olms, 1967.

Bamberger, Carl. *The Conductor's Art.* New York: McGraw-Hill, 1965.

Barker, Andrew, trans. *Greek Musical Writings.* Cambridge, MA: Cambridge University Press, 1989.

Bezold, Carl. *Ninive und Babylon.* 4th ed. Bielefeld: Velhagen & Klasing, 1926.

Buck, Craig. "Knowing the LEFT from the RIGHT." *Human Behavior* (June 1976).

Caesar, Julius. *Civil Wars.*

Chamberlin, Henry Harmon. *Last Flowers: A Translation of Moschus and Bion*. Cambridge, MA: Harvard University Press, 1937.

Chappell, William. *The History of Music: Art and Science*. London: Chappell, 1874.

Chase, Stuart. *The Tyranny of Words*. New York: Harcourt Brace, 1938.

Cicero, Marcus. *Academica*.

———. *Cato Maior de Senectute* [Cato the Elder On Old Age].

———. *De Divinatione*.

———. *De Finibus Bonorum et Malorum* [Abouth the Ends of Goods and Evils].

———. *De Natura Deorum* [On the Nature of the Gods].

———. *De Officiis* [On Duties].

———. *De oratore ad Quintum fratrem libri tres* [On the Orator, three books for his brother Quintus].

———. *Epistulae ad Atticum* [Letters to Atticus]. New York: Penguin Classics, 1978.

———. *Epistulae ad Brutum* [Letters to Brutus].

———. *Letters of Cicero*. Translated by L.P. Wilkinson. New York: Norton, 1966.

———. *Paradoxa Stoicorum*.

———. *Pro Archia Poeta* [In Defense of Aulus Licinius Archias the poet].

———. *Pro Balbo*.

———. *Pro Caelio* [In Defense of Marcus Caelius Rufus].

———. *Pro Milone* [In Defense of Titus Annius Milo].

———. *Pro Murena* [In Defense of Lucius Licinius Murena].

———. *Pro Roscio Amerino* [In Defense of Sextus Roscius of Ameria].

———. *Pro Sestio*.

———. *Tusculanae Quaestiones* [Questions debated at Tusculum].

Collingwood, Robin George. *The Principles of Art*. Oxford: Clarendon Press, 1938.

Croce, Benedetto. *Aesthetic*. New York: Noonday Press, 1958.

Davenport, Guy. *Archilochos, Sappho, Alkman: Three Lyric Poets of the Late Greek Bronze Age*. Berkeley: University of California Press, 1980.

Demosthenes. *Demosthenes I: Olynthiacs, Philippics, Minor public speeches, Speech against Leptines*. Translated by James Herbert Vince. Cambridge, MA: Harvard University Press, 1954.

Diogenes, Laertius. *Lives of the Eminent Philosophers*. Translated by Robert Drew Hicks. Cambridge, MA: Harvard University Press, 1950.

Dole, Nathan Haskell. *Odes of Anacreon, Anacreontics, and Other Selections from the Greek Anthology*. Translated by W. Shepard. Boston: Priv. Print. by N. H. Dole, 1903.

Durant, Will. *Our Oriental Heritage*. New York: Simon and Schuster, 1954.

———. *The Story of Philosophy: The Lives and Opinions of the Great Philosophers of the Western World*. 2nd ed. New York: Simon and Schuster, 1961.

Else, Gerald Frank. *Aristotle's Poetics: The Argument*. Cambridge, MA: Harvard University Press, 1967.

Engel, Carl. *The Music of the Most Ancient Nations, Particularly of the Assyrians, Egyptians and Hebrews with Special Reference to Recent Discoveries in Western Asia and in Egypt*. London: W. Reeves, 1909.

Epictetus. *The Discourses of Epictetus.* Translated by Percy Ewing Matheson. New York: Random House, 1957.

Epicurus. *Epicurus: The Extant Remains.* Translated by Cyril Bailey. Oxford: Clarendon Press, 1926.

Euripides. *The Phoenician Women.*

Farmer, Henry G. "The Music of Ancient Egypt." *The New Oxford History of Music.* London: Oxford University Press, 1966.

———. "The Music of Ancient Mesopotamia." *The New Oxford Dictionary of Music.* London: Oxford University Press, 1966.

Galpin, Francis William. *The Music of the Sumerians and Their Immediate Successors, the Babylonians & Assyrians.* Westport, CT: Greenwood Press, 1970.

Grove, George. *The New Grove Dictionary of Music and Musicians.* Edited by Stanley Sadie. London: Macmillan, 1980.

Guthrie, Kenneth. *The Pythagorean Sourcebook and Library: An Anthology of Ancient Writings Which Relate to Pythagoras and Pythagorean Philosophy.* Grand Rapids: Phanes Press, 1987.

Heraclitus. *Fragments.* Translated by Thomas M. Robinson. Toronto: University of Toronto Press, 1987.

Herodotus. *The History.* Translated by David Grene. Chicago: University of Chicago Press, 1987.

Hesiod. *Theogony; Works and Days; Shield.* Translated by Apostolos Athanassakis. Baltimore: Johns Hopkins University Press, 1983.

Hindemith, Paul. *A Composer's World: Horizons, and Limitations.* Garden City, NY: Doubleday, 1961.

Homer. *The Homeric Hymns.* Translated by Apostolos Athanassakis. Baltimore: Johns Hopkins University Press, 1976.

———. *The Odyssey.* Translated by Augustus Taber Murray. London: W. Heinemann, 1960.

Horace. *Carmina.*

———. *Epistles.*

———. *Epodes.*

———. *Odes.*

———. *Satires.*

———. *Satires, Epistles, and Ars poetica.* Translated by H. Rushton Fairclough. Cambridge, MA: Harvard University Press, 1955.

Josephus. *Jewish Antiquities.*

———. *The Jewish Wars.*

Juvenal. *Satire X.*

Kastner, Jean Georges. *Manuel général de musique militaire à l'usage des armées françaises.* Paris, 1848.

Kimura, Doreen. "The Asymmetry of the Human Brain." *Scientific American* 228, no. 3 (March 1973): 70-8.

Kirchner, Walther. *Western Civilization to 1500.* New York: Barnes & Noble, 1960.

Kirk, Geoffrey S. *The Presocratic Philosophers.* Repr. Cambridge: Cambridge Univ Pr., 1983.

———. *The Songs of Homer.* Cambridge: University Press, 1962.

Lang, Andrew, trans. *Theocritus, Bion and Moschus.* London: Macmillan, 1920.

Lang, Paul Henry. *Music in Western Civilization.* New York: Norton, 1941.

Langer, Susanne K. *Philosophy in a New Key.* New York: Mentor, 1948.

———. "The Cultural Importance of the Arts." *Journal of Aesthetic Education* 1, no. 1 (April 1, 1966): 5-12.

Liszt, Franz. "Berlioz and his 'Harold' Symphony." *Neue Zeitschrift fur Musik* 43 (1855).

———. *F. Chopin: A Biographical and Critical Notice.* Paris, 1852.

Livy. *History of Rome.*

Los Angeles Philharmonic Notes, April 1989.

Lucian. *A Second-Century Satirist.* Translated by Winthrop Dudley Sheldon. Philadelphia: Drexel Biddle, 1901.

———. *Icaromenippus.*

Lucretius. *The Way Things Are.*

Mahler, Alma. *Gustav Mahler: Memories and Letters.* New York: Viking Press, 1969.

Manniche, Lise. *Music and Musicians in Ancient Egypt.* London: British Museum Press, 1991.

Martial, Valerius. *Epigrams.*

Maximus, Valerius. *Factorvm et Dictorvm Memorabilivm.*

McLuhan, Marshall. "An Interview." *Playboy,* March 1969.

Menander. *Plays and Fragments.* Translated by Norma Miller. London: Penguin Books, 1987.

Meyerowitz, Jan. "Do We Overestimate Beethoven?" *High Fidelity Magazine,* January 1970.

Murphy, Gardner. *Human Potentialities.* New York: Basic Books, 1958.

Nagy, Gregory. *Pindar's Homer: The Lyric Possession of an Epic Past.* Baltimore: Johns Hopkins University Press, 1982.

Nahm, Milton C. *Selections from Early Greek Philosophy.* 4th ed. New York: Appleton-Century-Crofts, 1964.

Oates, Whitney Jennings. *The Complete Greek Drama: All the Extant Tragedies of Aeschylus, Sophocles and Euripides, and the comedies of Aristophanes and Menander.* New York: Random House, 1938.

Ornstein, Robert. *The Evolution of Consciousness: The Origins of the Way We Think.* New York: Prentice Hall Press, 1991.

Ovid. *Amores* [The Loves].

———. *Ars Amatoria* [The Art of Love].

———. *Fasti* [The Festivals].

———. *Letters in Exile.*

———. *Metamorphoses* [Transformations].

———. *Poetry of Exile.*

———. *Remedia Amoris* [The Cure for Love].

———. *Tristia* [Sorrows].

Persius. *Satire I.*

Philostratus. *The Life of Apollonius of Tyana.*

Pickard-Cambridge, Sir Arthur Wallace. *The Dramatic Festivals of Athens.* Oxford: Clarendon Press, 1953.

Pindar. *The Odes of Pindar.* Translated by Geoffrey S. Conway. London: J. M. Dent, 1972.

Plato. *Hippias minor.*

———. *Laws.* Translated by Benjamin Jowett. Oxford: Clarendon, 1953.

———. *The Dialogues of Plato.* Edited by Benjamin Jowett. 5 vols. Oxford: Clarendon Press, 1953.

Plautus. *Casina.*

———. *Epidicus.*

———. *Pot of Gold.*

———. *The Haunted House.*

Pliny the Elder. *Natural History.* Translated by Harris Rackham. Cambridge, MA: Harvard University Press, 1942.

Pliny the Younger. *Letters of Marcus Tullius Cicero and Letters of Gaius Plinius Caecilius Secundus.* Translated by William Melmoth. New York: Collier, 1909.

Pliny the Younger. *The Letters of The Younger Pliny.* Translated by Betty Radice. New York: Penguin Books, 1969.

Plotinus. *The Enneads.* Translated by Stephen MacKenna. 3rd ed. London: Faber & Faber, 1962.

Plutarch. *Lives.*

Polybius. *The Histories.* Translated by William Roger Paton. Cambridge, MA: Harvard University Press, 1954.

Propertius. *The Poems.*

Quintilian, Marcus Fabius. *Institutio Oratoria* [The Education of an Orator]. Translated by H.E. Butler. London: Heinemann, 1938.

Reale, Giovanni. *A History of Ancient Philosophy.* Albany: State University of New York Press, 1985.

Reese, Sam. "Discovering the Nonintellectual Self: Abraham H. Maslow's Humanistic Psychology." *Music Educators Journal* 60, no. 9 (May 1, 1974): 46-75.

Roszak, Theodore. *Where the Wasteland Ends: Politics and Transcendence in Postindustrial Society.* Garden City, NY: Doubleday, 1972.

Sachs, Curt. *The History of Musical Instruments.* New York: Norton, 1940.

Sadie, Stanley, ed. *The New Grove Dictionary of Music and Musicians.* Vol. 6. London: Macmillan, 1980.

Sallust. *The Conspiracy of Catiline.*

———. *The Jugurthine War.*

Scholes, Percy. *The Oxford Companion to Music.* 7th ed. London: Oxford University Press, 1947.

Sendrey, Alfred. *Music in the Social and Religious Life of Antiquity.* Rutherford, NJ: Fairleigh Dickinson University, 1974.

Seneca, Lucius Annaeus. *Apocolocyntosis divi Claudii* [The Pumpkinification of the Divine Claudius].

———. *Epistolae.*

———. *Medea.*

———. *Oedipus.*

———. *Phaedra* or *Hippolytus.*

———. *Trojan Women.*

Sharpe, Samuel. *Egyptian Antiquities in the British Museum.* London: J. Russel Smith, 1862.

Siculus, Calpurnius. *Eclogue VII.*

Sophocles. *Ajax.*

Sprague, Rosamond Kent. *The Older Sophists: A complete translation by several hands of the fragments in Die Fragmente der Vorsokratiker.* Columbia: University of South Carolina Press, 1972.

Statius, Publius Papinius. *Silvae.*

———. *Thebaid.*

Stipp, David. "What Happens When Music Meets the Brain." *Wall Street Journal,* August 30, 1985.

Strabo. *The Geography of Strabo.* Translated by Horace Leonard Jones. Cambridge, MA: Harvard University Press, 1959.

Stravinsky, Igor. *Chronicle of My Life.* London: Victor Gollancz, 1936.

Suetonius. *Lives of the Caesars.*

Sullivan, John, and Anthony Boyle. *Roman Poets of the Early Empire.* Translated by Peter Green. London: Penguin, 1991.

Tacitus. *Annals.*

———. *The History.*

Terence. *The Brothers.*

———. *The Eunuch.*

The Holy Bible, Revised Standard Version. New York: Nelson, 1957.

The Report of the National Commission on Music Education. Reston: MENC, 1991.

Theocritus. *Theocritus, Idylls and epigrams.* Translated by Daryl Hine. New York: Atheneum, 1982.

Theophrastus. *Metaphysics.* Translated by William David Ross and Francis Howard Fobes. Hildesheim: Georg Olms Verlag, 1967.

Thucydides. *The History of Thucydides.* Translated by Samuel Thomas Bloomfield. London: Longman, Rees, Orme, Brown and Green, 1829.

———. *The Peloponnesian War.*

Tibullus. *The Poems.*

Trevor, Albert. *History of Ancient Civilization.* Vol. 2. New York: Harcourt Brace, 1939.

Varro, Marcus. *On the Latin Language.*

Virgil. *Aeneid.* Translated by L.R. Lind. Bloomington: Indiana Univeristy Press, 1958.

———. *Georgics.*

Wagner, Richard. *Richard Wagner's Prose Works.* Translated by William Ashton Ellis. 8 vols. New York: Broude Brothers, 1966.

Wilmanns, E, ed. *Corpus inscriptionum latinarum.*

Wolf, Friedrich A. *Prolegomena ad Homerum,* 1795.

Xenophon. *Anabasis.* Translated by Carleton L. Brownson and O. J. Todd. Repr. Cambridge, MA: Harvard University Press, 1947.

———. *Cyropaedia.* Translated by Walter Miller. Cambridge, MA: Harvard University Press, 1960.

———. *Memorabilia and Oeconomicus.* Translated by Edgar Cardew Marchant. Cambridge, MA: Harvard University Press, 1953.

———. *Scripta minora.* Translated by Edgar Cardew Marchant. Cambridge, MA: Harvard University Press, 1956.

INDEX

A

Aaron, Old Testament figure, 92

Aelianus, Claudius, 175–235 Greek writer living in Rome, 345 (fn. 16)

Aeschines, 389–314 BC, Greek statesman and orator, 397

Aeschylus, 525–456 BC, Greek playwright, 105, 169ff, 343

Aesop, 620–560 BC, writer of fables, 169

Agathon, 448–400 BC, Greek tragic poet, 259

Aglais of Megacles, ancient Olympic trumpet winner, 110

Aglaophon, ancient Greek painter mentioned by Cicero, 373

Alcaeus, 170, 424

Alcibiades, 450–404 BC, Greek general, 109 [on music education]

Alexander the Great, 356–323 BC, of Macedon, 104, 111, 249

Alkman, ca. 640–550 BC, Greek lyric poet, 123ff

Amenemhib, 18th dynasty Egypt, overseer of the singers, 79

Amenophis, IV, 18th dynasty king of Egypt, 76

Ammianus Marcellinus, 4th century AD Roman writer, 470

Amphion, 426

Amunoph III, 15th century BC Egyptian leader, 103

Anacreon of Teos, 550–500 BC, Greek lyric poet, 124ff, 170, 294, 298, 423, 466

Anaxenor, Rhapsodist honored by Mark Anthony, 323

Anaxeron, kitharode player honored by Mark Anthony, 467

Anderson, Hans Christian, 1805–1875, Danish author, 45

Andron of Alexandria, 2nd century BC, 273

Andronius, music teacher to Marcus Aurelius, 463

Annarus, Viceroy under Cyrus the Great, 6th century BC, 69

Antef, King, old kingdom, Egypt, 75

Antiphon, 5th century BC Greek orator, 157

Antisthenes, 446–366 BC, Greek orator, 109

Apelles, 12–41 AD, Roman popular singer, 459

Apelles, ancient Greek painter mentioned by Cicero, 373

Aphrodite, ancient Greek goddess, 445

Apollo [also known as Phoebus], mythical Greek figure, 103, 106, 111, 117, 119, 125, 128, 143, 146, 171, 208, 245, 295, 428ff, 424, 432, 434, 440, 442, 448, 451, 460ff, 500, 507

Apollonius, 1st century AD account of the aulos player, Canus, 467

Apollonius, ancient Greek Rhapodist murdered by Ptolemy, 323

Arcesilaus, 318–242 BC,

Alexandrian philosopher, member of Skeptic School, 286

Archilochus, 7th century BC, Greek lyric poet, 123ff, 293, 406, 424

Archytas, 400–350 BC Greek musician, philosopher, School of Pythagoras, 153ff, 165ff

Ardalius the Troezenian, said to have invented the Prosodia, 130

Arion, mythical musician saved by a dolphin, 141 (fn. 1)

Aristhenes, 260

Aristides Quintilianus, late 3rd – early 4th century AD, historian and philosopher on music education, 326ff, 472ff

Aristippus of Cyrene, Greek philosopher, 337

Aristippus, early Alexandrian school teacher, 299

Ariston, 320–250 BC, Alexandrian philosopher, student of Zeno, 284

Aristophanes, 448–380 BC, Greek playwright, 126, 169ff

Aristotle, 384–322 BC, Greek philosopher, 7, 43, 104, 105ff, 163ff [on Pythagoras], 172, 224, 249ff, 511

Aristoxenus, fl. 335 BC, pupil of Aristotle, Alexandrian philosopher and author of a music treatise, 104, 173, 274, 281ff, 314

Artemis, mythical Greek goddess of childbirth, 196

Artemon, fl. ca. 230 AD, a painter mentioned by Athenaeus, 129

Asaph, Old Testament singer, 90

Ashur-Idanni-Pal, 668–626 BC Elamite king, 67

Asopodorus of Philius, ancient Greek professional aulos player, 274

Ateas, 4th century BC, king of the Scythians, 135

Athenaeus, late 2nd – early 3rd AD, Greek historian, 69, 79, 81, 106, 118ff, 171ff, 222 (fn. 69), 273, 276ff, 291, 293ff, 309ff, 315ff [on the development of modes], 317ff, 320ff, 323ff, 336ff

Augustus, Caesar, Roman emperor from 27 BC to 14 AD, 412, 416, 450ff

Aulus Gellius, 117–180 AD, Roman writer and grammarian, 466

B

Bacchus, mythical Greek figure, 453ff

Bacchylides, 6th century BC, Greek lyric poet, 123ff

Bach, J.S., 1685–1750, German composer, 15

Bathyllus, 424

Beethoven, Ludwig, van, 1770–1827, German composer, 16, 21, 25, 29

Bion, fl. 105 BC, Alexandrian poet, 293ff

Brendel, Alfred, b. 1931, Austrian pianist, 37

C

Caius Calpurnius Piso, Roman senator, conspirator against Nero in 65 AD, 459

Caligula, 12–41 AD, Roman emperor, 459

Calliope, mythical Greek goddess, 426ff, 440, 442, 447, 448, 451

Calpurnius Siculus, fl. ca. 50 AD, Roman lyric poet, 499, 502ff

Canus, most famous aulos player of the first century AD in Rome, 467

Caphisius, 4th century BC aulos teacher mentioned by Zeno, 292

Caracalla, 188–217, Roman emperor and kithara player, 463

Carinus, d. 285, Roman emperor, 466

Cassius, ancient Roman poet mentioned by Horace, 408

Cato, 95–46 BC, Roman writer, 355

Catullus, Gaius Valerius, 84–54 BC, Roman poet, 355, 363, 364, 355, 358ff

Celibadache, Sergiu, 1912–1996, Romanian conductor, 7, 46

Chenaniah, Old Testament conductor, 88

Chesterfield, Earl of, 1694–1773, of 'Letters to his son,' 108

Chrysogonos, Roman aristocrat, 352

Cicero, Marcus Tullius, 106–43 BC, Roman philosopher, 351ff 354 [on music of the theater], 356ff [on music education], 358ff, 363ff, 369ff, 384 [against the Epicurians], 389 [on music in ancient plays]

Claudius, Tiberius Caesar, 10 BC – 54 AD, Roman emperor, 363, 475, 490

Cleisthenes, leader of Athens, creates first democracy in 508 BC, 141

Clonas, elegiac and epic poet, invented the Prosodia, according to Plutarch, 130

Cratinus, ancient Greek playwright, dance teacher mentioned by Athenaeus, 171

Croce, Benedetto, 1866–1952, Italian philosopher, 3ff

Cybele, ancient Greek goddess, 443

Cyclops, ancient Greek god, 435 [playing a giant panpipe]

Cyrus, 600–529 BC, Persian emperor, 68, 147 [tells anecdote about music]

D

Damomenes, ancient Alexandrian choir conductor, 297

Damon of Athens, the music teacher of Pericles and Socrates, 145, 220, 229

Damonidas, 6th century BC choral member, 126

Danaus, d. 1,425 BC, Egyptian noble founded Argos in Greece, 103

Darius III, King of Persia in 336–330 BC, 69

Darwin, Charles, 1809–1882, English naturalist, 12

David, ca. 1,000 BC, Old Testament musician and king, 89, 91, 96

Davison, Archibald T., Conductor, Harvard Glee Club, 1919–1933, 26

Debussy, Claude, 1862–1918, French composer, 17

Demetrius, 337–283 BC, 106 [music at the funeral of]

Democritus, 460–370 BC Greek philosopher, 153ff, 390

Demodocus, blind singer in Homer, 115, 121

Demosthenes, 385–322 BC, Alexandrian orator, 287, 391, 396ff

Dexitheus, lyre player mentioned by Aristophanes, 175

Diana, mythical Greek goddess, 428, 432, 437

Diodorus Siculus, ca. 60–30 BC, Greek philosopher, 78

Diodorus, 1st century Roman lyre player, 467

Diogenes Laertius, 3rd century AD philosopher, 286, 292ff

Diogenes, 412–323, Greek philosopher of the Cynic School, 292

Dionysus, mythical Greek god of the harvest, 110, 156, 175, 182, 208, 244ff, 296, 321, 359

Diotogenes, ca. 6th century, follower of Pythagoras, 161

Dioysius, 'legendary ancient musician,' mentioned by Cicero, 393

Dorion, ca. 323–146 BC, professional Greek aulos player, 276ff

Duellius, Gaius, ca. 1st century BC, Roman admiral, 353

E

Elagabalus, 205–222, Roman emperor and aulos and trumpet player, 463

Emhab, 17th dynasty, Egyptian percussionist, 81

Emprepes, a member of the Ephors, mentioned by Plutarch, 129

Enlulim, shepherd flutist, 2600 BC at Eninnu, Sumeria, 62

Ennius, 236–169 BC, Roman poet, 358

Epictetus, 55–135 AD, Greek philosopher, 305ff, 320

Epicurus, 341–270 BC Greek philosopher, founder of Epicurian school, 278, 283ff, 356, 316 [on the physics and acoustics of music], 375, 384

Eratosthenes, 276–194 BC, Alexandrian philosopher, 288

Eupolis, 318

Euripides, 480–408 BC, Greek playwright, 169ff, 298, 343

Euryphamus, ca. 6th century BC, follower of Pythagoras, 161

F

Flaccus, 'freedman of Claudius,' according to Terence, Roman composer, 353

Flavius Philostratus, 1st century, Roman biographer, 467

G

Geminus, lyre and singing teacher to Marcus Aurelius, 463

Genthius, King of the Illyrians, 354

Gideon, Old Testament figure 93 [use of trumpet in battle]

Glaucon, a brother to Plato, 221

Gorgias, fl. ca. 425 BC, Greek philosopher, 155ff

Gracchus, Caius, 154–121 BC, Roman orator, 365

Gudea, Sumerian king of Sumeria, 2600 BC, 62

H

Hadrian, Roman emperor, 76–138 AD, played harp, 463

Handel, Georg, 1685–1759, German composer, 15

Hannibal, 472

Heman, Old Testament choral leader, 88, 90

Heracleides of Cumae, ca. 221–205 BC, Persian historian, 69

Heracleitus, 210, 310

Heraclides, ancient Greek author of a Compendium of Music, 128

Heraclitus, fl. ca. 513 BC, Greek philosopher, 156ff

Heradorus of Megara, 396 BC Olympic trumpet winner, 110

Hermes, mythical Greek god, inventor of the lyre 117, 127

Hermesianax, early 3rd century BC, Alexandrian poet, 293ff

Hermippus, 2nd century BC, famous Roman aulos player, 354

Herodotus of Halicarnassus, 484–425 BC, Greek historian, 68, 77, 80, 141ff

Hesiod, ca. 800 BC, Greek epic poet, 113, 118 [on competition], 121, 156 (fn. 13)

Hiero, 4th century BC Greek political leader, 142 [on competition]

Hieron, ruler of Syracuse in 478 BC, 135

Hindemith, Paul, 1895–1963, German composer, 11, 42

Hippias, fl. ca. 450 BC Greek philosopher and composer, 157

Hippocleides, 5th century BC [danced away his marriage], 148

Hirtius, Aulus, Roman consul, 90–43 BC, 473

Homer, ca. 850 BC, Greek epic poet, 113ff, 206, 146, 156, fn. 13, 186, 194, 293, 309, 399, 437

Horace, 66–8 BC, Roman philosopher, composer, singer, 352, 401, 423, 451 [on his patron, Maecenas], 454ff

I

Iamblichus, 250–325 AD, biographer of Pythagoras, 160ff
Ibis, mythical Egyptian god, 417
Ibycus of Rhegium, ca. 550–500 BC, Greek lyric poet, 124ff, 170
Ion of Ephesus, a Rhapsodist, 193, 212ff
Isaeus, 415–340 BC, orator, 487ff
Ismenias, 4th century BC, excellent Greek aulos player, 109
Ismenias, musician under Ateas, King of the Scythians, 135
Isocrates, 436–338 BC, Greek rhetorician, 388, 395

J

Jeduthun, Old Testament singer, 90
Jehoshaphat, Old Testament King of Israel, 91
Jephthah, Old Testament figure, 97
Jeremiah, 7th century BC, Old Testament figure, commanded to teach music, 88
Jesus, 111 [on the Greek myth of special Hell for music lovers]
Jochum, Eugen, 1902–1987, German conductor, 40
Jonathan, Old Testament figure, 91
Josephus, 1st century AD, historian of Jewish history, 472
Joshua, Old Testament religious figure, 86

Julius Caesar, 100–44 BC, Roman general and statesman, 352, 359, 473
Jupiter, 430, 455, 457
Juvenal, 2nd century AD, Roman poet, 488, 502ff

K

Khesuwer, middle kingdom Egyptian choral instructor, 77
Koussevitzky, Serge, 1874–1951, Russian-American conductor, 36, 39
Kraton of Chalkedon, 4th century BC famous aulos player, 172

L

Lamia, 3rd century BC, single-pipe playing prostitute, 278
Leaena, 4th century AD, famous prostitute harp girl, 475
Liszt, Franz, 1811–1886, Hungarian pianist, 26, 35, 37, 39, 45, 49, 56
Livius Andronicus, fl. ca. 240 BC, Roman actor and producer, 353
Livy, [Titus Livius] 59 BC – 17 AD, Roman historian, 344ff, 359ff, 364, 366
Lucanus, Roman poet, 469
Lucian of Samosata, 125–180 AD satirist, 310, 322, 337, 464, 500
Lucius Anicius, 2nd century BC, Roman general, 354
Lucius Flaccus, fl. ca. 19 AD, Roman Consul, 352
Lucretius, 99–55 BC, Roman poet and philosopher, 347, 357, 369ff, 392
Lycurgus, 9th century BC Greek general, 111
Lysimachus, 2nd century BC, famous Roman aulos player, 354

Lysippus, ancient Greek sculptor mentioned by Cicero, 373

M

Mahler, Gustav, 1860–1911, Austrian composer, 39, 55
Marcus Aurelius Roman emperor, 121–180 AD, had several music teachers, 323, 463, 480, 487ff, 494
Marcus Marius, d. 82 BC, Roman politician, 398
Maximian, 286–305 AD, head of the first music guilds in Rome, 463
McLuhan, Marshall, 1911–1980, Canadian philosopher [on ancient languages], 30
Menander, 342–291 BC, Greek playwright, 111, 179, 184
Mendelssohn, Felix, 1809–1847, German composer, 12ff, 14, 26, 37
Mercury, mythical Greek god, 426, 430, 432
Mesomedes, 3rd century kithara teacher to emperor Caracalla, 463
Metopus, 5th century BC Greek philosopher, 153
Meyerbeer, Giacomo, 1791–1864, German composer, 26
Michelangelo, 1475–1564, Italian artist, 5, 6
Midas of Acragas, winner of the Aulos playing, Pythian festival, 490 BC, 126
Minerva, mythical Greek goddess, 109
Miriam, Old Testament figure, 92
Moschus, fl. 100 BC, Alexandrian poet, 293ff
Moses, 13th to 12th century BC, Old Testament religious figure, 86, 88, 90, 92 [on trumpet construction]

Moussorgsky, Modest, 1839–1881, Russian composer, 42

Mozart, Wolfgang Amadeus, 1756–1791, Austrian composer, 17, 21ff, 410

Myron, ancient Greek sculptor mentioned by Cicero, 373

N

Narcissus, ca. 206 BC, slave in Rome [contract with music teacher], 356

Nebuchadnezzar, ca. 1000 BC [his court music in the Old Testament], 65

Nepos, Cornelius, 100–22 BC, Roman biographer, 352

Neptune, mythical Greek god, 430

Nero, 37–68 AD, Roman emperor, 459, 468, 474

Nikaure, choral instructor for King Userkaf, 2494–2487 BC, 77

Numa Pompilius, 7th to 8th century BC, Roman king, 347

O

Olympus, mythical Greek god, and aulos player, 130

Orpheus, mythical Greek god, 420, 431, 437, 447, 500, 507

Ovid, 43 BC – 17 AD, Roman poet, 103, 347, 402, 405, 416ff, 420, 423ff, 344, 435ff, 446ff, 455ff

P

Paculla Annia, Roman priestess, mentioned by Livy, 360

Pan, mythical Greek figure, 103, 121, 295, 357 [origin], 420, 432ff, 440

Parmenides, 5th century philosopher, founder of the Eleatic School, 155

Parrhasius, ancient painter mentioned by Horace, 403

Paulus Maximus, friend of Ovid, 435

Pericles, 5th century BC political leader and musician, 144, 150 [on public entertainment]

Persius, 35–62, Roman poet, 466

Petronius, Gaius, 7–66 AD, Roman courtier, 357, 474

Pherecrates, 5th century BC Greek playwright, 274

Philataerus, 4th century BC, Greek writer, 111 [on 'special Hell' for music lovers]

Philip of Macedonia, 273 [the defeat of the Greeks]

Philoxenus, ancient Greek poet, 289

Photius, 5th century BC philosopher, 155

Phrynichus, ancient Greek playwright, dance teacher mentioned by Athenaeus, 171

Phrynis, fl. 230 AD, ancient Greek musician mentioned by Plutarch, 129

Pindar, b. 518 BC, Greek lyric poet, 123ff, 146, 289

Pino, Marco, 1521–1583, 1521–1583, Italian artist from Siena, 5

Plato, 429–347 BC, Greek philosopher, 78 [on Egyptian educational system], 103ff, 108, 130, 157, 181, 191ff, 391, 495, 512

Plautus, 254–184 BC, Roman playwright, 354, 362, 366ff [on single-pipe girls], 412

Pliny the Elder, 23–79 AD, Roman writer, 464, 477ff, 480 [dates the invention of instruments], 488, 493, 498ff

Pliny the Younger, 61–112 AD, Roman lawyer and writer, 355, 465, 475, 482, 487ff, 499ff, 508ff

Plotinus, 204–270 AD, last Greek philosopher of antiquity, 303ff

Plutarch, fl. ca. 46 BC – 120 AD, Roman historian, 68 (fn 25), 69ff, 105ff, 111, 113, 118, 124, 126ff, 135, 144, 156, 158, 164, 172, 260, 275, 289, 306ff, 316, 318ff, 321, 324ff [on the decline of music education], 336, 348, 365, 473, 512

Pollux, Greek writer, 2nd century BC, 472

Polybius, 200–118 BC, Greek historian, 289ff, 354

Polyclitus, ancient Greek sculptor mentioned by Cicero, 373

Pomponius Secundus, 1st century AD, tragic poet, 491

Porphyry, 233–305 AD, biographer of Pythagoras, 158ff, 303

Pratinas of Phlius, 321

Pratinas, ca. 500 BC, Greek tragic poet of Athens, 130

Pronomus of Thebes, c. 440 BC, professional aulos player, teacher of Alcibiades, 274

Propertius, 50–16 BC, Roman poet, 419, 423, 423, 437ff, 439 [poems of Cynthia], 448ff, 455

Protagoras, 490–420, early Greek philosopher, 271

Psammetichus I [Psamtik I], 26th dynasty of Egypt, 103

Ptolemaeus Philadelphus, 283–246 BC, Egyptian king, 352

Ptolemy Auletes, 81–52 BC, King of Egypt and aulos player, 76

Ptolemy, 285–246 BC, Egyptian leader, 81

Purcell, Henry, 1659–1695, English composer, 15

Pyrrho, 360–270 BC, Alexandrian philosopher of the Sceptic School, 283ff

Pythagoras, 580–500 BC, Greek philosopher, 76, 83, 158ff, 191, 250ff, 299, 304, 307, 322, 334, 477, 495

Q

Quintilian, 35–100 BC, Roman rhetorician, 365, 467, 477ff, 483ff [on communicating the emotions], 489, 495ff [on music education], 499

Quintus Fabius, 280–203 BC, Roman general and politician, 349

R

Rewer, choral instructor, 5th dynasty, 2563–2423 BC, 77

Roscius, Sextus, 126–62 BC, famous Roman actor, 388, 396

Rossini, Gioachino, 1792–1868, Italian composer, 25

S

Sacadas, ancient Greek composer mentioned by Plutarch, 129

Sallust, 86–34 BC, Roman historian, 353, 369, 382

Sappho, 640–550 BC, Greek lyric lady poet, 124ff, 294, 298, 423, 466

Saturn, mythical Greek god, 416, 457

Saul, Old Testament figure, 91, 96

Schumann, Robert, 1810–1856, German composer, 27, 50

Scopas, ancient sculptor mentioned by Horace, 403

Seneca the Elder, 1st century AD Roman writer, 470

Seneca the Younger, Roman writer, 471, 500, 508

Severus Alexander, 208–235, Roman emperor and aulos player, 463

Silanion, Roman sculptor mentioned by Pliny the Elder, 498

Simonides, b. ca. 556 BC, Greek lyric poet, 125ff, 310, 355

Socrates, 469–399 BC, Greek philosopher, 108, 191ff, 281 (fn. 86), 495

Solomon, ca. 1,000 BC, Old Testament religious figure, 86 [his 245 singers] , 91, 94ff

Solon, 630–558 BC, Greek philosopher, 103

Sophocles, 495–406 BC, Greek playwright, 169ff, 298, 343

Statius, 45–96 AD, court poet to the Emperor Domitian, 506ff

Stesichorus of Himera, ca. 610–550 BC, Greek lyric poet, 123ff

Stokowski, Leopold, 1882–1977, English conductor, 30

Strabo, 64 BC – 23 AD, Greek philosopher and geographer, 68, 76ff, 104, 108, 110, 128, 288ff, 317, 320, 323, 325 [on education]

Stratonicus of Athens, fl. 336–323, Greek harpist and teacher, 276ff

Stravinsky, Igor, 1882–1971, Russian composer, 11

Suetonius, 69–130 AD, roman historian, 364, 422, 459, 468, 475

Sulla, Lucius Cornelius, 138–78 BC, Roman general and statesman, 352

T

Tacitus, 56–117, AD, Roman senator and historian, 460, 470ff, 501

Tegula, Publius Licinius, ca. 205 BC, Roman composer, 362

Telemann, Georg Philipp, 1681–1767, German composer, 15

Terence, 195–159 BC, Roman playwright, 353, 356, 363

Terpander of Antissa in Lesbos, 127, 710–670 BC poet and musician, 127ff

Terpnos, music teacher of the Emperor, Nero, 459, 467

Terpsichore, mythical Greek god of dance, 134, 209

Thales, c. 624–547 BC, Greek philosopher, 103, 156

Theages, 5th century BC Greek philosopher, 153ff

Theocritus, ca. 315–264 BC, Alexandrian poet, 293ff

Theodoric, 489–526 AD, Roman emperor, 463

Theodorus of Boeotia, 2nd century BC, famous Roman aulos player, 354

Theodosius, Roman emperor in 385, 475

Theophrastus of Eresus, 372–287 BC, Alexandrian philosopher, student of Aristotle, 105, 284

Theopompus, 2nd century BC, famous Roman aulos player, 354

Thespis, ancient Greek playwright and dance teacher mentioned by Athenaeus, 171

Thucydides of Athens, ca. 470–398 BC, historian of the Peloponnesian Wars, 141ff

Tibullus, 54–18 BC, Roman poet, 421, 423ff, 451 [on his patron, Messalla]

Timosthenes, fl. ca. 270 BC, Alexandrian composer, 288

Timotheus of Miletus, ancient Greek lyre player, 129

Titus, Roman emperor, and musician, 79–81 AD, 462

Trajan, Roman emperor, 52–117 AD, built a concert hall on the Forum, 463

Triton, mythical Greek figure, 104

Tullius, Servius, Roman king, 6th century BC, 345

Tutankhamun, 1341–1323 BC, pharaoh of Egypt, 81

V

Valerius Marial, 38–102 AD, Roman poet, 509

Valerius Maximus, 1st century AD, Roman writer, 471

Varro, 116–27 BC, Roman philologist and philosopher, 351, 369, 357ff, 363ff, 381

Venus, mythical Greek goddess, 435

Vespasian, Roman emperor, 69–79, 467

Vinci, Leonardo da, 1452–1519, Italian artist, 5, 23

Virgil, 70–19 BC, Roman poet, 402, 415, 419, 421, 423, 432, 449, 451 [on his patron, Maecenas], 452ff, 456ff, 499

Volso, Gnaeus Manlius, c. 2nd century BC, Roman admiral, 366

W

Wagner, Richard, 1813–1883, German composer, 26ff [criticism of Meyerbeer], 37, 31ff, 36, 39, 43, 48, 55ff

Walter, Bruno, 1876–1962, German conductor, 39, 43

Weingartner, Felix, 1863–1942, Austrian conductor, 39

X

Xenacles, ancient Alexandrian lyric poet, 296

Xenocrates, 325 [on protecting children's ears from music]

Xenodamus, ca. 6th century BC Greek poet and leader of a school of music, 131

Xenophanes, 576–480 BC, Greek philosopher, 156

Xenophilus, 4th century BC, lived 105 years without aging [attributed to music], 481

Xenophon of Athens, ca. 434–355 BC, soldier, historian, friend of Socrates, 141ff

Z

Zeno, 333–261 BC, Alexandrian philosopher, founder of the Stoic School, 283ff, 374

Zeus, mythical Greek god, 125, 267, 309ff, 323, 430, 437

Zeuxis, ancient Greek painter mentioned by Cicero, 373

ABOUT THE AUTHOR

Dr. David Whitwell is a graduate ('with distinction') of the University of Michigan and the Catholic University of America, Washington DC (PhD, Musicology, Distinguished Alumni Award, 2000) and has studied conducting with Eugene Ormandy and at the Akademie fur Musik, Vienna. Prior to coming to Northridge, Dr. Whitwell participated in concerts throughout the United States and Asia as Associate First Horn in the USAF Band and Orchestra in Washington DC, and in recitals throughout South America in cooperation with the United States State Department.

At the California State University, Northridge, which is in Los Angeles, Dr. Whitwell developed the CSUN Wind Ensemble into an ensemble of international reputation, with international tours to Europe in 1981 and 1989 and to Japan in 1984. The CSUN Wind Ensemble has made professional studio recordings for BBC (London), the Koln Westdeutscher Rundfunk (Germany), NOS National Radio (The Netherlands), Zurich Radio (Switzerland), the Television Broadcasting System (Japan) as well as for the United States State Department for broadcast on its 'Voice of America' program. The CSUN Wind Ensemble's recording with the Mirecourt Trio in 1982 was named the 'Record of the Year' by The Village Voice. Composers who have guest conducted Whitwell's ensembles include Aaron Copland, Ernest Krenek, Alan Hovhaness, Morton Gould, Karel Husa, Frank Erickson and Vaclav Nelhybel.

Dr. Whitwell has been a guest professor in 100 different universities and conservatories throughout the United States and in 23 foreign countries (most recently in China, in an elite school housed in the Forbidden City). Guest conducting experiences have included the Philadelphia Orchestra, Seattle Symphony Orchestra, the Czech Radio Orchestras of Brno and Bratislava, The National Youth Orchestra of Israel, as well as resident wind ensembles in Russia, Israel, Austria, Switzerland, Germany, England, Wales, The Netherlands, Portugal, Peru, Korea, Japan, Taiwan, Canada and the United States.

He is a past president of the College Band Directors National Association, a member of the Prasidium of the International Society for the Promotion of Band Music, and was a member of the founding board of directors of the World Association for Symphonic Bands and Ensembles (WASBE). In 1964 he was made an honorary life member of Kappa Kappa Psi, a national professional music fraternity. In September, 2001, he was a delegate to the UNESCO Conference on Global Music in Tokyo. He has been knighted by sovereign organizations in France, Portugal and Scotland and has been awarded the gold medal of Kerkrade, The Netherlands, and the silver medal of Wangen, Germany, the highest honor given wind conductors in the United States, the medal of the Academy of Wind and Percussion Arts (National Band Association) and the highest honor given wind conductors in Austria, the gold medal of the Austrian Band Association. He is a member of the Hall of Fame of the California Music Educators Association.

Dr. Whitwell's publications include more than 127 articles on wind literature including publications in Music and Letters (London), the London Musical Times, the Mozart-Jahrbuch (Salzburg), and 39 books, among which is his 13-volume *History and Literature of the Wind Band and Wind Ensemble* and an 8-volume series on *Aesthetics in Music*. In addition to numerous modern editions of early wind band music his original compositions include 5 symphonies.

David Whitwell was named as one of six men who have determined the course of American bands during the second half of the 20th century, in the definitive history, *The Twentieth Century American Wind Band* (Meredith Music).

A doctoral dissertation by German Gonzales (2007, Arizona State University) is dedicated to the life and conducting career of David Whitwell through the year 1977. David Whitwell is one of nine men described by Paula A. Crider in *The Conductor's Legacy* (Chicago: GIA, 2010) as 'the legendary conductors' of the 20th century.

'I can't imagine the 2nd half of the 20th century—without David Whitwell and what he has given to all of the rest of us.' Frederick Fennell (1993)

Made in the USA
San Bernardino, CA
03 October 2013